Critique of Everyday Life

THE ONE-VOLUME EDITION

HENRI LEFEBVRE

VERSO
London • New York

Liberté · Égalité · Fraternité
RÉPUBLIQUE FRANÇAISE

This book is supported by the French Ministry for Foreign Affairs as part of
the Burgess Programme, headed by the French Embassy in London by the
Institut Français du Royaume Uni

This one-volume edition published by Verso 2014

Critique of Everyday Life, Volume I: Introduction
First published by Verso 1991
Translation © John Moore 1991, 2008, 2014
Preface © Michel Trebitsch 1991, 2008, 2014
First published as *Critique de la vie quotidienne I: Introduction*
© Grasset 1947; second edition with new foreword © L'Arche Editeur 1958.

Critique of Everyday Life, Volume II: Foundations for a Sociology of the Everyday
First published by Verso 2002
Translation © John Moore 2002, 2014
First published as *Critique de la vie quotidienne II: Fondements d'une sociologie de
la quotidienneté*
© L'Arche Editeur 1961
Preface © Michel Trebitsch 2002, 2014
Preface translation © Gregory Elliott 2002, 2014

*Critique of Everyday Life, Volume III: From Modernity to Modernism (Towards a
Metaphilosophy of Daily Life)*
First published by Verso 2005
Translation © Gregory Elliott 2005, 2014
Preface © Michel Trebitsch 2005, 2014
First published as *Critique de la vie quotidienne III: De la modernité au modernisme
(pour une metaphilosophie du quotidien)*
© L'Arche Editeur 1981

3 5 7 9 10 8 6 4 2

Verso
UK: 6 Meard Street, London W1F 0EG
US: 20 Jay Street, Brooklyn, NY 11201
www.versobooks.com

Verso is the imprint of New Left Books

ISBN-13: 978-1-78168-317-0 (PBK)
ISBN-13: 978-1-78168-318-7 (HBK)
eISBN-13: 978-1-78168-319-4 (US)
eISBN-13: 978-1-78168-650-8 (UK)

British Library Cataloguing in Publication Data
A catalogue record for this book is available from the British Library

Library of Congress Cataloging-in-Publication Data
A catalog record for this book is available from the Library of Congress

Printed in the US by Maple Press

Critique of Everyday Life

Contents

Contents

VOLUME I

Introduction

Translator's Note

Except when prefixed (*Trans.*), footnotes are from the original. Translations of quotations in the text are mine, except when the source title is given in English. Bibliographical details are presented in the original in a partial and unsystematic way, and wherever possible I have endeavoured to complete and standardize this information, a frequently difficult task, since the author uses his own translations of Marx. I wish to thank my colleagues Robert Gray, John Oakley and Adrian Rifkin for the advice and encouragement they have given me during the preparation of this project.

Preface

by Michel Trebitsch

What a strange status this book has, and how strange its destiny has been. If Henri Lefebvre can be placed alongside Adorno, Bloch, Lukács or Marcuse as one of the main theoreticians of 'Critical Marxism', it is largely thanks to his *Critique of Everyday Life* (*Critique de la vie quotidienne*), a work which, though well known, is little appreciated. Perhaps this is because Lefebvre has something of the brilliant amateur craftsman about him, unable to cash in on his own inventions; something capricious, like a sower who casts his seeds to the wind without worrying about whether they will germinate. Or is it because of Lefebvre's style, between flexibility and vagueness, where thinking is like strolling, where thinking is *rhapsodic*, as opposed to more permanent constructions, with their monolithic, reinforced, reassuring arguments, painstakingly built upon structures and models? His thought processes are like a limestone landscape with underground rivers which only become visible when they burst forth on the surface. *Critique of Everyday Life* is one such resurgence. One could even call it a triple resurgence, in that the 1947 volume was to be followed in 1962 by a second, *Fondements d'une sociologie de la quotidienneté*, and in 1981 by a third, *De la modernité au modernisme (Pour une métaphilosophie du quotidien)*. At the chronological and theoretical intersection of his thinking about alienation and modernity, *Critique of Everyday Life* is a seminal text, drawn from the deepest levels of his intellectual roots, but also looking ahead to the main preoccupation of his post-war period. If we are to relocate it in Lefebvre's thought as a whole, we will need to go upstream as far as *La Conscience mystifiée* (1936) and then back downstream as far as *Introduction à la modernité* (1962).

5

'Henri Lefebvre or Living Philosophy'

The year 1947 was a splendid one for Henri Lefebvre: as well as *Critique of Everyday Life*, he published *Logique formelle, logique dialectique, Marx et la liberté* and *Descartes* in quick succession. This broadside was commented upon in the review *La Pensée* by one of the Communist Party's rising young intellectuals, Jean Kanapa, who drew particular attention to the original and creative aspects of *Critique of Everyday Life*. With this book, wrote Kanapa, 'philosophy no longer scorns the concrete and the everyday'. By making alienation 'the key concept in the analysis of human situations since Marx', Lefebvre was opening philosophy to action: taken in its Kantian sense, critique was not simply knowledge of everyday life, but knowledge of the means to transform it. Thus in Lefebvre Kanapa could celebrate 'the most lucid proponent of living philosophy today'.[1] Marginal before the war, heretical after the 1950s, in 1947 Lefebvre's recognition by the Communist Party seems to have been at its peak, and it is tempting to see his prolific output in a political light. If we add *L'Existentialisme*, which appeared in 1946, and *Pour connaître la pensée de Marx* and his best-seller *Le Marxisme* in the 'Que sais-je?' edition, both of which appeared in 1948, not to mention several articles, such as his 'Introduction à l'esthétique' which was a dry run for his 1953 *Contribution à l'esthétique*, then indeed, apart from the late 1960s, this was the most productive period in his career.[2]

Critique of Everyday Life thus appears to be a book with a precise date, and this date is both significant and equivocal. Drafted between August and December 1945, published in February 1947, according to the official publisher's date, it reflected the optimism and new-found freedom of the Liberation, but appeared only a few weeks before the big freeze of the Cold War set in. 'In the enthusiasm of the Liberation, it was hoped that soon life would be changed and the world transformed', as Henri Lefebvre recalled in 1958 in his Foreword to the Second Edition. The year 1947 was pivotal, Janus-faced. It began in a mood of post-war euphoria, then, from March to September, with Truman's policy of containment and Zhdanov's theory of the division of the world into two camps, with the eviction of the Communist ministers in France and the launching of the Marshall Plan, in only a few months everything had been thrown in the balance, including the fate of the book itself. The impact was all the more brutal in that this hope for a radical break, for the beginning of a new life, had become combined with the myth of the Resistance, taking on an eschatological dimension of which the Communist Party (which also drew strength from the Soviet aura), was the principal beneficiary. With its talk of a 'French Renaissance' and a new cult of martyrs (Danielle Casanova, Gabriel Péri, Jacques Decour) orchestrated by Aragon its high priest, this 'parti des 75,000 fusillés' momentarily embodied both revolutionary promise and continuity with a national tradition stretching back from the Popular Front to 1798. Between 1945 and 1947 the PCF's dominance was both political and ideological. Polling more than 28 per cent of the votes in the November 1946 general election, it appeared to have confirmed its place as the 'first party of France', without which no government coalition seemed possible. Its ideological hegemony, strengthened by the membership or active sympathy of numerous writers, artists and thinkers – Picasso, Joliot-Curie, Roger Vailland, Pierre Hervé – put Marxism at the centre of intellectual debate. Presenting itself as a 'modern rationalism' to challenge the 'irrationalism' and 'obscurantism' brought into disrepute by collaboration, its only rival was existentialism, which made its appearance in the intellectual arena in 1945. But existentialism also located itself with reference to Marxism, as we can see from the controversy which raged for so long in the pages of *Les Temps Modernes* and *L'Esprit*, and which began in that same year with Jean Beaufret's articles in *Confluences* and above all with the argument between Sartre and Lefebvre in *Action*.[3]

In a way both were after the same quarry: Lefebvre's pre-war themes of 'the total man' and his dialectic of the conceived and the lived were echoed by Sartre's definition of existence as the reconciliation between thinking and living. At that time Lefebvre was certainly not unknown: from the beginning of the 1930s the books he wrote single-handedly or in collaboration with Norbert Guterman had established him as an original Marxist thinker. But his pre-war readership had remained limited, since philosophers were suspicious of Marxism and Marxists were suspicious of philosophy. Conversely, after 1945, he emerged as the most important expert on and vulgarizer of Marxism, as an entire generation of young intellectuals rushed to buy his 'Que sais-je?' on Marxism and the new printing of his little *Dialectical Materialism* of 1939; when he brought out *L'Existentialisme*,

7

the Party saw him as the only Communist philosopher capable of stemming the influence of Sartre. With his experience as an elder member linking the pre-war and the post-war years and his image as a popularizer of Marxism, Henri Lefebvre could be slotted conveniently into a strategy by which the Party would exploit its political legitimacy to the full in order to impose the philosophical legitimacy of Marxism. He introduced Marxism to the Sorbonne, where he gave a series of lectures, on such topics as 'the future of capitalism' (March 1947) and 'the contribution of Marxism to the teaching of philosophy' (November). The latter was reported in *La Pensée*, 'the review of modern rationalism', in glowing terms:

> Our friend Henri Lefebvre gave a brilliant demonstration of how dialectical materialism can and should rejuvenate and bring new life to the way philosophy is traditionally taught at university. We were expecting his lecture to be a success; the extent of that success took us by surprise. We had scheduled his lecture for the Amphithéâtre Richelieu, but in the event we had to use the Sorbonne's Grand Amphitheatre, which was flooded with an expectant crowd of almost 2000 people, made up mostly of university staff, students and *lycéens*, who followed Henri Lefebvre's brilliant talk with passionate attention and frequent applause.[4]

But if we take a closer look, things were less simple. The idyllic relationship between Henri Lefebvre and orthodoxy in 1947 was to be little more than a brief encounter, an illusory and ephemeral marriage of convenience that was not without its share of opportunism, and which was soon to be shattered by the watershed of Zhdanovism. And in any event, at the precise moment when, as he himself admitted, he had been 'recognized as the best "philosopher" and French "theoretician" of the day', Lefebvre's material situation had become 'appalling', as he put it bluntly in September 1947 in a letter to his friend Norbert Guterman, whom he had just contacted again for the first time since the war.[5] His poor health made the future look rather bleak, and for a while he was even out of work – a compounding difficulty as he already had numerous offspring to support, scattered over several different homes. He had been working for Radio-Toulouse, where Tristan Tzara, in charge of cultural broadcasts, had found him a job in 1945, but the change in the political climate forced him to step down, and also to give up the classes at the Ecole de guerre which General Gambier, whom he had met during his military service, had managed to secure for him. In fact when the war ended he had the grade of officer in the Forces françaises de l'intérieur in recognition for his Resistance work in the Toulouse region, but the Vichy administration had dismissed him from the teaching profession, and he was wary of asking to be reinstated for fear of being packed off to some provincial backwater. His frenzied rush to print, some of which was purely commissioned material, can be explained in part by his financial worries, though he was finally reinstated as a teacher and appointed in Toulouse in October 1947, and then seconded to the Centre National de la Recherche Scientifique (CNRS) in 1948. Of the seven works he brought out between 1946 and 1948, six were with commercial publishers or beyond the purview of Communist publications. We should nevertheless note that although *Critique of Everyday Life* was published by Grasset, this was for distinctly political reasons. (The 'Grasset affair' was then at its height. Prosecuted for suspected collaboration, Grasset had just been acquitted by the investigative committee, but was still under attack from the Communist Party. After an unsuccessful attempt to bring in a compulsory purchase order in 1945, the Party backed a formula for control of Grasset dreamt up by René Jouglet and Francis Crémieux, who was in charge of the 'Témoins' collection, in which Lefebvre's book appeared; the aim was to take over the house on a very broad basis, 'with very "old school" Communists such as Pierre Hervé, leader writer with *L'Humanité*, but also independent personalities like Druon, Martin-Chauffier, Cassou'.)[6]

Though himself a Communist 'of the old school', Henri Lefebvre had not been integrated into the network of intellectuals 'in the service of' the Party who, with Aragon and several others as their focal point, were now dominating the stage. Indeed, according to his letters to Norbert Guterman, had this been proposed to him, he would have refused. Not that now and again he did not offer evidence of his allegiances, as for example when he took advantage of the campaign that had been mounted against 'the traitor' Nizan, his old associate of the 1920s, to settle some old scores *post mortem* in *L'Existentialisme*.[7] It is also true that he joined the editorial committee of *Nouvelle Critique*, the 'review of militant Marxism' that was founded in 1948, but, in the words of Pierre Hervé, his presence at the journal was just 'icing on the cake', an intellectual gesture rather than a genuine creative force. His contributions were few, his main articles being responses to accusations of 'Neo-Hegelianism': in March 1949 he wrote an 'Autocritique' in which he denied having used his so-warmly received lecture of 1947 to present Marxism simply as a 'contribution' to philosophy.[8] Behind all the circumlocutions, however, Henri Lefebvre held firm on three essential issues: the relations between Marxism and philosophy, those between Marxism and sociology, and the central role of the theory of alienation. Predictably, therefore, he very quickly began to fall out of favour. Between 1948 and 1957 he did not publish a single work of Marxist theory, unless one takes the view that his 'literary' studies on Diderot, Pascal, Musset and Rabelais were in fact indirect reflections on the dialectic of nature, alienation and the individual. In any case, from 1948 onwards, the Party put a stop to most of his projects.[9] *Logique formelle, logique dialectique*, which Kanapa acclaimed in 1947 as a fundamental work, was to have been the first volume in a vast general treatise on Marxist philosophy, in a consciously academic format, to be called *A la lumière du matérialisme dialectique*. The second volume, *Méthodologie des sciences*, was not only drafted, but in March 1948 it was actually printed, only to be blocked by order of the Party directorate, which was then involved in defending Lysenkoism and 'proletarian science'. Similarly, Lefebvre would not publish his *Contribution à l'esthétique*, drafted in 1949 from articles he had written in 1948, until 1953, and then it was only thanks to the subterfuge of a false quotation from Marx which was intended to reassure the Party censors.[10] As for *Critique of Everyday Life*, it was to be followed by *La Conscience privée*, but this never saw the light of day. This final failure leads us back, however, to a much earlier moment in Lefebvre's life; a moment which in turn will lead us by a series of regressions to the earliest moments of Lefebvre's life as a philosopher.

Mystification: notes for a critique of everyday life

As we have attempted to demonstrate elsewhere, Henri Lefebvre's originality, not to say marginality, lies in an unshakeable determination not only to reconcile Marxism and philosophy and to endow Marxism with philosophical status, but also to establish Marxism as critical theory, i.e. as both philosophy and supercession of philosophy.[11] We should not be fooled by the expedient eulogies of a Kanapa: *Critique of Everyday Life* is an essential document on the construction of a *critical* Marxism of this kind, and completely out of line with official arguments. If we are to believe the note in which Henri Lefebvre links the book explicitly with the ones which preceded it, it would seem to belong to a vast master plan, one whose purpose was to 'rediscover authentic Marxism', defined as 'the critical knowledge of everyday life'. He notes that the *Morceaux choisis* of Marx had drawn attention to economic fetishism, that *La Conscience mystifiée* had presented 'the entire scope' of modern man's alienation, and that *Dialectical Material-ism* had developed the notion of 'the total man', liberated from alienation and economic fetishism.[12] Far from being an a posteriori reconstruction, this note allows us to rediscover the genesis of *Critique of Everyday Life*, and even to date its birth. Although it appeared after the war, it seems to be the result of a train of thought – perhaps to call it a lengthy and determined meditation would be more accurate – which began at the start of the 1930s with the discovery in Hegel and Marx's early writings of the concept of *alienation*, and which was mapped out by the publication of several works written in collaboration with Norbert Guterman.

The plan to write a *Critique of Everyday Life* began at least as early as *La Conscience mystifiée*. The title appears among the 'Cinq essais de philos-ophie matérialiste' which are mentioned there as being 'in progress' – few of which were ever to appear.[13] But to date the birth of the *concept* of a critique of everyday life, we must go back even farther. Published in 1936, but drafted in 1933/4, *La Conscience mystifiée* reworks, sometimes verbatim, themes that had appeared as early as 1933 in the small review *Avant-Poste*. The brief history of this review, which lasted for only three numbers, is quite remarkable in its own right.[14] Pasted together in an attic room, supported by Malraux, who at that time was presiding over the *Nouvelle Revue Française*, it came out independently of Communist Party control, edited by a Communist, Henri Lefebvre, with two excluded members, Pierre Morhange and Norbert Guterman, as his assistants. A 'review of literature and criticism', it took as its main aim the analysis of Fascism as an ideological corpus – a quite daring project in view of the positions taken officially by the Party at that time. Fascism was defined less as a metamorphosis of capitalism than as a *mystification* of the revolution. Using this philosophical reading of politics as a starting point, and working closely together, Norbert Guterman and Henri Lefebvre now proceeded to develop the concept of alienation, notably in two profoundly innovative texts which were the matrices of their later contributions: 'Individu et classe' and, more particularly, 'La mystification: notes pour une critique de la vie quotidienne'.[15] Even more than *La Conscience mystifiée*, it is these texts from *Avant-Poste* to which we should return if we want to understand the confused processes by which the concept of a critique of everyday life came into being, and the extent to which it is intimately linked in Henri Lefebvre's thought with the concepts of alienation and mystification.

When Fascism calls itself revolution, 'its unreality disguises itself as the supreme reality, and tries to make true reality definitively unreal'. Starting from this extreme case of political mystification, Lefebvre and Guterman say that they intend to contribute to a 'theory of materialist knowledge by analysing, under the general heading of "Mystification", certain forms of bourgeois thinking – and even to identify a kind of general law of this thinking'. The first article attacks individualism as a mystification, and concludes with the idea that the individual consciousness cannot be explained by itself, that there is no consciousness in itself. In bourgeois society, the individual thinks he 'knows who he is', and perceives his self as 'his goods and his property'; when this illusion is shattered, the individual sinks into the anguish of 'unhappy consciousness' as he discovers the chasm which separates him from his self. Just as the subject (the individual) is *separated* from its self, the object, by becoming a commodity, becomes detached, so to speak, from itself, and the relations between men are masked by relations between objects. The second text, inspired by the Marxist theory of fetishism, leads to the idea of 'the progressive distancing of the object': alienation is not only economic, it is the inability in all areas of life to grasp and to think the *other*. It renders bourgeois thinking 'incapable of grasping the world as a totality, and distances it from the real'. The *values* it dreams up for itself make this distancing worse: 'It is when a reality has been devoured by bourgeois life that it becomes a "value".' Bourgeois life is thus alienated because it is not only *fragmented*, but *artificial*, and it is this artificiality which makes mystification possible. In *La Conscience mystifiée* Lefebvre and Guterman rework and broaden this problematic of mystification, defining the conditions for a Marxist critique of bourgeois ideology. 'How are we to proceed in order to effect a necessary rehabilitation of the mystified consciousness?' they ask. The answer is, 'by starting with the portrait of the most prosaic of men in his everyday life'.[16] The construction of the concept of mystification as a generalized process of disguise and inversion of reality derives, then, from a global reading of alienation as man's falsified relationship to the world. The sources here are well known: above all Hegel and his 'unhappy consciousness', but also Marx's early writings, in particular his 'Critique of the Hegelian Dialectic',[17] which was first published in France by *Avant-Poste*. How this led to the actual formulation of the concept of a critique of everyday life, which was only present by implication, is a more complex question.

In February 1936, a few days after their book had appeared, Lefebvre wrote to Guterman: 'Is it true what a chap who has looked through *La Conscience mystifiée* tells me: that the book just repeats what has already been said in Germany by Lukács?'[18] Indeed, how can we avoid thinking of Lukács here? It was, after all, the young pre-Marxist Lukács who first formulated the concept of *Alltäglichkeit* in 1911, in a frequently-quoted passage of *Metaphysik der Tragödie* which every Lukácsian, from Lucien Goldmann to the members of the 'Budapest School', led by Agnes Heller, would still be invoking many years later.[19] *Alltäglichkeit* designates the 'trivial life' of the human being, indistinguishable from the world of objects – the dreary, mechanical and repetitive unfolding of the everyday, which Lukács contrasts with an 'authentic life' thanks to which this being accedes to himself through the work of art, or even better, turns himself into a work of art. In 1923, as we know, *History and Class Consciousness*[20] made a radical break with this ontology of consciousness by relocating consciousness in historicity on the basis of the Marxist theory of alienation. The reversal thus effected by Lukács consisted in the transfer of the antagonism between authentic and inauthentic life to the history of class society: alienation is not simply inauthentic life, but rather that 'reification of consciousness' produced by the fetishism of commodities, which only proletarian class consciousness will be able to overcome. Here is a second sign of the curious affinity between Lefebvre and Lukács. Like *History and Class Consciousness*, *La Conscience mystifiée* offered a Marxist theory of consciousness breaking with the theory of transparency of being which had informed the philosophical tradition. Built around the theory of alienation, their Marxism is drawn from the same Hegelian source, although the concept of 'reification of consciousness', central to Lukács, is missing in Lefebvre, while the Lukács of 1923 was unaware of Marx's early writings. Moreover we must stress that when Lefebvre insisted that all consciousness is mystified, even proletarian class consciousness, he seems to be refuting aspects of the holist dream that are still present in Lukács. In this sense, his *critique* of everyday life is more of a prefiguration of Adorno's *Negative Dialectics*,[21] which, by building its critical theory on the way the negative is at work in present reality, acknowledges that this negativity embodies another 'colour' – a difference in what is possible which will allow us to stand back from the greyness of the 'already there' in order, precisely, to criticize it.

If anyone is tempted to infer from this similarity that Lukács may have influenced Lefebvre, then the letter to Guterman is material proof to the contrary, all the more so because Lefebvre, who in any case did not meet Lukács until after the war, has always insisted that he had no knowledge of *History and Class Consciousness* until after *La Conscience mystifiée* was completed. On the other hand, returning to these similarities in volume three of *Critique of Everyday Life*, he admits his debt to Heidegger, whom he mentions several times and takes to task in *La Conscience mystifiée*.[22] In *Being and Time*,[23] Heidegger also calls upon the concept of *Alltäglichkeit*, using it to characterize the inauthentic existence of *Dasein*. In so much as it is Being-with-one-another, *Dasein* stops being itself and the ascendancy of others rids it of its Being, all the more so because the other is *They*, the indeterminate, neuter *Man*:[24] in Heidegger, *Alltäglichkeit* opens the way to a loss of direction, to dereliction and disquiet. Was it then on the basis of his acquaintanceship with Heidegger – who knew Lukács's early writings, and whose *Being and Time* owes so much, as Lucien Goldmann was the first to show, to *History and Class Consciousness* and the concept of reification – that Lefebvre developed a problematic of the concept of everyday life that was unwittingly every close to Lukács'[25] If so, we must pause to examine the conditions under which, very early on, Lefebvre became acquainted with *Being and Time* via Jean Wahl, and probably even as early as 1928 via Nizan, who in 1931 published an extract from *Introduction to Metaphysics*,[26] the first Heidegger text to be translated into French, in *Bifur*. It is less a matter of attributing some kind of precedence to Henri Lefebvre in the development of the concept of a critique of everyday life, than of grasping the conditions which brought this concept forth from the heart of 'Western Marxism' in the overall context of the philosophical investigations of the 1930s.[27]

The full significance of the relationship between Lukács and Lefebvre emerges quite clearly if we think not in terms of influence but rather in terms of two parallel but chronologically separated intellectual journeys, both leading from ontology to Marxism. In *La Somme et le reste* Lefebvre recalls that his discovery of the theory of alienation was like a 'flash of inspiration': to arrive at his own concepts of mystification, of the total man and of the critique of everyday life, he had to work a reversal of the same kind as Lukács while he passed from the concept of inauthentic life to the concept of the reification of consciousness.[28] For Lefebvre, the 'path towards Marx' would lead 'from the cult of "spirit" to dialectical materialism', as he explained as early as December 1932 in a reply to Denis de Rougemont's survey of young intellectuals in the *Nouvelle Revue Française*. He writes that there had been a few young people, himself included, who believed they could refuse 'a life in which the sole act is: buying and selling, selling oneself' by following 'a call to the life of the spirit, of poetry, of eternity'. But with the onset of the economic crisis, with all its attendant perils, 'the problem was reduced to its most basic elements': 'for many people it's a question of staying alive, purely and simply of staying alive'. Thus one must 'attack the base, come to grips with the conditions of the diabolical universe of *capitalism*', and only political revolution would be capable of changing life.[29] To justify joining the Communist Party, Lefebvre challenged the very idea that Rougemont had proposed – that 'spiritual revolution' could be 'the common cause of young intellectuals' – by describing his own experiences in the 1920s. His call to revolution was both the culmination and the supersession of that romantic rejection of the world which he had espoused, in common with the avant-gardes, as a member of the *Philosophies* group.

Life is unique

'Man must be everyday, or he will not be at all': in the first pages of *Critique of Everyday Life*[30] Lefebvre uses this aphorism to show that from its starting point in everyday life the *critique* of everyday life can lead to the *revolution* of everyday life. 'Everyday man' is the man of praxis, and praxis alone will enable him to free himself from alienation and attain the concrete totality of the 'total man', at one and the same time the subject and the object of his becoming, a theme which was to become central to Lefebvre from *Dialectical Materialism* onwards (1939). In other words, the only means of acceding to totality is via revolution. This quest for totality, which was to lead Lefebvre from 'philosophical revolution' to Marxism, is none other than the quest for a theoretical method capable of reconciling thought and life, of changing life completely, of producing one's life as one creates a *work*. So, when Lefebvre defines his critique of everyday life as the 'revolutionary' way, as opposed both to the 'poetic' way embodied by the Surrealists and to the Heideggerian-style 'metaphysical' way, he is merely describing the various ups and downs within the *Philosophies* group which led him to effect his own 'reversal' of ontology and Marxism.

The first stage of this reversal was via the avant-garde. When Lefebvre accused the Surrealists of not having followed their radical ideas through to their logical conclusion, of having offered a merely 'magical' critique of the everyday, he was distancing himself from his own experiences as an avant-gardist. When in 1924, in the review *Philosophies*, Henri Lefebvre took his first steps as a philosopher alongside Pierre Morhange, Norbert Guterman and Georges Politzer, it was in the name of 'philosophical revolution'. This is not the place to give a detailed account of the history of the *Philosophies* group, of its call for a 'new mysticism' and its subsequent progressive radicalization which was to end in its fleeting rapprochement with the Surrealists, sealed in the summer of 1925 by the joint manifesto *La Révolution d'abord et toujours*.[31] For a brief moment the avant-gardes thought it would be possible to reconcile their 'revolt of the spirit' – a total revolt against the logos, the world, existing reality – with the political revolt embodied by the Communist Party. We all know Breton's famous formula: 'Marx said "Change the world", Rimbaud said "Change life": for us these two watchwords are one.' In the Surrealist experience, in the revolt of the poetic against 'the prose of the world', there is the idea that subverting the everyday will open the way to what, on its very first page, the *Manifesto of Surrealism* called *real* life. But at the same time, the modern *merveilleux*, automatic writing, the call on the unconscious and on objective chance, were being reduced to mere literary techniques. It is in this light that we must see the virulent exordium in *Critique of Everyday Life*:

> The attack on life led by poetry is just one episode, and literature is only the active-service unit of a much larger army. Like the poets, philosophers are wavering between the familiar, the trivial, the 'inauthentic', and the anguishing, the mysterious – between bourgeois reality and mystical unreality – and are pushing human reality to one side.[32]

Concord between the avant-gardes was short-lived and the choice between Marx and Rimbaud had to be made. But, stung by the initial politicization of 1925, the young *philosophes* went in the opposite direction to that of the Surrealists, who placed themselves 'in the service of the revolution' before breaking completely with the Communist Party. Between 1926 and 1927 *Philosophies* was replaced by the review *L'Esprit*, and this marked a phase of political withdrawal and sidetracking into philosophical stances that Lefebvre himself was to refer to as 'pre-existentialist'. Total revolt was replaced by the 'return to the concrete'. Only the 'return to the concrete' could reconcile thought and life, because life itself must be defined as the unity of thought and action. 'Life is unique', proclaimed the young *philosophes*, using a watchword conjured up by Pierre Morhange. They found father-figures in Spinoza, Schelling and Kierkegaard, and their guru in Jean Wahl, who published extracts from his *Malheur de la conscience dans la philosophie de Hegel* in *L'Esprit*.[33] As we have already mentioned, when Lefebvre read Hegel and discovered the theory of alienation as interpreted by Heidegger (rather than discovering Heidegger as such), it was thanks to Jean Wahl. In the 'Hegel debate' which flared up during the 1930s in France the stakes were considerable, for it was in opposition to the successful Kierkegaardian and Heideggerian Hegel introduced by the phenomenological reading of Kojève and Jean Wahl that Lefebvre vainly launched his logical and dialectical Hegel. We should note that the same refusal of both a purely phenomenological attitude towards consciousness and of Heideggerian pessimism was to power Lefebvre's post-war challenge to existentialism. In any event the 'pre-existentialist' sidetrack was curiously decisive in the encounter with Marxism, which was to culminate in Lefebvre and several members of the *Philosophies* group joining the Communist Party in 1928. Although the phase of ideological Stalinization was in full spate, the group was still impregnated with the paradoxical illusion that an autonomous theoretical development was feasible, and their final experiment was *La Revue marxiste*, which was launched in 1929, only to be immediately crushed in grotesque circumstances by the brutal intervention of the Party.[34]

In a sense it might be said that Lefebvre's plan for a critique of everyday life is the Marxianization of the slogan 'Life is unique'. It was only in 1928–29, after a long but vain search in the *philosophy of consciousness*, that Lefebvre felt that through the theory of alienation and in dialectical *method* he had discovered how to link the categories of unity, totality and reality. 'We intend to return primacy in consciousness to the object as such. The first article of our thought completely and deliberately reintegrates the external world, the concrete world, present, perceived as itself, into our consciousness.' From a text on the 'new mysticism', which in 1925 was taken as the group's first philosophical manifesto, to the affirmation in an article written in 1926 that 'to represent being to oneself is to cease to be', all the articles Lefebvre published in *Philosophies* and *L'Esprit* were – to use the title of the first of them – just so many 'Fragments of a philosophy of consciousness'.[35] In these texts, the stated aim of which was to tackle the aporias of traditional philosophy – being and representation, subject and object – when Lefebvre defined consciousness as an 'act' and as a 'relation' to the other qua other, he was in effect saying that consciousness was consciousness of the other. By recognizing the other as a mixture of presence and absence, the relation between 'the same and the other' as identity in difference and difference in identity, consciousness becomes the means of acceding to totality, i.e. to Spirit, which 'reunites and concentrates the diversity spread out through space'.[36] Lefebvre's quest for the totality, which took him as far as Schelling, had in fact begun well before he joined the *Philosophies* group, and the fragments he published were from a lengthy early manuscript, 'Esquisse d'une philosophie de la conscience', which constitutes not so much the matrix as the prehistory of his critique of everyday life. We must go back to this prehistory, which even predates the impact which the Blondelian philosophy of action was to make on him, in order to witness the emergence, from the very depths of his initial Christian experience, of the themes of unity and totality. In the beginning was his quest for *origins*: right from the start he saw the mysterious and the holy as something deeply human, and it was only after arduously searching for this original unity, forever lost, in religion and in philosophy that Lefebvre realized that it could be found in Marxist *supersession*. In the theme of 'philosophical revolution' of 1925, in the idea he took from Schelling that the philosopher lives 'not by observing his life but by producing it', we can already see the underpinnings of the 'realization' of philosophy as promised by Marxism. It was because he failed in his quest for a lost totality that Lefebvre was able to turn his attention to 'the total man'; but this failure also explains why his very definition of alienation has antecedents in the Christian thematic of the Fall and of original sin (profoundly transformed, needless to say).

'O Church, O Holy Church, when I finally managed to escape from your control I asked myself where your power came from.'[37] This is the moment to take a long look at what is certainly the most spellbinding chapter in *Critique of Everyday Life*, the enigmatic 'Notes Written One Sunday in the French Countryside', where Lefebvre describes in such detail and with such emotion the little church near Navarrenx (his 'native village'), in which the fundamental gestures of the Christian mystery are performed. The chapter closes, however, with the assertion that only Marxist method will enable us to understand these 'secrets' – these obscure aspects of the 'social mystery' and of history. He says that we can travel back in our minds to the origins of our civilization by studying the communal traditions which have persisted up to the present day in rural life. In his analysis of peasant festivals, he emphasizes that 'festivals contrasted violently with everyday life, *but they were not separate from it*'.[38] In this chapter, which is very similar to a long passage in *La Conscience mystifiée* about *lack of differentiation* in primitive societies, he defines traditional everyday life in a general way as based on non-separation, on the absence of differentiation in the cosmic order which formerly bound man and nature together. Thus *alienation* appears as a *historical* process of down-grading, of loss of this ancient 'human plenitude', by virtue of a dual movement of separation and abstraction: on the one hand, a separation of the social and the human, culminating in the division of labour and specialization of spheres of human activity; on the other hand, an increasing abstraction of human actions stripped of their living substance in favour of signs and symbols. Alienation thus leads to the impoverishment, to the 'despoliation' of everyday life; and yet for Lefebvre everyday life is not reduced to the inauthenticity of *Alltäglichkeit*, as in Heidegger or Lukács. It is not simply a residuum, or rather, its residual aspect bespeaks one or several strata of deeper meanings; it is both a parody of lost plenitude and the last remaining vestige of that plenitude. Even if Lefebvre's distinction between 'everyday life' and 'the everyday' only appears later, and is never fully developed, his critique of everyday life is a dual reading, at once a rejection of the inauthentic and the alienated, and an unearthing of the human which still lies buried therein. These 'Notes Written One Sunday in the French Countryside' may be set alongside Lefebvre's commentary on a passage from a book by Marc Bloch:

> But we are unable to seize the human facts. We fail to see them where they are, namely in humble, familiar, everyday objects: the shape of fields, of ploughs. Our search for the human takes us too far, too 'deep', we seek it in the clouds or in mysteries, whereas it is waiting for us, besieging us on all sides.[39]

This *archeological* mode of reading the everyday is also what characterizes Lefebvre's specifically sociological aims, and the consequences of this reach much farther than *Critique of Everyday Life*.

Everyday Life in the Modern World

If it was essential to recall the philosophical foundations, not to say the metaphysical prehistory, of *Critique of Everyday Life*, we should not lose sight of the fact that the book was intended first and foremost as a contribution to sociology, even if the originality of Lefebvre's sociology lies precisely in its philosophical roots. True, Lefebvre has a nostalgia for original *community*, but this is not so much the basis for his Communism as the inspiration for his early, partly empirical, research into rural sociology. We could go back as far as his youth, when while walking in the Pyrenees he came across some strange crosses with discs on them, and thought he had discovered the 'sun crucified', a primitive solar myth overlain by Christianity.[40] Above all, *Critique of Everyday Life* is contemporaneous of the research on the valley of Campan and agro-pastoral communities on which he was to base his doctoral thesis a few years later; he had begun this during the war, somewhat by chance, when he was hiding out in the Pyrenees, and spent his time rummaging through abandoned municipal archives. The conscious decision to study rural sociology dates, however, from 1948, when he joined the Centre National de la Recherche Scientifique (CNRS). Even if, apart from his doctorate in 1954 and a couple of articles, Lefebvre has not completed the ambitious projects he set himself in this sphere – like the *Traité de sociologie rurale* which was mysteriously stolen from a car, or the *Histoire rurale de la France* he was to have written in collaboration with Albert Soboul – the choice of sociology undoubtedly had a strategic significance.[41]

Lefebvre's critique of everyday life took up arms on two fronts: the first aim was to convince Marxists – at a moment when Zhdanovism was in full spate – of the value of an analysis of superstructures based on the concept of alienation; the second, to demonstrate to philosophers that the trivial should not be exempt from philosophical scrutiny. 'In so far as the science of man exists, it finds its material in the "trivial", the everyday.'[42] If the choice of the sociological field was strategic, this was above all because it was made at a moment when the entire range of the social sciences was witnessing a veritable explosion, whether in the domains of anthropology, demography and sociology, or in the shape of the revival of history by the history of 'mentalities'. A few key dates should suffice to prove this. The period between 1945 and 1949 saw the publication of major works by Friedmann, Dumézil and Bataille, as well as Braudel's *The Mediterranean* and Lévi-Strauss's *The Elementary Structures of Kinship*.[43] During the same period the institutions which were to assure the hegemony of this revival were set in place: the Institut Nationale des Études Démographiques and its review *Population*; the Centre d'Études Sociologiques at the CNRS, where Gurvitch produced the *Cahiers internationaux de sociologie*; and Section VI of the Ecole Pratique des Hautes Etudes, founded by Lucien Febvre, who, significantly, had just renamed his journal *Annales* (*Economies, Sociétés, Civilisations*). This explosion has been described as a 'change of paradigm in the social sciences' – even as a *critical* paradigm, and it is true that the social sciences were mounting a critique of speculative philosophy and of its abstract categories, thus making reflection on the destitution of the subject a possibility. At the same time they were leaning, if not to a directly political critique, then at least to a critique of society and history which sought to tear the veil from concealed or unconscious structures: *longue durée* economic cycles, collective psychology, the mythic and the symbolic. It is true that Lefebvre would launch an extremely violent attack on most of these trends in 1953 – the only moment in his career when opportunism led him to pay his political dues in this fashion – and denounced the 'police-force sociology' of the likes of Friedmann and Varagnac. It is a murky episode, but it should not deflect us from the fact that from Friedmann, whom he knew at the time of the *Philosophies* group, to Gurvitch, who secured him his place at the CNRS, Lefebvre was partly involved in the network which was to guarantee the expansion of the social sciences right up until the 1960s.[44]

But these French post-war years – the 'Trente Glorieuses' – were also the context for the impact of new technology and the consumer society as well as for the gradual disappearance of that rural world which had still been so dominant in the years between the wars. The period when André Varagnac was puzzling over traditional civilization and the spiritual world we have lost, when Gurvitch was sending his teams of sociologists out to investigate rural communities or religious behaviour, also saw the appearance of the first 4 CV, the first issue of the magazine *Elle*, the first Cannes Film Festival. Here we should compare the 'Notes Written One Sunday in the French Countryside' with 'Notes sur la ville nouvelle (Mourenx)' in *Introduction à la modernité*. When Henri Lefebvre moved from rural sociology to urban sociology, his thinking on the everyday was to become inseparable from his thinking about modernity. As he wrote in 1968 in *Everyday Life in the Modern World*, 'the quotidian and the modern mark and mask, legitimate and counterbalance each other. Today the universal quotidian ... is the verso of modernity, the spirit of our time'.[45] If modernity is the brilliant, even gaudy, side of the new, the everyday is its insignificant side, 'what is humble and solid, what is taken for granted and that of which all the parts follow each other in such a regular, unvarying succession that those concerned have no call to question its sequence'.[46] In other words, it is modernity which has *despoiled* the everyday life of former times, which never appeared save in its metamorphoses, as in *festival*, which embodied a genuine 'auto-critique' of the everyday; it is modernity which has caused everyday life to degenerate into 'the everyday'. Lefebvre's conception of modernity is both complex and contradictory, inscribed like Marx's in historical time, leading to a philosophy of progress, and, like Baudelaire's and Nietzsche's, anti-nomic to historical time, 'untimely' vis-à-vis its own present moment, leading to death and to the tragic. Modernity is the movement towards the new, the deployment of technology and rationality (which Lefebvre calls 'modernism'), but it is also the absence of any real transformation of social relations, and leads from the human towards the inhuman, towards barbarity. For Henri Lefebvre modernity and the everyday are historical categories, and if they cannot be dated precisely, at least they can be located at a moment of fundamental historical trauma: the failure of revolution, which was completed, at the very moment of the world crisis, by the advent of Stalinism and Fascism. With this failure of the world revolution, the moment of philosophy's 'realization' was gone, and it was modernity which, *in its own way*, was to complete the tasks that the revolution had been unable to bring to fruition; it was modernity that took on the responsibility of 'transforming the world' and 'changing life'.

Seen in this light, *Critique of Everyday Life* opens up yet another avenue, one that leads beyond rural sociology, beyond urban sociology, and beyond Lefebvre's later thinking on the production of space: the theme of the production of the everyday, of revolution as the revolution of everyday life. Producing the everyday, i.e. producing one's life like a work, is a thematic which in the 1960s led to Lefebvre's involvement with radical protest. In fact we need perhaps to go back here to 1948, when the Cobra group was founded, and to Constant, whose manifesto for an architecture of situations was explicitly inspired by *Critique of Everyday Life*. But above all we must offer some account of Lefebvre's relations with the situationist movement. They date back at least as far as the Research Group on Everyday Life which he organized at the Centre d'Etudes Sociologiques and, in particular, to the 'Department of Applied Sociology' which he created as a lecturer at Strasbourg University in 1961, and which in turn became the model for his Institute of Sociology at Nanterre in 1965. Before their brutal break with Lefebvre, the situationists, and first and foremost Guy Debord, acknowledged their debt to him; more precisely, they continued a dialogue with him from 1958 until the break in 1963. Conversely, the second volume of *Critique of Everyday Life*, *Fondements d'une sociologie de la quotidienneté*, in 1961, and equally his *Everyday Life in the Modern World* in 1968, were stimulated by the debate with the situationists. Subsequently Lefebvre and the situationists accused each other of plagiarism. Let us simply note the parallelism of their positions on certain crucial points, all present either explicitly or in embryo in *Critique of Everyday Life*. Most important among them is the idea that the use of everyday life is governed by the rule of scarcity, i.e. that it was detached from historicity at the height of the period of industrialization and accumulation. As Debord put it, 'everyday life is literally "colonized"' – a theme taken up again in the situationists' *De la misère en milieu étudiant*. This leads to the call for revolution in terms of 'revolutions in individual everyday life', a notion which is at the very origins of the theory of situations, and which subtends the identification of festival and revolution in Lefebvre's *Proclamation de la Commune* of 1965. In this book, which is the one the situationists accuse of plagiarizing their own writings, the idea that festival, like revolution, marks both a break in everyday life and a rehabilitation of the everyday, stems directly from *Critique of Everyday Life*.[47]

Of course it is impossible to deny Lefebvre's impact on the ideology of May 1968 itself, and it is astonishing that in France at least most studies should have underestimated Lefebvre's themes in favour of Marcuse or other even more exotic thinkers. Anglo-Saxon scholarship has concentrated on Lefebvre in a more serious and more sustained manner. We have written elsewhere of how the work of Perry Anderson, Mark Poster, Michael Kelly, etc., has restored Lefebvre to his rightful place among the great Marxist theoreticians of the twentieth century. We should mention, however, that it was in Germany during the 1970s that the debate on everyday life which sprang up in the context of the 'alternative' movement was the most firmly rooted in Henri Lefebvre's thought.[48] So much so that one might even begin making links with Habermas's distinction between *System* (specialized culture controlled by experts), for example, and *Lebenswelt* (lived experience and everyday life). Thus it becomes clear why we cannot fix our reading of *Critique of Everyday Life* in the context of 1947: it is not only an essential marker in Henri Lefebvre's philosophical and political evolution, but also one of the crossroads in the reorganization of the intellectual field of the second half of the twentieth century.

CNRS, Paris, March 1991

Foreword to the Second Edition

I In Retrospect

As it stands, this book[1] did not strictly speaking offer a new interpretation of Marxism. The following quotation from Lenin would have made an appropriate epigraph:

> The whole point, however, is that Marx ... did not confine himself to 'economic theory' in the ordinary sense of the term, that, while *explaining* the structure and the development of the given formation of society *exclusively* through production relations ... [he] clothed the skeleton in flesh and blood. The reason *Capital* has enjoyed such tremendous success is that this book by a 'German economist' showed the whole capitalist social formation to the reader as a living thing – with its everyday aspects ...[2]

In this very important text, Lenin shows that Marx created scientific *sociology*. He expressed similar ideas in many other places in his writings:

> In his *Capital*, Marx first analyses the simplest, most ordinary and fundamental, most common and everyday *relation* of bourgeois (commodity) society, a relation encountered billions of times, viz. the exchange of commodities. In this very simple phenomenon ... analysis reveals *all* the contradictions (or the germs of *all* the contradictions) of modern society.[3]

The fact remains that the *Critique of Everyday Life* was built entirely around a concept which Lenin had left aside or neglected, the concept of *alienation*.

The fact also remains that this book developed a generally neglected aspect of Marxism, the specifically *sociological* aspect.

When it appeared, the book was inadequately substantiated on both the philosophical and the sociological level. In the first place, it should have formulated and attempted to resolve the problem posed by the concept of alienation. It should also have explained what a Marxist sociology considered as a specific science could be (as method and object) in its relation with the other sciences (political economy, history, etc.) as well as with historical and dialectical materialism.

The fact is, however, that ten years ago these various problems were not sufficiently ripe. It was more or less impossible to formulate them correctly, let alone resolve them.[4]

Today we are only just beginning to glimpse the complexity of the questions the theory of alienation poses. These questions fall into several categories. *Historically*, we must discover what role this concept played in the development of Marxism, how (in his early writings) Marx took it from Hegel and Feuerbach, how he transformed and redirected it, and at what date. Thus it is appropriate to follow this transformation through the texts, and this means that a rigorous examination of the early writings, and notably of the celebrated *1844 Manuscripts*, is required.[5] *Theoretically*, we must determine what becomes of the *philosophical* concept of alienation in Marx's scientific and political works, notably in *Capital*, and understand whether the economic theory of fetishism is truly an extension of the philosophical theory of alienation onto an objective (scientific) level.[6]

Finally, the problem *philosophically* is of knowing what meaning and (critical or constructive) importance should be given at the present moment to the concept of alienation. To what extent should a philosopher take it up again, perhaps in a modified form, and put it at the centre of his thinking? This problem cannot be separated from the others although it can be distinguished from them. If it were true, as certain Marxists argue, that Marxism as such radically rejects earlier concepts, including those which helped to develop it – so that there was an absolute caesura in human thought at the moment of Marxism's emergence, and in Marxism at the moment when Marx became conscious of his doctrine – the problem of what the concept of alienation means now would not even arise. To take this position implies further positions, notably that Marxism is a completed system, and that philosophy's role and function are at an end. Such arguments must be deemed dogmatic and false.

Such vast and difficult questions had to ripen before they could be posed.

In particular it had to be possible to ask the question: 'Is alienation disappearing in socialist society? In the USSR or the countries which are constructing socialism, are there not contradictions indicative of new – or renewed – forms of economic, ideological and political alienation?'

As far as sociology as a specific science is concerned, there have been many moments of uncertainty to live through. The question of whether the Stalinist interpretation of Marxism was not mutilating it and depriving it of one of its dimensions has had to be faced; as has that of whether the Marxist notion of *socio-economic formation*[7] is not richer and more complex – since it involves the sociological study of social relations – than the currently favoured concepts of (economic) base and (ideological and political) superstructures.

The fact that these questions were absent from its argument explains to a certain extent the way the book was received when it was first published. What was the official, academic response? Utter silence. At that moment, in 1946, French philosophy had suffered a series of shocks from which it was only slowly recovering. The war and the Occupation had killed off several important currents of thought, notably Bergsonian anti-intellectualism, compromised by a vague relationship with German irrationalism, and Léon Brunschvicg's intellectualism,[8] which was poorly equipped to resolve the new problems. The generation of Hegelians[9] and existentialists was on the rise. But there were those who, though perfectly willing to respect and accept the notion of alienation on a speculative level, were probably less prepared to see it soiled by confrontation with actual human reality, with everyday life.[10]

So the professional philosophers generally ignored the book; for – starting with its title – it entailed relinquishing the traditional image of the philosopher as master and ruler of existence, witness and judge of life *from the outside*, enthroned above the masses, above the moments lost in triviality, 'distinguished' by an attitude and a distance. (There is nothing really exaggerated about these metaphors. The distance is called 'spiritual life' and the philosopher's attitude is called contemplation, detachment, 'epoche',[11] parenthesizing, etc.)

What about Marxism? If the traditional philosophers, still saturated with pure speculative thought or attracted by it, gave the book a cool reception, so did the Marxists.

In the enthusiasm of the Liberation, it was hoped that soon life would be changed and the world transformed. More than that: life had already been changed; the peoples were on the move, the masses were in a ferment. Their movement was causing new values to 'rise to the surface'. What was the point of analysing bourgeois everyday life, the style (or absence of style) imposed by the dominant class? What was the point of a philosophical or sociological critique? The weapon of criticism was about to be replaced, had already been replaced, by the criticism of weapons. In France, in the rest of the world, the proletariat was no longer an oppressed class. It was imposing itself on the nations as the ruling class. To talk about alienation was no longer possible, no longer permissible. The concept was just as outdated in France as it was in the USSR, in countries where socialism was on the march, or where the rumble of revolution could already be heard.

Thinking people were obsessed with the political drama. Rightly so. But they were forgetting that although the political drama was being acted out or decided in the higher spheres – the State, parliament, leaders, policies – it still had a 'base' in matters relating to food, rationing, wages, the organization or reorganization of labour. A humble, everyday 'base'. Therefore many Marxists saw criticism of everyday life as useless and antiquated; they perceived it as a reworking of an old-fashioned, exhausted critique of bourgeois society, little more than a critique of triviality – therefore a trivial critique.

For this reason philosophers today are experiencing difficulties of a kind unknown to their predecessors. Great or small, profound or superficial, their lives have lost that simplicity and elegance of line they attribute (fictitiously, no doubt) to the lives of their illustrious models. Philosophers and philosophy can no longer be isolated, disguised, hidden. And this is precisely because everyday life is the supreme court where wisdom, knowledge and power are brought to judgement.

II   What Has Changed in the Last Ten Years?

Under these circumstances, what is the point – after ten years of interruption – of resuming this task?

Firstly, during these years a certain number of young intellectuals have read the book with interest – with passion. Their expressions of appreciation have alleviated any feelings of bitterness the author may have had about the coolness of the book's 'official' reception.

But that is not all. During the last ten years the development of research in the social sciences has shown that the book was on target, that its point of view is well-founded. Problems of everyday life and studies of everyday life have become increasingly important in the minds of historians, ethnographers, philosophers, sociologists, as well as of writers, artists and journalists. Our very best informed and most 'modern' publications – daily and weekly newspapers, reviews – have started columns dealing with everyday life. There has been a proliferation of books about everyday life, and bit by bit a method to confront everyday life with ideas apparently far removed from it, such as myths, ceremonies, works of art, is being developed.[12]

For the historian of a specific period, for the ethnographer, for the sociologist studying a society or a group, the fundamental question would be to grasp a certain quality, difficult to define and yet essential and concrete, something that 'just a quarter-of-an-hour alone' with a man from a distant or extinct culture would reveal to us.[13]

Let us consider some areas very remote from the social sciences. Recently I read an article[14] which was something of a manifesto or policy statement for the idea that the modern theatre can only be 'a place where everyday life attains its highest degree of intensity; where the words and gestures of everyday life at last take on meaning'. A Soviet critic has made the same assertion about Chekhov's theatre: 'He [Chekhov] considers that theatre ought to represent everyday life'.[15]

We shall return to this idea.

Again, the monumental volume of *L'Encyclopédie française* devoted to *Everyday Life* was published recently. It is a considerable piece of work,[16] but one in which the descriptive and the technological points of view push the *critical* point of view into the background, and even obliterate it.

Indisputably the last few years have witnessed the application of the most modern of techniques to the way everyday life is organized, that is to say, to a sector which up until now has been paid scant attention. The way in which everyday life lags behind what is technically possible is and should be one of the themes of the *Critique of Everyday Life*. How could this theme possibly have lost its foundation or its meaning?

In *L'Express* of 8 June 1956 (p. 21) the following information was given on the 'interesting novelties' which its special New York correspondent had noticed, and which 'will inevitably end up coming to France':

> Kitchens are becoming less like kitchens and more like works of art ... The latest technique is the electronic oven.... The intercom (a system of loudspeakers linking every room) is becoming a standard piece of equipment in the home, while everyone is talking about a personalized little television network which will enable the lady of the house to attend to her chores while keeping an eye on the children playing in another room or in the garden ... The remarkable ubiquity of 'do it itself' [sic], the latest craze for the American husband ... includes all the household gadgets that go with it ... the latest development in the household industry? Swimming pools, which the manufacturers say they are about to mass-market ... Popular requirements as far as houses are concerned: at least seven rooms, with two bathrooms ...

In the next column, 'Madame Express' informs anyone who was unaware of it that:

> a woman needs cast-iron will-power to stop her hairdresser from cutting her hair short. Nothing is more persuasive than a hairdresser who has made his mind up. And they have some powerful allies: cover-girls, actresses, all the women for whom money is no problem and whose pictures, distributed every day, are more persuasive than any words could be ...

The remarkable way in which modern techniques have penetrated everyday life has thus introduced into this backward sector *the uneven development* which characterizes every aspect of our era. Manifestations of the brilliant advances in the 'ideal home' constitute sociological facts of the first importance, but they must not be allowed to conceal the contradictory character of the real social process beneath an accumulation of technological detail. These advances, along with their consequences, are provoking new structural conflicts within the concrete life of society. The same period which has witnessed a breathtaking development in the application of techniques of everyday life has also witnessed the no-less-breathtaking degradation of everyday life for large masses of human beings. All around us, in France, in Paris itself, there are hundreds of thousands of children, youngsters, students, young couples, single people, families, living in conditions undreamed-of by anyone who does not bring a sociologist's interest to bear:[17] furnished rooms (increasingly expensive and squalid), slums, overcrowded flats, attic rooms, etc.

The deterioration of the conditions of existence is spreading to a great many French rural areas (notably in the southern half of the country), to a large proportion of craftsmen, small shopkeepers and the working class.

Agreed, it is not unusual to find peasants owning electric cookers, but the houses they live in are still dilapidated; they manage to buy gadgets, but cannot afford to repair their houses, and even less to modernize their farms. In other words, the latter are given up for the sake of the former. In the same way quite a large number of working-class couples have a washing machine, a television set, or a car, but they have generally sacrificed something else for these gadgets (having a baby, for example). In this way problems of choosing what to buy – or problems associated with hire-purchase, etc. – are posed within working-class families, and these problems modify everyday life.[18] That relatively poor peasants, or workers, should buy television sets proves the existence of a new *social need*. The fact is remarkable. But it does not tell us the size or the extent of this need, nor the extent to which it is satisfied. Nor does it prove that this need has not been satisfied to the detriment of another.

Far from suppressing criticism of everyday life, modern technical progress *realizes it*. This technicity replaces the criticism of life through dreams, or ideas, or poetry, or those activities which rise above the everyday, by the critique of everyday life from within: the critique which everyday life makes of itself, the critique of the real by the possible and of one aspect of life by another. Compared with lower or degraded standards of living, everyday life with all the superior mod cons takes on the distance and remoteness and familiar strangeness of a dream. The display of luxury to be seen in so many films, most of them mediocre, takes on an almost fascinating character, and the spectator is uprooted from his everyday world by an everyday world *other* than his own. Escape into this illusory but present everyday world, the fascination of ordinary objects which scream wealth, the seductive powers of the apparently profound lives led by the men and women who move among these objects, all this explains the momentary success these films enjoy.

Happily, contemporary cinema and theatre have other works to offer which reveal a truth about everyday life.

III   On Charlie Chaplin, Bertolt Brecht and Some Others

It is not Chaplin's clowning contortions and funny faces that make people burst out laughing. From his very first films, he stood out from such other film comedians as Fatty Arbuckle and Harold Lloyd. The secret of his comic powers lies not in his body, but in the relation of this body to something else: a social relation with the material world and the social world. Naïve, physically adept but spiritually innocent, Chaplin arrives in a complicated and sophisticated universe of people and things with fixed patterns of behaviour (where people behave like things – and in conjunction with things). The clown's physical suppleness, and his concomitant ability to adapt himself and his gestures with an almost animal rapidity, become humanized as they give way to an extreme awkwardness which both proves and signifies his naïvety. However, this awkwardness is never permanent; the original situation is reinstated; the clown has his revenge, he defeats the hostile objects – and the hostile people – only to fall back into momentary disarray. Hence visually comic moments when he cannot adapt are followed by moments of victory when he can, and this stops the 'mime–audience' relationship from breaking down, producing fresh gusts of laughter and assuring that the humour never becomes awkward or embarrassing. Like pleasure, like harmony in music, laughter is stimulated by a series of resolved tensions, in which moments of relaxation are followed by even higher tensions.

The point of departure for the 'vis comica' peculiar to Chaplin is therefore the simplicity of a child, a primitive and a wonderfully gifted barbarian, suddenly plunged (as we all are at every moment) into an everyday life that is inflexible and bristling with ever-new difficulties, some foreseeable, others not. In his first films Chaplin takes up battle – a duel which is always different and yet always the same – with objects, everyday objects: an umbrella, a deckchair, a motorbike, a banana skin ... Always surprised, always delighted by the strangeness and richness of things, always awkward when faced with ritualized practices (essential behaviour, necessary conditioning), Chaplin captures our own attitude towards these trivial things, and before our very eyes. He makes it appear suddenly amazing, dramatic and joyful. He comes as a stranger into the familiar world, he wends his way through it, not without wreaking joyful damage. Suddenly he disorientates us, but only to show us what we are when faced with objects; and these objects become suddenly alien, the familiar is no longer familiar (as for example when we arrive in a hotel room, or a furnished house, and trip over the furniture, and struggle to get the coffee grinder to work). But via this deviation through disorientation and strangeness, Chaplin reconciles us on a higher level, with ourselves, with things and with the humanized world of things.

Thus the essence of this humour is not to be found in pity, nor even in strangeness (alienation), but on the contrary in a triumph which is forever being renewed and forever threatened. The dog, the pretty girl, the child, are not cinematic props, but elements necessary to the more or less complete final victory.

Therefore Chaplin's first films may be seen as offering a critique of everyday life: a critique in action, a basically optimistic critique, with the living, human unity of its two faces, the negative and the positive. Hence its 'success'.

In Chaplin's feature films, the critique becomes broader, taking on a higher meaning. They confront the established (bourgeois) world and its vain attempts to complete itself and close itself off, not with another world but with a *type*. This type (a down-and-out) is the emanation of that other world, its expression, its internal necessity, its essence externalized and yet still internal (to put it abstractly and speculatively, which after all is how Marx expressed his discovery of the proletariat as a class).

As necessarily as it produces machines and men-machines, the bourgeois world produces deviants. It produces the Tramp, its *reverse image*. The relation between the Tramp and the bourgeois order is different to the relation 'proletariat–bourgeoisie'. In particular it is more immediate, more physical, relying less on concepts and demands than on images.

By its false and illusory and euphoric and presumptuous insistence upon the self, the 'free world' immediately creates its pure negative image. Thus the Tramp-figure contains certain characteristics of the image Marx presents of the proletariat in his philosophical writings: the pure alienation of man and the human which is revealed as being more deeply human than the things it negates – negativity forced by its essence to destroy the society to which at one and the same time it belongs and does not belong. And yet the 'positivity' of the proletariat, its historic mission, is not accomplished on the philosophical or aesthetic level; it is accomplished politically, and philosophical criticism becomes political criticism and action ... In the type and the 'myth' presented by Chaplin, criticism is not separable from the physical image immediately present on the screen. If therefore it remains limited, it is nevertheless directly accessible to the masses; it does not lead to revolutionary action or political consciousness, and yet it uses laughter to stir up the masses profoundly. Thus in his best films Chaplin's humour takes on an epic dimension which comes from this deep meaning. 'The image of alienated man, he reveals alienation by dishonouring it.'[19]

Here for the first time we encounter a complex problem, both aesthetic and ethical, that of the *reverse image*: an image of everyday reality, taken in its totality or as a fragment, reflecting that reality in all its depth *through* people, ideas and things which are apparently quite different from everyday experience, and therefore exceptional, deviant, abnormal.[20]

The type created by Chaplin achieves universality by means of extremely precise elements: the hat, the walking stick and the trousers, all taken from London's petty bourgeoisie. The transition from the mime to the Type marks a date and an expansion in Chaplin's work, an expansion within the work itself and one made possible by that work alone; suddenly he puts his own previously constructed figure (or image) at the centre of his films. In a very strong sense, he puts himself on the stage; as a result, a new development takes place.

Thus the critique of everyday life takes the form of a living, dialectical pair: on the one hand, 'modern times' (with everything they entail: bourgeoisie, capitalism, techniques and technicity, etc.), and on the other, the Tramp. The relation between them is not a simple one. In a fiction truer than reality as it is immediately given, they go on producing and destroying one another ceaselessly. In this way the comical produces the tragic, the tragic destroys the comical, and vice versa; cruelty is never absent from the clowning; the setting for the clowning is constantly being broadened: the city, the factory, Fascism, capitalist society in its entirety. But is the comedy defined by its underlying tragedy, or by its victory over the tragic? It is in the spectator personally that Charlie Chaplin constantly manages to unite these two ever-present and conflicting aspects, the tragic and the comical; laughter always manages to break through; and like the laughter of Rabelais, Swift and Molière (i.e. the laughter of their readers or audiences) it denies, destroys, liberates. Suffering itself is denied, and this denial is put on display. In this fictitious negation we reach the limits of art. On leaving the darkness of the cinema, we rediscover the same world as before, it closes round us again. And yet the comic event has taken place, and we feel decontaminated, returned to normality, purified somehow, and stronger.

To sum up, our analysis has seen Chaplin as a *type* rather than a *myth*, based on general characteristics (poor but full of vitality – weak but strong – ruthlessly seeking money, work, prestige, but also love and happiness). How can an image which so directly reveals what is significant about the so-called 'modern man' be called *mythical*?

In any case the interesting thing here is not a discussion of the Chaplin 'myth' and the mythical character of the image of life he presents; it is the very fact that an image with its roots deep in everyday life can be seen as *mythical*, and that the word 'myth' can be used to describe it.

Might this illusion be significant on a more general level? The most extraordinary things are also the most everyday; the strangest things are often the most trivial, and the current notion of the 'mythical' is an illusory reflection of this fact. Once separated from its context, i.e. from how it is interpreted and from the things which reinforce it while at the same time making it bearable – once presented in all its triviality, i.e. in all that makes it trivial, suffocating, oppressive – the trivial becomes extraordinary, and the habitual becomes 'mythical'. In the same way, a humble plant taken from the soil and from the plants around it, seen up close, becomes something marvellous. But then, once images like this have been separated from their everyday context, it becomes very difficult to articulate them in a way which will present their essential everyday quality. This is the secret of talents like Fellini's (*La Strada*) or that of the directors of *Salt of the Earth*,[21] and (perhaps) it offers a potential way ahead for realism . . .[22]

Brecht – that great man of the theatre who recently passed away – tried to renew realism by proposing a revolutionary formula: *epic* theatre.

This formula has provoked more than one misunderstanding. On reading those words – in a country whose culture is traditionally referred to as 'humanist' – it is easy to imagine noble, violent actions unfolding majestically, and protagonists fighting for the crown, for their dynasty or their loves.

In fact what Brecht meant was a theatre in which action (and poetry) would be expressly and deliberately brought close to everyday life. When he tried to explain the meaning of the word 'epic', he used the example of a traffic accident, with witnesses discussing what happened and giving biased accounts of it, each implying a judgement (taking a stand, taking sides) and an attempt to make the listener share that judgement. 'The epic theatre wants to establish its basic model at the street corner . . .'[23]

Brecht's great play about Galileo – that hero of knowledge – begins with a 'de-heroization':

GALILEO: (*washing the upper part of his body, puffing, and good-humoured:*) Put the milk on the table . . .[24]

To understand this properly, we need to think about what is happening around us, within us, each and every day. We live on familiar terms with the people in our own family, our own milieu, our own class. This constant impression of *familiarity* makes us think that we know them, that their outlines are defined for us, and that they see themselves as having those same outlines. We define them (Peter is this, Paul is that) and we judge them. We can identify with them or exclude them from our world. But the familiar is not necessarily the known. As Hegel said in a sentence which could well serve as an epigraph for the *Critique of Everyday Life*, 'Was ist bekannt ist nicht erkannt.' Familiarity, what is familiar, conceals human beings and makes them difficult to know by giving them a mask we can recognize, a mask that is merely the lack of something. And yet familiarity (mine with other people, other people's with me) is by no means an illusion. It is real, and is part of reality. Masks cling to our faces, to our skin; flesh and blood have become masks. The people we are familiar with (and we ourselves) *are* what we recognize them to be. They play the roles I have cast them in and which they have cast for themselves. And I myself play a role for them and in them (and not only while they are watching), the role of friend, husband, lover, father which they have cast me in and which I have cast for myself. If there were no roles to play, and thus no familiarity, how could the cultural element or ethical element which should modify and humanize our emotions and our passions be introduced into life? The one involves the other. A role is not a role. It is social life, an inherent part of it. What is faked in one sense is what is the essential, the most precious, the human, in another. And what is most derisory is what is most necessary. It is often difficult to distinguish between what is faked and what is natural, not to say naïve (and we should distinguish between a natural naïvety and the natural-ness which is a product of high culture).

The waiter in a café is not playing at being a waiter. He *is* one.[25] And he is not one. He is not selling his time (for working and living) in exchange for the role of a waiter. And it is precisely when he is playing at being a waiter (and a virtuoso in the art of carrying overladen trays, etc.) in front of his customers that he is no longer a waiter; by playing himself he transcends himself. Moreover, it is certain that a worker does not play at being a worker and could not transcend himself if he did. He is completely 'that', and at the same time he is completely other and something else: head of the family, or an individual eager to enjoy life, or a revolutionary militant. For him and within him, at his best moments and his worst, contradictions and alienations are at a maximum. For us, in our society, with the forms of exchange and the division of labour which govern it, there is no social relation – relation with the other – without a certain alienation. And each individual exists socially only by and within his alienation, just as he can only be for himself within and by his deprivation (his *private* consciousness).[26]

It would be too simple to tear off the masks and shatter the roles; to cry 'faces are nothing more than masks' is the answer of cynical irony, the solution a cartoonist might come up with. An irrelevant solution, since *they* are that – and *they* are not that – and thus *they* escape irony on two counts. Still, the very fact that irony is possible immediately reveals the impossibility of any true identification with 'beings' who are not identical with themselves. Now familiarity relies upon apparent identification, upon a belief in identification: upon a practical credulity. Irony begins breaking this belief up; without necessarily putting *a reasonable distance* between us and the people we live with, it allows us to begin appreciating the distance between them and their own selves, between them and us. Irony is necessary, it is a powerful weapon ethically and aesthetically, but it is not enough. It plays a momentary role in the critique that everyone makes – more or less – of their own everyday lives and it cannot be disregarded. In Brecht – in his poetry as in his plays – there is a constant underlying irony, yet this irony is always transcended by a more deeply serious intent.

There is an intense feeling which can be rare or frequent in life, according to who one is, but which is certainly frequent in narrative fiction, and which can be put more or less in the following way: 'He realized that this woman who had been sharing his bed for the last ten years was nothing more than a stranger to him ... Germaine looked at Roger in amazement; it was as though she was seeing him for the first time ...'

For the audience in a theatre, this surprise must be made to last. And the distance between the characters, as between the characters and their own selves, must be determined by the distance between the audience, the stage and the actors. They must be placed at a reasonable distance. But this is just a technical problem, at least as far as Brecht is concerned. No doubt the essential thing is that in the twentieth century the people we live with have nothing in common with classical *characters*, precisely because they play a *role* in life.

In the great classical dramas, by virtue of a contradiction for which they offer a magnificent solution, *characters* are not *characters*. They are utterly sincere, authentically sincere, even when they are pretending. They are not acting, and this is why actors are able to impersonate them completely. The audience can identify with well-defined 'beings' and 'natures'. Conversely, all around us, in real life, characters really are characters; plays which attempt to represent them (in other words to present what is hidden in life in a clear way and at a reasonable distance) must go beyond the classical concept of *character*. We are dealing with people about whom it is impossible to say either what they are or what they are not; about whom we cannot say that they are not – that they only appear to be – what they are, nor that they are or appear to be what they are not. They are undefined and yet they are, and with a vengeance. Presence–absence does not function on the level of the image or the imaginary, but in life. This is precisely why an awareness of what is familiar becomes transformed into an awareness of something strange. As soon as we get really close to someone, we say to ourselves: 'He's an odd type of chap ... She's an odd type of girl.' Every 'type', by which we mean every individual (the opposite of *typical*) is an odd type of person.[27] The following conversation could be about anyone: 'You're exaggerating. I don't think he's nearly as complicated as that.' 'That's because you don't know him well enough.' 'Honestly, he's really very nice.' 'Who to? His friends. His little clique. But as far as I'm concerned ...' 'It's her fault, the bitch.' 'Come on, don't be so hard on her ...' And so on ...

One possible outcome of this is Pirandelloism, which has been fashionable for so long that it must have a deep meaning. Pirandello initiated a theatre which is almost perfectly *static*, and which recently has become even more so.[28] Nothing happens but a series of interpretations and points of view which shed light on a past, absent or unknown event. Pirandelloism expressed in terms of the theatre the relativity – the absolute relativity – of characters and judgements, an important discovery of 'modern times' in bourgeois society. There are only points of view, perspectives, masks and roles. Truth is draped in veils; it can be defined only by an endless succession of points of view.

And yet there is something in life which Pirandelloism cannot contain and which escapes it: the action, the event, the decision, the final outcome and the necessity for a final outcome; actions, and judgements about actions, in the sense in which they involve decisions. Even when we are playing, or above all when we are playing, we have to make decisions.[29] To play is to transform our point of view into a decision by confronting chance and determinism in the absence of adequate information about our opponent's game. We must lay our cards on the table, make our play. And quickly. We must make a decision. We do not have all the time in the world, either to shuffle the pack or to think about our partner's hand. In any case, would all the time in the world supply us with complete information? Would it exhaust chance and determination? Would it come anywhere near uncovering their unity? When we are not playing (in other words when we are living seriously) we also come to decisions in the absence of adequate information, confronting chance and determinism and therefore playing in the deepest meaning of the word.

At this point we may at last be defining and grasping something that Brecht understood profoundly. We are never really sure where actions, decisions or events spring from.[30] But, in all their stark reality, the results are *there*. What lies hidden within men and women is beyond our grasp; maybe these hidden depths are only an insubstantial mist, and not a profound substance (a *Grund*, a nature, an unconscious belonging to the individual or a group); it may only be a myth. Men and women are beyond us. But the battle, however confused, always has an outcome. There, before us, lies a child, a casualty, or a corpse; a marriage, a life together to organize or to disrupt, a place to live to be found; suffering to endure or avoid – pleasure to enjoy or spoil; a decision to hazard and accept with all its consequences (and this without adequate information, or having lost information en route, etc.).[31] Uncertainty is not without its charm or interest; it can never last long. It maintains ambiguity, keeping what is possible in a state of possibility, allowing us to take our pleasure in what Valéry called the whorehouse of possibilities; it can even oscillate between the comical and the dramatic, but we must choose. We weigh the pros and the cons, but there is no telling when something new on one side of the scales will come to outweigh the other. So decisions may ripen like fruit on a tree, but they never fall of their own accord; we must always cut the stem, we must even choose the moment of choice . . .[32] Hence the infinitely complex, profound and contradictory character of life is given an element which is always new, and which is indeed constantly being renewed by knowledge.

To put it more clearly or more abstractly, *ambiguity* is a category of everyday life, and perhaps an essential category. It never exhausts its reality; from the ambiguity of consciousnesses and situations spring forth actions, events, results, without warning. These, at least, have clear-cut outlines. They maintain a hard, incisive objectivity which constantly disperses the luminous vapours of ambiguity – only to let them rise once again.

Philosophers and psychologists have confused the issue by sometimes attributing this 'being-there' of results to consciousness or being, rather than to actions and decisions, and sometimes attributing ambiguity to philosophically defined existence rather than to the everyday as such.

Feelings and desires can hardly choose. They would like to choose, they would like not to choose, to possess incompatibles all at the same time: several skills, several possibilities, several futures, several loves. Practically, the requirement to act and to make decisions imposes choice. But to choose is to *make a judgement.* We have no knowledge of the human actions which go on around us; they escape us just as our own selves escape us. And yet we must *make judgements.* And even before or after the epic moment of decision or action, we must go on making ever more and more judgements. It is the only solid ground, the only unchanging requirement amid all life's ups and downs, its one axis. Such are the varied aspects of the everyday: fluctuations beneath stable masks and appearances of stability, the need to make judgements and decisions. But nothing is as difficult and as dangerous as making judgements. 'Judge not.' From the very beginnings of social life, men have been obsessed by the function of the Judge, and the powerful fight among themselves to exercise it. The Judge pronounces, makes irrevocable decisions according to the law as it stands, or in the court of appeal. He must embody justice, or Law, or the force of Truth. God passes for supreme judge, and the myth of the Last Judgement is a mighty image, the most striking in the most elaborate of all religions. The human masses sustain this great hope: the Judge will come. For ordinary men, every one of the innumerable little judgements required in life implies a risk and a wager. We are so used to making mistakes about our fellow man that good sense tells us to be wary of passing judgement, disapproves of hasty verdicts, and, quite rightly, denounces prejudice. As a result we find it easier to judge a global society than to judge men. Every capitalist is a man; within him, up to a point, the man and the capitalist are in conflict. Extreme cases – the capitalist who is the complete incarnation of money and capital – are rare. Generally, there are two or more contradictory spirits living inside the capitalist (in particular, as Marx noted, the coexisting needs of enjoyment and accumulation tear him apart). It is therefore both easier and more equitable to condemn a society than to condemn a man.

Brecht perceived the epic content of everyday life superbly: the hardness of actions and events, the necessity of judging. To this he added an acute awareness of the alienation to be found in this same everyday life. To see people properly we need to place them at a reasonable, well-judged distance, like the objects we see before us. Then their many-sided strangeness becomes apparent: in relation to ourselves, but also within themselves and in relation to themselves. In this strangeness lies their truth, the truth of their alienation. It is then that consciousness of alienation – that strange awareness of the strange – liberates us, or begins to liberate us, from alienation. This is the truth. And at the moment of truth we are suddenly disorientated by others and by ourselves. To look at things from an *alien* standpoint – externally and from a reasonable distance – is to look at things *truly*. But this strange and alien way of looking at things, disorientated but true, is the way children, peasants, women of the people, naïve and simple folk look. And they are afraid of what they see. For this many-sided alienation is no joke. We live in a world in which the best becomes the worst; where nothing is more dangerous than heroes and great men; where every thing including freedom (even though it is not a thing) and revolt, changes into its own opposite.

Brecht gave examples borrowed from everyday life. His *Verfremdungs-effekt* has become famous, but some technically inclined stage directors tend to turn it into a theatrical device; they achieve a specific effect with a couple of tricks of light and shadow, or with incidental music out of keeping with the real spectacle. When Brecht showed the strangeness of the everyday, pointing up that contradiction within the familiar, whereby it embraces both the trivial and the extraordinary, he was already protesting against this kind of technocratic interpretation. A lorry has just run over a passer-by. Policemen run to the scene, people gather round, discussing what has happened. They try to reconstruct the event, but are unable to do so. The witnesses disagree. The driver tries to exonerate himself, throwing the blame on the victim. The fact, the event, is there, in all its stark and gory reality. Everyone judges or tries to judge, everyone takes sides and makes his decision.

This is the approach historians – who must make judgements

sooner or later – still have towards criticizing evidence.

Brecht's epic theatre rejects classical transparency (as it happens, a deceptive transparency which in principle extends to the conflicts and problems presented, to the logical unfolding of the actions and events). If he starts from a 'commonplace', it is the opposite of the classical 'koinon',[33] and is taken from the everyday. He starts from disagreement, divergence, distortion. The play – or the scene – poses a complete problem which has not been resolved in advance, and which is consequently irritating, embarrassing. To begin with, Brecht confronts the spectator with an action or an event (the quarrel between the Kolkhozians in *The Caucasian Chalk Circle*, for example). He leaves the spectator in a (for him) disturbing externality. Instead of making him participate in an action or with defined 'characters', the stage action liberates him: it 'arouses his capacity for action, forces him to make decisions ... he is made to face something [by] argument'.[34] Called upon to make a judgement, obliged to come to a decision, the audience hesitates. And in this way the action is transferred to within the spectator. Without being aware of it, and although everything is clearly happening in full view, the spectator becomes the living consciousness of the contradictions of the real.

And is it really accurate to say that this theatre excludes emotion? It excludes emotion of a magical nature, the kind that allows or implies participation and identification. But maybe Brecht's theatre is aiming to bring forth new forms of emotion and images by actually ridding them of whatever magic the imagination has retained.[35] If this were not the case, if Brecht's theatre were restricted merely to evoking states of mind, this is where it would come up against its own limitations, and fairly severe limitations they would be. As it happens, it provides a model for art liberated from magic.[36] And that is a great innovation. Brecht unravels the contradictions of everyday life and liberates us from them. For magic plays an immense role in everyday life, be it in emotional identification and participation with 'other people' or in the thousand little rituals and gestures used by every person, every family, every group. But in practical life as in ideology, this magic only signifies the illusions men have about themselves, and their lack of power. And everyday life is defined by contradictions: illusion and truth, power and helplessness, the intersection of the sector man controls and the sector he does not control.

In Brecht's theatre, the protagonists are placed in the full glare of the stage-lights, but the very brilliance of the lights and the bareness of the dramatic space deliberately isolate and distance them. Thus the audience can identify neither with the dramatic development nor with such-and-such a 'hero' or 'character'. It is not even a bad thing – at least now and then – for the protagonist to be unsympathetic, irritating; this helps to accentuate the distance. The spectator weighs the pros and the cons; he waits for the play to offer him arguments, but it does so only in a way which delays judgement, or provokes judgement without laying down what it should be. A dialogue between the spectator and the spectacle (one dare not say author) is established which brings a growing tension, relieved by musical interludes (the 'songs').[37] The spectator cannot relax. He is not allowed to. He must take sides. Political, public, contradictory, the play is fundamentally no different from a meeting. The paradox here is that Brecht – who was never a politician, who was never a member of the Communist Party, who had difficulties with the East German authorities – nevertheless offers a model for a political art to which taking sides and making a stand are fundamental. Genuinely so: making the audience do so, without presenting it as a *fait accompli*, without explaining it or imposing it dogmatically. Hence the misunderstandings about him, which were as painful as they were ridiculous.

Far from attempting to purify passions and emotions – except in the most fundamental sense of delivering them from the realm of magic – Brechtian stage narrative stirs them up. Thus it condenses a becoming analogous with practical becoming: the exploration of potentialities, the transition from possibilities to actions and decisions. The denouement is the moment when a judgement is passed, a stand made, a side taken. Therefore the object of the play is something unknown and something strange: an event in the historical sense, a social man, rather than a 'plot' or 'situation' given or determinable in the relationships between the characters. Thus the action can very easily be cut up into distinct moments, into relatively independent 'scenes'. It loses the classical characteristics of unity and continuous movement, where a *coup de théâtre* is like a sudden blow on the kettledrums in a symphony: neither interrupts the unity of the whole. There is no internal conflict resolved by the supreme moment of denouement or death. The action is happening more inside the spectator than physically on the stage.

Let us sum up. Classical theatre transcended everyday life: by using heroes, situations, the formal logic of the Unities. It purified it; it represented it while filtering its impurities, investing it with noble, majestic outlines. It projected it along a continuous line and within a rigorous framework. It criticized it from outside, using metaphysical or religious norms (which historically were basically the 'values' of the dominant classes). It imposed an identification between the spectator and the Hero, his will, his conflicts, his struggle – an identification which included the espousal of accepted norms and values. It is precisely in this way that classical art sanctioned and consecrated one particular aspect of everyday life, a negative one: the magic of participation and ritual.

Brecht's epic theatre immerses itself in everyday life, at the level of everyday life, in other words at the level of the masses (not simply the masses of individuals, but the masses of instants and moments, of events and actions). Thus it appears as a democratic revolution in the art of the theatre. It breaks with the theatre of illusions as it does with the (Naturalist) theatre which imitates life. It does not purify the everyday; and yet it clarifies its contradictions. In its own way, it filters it. It throws its weak part away: the magical part. Thus the Brechtian dramatic image differs from what we called the *reverse image* in Chaplin. Brecht aims (and he has said so) at an image which will *master* the facts. Nevertheless he has used the reverse image procedure on occasion (in *Mahagonny*, for example).

Are Brecht's high ambitions justified? Did he achieve his goal?

There is no shortage of objections. In the first place his theatre is intended to be physical, direct, and thus popular, but parts of it appear to be excessively intellectual. Nowhere – even in Germany – does it seem to have become truly popular. The spectator wavers between an externalized judgement – an intellectual state which implies high culture – and an immersion in the image proposed. Perhaps this is what the dialectic of the *Verfremdungseffekt* is. The spectator is meant to *disalienate* himself in and through the consciousness of alienation. He is meant to feel wrenched from his self but only in order to enter more effectively into his self and become conscious of the real and the contradictions of the real. Unfortunately, there is a risk that this process will take on the disturbing form, worse even than classic identification, of *fascination*. Whether it be to compare them or contrast the two,

French partisans of Brecht's theatre nearly always refer to Antonin Artaud's theatre of cruelty. The violence of dramatic effects, of the lighting, of the images, make it even more impossible for the spectator to relax his mind and momentarily resolve his inner tension by identifying with the hero or by escaping into a kind of dream. There is a danger that unity will be re-established momentarily in the spectator's disorientated mind, caught up as he is by the image; for tension needs moments of respite; expectation demands to be satisfied, if only fleetingly. Unable to find this in a 'classic' completeness, there is a danger that he will look for them in a sort of bloody ecstasy. Therefore generalized strangeness entails a danger (which was avoided by Brecht, but not necessarily by the people who produce his plays or write about them). An art based on alienation must struggle against alienation; if not it sanctions it. Significantly some of his French commentators translate *Verfremdungseffekt* as 'effet d'aliénation'.[38] It would be another paradox, and a very strange one, if this new art were to sanction alienation by giving it all the glamour of violence. In *Danton's Death*, tragedy and fascination are grounded in the irremediable triviality of everyday life:

> DANTON: Time loses us. – This is very tedious – we put the shirt on first, then we pull the trousers up over it, and every night we crawl into bed, and every morning we crawl out again, and we always put one foot down in front of the other. And it doesn't look as if it's ever going to be any different.[39]

Criticism of life by death – surely the last word in lucidity.

We should add that the spectator cannot effectively be transformed into a historian of the event (or action or decision), since the historian's attitude is defined in terms of knowledge and not of art. Moreover, to make judgements – in life – is not the same as adopting the attitude of a Judge. The Judge's attitude excludes sudden surprises, amazement, expectation. The professional Judge pronounces according to written evidence, he applies the law, he takes the event as having actually happened. Impassive by definition, impartial by principle, he decides without taking sides. Such is his duty. And if he behaves otherwise, it is because he has fallen foul of the contradictions of the Law, of Justice, of truth. In which case it is the Judge's turn to be put on trial.

Thus it is that the functions of the critique of everyday life can be determined by reference to an art which immerses itself in everyday life. To be creative in art one must seek a certain pathway, committing oneself to it and pointing the way towards it. The philosopher still has a part to play, by pointing out the risks, the dangers; and how a straight line – a linear orientation, without deviations, without meanders – is generally a practical impossibility.

This is the place, or the moment, to mention one of the most gifted up-and-coming French authors: Roger Vailland.[40] This is not only because he has defended classicism against Brecht,[41] but also and above all because Vailland the novelist has his own problem: that of confronting everyday life with a 'vision', or with images, from somewhere else. Roger Vailland's formative reading was Stendhal and Laclos. He modelled himself on them, and still carries them in his head, even when he is no longer actually using them as models. Thus his attempts to grasp everyday triviality (real, apparent, or both) are honed by a sensibility derived from classical humanism, a carefully cultivated eroticism, an almost Romantic novelistic 'vision'. On top of that, he has read the Marxists. Such are the analytic tools with which he hopes to come to grips with the everyday. The resultant – fruitful – contradictions give his attempts great interest beyond whatever specifically literary qualities his books may have.

Thus *325,000 francs*[42] is a novel which is very close to the (apparently) most ordinary kind of everyday life: that of a moulder in a plastics factory. Someone has said that he wrote it for a bet: to write a romantic novel about overtime.

A simple, solid, healthy proletarian is in love with a girl (a working girl, but an isolated one, a dressmaker) who, after playing the field, uses her rather advanced feminine wiles to trap a husband. She teases him, and leads him on through the *classic* stages of courtship – almost of the *pays du Tendre*[43] – to force him to marry her. Roger Vailland thus manages to situate his refined eroticism at the centre of a novel dealing with the everyday life of the proletariat . . .

Aroused, and very much in love (and yet aware of what the girl really is – and in this respect reminiscent of the hero of a classical play), the boy knows that to have the woman he loves he will have to marry her, and that to marry her he will have to leave his class. He would probably aspire to leave it anyway, but surely not at the risk of his life or health. Thus the woman plays the traditional female role – a role which is certainly still a real one – of an ambiguous figure who excites contradictory actions and thoughts.

The boy seeks fame and fortune in sport and becomes a racing cyclist. When this fails, he is forced to work night and day to earn enough to 'settle down' with his beautiful but demanding lady. It costs him a hand, his health, and his physical mobility.

The drama of everyday proletarian life is treated here with true artistry, and this makes the book a work of art. Roger Vailland has captured his subject in such a way as to make it at once flimsy, transparent and profound. The book is written like a musical composition, an opera, with an overture to whet our appetites, containing the themes, presenting the characters and foreshadowing the continuation and conclusion: a cycle race, watched by the girl who is also the prize, in which the boy makes a heroic effort, only to fall, injure himself, and lose.

In this book, as in Vailland's earlier novels, the author appears as such. He says: 'I'. He intervenes as a witness, designating the characters and situating them, entering into a dialogue with them, inviting the reader to decide what attitude to adopt towards them: what judgement to make. Here judgement is inseparable from event; it is rigorously included in the story. This authorial presence has various meanings, and not simply on the level of technique. It is Roger Vailland's way – and a very simple way it is – of resolving a difficult literary problem, that of novelistic consciousness or of consciousness in the novel. Who is speaking? Who is seeing, who saw the actions in the story? Who bridges the gap between the lived and the true? How has the speaker seen or heard about the things he narrates? How has he been able to foretell or sense what will happen next? Who has detected the characters' motives (hidden even to themselves)? And as he is drawn on by the great movement called 'reading', with whom does the reader identify, in whose consciousness does he participate?

Roger Vailland's solution, the novel as first-person evidence, is not without its drawbacks. It corresponds too closely to the general tendency to bring the novel nearer to journalism and autobiography. Inevitably, as soon as he begins extending his narration, the author will start introducing scenes from which he was absent; or else he will write sentences which are incompatible with his main guidelines and techniques. 'At the same instant, she saw her father's face again ...'[44]

The presence of the author situates the characters, placing them constantly before our eyes, not too near and not too far away: *at a reasonable distance*. For Roger Vailland this has the advantage of piquing the reader's interest. And yet the use of his own consciousness as a witness – and virtually as a judge – would remain contemplative and formal if it did not have a solid content: the totality of human and social relations as manifested in the everyday life of a village, a factory, a small industrial town. Conversely, this knowledge of 'modern' everyday life, superimposed as it is upon a great familiarity with classical culture, is characterized by a certain externality of consciousness on the part of the 'knower' or witness. The author's use of the first person thus has a deeper meaning than simply the solving of a problem of novelistic technique. The author is present because in himself he contributes something irreplaceable; because he comes from somewhere else; because he introduces into a certain kind of everyday experience a lucidity and a recognition which it did not previously contain. Consciousness presents itself in the novel in this way because this is how it occurs in life: at one and the same time *from without and from within.*

We could show here, not without a certain irony, that Roger Vailland the novelist is to some extent doing what Roger Vailland the writer on drama and the critic of Brecht is rejecting. He composes his novels in an 'operatic' mode. He inserts scenes which are almost independent, and which as it happens are virtually scenes from a play: weddings, dances, arguments or brawls in pubs, jealous rows, etc. As a witness he passes judgement, and makes the reader take sides: making him pass judgement. Supported by details borrowed from everyday life,[45] the narrative has a spontaneous tendency to become epic. As the critic of *L'Express* observed on 27 November 1954, *Beau Masque* is 'an excellent epic narrative'.

That Roger Vailland, with all his idiosyncratic qualities and faults, should be much closer to Brecht than he thinks is really rather curious. It must surely be indicative of one of the requirements of everyday life – or more exactly of the aesthetic representation – in drama or in the novel – of everyday life.

Ulysses demonstrates that a great novel can be boring. And 'profoundly' boring. Joyce nevertheless understood one thing: that the report of a day in the life of an ordinary man had to be predominantly in the epic mode.

Finally, to clarify a few ideas, and above all to amuse the reader, here are two extracts from modern Anglo-Saxon authors. The first attacks American everyday life with a black and chilling irony. By contrast the second, by a famous and talented English woman writer, uses an acute sensitivity to show the subtle richness of the everyday:

> The subway, Archer thought, was the only place to read today's newspapers. Underground, in a bad light, at an increased fare, with all the passengers fearing the worst about each other. Everyone suspecting the man next to him of preparing to pick a pocket, commit a nuisance, carry a lighted cigar, pinch a girl, ask for a job, run for a vacant seat, block the door at the station at which you wanted to leave the train. Archer put the paper down and looked around at his fellow passengers. They do not look American, he thought; perhaps I shall report them to the proper authorities.[46] ... Archer walked down Fifth Avenue, past the shops with their windows full of dresses, coats and furs, and the women rushing in and out of the doors, their faces lit with the light of purchase. It is the new profession of the female sex, he thought – buying. If you wanted to set up an exhibition to show modern American women in their natural habitat, engaged in their most characteristic function, he thought, like the tableaux in the Museum of Natural History in which stuffed bears are shown against a background of caves, opening up honeycombs, you would have a set of stuffed women, slender, high-heeled, rouged, waved, hot-eyed, buying a cocktail dress in a department store. In the background, behind the salesgirls and the racks and shelves, there would be bombs bursting, cities crumbling, scientists measuring the half-life of tritium and radioactive cobalt. The garment would be democratically medium-priced and the salesgirl would be just as pretty as the customer and, to the naked eye at least, just as well dressed, to show that the benefits of a free society extended from one end of the economic spectrum to the other.[47]

> One goes into the room – but the resources of the English language would be much put to the stretch, and whole flights of words would need to wing their way illegitimately into existence before a woman could say what happens when she goes into a room. The rooms differ so completely; they are calm or thunderous; open on to the sea, or, on the contrary, give on to a prison yard; are hung with washing; or alive with opals and silks; are hard as horsehair or soft as feathers –...[48]

IV Work and Leisure in Everyday Life

Throughout history, criticism of everyday life has been carried on in a number of ways: by philosophy and contemplation, dream and art, violent political or warlike action. By flight and escape.

These criticisms have a common element: they were the work of particularly gifted, lucid and active *individuals* (the philosopher, the poet, etc.). However, this individual lucidity or activeness concealed an appearance or an illusion, and therefore a hidden, deeper reality. In truth their work belonged to a time and a class whose ideas were thus raised above the everyday onto the level of the exceptional and the dominant. Hence the criticism of everyday life was in fact *a criticism of other classes*, and for the most part found its expression in contempt for productive labour; at best it criticized the life of the dominant class in the name of a transcendental philosophy or dogma, which nevertheless still belonged to that class. This is how we must understand the criticism of the 'world' and the 'mundane' carried out from the Middle Ages until the era – the bourgeois eighteenth century – when the 'mundane' element burst forth into art and philosophy.

In our era, one of the most recent forms which criticism of everyday life has taken is criticism of the *real* by the *surreal*. By abandoning the everyday in order to find the marvellous and the surprising (at one and the same time immanent in the real and transcending it), Surrealism rendered triviality unbearable.[49] This was a good thing, but it had a negative side: transcendental contempt for the real, for *work* for example (the long-inevitable rift between Surrealists and Marxists took place during a memorable meeting of the Association of Writers and Revolutionary Artists (AEAR) over the Soviet film *Road to Life*).[50]

And yet, be he an author or not, the man of our times carries out in his own way, spontaneously, the critique of *his* everyday life. And this critique of the everyday plays an integral part in the everyday: it is achieved in and by *leisure activities*.

The relation between leisure and the everyday is not a simple one: the two words are at one and the same time united and contradictory (therefore their relation is dialectical). It cannot be reduced to the simple relation in time between 'Sunday' and 'weekdays', represented as external and merely different. Leisure – to accept the concept uncritically for the moment – cannot be separated from work. After his work is over, when resting or relaxing or occupying himself in his own particular way, a man is still the same man. Every day, at the same time, the worker leaves the factory, the office worker leaves the office. Every week Saturdays and Sundays are given over to leisure as regularly as day-to-day work. We must therefore imagine a 'work–leisure' unity, for this unity exists, and everyone tries to programme the amount of time at his disposal according to what his work is – and what it is not. Sociology should therefore study the way the life of workers as such, their place in the division of labour and in the social system, is 'reflected' in leisure activities, or at least in what they demand of leisure.

Historically, *in real individuality* and its development, the 'work–leisure' relation has always presented itself in a contradictory way.

Until the advent of bourgeois society, individuality, or rather personality[51] could only really develop outside productive labour. In Antiquity, in the Middle Ages, and even during the period when bourgeois social relations still retained aspects of the social relations bequeathed by feudalism – in the seventeenth century of the *honnête homme* – the man who was able to develop himself never worked.

However, whether they were aristocrats, clerks still tied to feudalism, or bourgeois *honnêtes hommes*, such men only *appeared* to remain outside the social division of labour and social practice. In reality they were prisoners of the separation of manual and intellectual work. Moreover, directly or not, consciously or not, they had a social function, if only on the ideological level. Leonardo da Vinci was an engineer as well as an artist. Rabelais was a doctor and then a writer, at once an encyclopedic brain and an epic novelist. Montaigne worked in local government. And Descartes was an army officer before becoming a scholar ... In so far as the man of those times was *genuinely* separated from social practice and devoted to leisure alone – to laziness – he was doomed both in a personal sense and from the point of view of class.

Another element must be considered which makes the question even more complicated. In those eras, in those modes of production, productive labour was merged with everyday life: consider the lives of peasants and craftsmen, for example. What distinguishes peasant life so profoundly from the life of industrial workers, even today, is precisely this inherence of productive activity in their life in its entirety. The workplace is all around the house; work is not separate from the everyday life of the family. Formerly the imperatives of the peasant community (the village) regulated not only the way work and domestic life were organized, but festivals as well. Thus up to a point a way of living which strictly speaking did not belong to any one individual, but more to a group of men committed to the ties – and limits – of their community or guild, could be developed.

With bourgeois society these various elements and their relations were overturned: in one sense they became differentiated, separate, in another they came to constitute a unified whole. Bourgeois society reasserted the value of labour, above all during the period of its ascendancy; but at the historical moment when the relation between labour and the concrete development of individuality was emerging, labour took on an increasingly fragmented character. At the same time the individual, more and more involved in complex social relations, became isolated and inward-looking. Individual consciousness split into two (into the private consciousness and the social or public consciousness); it also became atomized (individualism, specialization, separation between differing spheres of activity, etc.). Thus at the same time a distinction was made between man 'as man' on the one hand and the working man on the other (more clearly among the bourgeoisie, of course, than among the proletariat). Family life became separate from productive activity. And so did leisure.

As a result there is a certain obscurity in the very concept of *everyday life*. Where is it to be found? In work or in leisure? In family life and in moments 'lived' outside of culture? Initially the answer seems obvious. Everyday life involves all three elements, all three aspects. It is their unity and their totality, and it determines the concrete individual. And yet this answer is not entirely satisfactory. Where does the living contact between the concrete individual man and other human beings operate? In fragmented labour? In family life? In leisure? Where is it acted out in the most concrete way? Are there several modes of contact? Can they be schematized as representational models? Or must they be reduced to fixed behaviour patterns? Are they contradictory or complementary? How do they relate? What is the decisive essential sector? Where are we to situate the poverty and wealth of this everyday life which we know to be both infinitely rich (potentially at least) and infinitely poor, bare, alienated; which we know we must reveal to itself and transform so that its richness can become actualized and developed in a renewed culture? . . .

The discreteness of the elements of the everyday (work – family and 'private' life – leisure activities) implies an alienation; and perhaps at the same time a differentiation – certain fruitful contradictions. In any event, like all ensembles (or totalities), it must be studied in terms of the interrelation of its elements.

The social history of leisure shows that during the course of a development in which its various stages may have overlapped or contradicted each other, it has been transformed in fact as well as in theory,[52] and new needs have come into being.

At first, leisure gives rise to an undifferentiated global activity which is difficult to distinguish from other aspects of the everyday (family strolls on Sunday, walking).

On a higher level, leisure involves passive attitudes. Someone sitting in front of a cinema screen offers an example and a common model of this passivity, the potentially 'alienating' nature of which is immediately apparent. It is particularly easy to exploit these attitudes commercially.[53] Finally, on the highest level of all, leisure produces active attitudes, very specialized personal occupations, linked to techniques and consequently involving a technical element independent of any professional specialization (photography, for example). This is a cultivated or cultural leisure.

This brief examination immediately reveals the contradictory character of leisure, both in terms of itself and in relation to the everyday. Leisure embraces opposing possibilities and orientations, of which some tend to impoverish through passivity while others are more enriching. Some are undifferentiated (although they may still be worthwhile on a certain level), others very much the reverse. And while some involve escape into a vacuum, others rediscover 'nature', an immediate, sensory life, through what is sometimes a highly developed technical expertise (organized sports or amateur films, for example).

Therefore, with its fragmentation of labour, modern industrial civilization creates both a *general need for leisure* and differentiated *concrete needs* within that general framework.

Leisure is a remarkable example of a new social need with a *spontaneous* character which social organization, by offering it various means of satisfaction, has directed, sharpened, shifted and modified. In response to such new needs, our civilization creates techniques which nevertheless have an 'extra-technical' meaning and character. It produces 'leisure machines' (radio, television, etc.). It creates new types of play which transform the old ones, sometimes conflicting with other activities, sometimes overlapping (in the camping holiday, work and leisure are barely distinguishable, and everyday life in its entirety becomes play). Concrete social needs are determined in a way which increasingly differentiates them according to age, sex and group. They also fall spontaneously into the categories of individual needs and collective needs (for example, the distinction between individual sports and team sports).

There is no doubt that today – in capitalist, bourgeois *society*, which has its own way of manipulating the needs arising from a specific level of *civilization* – the most striking imperative as far as the needs of leisure among the masses are concerned is that it must produce a *break*. Leisure must break with the everyday (or at least appear to do so) and not only as far as work is concerned, but also for day-to-day family life. Thus there is an increasing emphasis on leisure characterized as distraction: rather than bringing any new worries, obligations, or necessities, leisure should offer liberation from worry and necessity. Liberation and pleasure – such are the essential characteristics of leisure, according to the parties concerned.[54] There is no more of a sense of genuine 'leisure' about a family get-together than there is about gardening or doing odd jobs around the house. So those involved tend to reject ambiguous forms of leisure which might resemble work or entail some kind of obligation. The cultural aspect strikes them as being irrelevant (which is not to say that *it really is so*). They mistrust anything which might appear to be educational and are more concerned with those aspects of leisure which might offer *distraction*, *entertainment* and *repose*, and which *might compensate* for the difficulties of everyday life. If we are to believe the subjective opinions revealed by surveys, this is as true for workers (proletarians) as it is for the other social classes.

It is thus not the work of art, in so far as it has a role to play in everyday life (the picture or the reproduction hanging in the bedroom), that is liable to constitute an element of leisure. Nor armchair reading, unless it provides thrills or escapism (travel books, stories about exploration, or crime novels), or relaxation (picture books, strip cartoons, or 'readers' digests' – evoking nothing so much as pre-digested food). The constitutive elements of leisure are more likely to be images and films. And images and films which are (or at least appear to be) as far away from *real life* as possible.

The first obvious thing that the so-called 'modern' man around us expects of leisure is that it should stop him from being tired and tense, from being anxious, worried and preoccupied. To use a term which is now very widely used by the public at large, he craves *relaxation*. There is a veritable ideology, and a technicity, and a technocracy of relaxation (which is obtained by a variety of procedures, some passive, ridding life of its content, creating a vacuum – others active, exerting control over actions and muscles). Thus the so-called 'modern' man expects to find something in leisure which his work and his family or 'private' life do not provide. Where is his happiness to be found? He hardly knows, and does not even ask himself. In this way a 'world of leisure' tends to come into being entirely outside of the everyday realm, and so purely artificial that it borders on the ideal. But how can this pure artificiality be created without permanent reference to ordinary life, without the constantly renewed contrast that will embody this reference?

There are plenty of examples in the past of art aiming to embellish everyday life by skilfully transposing it: presenting it in a flattering light, imposing a style on it while acknowledging its real achievements – Flemish and Dutch painting, for example. What is new today in bourgeois society is that a complete break has become imperative (a fact that constitutes a serious obstacle for any attempt at realism in art). Consequently the art of obtaining this break is now a specific and eagerly exploited commercial technique. Clever images of the *everyday* are supplied *on a day-to-day basis*, images that can make the ugly beautiful, the empty full, the sordid elevated – and the hideous 'fascinating'. These images so skilfully and so persuasively exploit the demands and dissatisfactions which every 'modern' man carries within himself that it is indeed very difficult to resist being seduced and fascinated by them, except by becoming rigidly puritanical, and, in rejecting 'sensationalism', rejecting 'the present' and life itself.

The sudden eruption of sexuality in the domain of the image – and more generally in leisure – calls for an investigation in its own right. Our era has witnessed the demise of a certain number of ridiculous taboos – which before becoming ridiculous were very serious indeed – which had imposed a ban on sexual matters, on clothes that external-ized sexual characteristics, on bodies, on nudity. And yet it still produces a shock whenever this ban is transgressed, as though it were still in force. Images with a (more or less explicit) erotic meaning, or simply the display of a woman's body, are violently attractive. The excessive use of such images in advertising has not yet exhausted the effect they have on us, and we may conclude that they correspond to something profound. Displays of sexuality and nudity break with everyday life, and provide the sense of a break which people look for in leisure: reading, shows, etc.[55] On posters, in shop windows, on the covers of magazines, in films, everywhere there are unclothed women. It is a kind of escapism which from certain angles is more like a generalized neurosis: this sexuality is depressing, this eroticism is weary and wearying, mechanical. There is nothing really sensual in this unbridled sexuality, and that is probably its most profound characteristic. From this point of view, we will not criticize eroticism for being immoral, or immodest, or corrupting to children, etc. We leave that to other people. What we will criticize 'modern' eroticism for is its lack of genuine sensuality, a sensuality which implies beauty or charm, passion or modesty, power over the object of desire, and fulfilment. With 'modern' eroticism we step outside of the everyday, without actually leaving it: it shocks, it seems brutal, and yet this effect is superficial, pure appearance, leading us back towards the secret of the everyday – dissatisfaction.

Chaplin gave us a *genuine reverse image* of modern times: its image seen through a living man, through his sufferings, his tribulations, his victories. We are now entering the vast domain of the *illusory reverse image*. What we find is a false world: firstly because it is not a world, and because it presents itself as true, and because it mimics real life closely in order to replace the real by its opposite; by replacing real unhappiness by fictions of happiness, for example – by offering a fiction in response to the real need for happiness – and so on. This is the 'world' of most films, most of the press, the theatre, the music hall: of a large sector of leisure activities.

How strange the split between the real world and its reverse image is. For in the end it is not strange at all, but a false strangeness, a cheap-and-nasty, all-pervasive mystery.[56]

Of course, the fictional and mystifying 'world' of leisure is not limited to the exploitation of sex, sentimentality and crime. Sport too will have to be scrutinized.

Sport has developed by presenting itself as the culture of the body, of individual energy and team spirit: as a school for health. What have these lofty ambitions achieved? A vast social organization (commercialized or not) and a great and often magnificently spectacular *mise en scène* devoted to competitiveness. The vocabulary is not without its humour. People who go to the races and bet on their favourite horse are known officially as 'sportsmen'. Every football club has its 'supporters'[57] and a supporter can be someone who has never kicked a ball in his life. He goes to the match in his car, or by bus or the metro. He participates in the action and plays sport via an intermediary. He quivers with enthusiasm, he fidgets frenetically, but he never moves from his seat. A curious kind of 'alienation'. Sport is an activity which is apparently incompatible with illusion, and yet in fact it confronts us with a reverse image, a compensation for everyday life.

So the analysis of the relation between the needs of leisure and the other areas which globally make up everyday life presents many difficult problems. It is not sufficient simply to describe the facts. To obtain an analysis of content, we need a conceptual apparatus to supplement description. In particular the philosophical concept of alienation is essential. In a sense it has been introduced from outside, but placed in the context of sociology it becomes scientific and allows the sociology of everyday life to become a science as well as a critique.

Georges Friedmann[58] has undertaken a long and very richly documented investigation into human labour in which he has attempted to pose the problem of the relations between leisure and work.

In substance, this work (*Où va le travail humain*) identifies leisure with freedom and work with necessity. Every day the sum total of techniques is transforming the conditions of existence. 'Every instant of life is more and more penetrated by them' and the *technical environment* surrounding man is becoming more substantial by the day.[59] The notion of a technical environment generalizes the relation between man and machine and extends it to everyday life. However, the sciences of man, whose right to examine mechanization and its effects cannot be contested,[60] themselves modify the technical environment. They do this by an intellectual, moral and social reassertion of the value of labour which 'tightens the link of interest between the worker and society, by strengthening the incentives which justify his work, even if it is fragmented, and integrate him within a collectivity'.[61] The human problem is therefore a dual one: on the one hand how to organize labour rationally, and on the other how to organize leisure rationally – especially 'compensatory leisure', in which the workers can express their personality.[62] It would seem therefore that freedom in and through work comes principally from the intervention of psycho-technical or sociological theoreticians, in a word from an intervention of the 'sciences of man applied to industrial labour',[63] which assures freedom 'in so far as it exists in this domain' – which according to Friedmann is not very far. For the technical environment is following its destiny. It characterizes not only capitalist society,[64] but also industrial civilization as a whole.

Only the domain of leisure escapes the technical environment, escapes necessity, in other words, escapes depersonalization. In our leisure activities we are already beyond techniques. We achieve a leap from necessity into freedom, from the enslavement of the individual into whatever will permit his self-development.

Georges Friedmann has had the indisputable merit of posing problems and posing them in a wide-ranging way. He takes Marx's arguments about the worker alienated by a labour which is itself alienated and renders them concrete in terms of the era we live in. (For Marx, however, the alienation of the worker by fragmented labour and machines is only one aspect of a larger – a total – alienation which as such is inherent in capitalist society and in man's exploitation of man.)

It is certain that the development of the productive forces (in other words of techniques) has consequences within the *social relations* structurally linked to these techniques. Many Marxists have shut themselves away in a class subjectivism; their understanding of the social relations of production (in capitalist regimes) is restricted to and blinkered by the notion of class struggle. They have thus neglected to study the relations of production in so far as they are linked with the development of the productive forces. And this despite what Lenin had to say on the subject. Analysing monopoly capitalism, he demonstrated that 'underlying this interlocking ... its very base, are the changing social relations of production ... it becomes evident that we have socialisation of production ... that private economic and private property relations constitute a shell which no longer fits its contents'.[65] By starting from an abstract notion of the class struggle, some Marxists have neglected not only to study the recent modifications of capitalism as such, but also the 'socialization of production', and the new contents of specifically capitalist relations. Such a study could perhaps have modified the notion of class struggle, leading to the discovery of new forms of struggle.

These questions have been put by 'industrial sociology'. Has it resolved them accurately and completely? That is another matter. The undisputed fact is that since Marx's analyses, and since Lenin's, the productive forces have developed, and this economic fact cannot but have had consequences on the level of social phenomena.

Rather than resolving all the problems, Marx's statements about labour and its relation with leisure inaugurated an area of research. He predicted that work would become man's foremost need. The formula is only superficially clear. Objectively, for society, for the social man, for the 'collective worker', work has always been the foremost need. Does Marx mean that the *individual* man will transform this objective need into an essentially subjective one? So that by and in this work he will eliminate alienation? No doubt, but the formula is difficult to accept in relation to 'modern' fragmented labour. Moreover, if we put ourselves at the vanguard of technique and the modern productive forces, and consider the implications of automation, then we will need to interpret it afresh. For automation and transfer-machines tend to differentiate labour by splitting it into very highly skilled work and work for which no skill at all is required.

We may certainly affirm that work is the foundation of personal development within social practice. It links the individual with the other workers (on the shop floor, in the social class, in the social system) and also with knowledge; it is through work that the multi-technical education which controls the sum total of the productive processes and social practice is made possible, and necessary. And yet the fulfilment of these possibilities presents considerable difficulties. And under no circumstances can the 'bitty' character of labour be seen as conducive to the development of personality: whatever its social and political context, it is 'alienating'.

Elsewhere Marx wrote that 'this always remains a realm of necessity. *The true realm of freedom, the development of human powers as an end in itself, begins beyond it, though it can only flourish with this realm of necessity as its basis.* The reduction of the working day is the basic prerequisite.'[66] Therefore, according to Marx, the development of the need for leisure and the needs of leisure is deeply significant. Recent French sociology, and Georges Friedmann, have been right to bring this to the fore. But once that has been said, ought we to accept unreservedly the notion of leisure as the breakthrough of freedom into necessity? Or as a leap from necessity into freedom? As Marx said (and as Hegel said before him), necessity does not disappear in freedom, and freedom relies upon necessity. We cannot conceive of them as external to one other, except relatively. The notion of free leisure is valid up to a certain point. Beyond that point it is inadequate. If we push it too far we run the risk of forgetting that there can be *alienation in leisure just as in work* (and alienation precisely in so far as the worker is trying to 'disalienate' himself!).

Thus the dialectical analysis of leisure and its relation with work (an analysis which is an integral part of the critique of everyday life) would seem in some ways to complement the investigations of both the 'industrial sociologists' and the 'sociologists of leisure'.

Within the framework of bourgeois society (and the capitalist regime) work is lived and undergone by the worker as an alien and oppressive power. Not only do the technical division and the social division of labour overlap and impose themselves on him without his knowing the reasons why, but also he knows that he is not working for himself, either directly or indirectly. Moreover the fragmented character of individual labour is in fact interdependent with the increasingly complete socialization of productive labour. Fragmentation and socialization are the dialectically contradictory aspects of the labour process wherever the productive forces are highly developed. Fragmented labour can only be meaningful and productive within global or total labour. Thus for the worker a dual need develops in respect of his own labour.

On the one hand, the worker aspires to a *knowledge* of the system in which he plays an integral part: a firm, and also a global society. And this is already a means of not submitting, a freeing himself from imposed constraints, of mastering necessity. In capitalist firms this confused but real aspiration is answered in a mystifying way by 'human relations' and 'public relations'.[67] Marxists who have criticized these recent, originally American, institutions have made the mistake of merely seeing the ideology they embody, and of ignoring the fact that they correspond to a real *social need*, born precisely from the socialization of labour. They have disregarded this socialization of labour, imagining that it happens only in socialist regimes, whereas it is in fact also a function of the development of the productive forces. They have not understood that in socialism knowledge satisfies a need which under capitalism is answered by an ideology. Reciprocally, the mistake of the non-Marxist industrial sociologists has been that they have not always shown that these innovations (human relations, etc.) were responding to needs purely in order to harness them, twist them, deflect them from their meaning, by reducing them to the dimensions of the firm and to cooperation with the employers.

Moreover, the worker craves a sharp break with his work, a compensation. He looks for this in leisure seen as entertainment or distraction.

In this way leisure appears as the non-everyday in the everyday.

We cannot step beyond the everyday. The marvellous can only continue to exist in fiction and the illusions that people share. There is no escape. And yet we wish to have the illusion of escape as near to hand as possible. An illusion not entirely illusory, but constituting a 'world' both apparent and real (the reality of appearances and the apparently real) quite different from the everyday world yet as open-ended and as closely dovetailed into the everyday as possible. So we work to earn our leisure, and leisure has only one meaning: to get away from work. A vicious circle.

Thus is established a complex of activities and passivities, of forms of sociability and communication which the sociologist can study. Although he cannot describe or analyse them without criticizing them as being (partially) illusory, he must nevertheless start from the fact that they contain within themselves their own spontaneous critique of the everyday. They *are* that critique in so far as they are *other* than everyday life, and yet they are *in everyday life*, they are *alienation*. They can thus hold a real content, correspond to a real need, yet still retain an illusory form and a deceptive appearance.

Thus leisure and work and 'private life' make up a dialectical system, a global structure. Through this global structure we can reconstruct a historically real picture of man and the human at a certain step in their development: at a certain stage of alienation and disalienation.

Examples? Some are to be found in the present volume. Others will be analysed in the next. Let us list them briefly:

The café: generally an extra-familial and extra-professional meeting place, where people come together on the basis of personal affinities (in principle and at least apparently), because they have the same street or the same neighbourhood in common rather than the same profession or class (although there do exist cafés where the clients are predominantly of the same class or profession). It is a place where the regulars can find a certain luxury, if only on the surface; where they can speak *freely* (about politics, women, etc.), and where if what is said may be superficial, the freedom to say it is fiercely defended; *where they play.*

The funfair: a people's event whose survival and indeed industrialization have occasioned much astonishment. The noise and the deafening music supply the required break. Here we enter a humble, restless microcosm, extraordinary and vulgar. And apparently cheap. Only things which might remind us of work are excluded from this microcosm. In it we find knowledge (the aquarium, anatomical displays), eroticism (naked dancers), travel, wonders, departures, sport, etc.

Radio and, even more so, television, the sudden violent intrusion of the whole world into family and 'private' life, 'presentified' in a way which directly captures the immediate moment, which offers truth and participation, or at least appears to do so ...

Here again we come up against certain characteristics specific to cultural or cultivated leisure. These forms of leisure have functions which are both new and traditional (comparable with reading books, listening to songs and poems, or perhaps dancing as it used to be). Their content is not only entertainment and relaxation, but also knowledge. They do not exclude productive activities – specialized techniques – but they control them. Sometimes it is a matter of techniques which have been rendered obsolete by production and which have become or are in the process of becoming sports (sailing, for example). Finally, as we have already mentioned, the ultimate characteristic of such cultivated leisure activities is that they lead us back towards the feeling of presence, towards nature and the life of the senses (or, as the experts would say, towards an audio-visual milieu revitalized by modern techniques).

Of all the leisure activities concrete sociology should scrutinize, there is one which nowadays seems particularly remarkable.

Everyone knows that for more than a century the French school of painting has enjoyed world-wide renown. But do enough people realize that in France painting is becoming a mass art? That France – for reasons which as yet remain obscure – is becoming a nation of painters? 'Sunday painters', people who spend their leisure time painting, exist in their tens and perhaps hundreds of thousands. Innumerable local or corporate 'art exhibitions' are held. Thus, at a very high cultural level, leisure transcends technical activity to become art. On this level it seems to be using a certain means of expression in order to re-establish a hold on life in its entirety. In this context leisure involves an original search – whether clumsy or skilful is unimportant – for a style of living. And perhaps for an art of living, for a kind of happiness.

To sum up, work, leisure, family life and private life make up a whole which we can call a 'global structure' or 'totality' on condition that we emphasize its historical, shifting, transitory nature. If we consider the critique of everyday life as an aspect of a concrete sociology we can envisage a vast enquiry which will look at professional life, family life and leisure activities in terms of their many-sided interactions. Our particular concern will be to extract what is living, new, positive – the worthwhile needs and fulfilments – from the negative elements: the alienations.

V Some Overviews on the 'Modern World'

As I look up from writing these pages, I see before me one of the loveliest landscapes in the suburbs of Paris. In the distance, the long, lazy curve of the Seine, calm and blue, with its strings of barges. Rows of sparkling cars are driving across the pont de Saint-Cloud. A hill to the left, another to the right. On these hills, groves of trees, gardens, meadows, the last remnants of royal or princely domains. On their island, between the noble lines of these hillsides, I can see the concentrated power of the Renault factories. But nearer, tumbling down the groove of the valley of the Sèvre like insects, in a prosaic disorder, little houses separated by kitchen gardens where guard-dogs bark and cats wail at night. They are called 'pavilions', but no irony is intended. Between these pavilions lie alleyways, muddy paths where the puddles are never dry. Their owners' superficiality oozes forth in an abundance of ridiculous details, china animals on the roofs, glass globes and well-pruned shrubs along the miniature paths, plaques adorned with mottos, self-important pediments. From my window I can see a huge notice nailed to a tree in one of the kitchen gardens, proclaiming: 'Danger of death. Keep out.' On Sunday mornings, especially when the weather is fine, these little houses open their entrails to the sun with strings of red eiderdowns, sheets, blankets. They spread over the hillside like hundreds of dead chickens in an immense shop window.

Not much poverty here. The slums are farther down. And yet not only bourgeois and petty bourgeois live on these hillsides; there are also factory employees, workers. Your neighbour could be a taxi driver.

In the distance, tumult, power, creation, luxury – and poverty as well. Here the city has grown itself an appendix. In among the remnants of a mighty past it has established something terrifying: mediocrity. But for the Algerian workers at Renault, and for many others besides, going into one of these little houses would be like entering heaven.

Why should I say anything against these people who – like me – come home from work every day? They seem to be decent folk who live with their families, who love their children. Can we blame them for not wanting the 'world' in which they feel reasonably at home to be transformed?

Platitude. There are still contrasts here which give it a certain charm. A few more little developments, and even that will disappear. Mediocrity will have swamped this Parisian suburb just as it has swamped villages as much as ten kilometres away from the city. One has to go back to the office buildings in the centre of Paris to rediscover something of the beauty or charm of times gone by.

Will there ever be anything great which is not dehumanized – or a form of happiness which is not tinged with mediocrity?

The picturesque is disappearing with a rapidity which provides the

reactionaries with an ample supply of ammunition for their pro-
clamations and jeremiads. Above all it is being reduced to its vile
essence: poverty. What used to be its spark of beauty – the primitive
diversity of everyday man, the generosity of his nature, the many-
faceted local eccentricities, the brutal, swarming tumult – that beauty
has disappeared. It has become congealed into so many museum
pieces floating on the muddy ocean of destitution. What disappointments await the naïve traveller to the famous cities of the fabulous East!
Were all those old story-tellers lying? Did they see things differently
then? Can things and people have changed so much? The eagerly
awaited wonders, the marvellous surprises, the ruins, the monuments,
the stories from the Thousand and One Nights, the folksongs and
dances – they are no longer enough to colour the spectacle and
transform it for us. Naples, Baghdad, Calcutta: the same sun shines
down on the same rags, the same running sores. The myths have
disappeared, the rituals and magic spells have lost their glamour. All
we can see now are the destitute masses, and the ignoble apparatus of
domination which lies over them, the unlovely art of power. There is
nothing left to seduce us. Everywhere a bare-faced display of force:
rifles, armoured cars, policemen.

Wherever people are in the throes of liberation from the old
oppressions, they are also sacrificing – there is no way they can avoid it
– certain ways of life which for many years were great and beautiful.
The tractor and the mechanical seeder must replace the gestures of the
ploughman. Thus when backward countries move forward they
produce ugliness, platitude and mediocrity as though that meant
progress. And the advanced countries which have known history in all
its greatness, produce platitude as though its proliferation were inevitable.

So the New China, from the lowliest peasant girl to the highest Party
chief, dresses up in blue overalls. She has given up the mandarins' silks,
for hundreds of millions of peasants the direct opposite of their own
rags. She has relegated them to museums or turned them into export
items, along with the magic dragons and ivory buddhas. She is
becoming austere, her mind bent on being victorious on the labour
front. Solid Republics are founded on virtue.

In the USSR in September and October 1954 various articles
appeared which presented some new problems. The *Kommunist* of 14

October suggests that the standard of culture in the Soviet Union and the handling of dialectical analysis were reaching a point where the simplified black-or-white, good-versus-bad view of reality which had been generally accepted hitherto would have to be abandoned. Thus writers, artists and philosophers needed to set about examining reality and life in all their aspects, distinguishing between their various elements, discerning the seeds of the new germinating in the old, separating the positive from the negative, but also grasping all the contradictions, even in what was new.

At the same time (and, to borrow a time-hallowed formula, this was no coincidence) the problem of *taste* was raised in the USSR for the first time. On 10 October the review *Novy Mir* writes: 'During the period of the construction of Communist society, the problem arises of how to elaborate a style of living in material culture which will best satisfy popular requirements.' There follows a comparison between 'the industrial aesthetic' of cars and railway engines, and the aesthetic anachronism of the objects on sale in the Moscow stores: sofas with fringes, beds with fruit-and-flower decorations, imitations of the mirrors and knick-knacks to be seen in the Savoy (a restaurant frequented by tradesmen under the old regime).

And the philosopher Alexandrov, who was then Minister of Culture, is quoted for his part as follows: 'everything surrounding man in his everyday life – houses, architecture, the organization of living space, furniture and household objects – is also part of culture, and influences taste ...'

The Soviets are thus discovering problems which we, who live in a capitalist country, have been aware of for a long time (which does not mean that we have solved them). As far as the style of everyday life is concerned, the Soviets have not progressed far beyond 1900. They are discovering *social needs* which are already known and which have already been explored (which is not the same thing as saying that they have been satisfied or fulfilled). They have attained petty-bourgeois mediocrity as though that were progress. How easily and quickly will they leave it behind them? Today the latest stop is the 'industrial aesthetic', an old chestnut which is liable to involve them in more than one lapse of taste ...

These observations are not intended to imply any hostility or even mistrust of the USSR, which remains the *objective* support of the democratic forces and the socialist movement. On the contrary: that a great civilization in the process of formation should express such problems frankly and lucidly can be considered a sign of its vigour and innovativeness. But nevertheless these facts give food for thought; we observe that socialism and the construction of socialism also involve criticism of everyday life. While not necessarily agreeing with Jean-Marie Domenach's conclusions, we can accept what he has to say on the subject of Yugoslavia:

> We have failed to pay enough attention in our analyses to this more immediate and less easily grasped reality of everyday life; let us not forget it, Marxism started from a concrete observation of alienation, and aimed to eliminate it. Nothing would be more useful today than a sociology of everyday life, separate from proclamations and official statistics, a sociology of the conditions of real existence in a socialist country: we could take a fresh look at the shortages and the sufferings which lead to unexpected explosions of unrest; by studying new alienations we could achieve a newly conceived revolutionary theory which would no longer be based exclusively on the poverty of the workers in 1850, but on the concrete sufferings of the men of 1956. Sadly, no such sociology exists as yet, in any of the popular democracies (although objective surveys on work, youth, etc. would help to avoid a good many wrong turns), and we have to make do with fragmentary impressions, naturally subject to chance, mood, and therefore extremely questionable . . .[68]

This leads us in turn to pose yet more problems.

A few years ago, 'the new man', the socialist or Communist man, seemed radically and infinitely different from what 'we' are, 'we' who are immersed in capitalism and contaminated by the bourgeoisie even in terms of the way we struggle against it. This is how literature presented the new man: entirely positive, heroic, fearless and blameless in work, war or love. He was defined by his wholehearted devotion to (socialist) society and by the way he discovered the meaning of his individuality in dedication and self-sacrifice. That the individual was dedicated to society, that he was defined as well as determined by society, was never doubted for one minute, and this affirmation formed the basis for both an ethic and an aesthetic.

However neither this ethic nor this aesthetic was ever successfully or clearly formulated. Even less was anything definitive written, or a style of living developed, which might have imposed them. Is that not an indication, the visible sign of a flaw? The symptom of something lacking? In fact it became clear that the exaltation of the social man in socialist society was ending up as a set of perfunctory images of limited interest and certainly of limited use once they had outlived certain specific circumstances (the struggle for the Plan, production goals, or the war effort). So in ·place of the monotonous display of 'positive heroes' there was a demand for images of the real man, diverse, individual, complete with his conflicts and contradictions, and exemplified in his different types. There was even an official statement to the effect that certain negative types were not without interest – and that there were a great many men and women who experience within themselves the clash between the old and the new, the positive and the negative. Men and women in transition ...

Thus it is in his similarities with how men used to be that the new man becomes humanized. And we find the socialist or Communist man much more interesting when the distance between him and 'us' is reduced. He gains in sympathy and interest what he loses in terms of his ability to impress the naïve and the stupid. Even if the contradictions are different, even if they must be emphasized in different ways, even if over there they are fruitful while back here they are devastating, even if the attitude of the socialist man towards his work and society is totally different to 'ours', the contradictions allow us to understand, to know, to communicate. They enlighten 'us'. In the past an over-facile rhetoric has taken the 'socialist man' and the 'Communist man' over, comparing them to saints, to knights in shining armour. From our lowly positions we looked up in admiration at the Positive Hero. It was not possible to love him. Now that he has become contradictory, the socialist man is no taller than we are.

But this means we can ask him questions. But this means we become more demanding. We ask ourselves: 'What is socialism exactly? How does it intervene in everyday life? What does it change?' And the answer is unclear. The elimination of the bourgeoisie and class antagonisms? The suppression of capitalist relations of property and production? These are only negative definitions. We find the picture of a bourgeois society without a bourgeoisie neither reassuring nor satisfying. We think that there is, or will be, something else. But what? Accepting one's work, making it – willingly if possible – one's first priority, working harder, willing productivity to increase rather than merely putting up with it? These ideas are fine as far as they go. Admittedly they are probably all essential, very important for the social relations of production, and perhaps they would go some way towards defining a mode of production economically. But as a definition of a culture, a civilization, a humanity, a joy of living which are really *new*, they are inadequate. Nor can they define a worthwhile way of living which could come into being thanks to its own powers of persuasion.[69]

The problem is not limited to ethics and aesthetics. It forces us to return to the theoretical and scientific principles of Marxism. What is the exact role of the productive forces in society? Unquestionably production in the USSR and in the other countries of the socialist camp is growing at an increasingly rapid rate, and above all so are the means of production (Marx's Department I).

It is ludicrous to define socialism solely by the development of the productive forces. Economic statistics cannot answer the question: 'What is socialism?' Men do not fight and die *for* tons of steel, or for tanks or atomic bombs. They aspire to be happy, not to produce. What is more, both production (global or per capita) and labour productivity are even higher in the USA than they are in the USSR.

The productive forces do not define socialism. For socialism, it is necessary for the productive forces to be at a high level, as the example of the USSR shows, but that is not enough to institute it, as the example of the USA shows. And yet if 'life is to change' it is essential for the productive forces to reach a certain level. Moreover, change in the political superstructure (in its class nature: here the bourgeois State – there the proletarian State, controlling the means of production, the dictatorship of the proletariat, its leading role embodied in and exercised by the Party) does not *ipso facto* imply a concrete change in the way people live. In the capitalist countries, the superstructures (the 'shells' in the sense Lenin used the word in the text quoted earlier) are in contradiction with the living contents, because they *lag behind* them, whether it be the State or legal relations of property. This super-stuctural backwardness acts as a brake. And it will be the task and the meaning of the political Revolution to destroy these shells, to release their contents, and to rebuild new superstructures from the bottom up. In the countries which are building socialism today, the political and ideological superstructures start off *ahead of* the social relations and the economic base. In the backward countries this is what the Revolution is all about. But how is the contradiction resolved? How is a change which in these backward countries begins at the top, in the stratosphere of society, passed downwards through an immense apparatus into the humble depths of everyday life? Will it not sometimes come to a halt on the way? Will not whatever comes between the base and the apex slow it down or divert it?

To put it another way, socialism (the new society, the new life) can only be defined *concretely* on the level of everyday life, as a system of changes in what can be called lived experience.[70] Now, half a century of historical upheavals have taught us that everyday relations between men – 'lived experience' – change more slowly than the structure of the State. And in a different way, at a different rate. Thus in the history of societies modifications in the different sectors take place unevenly, some ahead of their times, others lagging behind. The fact that one sector is ahead does not mean that there is immediate progress in another. And vice versa. According to the productive and technical forces, certain social needs arise in bourgeois society which capitalism is unable to satisfy; they modify everyday life in a positive way, while at the same time introducing negative elements such as dissatisfaction, disappointment, alienation. On the other hand, in the socialist countries, or in the countries in which socialism is being built, the real social needs – which socialism should both stimulate, detect and satisfy – lag behind ideology and the superstructures.

Let us summarize and put what we have said into perspective. Today, the Revolution has lost its mythical meaning and the now-outmoded aspects of its former romanticism. In 1917, as in 1789, the revolutionaries thought they were entering straight into another world, an entirely new one. They were passing from despotism to freedom, from capitalism to Communism. Just one sign from them and life was going to change like a stage set. Today we know that life is never simple. There are no magic wands. We have been taught to look at necessary Revolution in a hard, realistic light. Still inadequately controlled by human will and freedom, necessity has produced a historical result that Marx did not foresee. The political Revolution which is a necessary condition for the transformation of the world, was first accomplished in the backward ('under-developed') countries. The incalculable consequences of this fact are springing up all around us, filling our era inexorably with tension and discord. This relationship of confrontation between two politically opposed 'camps' or 'worlds' is extending and amplifying the class struggle to world-wide, historical dimensions. But only a shamelessly absurd logic could mistakenly conclude from this contradiction, this 'coexistence' in antagonism, that the men in these two camps, and the way they actually live, had nothing in common.

In his lectures at Sverdlovsk University in 1924, Stalin defined the spirit of Leninism as the synthesis of Russian revolutionary enthusiasm and American pragmatism. Since then, now that the romanticism has faded away, the balance has possibly tipped in favour of the American sense of business, yield, results. Is this a bad thing? Certainly, if it is, it has its positive side. It is true that one of the camps is on the decline while the other is expanding; the latter may well be able to incorporate whatever is best or more effective in the former.

But to define 'the new' by sifting out everything that distinguishes it from the old is not as easy as the dogmatists with their lack of dialectic used to believe. Our era is truly an era of transition; everything about it is transitory, everything, right down to men and their lives. The informed observer will be as struck as much by similarities as by differences, as much by the unity within contradiction as by contradiction itself. The one must not eliminate the other! (A little example, quoted from a comedian: there are secret police in democratic countries as well as in reactionary or Fascist countries. In the democratic countries police chiefs are changed very often; in the socialist countries sometimes they even shoot them. Under Fascism they last as long as the regime!)

Today, despite the extreme unevenness of development, a sort of vast world-wide levelling process is taking place. The myths and the ideologies are falling; they are nothing more than shells concealing – very badly – facts, results, needs. Backward social structures are collapsing, giving way to demands that the social average be raised to the average level achieved in the developed countries. From one side of the world to the other questions are being asked about production and productivity, power of consumption, distribution of the gross national product, diversification of investments (and the 'socialist' countries realize that one day or another they will be obliged to do voluntarily and consciously what the capitalist countries have done involuntarily and blindly: invest in the production of consumer goods). So everywhere we see that advanced automated machines, power stations and atomic energy, tractors and combine harvesters are being perceived as a hope and a solution. But the 'man–machine' relation is only one aspect of the question. Men and women everywhere are aspiring to build their everyday lives on a solid basis, to escape from insecurity and poverty. These are mass problems, problems of social aspirations and social needs. The face of the world is changing; everywhere the everyday nature of life asserts itself, conscious now of its own weakness and its own value. Life is appearing in all its nakedness. The result for this period of transition is an appalling outburst of platitude which is in singular contrast to the other characteristics of this self-same period: inordinate ambitions, failures on a par with those ambitions, tragedies, threats, an ocean of blood and mire – and with brutal stupidity and platitude thrown in for good measure.

Should we attempt to escape from platitude through the past, the tragic and the mythical, the surreal or the transcendental? Or through the marvellous, in other words through the trumpery of lost illusions and miracles? In the course of our study we will attempt wherever possible to demonstrate the new marvels which are being born at the very heart of mediocrity. They are simple, human marvels. Let us name one of them without further ado: *trust.*

It is as old as social life itself; very close to naïvety, to foolishness; always abused from childhood on (trust in one's parents, in masters and bosses, priests and gods, faith and destiny, love); always changed into a distrust which is almost as unexpressed as the initial naïvety – today trust in life is taking root in life and becoming a need. In the contradictory dualism 'trust–distrust' – contradictory in an embryonic, suppressed way, more ambiguous than antagonistic – trust is slowly getting the upper hand. In spite of the most dreadful trials, the most awful illusions, it is getting stronger. Today trust is bursting forth, today trust is growing. We will see how it is at work deep in the heart of the everyday, and how it works through its opposite, doubt – the restless need for material security. This will be one of the themes of the second volume of *Critique of Everyday Life.*[71]

VI   Once Again, the Theory of Alienation . . .

Now let us return to several questions which we touched upon at the beginning and elucidate them more thoroughly. A certain number of Marxists, and notably the 'official' Marxists, gave this book a rather bad reception when it was first published. Why? In the first place, at that time in France there was a widespread prejudice against *sociology*. Due to the fact that certain theoreticians of the kind generally described from the political point of view as 'right-wing socialists' had reduced Marxism to a sociology, Marxist revolutionaries had drawn the hasty conclusion that sociology does not exist as a science. Indeed, in the USSR sociology is not included among the social sciences. When the term is used there, it is in reference to societies generally, either ethnographically or ethically, or even simply administratively. That there are ideologues – notably in Germany (Weber, Mannheim, etc.) – who have reduced the historical and social sciences, together with philosophy and the theory of knowledge, to sociology, is offered as an irrefutable argument; but this is merely a way of avoiding, by pure and simple negation, the real difficulties the sociologist encounters when he wants to situate and determine the object and method of his discipline.

We should add that the disappearance of sociology from the USSR and from revolutionary Marxism surely has another, deeper significance. We have already quoted an important text by Lenin which demonstrates how the materialist analysis of social relations in Marx goes beyond political economy (by renewing it). Far from excluding a scientific sociology which would study social relations (or certain aspects of them), the notion of *socio-economic formation* demands and requires it. We may note that the concept of *socio-economic formation* has almost disappeared from Marxist writing, to be replaced by the simplified scheme: '*economic base – political superstructure*'. Theoretically, Marxist thought and method have become impoverished. Practically, neither capitalist society nor socialist society in the process of formation has been studied in a concrete way. Economic statistics on the one hand, and observations attacking or defending ideology and the political apparatus in the two 'camps' on the other, have been deemed sufficient. This reveals an extremely serious development: *the growing break with objectivity* which in our view characterizes the Stalinist interpretation of Marxism.

This dogmatic and schematic simplification of Marxism, with its elimination of sociological research, went hand in hand with a simplification of philosophy. Why was the concept of *alienation* treated with such mistrust? Why was the Hegelianism in Marx's early writings rejected? Where does the tendency to separate Marx from his roots, and his mature scientific works from his early writings, come from? Or the tendency to date and determine the formation of Marxism from his political writings? Analysis shows that behind all this lies that murky mixture of simplistic empiricism, pliant subjectivism and doctrinaire, authoritarian dogmatism which is the philosophical basis of the Stalinist interpretation of Marxism. In Soviet society, *alienation could and must no longer be an issue*. By order from above, for reasons of State, the concept had to disappear. Why? Was it because alienation (economic, ideological, political) really had disappeared? The divorce between Stalin's decree and the reality, between ideology – brought into line with propaganda – and the objective truth, could only get wider.

This was why the Marxists who imported this Stalinist interpretation into France – not merely uncritically, but actually shooting down the slightest hint of criticism as though it were treason – could not accept sociology as a science, or the philosophical concept of alienation, or even philosophy as such. They had to be reductive, simplistic, schematic, dogmatic. And of course the Stalinist interpretation of Marxism,[72] which had already been pedagogically and politically simplified, and bent in the direction of a State ideology, could only become even more desiccated. So dogmatic was their attitude that all they could see in the *Critique of Everyday Life* was an attempt to analyse certain aspects of bourgeois society *sociologically*, without actually making a stand against it. They imagined it was taking a step backwards, that it was giving up political economy, and even dialectical and historical materialism. (Sectarian and dogmatic Marxist criticism frequently begins by isolating texts from their context, and then from the author's other works, in order to pin down some 'formula' or other.) They considered my sociological point of view to be narrow and depoliticized; as if the sociology annihilated all ideological or political criticism. (Sectarian Marxists have nothing much to say – and everything they have to say they say over and over again; when they were unable to find what they were looking for immediately in my book, they insisted that I had deliberately left it out!)

These attacks were spoken rather than written, and took place more by word of mouth behind my back than in actual discussions with me. Here are some extracts from a letter written by a young Marxist who was otherwise sympathetic towards the book:

> Your critique ends up being a theory of the decline of everyday life, of the growing alienation of a naïve way of life in which you sometimes appear to see the remains of a golden age for humanity ... Alienation in production consists above all in the fact that the worker is deprived of a share of the product of his labour. Mystification (the superstructure) also deprives the workers of an objective vision of the relations of production. This superstructure, this ideological alienation is complex (human relations hypostatized in religion – justified in ethics – explained by the pseudo-social sciences, by the political ideology of the dominant classes, etc....). But it cannot be said that social man has undergone a process of increasing alienation, for example by passing from slavery to serfdom and the proletariat ... Some of your propositions suggest that you believe that the analysis of everyday life can only begin with the theory of ideological mystification ... You say that the scientific study of society and of the proletariat begins by tearing away the veil of ideologies, and that Marxism describes and analyses the everyday life of society. But this is all grist to the mill of those who maintain that you are limiting Marxism to a sort of materialist phenomenology of the superstructures ... It would be worth your while to actually say that you are writing a theory of the super-structures ... You also seem to be saying that all the parts of Marx's writings are of equal importance. Your enemies have used this declaration that Marxism constitutes a whole, and is therefore a science and a philosophy, to conclude that you see economic facts and ideologies as having equal importance. That accusation of phenomenology again ... And it is telling!

This letter is a good illustration of how confused the ideas and discussions were (moreover they were never openly discussed in public or explored in any depth).

Before replying briefly, this is an appropriate place to emphasize another shabby polemical procedure associated with sectarian Marxism. In fact, whether historically or today, Marxist thought and the Marxist thinker cannot exist in isolation from each other. Absolute Marxism and the purely Marxist manner of thinking are intellectual entities created by dogmatism; this dogmatism has become entangled in the very contradictions it has unwittingly created; in fact Marxism asserts that thought – all thought – can only express itself historically, socially, contextually. I (using the pronoun generically) am a French Marxist who writes and thinks in French; who has been formed by French culture. One would not have to go very deeply into my dialectical thinking to find a predilection for lucid, well-organized, clearly articulated ideas, for *analysis*. Clearly I have a rationalist and Cartesian background. It is indeed conceivable that at one time or another these tendencies of mine may conflict with the materialist and dialectical thinking which, despite its differences with my background, is my starting point; and I know this. It is equally conceivable that I have resolved this conflict, or that I will resolve it, in a creative way. And what could be more natural than such a conflict, given that everything is contradictory and that we only move ahead in and through contradictions? But here comes the sectarian, dogmatic Marxist. Frowning, threatening, contemptuous, or indifferent, he smells something he disapproves of, something incompatible, something impossible: one cannot be both a Cartesian and a Marxist; Marxism is radically different from Cartesianism in respect of its theory, its content and its aims. Therefore he will define me as a Cartesian, fixing me for ever, labelling me, nailing me to the whipping post of Cartesianism. And he will be very pleased with himself: he will have served the cause of Marxism and the proletariat. And if I answer back, he will brand me with other labels, other epithets. In fact he will have transformed a problem, in other words a real conflict – and therefore a creative one in so far as I am able to resolve it – into an irresolvable, unproductive antinomy. He will have burdened living reality with a parasitic growth: his interpretation. And he will have been drawn unwittingly into a contradiction between the 'point of view' of Marxism and the proletariat, and the 'point of view' of acquired culture and national tradition; between the point of view of the 'new' and that of the 'old'. It is true that subsequently the sectarian can save face by jumping nimbly from one point of view to the other. He can even maintain that there is no contradiction between the 'points of view'; which is true, since it is he who introduced the contradiction in the first place, exaggerating it to the point of antagonism when necessary, and dismissing it when no longer required! And now we are gradually isolating a process of degeneration in dialectical thought: 'points of view' and the jump from one point of view to the other.

Thus it is fashionable for the dogmatists to use dominant modes of thought from outside Marxism against anyone who attempts to introduce new ideas. If phenomenology is fashionable, then they see phenomenology in every idea which does not duplicate the proven 'formulas'. If Hegelianism is in fashion, then they will find Hegelianism wherever they want to find it, etc. And maybe, indeed certainly, there is something true in all this, since, after all, phenomenology, Hegelianism or Cartesian analysis also correspond to something around us and within us. If not they would have lost all meaning, or would not have meant anything in the first place! And this is one of the worst aspects of dogmatism: as soon as it touches a sore point it turns it only too easily into a global condemnation, using a constant process of superfluity and imperturbable logic instead of analysing works, situations and men dialectically.

Dogmatism is a great evil which comes in countless forms. If we are to exterminate it we must hunt it down in every nook and cranny and drag it from its hiding place by the tail like a rat.

The amusing thing is that the man who wrote the letter quoted above begins by rejecting this form of criticism; then he appears not only to accept it but actually to overshoot the mark by seeming to embrace a theory of superstructures which is a theory of superstructures and nothing else. Thus he wavers between dogmatism and theoretical opportunism or eclecticism.

Sectarian criticism also forgets that the economic and the ideological as they are expressed in everyday life only attain the level of political consciousness at moments of revolutionary crisis. This is something Lenin wrote about at length in his analyses of the political crisis. At such moments all the elements of social practice, of spontaneous consciousness, and of the life of the masses and the classes are condensed and concentrated in political life. Outside of such moments, social practice splits up into discrete and even divergent areas; notably into the economic and the political. In everyday life, from that point on, the immediate and the ideological join forces to form a shell in which economic reality, the operation of the existent political superstructures, and revolutionary political consciousness are all contained and concealed.

So to reach reality we must indeed tear away the veil, that veil which is forever being born and reborn of everyday life, and which masks everyday life along with its deepest or loftiest implications.

There is no reason not to quote Lenin again: 'The beginning – the most simple, ordinary, mass, immediate "Being": the single commodity ('Sein' in political economy). The analysis of it as a social relation. A *double* analysis, deductive and inductive – logical and historical ...'[73] Thus the simplest event – a woman buying a pound of sugar, for example – must be analysed. Knowledge will grasp whatever is hidden within it. To understand this simple event, it is not enough merely to describe it; research will disclose a tangle of reasons and causes, of essences and 'spheres': the woman's life, her biography, her job, her family, her class, her budget, her eating habits, how she uses money, her opinions and her ideas, the state of the market, etc. Finally I will have grasped the sum total of capitalist society, the nation and its history. And although what I grasp becomes more and more profound, it is contained from the start in the original little event. So now I see the humble events of everyday life as having two sides: a little, individual, chance event – and at the same time an infinitely complex social event, richer than the many 'essences' it contains within itself. The social phenomenon may be defined as the unity of these two sides. It remains for us to explain why the infinite complexity of these events is hidden, and to discover why – and this too is part of their reality – they appear to be so humble.

Is it truly a question of the superstructures? Is it the superstructures alone that matter? No: it is a question of superstructures only in so far as they are created at each instant of everyday life and social practice – in so far as they are constantly coming down to penetrate these realms from above. And also only in so far as the superstructures are linked to society as a whole, to social practice as a whole, although everyday practice is dispersed, fragmented – be it in terms of an individual or a specific and determined social activity: in them the whole is represented by the part, and vice versa.

It is therefore not only a question of the superstructures. In truth it is a question of *sociology*, in other words of a science which studies an aspect or sector of social relations.

And now the new reader – or the old one who reads this book again – will be able to judge for himself. Did it contain a theory of *increasing*

79

alienation, based upon a fundamental naïvety, and with archaic contents left over from some golden age (to put it more scientifically: from primitive community – or from direct, immediate person-to-person relationships)? If it did, then the author must have expressed his thoughts badly. He believes that philosophically the process of social development involves two sides: *the increasing fulfilment of man* – and also an *increasing alienation* up to and including capitalist society. The one in the other. The one via the other. On the one hand *objectification*, in other words the more-and-more real, objective existence of human beings, both in the human world of products and works, and in the human strengths and powers developed throughout history; and on the other hand, and equally on the increase, externalization, an uprooting of the self, a split, an estrangement.

In capitalist society this contradictory process – this tearing – is at its maximum. This society and the concepts which express it (for example the idea of *social labour* discovered by classic bourgeois economy) shed light on the march of history, the past and the future. And this is why the objective analysis of it as a totality[74] undertaken in *Capital* is a decisive one.[75] The ever-unfinished development of the productive forces – in economic terms – has the philosophical implication of a new stage in human fulfilment, of limitless possibilities. But the corresponding alienation here is just as all-encompassing. It encompasses life in its entirety.

In capitalist society, money – the externalization of relations between human beings by means of commodities – takes on an absolute power. But this is merely economic alienation: *money-as-fetish*, objectified outside of men, functioning by itself, and as such one of the objects studied by the science called political economy. This economic alienation, though an integral part of total alienation, is but one of its aspects. Although the volume which follows contains certain quotations, let me clarify matters now by quoting some long extracts from the most important text by Marx on this question.[76] Obviously some of Marx's observations were only valid for his own times. One may still find workers living in hovels – even in France. But it cannot be said that this is the general rule, much less a law.

VII   Alienated Labour

The worker becomes poorer the more wealth he produces, the more his production increases in power and extent. The worker becomes an ever cheaper commodity the more commodities he produces. The *devaluation* of the human world grows in direct proportion to the *increase in value* of the world of things. Labour not only produces commodities; it also produces itself and the workers as a *commodity* and it does so in the same proportion in which it produces commodities in general.

This fact simply means that the object that labour produces, its product, stands opposed to it as *something alien*, as a *power independent* of the producer. The product of labour is labour embodied and made material in an object, it is the *objectification* of labour. The realization of labour is its objectification. In the sphere of political economy this realization of labour appears as a *loss of reality* for the worker, objectification as *loss of and bondage to the object*, and appropriation as *estrangement*, as *alienation [Entaüsserung]* ...

It is the same in religion. The more man puts into God, the less he retains within himself. The worker places his life in the object; but now it no longer belongs to him, but to the object ... What the product of his labour is, he is not ... The externalization [*Entaüsserung*] of the worker in his product means not only that his labour becomes an object, and *external* existence, but that it exists *outside him*, independently of him and alien to him, and confronts him as an autonomous power; that the life which he has bestowed on the object confronts him as hostile and alien ...

Political economy conceals the estrangement in the nature of labour by ignoring the direct relationship between the worker (labour) *and production.* It is true that labour produces marvels for the rich, but it produces privation for the worker; it produces palaces, but hovels for the worker ... It produces intelligence, but it produces idiocy and cretinism for the worker ...

After all, the product is simply the résumé of the activity, of the production. So if the product of labour is alienation, production itself must be active alienation, the alienation of activity, the activity of alienation. The estrangement of the object of labour merely summarizes the estrangement, the alienation in the activity of labour itself.

What constitutes the alienation of labour?

Firstly, the fact that labour is *external* to the worker, i.e. does not belong to his essential being; that he therefore does not confirm himself in his work, but denies himself, feels miserable and not happy ... Hence the worker feels himself only when he is not working; when he is working he does not feel himself. He is at home when he is not working, and not at home when he is working ... [His labour] is therefore not the satisfaction of a need but a mere *means* to satisfy needs outside itself ... Just as in religion the spontaneous activity of the human imagination, the human brain and the human heart detaches itself from the individual and reappears as the alien activity of a god or of a devil, so the activity of the worker is not his own spontaneous activity. It belongs to another, it is a loss of his self.

The result is that man (the worker) feels that he is acting freely only in his animal functions – eating, drinking and procreating, or at most in his dwelling and adornment – while in his human functions he is nothing more than an animal.

It is true that eating, drinking and procreating, etc., are also genuine human functions. However, when abstracted from our other aspects of human activity and turned into final and exclusive ends, they are animal ...

This relationship is the relationship of the worker to his own activity as something which is alien and does not belong to him, activity as passivity [*Leiden*], power as impotence, procreation as emasculation, the worker's *own* physical and mental energy, his personal life – for what is life but activity? – as an activity directed against himself, which is independent of him and does not belong to him. *Self-estrangement*, as compared with the estrangement of the *object* [*Sache*] mentioned above ...

Nature is man's *inorganic body*, that is to say nature in so far as it is not the human body. Man *lives* from nature, i.e. nature is his body, and he must maintain a continuing dialogue with it if he is not to die. To say that man's physical and mental life is linked to nature simply means that nature is linked to itself, for man is a part of nature.

Estranged labour not only (1) estranges nature from man and (2) estranges man from himself ... it also estranges man from his *species*. It turns his *species-life* into a means for his individual life. Firstly it estranges life-species and individual life, and secondly it turns the latter, in its abstract form, into the purpose of the former, also in its abstract and estranged form.

For in the first place labour, *life activity, productive life* itself appears to man only as a *means* for the satisfaction of a need, the need to preserve physical existence. But productive life is species-life. It is life-producing life. The whole character of a species, its species-character, resides in the nature of its life activity, and free conscious activity constitutes the species-character of man. Life itself appears only as a *means of life*.

The animal is immediately one with its life activity. It is not distinct from that activity; it *is* that activity. Man makes his life activity itself an object of his will and consciousness. He has conscious life activity. It is not a determination with which he directly merges. Conscious life activity directly distinguishes man from animal life activity. Only because of that is he a species-being. Or rather, he is a conscious being, i.e. his own life is an object for him, only because he is a species-being. Only because of that is his activity free activity. Estranged labour reverses the relationship so that man, just because he is a conscious being, makes his life activity, his *being* (*Wesen*], a mere means for his *existence* ...

It is true that animals also produce ... But ... they produce one-sidedly, while man produces universally; they produce only when immediate physical need compels them to do so ... while man is capable of producing according to the standards of every species ... hence man also produces in accordance with the laws of beauty.

It is therefore in the fashioning of the objective that man really proves himself to be a *species-being*. Such production is his active species-life. Through it nature appears as *his* work and his reality. The object of labour is therefore the *objectification of the species-life of man*: for man reproduces himself not only intellectually, in his consciousness, but actively and actually, and he can therefore contemplate himself in a world he himself has created. In tearing away the object of his production from man, estranged labour therefore tears away from him his *species-life*, his true species-objectivity, and transforms his advantage over animals into the disadvantage that his inorganic body, nature, is taken from him ...

An immediate consequence of man's estrangement from the product of his labour, his life activity, his species-being, is the *estrangement of man from man*. When man confronts himself, he also confronts *other* men ...

In general, the proposition that man is estranged from his species-being means that each man is estranged from the others and that all are estranged from man's essence ...

The *alien* being to whom labour and the product of labour belong ... can be none other than *man* himself ... a *man other than the worker.*

Thus Marx does not limit alienation to exploitation, to the fact that a share of the product is taken away from the worker individually or collectively (the working class) by the individual and the class which controls the means of production. He analyses alienation under several headings:

(a) the alienation of the worker as an *object* (the alien power which turns him into an object);

(b) the alienation of productive activity, in other words of labour itself (which is divided and split up by it);

(c) the alienation of man as species-being, member of the human species – as a system of *humanized species-needs*;

(d) the alienation of man as a being of nature, as a set of *natural needs*.

A little farther on, in other texts, Marx introduces some new elements: 'The machine accommodates itself to man's *weakness*, in order to turn *weak* man into a machine.'[77] Or again: 'The *division of labour* is the economic expression of the *social nature of labour* within estrangement.'[78] And again:

> *just as* society itself produces *man* as *man*, so it is *produced* by him ... The *human* essence of nature exists only for *social man*.[79] ... Each attempts to establish over the other an alien power, in the hope of thereby achieving satisfaction of his own selfish needs.[80] Estrangement appears not only in the fact that the means of *my* life belong to *another*, but also in the fact that *my* desire is the inaccessible possession of *another*, and also in the fact that all things are *other* than themselves, that my activity is *other* than itself, and that finally – and this goes for the capitalists too – an *inhuman* power rules over everything.[81]

These texts make the polyscopic, omnipresent character of alienation as a concept, a reality and a *philosophical* theory linked to the social *sciences*, more than abundantly clear, and this as much in regard to productive forces and social relations as in regard to ideology, and even more profoundly in regard to man's relation *with nature* and with *his own nature*.

The main quotation (from 'Estranged Labour') shows that for Marx work constitutes man's essence as a creator: a being of needs who creates his own needs; and it is precisely work that alienation humiliates, atomizes, overpowers.

The theory of impoverishment is an integral part of Marx's theory of alienation. And yet the two concepts are discrete; thus the facts relating to them must be studied separately, the latter being a more extensive area than the former. Therefore if one emphasizes the idea of alienation it means that one does not reject a priori the theory of the *tendency* towards impoverishment. The economic laws formulated by Marx always deal with tendencies, and are thwarted by other forces, other activities and other laws. As long as it is not backed up by scientific analyses of the life and the needs of the proletariat, compared by region, type of industry, and country, the analysis of impoverishment, like the analysis of alienation, is just so much hot air. A priori it is probable that here, as elsewhere, differences in development play an important role. It is becoming essential to undertake not only an economic analysis, but also a sociological one (dealing with basic or differentiated needs, the degrees and the structures of those needs, be they old or new, hidden or unsatisfied, etc.).

There are other texts by Marx which show clearly that in his view the crowning element in the inhuman power which reigns over all social life is the State; it consolidates that power, and sanctions it. In one sense *political* alienation (with the *political superstition* by which the State is actually endowed with a life superior to the life of society) is the most serious type of alienation. In another sense, it also determines the sphere in which the struggle against alienation ('disalienation') and radical criticism, its auxiliary, will be most effective, most necessary and most directly possible.

It is equally clear that Marx sees the *division of labour* as the cause of alienation. Now he never suggested that the political Revolution, on the level of the superstructures – nor socialism, on the level of the relations of production – could bring an end to the division of labour. He merely imagined that after a transitional period of unspecified length, Communism could supersede the division of labour. During this transition, the forms of alienation (the law, for example, and of course the division of labour) would carry on. Therefore Marx never limited the sphere of alienation to capitalism; and never did he suggest that socialism, or the proletarian Revolution, would bring alienation to an absolute and immediate end.[82] Alienation persists, or is even born again in new forms, along with its contradictory process, the process of 'disalienation'. But here we are broaching new problems which go beyond our immediate concerns, and maybe beyond the concerns of the book itself. For these are philosophical problems: the philosopher may well go so far as to ask himself whether all realization, all objectification, does not involve an alienation as its own deep-seated negativity.

And so there is still more to be said about the theory of alienation.

But before we proceed, we should clear up a difficulty which is linked to this theory, but distinct from it. A letter the author received shortly after the book was published said:

You demonstrate an analogy between acting, theatre and life ... You emphasize the importance of mask and character ... But what about the new man? Doesn't he supersede the opposition between acting and being serious? ... In my opinion, he no longer wears a mask for other people, not even the mask of irony ...

Oh, how wonderfully optimistic we were after the Liberation! It was zero hour for history, the man of old was disappearing, the new man was bursting forth in all his beauty and undeniable authenticity! What has become of this beautiful and naïve image? And this beautiful and naïve confidence? The new man, the new life, these were the images, the hopes, the myths at the moment of the Liberation, replacing the myth which had inspired the struggle in October 1917: the (almost) immediate transition to Communism. Significantly, the hope of the Liberation focused itself on everyday life and expressed the need to make a break – which we have encountered at the microscopic level of day-to-day worries and preoccupations – at the level of society. Indeed we could ask ourselves why this naïve expectation expressed itself as it did on the ethical level. And why it found it so easy to abandon the aesthetic level, where masks and acting are not considered necessarily bad. Would there still be theatre in art if there was no longer any theatre in real life? And if 'personalities' no longer put on their act – for themselves and for other people? The naïve belief that the new was at hand made it easy to sacrifice the aesthetic for the ethical. For better and for worse, this expectation of an absolute ethical authenticity was completely disappointed, a misfortune from which aesthetics came out very well – proving that the best things come to those who wait. Events have surpassed even Shakespeare for buffoonery and tragedy; history has gone even farther than the trials in Brecht's plays. What theatrical production could compete with the Rajk trials? What stage effect could rival the Khrushchev report?[83] What mask, what character in fiction, could compare with Stalin's?

The *new man* was not completely absent from this book. However, he only appeared in the conceptual and philosophical shape of the *total man*, entirely developed, entirely won back from alienation. In my critique of everyday life I was wary of bringing this concept too closely into confrontation with given everyday life. The philosopher's vocation is such that he is almost entirely and almost always above the naïvety of the passing moment. The new man, the Communist man, the total man: it would have been only too easy to confuse these terms. And in fact we have seen people who excel at sticking what they consider to be appropriate labels on others sharing these titles out amongst themselves. For all their assaults on huge historical truths, such dogmatists insist that they are world-historical men, contemporaries of the future. Because they are Communists in the mid-twentieth century, they see themselves as members of the Communist society of the future, with all the qualities of the Communist man (sometimes, in fits of critical and autocritical sincerity or self-deception, they reproach themselves for *not* having these qualities, and beneath the seriousness of their masks a set of new comic characters is born).

The concept of the *total man* comes from some brief comments Marx made. Notably this one: 'Man appropriates his integral essence in an integral way, as a total man.'[84]

In this brief phrase Marx limits himself to defining the philosophical problem of universality as a function of human development and of another fundamental concept, that of appropriation. This means that his observation would need to be much elucidated and developed before being treated as a genuine philosophical theory.[85]

It is particularly important to note that the famous theory of the leap from necessity into freedom offers an all-too-easy justification for the new strain of utopianism and idealism we have briefly outlined above. This theory tends to support the great modern myth of the Revolution as total act, radical break, absolute renewal. It is therefore appropriate to emphasize that the shift from necessity to freedom and from alienation to fulfilment requires a lengthy period of transition. What the classic Marxist theorists have somewhat laconically called a 'leap' occupies a vast period in history and implies the resolution of numerous problems and contradictions. The end of non-human history and the beginning of human history inform a process of becoming in which elements of discontinuity and continuity, a multitude of factors on the decline or on the rise, and complex quantitative questions are all interwoven. The classic account based on quantity and quality is too simple – as if in reality everything could always be reduced to a confrontation between quantity and quality. The transitional man cannot be avoided. And the transition is evident all around us. As much in capitalist society (and the reader is directed to the final pages of *Imperialism, the Highest Stage of Capitalism*) as in socialist society. It is impossible to cross over this period in a single bound. The critique of everyday life analyses 'life', as it is, without making an obscure entity of it; it studies the negative and positive elements which confront one another; it studies the new conflicts and the new contradictions in what is new, knowing that the new is (more or less) everywhere ... Thus it knows that the new man must resolve his own contradictions in order to develop as a man.

Man and the human have always constituted a whole: in and through contradictions, i.e. alienations. As for the total man – *universal, concrete* and alive – he can only be conceived of as a limit to the infinity of social development.

To what extent do the stages of transition fall into the philosophical category of alienation? Merely to ask the question shows that interest is shifting towards transition and man in transition, but in so far as he is moving towards the total man, in other words crossing through alienation – and perhaps alienation at its maximum – the transitional man is 'disalienating' himself. So we can keep our philosophical concepts, as long as we make them concrete and see them historically and sociologically, thus extending the developments undertaken by Marx, who concretized the initially philosophical concept of alienation by situating it in economic objects. This obliges us to search documents and works (literary, cinematic, etc.) for evidence that a consciousness of alienation is being born, however indirectly, and that an effort towards 'disalienation', no matter how oblique and obscure, has begun. For the era of transition should be the one in which the philosophical concept enters life and consciousness, whether spontaneously or introduced from outside; otherwise, that concept will remain philosophical and nothing more.

In any event, it is very important for the critique of everyday life to know (and to know that the masses know) that the transcendence of the internal splits and contradictions in the human realm (intellectual versus manual work, town versus country, private versus social) can no more be reduced to a simple act, to some decisive and 'total' moment, than revolution itself. The *total man* is but a figure on a distant horizon beyond our present vision. He is a limit, an idea, and not a historical fact. And yet we must 'historicize' the notion, thinking of it historically and socially. And not naïvely, like those who believed that the new man would suddenly burst forth into history, complete, and in possession of all the hitherto incompatible qualities of vitality and lucidity, of humble determination in labour and limitless enthusiasm in creation.

However, the dialectic of knowledge shows us a 'historicity' and a becoming united with universality. All historically acquired knowledge is approximate, reversible, provisional: *relative*. And yet only the notion of the *absolute* gives this partial, divided, contradictory knowledge a meaning. The absolute is present in the relative (and the relative in the absolute) in a dual way. On the one hand, the absolute is *in* the relative as we receive it historically: every piece of knowledge (every concept, every proposition, every statement) contains a grain of truth, which can only become clear in the context of an ongoing evolutionary process; though an integral part of this process, it will retain a degree of invariability even as the contradictions immanent to historical development are successively confronted and resolved. On the other hand, the absolute is *outside of* the relative: this is the idea that there will be a completion of knowledge, a fulfilment which is impossible and yet implied by the total becoming of knowledge, therefore placing a limit to infinity (the asymptote of the total process). Dialectically, the absolute is a limit to the infinity of the relative – and yet there is *already* something of the absolute in the relative. In all limited, contradictory and subjective knowledge there is already an element of total objectivity. Only the notion or idea of the absolute gives a *sense* (in other words both a *meaning* and a *direction*) to historically acquired knowledge. Only the (materialist) dialectic enables us to demonstrate the *historical* character of knowledge without making it entirely relative. Only the dialectic will enable us to define an advance (a progress) while at the same time criticizing the illusions which arise whenever progress is made, and which cause us to take every step forward, every discovery, every new law or theory for the finished form of some particular sector of knowledge. (This is another 'gnosiological' underpinning of the dogmatic approach.)

It is the same for the human. Either one thinks philosophically in order to found humanism, or else one neglects and rejects such an intellectual development, thus abandoning humanism to contingency and chance. Human advance and progress only take their sense (in other words both their *meaning* and their *direction*) from the notion of the *total man.* Every moment of history, every stage accomplished through history, constitutes a whole; so does every partial activity, every power which has been achieved practically; every *moment* also contains its grain of human reality which will appear more and more clearly during the subsequent process of development. At the same time the *total man* is a limit to infinity.

Only if we posit this limit as a universality can we assert that, despite the conflicts and the contradictions, there is a profound if still unrealized unity between domains of activity, poetry and science, art and knowledge, etc. Just as learning, without the idea of the absolute, falls into pure relativism – so, without the notion of the total man, humanism and the theoretical conception of the human fall back into an incoherent pluralism. Thus the theory of the fundamental *is* and *is not* in history. It integrates history, and integrates with history, in a coherent dialectical way.

Is this theory Hegelian, or neo-Hegelian? Let us look at it more closely. It is certain that for Hegel the absolute foundation of existence, of history, of the dialectic, was the alienation of the Idea. In his system this alienation is the initial and absolute condition for development. The Idea leaves its self, becomes alienated, the dispersed *Other*, itself a constantly alienated existence, incapable of apprehending itself without entering into opposition with itself. The ascending stages of Being (nature, mechanism, society, art, religion, philosophy) establish themselves by the Idea successively regaining control over itself. None of these stages, none of these shapings or configurations of consciousness, succeeds in being its own truth in itself and for itself. They thus remain in the domain of alienation. *In Hegel, then, contradiction is nothing more than an implication of alienation.* To know and to understand oneself, to reflect upon oneself, is to resolve contradictions while provoking new alienating contradictions.[86] The Idea is at once the motive force of contradiction and its outcome. It is both that which opposes itself and that which uses contradiction to rediscover – and to recognize through reflection – its unity with itself.

The movement of Logic appears to reconstruct the universe: in fact, it rediscovers and recognizes the descending and ascending emanations of the Idea. The Being which seems the absolute beginning of the real and of reflection (of consciousness) is in truth only the absolute limit of the Idea, at once inferior and superior, from below and from above, from the side of nature, feelings, abstraction – and from the side of Spirit. Thus Logic, which in Hegel appears at first to produce the world, is in truth only the human method for attaining the Idea (which is why it can rid itself of the Idea and the absolute in the Hegelian sense, and change course so as to enter Marxism). And yet in Hegel the absolute tearing apart of the Idea – its alienation – is indispensable if this Idea is to create self-consciousness and to become conscious of itself as it creates (by means of its reflection, in which it *is reflected*). Hegelianism likewise views the tearing apart of reality, of life, of consciousness (and its *unhappiness*) as irreducibly given.[87]

By abandoning the concrete analysis of these divisions, these separations, that tearing apart of actions and consciousness which are the real facts of real life, certain of Hegel's exponents have ended up in mysticism. They maintain that the tearing apart is an absolute drama: a drama within the absolute. In their view human actions illustrate this absolute drama, and can only be understood in terms of its image. Post-Hegelian mysticism develops the vision of the 'Speculative Good Friday'; it starts with the hypothesis that Hegel developed a new series of concepts in order to rationalize the irrational, that he succeeded up to a point, but that beyond that point he failed, thus authorizing them to resume the task from where he left off, precisely by giving prominence to the mystical essence of the residue of irrationality.

Yet it is also possible to show that in Hegel – and this even in his system-building – there was an attempt to enclose totality within the reflecting Individual, and that for him this attempt involved an explicit struggle against mysticism. For this is the sense and the goal of the Hegelian system: to allow an individual – the philosopher and his followers – to dominate the universe by thought; and the system is also the justification for this goal, the history of this Individual. Marx extended Hegel's contradictory attempt to rationalize, resolving its contradiction and breaking his system while at the same time retaining its element of rationality. Marx has demonstrated how dialectical reason arises precisely from the supposed irrationality constituted by nature, by practical and social activity, by man as he is in everyday life.

It is thus that the residue of irrationality in Hegel – the theory of alienation – becomes integrated within historical and dialectical materialism, and is transferred onto a level which is both practical and rational. In Marxism, *alienation is no longer the absolute foundation of contradiction. On the contrary: alienation is defined as an aspect of contradiction and of becoming in man.* Alienation is the form taken by dialectical necessity in human becoming. Thus Hegel explained contradiction by alienation, while Marx explains alienation by dialectical contradiction. This is what the well-known reversal whereby the Hegelian dialectic has been 'set back on its feet' consists of. This transformation does not exclude the theory of alienation, it encompasses it.

Feuerbach thought he had brought human alienation to an end in one fell swoop (by a radical and total philosophical act or decree). He proclaimed that theology, religion, metaphysics, are all alienations of man (and no longer of the Idea). But by defining man once and for all as an individual physiological entity – by rejecting the dialectic and the historicity of the human – he was destroying the foundation for a concrete theory of alienation. And he was also admitting the bourgeois individual as an anthropological principle – as an unconsidered presupposition.

Marx rejects the form taken by Feuerbach's materialism: his anthropological postulate. He does not think that man as such is a simple fragment of nature. But, on the other hand, he rejects the idealist postulate that thinking man emerges from nature and sets himself up above it by virtue of his thought, of the mere fact that he thinks. In this way he succeeds in superseding previous philosophies, the picture of man they presented and the relation they defined between man and the universe. Marx wants to think of man's essence dialectically: for him man is a being of nature in the process of self-transcendence, a being of nature struggling with nature in order to dominate it, a being emerging from nature, but doing so in such a way that in the very process of emerging from and dominating nature its roots are plunged ever more deeply therein.

In the prehistory of man (therefore up until the present) man was first of all a being of nature. Now in material and biological nature, becoming appears as fragmentation, dispersion, externalization, exclusion and reciprocal destruction. The natural *other-being* is essentially the enemy-being. In this prehistory, which was his natural history, man was precisely *that.* But in so far as he was a social being he was already becoming *something else*, in such a way that in his natural history nature within him was the profound reason and ever-present cause for his alienation, constantly renewed; for his internal contradiction.

This history of humanity presents us with a collection of strange facts and events. Institutions and ideas were external to the human, oppressive, exclusive, mutually contradictory. They were mutually destructive, and it was necessary to destroy them if they were to be superseded. And yet these institutions and these ideas were the indispensable expression of the development and the acquisition of human practice and human powers, essential in order to organize and formulate these and to render them conscious.

This contradiction is at the heart of Marxist thought as far as the historical development of man is concerned. But it is not a contradiction in Marxist thought itself.[88] It is an internal contradiction in history itself, and only the general theory of alienation can elucidate it. It alone can help us to understand how men constructed history while being caught within history, within their own history; and how they constructed it without knowing they were doing so, blindly at first, but more and more consciously, on several differing but convergent levels (economic, political and ideological struggles); and how finally revolt and violence and chance were only apparently an irrational and absurd factor in history. Things progress (in other words certain things disappear) with their bad side forward.

This tearing apart shows that in the growing control that man has over nature, nature as such keeps control over man. His products and his works function like beings of nature. He must *objectify* himself, and social objects become things, fetishes, which turn upon him. Man as a collective subject exists after the fashion of nature, yet man tends to supersede nature and to build a specific environment in which contradiction in its natural form (spontaneous, blind, necessary) will itself be superseded, controlled, known and mastered. The moment man invented tools and began to work he stopped being an animal, and entered the realm of historical and human contradictions. But these contradictions extend the contradictions of nature, and particularly in their necessary, blind aspect; if man has humanized himself, he has done so only by tearing himself apart, dividing himself, fragmenting himself: actions and products, powers and fetishes, growing consciousness and spontaneous lack of consciousness, organization and revolt.

Alienation may be defined philosophically as this single yet dual movement of objectification and externalization – of realization and derealization. But this movement must be seen in its dialectical profundity. *That which realizes is also that which derealizes. And vice versa*: whatever derealizes – dissolves, destroys, negates – also realizes by supersession. Obstacles, uncomfortable difficulties, disquiet, apparently insoluble problems, contradiction pushed to the point of antagonism, these are moments of progress: the step forward, the birth of a reality and a higher reflecting consciousness through the dissolution of what exists. *The positive is negative, but what is most negative is also what is most positive* ....

And this becoming may be expressed, in a way which is all the more striking for being concrete, practical and alive, as *the discreteness yet inclusiveness of the individual and the social.*[89]

This unity is the foundation of all society: a society is made up of individuals, and the individual is a social being, in and by the content of his life and the form of his consciousness. Now from the direct and physical rituals of primitive societies to the lived abstraction of self-consciousness (*private* consciousness) this unity has only expressed itself in mutilated, fragmented, singular ways.

It cannot be expressed outside of the contradictions which have ensnared it, splitting it and making it problematic, unstable, destined to be superseded. The social, for and in the individual, is always embodied in rituals, in particular words or expressions,[90] which are full of meaning and at the same time relatively meaningless in themselves, thus insignificant and symbolic.

According to the moment and the angle from which we perceive him, the individual is at one and the same time what is most highly concrete and most remotely abstract. He is what is most changing historically and what is most stable, what is most independent from the social structure, and most dependent upon it. Conversely, the social is abstract, since it is defined only by the individuals who make it up; and it is what is most supremely concrete, since it gives these individual existences their unity, their totality, and since it determines the content of their lives and their consciousness. For each individual, the unity of his consciousness and unity with his consciousness is his reality, and the rest is mere destiny, externality, necessity. However, from the point of view of its foundation and social content, the very unity of the most intimate individual consciousness is determined from outside. Thus what is most internal is also what is most external (*private consciousness* for example) – and conversely, what is most external is what is most internal (the sense of a 'value', for example).

Past ideologies tried to find answers to some very diverse questions and problems, to offer solutions to a multitude of contradictions, but most of all they addressed the problem of, and the contradiction between, individual and social. They recreated it in new forms, deeper and more hopeless, until such time as these were eliminated by violence or by gradual erosion, in the name of a new social content. Thus religions, theological or metaphysical projects, were *authentic* attempts to reconcile man with himself, the human with nature, the individual with the social. They achieved both their internal coherence and their entry into life from these attempts, in the form of actions, and the search for a style. Religious fervour and belief in a God gave symbolic expression to the unity of the elements of the human, and projected this unity outside man.

In fact, however, at the very moment ideology was creating this unity by becoming a coherent doctrine and discovering a style of living, it was also perpetuating the inner division, in the form of good and evil, sin and salvation, God and the Devil. Religion as institution maintained a social unity by separating the sacred and the profane, and by oppression. As for direct or indirect communion with nature, ecstatic contemplation, for the oppressed and even for a proportion of their oppressors, was merely a diversion; the intensity of the mystical states attained was an index of nothing but real powerlessness, and an absence of any creative appropriation.

As soon as the unity between the individual and the social begins a process of renewal, alienation takes the form of an antagonism between the private consciousness and the social consciousness. In modern society this self-same alienation has taken other forms. Every time it is possible to proclaim the externality of the whole and of the part – either that the part is superior to the whole, or that the whole transcends the part – there is always an ideologue on hand to do the job. And the resultant ideology is always influential: machines for machines' sake, or conversely man versus machine – reason for reason's sake, or conversely art reduced to a mere utilitarian technique, etc.

Man's unity with himself, in particular the unity of the individual and the social, is an essential aspect of the definition of the total man.

In these circumstances we must either abandon trying to formulate a coherent theory and proclaim pluralism – which is simply the expression of this abandonment – or instead construct a system of categories which will grasp *nature and man* at the same time, in their movement, in their contradiction and in their interpenetration.

Before dialectical materialism every 'system' which wanted to be total (which wanted to be philosophical, thus systematic and coherent) merely used unconscious social categories to grasp the universe. For the philosopher, for the ideologue in general, society was a given accepted naïvely along with its content and in the ideological forms it had spontaneously adopted at the moment the thinker started to reflect; in other words, he accepted it together with its profoundest assumptions. Thus Plato accepted slavery, Descartes and Spinoza accepted commerce and mercantile capitalism and Hegel accepted the bourgeois individual. So in these doctrines, and in their search for internal coherence, there was a radical duplicity, more often than not concealed by sophistry or mysticism: *thoughts based on unconsidered data and presuppositions.* Certainly throughout the history of philosophy we can see the (ambiguous and contradictory) pathways which in the eighteenth century crystallized as materialism and idealism. But that is just one aspect of the history of ideologies and philosophies in relation to the development of history and society. In our view past philosophies and their history, on the one hand, and Marxist philosophical thought on the other, cannot be reduced to a few glibly systematized observations on matter and spirit. They are richer and more complex than that. The elaboration of categories constitutes another aspect of the development, one which has its own complexities. For the categories had practical, historical and social origins; at the same time they underwent a theoretical elaboration aimed at formulating and defining them, and determining the connections between them. Specifically philosophical categories can only be separated from social categories a posteriori. In the wake of Marx (in *A Contribution to the Critique of Political Economy*), we have already noted the importance of the objectivity of the categories by which bourgeois society expresses itself and its criticism of previous socio-economic structures. For example, the category of *social labour.* At a certain stage in its development, society began to examine critically the categories which expressed it: this was when Marx inaugurated (as a function of bourgeois society seen in its becoming and its totality, and therefore as a function of the existence of the working class) the critique of the categories of bourgeois society itself. Thus Marx defined the bourgeois nature of the Individual, which hitherto had been taken as an absolute. For Marx the category of social labour discovered by the classic economists became that of *alienated* labour; need was revealed as *alienated* need; it was through critical reflection that the *fetishistic* character of commodities and money was arrived at; in this way a higher and decisive stage in objectivity was reached. Once the origins of these categories were made conscious, it became feasible to represent the universe and history coherently and in a way which really allowed the elements of the human their unity. In a way in which society and the human were consequently no longer in opposition, but integrated in a whole, each retaining its specificity.

If this unity is to be fully developed a painstaking and extensive critical analysis of the categories in every sphere of art and science will therefore be needed. In philosophy as well. This immense undertaking will provide us with a better grasp of what is still only abstract, and will enable us to introduce what is still only theoretical and ideological into *everyday* life and consciousness. Marx merely set this task in motion. Notably in the *Contribution to the Critique of Political Economy*, the importance of which is often totally neglected in favour either of his earlier writings, or else of *Capital.* His work is a model, a guide, a beacon. In no respect is it a completed system, a vision or a conception of the world in the traditional meaning of the terms!

At the same time this examination of categories and the elaboration of their relations and of their theoretical unity constitutes a critique of superseded ideologies, their concepts and categories; notably of those ideologies that sanction the directly experienced discreteness of the individual and the social (their real contradiction) by hypostasizing it in the form of an imagined discreteness which puts all the stress either on the one or on the other.

The profound Hegelian distinction between *understanding* (or in-telligence) and *reason* takes on a new meaning. Understanding must be defined as a historical and theoretical stage in thought and conscious-ness. It analyses, separates and situates determinations in a reciprocal externality; it determines properties and relations in isolation. It undergoes determinations; it accepts them according to a given culture, a given society, with its class struggles and its social structure and its oppressive institutions. It seeks unsuccessfully to work out a coherent (logical) discourse on the universe.

Dialectical reason criticizes understanding and dispels its determinants but only so as better to grasp the unity behind its contradictions. It understands categories in their real historical development and their connections. It is defined by the *critical movement* of these categories. *It is the function of the universal* and of the *totality* operating through negation, and through contradictions, that are known and dominated. It relativizes categories in order to grasp the universal within them more surely. At the same time, whereas understanding always hopes to close and conclude its discourse on the universe, dialectical reason knows that *its* work can never be completed.

The notion of alienation may be grasped on the level of understanding. And that is the level on which we all receive it and grasp it initially, then try to conceptualize and apply it. But the problem is to move to the highest level of dialectical reason: to think the notion dialectically, in a universal and concrete way, in other words by determining it in all the breadth of its universality and by grasping it in the minutiae of everyday life.

Moreover, the effort of the philosopher does not and cannot stay on an isolated philosophical level, in a separate consciousness, sphere or dimension; the source of his theories is social practice, and he must direct them back towards life, be it through his teaching or by other means (poetry? literature?). Dialectical thought can and must transform itself into dialectical consciousness of life, in life: unity of the mediate and the immediate, of the abstract and the concrete, of culture and natural spontaneity. In this way it will pass from ideology and specific knowledge into culture, language, perhaps into direct perception of the world – in any event, into everyday life!

Conclusion: the theory of alienation and of the 'total man' remain the driving force behind the critique of everyday life. They allow us to represent social development as a whole and to determine the direction in which it is going. They also allow us to analyse this becoming, boring down within it for samples, penetrating its details and linking it with the overall system. These notions must be handled with extreme caution, however. We cannot give them an ontological meaning like the concepts in use in traditional philosophy. To use them inconsiderately – speculatively – is extremely hazardous; for example an *idea* (which expresses all the parts of the process and its limit to infinity) can become an *image of the future* or, even worse, an already accomplished *reality*. There is a perfunctory kind of Marxism which believes itself capable of seeing into the future or of asserting that the present – a given individual man in particular conditions, such as socialist society or militant action – represents the future.

And yet non-Marxist philosophers, psychologists and sociologists carry out exactly the same operation, even though they do so – apparently – in a more abstract way. They declare that man, or the human, or the social, or the historical, make up a whole. At the same time they declare that this totality is already with us, present, describable and fully graspable. They use the category of *totality*, a philosophical category, in a non-critical manner. They use it non-dialectically, in a way that is both logical and speculative. Thus investigations which ought to be pursued coherently using the category dialectically end up at sixes and sevens, pulling in different directions, representing themselves as opposing systems. Sometimes man and the human appear to be wandering aimlessly and endlessly through history; history and everyday life appear complex, but ambiguous, at the mercy of radical contingency and pure relativism; the concrete face of freedom is reduced to the minuscule dimensions of individual choice, and disappears as far as the meaning of history is concerned. At other times history is given a goal and personality a meaning according to a traditional theology: God and religion are the foundation of totality, of total life. And at other times again the hypothesis that totality is effectively present is used to certify its absence; and so it becomes a question of 'detotalized totality', something which emphasizes splitting and breaking, separation and the tragic, as a way of consecrating them.[91]

Thus, when taken *in isolation*, in other words speculatively, outside of *praxis*, the theories of alienation and totality become transformed into systems which are very remote from Marxism – into neo-Hegelianism. The operation which consists of leaving social practice and its analysis in order to engage in speculation, only to come back to reality armed with a pseudo-concept, leads to a variety of contradictory representations; their externality creates an illusion, and makes us believe in the richness of philosophy, whereas what we have before us is the image of its incoherence, its powerlessness, its poverty.

Another aspect of the question. Taken in isolation, non-dialectically, the concept of alienation is open to strictly individual manipulation.

Anyone at all can take it over and declare that such-and-such an activity alienates and externalizes him, and turns him into a thing – work, for example, or a profession, or love, marriage, children. There may be an element of truth in this, but the person concerned will use this partial truth to construct superfluities, exaggerations, disturbing interpretations. From this false point of view, it is no longer consciousness which is alienated, it is consciousness which does the alienating; and the first schoolboy who comes along will be able to say that the way he is taught at school (especially if he really is being badly taught) and the work he has to do there are turning him into a thing. In the same way, it will no longer be a particular type of work which is alienating, or social labour which is alienated, but work in general which will appear alienating. And the theory of everyday life, together with its critique, will be metamorphosed into a philosophy of idleness.

Thus this difficult and rigorous theory can become a principle of facileness; the implement for a positive critique becomes the implement for hypercriticism, for entirely negative pseudo-criticism. What form of life, what partial content is there, which could not be taken as being totally alienating? Not only religion, but love too; every form of art, not simply purely abstract art, or art for art's sake; not only State oppression, but any discipline within society; not only the *private* man, but the citizen; not only the systematic disordering of the senses,[92] but knowledge itself. Thus all self-realization – which can only be partial, and must therefore involve alienation at a more-or-less deep level – appears to be, and becomes, total alienation. Thus in recent years the theory of alienation has become widely available in a form which is both speculative and arbitrary; this is above all because in this guise it permits the 'free' and empty affirmation of the self – in other words a return to the bourgeois individual, as well as to pessimism, to individualism. But despite appearances, we are still within the parameters of neo-Hegelianism. I say 'despite appearances' because this interpretation does conflict with the political and state-controlled claim that only by political action and activity on the level of the State can alienation be avoided, the human realized and the individual humanized. The fact is that the two interpretations (individualist or political, anarchistic or state-centred) are interdependent; the one relies on the other, the one justifies the other, and neither goes beyond the Hegelian framework.

Thus of necessity theory and concepts (such as alienation, totality, the total man) become meeting points and areas of discussion for divergent doctrines; and an excuse for polemics. On the theoretical and ideological level it is a situation which calls for extra vigilance. We have reached the core of the problems of our era: the core of all our problems.

The danger is that we may use philosophical concepts and categories speculatively. But how can we determine how to use them legitimately?

Marx gives us the example and the model. In his writings the theory and the concept of alienation are integrated into the development of his thought while retaining their philosophical meaning. They become transformed. Though no longer discernible *as such* in economic science, they nevertheless constitute its basis and its philosophical meaning. The theory of alienation becomes transformed into the theory of fetishism (fetishism of commodities, money, capital). Social relations are enclosed and concealed within these economic objects, which are also objects of political economy. Taking on the appearance of things, the products of social activity in effect become things invested with power over men.

In my opinion, in his early writings, particularly in the *Economic and Philosophical Manuscripts of 1844*, Marx had not yet fully developed his thought. It is there, however, germinating, growing, becoming. Certainly, the interpretation of these texts is problematic, but the problems need to be properly formulated. My view is that historical and dialectical materialism *developed*. It did not come into being abruptly, with an absolute discontinuity, after a break, at *x* moment, in the works of Marx (and in the history of humanity), and to think that it did produces false problems. To begin with, Marxism is made to appear like a system, a *dogma*.

This is not to challenge the newness of Marxism. On the contrary, it represents it in a more profound manner. Any radical newness must be born, must grow and take shape, precisely because it is a new reality. A brutal break is highly unlikely to produce something with genuine life; rather it creates a pure, abstract idea, or a dogmatic decree. The thesis which puts a date on Marxism, or tries to, seriously runs the risk of desiccating it, and of interpreting it in a one-sided way. What is more, how can Marxism be envisaged outside of its own categories –

becoming, development? This would be to enclose it in a contradiction; or worse: to represent it as external to the reality for which it
provides the key; to apply it from outside, dogmatically.

These problems have their philosophical side; they involve exegesis,
scholarly apparatus, but they also contribute to living research. It
cannot be simply a matter of confronting text with text; the texts must
also be confronted with living reality. Therefore there is generally no
ready-made solution to the problems presented; or else the problem
presented is not the real one, but a prefabricated, dogmatic schematization. The mistake, the false option which must be avoided, is to
overestimate or else to *underestimate* Marx's early writings. They already
contain Marxism, but as a potential, and certainly not *all* Marxism (a
term which in any case has no clearly defined meaning). It is false (and
anti-dialectical, and anti-Marxist) to consider that Marx's thought was
born like Minerva springing forth from the head of Jupiter; and it is
absurd to consider that Marxism begins with the *Manifesto* or *Capital*.
The early writings contain great riches, but riches still confused, riches
half mined and scarcely exploited. That Marx should subsequently
abandon or transform such philosophical concepts as alienation does
not prove them to be meaningless, nor does the advent of political
economy mean that the role of philosophy is at an end. We may take
them up again and use them – as Marx did – to criticize their social
origins and speculative interpretations of them. What is more, Marx
shows us the dangers of using them metaphysically. He integrates them
within a specific science, political economy. Thus the problem is as
follows: there is more to *Capital* than political economy. It contains
history; it contains deep insights into *sociology* (notably the fundamental
concept of 'socio-economic formation'). Are we really betraying Marx's
work if we integrate the concept of alienation into a sociology which
has been explicitly constituted as a science?

Certainly, it is not clear what use the concept of alienation can have
for the historian. But in fact that proves nothing; maybe historians will
have something to say about this, and they are perfectly entitled to do
so. The same question goes for psychologists and psychiatrists. But if
we can form a clear idea of the use the *sociologist* may make of the
concept, then we can *legitimately* conclude that such a use follows the
fundamental tendencies of Marxist thought.

Let us make an even more general point. The content of concrete life has produced forms which conflict with it, smother it, and which consequently collapse from this self-inflicted lack of substance and roots. The separation of form and content does not date from today or yesterday; it turns up in most ideological mystifications. And it produces an error which dialectical thought must carefully avoid. The danger in separating form and content is that their unity will be forgotten. There is no form without content, no content without form. It is impossible to grasp a content *as such* without giving it a form, or without using an existing form as a starting point in order to come to grips analytically with its content. Any separation of form and content involves a certain amount of illusion and superficiality; for form it means not an absence or formal purity, but rather a loss of content. Conversely, to determine content in terms of itself is an indication of dogmatism, and more often than not a confidence trick. This having been said, nowadays (needless to say, in the speeches and writings of 'thinkers' and authors) forms do appear as purified and purely formal, as striving to become self-sufficient, to supplant content, to take its place; which, being translated, means the destruction of content. This active formalization becomes an attack on form itself, which is destroyed by its consequent emptiness; unless, of course, it can still be used to present a 'content' outside of itself, which has no relation to the form, but which needs a deceptive language in order to appear as a figure.

Let us make a (provisional, incomplete) list of these conflicts:

(a) *rationalism versus reason* (formal rationalism, bourgeois intellectualism, never going beyond the level of understanding – versus living, concrete, dialectical reason);

(b) *nationalism* (the old, 'classic', right-wing variety) *versus nations and versus its own nation* as a living thing, on the march towards democracy and socialism;

(c) *individualism* (the individualism of the bourgeois individual isolated and isolating himself in his *private* consciousness and his own aloofness) *versus the individual,* the real individual, active, alive, solving problems, starting with his own;

(d) *objectivism* (the kind which thinks 'neutrally' and 'impartially', which endlessly weighs the pros and the cons or jumps from one point of view to another, which takes facts in isolation and information out of context) *versus thorough objectivity*, where thought is allied with practice to grasp every aspect of a contradictory reality, its complex becoming, its hidden tendencies ...;

(e) *aestheticism of pure form* (technicality in art, the pursuit of pure style and pure plasticity), completely detached abstraction or formalism, *versus form*;

etc.

This list of 'isms' could go on and on. We have given enough examples to demonstrate the general present tendency of thought, ideology and culture in bourgeois society; a tendency which is concealed by the technical and technocratic airs adopted by most activities in a specific area — and also by the existence of conflicting aspirations, procedures and efforts to rediscover or create a content.

Surely this general formalism means that human activities and capabilities are being alienated in a multiplicity of ways, heterogeneous and yet drearily monotonous, that while shapes external one to the other and external to living man are being projected, human activities and capabilities are being split apart. It is a general alienation, coming to the surface in the overall structure of society and brought forth by the movement of that structure, but constantly turning back towards and into day-to-day living. Might this not give us a potentially vital guide to the critique of everyday life?

We began by showing the danger of using the notion of *alienation* in an abstract (isolated, speculative) way. The philosopher has no right to elaborate this notion in itself, to examine it outside actual alienated or alienating situations. He has no right to isolate the domain of philosophy. Once he has established the notion and its universal significance, he must move over into other well-defined areas — political economy, sociology — and above all he must confront the notion with concrete situations in everyday life. Here, however, basing ourselves upon practice, and on the real — contemporary — situation, we may rediscover generalities — and thus halt the decline of knowledge into the mere observation of facts, into mere empiricism or mere pragmatism.

This theoretical development does not give us the right to postulate — by decision or 'option' — one activity as essentially human and another (which we find unpleasant or boring) as dehumanized, alienated or alienating. The critique of everyday life does not make life's problems any simpler. It requires and determines a critical and self-critical consciousness which is higher than the consciousness exerted when we make the occasional uncomplicated choice. Anyone who wishes to found an ethic – and his personal ethic – on the notion of alienation needs to have a precise and analytic tool and a consciousness that has been finely honed by the dialectic at his disposal. Only then will he be able to find his way through the labyrinth which is all social life and through the jungle which is bourgeois society; only then will he distinguish between what is 'life-enhancing' and what is obscurantist and static in his life. Thus everyone may perhaps be able tightly to embrace *their own* lives, and to love them, without evading any task, fruitful conflict, or useful risk.

In short, we have returned to the level of philosophy, a philosophy tested by life. It is as much a question of ethics as it is of sociology. But before we can broach the ethical problems we will need to put our concepts to the test, to verify them and develop them more thoroughly, and not just once.

VIII   Philosophy and the Critique of Everyday Life

Philosophy is going through a very difficult period; and so is the philosopher. He draws comfort from the thought that he is not the only one. One wonders: 'Is it growing pains, an adolescent crisis, or a terminal illness?', ('one' being first and foremost the philosopher).

One of the most curious symptoms of this crisis is philosophy's increasing importance. Who is there who does not long to have his say about 'important problems'? Specialists from the various sciences, men of action, men of state – they all yearn to launch into vast reflections, and by doing so to justify themselves in grandiose terms. This is an outpouring of philosophy in which the philosopher himself disappears; and the more obscure he becomes, the more disturbing he is (assuming always he perseveres in being a philosopher). It becomes easier and easier for him to inspire fear in people. The promotion of philosophy to the status of an ideology – of a weapon in the great struggles between classes, nations, peoples – is not without its drawbacks. It is subjected to appalling pedagogic or political simplifications. Over a period of twenty or thirty years we have been forced to witness the schematization of the dialectic: the Stalinist interpretation has reduced this subtle way of thought first to a robust and popular common sense (and that was the heyday of Stalinist interpretation, the era of *Anarchism and Socialism*), then to the permanent seven-point plan: four points for the dialectic, three for materialism. With the definition of matter, and of consciousness as a reflection of it, philosophy comes to an end. Everyone thinks he is a philosopher, and sets off cheerfully for life's fray armed with this possibly useful but somewhat light-weight equipment. The role of philosophy is over. The general, world-wide crisis has certainly not spared non-Marxist philosophy (that was the sector where it began); it has also affected Marxist philosophy. But the symptoms are different. On one side, the non-Marxist side, the symptoms are obscurity, jargon, technicality, illusory profundity. On the Marxist side they are false clarity, pedagogy which takes itself as a measure of thought, desiccated dogmatism and skeletal schematization, propagandist exploitation of ideological themes. Philosophy is in its death throes: it is being killed off, or perhaps it is the philosopher who is committing some second-rate hara-kiri.

In the period of the last twenty-five years, have the philosophers in the Soviet Union been blind or merely unwilling to see? Have they been in hiding? What analysis of the real, or what elements for an analysis of the real, have they contributed? What worthwhile books have they produced? Certainly not the glossaries, dictionaries or encyclopedias, in which the 'formulations' have changed only according to the political situation. We cannot even say to their credit that these official or semi-official philosophers used the kind of ruses by which other philosophers (Lukács, for example, but not only him, since the reader may enjoy looking for a few such ruses here in this book!) managed to introduce a few new ideas into the general debate. Today, even the most prudent, the most official 'Marxists' admit that a new analysis of this period is needed. Now the aridity of Marxist philosophy – and that in the very countries where it should have grown and developed – cannot be separated from the sum total of the events that have taken place. It is an aspect of the situation, and must be analysed and studied. Marxists must open their eyes and examine the fact closely: Marxism has become *boring*. It has been a disappointment;

young people are disappointed with it because it bores them.

If the philosopher can no longer be accepted as typifying man, or as the mediator between heaven and earth – between the relative and the absolute – then what role has he to play? If in the last analysis it is the masses which judge, if philosophy becomes accessible and turns into a force, if the political leader speaks (legitimately when like Lenin he has attained authentic and incontrovertible greatness) as a philosopher, what use can the philosopher have? As a funeral director, a pall-bearer for the past, in other words as a historian for out-of-date philosophy? As a secondhand scholar, following painfully in the footsteps of genuine scholars? As a latter-day encyclopedist? As a vulgarizer, compiling glossaries and manuals? None of this is worth even an hour's effort. So the philosopher is beset with self-doubts. He lets himself be outclassed by literary hacks whose best-sellers bring them fame and fortune. He gives in to the temptations of literature or politics, and abandons philosophy – yes, philosophy too – to platitude and mediocrity.

This leads us to the point when we need to ask ourselves what the 'critique of everyday life' means. To confront philosophers with life – simple life – and its problems, to immerse them in this human raw material and to ask their help in mastering it, in scraping away the coating of mud to reveal the gems within, would that be a breakthrough, a new direction? How should we situate the critique of everyday life in relation to classic philosophy? Is there room in Marxist philosophy for a critique of everyday life considered as a philosophical discipline? Are we dealing with a *sociological* undertaking in the narrow sense of a specialized discipline, or of an undertaking with a *philosophical* meaning and a set of concrete contents and social objects to support it?

It is not enough simply to examine the concept of alienation and its *actuality* (in the dialectical meaning of the word). For here we are talking about philosophy as an activity, and of the philosopher as such – of his function, his situation – rather than about philosophy as a set of concepts and as the development of those concepts.

As an activity, philosophy used to be precisely one of those exceptional and superior activities through which men who could devote their lives to leisure[93] could step outside of everyday life, and which involved criticism of everyday life, implicitly or explicitly. Among these activities we can also include: dreams, the imaginary, art, play, ethics, political life, etc.

In terms of these activities, the first definition of everyday life is a *negative* one. If in our minds (by a sort of abstraction) we remove the highly specialized occupations from man and from the human, what is left? An apparently very scanty residue. In reality this so-called residue contains a 'human raw material' which holds hidden wealth, as our study shows. The higher activities derive from it, they are at one and the same time its ultimate expression, its direct or indirect critique and its alienated form – albeit an alienation embodying a more-or-less conscious and successful attempt to achieve 'disalienation'.

Would the aim of a critique be to systematize the various perspectives offered by these higher activities and by the indirect criticisms they imply? Or conversely to exclude them systematically and to separate the exceptional moments from the everyday by way of an apology for the latter? Neither. The second of these objectives would abandon everyday life to vulgarity; it would bring back a sort of populism into philosophy; thus it would grant art, science, ethics and philosophy the inordinate privilege of constituting superhuman – and therefore inhuman – 'worlds'. It is therefore an interpretation we must formally reject. On the other hand the first objective would limit itself to confronting what is possible with what was been accomplished. It would delve into poetry, or play, or ethics, in search of images from beyond everyday life which could be used in evidence against it. It would add little to works of the past, which can be looked upon as indirect criticisms of everyday life. So neither objective is valid. And yet they both are. For we must be careful neither to abandon the (acquired or potential) wealth of the content, of the 'human raw material'; nor to lose whatever was achieved in the highest, most intense moments. The problem is therefore to define the reciprocal relation of these activities and realities: the simple moments and the highest moments of life.

Superior, differentiated and highly specialized activities have never been separate from everyday practice, they have only appeared to be so. Their consciousness of being separate from it was in itself a link; they implied an indirect or implicit criticism of the everyday only inasmuch as they raised themselves above it. Thus French eighteenth-century philosophy, literature, art, ethics and politics corresponded to *the everyday life* of the bourgeoisie: the new pursuit of happiness, pleasure, luxury, profit and power. In the same way eighteenth-century rationalism corresponded to the everyday attitude expressed in 'commonplace books'. And every time a scientist comes up with a formula or a law, he is of necessity condensing a long experience in which the lowliest assistant and the simplest tool have had their part to play.

And yet these appearances (like all appearances) contain a certain reality. Specialized activities (considered *as* activities, with their 'products', or works) genuinely did develop outside and above the everyday. Only by controlling it through this externality were they able to condense it, to concentrate its meanings and achievements. There is a cliché which with a certain degree of justification compares creative moments to the mountain tops and everyday time to the plain, or to the marshes. The image the reader will find in this book differs from this generally accepted metaphor. Here everyday life is compared to fertile soil. A landscape without flowers or magnificent woods may be depressing for the passer-by; but flowers and trees should not make us forget the earth beneath, which has a secret life and a richness of its own.

The indirect criticism of the everyday in works of the past which emerged from that everyday appeared only too frequently to *devalue* it. People who gather flowers and nothing but flowers tend to look upon soil as something dirty. Practical activities were always the basis and the foundation for 'pure' thought, and even for its most extreme form, pure contemplation. What does the contemplator contemplate, if not – from afar – the everyday, the crowd, the masses, all the things from which his 'epoche'[94] holds him aloof, and which he will try in vain to rediscover?[95] And yet the situation is eventually reversed. The day dawns when everyday life also emerges as a critique, a critique of the superior activities in question (and of what they produce: *ideologies*). The devaluation of everyday life by ideologies appears as one-sided and partial, in both senses of the word. A direct critique takes the place of indirect criticism; and this direct critique involves a rehabilitation of everyday life, shedding new light on its positive content.

We have already demonstrated how the worker, as a human being, constitutes a whole. To consider him as such means that the *separation* between the human factor and the technical factor in private life and in leisure is ruled out, but not as a result of analysing the *contradictions* between the elements which make up the whole. The fragmented character of modern industrial labour both encloses and conceals the social character of all the work done in any one firm and of the total labour in society (the growing *socialization* of labour and the relations of production). Thus the worker's consciousness of the *social* character of labour comes to him largely from outside rather than from *his own* individual work, notably from his political life. It is a consciousness which he expects and demands from *his own* work, which he needs in order to understand that work and the place it holds, and yet it does not come from his work alone. We need to study the life of the worker in its varied aspects, its conflicts, its contradictions. The consciousness of the worker involves – together with the content of his own practical experience – numerous ideological elements, some justified, others illusory; some atavistic (coming for example from the peasant or artisan classes); others deriving from objective but partly outmoded conditions of capitalism (the 'free' labour contract in competitive capitalism, the 'classic' forms of the class struggle); still others derived from the new conditions within capitalism (monopolies, and new content contradicting the monopolistic form of capitalism; trade union action and new forms of class struggle); others deriving from socialism, and finally others coming from individual limits or the limits of the group the worker in question belongs to (corporatism, professional solidarity, etc.). If we consider the overall life of the worker, we will see that his work and his attitude towards work are linked to social practice *as a whole*, to his experience as a whole, his leisure activities, his family life, his cultural and political goals, as well as to the class struggle. What is more, this 'whole' must be taken in the context of a specific country and nation, at a specific moment of civilization and social development, and as involving a certain set of needs. And this brings us back to the critique of everyday life.

Let us turn to another very precise example: *political* activity. It can be founded on already established authority, or on constituted law, on mystification and violence, or on knowledge. In so far as it is founded on knowledge, it requires the most scrupulous attention to everyday life. The progressive or socialist politician must know the life and the needs of the people whose immediate or essential interests he is defending. If he strays from this duty, he is no longer qualified for the task. He is progressive or socialist only in so far as he has this knowledge. The simplest matters concerning housing, roads, children's playgrounds, public transport etc., have their place in a hierarchy of requirements which may lead to the transformation of the State. The politician's talent rests on his ability to grade the elements in this hierarchy, and to address whatever is essential at any given moment.

And yet if true politics involves a knowledge of everyday life and a critique of its requirements, conversely everyday life involves a critique of all politics. Political life is by definition lived out in the stratosphere of society: in the sphere of the State and on that level. The problems posed in political life are both abstract and concrete, but they have an aura of technicality which makes them appear totally concrete (questions of law, finance, budget, etc.). However, their abstraction can conceal both the fact that they will influence many human lives and interests, and that any solution proposed will be class-specific.

More generally, in the modern State, the *citizen*, in so far as he is separate from the *private* man and the *productive* man, becomes externalized in terms of his own self. He plays a part in a political community in which he sees himself as social. Whereas he is also social, and more so, in another context. The citizen – the man who is well-informed about public matters, who has reasoned opinions, who knows the law – has become a political fiction; for there are necessarily political fictions just as there are necessary legal ones ('ignorance is no defence in law'). At this point we could define concrete democracy as the reduction of the role of political fictions to a minimum. The externality of the citizen in relation to his own everyday life becomes of necessity projected outside of himself: in models, in fanaticisms, in idolizations, in fetishisms. Wherever it appears, the cult of personality has a political sense and can never be reduced to a peripheral ideology; it is bound up with the nature of the State; it signifies both a democracy and a lack of democracy: a political fiction which is in danger of becoming a crushing reality. The externality of the citizen and his projection outside of himself in relation to his everyday life is part of that everyday life.

'[The] *German*[96] conception of the modern state, which abstracts from *real man*, was only possible because and in so far as the modern state itself abstracts from *real man* or satisfies the *whole* man in a purely imaginary way',[97] wrote Marx, in one of the rare and precious texts in which he talks to us about *the total man*; and what was valid for the monarchical State, for enlightened despotism and for Hegel's ethically based State remains valid for any State which establishes itself above society. The man who holds power becomes the only 'total man' and at the same time embodies the fiction of the total man in the eyes of every individual: its deceptive image. From this analysis Marx drew a decisive conclusion about the State:

> Only when real, individual man resumes the abstract citizen into himself and as an individual man has become a *species-being* in his empirical life, his individual work and his individual relationships, only when man has recognized and organized his *forces propres* (own forces) as *social forces* so that social force is no longer separated from him in the form of *political* force, only then will human emancipation be completed.[98]

Wherever there is a State, it is in the State that individual man will find his generality, his generic existence as a man, and this he does by becoming an imaginary member of a fictitious community. Within every class-based society the constraints that one class imposes upon another are always a part of the inhuman power which reigns over everything. On that level, the individual sees himself 'divested of his real individual life and filled with unreal universality'.[99] How does the individual see himself when faced with the enormous mass of the State? Like a minute speck, like a shadow. He becomes *for himself* an unreal appearance; but at the same time, by an absolute contradiction, the political fiction sanctions the *private* man, *qua* selfish individual with personal interests, as the supreme reality. This division assigns reality to egoism and abstract form to the citizen. Therefore a political revolution can take place without the State's natural basis, real social life – the 'world of needs' or of private law – being submitted to a critique and completely transformed. And if the political transformation subsequently 'revolutionizes' certain of these elements – after having dissociated them and thus particularized them *as* elements – it may leave certain others intact. For example, it might leave the world of needs to one side, or likewise the law, despite having transformed 'private' interests or the way labour is organized. Thus there is alienation by politics wherever the State has not yet withered away, for the Marxist critique of the State attacks all States. If certain texts are specifically directed against the Hegelian State or the bourgeois democratic State, others specify the 'political State' in general, in its relation with civil society. In no respects do the texts quoted by Lenin (in *The State and Revolution*) on the smashing of the bourgeois State apparatus, the constitution of a new State and its decline, invalidate the earlier texts. Rather, they confirm them as a function of concrete political situations. But if politics alienates, and contains alienation, it can also be disalienated, and this through political activity – in and through struggle on the political level and in and through the conflict between life and politics. Here again we recognize a complex of contradictions within a unity. In a sense bourgeois democracy in capitalist society, for example, entails a maximum of alienation: total alienation, complete political alienation. It perfects the opposition between the public and the private, between community and slavery. It mystifies every individual by granting him a place both in slavery and in community, in fiction and in reality. It allows him an apparent independence, because he takes 'the *unbridled* movement of the spiritual and material elements which form the content of his life'[100] for total freedom. The individual becomes totally subservient, and totally dehumanized. At this point the only link between all these social atoms and fragmented activities seems to be the State. It is not irrelevant to point out here that right from the start of his career, Stalin fell foul of what Marx calls political superstition: the illusory idea that the State cements society together, whereas it is the functioning of civil society and its cohesion, even in the apparent anarchy of its activities, which support the State.[101] The individual realizes that in bourgeois society the way he represents himself, for others and for himself, is contradictory, in that it splits him in two. On the one hand it isolates him as 'private' , atomizing him, dividing him; and this is a false image: atoms have no needs, they are self-sufficient, without needs, contented, perfect. Then on the other hand the individual realizes that each of his activities, his 'properties', his impulses, involves a *need.* This need brings him into relationship with other people. No matter how alienated need, natural necessity and man's essential properties may become, they still form a link between the members of this society. Thus these needs in everyday life are a cohesive force for social life even in bourgeois society, and they, *not political life,* are the real bond. So the individual tends to transcend his own separation from his self, his illusory image, his real appearance and false reality, his artificial atomization, his duplicity. He recognizes himself, and even by recognizing himself as an egoistic individual he has transcended political superstition.

Let us sum up. There is a set of elements to consider, and to the ones we have already examined we must add this complex contradiction: the citizen, the public man, the member of a State versus the real man, the private man. It is a complex system, for the public man and the citizen are at one and the same time fictitious and real; in so far as they are real, they pull the reality of man into the fictitious realm. As for the 'private' man, he is also both real and fictitious.

Everyday life includes political life: the public consciousness, the consciousness of belonging to a society and a nation, the consciousness of class. It enters into permanent contact with the State and the State apparatus thanks to administration and bureaucracy. But on the other hand political life detaches itself from everyday life by concentrating itself in privileged moments (elections, for example), and by fostering specialized activities. Thus *the critique of everyday life involves a critique of political life, in that everyday life already contains and constitutes such a critique*: in that it *is* that critique.

Let us now consider the structure of consciousness. A man's consciousness is determined by his (social) being. To coin a phrase, it *reflects* it. The word 'reflection' can lead to many confusions, and above all to many simplifications. If we are to avoid them, all we need do is notice that in nature reflections are profoundly different from what they reflect; and the image in the mirror only appears to be a reproduction of whatever is in front of it. The theory which maintains that on the one hand there are things and on the other their reflection in men's minds, and that the one reproduces the other, is philosophically puerile. A reflection in a consciousness, or a reflection which constitutes a consciousness, can be incomplete, mutilated, inverted, distorted, mystified; it is a reflection and yet in the generally accepted sense it is not a reflection. Let us consider the individualist individual's consciousness – under classic capitalism: the bourgeois individual's consciousness. In no way does it reflect the social complex to which he belongs: bourgeois society, capitalism. It is in the very nature of 'free competition' that an overview of phenomena and their laws is beyond the scope of the individual consciousness; and that is why there had to be economists, and Marx, to discover and understand these laws! The bourgeois's (the capitalist's) individual consciousness *reflects* his private interests in competition; it therefore conflicts with society as such, in that it is a *social consciousness*. The capitalist individual sees the other members of society – be they bourgeois or not – as outside of himself, and in opposition to himself. His consciousness only reflects the fact that competition separates one individual from another in such a way as to constitute a society which is beyond the grasp of any individual consciousness. But having said that, we should add that up to a point the capitalist embodies Capital and its functions, and this personification may be more or less successful. The *typical* bourgeois would be the perfect incarnation of Capital. But Capital is an economic fetish, and cannot in itself define a human being, with a human being's consciousness. Every bourgeois is *also* something else: a private man, with private passions – a father, who loves horses, or music, etc. As Marx has said, within every bourgeois two souls are locked in Faustian combat: the need to enjoy and the need to accumulate, thus on the one hand man's 'private' needs, and an aspect of his 'private' consciousness which now and again he gives in to – and on the other the need imposed upon him by the requirements of his money, his capital. What is more, in so far as he is a private man, or a father, or even a sensualist (in other words an egoist), he needs other people; now his consciousness reflects this tendency, now it reflects his secret or avowed opposition to it. Thus consciousness joins forces with the need for other people which is determined by the situation the individual is in; together they transform needs into desires, decisions into actions; or, conversely, the one inhibits the other.

This consciousness is therefore determined by *objective* conditions (economic, social, but also physiological, etc.); however, it is unaware of these conditions; and it is, precisely, inasmuch as it is unaware of them that it is determined. Such a complex and contradictory situation gives rise to a multitude of problems. The individual (in this case the bourgeois individual) must solve them; he looks for a solution, consciously. He looks to ideologies and moral doctrines for an image of himself. The solutions and possibilities thus revealed and represented – through a mixture of ideological fictions and moments of awareness – are true or false, illusory or valid; they lead to more-or-less complete failures or successes, and also to combinations of success and failure. It is possible for the success to have no objective relation with ideology. For example, take a believer who is a successful businessman; he is supported by his faith; he will see his success as a blessing from God (which is how religion is generally perceived in the USA: as a factor in success). Thus activities of an exceptional nature only *appear* to be beyond everyday life; they are used to solve problems – or not to solve them. The externality of ideology involves a measure of illusions.

All this means that the simplified notion of reflection is inadequate as an analytic tool. Consciousness reflects and does not reflect: what it reflects is not what it seems to reflect, but *something else*, and that is what analysis must disclose. Precisely because the activity that produced ideologies was exceptional and specialized, they came out of social practice – of everyday life – in two senses: it produced them and they escaped from it, thus acquiring in the process an illusory meaning *other* than their real content. The problem of ideologies is as follows: how can consciousness at all levels (individuals, groups, classes, peoples) be mistaken about itself and its content – its being – when it is that very content and that very being which determine it? Only by taking the formal structure of consciousness and its content as inseparables and submitting them to a complex analysis will we be able to understand any particular form of consciousness, or any particular ideology.

And here we are faced once again with a problem which is fundamental for the critique of everyday life. It is a problem which the first volume of this study failed to pose clearly. Many men, and even people in general, *do not know their own lives very well, or know them inadequately.* This is one of the themes of the critique of everyday life, confirmed by the spectacular failures of subjectivist sociology (based solely on interviews, questionnaires or surveys). Men have no knowledge of their own lives: they see them and act them out via ideological themes and ethical values. In particular they have an inadequate knowledge of their needs and their own fundamental attitudes; they express them badly; they delude themselves about their needs and aspirations except for the most general and the most basic ones. And yet it is their lives, and their consciousness of life; but only the philosopher, and the sociologist informed by the dialectic, and maybe the novelist, manage to join together the *lived* and the *real, formal* structure and *content.* Thus ideology is at one and the same time within everyday life and outside of it. It is forever penetrating everyday life, forever springing forth from it, uninterruptedly. Yet at the same time it interprets it, adds to it, transposes it, refracts it (more or less clearly, more or less deceptively).

Man's being is at once natural and historical, biological and social, physiological and cultural (which does not exclude possible or real conflicts between these elements and aspects – on the contrary, it involves them). Man thinks because he has a brain (a superior activity of the nervous system), and because he has hands, and because he works and because he has a language. Therefore consciousness *reflects* these manifold interactions; it not only 'reflects' the outside world, and things, but also human activity, practical power over nature. It not only reflects a given objective environment, but the equally objective conflicts between man and the 'environment', between the human world and nature, between individuals in the human world. A thing in isolation can only be defined as a *product*, and consequently as corresponding to a more-or-less consolidated *power*. Even when a consciousness reflects a thing, in truth it is reflecting a power together with the imperatives of action and its *possibilities*. And this involves the leap forward, the unending escape from what has already been accomplished towards images and the imaginary, towards a realm beyond the everyday, and thence indeed back into the everyday so as to take cognizance of it.

And yet it is in everyday life and in everyday life alone that *the natural and the biological are humanized* (become social), and, further, that *the human, the acquired, the cultivated, become natural.* Here there is a constant interaction between *the controlled sector* (controlled by knowledge and practice) and *the uncontrolled sector* (unknown, or unbounded by knowledge, so that blind necessity holds sway over man's helplessness and ignorance). It is in everyday life and everyday life alone that those interpenetrations which philosophers and philosophy define in general and abstract terms are concretely realized. Thus when the philosopher turns back towards real life, general concepts which have been worked out by means of a highly specialized activity and abstracted from everyday life are not lost. On the contrary, they take on a new meaning for lived experience. The philosopher discovers that exceptional activities benefit from the richness acquired on the level of everyday life; sometimes they contribute to that richness, at other times they prey upon it and suck it dry; they do not produce it. It is in and through everyday life that organs (eyes, genitals) are humanized. They have been transformed by history, by work, by social life and culture. This transformation operates in the everyday realm, it flows from the everyday and concludes within it. Otherwise it cannot exist.

Here the fundamental notion becomes appropriation, a philosophical notion which Marx extracted from the work of the economists, and criticized; he then integrated notion and criticism and incorporated them in the theory of Capital and property, but without ever fully developing them. Through social practice, man appropriates nature (an elementary thesis of Marxism); he also appropriates *his own nature*. Thus the human eye is no longer the organ with which an animal, nervous or replete, always on the look-out, explores a nature ever filled with danger, ever filled with prey. It becomes the mediator between a consciousness and a formed, welcoming world. By thus becoming a means, it becomes an end: joy, rest, fulfilment. And communication.

Rest can only be regarded simply as an interruption of activity – or the opposite of activity – in a fragmented and alienated life, and within a non-dialectical conception of life. In fact, the totality of the conscious being – even while he is resting, even in his exceptional activities – benefits from work, itself considered as a total activity, in other words as the power of man over nature (and his own nature).

Material labour (to which intellectual work contributes the essential tools – techniques, concepts, knowledge) creates *products*. Some of these products are means of production, others are objects or consumer goods. Taken together, products and works make up the 'human world'. But where and in what sphere is the relation between living men and objects of consumption actualized? Where do they become *goods* in the concrete sense of the term? How are they *appropriated*? In everyday life, that sphere where needs and goods meet.[102] And yet, where do needs come from? Where are they formed? How? And how do they find what they are looking for? Do needs make up a system? Is there a 'system of needs' or a structure of needs? What is this structure?

Alongside the scientific study of the relations of production which is the province of political economy, there is thus a place for a concrete study of *appropriation*: for a theory of needs. Such a study enfolds philosophical concepts and makes them concrete; in a sense it renews philosophy by bringing it back into the sphere of real life and the everyday without allowing it to disappear within it. But it also belongs to a specific science which we have called *sociology*.

The social relation between individuals and products (and works) embodies modalities and various aspects which can be distinguished by analysis. It cannot be reduced to the economic study of the processes of production and circulation (or as vulgar economics has it: distribution). It involves a sociology and even a psychology. It has ideological, cultural and even ethical aspects which the economist may glimpse but which he is unable to grasp. The notions of *need* and of *good* affect political economy on the one hand, and ethics, the theory of social classes, the critique of society and the definition of society, culture and civilization on the other. Thus they affect concrete philosophy.

Therefore we need to develop the notion of need and to formulate a theory of needs. This will be one of the aims of the next volume of this *Critique of Everyday Life*.

Everyday life, in a sense residual, defined by 'what is left over' after all distinct, superior, specialized, structured activities have been singled out by analysis, must be defined as a totality. Considered in their specialization and their technicality, superior activities leave a 'technical vacuum' between one another which is filled up by everyday life. Everyday life is profoundly related to *all* activities, and encompasses them with all their differences and their conflicts; it is their meeting place, their bond, their common ground. And it is in everyday life that the sum total of relations which make the human – and every human being – a whole takes its shape and its form. In it are expressed and fulfilled those relations which bring into play the totality of the real, albeit in a certain manner which is always partial and incomplete: friendship, comradeship, love, the need to communicate, play, etc.

The substance of everyday life – 'human raw material' in its simplicity and richness – pierces through all alienation and establishes 'disalienation'. If we take the words 'human nature' dialectically and in their full meaning, we may say that the critique of everyday life studies human nature in its concreteness.

So then how are we to define the function of the philosopher? Will philosophy still retain a meaning as a specialized activity?

Yes, it will. Once the philosopher is *committed to life*, he will watch over its meaning and its development from within. He will not set himself up above the everyday, in the sphere of exceptional activities, in the domain of ideologies and of the State. At the very heart of the everyday, he will discover what is hindering or blocking the march forward. He will remain a witness to alienations, and their judge. Keeping his vigil by night and day, the philosopher will not be satisfied simply to study the development of 'human nature'; he will want to help it, negatively at least – but the negative is also positive – by removing whatever may obstruct its fragile seeds. And the more life is in jeopardy, the more vigilant he will be. An overall picture of the universe? A cosmology? An ontology? A theory of knowledge? It is not on such a traditional level that the philosopher will rediscover his lost concrete universality. To rediscover it he must confront looming alienations as a critic and an implacable enemy. Wherever they come from.

This duty has its dangers, both for the philosopher as individual, and also for the effectiveness of his role, in that it will always run the risk of turning into an aberrant activity and an irrelevant by-product The philosopher must accept these risks. The critique of everyday life does not mean exemption from self-criticism.

IX   Plans and Programme for the Future

In principle this present volume was only intended as an introduction to the *Critique of Everyday Life*.

The first draft of the second volume was abandoned for a number of reasons.[103]

The second volume was intended to include a methodical study of little magic spells in everyday life: words, sayings, interjections – familiar gestures, rituals – minor superstitions, archaisms, countless relics of ideologies and customs whose 'base' has disappeared. These detailed observations were to have been the starting point for an analysis of myths and remains of myths in emotional, erotic and sensual life, and even more generally in images of the cosmos, as well as in the sphere of human relations in general, in literature (including bad literature, melodrama, serials), on the radio, etc.

The plan had one serious drawback: the external – and therefore arbitrary – way it was systematized. The book ran the risk of becoming a work of philosophy rather than a piece of concrete sociological research.

One fine day, once I had become aware of this objection and the risk involved, I realized that I had at my disposal a vast amount of material in which my object of study was concretely embodied: the *romantic press*, the so-called *women's* press. In it we find survivals, superstitions, rituals, myths and modern mythology, formulated and systematized in accordance with new (and obscure) needs; and that in the fullness of the everyday, in a direct expression of the preoccupations and aspirations of the most immediately practical kind of everyday life. Moreover, this press represents an extraordinary sociological fact, which cries out to be analysed. It is precisely over the last ten years that it has achieved its world-wide success and importance. In France its three million copies per week are read by ten million women (and men ...). What does this enormous success mean? What new need does it reveal? Is it profound or superficial, valid or spurious? What structure of consciousness does it reveal? What contents?

Thus the second volume of *Critique of Everyday Life* will include:

(a) an attempt at a *theory of needs* which will develop the observations included here, and in the works of contemporary sociologists, economists and demographers;

(b) an *analysis of the romantic press*, not on the economic level, as a commercial organization, but on the *sociological* level (an analysis of the formal structures of consciousness, of ideologies, and more profoundly of the contents and the needs in so far as one can grasp them through their public expression);

(c) the outline of an analysis of *class* relations and attitudes in everyday life – of the contents and needs which these attitudes and conflicts reveal.

Obviously I will not be able to isolate these different 'chapters'. Moreover, the final section – on class relations – could become the subject of a special volume if it at last became possible to carry out precise, concrete and broad-based surveys in France.[104]

Paris, December 1956 to February 1957

1

Brief Notes on some

Well-Trodden Ground

Numbers have lost nothing of their mystical glamour. Between 1880 and 1900, in a confusion worthy of the panic which greeted the year 1000, most artists and writers considered themselves to be 'fin de siècle' and 'decadent'. By the same confusion the writers who appeared on the literary scene after the 1900 Exhibition slipped effortlessly into the role of renovators. For the public, and in their own eyes, they represented the 'New Century'. Decadence was no longer in fashion.

But decadence stopped being a fashion at the very moment it was becoming a reality, when so-called 'modern' civilization was entering its convulsive death-throes. Peacefully and blissfully nurtured during the years before the First World War, this 'New Century' generation was nevertheless able to dominate the tormented times which followed, and at this moment in time (1945) it is still peddling its 'values' – so that for more than half a century France has suffered a 'spiritually' stultifying continuity in which until now wars and defeats have seemed mere episodes, untroubling to philistine and aesthete alike.

To this generation we owe a certain worldly *awareness*. Although we have become extremely *cynical*, on the positive side we see things more sharply, more lucidly, and we have refined our intellectual and literary techniques.

Most of the pharisees of political and social life come from the petty bourgeoisie: as oppressor or victim, the petty bourgeois likes situations he can vindicate. By 1900 (and the coincidence between the number and the historical significance of the date is purely fortuitous) the haute bourgeoisie no longer needed to vindicate its political actions to itself (although it still knew how to pull out all the stops when rehearsing the gamut of its 'values'), and it won a decisive victory over the petty bourgeoisie, which ceased to play any determining political role.

The minds of the petty bourgeois were crammed with prejudice, boredom, ideals. But after 1900 immoralism became the order of the day. It was immoralism, not the invention of a new morality, that replaced outgrown moral categories. To a certain extent questions of sexuality became less shrouded in secrecy. Clarity and abstraction took over from preaching. A kind of intellectualized sensuality made its appearance; intellectuals and aesthetes began to discover – and to disinterested eyes the spectacle was one of high comedy – that they could be thirsty, that they could be hungry, that they could feel desire. This discovery was greeted with demonstrations of joyful and emotional surprise: poetic hymns to thirst, to hunger, to desire, to fountains, to taverns, to fruits of the earth ...[1]

At the same time, from its very beginnings the era of finance capitalism was characterized by the extreme abundance of unfixed capital on the move, seeking investments – or avoiding them in a series of *exoduses*, some unobtrusive, some turbulent, towards some safe haven.

This wealth of availabilities, whether pecuniary or human, proved very profitable for the literary hacks and the artists. Shortly after 1900 the boom in paintings, rare books and luxury editions coincided with a revival in snobbery. Writers and artists began to find life more beautiful, more 'free'. Almost totally indifferent to the fact that they were putting themselves up for sale along with their works – theirs was an alienated consciousness transformed into commodities without their even knowing it – they disregarded the terrible events which were looming on the horizon, even and above all when they brought the new, abstract, metaphysical themes of 'adventure' and 'risk' to the fore. It is of little importance here whether or not we would deem this irresponsible. The important thing is to establish that the underlying themes had not changed, and that the literary twentieth century is a myth, an illusion. Had the themes of adventure, risk, immoralism and sexual freedom in any way modified those far more serious and tenacious themes and realities – pessimism, doubt, weariness, despair, loneliness – which first appeared in our literature towards the middle of the nineteenth century? No, on the contrary, in the 'new' climate of dry lucidity, improved verbal technique and icy cynicism, the resonance of these themes merely grew stronger, deeper and more clear-cut. What does the theme of adventure really imply? The dissolution of social relations in decadent capitalist society.

If he avoids complicity in the deceptions, the complacent optical illusions, the self-interested mutual congratulations and the posturings of critics who pronounce on the 'importance' of works which have only been out a week, the objective critic will be able to unravel the deeper network of themes lying beneath the surface decorations. His conclusion will be that:

the literary and 'spiritual' nineteenth century began with Nerval and Baudelaire and Flaubert. Romanticism goes back to Rousseau with his sentimental rhetoric and an individualism which he could still be complacent about, since it perceived no barrier between itself, nature and the divine, and since it had not been seriously tested as yet by loneliness and anguish. Stendhal too was an eighteenth-century man, optimistic and full of confidence in mankind, nature and the natural. With Baudelaire and Flaubert we enter another era, in which we are still living . . .

According to this objective critique, what are the characteristic themes of that intelligent but sombre nineteenth century? We will limit ourselves to three, only one of which — the third — need concern us here, and all of which are linked by more than one painful thread.

THE THEME OF FAILURE AND DEFEAT

Cf. *Sentimental Education*, 'Fusées',[2] 'My Heart Laid Bare', etc.

THE THEME OF DUALITY

Spleen and ideal, action and dream, flesh and soul, etc.[3]

THE THEME OF THE MARVELLOUS

Under the banner of the marvellous, nineteenth-century literature mounted a sustained attack on everyday life which has continued unabated up to the present day. The aim is to demote it, to discredit it. Although the duality between the marvellous and the everyday is just as painful as the duality between action and dream, the real and the ideal — and although it is an underlying reason for the failures and defeats which so many works deplore — nineteenth-century man seemed to ignore this, and continued obstinately to belittle real life, the world 'as it is'.

It was Chateaubriand who invented 'the Christian marvellous',[4] which was as coldly academic as the antique marvellous had become, constructed as it was of gods borrowed from Homer's pantheon. Then came Romanticism, which had to make do with a mediocre compendium of witches, ghosts and vampires, of moonlight and ruined castles, a vast petty-bourgeois waxworks. It remained for Victor Hugo to invent the most inept brand of the marvellous yet, the *moral*, which only his extraordinary poetic vitality rescued from total risibility: 'As you are my witness, O mountains clad in the candid purity of ageless snows, I say this man is wicked!', exclaims the Aigle du Casque, in a sudden burst of moral energy.[5]

With Baudelaire, and with him alone, the marvellous takes on a life and intensity which were totally original: this is because he abandons the metaphysical and moral plane to immerse himself in the everyday, which from that moment on he will deprecate, corrode and attack, but *on its own level* and as if from within. His insight into man's failures, his duality, his loneliness and ultimate nothingness is not merely intellectual, it is intensely physical.

Take for example 'The Painter of Modern Life', which more than one commentator has singled out as being particularly important. In it Baudelaire announces the presence in each object – even the most familiar – of a second nature, abstract, symbolic:

> If an impartially-minded man were to look through the whole range of French fashions, one after the other from the origins of France to the present day ... and if to the illustration representing each age he were to add the philosophical thought which that age was mainly preoccupied by or worried by, a thought which the illustration inevitably reflects, he would see what a deep harmony informs all the branches of history ...[6]

To Baudelaire the unity of the world appears in the narrow, abstract form of the symbol hidden behind the thing. He says elsewhere that beauty always has 'a double composition'.[7] This duality of art is a consequence of the duality of man: on the one hand an eternal element, on the other a 'circumstantial' element, which will be separately or at one and the same time 'the period, its fashions, its morals and its appetites'. When the eternal appears in the circumstantial – the marvellous in the familiar – the result is a beautiful work of art. According to Baudelaire, who wrote the article as a eulogy to his work, Constantin Guys had the ability to extract the phantasmagorical from within nature.

Among the various aspects of man's duality, that of art and nature corresponds to those of town and countryside, make-up and unpainted skin, clothes and body. The duality of the eternal and the circumstantial, of spirit and matter, is also the duality of good and evil, of the individual and the crowd. Baudelaire, who did not discover duality and who never pretended to have done so, is mainly concerned with intensifying it until it reveals a sort of unity within its extreme and painful tensions: a confused unity – not conciliation, or synthesis, or supersession, but more of a scholarly confusion where contradictions are resolved through a painful, relentless struggle so intense that it leaves the mind in ruins. What does he expect of the painter of modern life? That he should embrace the hostile crowd, contemplate the 'stone landscapes' of great cities as though they were a new nature at the heart of art and artifice, that he should perceive the eternal in the transitory, and above all in the most fleeting of moments. He wants the artist to confront the everyday – and even if necessary to tear through it to reveal the living spirit enshrouded within, not above, or beyond, but within – and in doing so to liberate something strange, mysterious and bizarre ... And then, confusing the most differing categories and groupings, and becoming the first writer to eulogize mental illness, Baudelaire calls on thought itself to supply the shock, the physical spasm which will give birth to the Bizarre. And in the process he rejects Man, maturity, strength, in favour of the myth of Childhood, which is the corollary of the Marvellous:

> Let us hark back, if we can, by a retrospective effort of our imaginations, to our youngest, our morning impressions, and we shall recognize that they were remarkably akin to the vividly coloured impressions that we received later after a physical illness ... The child sees everything as a novelty; the child is always 'drunk' ... But genius is no more than childhood recaptured at will, childhood equipped now with man's physical means to express itself, and with the analytical mind that enables it to bring order into the sum of experience, involuntarily amassed. To this deep and joyful curiosity must be attributed that stare, animal-like in its ecstasy, which all children have when confronted with something new.[8]

The power of seeing the mystery traced like a watermark beneath the transparent surface of the familiar world is only granted to the visionary. The Angel of the Bizarre merely brushes the surface of the child's mind, but for the invalid or the convalescent he penetrates the very soul, opening the world up to reveal its secret treasures. Is it an illusion, or is it reality become more real? For Baudelaire, as yet, this is not a question that needs asking.

All he asks is the pleasure, the organized confusion of the mind which words can so delightfully supply, particularly words of different natures: 'These great and beautiful ships ... with their out-of-work, homesick air'[9] – 'Spiritual and physical pleasure.'[10] Baudelaire demonstrates a kind of dialectic of opposites[11] which always ends abortively: 'a sketch for a lyrical or fairy extravagance for a pantomime ... Supernatural, dream-like atmosphere of the *great days*. That there should be something lulling, even serene, in passion. Regions of pure poetry.'[12] Or again: 'Cruelty and sensual pleasure are identical.'[13] This explains the admission: 'I have cultivated my hysteria with delight and terror.'[14]

In this confusion (at the basis of which we may discern not an anti-intellectualism, but on the contrary an excess of intellectualism, a cerebralism, an over-excitement of the mind whereby he tried to *think* the everyday world of the senses instead of merely perceiving it, and so to uncover its second, abstract truth), words still have power, they are the only remaining support, the last social reality. In Baudelaire may be found all the formulae which were henceforth to become ever-repeated passwords for successive clans of turbulent and neurotic poets – but from his pen they have an honesty which can produce such thoughts as 'only the brute gets a proper erection'.[15] 'Of language and writing, considered as magical operations ...'; 'A magic art'; Magic 'as applied to ... evocation', he announces in 'My Heart Laid Bare'.[16] And in his essays on the theatre he is careful not to forget 'drama, the marvellous – the magical and the romanesque'.[17]

When Flaubert set out for the Orient – Flaubert the petty bourgeois who hated the petty bourgeoisie (they all hated and despised one another) – he was unaware that the journey would change nothing, that he would end up once more living on his private income in some provincial backwater – with his ageing mother – and with nothing to show for it but oriental bric-à-brac and incipient syphilis – just as Baudelaire, that half-starved bohemian clown, lived with his memories of tropical islands, black women and a pampered childhood. The theme of failure is no less poignant in Flaubert's books and letters than it is in Baudelaire's intimate notebooks. Failure of one love, of one man: *Sentimental Education*; failure of one woman, failure of love itself: *Madame Bovary*. The contrast between the oriental splendour of *Salammbô* and the bitter, ludicrous precision of *Bouvard and Pécuchet* is a striking example of duality (even though Flaubert's genius was not sufficiently lucid to realize it). Thus it is that Flaubert shares with Baudelaire the thankless distinction of having inaugurated the literary nineteenth century.

But the denunciation of reality and its transposition into literary themes – in particular childhood illness and the dissolution from within of a type of individuality which corresponds to so-called 'modern individualism' – does not concern us for the moment. The call to unconscious, elemental, primitive forces which were supposedly capable of freeing this individuality from its impasse by offering it a content and a meaning and revealing hidden 'depths' was but one aspect of its decay.

After Baudelaire, after Flaubert, literature became increasingly involved in cerebralism and hyper-intellectuality.[18] There was no need for Rimbaud to return to childhood: he was a genius as a child, and when he was no longer a child, the genius left him. He never reached maturity, the sphere of distinctions between intelligence and reason, the senses and the mind, things and concepts.

It has been said time and time again that Rimbaud – like many children – practised simple hallucination. He poeticizes the real by directly seeing one thing in the place of another. Where his eyes perceive faces, clouds or landscapes, he 'sees' animals, angels, incredible cities. He casts aside any halfway stages between the thing and the other thing (the image). He eliminates the comparative conjunction which was traditionally used in classical and romantic writing to introduce metaphors, similes and 'images'. With Rimbaud the word 'image' takes on a new meaning, working on two levels, that of the senses and that of the mind or the dream. In this heightened confusion of the abstract and the concrete, symbol and sensation are no longer distinguishable, although Rimbaud's symbols are so intellectually refined that they take on a metaphysical dimension; and he identifies himself boldly with the thing, with the symbol: 'Sweeter than the flesh of sour apples to children, the green water penetrated my pinewood hull ... and sometimes I saw what men thought they saw ...'[19]

In this way 'The Poet becomes a seer by a long, prodigious and rational disordering of all the senses . . .'[20]

The poet splits into two, intolerably, for 'I is someone else',[21] and he knows it. But on the level of basic, physical life, and in confusion – in cultivated neurosis – he regains a kind of formless unity. 'Unspeakable torture', as he calls it in the famous letter, since the poet 'searches himself and consumes all the poisons within',[22] and every form of suffering and madness.

The alchemy thanks to which the real becomes transformed into poetry by means of words operates on the level of everyday reality. And in the *Songs of Maldoror*, it is precisely the unexpected juxtaposition of two familiar objects – for example an umbrella and a sewing machine on an operating table – which provokes the effect of surprise, of simultaneous shock to the mind and the nervous system, wherein Lautréamont discovers what he still calls beauty.

But subsequently the modern theme of the marvellous underwent a curious and rather confused disassociation.

Magic realism[23] attempted to express the mysterious meaning of the real world in a way that would make it appear insubstantial, like a perfume. Thus in *Le Grand Meaulnes* the apparently trivial life of a penniless schoolboy gradually reveals a mystery, a magic spell. In this way the real becomes 'transfigured', or, to put it more simply, more decorative and acceptable, at least on a literary level.

More explicitly, *Surrealism* set out to divert interest away from the real and, following Rimbaud's lead, to make the other world, the imaginary infinite, spring forth from within the familiar.

The magic realists had rather reactionary aims, whereas the Surrealists thought themselves to be revolutionaries, but both shared a common desire to belittle the real in favour of the magical and the marvellous. This coincidence of aims, this complicity, is very significant. In each case the concerted attack directed against everyday life and human reality is identical. The paths of literary and political reaction – and pseudo-revolution – have converged.

'The marvellous is always beautiful, anything marvellous is beautiful, in fact only the marvellous is beautiful', proclaimed Monsieur Breton in the *First Manifesto of Surrealism*.[24] The tone is characteristic: solemn, authoritarian and intimidating – to impressionable adolescents, that is. The aim of the Surrealists was to ensure that no form of the marvellous would be neglected. But Antonin Artaud's preface to his translation of Matthew Lewis's *The Monk* puts it better than I ever could:

> Yes, let them all slip back once again into that closed world where, like their excreta, only what is organically and sensuously demonstrable is valid, let them feed off the routine detritus and mental excrement of what they call *reality*, for my part I will continue to regard *The Monk* as an essential work, one which vigorously challenges that reality, dragging sorcerers, apparitions and phantoms before me in the most perfectly natural fashion, making the supernatural a reality like any other ... I know that I believe in ETERNAL LIFE, and that I believe in its complete meaning. I regret living in a world where sorcerers and soothsayers must live in hiding, and where in any case there are so few genuine soothsayers ... as far as I am concerned, I find it astounding that fortune-tellers, tarot-readers, wizards, sorcerers, necromancers and other REINCARNATED ONES have for so long been relegated to the role of mere characters in fables and novels, and that, through one of the most superficial aspects of modern thinking, naivety is defined as having faith in charlatans. I believe whole-heartedly in charlatans, bonesetters, visionaries, sorcerers and chiromancers, because all these things have being, because, for me, there are no limits, no form fixed to appearances; and because, one day, God – or MY SPIRIT – will recognize his own.[25]

This attack on the real and on everyday life is energetic, agreed, but how compromising it is!

After all, it may well be that the historians of modern life will come to look upon 'Surrealism' as a great moment for the intellect, born in an era when events were many and thoughts so few.

Already there are some very impatient historians scrambling to get their hands on this little corpse. (Moreover, rather than being a proof of richness and creativity, the current plethora of biographies, appraisals, judgements and learned tomes devoted to illusory 'contemporaries' is an indication of poverty and exhaustion.)

Without a doubt, the young disciples of Surrealism brought with them *a great desire for purity*. They wanted to live, to live according to themselves – freely, in the purity of 'the spirit'. Revolt, protest against an insufferable reality, refusal to accept that reality, despair, hope that human redemption was immediately possible, ever-repeated departures in search of the marvellous, an imminent world of images and love, all this was mingled in a confusion from which lucid analysis was permanently absent. They maintained a desperate, deliberate and well-nurtured duality through which they tried to live outside of the real world, without it, against it. As a *symptom*, maybe Surrealism was important. The most unfortunate thing the Surrealists did was to condemn the abject reality of the inter-war years along with human reality itself – to brand man's potentiality and the degrading destiny of the bourgeoisie with the same mark of infamy.

Their second misfortune was to fall into the hands of someone – Monsieur Breton (André) – who was able to capture, to use and to degrade the purity of those who were drawn to him: he was not only the pope of Surrealism, he was its politician.[26]

Applying all the procedures of traditional political life to the 'management' of the 'Surrealist group' – flattery, divide and rule, attraction, provocation, calumny, exclusion – he was able to lead this clan of young poets as if they formed a party on the fringe of political parties as such. Surrealism's allegedly 'spiritual' discoveries were in fact *political* discoveries, that is to say they were determined according to the needs and perspectives of the group's policies, and to events which were totally external to it.[27] Dadaist anarchism had been born in the 'disorder' which followed the 1918 armistice. In this truly revolutionary period, all that was needed to overthrow this established disorder were thought, organization and the sense of a new order; but the anarchist intellectuals failed to realize this. Then, in the post-war years, at the moment Marxist economists call the period of relative stabilization of capitalism, Monsieur Breton, after having proclaimed: 'Leave everything ... Leave your wife ... Set out along the highways ...',[28] had the (political) shrewdness to perceive that there was a general need for a definite doctrine and for a system propped up by logic; the hour had come for a universal call: 'Snobs of the world, unite', as well as for a skilfully organized confusion between 'permanent revolution' and permanent scandal. As the momentary stability of established society continued for a while, the man who had previously adopted the slogan 'art is stupidity' pompously devised the possibility of Surrealist art – of Surrealist poetry, painting, sculpture, cinema. The hour had also come when the outrageous in art could be made socially acceptable and profitable. At the same time Monsieur Breton was able to exploit the persistent confusion between anarchism and Communism, between the 'spiritual' and the social transformation of man. The time had come for sibylline discussions about 'Spiritual Revolution' which offered much-needed support and sustenance to the declining prestige of 'Surrealist thought'.[29] Nowadays if we attempt to examine the content of this 'thought', we will observe that doctrinal Surrealism, which started off with such enormous pretensions – to be a new mysticism, a method of knowledge of the 'interior abyss' – ended up as nothing more than a lot of superstitious nonsense. Its only remaining interest is that it was a symptom. At one and the same time Surrealism marked the absurd paroxysm and the end of the methodical disparagement of real life and the stubborn attack on it which had been initiated by nineteenth-century literature.

Surrealism wanted to deal a death blow to 'directed thought'. It wanted to be 'dictated by thought, in the absence of any control exercised by reason, exempt from any aesthetic or moral concern ...'.[30] It even aimed to wreck 'all the other psychic mechanisms and to substitute itself for them in solving all the principal problems of life ...'.[31] And this enormous pretension (this 'great ambition', this 'overwhelming message', to use the fashionable jargon of twenty years ago, before it was a question of 'commitment' and of 'assuming' reality ...) justified itself in terms of a simple-minded Hegelianism: 'I believe in the future resolution of these two states, dream and reality, which are seemingly so contradictory, into a kind of absolute reality, a surreality ...'[32]

But disillusionment was just around the corner. And just about all that came out of these aspirations to renew thought, knowledge and reality was the theory of the 'modern marvellous':

New myths spring up beneath each step we take. Legend begins where man has lived, where he lives. All that I intend to think about from now on is these despised transformations. Each day the modern sense of existence becomes subtly altered. A mythology ravels and unravels ... How long shall I retain this sense of the marvellous suffusing everyday existence? I see it fade away in every man ... who advances into the world's habits with an increasing ease, who rids himself progressively of the taste and texture of the unwonted, the unthought of ...[33]

It is you, metaphysical entity of places, who lull children to sleep, it is you who people their dreams. These shores of the unknown, sands shivering with anguish or anticipation, are fringed by the very substance of our minds. A single step into the past is enough for me to rediscover this sensation of strangeness which filled me when I was still a creature of pure wonder ...[34]

The gateway to mystery swings open at the touch of human weakness and we have entered the realm of darkness. One false step, one slurred syllable together reveal a man's thoughts. The disquieting atmosphere of places contains similar locks which cannot be bolted fast against infinity. Wherever the living pursue particularly ambiguous activities, the inanimate may sometimes assume the reflection of their most secret motives: and thus our cities are populated with unrecognized sphinxes ...[35]

Rereading these Surrealist texts twenty years after they first appeared, it is impossible not to be surprised by their shortcomings both in form and content: an assertive, icy tone which passes from point to point, linking them but never establishing any real connections – an insensitivity, an almost nightmarishly inflexible dependence upon verbal automatism, an obvious disparity between alarming promises and what was actually accomplished.

The Surrealists promised a new world, but they merely delivered 'mysteries of Paris'.[36] They promised a new faith, but did that really mean anything? Oh Literature, what petty crimes are committed in your name!

In their *nouveau merveilleux* there was nothing new – and nothing marvellous. Nothing that had not already appeared in the mental confusion pursued by Baudelaire and Rimbaud. A bit of metaphysics and a few myths in the last stages of decay (no more or no less than in Giraudoux and Claudel); some psychoanalysis, some Bergson-izing (the return to the purity of childhood sensations); an eclecticism, an impenetrable doctrinal confusion, together with a remorseless Parisian-ism – such are the ingredients that the most cursory analysis will discern in the 'modern marvellous'. On closer inspection, we find a number of original elements as compared with the Baudelaire–Rimbaud period:

(a) In Surrealism, the morbid element (mental confusion) is brought to the fore and 'systematized'. A paranoiac may get to the stage where he 'regards the very images of the external world as unstable and transitory, if not actually suspect ...', and this is a proof of '*the omnipotence of desire*, which has remained since the beginning surrealism's only act of faith'.[37] To suppress any possible complicity with the real world, *duality* is exacerbated until even insanity is seen as acceptable.

(b) The 'new realm of the marvellous' is marvellous no longer. In so far as there ever was a poetry founded on the marvellous, it depended upon myths and religion (naïve myths, myths 'lived out' by simple souls); even then, there was a derivativeness about this metaphysical and moral sphere. With Surrealism (and the text by Aragon quoted above is full of tacit admissions of this), it is no longer really a question of the marvellous, but of the weird, the unexpected and the bizarre, of mere effects of surprise and exoticism.

(c) In fact, this so-called marvellous realm operates only on the level of everyday life. Not above it or outside it, as in the cases of magic, of myth or of the supernatural, where everything is really, and instantly, possible. The marvellous is supposed to turn everyday life inside out, to discover its other, infinitely more interesting side. To shift the sense of what is important in life, to throw it off centre. This explains the pedantically detailed descriptions, and the ridiculous importance Breton attaches to looking for 'Surrealist objects'. It was even proposed that practical Surrealist objects should be produced for ordinary use. For example:

> two solids: one in the shape of a quarter of an orange resting on its rind, the two upper planes forming a sharp ridge, the other solid a sphere split at its base and suspended by a thread over the first. This sphere was therefore mobile and swung over the lower solid so that the latter's ridge was in contact with the split base of the sphere. This contact was not a penetration. Now, everyone who has seen this object function has felt a violent and indefinable emotion, doubtless having some relation with unconscious sexual desires ...[38] [and any impartial psychologist might add: linked with infantile and neurotic desires].

Here, with unshakable naivety, Nadeau the historian/commentator adds that dreams, automatism and the unconscious thus enter 'the realm of everyday life ...' and that 'the Surrealists, acquiring an awareness of their new gifts, believed themselves to be capable, by launching an infinite number of such objects into the world, of putting life entirely in the service of the unconscious . . .'.[39]

This penetration – inevitable, logically determined – of everyday life by Surrealism produces the following results:

> Daily life abounds, moreover, in just this sort of small discovery . . . I am profoundly persuaded that any perception registered in the most involuntary way – for example, that of a series of words pronounced off-stage – bears in itself the solution, symbolic or other, of a problem you have with yourself . . .
>
> So that, in order to have a woman appear, I have seen myself opening a door, shutting it, opening it again – when I had noticed that it was not enough to slip a thin blade into a book chosen at random, after having postulated that such and such line on the left page or the right should have informed me more or less indirectly about her dispositions, confirming her immediate arrival or her nonarrival – then starting to displace the objects, setting them in strange positions relative to each other, and so on. This woman did not always come, but then it seems to me, it helped me to understand why she wasn't coming; I seemed to accept her not coming more easily. Other days, when the question of absence, of the invincible lack, was solved, I used to consult my cards, interrogating them far beyond the rules of the game, although according to an invariable personal code, precise enough, trying to obtain from them for now and the future a clear view of my fortune and my misfortune . . . The way of questioning the deck that I preferred and still prefer supposed from the beginning that you place the cards in a cross, placing in the center what I am asking about: myself and her, love, danger, death, mystery; above, what is hovering; on the left, what can frighten or harm; on the right, what is certain; below, what has been overcome. My impatience at too many evasive answers caused me to interpose, rapidly and within the figure, some central object, highly personalized, such as a letter or a snapshot, which seemed to me to bring better results. This time I alternated two little disturbing characters which I had taken in: a mandrake root . . .[40]

And so forth. But enough of these old wives' tales. If the inter-war period was impenetrably closed to any authentic attempts to renew thought, it was only too open to every conceivable type of spiritual charlatanism.

Worried at first, then panic-stricken, intellectuals ran headlong towards false solutions, taking any way out but one which might offer a real answer or demand a real 'commitment', a real responsibility, a real renewal. For almost twenty years Surrealism has provided amusement for some; for others, shocked by its outrageousness, it has helped to strengthen certain wavering convictions; but now its failure seems complete and incontrovertible. Objectively it can only appear as an ersatz Romanticism, a woeful literary 'fin de siècle'. And if Breton was right in his *First Manifesto* when he linked Surrealism essentially with *defeatism*, this was only half the story, for it was not just a question of temporary political defeatism but of a deep, lasting defeatism in respect of man, of thought, of love and of the totality of the real.

Nevertheless, the analysis of Surrealism allows us to formulate, or rather verify, one of the laws of the human mind: a law which will provide us with one of the guiding ideas for the critique of everyday life, and which will reappear several times in that critique in other forms and supported by other evidence:

The law of the transformation of the irrational

The mysterious, the sacred and the diabolical, magic, ritual, the mystical – at first all of these were lived with intensity. They were part of the real lives of human beings – thoroughly authentic, affective and passionate forces. Then, with the appearance and development of rationality, they were doubly modified, along with their relationship to everyday life.

(a) *Demotion* – Gradually ritual becomes gestural. The diabolical becomes shameful, ugly. Myth becomes legend, tale, story, fable, anecdote, etc.

Finally, *the marvellous and the supernatural fall inevitably to the level of the weird and the bizarre.*

(b) *Internal transformation and displacement* – Everything that once represented an affective, immediate and primitive relationship between man and the world – everything that was serious, deep, cosmic – is displaced and sooner or later gradually enters the domain of play, or art, or just simply becoms amusing or ironic verbalization.[41]

This internal transformation takes place at the same time as the 'demotion' mentioned above. It is inseparable from it. Thus as man develops and becomes rational, the old, primitive irrationality maintains its connections with his everyday life.

We already know (albeit in a way that is still too vague and general, since as yet these questions have not been adequately studied) that toys and games are former magical objects and rituals. Be it children's hoops or dolls, the simple ball or playing cards and chess, they are all 'cosmic' objects which have been demoted (in one sense) and (in another sense) transformed and clothed with a new social meaning. There are good grounds for studying playing cards, for example, not after the fashion of Monsieur Breton, who sinks to the level of old women who use them to tell fortunes, but in terms of their history, in order to determine the source and the nature of the passionate interest they excite in people. So deep is the fascination and so passionate the involvement of human beings in the various games they play that there must surely be a direct connection between playing games and life itself.

It is demonstrable, for example, that games of chance embody the possibility of becoming conscious of, and (in the imagination) dominating a double-sided situation: on the one side, chance and a non-dominated nature (including one's own nature); on the other side, freedom (but an empty freedom, the freedom to take advantage of chance). This situation is in fact *that of everyday life*, corresponding exactly to the residue of weakness, powerlessness and irrationality which the now partially rational human being still harbours. By virtue of their use of former magical objects, games of chance are the social expression and the consciousness of this situation – and in a sense a spontaneous criticism of it.

Let us return to the weird and the bizarre. What are they? The mysterious displaced, transformed (with the marvellous acting as a halfway stage) and demoted. This demotion has turned the mysterious into something *everyday*, at one and the same time familiar yet surprising. When brought into sudden contact with each other, perfectly trivial objects and ordinary words can produce an impression of weirdness and bizarrerie. All it needs is for the familiar routine to be upset – but not too much, for otherwise it will give way to anxiety or, at the very least, expectation. A word of our language pronounced by a foreigner – a creaking door which sounds like someone groaning – an unfamiliar expression which passes fleetingly across a familiar face – and we say: 'How bizarre ...' Abruptly, familiarity is transformed into something new, but nothing too disconcerting or 'upsetting'. An ambiguous mixture of the known and the unknown which confuses thought and meaning without actually revealing the unknown to the mind or the senses, without producing any real enigmas or problems, without ever really being disturbing or worrying, such is the momentary experience of the bizarre. The bizarre is a mild stimulant for the nerves and the mind – particularly recommended as risk-free for cases of nervous fatigue and mental impotence. It is both a stimulant and a tranquillizer. Its only use is as a spice for banality, a cosmetic for insignificance. It is a pseudo-renewal, obtained by artificially deforming things so that they become both reassuring and surprising. (As in so many so-called 'modern' paintings and poems, where although the meaning is quite obvious, well-known objects or ideas are presented in a way which provokes a slight nervous twitch, a feeble jolt from the reassuringly recognizable to the mildly surprising.) The bizarre is a shoddy version of the mysterious from which the mystery has disappeared. Oh, women with strange faces, portraits and poems with weird imagery, peculiar objects, all you prove is that there is no more 'feminine mystery', that mystery has disappeared from our world, that it has degenerated into something public, that it is a game, an art-form, that it has lost its ancient glamour founded on terror and wild hope, that it has become mere journalism, mere advertising, mere fashion, a music-hall turn, an exhibit . . .

It is most certainly impossible for a 'viable' feeling of life to be based upon the impression of the bizarre. Such a feeling can only have its basis in the consciousness of human *power*, that power which surrounds us, upon which we live, and in which we participate in all the acts of our everyday lives – and yet which escapes us in such a way that we are unable to live it, so that nearly all our ideas and feelings still come to us from a time when man was weak in the face of nature.

But it is extremely revealing that an attempt was made to do this, and that a new feeling of everyday life should have been sought through the weird and the bizarre. This attempt, this game for aesthetes, nevertheless provided a certain criticism of our everyday life, but a clumsy one, equivocal, dangerous and thoroughly negative. Considered as a symptom it reveals:

(a) A malfunction, a disorder of the senses and the brain which has become conscious and more or less normal (especially among intellectuals). The physiological functions of the 'modern' man's nervous and cerebral systems seem to have fallen victim to an excessively demanding regime, to a kind of hypertension and exhaustion. He has not yet 'adapted' to the conditions of his life, to the speed of its sequences and rhythms, to the (momentarily) excessive abstraction of the frequently erroneous concepts he has so recently acquired. His nerves and senses have not yet been adequately trained by the urban and technical life he leads. Modern concepts are like a kind of electrical supercharge to his brain (a natural consequence of the extreme complexity of these concepts and of the situations in which we struggle), and, to pursue the metaphor, his nerves and senses are frequently short-circuited. And so the 'modern' intellectual, an extreme example and a complete product of this situation, is no longer able to abstract the concept or idea which is both within things and *different* from them, and to perceive it as on another stage or level of consciousness. In his perception the abstraction and the thing are mixed together, merged, the concept is like the thing's double – distinct, ideal, 'mysterious'. Furthermore, it is a second-rate abstraction, not *a way of knowing*, a *rational* element, but a 'signifying' of things, a symbol, a second thing, a façade. The elements of consciousness, its 'functions' or its 'stages', are at once separated and reunited in a false, confused unity in which their relations, their order and their hierarchy are lost.

For a century now this state of *mental confusion* has been manifesting itself clearly in modern art. It is a state of 'hysteria' (Baudelaire), 'disordering' (Rimbaud), or 'paranoia' (Surrealism) – but it is an incipient state only, and one compensated for by very real considerations; if it presents no real dangers this is precisely because it is accepted, deliberate, exploited aesthetically (whereas for the genuine sufferer such states are involuntary, unconscious or resisted). This state of deliberate semi-neurosis, partly play-acting, often little more than an ambivalent infantilism, allows the 'modern' intellectual to push far from his lips the bitter chalice of an everyday life which *really is* unbearable – and will always be so until it has been transformed, and until new foundations for consciousness are established.

By his attempt to maintain such an incipient neurosis as a reflection of his detachment, the 'typical' intellectual is able to replace the trivial and the familiar with emotions and illusions which he finds more appealing, more bearable: the mysterious, the strange, the bizarre. He 'lives out' these emotions, and the element of play-acting is rarely significant enough to provoke accusations of insincerity.

(b) A perpetual expectation of something extraordinary, an ever-disappointed and ever-rekindled hope, in other words a dissatisfaction which seeps into the humblest details of day-to-day existence.

How can we fail to believe in the marvellous, the strange, the bizarre, when there are people who lead marvellous (or seemingly marvellous) lives full of departures and incessant changes of scenery, lives which we see carefully reflected in the cinema and the theatre and novels?

– when there are technical processes which bring things which are distant and inaccessible to our senses near to us, revealing the astounding shapes of crystals, organs and organisms, nebulae and molecules (so that to our unprepared senses the realest things seem unreal or 'surreal' ...)?

– when we know that there are so many beautiful, idle women in the world whose only aim in life is pleasure and the quest for novel experiences; so that each time the adolescent or the young poet hears a knock on the door, his heart beats faster, and if the telephone rings, he rushes to answer it in the belief that the miracle is about to happen, that at last that beautiful, unique, absolute, mysterious woman (who with a bit of luck may be rich and a virgin to boot) is about to appear ... (for many confirmed idealists betray a very real tendency towards parasitism or pimping ...)?

Everything – life, science, both the ideal and the idea of love, not to mention that arch-sorcerer of the Western world, money – conspires to instil in the sensitive, lucid, cultivated young man with a gift for 'belles-lettres' a feeling of unease and dissatisfaction which can only be assuaged by something strange, bizarre or extraordinary. If we add to this the fact that his nerves and senses require sudden shocks, that his heart needs novel thrills – that in his unbalanced mind each object of thought must be defined through a kind of nervous and sensorial spasm, that a certain laziness or even a revulsion towards work (so clearly, so brutally expressed by Rimbaud and the Surrealists) prevents him from broaching any investigation which might compromise his convictions, and confirms him in his decision to stick with a facile and immediately-saleable re-hash of ancient mysteries – then we will have a more than adequate explanation of the cult of the bizarre and its success.

The strange and the weird were never more than a cheap and contaminated substitute for mystery. Of what value is the bizarreness of *The Songs of Maldoror* when compared with the mystery which animates *The Divine Comedy* – or with the passions kindled in the catacombs by the first Christian ceremonies – or by the Eleusinian mysteries?

For while mystery had its specifically consecrated times and festivals, the attraction of the strange is all-pervading. This myth of the modern world – decaying like all our enchanters[42] and all our myths – has this particular characteristic: the rotting remnants of what once was grandiose, exceptional and solemn, it seeks to penetrate, it can penetrate, it does penetrate our every moment. Woe betide the bewitched adolescent! He is in danger of being lost for ever; he is in danger of no longer belonging to this world; polluted, fanatical, his blood has become tainted. Did he long for a mysterious woman. absolute love, 'ideal' beauty? Real love, real women, real beauty will never be his. (Baudelaire's concept of beauty loses nothing by this; do strong spirits and the drugs healthy people can safely take in small doses lose their virtues simply because we describe them accurately as poisons?) Dante, in love with Beatrice, was a healthy, social, political man; there was nothing morbid about Petrarch and his Laura. But Baudelaire, the man who dominates our culture poetically, who was a dandy, a little buffoon, a Second Empire bourgeois ham – who at the same time denounced the forms his class was imposing upon life – is an important dealer in narcotics; hence his success, for our day-to-day life makes us vulnerable to the thirst for drugs and intoxicants. He did not wish to kill life, to commit treacherous murder on all that is human. For he wrote in his notebooks: 'Even as a child I felt two conflicting sensations in my heart: the horror of life and the ecstacy of life.'[43] He simply wanted to *line* life with another, truer life, the life of the 'soul'. He wanted to live through the mind, giving the real world a lining of enigmas, strangeness, correspondences,[44] with every colour, every sound, every taste and every perfume concealing a host of perceptible and tangible meanings. He was one of the first (but alas! by no means the last) to try to reanimate the old category of mystery, but on the level to which it had declined, on the level of the perceptible and the everyday. So he compromised *this* world and *this* life even more effectively than any of the metaphysicians, theologians and mystics who were seeking 'another life' to replace the everyday; the only thing that interested him, seduced him, fascinated him, was the *lining*. (Only symbols, only the mind, and they alone, can 'fascinate' and 'seduce', for, as opposed to any feelings based upon man's power, they weaken man and then exploit that weakness, drawing him down into a vertiginous chasm of mental confusion.)

Since Baudelaire, the world turned inside out has been deemed better than the world the right way up. Its hinterland is no longer the realm of Platonic Ideas, which at least left life, matter and nature to run along according to their own movements, governing them from on high, from 'Eternity'. Baudelaire's satanism has brought this hinterland into the world like a supplementary 'dimension' (to use today's fashionable pseudo-scientific, confusionist jargon), like a 'spiritual dimension'. In other words, he has put the cat among the pigeons, the maggot in the fruit, disgust in desire, filth in purity; and not as stimulants, but as poisons, all mixed together in an unspeakable confusion.

Under cover of the sublime and the superhuman, all manner of dehumanization is being smuggled in. Under cover of purity and 'pure' beauty, we are being invaded by impurity and ugliness.

The result is that if this strange *duplicity* loses its power to shock the nervous system (a power dubbed 'spiritual' for the nonce), and if things are perceived in themselves and not in terms of their magical lining, then interest, desire, love, become aimless. If it is to seduce and fascinate, the real world must be metamorphosed, transfigured. If it is to be noticed, every object, every living being, must be exaggerated, rendered surprising. For those hearts and minds infected with this scourge, the result is nothing less than a 'spiritual' *inability* to live, to love, to understand any human being who fails to show ambiguous, equivocal or psychopathological characteristics – a fake, a façade. For us the *dualities* of mind and matter, the ideal and the real, the absolute and the relative, the metaphysical and the tangible, the supernatural and the natural, have become a living duplicity, a lining, a façade, a fake, just impotence and lies lived out under the pretence of thought, poetry and art.

Moreover it is clear that in the end, despite the intention to reject it, the real world is accepted, since it is transposed, instead of being transformed by knowledge!

The attack on life led by poetry is just one episode, and literature is only the active-service unit of a much larger army. Like the poets, philosophers are wavering between the familiar, the trivial, the 'inauthentic', and the anguishing, the mysterious – between bourgeois reality and mystical unreality – and are pushing human reality to one side.

'The temperate zones of universal and human life bear no resemblance whatsoever to the polar and equatorial zones ...', writes Chestov, a contemporary 'existentialist' mystic and irrationalist philosopher.[45] This comparison between the soul and the earth, which is intended to discredit man's 'temperate' zones, misses out a rather important fact: the polar and equatorial zones are scarcely fit for habitation, and all civilization has developed in the temperate zones – the zones of everyday life. The mystic metaphor ends up defeating itself.

Another mystic has recently expounded his theory of paroxysmal moments in even crueller terms:

> There are certain instants, minimal in the passing of time, but extremely important in terms of their plenitude, when the mind breaks through the circle in which it had been enclosed, and begins to contradict itself, to have intuitions, flashes of insight, which, try as one may, cannot be denied afterwards – they really happened ... There are masses of times, enormous and stupid, in which nothing happens; and short, marvellous moments in which lots of extraordinary events take place. So far no one has ever come up with anything to prove that truth is in proportion to abstract time, that what lasts for a long time is true and that what only lasts for an instant is false.[46]

We must emphasize that this theory, of mystical and religious origin, but scarcely tenable in its original forms nowadays, has become demoted to the rank of philosophical theory, a 'secular' theory of truth. For our contemporary mystical philosophers, paroxysmal instants have lost their unique, divine, revelatory character. According to them, privileged instants can *be repeated*: Heidegger's anguish, the heady charms described by Sartre,[47] no longer have the 'unique' character of a mystic vision; they fall to the level of common 'existence'; the philosopher can pass from trivial, everyday and 'inauthentic' existence to this moment of revelation by a process which can be analysed and described. And yet the paroxysmal moment dispossesses mundane, everyday existence, annulling it, denying it. *It is the very thing which denies life*: it is the *nothingness* of anguish, of vertigo, of fascination.

Thus metaphysical mystery is being demoted in parallel with poetic mystery. Reduced to the level of everyday life, it appears merely as everyday life turned inside out. Except that the philosophers, who are more lucid – more cynical perhaps – than the poets, proceed in a way which 'unveils' (fashionable vocabulary) the point of the operation. Average life is repudiated; human life is relegated to the rank of the 'enormous and stupid' masses. But there is more, and worse, to come: this life must be 'made nothingness' so that the secret of existence may be revealed, namely nothingness, the nothingness within every man, his 'infinite' ability to free himself from any instant, any moment, any state, any determined situation, in and through nothingness. The underside of life reveals itself to be its nothingness; and the confusion of nothingness and being is to be found at the heart of the confusion between the abstract and the concrete, the symbolic and the real.

The poets now only like beings for the forms in which they can be *expressed* – the existence of human beings, of women, of love, is paralleled by a 'poetic' existence (uncertain, hazy, unreal, because it is essentially verbal); similarly the philosophers only like human beings for what they *mean*: like poetic expression, philosophical 'meaning' is located on the level of real life, within it and yet above it, like a *lining* to its reality, which is the only thing about it which is interesting, attractive, seductive or fascinating. The philosophers go on to emphasize the nastiest aspects of everyday life so that they can clearly demonstrate the negation of this life, the nothingness which liberates, in the world of philosophy.

'Hell is other people', maintains one of Sartre's characters, with metaphysical 'profundity'.[48] But is not the hellish part of us rather this 'other-than-being', this hinterland (or rather, nothingness) which the mystics, the theologians, the poets, the philosophers, have maintained in their consciousness, and in which they obstinately continue to live their visionary lives without realizing the level to which it has been demoted?

But we should not take such 'profound' theories too seriously. Anguish and mystery (the feeling of mystery) cannot be reduced to a theoretical level, it is impossible to theorize them. Genuine anguish, the anguish of a lost child, of a primitive man lost in the jungle, of a being who feels utterly weak and helpless in the face of nature, such anguish escapes us. The feeling of human power (not the will to individual power, but the consciousness of the collective, social power of man over nature) penetrates our every thought and every sensation, albeit indirectly. 'But what about death?' ask the metaphysicians, 'your death – yes, yours, tomorrow, today, in a few minutes? Have you got time to wait until biologists find a way of delaying death (supposing that to be possible)?' Alas, no, I haven't the time. But so what? Do you think that is a reason for me to stop living, loving, being a man and participating in all man's possibilities? Even at this very moment action, work, love, thought, the search for truth and beauty are creating certain realities which transcend the transitory nature of the individual. And the fact that this assertion has become trivial, that it has been put to use too often – sometimes to the worst kind of ends – does not mean that it has stopped being true. On the contrary: let us reaffirm the certainties of human community; let us renew and re-establish these foundations of the human in all their strength and youth. Philosophers, metaphysicians, you are like dogs baying at death! Or rather – excuse me – I should say *pretending* to bay at death. For you death is like a perfect thought which you can recall, repeat and merge with every moment of your lives; and you are inviting us to follow you, to accept this final phantom from the other world, and it really is no more than a phantom. But this 'other', this absence, this 'tragic' feeling of existence, this consciousness of the absurd, I observe it in men who lead very skilful, successful lives; they hold forth on the subject of anguish to fashionable audiences in lecture halls, and it becomes a topic for scholarly essays; people sit in cafés and newspaper offices writing about anguish, cleverly, shrewdly, technically, and with verbal elegance. The floral tributes thrown to death are nothing more than rhetorical flourishes. No matter how profound, how inhumanly existent (or nonexistent!) 'existentialist' metaphysicians may be, they will never stop anguish from becoming demoted and displaced. Brute, primitive anguish is fading from our lives; to rediscover it is to experience a moment of weakness which in no way leads back to the 'authentic' or to 'the depths of the abyss'. Ancient wisdom knew that old age is an evil worse than death. Our metaphysicians, who go on so much about 'the other-than-being' (to use their jargon yet again), have little to say about old age. This is because it is not exciting to think about, there is nothing other-worldly about it. It is simply a sad reality; and yet thinking about it will tell us what we need to overcome, and immediately, within each of us, no matter how young we may be, and in every moment of our everyday lives. In any case we know only too well that old people do not need to make an effort to think about death, such thoughts come naturally and there is nothing positive about them. But if young people feel the need to think about death to stimulate their sense of being alive, if they proclaim their youth arrogantly in the belief that the simple fact that they are young suffuses their lives with truth – and if at the same time their youth becomes blighted by the obsessive thought of death – then one can only pity such premature senility.

Thus philosophy has joined forces with literature in this great conspiracy against man's everyday life. Even in our so-called 'modern' poets' and metaphysicians' most polished verbal and technical games we can find the elements of a certain criticism of everyday life, but in an indirect form, and always based upon the confusion between the real in human terms and the real in capitalist terms.

The true critique of everyday life will have as its prime objective the separation between the human (real and possible) and bourgeois decadence, and will imply a *rehabilitation of everyday life*.

It is not distinguished poets and philosophers who have plumbed contempt for man and his real life to its very depths, but the despicable and in a sense brilliant Louis-Ferdinand Céline.[49] We must reverse this slide into contempt and corruption. To rehabilitate the masses – the masses of instants that philosophers condemn to 'triviality' as well as the peoples that poets relegate to the shadows – are related tasks. Is it not in everyday life that man should fulfil his life as a man? The theory of superhuman moments is inhuman. Is it not in day-to-day life (not the life we lead now but a different one, already attainable) that the truth in a body and a soul must be grasped? If a higher life, the life of the 'spirit', was to be attained in 'another life' – some mystic and magical hidden world – it would be the end of mankind, the proof and proclamation of his failure. Man must be everyday, or he will not be at all. As one of the characters in Jean Cassou's novel *Le Centre du monde* exclaims: 'For that's what's important, don't you see, giving up believing in magic. And there comes a moment in every man's life when he has to, when he's got to throw all the tricks and mumbo-jumbo away for ever.'[50]

Cassou's novel poses a problem. The debate it engages between reason and irrationality grows into a debate between the real and the unreal, between the human and the inhuman, between the mysterious and reality. The title itself is vaguely cabbalistic, redolent of mysteries to come. Where is the Centre of the World? Everywhere, nowhere, within us, within each of us perhaps. Could it be the Secret, the famous secret of existence which we are supposed to look for night and day, even if we have to go to the ends of the earth to find it? But as soon as we begin reading we see a conflict growing between the attractions of magic, the expectation of a magical sense or aspect of life, and the desire, the necessity, of breaking the spell.

And yet the very *charm* of Cassou's book is the child-like magic which from the start transforms simple, everyday beings. A pretty girl becomes 'the Duchess of Montbazon', an old man becomes 'the Old Man of the Mountain'. And the father, the wizard, keeper of the secret and dispenser of good things, what is he really? A former bureaucrat, a poor old man with rheumatism and funny little habits who dies like everyone else, and whose corpse smells bad. Hélène is the magic, mysterious woman, the pure feminine myth sought by Raphaël, who finds her through a chance encounter, only to lose her again in the disappointment of her realness. Raphaël lives in a hermetic and mysterious world, an incomplete being, alone and powerless. Lost in the society he has rejected, he seeks refuge in a magical world where conflict has been eliminated, where everything is reassuring, and resolves his problems by denying that they exist. He comes down to earth again – at the moment of death. Then, as he slides into nothingness, everything he has lived through falls into place according to the perspectives and proportions of the real world. At last he understands, and wants to go on living. Too late. 'How long the night seemed, and yet it did not become fantastic. The fantastic had happened before. Outside, there was the street, not a meadow full of lunar horses. Everything fantastic was in the poor life he had led . . .'[51]

Here death no longer appears as the Muse of poets and metaphysicians, the 'great captain' and 'she who gives us life' (Baudelaire), but as the great disillusionment which puts everything back in place. Are we then condemned to hesitate, to waver between self-deception and awareness, between the illusion that confounds us and the reality which in its way is equally confounding?

Jean Cassou's book remains a novel about a defeat, an unresolved duality. It fails to resolve the problem of the marvellous, but poses it with a certain lucidity; it is almost a farewell to magic; such works announce the end of one era and the beginning of a new one.[52] 'Spiritually' we have not yet left the nineteenth century. When the new man has finally killed magic off and buried the rotting corpses of the old 'myths' – when he is on the way towards a coherent unity and consciousness, when he can begin the conquest of his own life, rediscovering or creating *greatness in everyday life* – and when he can begin knowing it and speaking it, then and only then will we be in a new era.

2

The Knowledge of Everyday Life

Therefore, in the contemporary period, art and philosophy have drawn closer to everyday life, but only to *discredit* it, under the pretext of giving it a new resonance.

This action against life resembles the 'right-wing critique' of institutions and things which was rife during the period of superficial freedom and abstract democracy preceding the collapse of 1940; for several decades Barrès, Maurras and their disciples – and many others as well – gnawed away at the structure and substance of democracy like termites, from within, both in thought and action.[1] They criticized its political economy, even appearing to attack capitalism and trusts in the name of precapitalist ideologies and institutions (guilds, the primacy of the spiritual realm, etc.).

The only real critique was and remains the *critique of the left.* Why? Because it alone is based upon *knowledge.*

Mystical or metaphysical criticism of everyday life, be it from poets or philosophers, ends up in a reactionary position, even if and above all when its arguments have *formal* similarities with those of the 'left'. Escape from life or rejection of life, recourse to outmoded or exhausted ways of life, nostalgia for the past or dreams of a superhuman future, these positions are basically identical. This is why extremist, 'far-left' critiques so closely resemble reactionary ones. In France, fortunately, the total, relentless rejection of life and the real world has had neither the time nor the opportunity to reap its harvest of Dead Sea fruits. The total rejection which, according to all available documentary evidence, gave the Hitler Youth movement strength until the very end, allowed it and perhaps still allows it to cope with the collapse of its 'superhuman' dreams by giving that collapse the value of a holocaust. Make the rejection of everyday life – of work, of happiness – a mass phenomenon, a malady of the decaying middle classes, a collective neurosis (where in France it was merely an individual phenomenon), and you end up with the Hitlerian 'mystique'.

At the same time as art, literature and philosophy were attacking everyday life so relentlessly, without discriminating between its two sides (the bourgeois and the human), the world of knowledge was also moving closer to it, but in order to study it as seriously as possible. Important discoveries were made in several scientific fields through the study of humble, everyday and (at first glance) insignificant objects. Let us recall the following passage, one of the most extraordinary Marc Bloch ever wrote, and a curiously moving one, even if one does not accept all the conclusions.

Nevertheless, in France, three main types of agrarian civilization may be distinguished which are all closely linked at once to natural conditions and to human history. First, a poor terrain which had been only half-heartedly, and for a long time intermittently, exploited, and the greater part of which – up until the nineteenth century – remained unchanged: a system of enclosures. Then two more intensive types of farming, both in principle involving the collective control of ploughing, which, given the extent of cultivation, was the only way to maintain the proper balance between arable and pasture necessary if everyone was to survive – consequently neither was enclosed. The first of these, which we may cal 'Northern', invented the plough and is characterized by the particularly strong cohesion between its communities; it can be recognized by the generally elongated shape of its fields, which are grouped in parallel strips . . . Finally, the second of these open types, which for the sake of convenience but with some reservations may be called 'Southern', combines a continued use of the swing plough and – in the Midi proper, at least – two-yearly rotation of crops, with noticeably less community spirit in the exploitation of the land and agrarian life itself. There is nothing to stop us thinking that these sharp contrasts between ways of organizing and thinking in the old rural societies did not have profound repercussions for the evolution of the country overall.[2]

How many times have we all 'strolled' through the French countryside without knowing how to decipher the human landscape before our eyes! We look with the eyes of unskilled aesthetes who confuse natural facts with human facts, who observe the product of human actions – the face that a hundred centuries of working the soil have given to our land – as though it were the sea or the sky, where the wake of man's passage quickly fades away. We do not know how to see this reality, so near and so vast, these forms creative labour has produced. City dwellers getting away from it all, intellectuals at a loose end, we wander through the French countryside simply for something to do, we look but we are unable to see. We are caught in a hybrid compromise between aesthetic spectacle and knowledge. When the flight of a bird catches our attention, or the mooing of a cow, or a shepherd boy singing, we think we are being very clever and very concrete. But we are unable to seize the human facts. We fail to see them where they are, namely in humble, familiar, everyday objects: the shape of fields, of ploughs. Our search for the human takes us too far, too 'deep', we seek it in the clouds or in mysteries, whereas it is waiting for us, besieging us on all sides. We will not find it in myths – although human facts carry with them a long and magnificent procession of legends, tales and songs, poems and dances. All we need do is simply to open our eyes, to leave the dark world of metaphysics and the false depths of the 'inner life' behind, and we will discover the immense human wealth that the humblest facts of everyday life contain. 'The familiar is not necessarily the known', said Hegel. Let us go farther and say that it is in the most familiar things that the unknown – not the mysterious – is at its richest, and that this rich content of life is still beyond our empty, darkling consciousness, inhabited as it is by impostors, and gorged with the forms of Pure Reason, with myths and their illusory poetry.

We have become too sensible for these myths, which imply naïvety; we no longer believe in mysteries, but pretend to believe in them; and there is nothing so tiresome as the false naïvety, the false stupidity of certain poets who in other respects have all the tactics, the tricks of the trade, the technical subtleties of literature at their fingertips (Claudel, Pierre Emmanuel, etc.).[3] But we are not sensible enough to get beyond abstract, formal, metaphysical reason in our lives and in our consciousness of them. Thus we are caught in a state of uncertain transition between old and new Reason; and our consciousness is still only a 'private' consciousness (individual and isolated, becoming universal only in its abstract form, thought – deprived of real contact with the

real and of any consciousness of its practical and everyday character).
We perceive everyday life only in its familiar, trivial, inauthentic guises.
How can we avoid the temptation to turn our backs on it?

Like the magnificent fruit and the beautiful creatures of temptation
– which crumble to ashes should we touch them – myths, 'pure'
poetry, mysteries, await us with open arms.

Who would have thought it possible a century ago that the first
hesitant words of infants or the blushes of adolescents – or the shape of
houses – could become the objects of serious scientific study? In so far
as the science of man exists, it finds its material in the 'trivial', the
everyday. And it is the science of man – knowledge – which has blazed
the trail for our consciousness. At all times and in all circumstances our
consciousness is tempted to believe in its own self-sufficiency, its own
self-awareness, its ability to possess itself and its objects. Now and
again real knowledge teaches it some hard lessons in modesty; and for
the foreseeable future such lessons will continue to be necessary, since
our consciousness always has its own ways of interpreting the results
knowledge itself produces; it always feels the need to believe that
science must deal with sublime, mysterious things – when it is quite
simply a matter of those first words of the child or the shape of that field
(or even, for the most up-to-date physicist, the blue colour of the sky or
the 'trivial' impact of two bodies upon each other).

Before we go any farther, one particular ambiguity must be
eliminated. In their arguments and reflections the historians of the old
school always made sure they introduced painstakingly detailed and
often repellently trivial descriptions of everyday life at a given period, of
royal illnesses and love affairs, of life in the medieval castle or of the
seventeenth-century 'peasant interior'. Such details have no relation
whatsoever with the idea we are likely to develop of a knowledge of
everyday life. They only appear to do so; and they are merely a mask
for whimsical interpretations of history. It is quite possible to move
from a 'realistic' description of the peasant at work, or of a worker's oil-
stained blue overalls, to a fanciful theory about peasant life or the
destiny of the working class. And such sleight of hand is the easiest
thing in the world; it is how many philosophical or political tricksters
work, substituting the concrete (the apparently concrete, and consequently false, deceptive and mendacious) by an abstraction (consequently a pointless abstraction), and relying solely on well-turned but

unconnected and intellectually stagnant phrases.

Knowledge and genuine thought pass methodically from the individual scale to the social and national scale (by a process of thought comparable to the mathematical integration of very small elements). Thus they succeed in establishing a scientific notion of the social whole – and in particular a scientific theory of *social labour*. In this way tools, and the way workmen handle them – be they peasants, craftsmen or factory workers – appear like elements, moments in the totality of labour; and we know that this totality of labour has modified and transformed the face of the world. In this context the nation ceases to be an abstraction, a 'moral person' (Renan), or a (national or racist) myth. We have learned how to perceive the face of our nation on the earth, in the landscape, slowly shaped by centuries of work, of patient, humble gestures. The result of these gestures, their totality, is what contains greatness.

Of course, details retain their brutal reality; this wheelbarrow is still creaky and cumbersome, this peasant's life is still harsh and that worker's life is still dull and joyless. Things have not been transfigured, and we do not get carried away by mystical joy. And yet our consciousness of these things becomes transformed and loses its triviality, its banality, since in each thing we see more than itself – something else *which is there* in everyday objects, not an abstract lining but something enfolded within which hitherto we have been unable to see. In fact if the harshness of peasant life and the squalor of the farmyard, or the sadness of life in a proletarian neighbourhood, appear intolerable, they seem even more so once we become aware of the magnificent, grandiose character of the works they have produced by their labour. Our awareness of this contradiction becomes more acute, and we find ourselves faced necessarily with a new imperative: the practical, effective transformation of things as they are.

Guided often unconsciously by these perspectives, the genuinely modern historian has abandoned those lofty spheres in which kings, generals and princes of the Church used to parade in their stately robes, uttering nothing but historical statements. Now the historian helps us to enter historical reality by showing us for example how the former kings of France turned themselves into large feudal landowners and established the solid foundations on which their 'grand policy' was built by buying fiefs and increasing their ownership of land. Unglamorous facts were actually the more important ones, and for us historians they are more revealing than sensational events. Here the shift from 'significant' facts to the sum total of everyday events corresponds exactly to the shift from appearance to reality – an operation which is as important for science as is the shift from individual elements to the totality. Only this certainty that we are moving from glamorous appearances to the essence saves us from the illusory perspectives with which individuals and groups have viewed themselves throughout their history, allowing us to see the beginnings of a science, rather than a bookish rehearsal of out-moded masquerades.[4]

The great scenes on the stage of history have never been 'representations' in the psychological and philosophical meaning of the word, as naïve people still believe; they were not the work of naïve people, expressing themselves 'with complete sincerity' and eager to speak the truth. They were more like theatrical 'performances' (and let us not forget the profound link that has always existed between theatre, acting and life itself); historical scenes have always been cleverly and cunningly 'staged' by certain men who were aiming for specific results. They were acts. Every word, every gesture constitutes an act, and acts must be understood according to their purpose, their results, and not merely in terms of the person speaking and acting, as though he could somehow express or 'externalize' his reality and sincerity. More exactly, words and gestures express an *action*, and not simply some ready-made 'internal reality'. When men speak they move forward along their line of action in a force field of possibilities. You need only watch a child to realize that whatever it says is intended to influence you, to obtain a specific result from you, and must therefore be understood in terms of yourself, the moment in time and the intention; it is the very essence of childhood: a weak being seeking to get results from stronger beings whom he sees as being terrible, grandiose, powerful ... and ridiculous.

A keener awareness of everyday life will replace the myths of 'thought' and 'sincerity' – and deliberate, proven 'lies' – with the richer, more complex idea of *thought-action*. Since words and gestures produce direct results, they must be harnessed not to pure 'internal consciousness' but to consciousness in movement, active, directed towards specific goals. Whether spontaneously or deliberately, we always get results by rapidly summing up the situation and the person we wish to influence. The effects we use will always have their share of play-acting and artistry, persuasion, seduction, oratorical display, intimidation, histrionics. It is not a question of that ready-made characteristic of sincere people, 'sincerity', on the one hand, and of 'lying' (planned and plotted by 'liars') on the other. In everyday life or in the full glare of the theatre footlights, human beings always behave like *mystifiers*, who manage to 'play a role' precisely by exaggerating their own import-ance. Sometimes the acting is crude, sometimes extremely subtle; and moreover the actor becomes committed, compromised; it is a serious business. The parts must be acted out until the end; they are not pure roles, which an actor can give up when he is tired or when he feels he is acting badly. They extend reality, and are equally as real; acting explores what is possible; in the abstract, play-acting does not exclude sincerity; on the contrary, it implies it, while at the same time adding something extra – something real: the knowledge of a situation, an action, a result to be obtained.

It is precisely in this way that everyday life resembles theatre – and that theatre is able to resume, condense and 'represent' life for real spectators.

If he fails to examine history in the light of everyday life, the historian is falling naïvely and of necessity into a trap laid for simpletons. There he is among the onlookers, open-mouthed, a minor intellectual too awe-struck to approach – on paper, that is – the great men of this world. Scenes were staged (with more than enough sincerity) with glory and prestige in view; the naïve historian is taken in, just as contemporaries were. He has no awareness, no irony, no craftsmanship. He is erudite to the *n*th degree, and yet he is without substance, weight, human consciousness. He is content to churn out the same old historical scenarios event by event. And the anecdotes pile up before him; he is all but ready to start believing in the divine nature of kings.

While taking care not to deny the importance of the leading players, more profound historical study takes the whole into account: specta-tors, situations, the canvas of the immense *commedia dell'arte.* Once the historian and the explorer of human reality realize they have been fooled, and begin consciously linking history and the knowledge of mankind with life – everyday life – in the past and in the present, they will have left their naïvety behind. Such historians denounce appearances, those appearances which use reality in a way that enables the 'great men of this world' cleverly to nurture their prestige and present their own reality to its best advantage – and hence to perpetuate that reality.

Thus bit by bit there is a growing conviction that *in one sense* lavish institutions and grandiose ideas were façades – theatrical costumes.

On the almost stagnant waters of everyday life there have been mirages, phosphorescent ripples. These illusions were not without results, since to achieve results was their very *raison d'être*. And yet, where is genuine reality to be found? Where do the genuine changes take place? In the unmysterious depths of everyday life! History, psychology and the science of mankind must become a study of everyday life.

Here and there, bit by bit, though sadly sporadic, fragmented and without an overall strategy, this conviction is dawning in the work of certain historians (Marc Bloch) – certain geographers (Demangeon) – certain psychologists. No one so far has attempted a synthesis.

3

Marxism as Critical Knowledge of

Everyday Life

Our age is, in especial degree, the age of criticism, and to criticism everything must submit. Religion through its sanctity, and law-giving through its majesty, may seek to exempt themselves from it. But they then awaken suspicion, and cannot claim the sincere respect which reason accords only to that which has been able to sustain the test of free and open examination.[1]

But after this magnificent declaration of the rights of Human Reason, Kant failed to grasp the essential. He was content to criticize 'Pure Reason'; thus he remained on that level. Only at certain moments and in certain places does his critique rise to the level of a *critique of man*. Wishing to eliminate dogmatisms, theologies and metaphysical systems in favour of a rational order, he failed to discover the human foundations upon which the speculative aberrations he was attacking are founded. This is why after Kant metaphysical explanations enjoyed a new lease of life; his critical tempest turned out to be just a storm in a teacup, a squall which uprooted some weeds only to bring forth others.

Why do some men go on pursuing a 'hidden world' with so conscious and so emotional a determination? They call themselves sincere; they have reduced their innate tendency to posture to a minimum (for it is a function of the philosophical and scientific mind to do so). But we can argue that, despite all their sincerity, their speculations still contain elements of intellectual play; and that the simple idea that the secret of the universe should reveal itself to them, and to them alone, implies an exaggeration of their own importance so extreme as to border on the burlesque, requiring hypocrisy, play-acting, even clowning. But just for the moment let us put to one side the consideration of *metaphysical* thought as dramatic posturing and hypocrisy. Let us just say that they are sincere.

Over there I can hear someone crying out to God – but why? He is the son of a merchant, of a parvenu. He is rich, he can live off his private income and dedicate himself to happiness, love, seduction, art. But the truth is that he is incurably bored. And yet he is very gifted, witty, even brilliant; he loves life, and at the same time hates it: 'All existence makes me anxious, from the smallest gnat to the mysteries of the incarnation; all life is a plague to me, most of all myself.' His thought and his intelligence merely serve to make him anxious about everything. He hates himself, and yet thinks more of himself than of anything else in the world: 'Basically only one quality exists, the individual, that is the axis of everything.' He is walled up within himself, trapped in the framework of his life like the bourgeois with a private income, the intellectual, the literary hack he is. But he values the very things which are destroying him, because he exists through them alone. He possesses everything it is possible to possess: money, property, leisure, talent, thought. And yet he possesses nothing, and knows it, and says it: 'I believe I am brave enough to doubt everything, to fight against everything; but I am not brave enough to recognize nothing, to possess nothing.'

He does not even possess his body, his flesh, his desires. His upbringing has killed everything inside him. We should realize that this man's father was not a run-of-the-mill shopkeeper. One lonely, hungry, painful evening, when still a young shepherd watching his flocks on the barren heath beside the sea, he cursed his God; and judged himself accursed and damned. Subsequently, thanks to his dourness and austere inflexibility, he managed to save money and to rise in the social hierarchy. But he carried within himself the consciousness of his sin – of his nothingness. Late in life (through humility, through shyness ...) he married (and terrorized) his servant. Sometimes he would take his son into an unlit room and talk to him in passionate terms about the world, ships, ports, faraway countries. At the same time he taught him to fear Sin, to recognize Sin within himself. This unfortunate son admits that 'if a child was told that it was a sin to break his leg, how anguished his life would be. And he would be all the more likely to break it.'

And so this young man suffocates in the narrow framework of his life and consciousness. He cries out for – what? Something different, something Possible. What of his thoughts? They bring him no deliverance, no future possibilities. Quite the opposite, they enable him to 'leap over life'. Although he falls in love, he is unable to sustain it. He leaves his fiancée, and spends the rest of his life regretting it, calling on God to bring her back, to bring his lost life back – like old Faust calling on the Devil. He believes in God, his hopes are in God. His faith 'struggles like one possessed' against the suffocation of everyday life. Only through madness, regret and the transposition of his despair into literature does he remain a man, or go beyond the suffocating limits of his life. He is a believer; no, he is a non-believer. He has hopes; no, he has no hopes. 'What is faith? A rope from which we dangle, unless we use it to hang ourselves with', and again: 'Faith is a category which is only to be found in distress', and 'my doubt is terrifying'. He hates sin, and yet all his literary skills gravitate around eroticism and an impotent lusting after sin and 'the secret of sinning'. His intense inner life is rotting away, lit by the phosphorescence of its own decay. He claims to place his own drama, his own case, at the centre of philosophy and religion – to found faith, all faith, on an anguish resembling his own. He claims that in his own internal microcosm he is behaving 'in the most macrocosmic manner', but writes: 'How awful when history becomes eclipsed by the morbid ruminations of our petty tales.' And wanting to base faith on anguish, on the cry for deliverance from subjective anguish, he acknowledges the dual, ambiguous, equivocal character of his anguish: 'Anguish is the desire for what we most dread ... it is an alien power which takes hold of the individual, who neither can nor wants to free himself, for he is afraid, but that very fear is a desire.'

The conflict between everyday life as it is – as it has been made by the bourgeoisie – and the life which a human being actually demands, begs for, cries out for with all his strength, that is the conflict which harrowed Søren Kierkegaard.[2] He resolved it in his own way – very badly. In psychology – although psychologists are not always able to discern the deep, historical, social and human sources of conflict within the individual – the term for an inner conflict which has been badly resolved is 'anxiety neurosis'. But the notion of a morbid condition does not fully explain the situation of someone like Kierkegaard. We must understand that his faith, and his appeal to the world beyond, are based on the demands of his earthly being; that his madness is based upon his reality and his rationality. Whenever he attempts to stop being a slave to necessity, and to revolt against reality as 'robust champion', he is making a protest against life as it is in existing society, and that is the reality he rejects. And if on the ideological level Kierkegaard's philosophy has functioned as a reactionary philosophy (in his appeal to the absurd, to the irrational, to faith without knowledge), when we see his work as a whole and in the context of the hopeless 'existence' he led we realize that it nevertheless offers an implacable criticism of bourgeois life: dissatisfied, suffocated, the individual feels as though he is dying before he has lived, and is forced into the insane situation of pleading for a 'repetition' of the life he has never had. Imprisoned by a necessity he cannot understand, and desperately doubting the power of reason which fails to bring him *another life* (a different life) but which seems instead to approve and justify that necessity, he appeals to the absurd. He even gives up expecting any world beyond, but makes do with asking for a 'repetition' of his life, a chance to start again.

Theological faith is dead, metaphysical reason is dead. And yet they live on, they take on new life – insanely, absurdly – because the situation and the human conflicts from which they were born have not been resolved. Now these conflicts are not in the realm of thought alone, but *in everyday life*. The works of Baudelaire, like Dostoevsky's or Rimbaud's, may take on a revolutionary meaning – provided that they are understood and situated by knowledge, by social criticism of men and ideas. This is also true of Kierkegaard's works, as long as they are understood and situated within a general critique of everyday life. Taken in themselves, in isolation, these works provoke absurd, illusory feelings; situated in the overall context of the human problems of our time, their character changes. This 'revision' of meanings and 'values', as brought about by knowledge, will surprise only those whose thoughts are petrified in an attitude of contemplation towards men and their works.

Rational criticism, when carried through to its logical conclusion, will deal not only with 'Pure Reason' but also with life in all its impurity. From an intellectual heaven where the ghosts of former gods battle on, critical thought will descend into everyday life. Criticism of ideas will not be abandoned, far from it: taken up on another level, it will become deeper, since it will have become criticism of men and actions.

In 'pure' ideas, as in the great ceremonies of royal courts, we can perceive a certain amount of ceremoniousness, etiquette, deliberate and pretentious grandness – of play-acting – which no longer fools us. Louis XIV's divine prestige may have disappeared, but this only enhances our appreciation of its expert staging, grandiose spectacle and delightful entertainments, so splendidly set among the halberds, muskets and canons. As with Louis XIV, so it is with Bossuet and his *Discourse on Universal History*;[3] but have no fear, we may appreciate its high style, construction and pace all the more now that we are no longer intimidated and that we can see it for what it really is – a display, a work of art! We do not have to believe in gods and 'pure' ideas in order to appreciate the true 'worth' of the spectacle they afford. Quite the contrary, it is when we stop believing in them that they take on a 'pure' aesthetic significance, and in general it is when our belief in gods and ideas starts to waver (when they can still move us, but not overwhelmingly so) that they become subject matter for great art. Religious dread, religious hope, divine 'presence', fear inspired by myths when myth is accepted as a part of life, all these preclude aesthetic considerations. Here the law of the displacement of the irrational[4] finds a new application.

'Pure' ideas have real meaning, as Marx and Engels so profoundly understood. As historians, they refused to be idle onlookers of history. As philosophers, they stopped being mere flies on the wall so far as politics was concerned. They were the first to perceive how thought is linked to *action*. They were able to get to the very roots of ideas, to the fundamental questions. With Marx and Engels philosophical thought at its most coherent and most methodical comes down to the level of life and penetrates it, reveals it. By refusing to leave the real world for the exile of a world beyond – by becoming the consciousness and the critique of mankind, of men and of human conditions – Critical Reason, the Critical Reason of Descartes and Kant, becomes concrete, active and constructive.

A modern proletarian is not first and foremost a man with a ready-made human soul or nature of which he is in full 'spiritual' possession, a man who leads a proletarian life simply because of an unfortunate conjunction of circumstances. His opinions and feelings as a worker are not something that the hazards of fate have superimposed upon an already acquired, 'deep' human essence, something external to it, and produced by questionable influences and theories. No. First of all he lives the daily life of a proletarian; and if he becomes humanized, it is because he has succeeded – by luck or by will-power – in transcending proletarian life.

But here the problem gets a little more complex. The proletarian 'condition' has a dual aspect – more precisely, it implies a dialectical movement. On the one hand it tends to overwhelm and crush the (individual) proletarian under the weight of the toil, the institutions and the ideas which are indeed intended to crush him. But at the same time, and in another respect, because of his incessant (everyday) contact with the real and with nature through work, the proletarian is endowed with fundamental health and a sense of reality which other social groups lose in so far as they become detached from practical creative activity. The petty bourgeois and the bourgeois, the intellectuals and the specialists – they all degenerate, decay and wither. Considered collectively as an oppressed class, the proletariat is as 'deprived' of consciousness and culture as it is of wealth, power and happiness. But this deprivation proves to be of a quite different kind to that which devastates the 'private consciousness', the 'private' life of the bourgeois or petty-bourgeois individual. The latter is not aware, or is only partly aware, of being deprived. He tends to become withdrawn and to conflate his 'deprivation' and his property, for the two go together: he thinks he owns his self, his ideas, his life, his family, his country, just as he owns his material 'assets'. The deprivation of the working class is rich in possibilities. For the individual proletarian to become conscious of the proletariat as a class, of its social reality, and thus of society as a whole, of its action, and therefore of its political future, is to have already superseded the proletarian condition. It is to have achieved a great and true thought: that of the social and human totality, of creative labour. On the other hand, the petty bourgeois and bourgeois who discover self-consciousness, but fail to reject the self (as they would if they came over to Marxism) become remote from this great truth; they stop being able to see man, society and human labour in their totality. Rather than superseding deprivation they withdraw into a 'private consciousness'; unless, that is, they are sufficiently aware and lucid to create a political machine designed to extend their control – and their spiritual and human poverty.

To put it another way, from the human point of view the 'proletarian condition' and the 'bourgeois condition' are fundamentally different.

The proletarian qua *proletarian can become a new man.* If he does so, it is not through the intervention of some unspecified freedom which would permit him to liberate himself from his condition. Such metaphysical freedom is nothing more than a survival from the former 'human nature' common to all men. It is *through knowledge* that the proletarian liberates himself and begins *actively superseding* his condition. Moreover in this effort to attain knowledge and awareness, he is forced to assimilate complex *theories (economic, social, political . . .)*, i.e. to integrate the loftiest findings of science and culture into his own consciousness.

On the other hand the petty bourgeois and bourgeois, *as such*, are barred access to the human.

For them to become humanized, they must break with themselves, reject themselves, an endeavour which on an individual level is frequently real and pathetic ... We should understand men in a human way, even if they are incomplete; conditions are not confined within precise, geometrically defined boundaries, but are the result of a multitude of obstinate and ever-repeated (everyday) causes. Attempts to escape from the bourgeois condition are not particularly rare; on the other hand, the failure of such attempts is virtually inevitable, precisely because it is not so much a question of *supersession* but of a complete *break.* (Among intellectuals, this notion of supersession is frequently false and harmful: when they *supersede themselves as petty-bourgeois or bourgeois intellectuals*, they are often merely continuing in the same direction and following their own inclinations in the belief that they are 'superseding themselves'. So far from gaining a new consciousness, they are merely making the old one worse. There is nothing more unbearable than the intellectual who believes himself to be free and human, while in his every action, gesture, word and thought he shows that he has never stepped beyond bourgeois consciousness.) In any event, a man's consciousness, his condition, his possibilities, do not depend upon a relation with some timeless Reason, a permanent human nature, a ready-made essence or some indeterminate freedom. His consciousness depends upon his real life, his everyday life. The 'meaning' of a life is not to be found in anything other than that life itself. It is within it, and there is nothing beyond that. 'Meaning' cannot spill over from being; it is the direction, the movement of being, and nothing more. The 'meaning' of a proletarian's life is to be found in that life itself: in its despair, or conversely in its movement *towards freedom*, if the proletarian participates in the life of the proletariat, and if that life itself involves continuous, day-to-day action (trade-union, political . . .).

The method of Marx and Engels consists precisely in a search for the link which exists between what men think, desire, say and believe for themselves and what they are, what they do. This link always exists. It can be explored in two directions. On the one hand, the historian or the man of action can proceed from ideas to men, from consciousness to being – i.e. towards practical, everyday reality – bringing the two into confrontation and thereby achieving *criticism of ideas by action and realities*. That is the direction which Marx and Engels nearly always followed in everything they wrote; and it is the direction which critical and constructive method must follow initially if it is to take a demonstrable shape and achieve results.

But it is equally possible to follow this link in another direction, taking real life as the point of departure in an investigation of how the ideas which express it and the forms of consciousness which reflect it emerge. The link, or rather the network of links between the two poles will prove to be complex. It must be unravelled, the thread must be carefully followed. In this way we can arrive at a *criticism of life by ideas* which in a sense extends and completes the first procedure.

Let us return to our earlier example. As soon as we stop being taken in by the spectacle of the royal court of Louis XIV, we can start looking for the social, political and economic realities which that spectacle concealed. We first move from ideologies – appearances, but somehow real, pretences, but effective ones – to the more concrete (and thus more human) underlying realities. Then, by moving in the opposite, complementary direction we will at first seek to grasp and to reconstitute the real life of that period, and to rediscover how the men who led that life could subscribe to certain forms of consciousness, certain prestigious ideologies, and find them valid despite their remoteness from their real lives. The contrast between ideas and life, the complex relationship between them, will then entail not just criticism of ideas by life but also, and more specifically, criticism of life by ideas (criticism of the real life of seventeenth-century peasants, craftsmen, country squires or bourgeois by reference to the 'representations' of the world and of themselves that they found acceptable). What does the fact that they accepted the divine right of kings without too much opposition tell us about their real lives? Why did all the pomp which was part and parcel of royal power prove so effective? What did this effectiveness correspond to in men's lives? How did those illusions which were formulated into ideas by official spokesmen take shape in the depths of the social sediments and 'strata', in the heart of the 'masses'? How and why did they accept them? In this instance criticism of life consists in studying the margin which separates what men are from what they think they are, what they live from what they think. It re-examines the notion of *mystification* more deeply. Most ideologies have been mystifications in so far as they have succeeded at certain periods in making men accept certain illusions, certain appearances, and in introducing those appearances into real life and making them effective there. We must first denounce mystifications, and then proceed to a study of how they could have begun, of how they were able to impose themselves, and of how ideological *transposition* can operate in men's consciousness; for ideologies and mystifications are based upon real life, yet at the same time they disguise or transpose that real life. A complete understanding of mystification presupposes that the link between ideas and the real has been followed in both directions, thus incorporating criticism of life by its own consciousness of itself.[5]

When a proletarian believes that he is simply a 'citizen' comparable to every other citizen, or that he is destined to work because it is written for all eternity that every man 'must earn his bread with the sweat of his brow', he is being *mystified*. But how, and why? Because for him, his work is a laborious, exhausting burden *in real terms*, and – under certain pressures – if he does not understand (or *know*) that work can and must become something else, he may well interpret it as a fatality of the human condition or as his own personal misfortune. But the belief in the political and legal equality of the individual, which is an illusory belief for any proletarian who takes it at face value, becomes transformed into an admirable means of action as soon as he begins insisting that democracy stop being a legal and political fiction. The study of mystifications reveals their ambiguity – an ambiguity which at first makes them acceptable but which subsequently makes it possible to supersede them. In mystification appearance and reality are confused, inextricably bound up together. But on the one hand, mystifications rebound upon the mystifiers themselves, notably when consciousness penetrates them by superseding them (and supersedes them by penetrating them), while on the other hand, they teach us something about the lives of the people who accept them. Appearance and reality here are not separated like oil and water in a vessel, but rather amalgamated like water and wine. To separate them, we must *analyse* them in the most 'classic' sense of the word: the elements of the mixture must be isolated.

In the first instance Marxism may be defined as the scientific knowledge of the proletariat: it is the 'science of the proletariat'. This expression must be understood in two ways: Marxism studies the proletariat, its life, its reality, its social function, its historical situation. At the same time, this science comes from the proletariat and expresses its historical reality and its social and political ascension.

Scientific knowledge of this social reality, of this *class*, implies knowledge of society and of the history of human consciousness in their totality. The one leads to the other; it is the only methodologically possible starting point. Of course, when a science develops it goes a considerable way beyond the point from which it began, while continuing to incorporate it. And the analysis of the proletariat, of its *practical, historical and social* reality, implies and involves the assimilation of the deepest and most subtle methods elaborated over the centuries by human thought in the course of its investigations and trial-and-error experiments (I refer, of course, to the dialectical method). Thus the problem of the proletariat encompasses all the problems of thought, of culture, of the human.

To study the proletariat scientifically is to begin tearing away the veil of ideologies by which the bourgeoisie has attempted to explain history to itself and to explain – to make acceptable – the proletarian situation to the proletariat. These ideologies tend to *deprive* the proletariat (as individuals and as a class) of consciousness, of the *new consciousness* it can attain and which is the proletariat's own achievement. These ideologies share a common characteristic. Whether it is a question of religion, of the theory of 'human nature' and 'pure' Reason, of the allegedly historical themes of the Human Spirit and immanent justice, or of the great 'Ideas which shape the world', they are all *idealist and metaphysical*. They are masks which shield men from their *real lives* (which in turn poses the question: how and why do men accept them? what does the repeated complicity with the forces which crush them implied by this acceptance consist of?).

Marxism describes and analyses *the everyday life of society* and indicates the means by which it can be transformed. It describes and analyses *the everyday lives of workers* themselves: separated from their tools, connected to the material conditions of their labour solely by the 'contract' which binds them to an employer, sold like commodities on the labour market in the (legal and ideological) guise of the 'free' labour contract, etc.

The real, everyday life of the worker is that of a commodity endowed, unhappily for him, with life, activity, muscles – and with a consciousness which the concerted pressure of his Masters seeks to reduce to a minimum or to divert into inoffensive channels (let it be said that this pressure is very often involuntary – for we should avoid falling into the proletarian myth of the sadistic bourgeois, rotten to the marrow, consciously and strategically mendacious, a myth which in point of fact only the Fascists made into a reality).

Thus Marxism, as a whole, really is a critical knowledge of everyday life.

It is not satisfied with merely uncovering and criticizing this real, practical life in the minutiae of social life. By a process of rational integration it is able to pass from the individual to the social – from the level of the individual to the level of society and of the nation. And vice versa.

This penetration of dialectical method into individual, everyday life is so unfamiliar that it is absolutely necessary at this point to offer a summary of Marxism considered as a critique of everyday life.

(a) *Critique of individuality* (Central theme: the 'private' consciousness)

The very things that make a man a social and human being, and not simply a biological creature that is born, grows up and dies steeped in natural life – namely his work, his social activity, his place and situation in the social whole – are the things that also limit him and confine him according to *the way labour is currently organized.*

Durkheim maintains that the division of labour is the foundation for individualization. Marxists reply that the fragmentation of labour provides only a *negative* foundation for individuality; in this world of production, individuals have an effective self-consciousness, but of a kind which makes them lead inward-looking lives, centred upon their particular skill and specialization. As regards the rest of social and human life, they are conscious of it only in so far as they reject it, despise it or transpose it to a level of unreality. They tend towards *individualism*. Now if human individuality must consist in a specific relationship between single beings and the universal – reason, society, culture, the world – then there can be no question here of real individuality, but merely of an abstract, empty, negative *form* of individualism. This form, with its minimal content, is what may be called the 'private consciousness'. It is a self-consciousness, but limited, restricted, negative and formal. Separated from the conditions in which it could flourish or even exist, it believes itself to be self-sufficient, and aspires to be so. It is in the process of degenerating. And the expression currently in use to designate the everyday life of individuals in this social structure – *private life* – sums this up perfectly.[6] When an individual life is shaped by individualistic tendencies, it is literally a life of 'privation', a life 'deprived': deprived of reality, of links with the world – a life for which everything human is alien. It is a life split into contradictory or separate poles: work and rest, public life and personal life, public occasions and intimate situations, chance and inner secrets, luck and fate, ideal and reality, the marvellous and the everyday. Instead of expanding, of conquering the world, this consciousness shrinks in upon itself. And the more it shrinks, the more it seems to be 'its own'. Crass and complacent, the individual settles down amid his familiar surroundings. Consciousness, thought, ideas, feelings, all are seen as 'property' on a par with 'his' furniture, 'his' wife and 'his' children, 'his' assets and 'his' money. In this way the narrowest, most barren, most solitary aspects of life are taken (and with such crude sincerity) for what is most human.

Thus everyone 'is' what he is and nothing more. We will find descriptions of these genera of bourgeois society, including not only usurers, gangsters and social climbers, but also all those fixed 'beings' who are determined solely by their function and established in their private lives, in *The Human Comedy*,[7] where Balzac offers probing accounts of this dual nature of bourgeois life, which was forming and consolidating during his lifetime but which holds no surprises for us: on the one hand, formal individualization (or as classic philosophy would put it, a greater subjectivity), thus an enhanced consciousness in increased isolation; on the other hand, an 'objectification', beings who are more 'involved' in their own physicality, weightier, thicker, more opaque. This dual character is beautifully reflected in Balzac's work, in its very style: so weighty, compared with the lightness of the eighteenth century, and so lucid. This dual character also corresponds to the dual character of bourgeois society: progressive in terms of technology, thought, consciousness – but otherwise retrogressive. And finally it corresponds to the dual character of capital: a brutal objective *reality* which eludes human will and drags it along towards a predestined fate for as long as human thought and action, straining towards another order, cannot reverse it – and yet at the same time an abstraction, an *unreality*, a complex of signs and concepts.

Before Balzac, in that epic of human consciousness in the ascendant which bears the name *The Phenomenology of Spirit*, Hegel had ironically described 'abstract animals', specialists, experts, imprisoned in a narrow field of practice or thought.

And nowadays we are still struggling with this deep – in other words *everyday* – contradiction: what makes each of us a human being also turns that human being into something inhuman. More biological than truly human, this organization smothers the individual, dividing him and stunting his development at the very moment it is striving to create him as a human individual. It is just one of the many painful contradictions our era is experiencing, and which we must resolve if we are to move forward. These contradictions are at the same time a measure of the greatness, the richness and the suffering of the age in which we live. We are all familiar with the drama of youth destroyed by this arrested state of the human being, as also with that drama of more mature, more conscious years, acted out within the asphyxiating strait-jacket of fragmented activities.

How can this organization be superseded? By practical and theoretical participation in work and in the knowledge of work, in the social and human totality. If the world is to be transformed, this is one of the fundamental problems.

We must supersede the 'private consciousness'.

(b) *Critique of mystifications*
(Central theme: the 'mystified' consciousness)

We should note that the proletarian does not escape the dangers of the 'private consciousness' completely. Agreed, his work is always collective, and this tends to reinforce his awareness of social activity and society as a whole.

However, the tasks of workers in workshops or even in factories are generally fragmented. The most tangibly collective work – assembly-line work – is also the most exhausting. Human contacts tend to be established after work, outside the factory, in cafés, sports teams, etc. Thus the forms in which these contacts are established are precisely those of the individualistic bourgeoisie (family, press, cinema, etc.).

Although the material conditions of modern production tend to form a social and human consciousness whose first stage is class consciousness, there is nothing inevitable about this formation. It is not *spontaneous*. (The theory of proletarian spontaneity came from intellectuals who had 'studied' the proletariat!) Consciousness must be gained over and over again through action and struggle as well as through organizations whose role is to penetrate everyday life and to introduce a new, more elevated element (from unions to sports and 'cultural' organizations . . .).

In life there are no absolute boundaries. The proletariat no more has a ready-made essence, soul or consciousness (clearly separate from 'bourgeois' realities) than does humanity taken as a whole. Hence the role of *knowledge* as both action and theory.

And so the bourgeoisie can exert permanent, and to a certain extent successful, pressures upon the proletariat – an influence which tends to split it up into individuals.[8] Individualism is not simply a theory, but also a fact and a class weapon. It is not simply through its ideas and its conception of the world that the bourgeoisie exerts this influence. Admittedly, its theoretical individualism, its 'social atomism', are by no means ineffectual, but the way it actually organizes everyday life, leisure, family life, etc., is infinitely more important.

Paradoxically – or apparently so – the bourgeoisie is a class of individualists. Its theory of social atomism tends to represent society as a collection of juxtaposed atoms, breaking the social body down into separate elements – fictitious, dead, inert elements: 'pure' individuals.

This representation is nothing more than an ideology, i.e. a means of action, an efficient illusion – and the consciousness of the average bourgeois, and above all of the petty bourgeois, is taken in by it. Not so the governmental, political and police arms of the bourgeoisie; on the political level, the bourgeoisie understands perfectly about masses and classes. Those who effectively 'represent' the bourgeoisie are kept very well informed, thanks to that class's political practice and Machia-vellianism – thanks, in other words, in the absence of guidance from general philosophy, to the police.

Moreover, this 'representation' in no way stops the most individual-istic social groups from having been or actually being classes, or masses, objectively, historically and socially. There is a remarkable image in Nietzsche which expresses this paradoxical situation well. Typically the middle classes are individualistic social groups made up of 'human sand'. Each grain is quite distinct and separable. And taken together they form a mass – indeed the heaviest and most impene-trable of masses. A sandbag can stop bullets!

What is comical about this is that each grain of human sand thinks itself to be not only distinct, but infinitely original. But nothing is more like a grain of sand than another grain of sand. Bourgeois individual-ism implies the dreary, ludicrous repetition of individuals who are curiously similar in their way of being themselves and of keeping them-selves to themselves, in their speech, their gestures, their everyday habits (meal times, rest times, entertainments, fashions, ideas, expres-sions).

Any objective anthropology or scientific description of the con-temporary man will have to begin with this obvious paradox – which constitutes the *comical mystery* of bourgeois life ...

In the modern world, mystifying ideologies presuppose and imply the *private consciousness.*

The individual who is deprived of human reality is also deprived of truth. He is separated from his concrete human and social reality, deprived of a consciousness of the practical, historical and social whole (even though, nowadays, given modern social structure, science and techniques, such a consciousness is both possible and necessary).

Turned back upon himself, secure within some imaginary inner fortress, he is the plaything of every hallucination, every spontaneous or deliberate ideological illusion. The 'thinker', self-taught or not, concocts his own little personal philosophy; the 'non-thinker' inter-prets what he reads in books (or preferably in newspapers) as best he can; and then one day individualism begins to collapse (and not as a result of a crisis of ideas or 'world views', but because of a *material* crisis, both economic and political), and these erstwhile individualists rush headlong to form a crowd, a horde, urged on by the most insane, most loathsome, most ferocious 'ideas', leaving the last vestige of human reason behind, caught up in a collective mental fever: and we have Fascism, the Fascist 'masses' and Fascist 'organization'.

The private consciousness and the mystified consciousness go hand in hand, reinforcing each other and becoming increasingly entrenched as a result of instabilities which have their origins in real life, and not in 'pure' ideas.

(c) *Critique of money*
(Central theme: fetishism and economic alienation)

There is a sentimental rhetoric, corresponding to the 'spiritual state' of the petty bourgeois who hates and envies people who are richer than he is, which readily waxes emotional about deserving paupers and unhappy millionaires alike, and which rails against money. The best things in life are free! And with women particularly in mind: she was poor, but she was honest! etc. These melodramatic and moral motifs are part of the everyday lives of poor people. Verbal propaganda of the rich, they make up the greater part of the average person's ideological baggage. Disguised as an indictment of money, they justify wealth by reducing it to a mere accident of the human condition (in itself moral or metaphysical). They give consolation to the poor and full satisfaction to people who are threatened by poverty but who nevertheless hope with all their 'soul' to become rich. These motifs have been raised to the dignity of philosophical and lyrical themes in the work of that demented petty bourgeois, Péguy.[9] Moreover, as proverbs which seem to contain eternal truths, they have penetrated the consciousness of the people, where they act as corollaries to the capitalist axiom: 'There will always be rich and there will always be poor.' Their aim is to consolidate, to crystallize those absurd concepts 'wealth' and 'poverty', to present them as opposites, to incarnate them in individuals, enclosing them so effectively within these sentimental and moral

173

categories that the most violent statement against 'the rich' will in no respect go beyond the parameters of capitalist ideology.

The result is a curious one. Today, for the Marxist, the first task in this area must be a *rehabilitation of wealth*. Wealth is neither an evil nor a curse. Wealth, like power, is part of man's greatness and of the beauty of life. The solution to man's problems is to be found not by sharing out weakness, poverty and mediocrity – but by seeking power and wealth; they alone have permitted and conditioned everything magnificent and brilliant that has ever been in culture, in civilization, in life – from palaces and stately homes and cathedrals to those slowly nurtured works of art whose creation used to demand and still demands long periods of leisure, silence, peace of mind and physical security.

And yet (and this is the essential point) the parameters of power and wealth are in the process of changing. It is impossible to go any further towards *individual* wealth. Today, wealth is becoming *social*; in fact, it has always been social; and within the framework of capitalist economy, under the guise of the individual acquisition of wealth, it was indeed society as a whole which was developing and to a certain extent progressing. Today this social wealth can develop no further within the framework of individual appropriation (of capitalist private property); it clearly needs reorganizing. But the aim is not to combat wealth with a view to achieving a general mediocrity, an 'equality' of mediocrity. The aim is still wealth: wealth that becomes progressively universalized, socialized wealth. This progressive expansion can only be achieved by degrees, by stages, by a series of measures suited to the complex, concrete, unpredictable circumstances of economic and political life.

Thus the Marxist finds himself impelled to criticize those *myths* of capitalist democracy which are still so widespread (though much less effective than their extension might suggest): the myth that wealth is immaterial or intrinsically bad, and the myth of egalitarianism (both obviously bound up with the myth of the 'private' individual, always identical to himself whatever the conditions or circumstances may be . . .).

Once this has been achieved, it becomes apparent that the Marxist critique of money is incomparably more radical than any moralizing rhetoric can be. And here, once again, it goes to the heart of the question.

Under capitalist regimes, 'to exist' and 'to have' are identical. 'The man who has nothing is nothing.'[10] And this situation is not a theoretical one, an abstract 'category' in a philosophy of existence; it is an 'absolutely desperate' reality; the man who has nothing finds himself 'separated from existence in general' and a fortiori from human existence; he is separated from that 'world of objects', i.e. the real world, without which no human existence is possible.

Spiritualism and idealism maintain that the loftiest situation for man is that of a spirit or a soul independent from the 'world of objects'. This situation is experienced, ironically, by the man who has nothing: 'Not having is the most despairing *spiritualism*, a complete unreality of the human being, a complete reality of the dishumanized being, a very positive having, a having of hunger, of cold, of disease, of crime, of debasement, of hebetude, of all inhumanity and abnormity.'[11]

Doubtless this is the 'profound' reason why spiritualism calls on people who have nothing at least to 'possess' their souls: this abstraction expresses their state of non-possession perfectly. Moreover it appears that objects are not simply important in so far as they are goods, but also as a shell for man's objective being, 'the *existence of man for other men*, his *human relation to other men*, the *social behaviour of man to man*'.[12] In this way, by arguing that non-possession is superior to possession, idealism situates 'profound' human reality – more profound than wealth – within the absence of real human relations, in other words within the loneliness and emptiness of abstraction.

Opposing this argument for non-possession is the argument which considers possession as an essential. If we accept the principle that the possession of objects constitutes the basis of human reality, it will lead us immediately to demand *equal possession for all.* This is exactly the principle of Proudhon's egalitarianism and petty-bourgeois socialism. The most cursory examination of this principle will reveal that it never goes beyond bourgeois ideology or the categories of bourgeois political economy; on the contrary, it places the category, the concept of 'possession', at the highest level. Thus it becomes involved in empty recriminations and moralizing, ineffectual anti-capitalist postures.

And how easy it is for bourgeois thinkers to demonstrate that this apology for ready-made equality of possession for all individuals is nothing more than an apology for boredom, uniformity, humdrum, day-to-day greyness! It really is petty-bourgeois mediocrity raised to the level of supreme truth and socialist 'ideal'!

But is this not precisely the same idealism that some people today[13] are proposing to restore in order to 'complete' Marxism and to take up the defence of the 'human being' against both capitalism and Marxist materialism? Is it not the hidden principle of the 'humanist socialism' with which they are trying to challenge Marxist humanism – which is Marxist not because Marxists have their own definition of man but because Marxist (dialectical materialist) method alone allows for the study of human reality and the creation of the new man who today is *possible* and implied in the *movement* of human reality?

According to Marxism, the relation between man and object is not the same as a relation of possession. It is incomparably broader. What is important is not that I have possession (be it capitalist or egalitarian) of an object, but that I can enjoy it in the human, total meaning of the word; that I can have the most complex, the 'richest' relationships of joy or happiness with the 'object' – which can be a thing or a living being or a human being or a social reality. Moreover it is by means of this object, within, in and through it, that I enter into a complex network of human relations.

Apropos of love, the term 'to possess' (e.g. to possess a woman) brings with it a long procession of feelings, aspirations, prejudices, myths and 'paroxysmal moments'. Still too frequently the myth of possession is countered by the myth of non-possession, according to which love is just a function, an inessential activity which does not involve the human being in his totality; so that promiscuity, infidelity, the absence of jealousy, become signs of freedom, of the new love, of the emancipated 'feminine personality'. This myth of non-possession remains firmly within the abstract category of the 'private' individual, allegedly endowed with an 'inner being' that is inaccessible and indifferent to (external) activities. The dialectical truth may be formulated roughly as follows: a man's (or a woman's) relationship will be richer, more human, more complex, more joyful (but also possibly more deeply painful) with someone who is free than with someone who allows him or herself to be 'possessed'. At last relationships will be humanized, and in the process will do away with those zones of indifference perpetuated as much by myths of possession as by myths of non-possession (either of accomplished and complete possession or of the inadmissibility of possession). By bringing together two complex free beings these physiological, psychological, 'spiritual' relationships will go infinitely farther than the merely sexual, although the sexual will be by no means marginalized. Their *tendency*, therefore, will be to enter everyday life; to allow their presence to impregnate the other human relations (social activities, thought, etc.), which henceforth will be accomplished through them, but not without them. The (humanized) object for me makes me into a (humanized) object for it; I thus enter the sphere where my human possibilities are totally, objectively realized. The object then will have accomplished the totality of its functions as an object.

Whereas Proudhon declares that 'possession is a social function',[14] the Marxist theory of the object expressly supersedes this kind of 'socialism' and moves in the direction of concrete, total humanism, affirming with Marx that 'what is "interesting" in a function, however, is not to "exclude" the other person, but to affirm and to realise the forces of my own being',[15] which is possible only by the other person, with the other person and in the other person.

In the social domain, capitalist theory and practice end up producing a mass of individuals deprived of any rights over objects of social importance such as large factories, large businesses, works of art, the spaces in which rest and leisure take on superior value and meaning (mountains, the sea, the air, etc.).

On the other hand, the 'socialist' apology for possession as a 'social function' creates some very strange illusions. For example, it might lead one to compare large social buildings – gigantic factories, palatial public edifices – with the pyramids of Egypt, for which the Pharaohs sacrificed innumerable slaves. The proletariat will appear to be making a decisive step towards freedom whenever it 'shares in the profits' of a business, or becomes a shareholder, or has a vote in the nomination of a management committee, etc. The possession of a minuscule square inch of property will be seen as a liberation of the individual – and of the sum total of individuals, the proletariat, the people.

In the first place this kind of 'socialism' omits an essential distinction, the distinction between consumer goods and the (social) means of production.

Consumer goods, the objects linked to my everyday life – this pen, this glass, these clothes, etc. – are obviously 'mine' and should stay so. The question is not one of taking 'my' objects away from me, but on

177

the contrary of giving me more of them. Only a few cranks, inspired by ascetic, monastic Communism rather than by scientific socialism, have gone so far as to criticize the principle of the *individual* appropriation of consumer goods. It is moreover evident that the motto of phalansterian Communism, 'what is mine is thine', neither eradicates nor supersedes the 'thine' or the 'mine', but on the contrary generalizes them as fundamental categories of everyday life.

What is more, the relation I have with the objects which are immediately 'mine' is not a *legal*, 'private'-property relation. I can break them, give them away, sell them, without drawing up a legal contract. The relation is therefore an immediate one, part of everyday life, and does not have to be altered when the economic, social and legal parameters of the social structure based on 'private' property are modified. But it is precisely this relation that egalitarian socialism tends to generalize into a legal category. This merely serves to reveal how far it lags behind the way the practicalities of life are organized even in bourgeois society; it takes us back to the days when slaves could only dream of being able to say of the most ordinary of objects: 'it's mine'.

The important thing is not that I should have the impression of possessing a minuscule interest in socially important concerns (the means of production) but that these concerns should strive objectively to increase social wealth, to make wealth universal.

The important thing is not that I should become the owner of a little plot of land in the mountains, but that the mountains be open to me – for climbing or for winter sports. The same applies for the sea and the air, regions of the world where the notion of 'private' possession becomes more or less meaningless, but whose appeal and attraction to the 'free' individual is all the more powerful because of that.

In this way and in this way alone the world becomes mine, my estate, because I am a man. In this way and this way alone is the world the future of (social) man.

Only in this way can the 'private' individual, the individualistic model of man, be superseded, and concrete and truly free individuality attained.

The movement of self-realization of the human proceeds from the subject (desires, aspirations, ideas) to objects, to the world – and equally from the object to the subject (liberation from any external determinism, from any destiny which has not been understood and controlled). In philosophical terms, this realization may be described equally as a deeper *subjectivization* – a more lucid awareness – and as an *objectification*, a world of material, controlled objects.

Subjectivization and objectification go hand in hand, inseparably.

The big disadvantage of traditional terminology is that there is one major aspect of the problem of man it fails to emphasize. No amount of theorizing will permit us to attain the total man, or even to define him. Humanized at last, this 'essence' of man, who up until now did not exist and who cannot exist in advance, is made real through action and in practice, i.e. *in everyday life*.

Theorizing has its part to play. If we are to define not so much the human, but the direction in which action must go, we need to call upon knowledge and science. And not just one science, but all of them. Man is not just economic, or biological, or physio-chemical, etc. And yet he is all of this. This is what makes him the total man. From each science, from each partial method of research, total humanism borrows elements for analysis and orientation (in varying proportions according to the moments and the problems ...). The most extensive method of all, the dialectic, is the only one capable of organizing the 'synthesis' of all these elements and of extracting from them *the idea of man*, which, rather than acting as a substitute for real achievement, as idealism does, actually provokes realizing action, strengthening it and guiding it forward.

A human being only is (only exists) through what he *has*; but the present form of 'having', the possession of money, is merely an inferior, narrow, limited one.

Conversely, a human being only completely has what he *is*. This is why 'to be' a social being, or a thinker, or a poet, etc., and to participate in human reality, *to be* as extensive a fragment as possible of that reality rather than to contemplate it, conceive it or control it from outside, is problematic.

On this point, money is a particularly untrustworthy master. Let us imagine a man with a certain amount of potential, a 'personality' as they say, devoting his activities and his talents to getting rich and succeeding (with a bit of 'luck' and above all *an absolute single-mindedness*, almost anyone, even an idiot, can manage to earn money), upon which he buys some paintings by Picasso or Matisse, some luxury editions of Valéry and the complete works of Monsieur Gide. As we all know, in a society where everything is for sale, and where consciousness is merely a commodity which costs just a little less than any other commodity, because it is in plentiful supply, money can buy anything. Thus our parvenu has everything at his fingertips: beauty, art, knowledge ... But he could have been a poet, or a painter, or a scientist, someone who would create beauty and knowledge. 'Everything which you are unable to do, your money can do for you.'[16] In the still-dehumanized life of bourgeois society, money symbolizes this tearing away of man from himself; it is more than the symbol of *alienation*, it is the alienation of man itself, his 'alienated essence'. In the capitalist human being it represents all the time devoted not to living (through creative labour or through leisure), but to saving or 'speculating' (in the financial sense of the word) instead. In the creative *belle époque* of ascendant capitalism, the bourgeois 'deprived' himself in order to accumulate capital, to build up his business concerns. At this stage, money had its ethic, its religion: asceticism, economy. It taught 'abnegation'; and thus it spoke to the bourgeois of the seventeenth century, and thus it speaks to the petty bourgeois even today:

> The less you eat, drink, buy books, go to the theatre, go dancing, go drinking, think, love, theorize, sing, paint, fence, etc., the more you *save* and the greater will become that treasure which neither moths nor maggots can consume – your *capital.* The less you *are* ... the more you *have*.[17]

The finance capitalist of the decadent period – the degenerate son of a family rich for generations or the parvenu made rich through speculation – speaks as follows:

> The stronger the power of my money, the stronger am I. The properties of money are my, the possessor's, properties and essential powers ... I am ugly, but I can buy the *most beautiful* woman. As an individual, I am *lame*, but money procures me twenty-four legs ... Through money I can have anything the human heart desires.[18]

To the proletarian money speaks a different language. Ceaselessly, at every moment of his everyday life, it whispers these threats:

> *You need me, and you'll have to swap your own self to get me. You've got to sell yourself. I am your life and the meaning of your life. You're nothing but a thing, a coarse,*

natural object like any other, a commodity among commodities. And what you're swapping for these objects you call coins is your time for activity and living. But in any case it's better for you to imagine that you're expiating original sin or sharing in the misfortunes of the human condition . . .

Although deprivation and alienation are different for the proletarian and the non-proletarian, one thing unites them: money, the human being's alienated essence. This alienation is constant, i.e. practical and everyday.

(d) *Critique of needs*
(Central theme: psychological and moral alienation)

The more needs a human being has, the more he exists. The more powers and aptitudes he is able to exercise, the more he is free.

In this field, (bourgeois) political economy creates a single need: the need for money. In the hands of the individual, money is the only power which gives him contact with the alien, hostile world of objects. The vaster this world of objects becomes, the greater the need for money. And it is thus that 'the *quantity* of money becomes more and more its sole *important* property'.[19] Every being becomes reduced to this abstraction: market value; man himself becomes reduced to this abstraction. Money, man's alienated essence, the projection beyond himself of his activities and his needs, is only a *quantitative* essence. And there is nothing to determine or limit it qualitatively. For this reason, functioning outside of men and yet produced by them, an 'automatic fetish', money becomes inflated out of all proportion, as does the fundamental need (in capitalist regimes) which bears witness to its presence in men's hearts. And every other need is adjusted and revised according to the need for money. As a set of desires, the human being is not developed and cultivated for himself, but so that the demands of this theological monster may be satisfied. The need for money is an expression of the needs of money.

On the one hand, therefore, every effort is made to create fictitious, artificial, imaginary needs. Instead of expressing and satisfying real desires, and of transforming 'crude need into human need',[20] the capitalist producer inverts the course of things. He starts with the

181

object which is the simplest or the most lucrative to produce, and endeavours – mainly through advertising – to create a need for it.

Satirically, Marx has demonstrated the 'idealist' character of this operation, which begins with the external, abstract concept of the object in order to stimulate a desire for it. This idealism culminates in fantasy, whims, the bizarre (as in the decadent aesthetic, for example!). Like the eunuch who panders to his rich master's every desire, or the priest who exploits every imperfection, every weak spot in the human heart and mind in order to preach about heaven, the producer becomes the pimp for the individual and his own self: he 'places himself at the disposal of his neighbour's most depraved fancies, panders to his needs, excites unhealthy appetites in him, and pounces on every weakness, so that he can then demand the money for his labour of love.'[21]

But at the same time, for all those unable to pay, needs die, degenerate, become more simple. As a result the worker stops feeling the simplest needs, which are also the most difficult needs for workers to satisfy: the need for space, for fresh air and freedom, for solitude or contemplation. Man the proletarian

> reverts once more to living in a cave, but the cave is now polluted by the mephitic and pestilential breath of civilization. Moreover, the worker has no more than a precarious right to live in it, for it is for him an alien power that can be daily withdrawn and from which, should he fail to pay, he can be evicted at any time. He actually has to *pay* for this mortuary.[22]

So man sinks even lower than an animal. Needs and feelings no longer exist in a human form; they no longer even exist in a dehumanized form, therefore 'not even in animal form'. Not only does man cease to have human needs, but he loses his animal needs: to move about, to have contacts with beings of the same species . . .

It is a state of affairs that the bourgeois economist finds eminently satisfactory; it means that all is well in the capitalist economy. Money reigns; everyone serves it in their particular way, according to the position they hold in 'human nature': the bourgeois worship it in a refined, even artistic, way, while the workers' homage is humble and austere.

The human being's many needs and desires have their foundation in biological life, in instincts; subsequently social life transforms them, giving this biological content a new form. On the one hand needs are *satisfied by society*; on the other, as history unfolds, society *modifies* them both in form and in content.

Thus as soon as the objects it perceives stop being crude objects immersed in nature and become social objects, 'the eye has become a *human* eye'.[23]

What psychologists call 'perception' or the 'perceptible world' is in reality the product of human action on the historical and social level. The activity which gives the external world and its 'phenomena' shape is not a 'mental' activity, theoretical and formal, but a practical, concrete one. Practical tools, not simple concepts, are the means by which social man has shaped the perceptible world. As regards the processes of knowledge by means of which we understand this 'world', torn as it is from the immensity of nature and rendered coherent and human, they are not 'a priori categories', or subjective 'intentions'; they are our senses. But our senses have been transformed by action. Capable of understanding and organizing certain wholes, certain forms, the human eye is more than just the natural organ of vision of a superior vertebrate, of a lone figure lost in the natural world, of a primitive man or a child.

Thus the 'world' is man's mirror because man makes it: it is the task of his practical, everyday life to do so. But it is not his 'mirror' in a passive way. In this his work man perceives and becomes conscious of his own self. If what he makes comes from him, he in turn comes from what he makes; it is made by him, but it is in these works and by these works that he has made himself.

Thus it is that our senses, organs, vital needs, instincts and feelings have been permeated with consciousness, with human reason, since they too have been shaped by social life.

The creation of these human feelings, along with the appropriation of objective reality (the constitution of a human 'world'), constitute *the fulfilment of human reality*.

And it is in everyday life, and through everyday life, that humanization is accomplished. Every moment of inspiration, of genius or of heroism must serve – and even despite itself, does serve – everyday man. Should any other claims be made for such moments, they must fall into the realm of 'alienation', where man is torn apart. Great things have been attempted in the name of 'alienation'; they have failed or have been subsumed, but in unpredictable ways everyday man and the everyday world have benefited from them. It is in this fact, which idealism uses to prove the inevitable failure of all 'greatness', that we must on the contrary see the forming of true greatness, the greatness of human life.

(e) *Critique of work*
(Central theme: the alienation of the worker and of man)

The relation of every humble, everyday gesture to the social complex, like the relation of each individual to the whole, cannot be compared to that of the part to the sum total or of the element to a 'synthesis', using the term in its usual vague sense. Mathematical integration would be a better way of explaining the transfer from one scale of greatness to another, implying as it does a qualitative leap without the sense that the 'differential' element (the gesture, the individual) and the totality are radically heterogeneous.

Within the parameters of private property, this relation of the 'differential' element to the whole is both disguised and distorted. In fact, the worker works for the social whole; his activity is a part of 'social labour' and contributes to the historical heritage of the society (nation) to which he belongs. But he does not know it. He thinks he is working 'for the boss'. And he is indeed working 'for the boss': he provides him with a profit. In this way the portion of the social value of his labour which does not come back to him in the form of wages is retained by the boss (surplus-value). The only *direct* relations the worker has are with the boss. He is ignorant of the overall or total phenomena involved. He does not know that the totality of surplus-value goes to the bosses as a group or capitalist 'class'. He does not know (at least, not spontaneously) that the sum total of wages go to the proletarian 'class'; he is even more ignorant of the fact that the way the sum total is distributed – surplus-value, wages, products, rates of profit, purchasing power, etc. – obeys certain laws.

Integration takes place beyond the will of individuals, outside of their 'private' consciousness. The individual capitalist is just as ignorant of the laws of capitalism as the individual proletarian. As an individual, a capitalist may be intelligent or stupid, good or vicious, active or inert. He does not know that his essential reality is that of a member of a class. Here again, his essence is outside of him. In good faith, the individual – be he bourgeois or proletarian – can deny the existence of social classes since objective social reality functions beyond his own 'subjectivity', beyond his own 'private' consciousness.

The direct, immediate relation between the wage-earner and the boss is therefore a rigged, ambiguous, formal relation which conceals a hidden content.

The wage-earner's relations with society as a whole pass via the employer, through the mediation of money and wages. But in everyday life the deep, objective relation is disguised by direct, immediate relations, apparently real – until knowledge begins to penetrate the real.

Here, therefore, *everyday life functions within certain appearances* which are not so much the products of mystifying ideologies, as contributions to the conditions needed for any mystifying ideology to operate.

The social whole is essentially constituted by the total activity of society – by work and by the various activities of society considered in its totality.

But within the parameters of 'private' property, labour is 'alienated'. The alienation of labour is many-sided. The wage-earner works for the employer and the proletarian class works for the capitalist class; but that is *only one aspect of alienation*, the easiest aspect to understand – above all for those who stand to gain from it! – and the one which will help to elucidate the others.

Alienated labour has lost its social essence. Though its essence is indeed social, labour assumes the appearance and the reality of an individual task. Moreover, as it is social labour, it takes the form of a buying and a selling of labour-power.

The individual ceases to feel at one with the social conditions of his activity. Not only do the tools of his trade loom up before him like an alien, threatening reality – since they do not belong to him (either as an individual, as in a craft, or as a member of a collectivity, as in socialism) – but also he becomes separated, disassociated from his own self, in his real, everyday life. On the one hand he is a human individual; on the other, he is 'labour-power', labour time which is up for sale like a commodity, a thing. For the worker, participation in the creative activity of the social whole takes the form of an external necessity: the necessity of 'earning a living', and it is thus that, for the individual, social labour takes on the appearance of a penalty, a mysterious punishment. The necessity of having to work weighs down on him from without as though he were an object. It turns him into an object, dragging him into a mechanism he knows nothing about. The wage-earner sells his labour-power like a thing – and becomes a thing, a base object. 'Man himself, viewed merely as the physical existence of labour-power, is a natural object, a thing, although a living, conscious thing, and labour is the physical manifestation (*dingliche Aüsserung*) of that power.'[24]

The human being – ceasing to be human – is turned into a tool to be used by other tools (the means of production), a thing to be used by another thing (money), and an object to be used by a class, a mass of individuals who are themselves 'deprived' of reality and truth (the capitalists). And his labour, which ought to humanize him, becomes something done under duress instead of being a vital and human need, since it is itself nothing more than a means (of 'earning a living') rather than a contribution to man's essence, freely imparted.

The wage-earner is confronted with the use of his labour-power 'as *something alien*'.[25] Not only is his labour-power bought from him, but it is also used in combination with other people's work (the technical division of labour) of which he has no knowledge; and no one really understands this division of labour; occasionally experts and specialists in the area might know about it *at the level of their own firms* (but it is well known that in France the level of design and planning is less efficient and productive than it could be); such experts know nothing about the division of labour *at the level of society*; only a *plan* for social labour could demonstrate how it functions and control it. Therefore, for every individual, worker or expert, the division of labour is imposed from without, like an objective process, with the result that each man's activity is turned back against him as a hostile force which subjugates him instead of being subjugated by him.

In this way a dehumanized, brutally objective power holds sway over all social life; according to its differing aspects, we have named it: money, fragmented division of labour, market, capital, mystification and deprivation, etc. 'This fixation of social activity, this consolidation of what we ourselves produce into an objective power above all, growing out of our control, thwarting our expectations, bringing to naught our calculations, is one of the chief factors in historical development up till now.'[26]

It is always changing shape, now appearing as the objective laws of political economy, now as the destiny of politicians, now as the State, or as the market, as historical fatality, as ideologies.

Only man and his activity exist. And yet everything happens as though men had to deal with external powers which oppress them from outside and drag them along. Human reality – what men themselves have made – eludes not only their will but also their consciousness. They do not know that they are alone, and that the 'world' is their work. (Here we are using the word 'world' to signify the coherent, organized, humanized world, not pure, brute *nature*.)

There is a name for this fixing of human activity within an alien reality which is at one and the same time crudely material and yet abstract: *alienation.*

Just as the creative activity of the human world is not theoretical but practical, a constant, everyday activity rather than an exceptional one, so too *alienation is constant and everyday.*

Alienation is not a theory, an idea or an abstraction – it is rather that the theories, the ideas or the 'pure' abstractions which induce man to obliterate his living existence in favour of absolute truth, and to define himself by a theory or reduce himself to abstractions, are part of human alienation.

Alienation appears in day-to-day life, the life of the proletarian and even of the petty bourgeois and the capitalist (the difference being that capitalists collaborate with alienation's dehumanizing power).

In every attitude which tears every man away from what he is and what he can do – in art, in the moral sphere, in religion – criticism will reveal alienation.

Certain gestures, certain words, certain actions, seem to come from an 'alien being', in the general, human sense of the term: it is not 'me', a man, who has spoken, but 'him', the artificial being, presumptuous, angel or devil, superman or criminal, created within me to stop me from being myself and from following the lines of force whereby action achieves *more reality.*

Appearance and reality intertwine. Appearances graft themselves onto reality, encompassing it, replacing it. For people who have been unable to overcome alienation, the 'alienated' world – social appearances, the theories and abstractions which express these appearances – seems the only reality. Thus any criticism of life which fails to take the clear and distinct notion of human alienation as its starting point will be a criticism not of life, but of this pseudo-reality. Blinkered by alienation, confined to its perspective, such a critique will take as its object the 'reality' of the existing social structure, rejecting it wholesale as it yearns for 'something else': a spiritual life, the surreal, the superhuman, an ideal or metaphysical world. This kind of criticism will therefore move more and more towards alienation, reinforcing it in the process.

Genuine criticism, by contrast, will expose an *unreality* in the 'reality' of the bourgeoisie, a system of phenomena which have already been refuted by life and thought, a group of appearances which seem real but which consciousness has overcome or is in the process of over-coming.

Genuine criticism will then reveal the human reality beneath this general unreality, the human 'world' which takes shape within us and around us: in what we see, what we do, in humble objects and (apparently) humble and profound feelings. A human world which has been torn away from us, disassociated and dispersed by alienation, but which still constitutes the irreducible core of appearances.

The notion of *alienation* is destined to become the central notion of *philosophy* (seen as criticism of life and the foundation for a concrete humanism) as well as of *literature* (seen as the expression of life in movement).

It is a key notion. It replaces out-moded ideological 'centres of interest' by a new interest in individual and social man. It enables us to discover how man (every man) gives in to illusions in which he thinks he can discover and possess his own self, and the self-inflicted anguish which ensues; or how he struggles to bring to light his 'core' of human reality. It enables us to follow this struggle through history: to see how appearances fade or become strengthened, and how truly human reality seeks to go beyond appearances and discover a reality 'other' than the one we live and yet which will still be that reality, brought to light at last in all its truth, and reinstated as the keystone of the very edifice beneath which it has been entombed.

The drama of human alienation is much more profound and enthralling than any of the phony cosmic dramas or divine scenarios which man is supposed to act out in this world.

The drama of alienation is dialectical. Through the manifold forms of his labour, man has made himself real by realizing a human world. He is inseparable from this 'other' self, his creation, his mirror, his statue – more: his body. The totality of objects and human products taken together form an integral part of human reality. On this level, objects are not simply means or implements; by producing them, men are working to create the human; they think they are moulding an object, a series of objects – and it is man himself they are creating.

But in this dialectical relation of man to himself (the relation between the human world and human consciousness), a new element emerges to confuse the situation and halt its development.

As he strives to control nature and create his world, man conjures himself up a new nature. Certain of man's products function in relation to human reality like some impenetrable nature, undominated, oppressing his consciousness and will from without. Of course, this can only be an appearance; products of human activity cannot have the same characteristics as brute, material things. And yet this appearance too is a reality: commodities, money, capital, the State, legal, economic and political institutions, ideologies – all function as though they were realities external to man. In a sense, they are realities, with their own laws. And yet, they are purely human products ...

Thus the human being develops through this 'other' self, half-fact, half-fiction, which becomes intimately involved with the 'human world' in its process of formation.

Analysis must therefore distinguish between the real 'human world' on the one hand, the totality of human works and their reciprocal action upon man, and, on the other, the unreality of *alienation*.

But this unreality appears to be infinitely more real than anything authentically human. And this appearance contributes to alienation; it becomes real, and as a result a great abstract 'idea' or a certain form of the State seems infinitely more important than a humble, everyday feeling or a work born of man's hands.

Thus the real is taken for the unreal, and vice versa. Moreover this illusion has a real, solid basis, for it is not a theoretical illusion; it is a practical illusion, with its basis in everyday life and in the way everyday life is organized. This real and this unreal are not speculative categories but categories of life, of practical activity – historical and even tragic categories. If the human is the fundamental reality of history, the inhuman is reduced to an appearance, a manifestation of man's becoming. And yet how well we know the terrible reality of the inhuman! Only a concrete dialectic which demonstrates the unity of essence and appearance, of the real and the unreal – a unity in the process of becoming, in which the two poles merge and act one upon the other – is capable of giving a meaning to the 'human' and the 'inhuman' in history.

Man attains his own reality, creates himself through, within and by means of his opposite, his alienation: the inhuman. It is through the inhuman that he has slowly built the human world.

This humble, everyday, human world has been taken as a crude façade for certain sublime realities. We know today that these 'higher realities' were simply the manifestation, the appearance, of man's attempt to create his own reality in everyday life – but possessing the monstrous power, peculiar to alienation, of absorbing human reality, of crushing it and throwing it off centre, so to speak.

Now it has reached its moment of highest intensity, the conflict between what is apparent and what is real is about to be resolved through a progress in consciousness and activity. Alienation, now made conscious, and thus rejected as mere appearance and superseded, will give way to an authentic human reality, stripped of its façade, and liberated.

(f) *Critique of freedom*
(Central theme: man's power over nature and over his own nature)

What does freedom consist in?

According to Article 6 of the 1793 Constitution: 'Liberty is the power which belongs to man to do anything that does not harm the rights of others'; and the Declaration of the Rights of Man of 1791 maintains that: 'Liberty consists in being able to do anything which does not harm others.'

Quoting these texts[27] gives Marx the opportunity of directing his irony against the idols of the bourgeoisie.

The limits within which each individual can move *without* harming others are determined by law, just as the boundary between two fields is determined by a stake. The liberty we are here dealing with is that of man as an isolated monad who is withdrawn into himself ... But the right of man to freedom is not based on the association of man with man but rather on the separation of man from man. It is the *right* of this separation, the right of the *restricted* individual, restricted to himself.[28]

It is therefore the right of the 'private' individual, and in its practical application consists essentially of the right to 'private' property (Article 16 of the 1793 Constitution).

So this bourgeois definition of freedom has something narrow and sordid about it. Yet its partisans see it as noble and profound; it protects the rights of 'individual conscience', of 'inner freedom', of the 'personality'. And it is not entirely false, in so far as the way the lives of individuals have been organized has allowed certain privileged people to develop an intellectually rigorous or morally sincere 'conscience'. But when we consider the sum total of results, the sum total of 'private lives' formed and established within the parameters of this bourgeois freedom, it is easy to see that its nobility and profundity are part and parcel of the process of mystification.

Even at best, freedom defined in this way is totally negative. One must never do anything for fear of encroaching upon one's neighbour, even if he needs help! When it attempts to be active and 'positive', this freedom becomes the art of twisting the (moral or legal) law, of interfering cunningly in other people's lives and property. But since by definition intermonadic relations cannot be organized and work to all intents and purposes haphazardly, any positive attempts to be free become nothing more than the skilful exploitation of chance in relations founded on money (markets, sales, inheritances, etc.) and the skilful use of money according to the whim of the 'free' individual.

The Marxist definition of freedom is concrete and dialectical.

The realm of freedom is established progressively by '*the development of human powers as an end in itself*'.[29]

The definition of freedom thus begins with the *power* man increasingly has over nature (and over his own nature, over his self and the products of his activity). It is not a ready-made freedom; it cannot be defined metaphysically by an 'all or nothing': absolute freedom or absolute necessity. It is won progressively by social man. For *power*, or, more exactly, *the sum total of powers* which constitute freedom belong to human beings grouped together in a society, and not to the isolated individual.

In the first place, then, freedom must be won; it is arrived at through a process of becoming: there are therefore *degrees of freedom*. (In the same way, to take a comparison from a political problem which is not unconnected with the general problem of freedom, there are *degrees* of democracy, more democracy, less democracy, a development in democracy ...)

In the second place, the freedom of the individual is founded upon that of his social group (his nation, his class). There can be no freedom for the individual in a subservient nation or class. Only in a free society will the individual be free to realize his full potential.

In the third place, there are *freedoms* (political and human, both on the social and the individual level) rather than 'freedom' in general. All freedoms imply the exercise of *effective* power. Freedom of expression, effective participation in the running of the social whole, these are political freedoms. The (complementary) rights to work and to leisure – the possibility of attaining the highest consciousness and development of the self through culture – contribute to *concrete* individual freedom. All power is liberating; thus, to take a very simple example, someone who can swim or run is attaining a higher level of freedom: he is free in relation to a material environment which he controls instead of being controlled by it. 'Spiritually' and materially, the free individual is a totality of powers, i.e. of concrete possibilities. Freedom reduced to so-called freedom of 'opinion', or to the open-ended possibilities of adventure or flight of fancy, is one of the illusions of the 'private' consciousness – mystifications accepted by the 'subject' who has been separated from the natural and human 'object'.

Nevertheless the notion of freedom in general retains a meaning. Dialectically it even takes on a new meaning, higher and more profound. It designates the *unity* of the different aspects of freedom, of the various freedoms. There can be no concrete freedom for the individual without social, economic and political freedoms. The power which will liberate is not the power which certain men have wielded over other human beings, but the power which man, considered as a whole, wields over nature.

There is no metaphysical dilemma of the order: 'Either absolute determinism – or else absolute freedom. All or nothing!' The universe is not an indifferent, immovable mass, an immediately available 'world' which unfolds according to inexorable 'Laws'. Such a vision, which deprives man of the world, has a name which situates it in the history of thought and which demonstrates how much and by what means we have superseded it: it is called 'mechanism'. This vision served a purpose by lending support to science, as a transitional stage, at the very moment when action founded upon science was demonstrating how erroneous an interpretation it was. The 'laws of nature' do not forbid effective action, they are its foundation. If we get rid of mechanism, we get rid of the inevitability of destiny. The way opens up for the conquest of the world. *The world is man's future.*

So long as man did not understand the laws of nature and history, they weighed him down; because he did not understand them, they inevitably seemed to be governed by a 'mysterious', oppressive, blind necessity.

Knowledge and action extend the 'dominated sector' of nature and man, taking this necessity over and transforming it into powers, i.e. freedoms: man dominates nature and his own social nature by 'understanding' them. Necessity is blind only in so far as it is not understood.

In the realm of necessity, human needs became degraded. They represented 'the sad necessities of everyday life'. People had to eat, drink, find clothes . . . and so they had to work. But people whose only reason for working is to keep body and soul together have neither the time nor the inclination for anything else. So they just keep on working, and their lives are spent just staying alive. This, in a nutshell, has been the philosophy of everyday life – and it still is.

And yet, every human need, conceived of as the relation between a human being and the 'world', can become a power, in other words a freedom, a source of joy or happiness. But needs have to be rescued from the realm of blind necessity, or at least its ascendancy must be progressively reduced.

'Man appropriates his integral essence in an integral way, as a total man.'[30] This 'essence' is not a metaphysical essence, but a set of needs and organs which become social, human, rational, as a result of the power of social man over nature (and over his own nature). Whether we are concerned with the eye or genitals, with rational consciousness or physical activity, it is always a question of the 'appropriation of *human* reality' of the 'approach to the object',[31] and this is what 'the *confirmation of human reality*'[32] consists in. On the one hand, man's 'essence' is factual: his body, his biological reality. But on the other hand, seen as practical activity which appropriates these biological realities and transforms them into freedoms and powers, the 'essence' of the human cannot be defined as a ready-made nature; it creates itself, through action, through knowledge – and through social becoming.

One particular aspect of art demonstrates this transformation well. In a painting, the human eye has found its 'appropriate object'; the human eye has formed and transformed itself first through practical and then through aesthetic activity, and by knowledge: it has become something other than a mere organ; for the painter at least, through this work which has been freed from all external constraints, truly prefiguring the realm of freedom, and producing the work of art, the eye partakes of that 'joy that man gives to himself'.[33] (Of course, such a sketchy analysis scarcely scratches the surface of the problem of art . . .)

It is perfectly obvious that the realm of 'private' property forms part of the realm of blind necessity. Every human activity which is controlled by this narrow and limited entity will devote itself to perpetuating it. In bourgeois ideology, it appears as an *inner part* of the individual, one of his fundamental 'rights', something his freedom is founded on. In fact, and consonant with the dialectical principle according to which what appears to be most internal is in fact most external, analysis shows that it is really an external, oppressive entity. When they are linked to this institution, 'individual' feelings and needs cannot attain a humanized level. '[An] object is only *ours* when we have it . . . Therefore *all* the physical and intellectual senses have been replaced by the simple estrangement of *all* these senses – the sense of *having*.'[34] Moreover Marx transforms this observation about human poverty into something hopeful, for he adds: 'So that it might give birth to its inner wealth, human nature had to be reduced to this absolute poverty.'[35]

The realm of blind necessity is retreating before the combined onslaught of knowledge and action. Liberated from sordid necessity, needs per se are becoming suffused with reason, social life, joy and happiness. Moreover people are having to spend less time working in order to satisfy these needs; in the past only the subjection of the masses allowed the upper classes that freedom which is to be found beyond the sphere of material production. In our era, especially in our era, the condition which restricted creative leisure and 'spiritual' activities to the oppressors has disappeared. It is a complex dialectic: needs are becoming more extensive, more numerous, but because the productive forces are broadening, this extension of needs *may* imply their humanization, a reduction in the number of hours worked to satisfy immediate needs, a reduction of the time spent at work generally, a universalization both of wealth and of leisure. If, in a sense, the realm of natural necessity is growing more extensive, since the needs of modern man *are tending towards* a greater complexity than those of primitive man, then the realm of freedom will only become greater and more profoundly rooted in nature as a result.

Nevertheless, first and foremost:

(a) 'The associated producers must ... govern the human metabolism with nature in a rational way, bringing it under their collective control instead of being dominated by it as a blind power.'[36]

(b) The material and moral parameters of practical (everyday) life, which are determined by private property, must be transformed.

(c) Through activities devoted to satisfying and controlling immediate necessities, there must be a growth in the sphere of '*the true realm of freedom, the development of human powers, as an end in itself,* [which] *begins beyond it, though it can only flourish with this realm of necessity as its basis*'.[37] This sphere, this 'spiritual' domain of man, consists in the first place in a social and rational organization of free leisure. As Marx asserts in *Capital*: 'The reduction of the working day is the basic requisite.'[38]

4

The Development of Marxist Thought

But in that case, one may say, Marxism *already* offers a complete critical knowledge of everyday life!

No.

The significance of the work of Marx and Engels is still far from being clearly elucidated.

Two obstacles have hindered a deeper elaboration of Marxist thought. Some take Marx's and Engels's texts *literally* – seeing each text in isolation, without link, without unity – rather than attempting to grasp and extend the evolution of the thought they contain. In this way certain Marxists have lost sight of its dynamic, living character. Although they are conversant with the texts, such theoreticians have become bogged down in literal exegeses which add nothing to Marxist thought (even though they are preferable, admittedly, to the flights of fancy of people who write or talk about Marxism without knowing anything about it); this is a doctrine about thought in movement and about movement in things, and they immobilize it. They are thus incapable of reconstructing the work of Marx and Engels in the integrality of its meaning.

On the other hand, attempts to develop Marxism 'freely' have too often involved deliberate modifications of its most solidly established foundations.

The genuine line of development of Marxist thought avoids both these dead-ends: literal dogmatism and the allegedly 'free' revision of first principles.

Dialectical materialism develops as a method of thinking which is neither empty nor formally separable from its object (an academic and scholastic way of conceiving method); instead it elaborates both itself and its content at the same time.

Before Marxist *humanism* could be fully reinstated, there were some fairly widespread errors which had to be refuted.

Marx and Engels began their work with philosophical research; then moved on to economics and political action.

Some – philosophers rather than economists – have concentrated exclusively upon the philosophical works. Conversely, others see Marx's economic works as eclipsing his philosophical works. In fact for a long time there was a widely held but fallacious theory that Marx's economics and politics had eliminated his philosophy. The fact that economic science and political action had *superseded* speculative philosophy fostered the false conclusion that Marx had abandoned any conception of the philosophical world.

This narrow, one-sided position was based on a traditional mistranslation. In the economic and political works of Marx and Engels, philosophy appears *aufgehoben*.[1] But there is no verb in French which translates this Hegelian term exactly; it means *at the same time* to abolish something (as it was) and to raise it to a higher level. From the first French translator of Hegel (Véra) onwards, the dialectical term *aufheben* has been repeatedly translated and traduced by the word 'supprimer'. The word 'dépasser', which is used nowadays, while nearer in meaning, still falls short of rendering the *double movement* Hegel's verb signifies; it fails to show clearly that the reality which has been *aufgehoben*, the dialectical *moment* which has been 'superseded' as such, takes on in the process of being 'superseded' a new reality, higher, more profound. Thus the philosophy must be rediscovered in the economy and the politics, and not as an 'eliminated' stage, but on the contrary as a moment and an essential element, which indeed only acquires *its full importance* in the higher reality.

Gradually the certainty has been reached that the *dialectical method* is an essential element of scientific sociology – indeed of all scientific thought.

But there is still more progress to be made. It still remains to be demonstrated clearly that this dialectical method is not one that is 'formally' separated from philosophical research and then subsequently applied to economic or social data. The dialectical method contains and implies a scientific, philosophical and human content. Thus philosophy ceases to be speculative and systematic; on the one hand it opens itself up to science, and on the other to the totality of human reality. Not only does it become 'committed' (a vague, abstract term), but it also becomes rationally (dialectically) articulated with the sciences and with the *movement* of scientific thought, with the human and with the *movement* of human reality, in other words with the action which transforms this reality, with the knowledge of its laws (i.e., precisely, its movement) as starting point.

We are still dealing with philosophy and with an *overall* conception of man and the world, but in a *renewed* sense: concrete, dynamic philosophy, linked to practical action as well as to knowledge – and thus implying the effort to 'supersede' all the limitations of life and thought, to organize a 'whole', to bring to the fore the idea of *the total man.*

In this way Marxism – a philosophy and a method, a humanism, an economic science, a political science – can be reconstructed in all its integrality. In this way and this way alone have certain major notions which had to be rediscovered and brought to light become apparent in Marx's works: the notion of *alienation,* of *fetishism* and of *mystification.*[2]

This preparatory work was absolutely vital if the methodical study of human reality was to continue, and if certain equally vital questions concerning concrete humanism were to be tackled.

The first principles and fundamental ideas which enable us to formulate and resolve these problems effectively are implicit in the work of Marx and Engels, provided this work is taken as a whole and understood in terms of its basic tendency. It is nevertheless true that the ideas in question are not dealt with comprehensively in the classic texts of Marxism, and that therefore they need not only clarifying but also developing.

Thus Marxism develops as a living whole (in economic, political and also *philosophical* research), without, however, ever emerging either as an 'orthodoxy' or scholasticism or, alternatively, as a shapeless eclecticism.

Where economy and philosophy meet lies the theory of *fetishism.*

Money, currency, commodities, capital, are nothing more than relations between human beings (between 'individual', qualitative human tasks). And yet these relations take on the appearance and the form of *things* external to human beings. The appearance becomes reality; because men believe that these 'fetishes' exist outside of themselves they really do function like objective things. Human activities are swept along and torn from their own reality and consciousness, and become subservient to these things. Humanly speaking, someone who thinks only of getting rich is living his life subjected to a thing, namely money. But more than this, the proletarian, whose life is used as a means for the accumulation of capital, is thrown to the mercy of an external power.

On the one hand, therefore, the economist observes *facts*; using *induction* and *deduction*, i.e. the procedures proper to the experimental sciences, he establishes laws to explain these facts – the law of value, of prices, of money, etc. The (dialectical) analysis of reality enables him to grasp the moments and the stages, the contradictions, the movement of this economic and social reality. It appears to be, and in one sense *is*, a reality independent of human consciousness and human will, developing according to a *natural and objective* process.

But in another sense, nothing else exists but human consciousness and human will. Only, they are 'alienated' – and alienated not merely in the domain of ideas or intuitions, but also in the domain of *practical* life. The theory of *economic fetishism* is fundamental because it enables us to understand the shift from human activities (individual, qualitative tasks) to economic 'things'; it also enables us to understand why economic and social truth is not immediate, how and why all the questions in this domain are veiled with a *social mystery*, namely, because economic 'things', fetishes, envelop and *disguise* the human relations which constitute them. When we handle money we forget, we no longer realize, that it is merely 'crystallized' labour, and that it represents human labour and nothing else; a deadly illusion endows it with an external existence ...

The theory of fetishism demonstrates the *economic, everyday* basis of the *philosophical* theories of mystification and alienation. We say of goods that are sold, that they are 'alienated'. We say of someone enslaved, that he has *alienated* his freedom. In its most extreme sense, the word designates the situation of people who have become estranged from themselves through mental illness. More generally, at certain stages of its development, human activity spawns relations which masquerade as *things*. Now these things and the way they function are beyond the grasp of action or consciousness, and permit interpretations, bizarre hypotheses and pseudo-explanations which are as remote from reality and truth as they could possibly be: ideologies ...

And that is precisely what human *alienation* consists in – man torn from his self, from nature, from his own nature, from his consciousness, dragged down and dehumanized by his own social products. This explains how there can be such a thing as a *social mystery*. Society becomes a mechanism and an organism which ceases to be comprehensible to the very people who participate in it and who maintain it through their labour. Men are what they do, and think according to what they are. And yet they are ignorant of what they do and what they are. Their own works and their own reality are beyond their grasp.

Man has been unable to avoid this alienation. It has imposed itself in everyday life, in social relations more complex than the immediate relations of kinship and primitive economy. Man has developed and has raised himself above the animal and biological condition of his lowly beginnings via socio-economic fetishism and self-alienation. No other way has been open to him. *The human has been formed through dehumanization* – dialectically. The division between the human and its self was – and remains – as deep, as tragic, as necessary as the division between man and nature. The one is the corollary of the other. Man, a being of nature, forever united inseparably with nature, struggles against it. He dominates it and imagines he can separate himself from it, through abstraction, through self-consciousness – something only attained by painful effort. Thus it is through the (theological and metaphysical) alienation which has allowed man to believe himself outside of nature and the world, through *idealism* itself, that we have successfully dominated nature. It is in contradiction and painful division, in the struggle against nature and against his own self, that man becomes what he *can* become.

Now the time of *rediscovered, recognized unity* is beginning, but at a higher level. Once more man recognizes himself as a being in nature, but now possessed of power and a consciousness which the immense and painful effort has afforded. Division, alienation – fetishism, mystification, deprivation – the formation of the total man, these *philosophical* ideas make up an organic, living whole. Man, his thought and his reality have developed *dialectically*. Dialectical method, the expression of all real processes, controls, organizes and illuminates this complex of ideas and confers on it the rigour of concrete logic.

Moreover, fetishism is *equally* a *scientific theory*, resulting from an analysis of data, from a series of inductions and deductions in the domain of economic science.

Thus Marxism cannot be reduced to being simply a *prise de conscience* of the world. When Marxists maintain that they are philosophers *as well,* what they mean is that they are not *only* philosophers, but something more: intellectuals on the one hand, men of action on the other. And this is where they part company with those philosophers who perpetuate the old tradition of metaphysical speculation. Marxism cannot be compared to a 'description' of the modern world, to a 'phenomenology of economic essences'. Without the work of the natural and social sciences, without the 'demystifying' influence of action, consciousness (the philosopher's) would come to an abrupt halt and become ensnared in alienation and mystification. Consciousness cannot free itself from existing illusions by its own strength alone; it will either atrophy in antiquated interpretations of the social structures inherited from the past, or else construct new 'ideological' interpretations.

Man is an infinitely complex being and his knowledge entails a multitude of aspects, investigations, techniques – all organically linked by dialectical method.

In the days when people wrote studies about 'human nature', moralists used to moan that there was not much left to say. Later, in the days of romantic idealism, this lament was repeated ad nauseam and transformed into a poetic dirge: we were born too late into a world too old. By proclaiming that man's youth is to be found in the future, dialectical materialism is also revealing the complexity of human reality, its richness. It renews and recreates interest in the human – and first and foremost by reintegrating the humbler reality of everyday life into thought and consciousness.

How could Marxism, which opens up a new horizon to consciousness and action, limit consciousness and tell it: 'Stop, there's nothing more to say!'? The founders of Marxism drew up the general guidelines for the criticism of life, but how could they possibly have completed that criticism? Marxism must move the knowledge of human reality forward, and this is what it is doing. Research and action reveal the human, and enrich it at the same time. Each new stage reveals new aspects of life – which we find increasingly complex, increasingly rich in the 'spiritual' sense of the word.

Dialectical method excludes the possibility that there can be nothing more to say about the human or about any domain of human activity. On the contrary, it supposes that the *knowledge* of man and his *realization* are mutually inseparable and constitute a total process. To penetrate ever more deeply into the content of life, to seize it in its shifting reality, to be ever more lucid about the lessons it has to teach us – this is the essential precept of research.

Lenin's analysis of historical situations has demonstrated the complexity of their elements and their interactions. For the transformation of the world to become possible, there must first be an *objective* crisis, a disassociation of the economic and the social structures (under the impetus of forces of production, caught between the mode of production and those legal relations which they are destined to shatter). This objective element is not enough. For a 'revolutionary crisis' to occur, however, a *subjective* element is equally necessary: revolutionary theory, upon which the action of a party, a class – as large and as well-informed a fraction of the social whole as possible – will be founded. But in the last resort the revolutionary solution to economic and social contradictions will only become possible when the human masses *are no longer able or willing to live as before*. Therefore Lenin calls upon everyone who wants to think like a man of action and to act like a man of thought to be open to what life can teach, and above all to look at everyday life. There is no such thing as the spontaneity of the masses, and theory by itself is not enough. And yet it is the awkward, tentative, spasmodic efforts of the human masses to free themselves from oppression – and the theory which understands, studies and illuminates mass movements – which quicken the idea of revolution. 'Unity of theory and practice' – this tenet dominates and sums up living Marxism. And it is in life that this unity is achieved and perpetuated, that this idea comes to maturity, that the union between its various elements – practical and theoretical, objective and subjective – is realized. None of these elements can be defined or can work effectively if separated from the others. The spontaneity of the masses is just an illusion, a myth created by people who expect 'history' to achieve its ends and to accomplish its task aided only by providence. Theory and knowledge outside of action are in themselves mere abstractions, and the myth of the 'vanguard' and the 'active minority' is no less harmful than the myth that the 'masses' can set themselves in motion spontaneously. Individuals and 'private' consciousnesses can only become a creative force through a theory and an action which unites them as a totality, an active mass, a lever for thought to lift the world with. Individual and mass are two opposing terms, but, like thought and action, they are bound together. And once more it is practical, everyday life which demands this unity, and develops it. It is in life – and in the light of previous knowledge and experience – that forms of organization and effective ideas are to be found. Only thus does the dialectic stop being an anti-dialectical abstraction to become the movement which unites opposing aspects and elements. It is no coincidence that Marxists repeat the word 'concrete' so frequently. Adversaries of Marxism refer ironically to the exaggerated and excessive use of the word (Malraux, for example, apropos of the Communist Pradas in *Days of Hope*); but talk of the 'concrete' is only truly ridiculous when it becomes an abstraction itself, an automatism. (Which in fact is what happens when people who believe they are acting and thinking dialectically stop looking at everyday life, stop learning from it, stop searching for its deeper significance. This is treachery, self-betrayal: in their mouths the dialectic reverts to being just so much metaphysical waffle; they become congealed in their own mystical speechifying about movement and history; they talk about the 'concrete', but they end up being more abstract than anyone!)

In the zone of clarity which precedes and follows action (or to put it more dialectically, *thought-action*), the theoretical themes of alienation, mystification, fetishism and deprivation spring suddenly to life. I see 'concretely' how human beings are mystified, hoodwinked, annihilated, confused; when I fight this many-sided alienation practically, I am better able to perceive how certain acts, certain words, split me from my self to feed the vampire of the non-human – that 'substance' which is, precisely, nothing, because from the point of view of the human, it is 'other', the negation of the human, the human cast to the winds and into the valley of death.

'Alienation' – I know it is there whenever I sing a love song or recite a poem, whenever I handle a banknote or enter a shop, whenever I glance at a poster or read a newspaper. At the very moment the human is defined as 'having possessions' I know it is there, dispossessing the human. I thus grasp how alienation substitutes a false greatness for the real weaknesses of man, and a false weakness for his true greatness.

Bombastic language, abstractions, deductions, every devilish device to vaporize man's will and man's thoughts – all vouchsafe me a glimpse of alienation in action.

This is not to say that I am able to separate what is human from the inhuman simply by thinking about it. The task is much more difficult, the division within the self and the waste of self are too deep-seated. If I have learned to think or to love, it is in and through the words, gestures, expressions and songs of thirty centuries of human alienation. How can I come to grips with my self, or how can we retrieve our selves once more? If I stay on my guard and strip myself of everything suspect, I am left naked, dry as dust, reduced to 'existing' like someone who refuses to be hoodwinked by anything; and what will become of me and my wariness? Nothing. Alienation is an ordeal that our era must undergo, there is no means of escaping it. Only later will future human beings, freed from alienation, know and see clearly what was dehumanized and what was worthwhile about the times we live in.

We are still learning to think via metaphysical, abstract – alienated – forms of thought. The danger of dogmatic, speculative, systematic and abstract attitudes lies ever in wait for us. How long will it take to create a *dialectical consciousness*, as long as our consciousness still feels it necessary to rise above its own self – in the metaphysical way – in order to think dialectically? It is impossible to fix a date; it may need generations before the dialectic can penetrate life by means of a regenerated culture.

And as for love – which for nearly all of us oscillates between coarse biological need and the fine abstractions of passion's rhetoric – what is there to say?

And so our entire life is caught up in alienation, and will only be restored to itself slowly, through an immense effort of thought (consciousness) and action (creation).

The word 'commitment' (commitment to the world – committed thought, etc.) has had its day. As a philosophical slogan, it had a certain meaning. The abstract intellectual, moving about in unreality, felt the need to 'commit' himself to life, to action. He ended up with action for action's sake – commitment for the sake of commitment! As great a folly as art for art's sake, or thought for thought's sake; a new alienation: the ludicrous situation of the 'thinker' who wants to commit himself and suddenly realizes that he was *already* committed in the first place!

Today it is much more a question of becoming *decommitted* from a singularly ambiguous, confused and equivocal era – from a many-faceted alienation. We need to gain control. 'Committed' people are up to their eyes in the mire, the nauseating quagmire of the time they live in, and they will never pull themselves free, never reclaim that time, and eventually will even cease understanding it. They are still grappling with the hoary problem of the intellectual who decides to 'leave his ivory tower' . . . (ah! how many times have we heard that old tale!). This intellectual 'gets involved' with life, wanders through the world, and discovers that thought is not everything. So, making an extra effort, he flirts with action, going on about 'commitment' amid applause and self-congratulation; but deep within him there is an unresolved contradiction: he wants to remain *available* while *appearing to be committed.* So he cheats, goes into reverse, starts play-acting. One step forward and two steps back!

Most of the 'important intellectuals' of the inter-war years were actors in this hackneyed old drama . . .

But there were some who, less arrogantly and without cheating, really did become 'committed', and who nowadays are faced with the opposite problem: to *decommit* themselves, not from action, not from militant thought, but from all the limited and immediate ways the times we live in are perceived; then, taking the lessons of action into account, *to take control of our era by grasping it in its totality* . . .

Action and action alone can guide critical thinking, because it detects deception – and because it is deception which deflects us from action. Many people might be tempted to see this guiding role in the investigation of life and human reality as falling to literature, for literature's importance is today much exaggerated. But literature itself needs to be confronted with life, to be thought out and criticized in the name of human reality, and enriched by action. Only the establishment of action's unassailable primacy, though it will certainly contribute much to literature, can assign its real place – which is neither first nor last.

Literature does not deserve to be held in excessively high esteem, but nor does it deserve the fate of being degraded by resentful, disappointed people. The idolatry of literature can only end in disappointment. Whatever its 'function' may be – testimony or aesthetic pleasure, or something else again – it has only one. It is puerile to expect the practice of literature, taken in itself, to throw any decisive light on life and human reality. Literature cannot bring us salvation, because it needs to be saved itself. Immobilized in the clichés of poetic Byzantinism or the *roman noir*, it too needs new men who will state simply and without bias what was hateful or disgusting about our era, what was good, joyful and sturdy, and by what means human beings managed to go on loving life and hoping for the future.

Action and action alone can bring this healthiness and this elementary equilibrium, this ability to grasp life in its varied aspects, without being deliberately gloomy or abstractly optimistic. Action alone can supersede the aesthetic or theoretic attitudes which allow people to see in the real only what they want to see: degradation, humiliation, stupidity, or conversely joy and greatness left, right and centre – either looking at life on the black side or through rose-tinted glasses.

Action as defined by Marxism – the transformation of the world by a political party which strives to guide the great human masses and carry them along in its path – has as its aim a new *type of human being*. This new man thinks, but on the level of the real, on an equal footing with the real. He thus has no need to *come out of* his own thoughts in order to belong to reality and 'commit' himself. Neither anguished like the self-centred intellectual, nor self-satisfied like the bourgeois, he can avoid this old dilemma (anguish or thoughtless self-satisfaction) because what he loves about the real today and about life at the present moment are the *possibilities* they offer, and not simply the *fait accompli* which can be easily grasped and which can only disappoint. Once he sees human beings as moving towards the future, and once he loves this movement, then this new man can leave the old attitudes of sentimental humanism and callous contempt behind; he can be demanding without being inhuman, because he wants man to show his full potential at long last. Thus today only a new man such as this can find the *appropriate level* for talking precisely about things (which does not exclude violence, indignation, or anger, far from it; for there is no longer any question of being impersonal, neutral, abstractly 'objective'; and the old dichotomies of objectivity and passion, impartiality and action, will also have been superseded and resolved ...). He alone will be able to *extricate himself from immediate reality, without, for all that, forgetting the real in general.*

Every ideology is an 'expression' of its time; but in fact the term has no predetermined meaning; in hindsight a critically minded reader will realize that a novel, a play or a book of poetry was an 'expression' of its times – one possible 'expression' among others. There can be all manner of spaces and distances, transpositions and metamorphoses, standing between reality and the ways reality is expressed, so much so that very differing works of art can equally and quite justifiably be regarded as 'expressing' the same moment in time (Balzac and Stendhal, for example). Here again the distance between what is expressed and the means of expression itself must be bridged by a double-edged line of thought: on the one hand, by explaining each work in the light of real life; and on the other by seeking to discover what we can learn about that life as it was, in the literary work which has 'expressed' it.

It is rather odd that our era, an era of contradictions if ever there was one, has been 'expressed' by works which swarm with weak and shapeless characters without conflicts, without fixed contours. For, to judge by the resounding success of such books as Céline's *Journey to the End of the Night* or Sartre's *Roads to Freedom*, they must indeed be significant. Must we conclude that there is a disjunction between literature and real life here, that books like these work solely in terms of conventions, or that there is something deeply erroneous about them? To a certain extent, yes, they are wrong, they do hold back, distort or ignore reality. But there is more to it than that. In an era when unbearable conflicts and contradictions *strive* to make themselves political and to resolve themselves on the political plane, everything in 'ideological life' finds itself in the business of camouflaging them (no coincidences here!); these contradictions are thus concealed, watered down, denied expression; their depth and their meaning are resolutely ignored. The origins of this tendency are to be found in the tactics of the ruling class, of the bourgeoisie, which is propped up by metaphysical systems or existing religions. It is succcessful because its accomplices are legion (it is so much easier and nicer not to feel beset by contradictions!), and it ends up producing spineless, shapeless literature. Simultaneously cause and effect, this literature *expresses* the situation and expresses it well.

Only action brings a clear awareness of how false this situation is. Action alone reinstates the conflicts and the sharp-edged contradictions in all their truth and violence. It gives us back the 'world' in all its truth. Thus action alone will enable literature to become renewed by giving it something it cannot attain unaided: a living awareness of human reality and its movement . . .

Old metaphysical reason deliberately excluded *the irrational* from its definitions and its sphere of influence. As a result it ignored individuality, instincts, passion, practical action and imagination: the living being in his entirety. Abstract Reason could thus approach the irrational only by such indirect and rather ineffectual means as the moralizing sermon. It was always possible, of course, to suppress the irrational (by 'repressing' it), and to condemn it from on high in the name of metaphysical truth.

But we know now that this 'irrationality' was the human, the entire living being. We know that, philosophically and humanly speaking, the irrational has rebelled, that because it was considered 'absurd', it has deliberately made its rebellion an absurd one, and that it has raised the flag of the absurd as a challenge to reason. And this is one aspect of the crisis of modern man and modern culture: they are split between abstract reason on the one hand and an absurdity which wants and believes itself to be 'vital' on the other, torn between two opposites which seem locked forever in a painful and apparently unresolvable confrontation.

Dialectical Reason (Marxism) answers the question by approaching it from another angle. For dialectical thought, it is not and never can be a question of some self-sufficient 'irrationality' doomed to eternal rejection by an equally changeless Rationality. The irrational can only be relative, momentary: it is whatever has not been subsumed, organized and categorized by active Reason.

More precisely, we must distinguish between two aspects of the irrational:

(a) The 'irrational' as such, in other words the sum total of the magical creations, ideological interpretations and fictions about the world that human weakness has produced. This irrational is 'nothing' since in truth it is 'other' to man, his alienation. It is 'nothing' in itself, although on the human level it has been appallingly active. In Chapter 1 we demonstrated the important law according to which this irrationality evolves: after a series of transformations and displacements it installs itself under a new form in the life of rational man. And it is in life and through everyday life that this displacement and transformation of the irrational take place.

(b) So far from constituting something irrational beyond the control of reason, the entirety of the human being's needs and instincts – his 'passions', vital activities – are the very basis and the content of Dialectical Reason. These vital activities are already involved in the processes by which they become the needs and the capabilities of a 'being of nature' with the ability to understand and control that nature – i.e. a rational being. In so far as they are part of man's practical activities, they form the first step in his struggle to control nature; they are thus very much a part of a dialectical process, and therefore rational, and even instrumental in the creation of concrete Reason.

And yet this process is a process of becoming, a process yet to be brought to completion. Human needs and activities do not contain 'a certain amount' of ready-made dialectical reason, which would in any case be meaningless. It therefore rests with methodically worked-out rational thought (dialectical thought) to get to know this rich *human raw material* – and to win recognition from it in turn. It must study and organize this material, and thus contribute to the process whereby men's lives produce living reason, and become rational.

Without being irremediably opaque and irreducible to reason, 'human raw material' is a given. It is a mixture of the *irrationality* generated by alienation (which is far from being completely elucidated and categorized) and the *potential rationality* of instincts, needs and activity of all kinds.

This human material is a fact of everyday life. To pursue the analysis of everyday life and distinguish as far as possible between its various elements, critical knowledge and action must work together.

Although according to this definition 'human raw material' offers no opacity, no absolute resistance to knowledge and action – since this is precisely where their content and their base of operations are located – it is nevertheless *ambiguous*. If on the one hand everyday life reveals the forces which work for and against man, on the other hand it has always been possible to erect the *immediate* as a barrier to wider and more far-reaching ways of seeing. It is in the name of the immediate (immediate demands, immediate needs, etc.) that people have opposed and continued to oppose wider visions, wider solutions to their problems. The immediate – the given human raw material of everyday life – at one and the same time reveals and disguises the deepest of realities, both implying them and concealing them. Thus the task facing active, constructive, critical thought becomes clear: to penetrate ever deeper into human raw material, into the immediate which is a fact of everyday life, and to resolve their ambiguities. Here is a major problem which Marxists know well: to find a link between the immediate and the solutions Marxism proposes, so giving the immediate a positive function as practical and historical intermediary between theory and reality. This is an essential problem for action, but it is equally so for humanist philosophy: to link the *idea* of the human to the human *as it is*. The problem is always a new one, its terms of reference are constantly changing; merely to formulate it requires an ever-watchful lucidity and a method that is both rigorous and flexible.

Let us try to look more closely at certain characteristics of given 'human raw material'.

There is an *average general standard*, specific to every region, to every country, to every moment of life and civilization. This standard of living is both a historical and a practical fact. It is based upon the technical characteristics of the economy (the level of material development, the social power of production) but also upon the extent to which the working masses can resist the pressure exerted by their adversaries.

In the theory of wages, this average standard of living helps to determine the 'lowest living wage' acceptable at any given moment, in other words to determine the *value of labour power* as sold on the market; like any other commodity, labour power is bought by capitalists, 'honestly', for what it is worth, in other words according to the socially necessary labour time required to produce and reproduce it. This labour time is determined by a practical and historical factor: the average standard of living, which as we know is higher in certain states of North America than it is in France, and higher in France than it is in Japan ... The average standard of living is explained by historical factors. (If it is higher in certain parts of the United States, a major reason is that from the start economic development has never been hindered by a pre-existing feudal and medieval economy; but this does not mean that it can avoid *colliding with the internal limits of capitalism*.) But in any event, no matter how precise the economic determinants may be (the value of labour power, wages, etc.), they cannot be used simply as some kind of algebraic calculation. They have a basis in practical, everyday life. What is in question, what must be defended and even improved, is the standard of living, at a given moment, in a given situation. And in this sense again, the study of life and of 'human raw material' is the great precept of dialectical method.

At the same time as a material standard of living there is an intellectual or 'cultural' standard of living. In a given civilization and among a given people there are a certain number of ideas which have been eliminated, superseded, rendered obsolete; and a certain number which are accepted as 'self-evident'. Thus, many people still take occultism, spiritualism, vegetarianism, a particular moral code or the Christian religion seriously; but nobody takes the Greek gods seriously any more. Those people who support a religion, or a moral code, or even a philosophy, demand that their belief be shown the respect owed to all 'sincere' opinions. But anyone who believed in Apollo or Venus would be regarded quite simply as a madman. Such a belief would seem to be completely out of touch with life. It is worth remarking, however, that it has never been proven that Apollo or Venus do not exist; it has simply 'become impossible' to believe in them. Why? The question is worth answering, not least because in our culture, in our 'humanities', Apollo and Venus are forever cropping up, much more frequently than Jehovah, or Christ, or astral bodies!

When an artist wishes to make himself understood, or to express certain feelings, he may still write plays about Apollo or Venus, or paint them, or sculpt them; but nobody or virtually nobody ever presents his ideas or his feelings by means of the Christian god, or the ectoplasmic spirits, which so many people believe in, and which moreover are taken so seriously.

What do these facts mean as far as our culture is concerned? That our art is not serious? Or that we do not address the things we take most seriously when we want to express our most serious ideas? In any event, this is one of the symptoms – a very minor one – of a paradoxical situation and a problem which can only be resolved by examining the ideas implied in our present standards of life and civilization more closely.

This standard of civilization is characterized by the extremely disparate and heterogeneous elements which help to compose it. In its structure, capitalist society brings with it all kinds of outdated forms which it raises to a 'modern level', being unable to eliminate them.

Thus in France itself we find every type of economic structure, from a quasi-primitive pastoral economy (in the Pyrenees, for example), and an almost patriarchal agrarian economy (the small peasantry to be found in many regions), up to the most modern techniques of large industry.[3] In the same way, and as a corollary, there are overlapping and intersecting ideas in our culture and our consciousness which correspond factually and historically to different stages of civilization: from agrarian myths and peasant superstitions to recently acquired scientific concepts. Our 'average standard' is made up of this inextricable tangle. Even in its apparent and pretentious 'modernity' (and what in fact does this 'modernity' consist of?) our culture drags in its wake a great, disparate patchwork which has nothing 'modern' about it . . .[4]

'Social milieux' are not separated into watertight compartments. Juxtaposed, without rigorous boundaries, the reciprocal influences between them – a 'spiritual' osmosis – is never-ending. This juxtaposition of socio-economic forms and human types from different ages and different stages in the embryology of the total man produces a curious situation. Seen from this perspective our era looks like a freak with a hypertrophic human brain, the body of an invertebrate and the cells of a protozoan. Or again one might compare it to a folly built to the specifications of some insanely eclectic architect in which Doric columns support Gothic vaulting or reinforced concrete slabs (effects like this are not unusual in the buildings which have sprung forth from the impoverished imagination of the bourgeoisie; and such eclectic imbecility is even less unusual in the ideological constructions of our era!).

Of course, the complex economic, social, legal and political relations which this situation produces are not of direct interest in the critique of everyday life. What it must concern itself with are the overall consequences for life and for the consciousness of life. Given the confusion of facts, actions and the practical conditions of consciousness, how could consciousness itself be anything but extremely confused? (And among the consequences of this confusion we must include the fact that although many individuals receive their ideas and their feelings via the influence of a social formation other than the one they immediately belong to, they nevertheless go on believing in the independence of ideas, feelings and consciousness!) This confusion reflects a fundamental disorder. There is nothing to arrange or organize the elements of life, culture and consciousness, composed as they are of a mixture of styles, types of life, and enthusiasms of very differing origins and meaning. There are certain sophisticated intellectuals who have all the verbal techniques, the entire bag of tricks of bourgeois thought at their fingertips, of whom it can be said: 'They are peasants' (Claudel, for example), or else: 'They are craftsmen' (Péguy). The one ferries the other: the verbal techniques of the era of advanced literary styles are merely a vehicle for agrarian myths or the craft ethic; and vice versa.

There can never be any question of denying anything that exists the right to exist. It is the movement within whatever exists which transforms the world, past, present or future, and not theories about what should be rejected and what should be preserved. The essential thing here is to denounce confusion with all its baggage of bad faith, guilty conscience, ideological duplicity, trickery and trumpery. Now this confusion is *lived* – in other words it intervenes in life and in the consciousness of life. It explains how that ideological representative of the most backward peasants and their myths, Monsieur Jean Giono, has managed to be so popular, even with the younger generation in industrial towns, even with mechanics. But it has paved the way for many more paradoxes and sophistries ... Here is a simple example: one can consider that in the West, and in advanced countries, a certain knowledge of the world and even of biological reality has become part of the average consciousness, of 'normal' culture (to use the very equivocal and confused term employed by sociologists ...). Various rather vague notions about health, sport, heredity, have been 'vulgarized', as they say, and in this way an 'average' stock of knowledge has been formed (although it is unequally distributed between the various groups and classes). In this way more-or-less scientific notions about heredity have merged in the 'average' consciousness with old models of peasant origin, and old group and class prejudices. This 'vulgarization' of science at its most modern has paved the way, in certain countries at least, for the propagation of a scientifically false theory – racism – which has all-too-easily permeated the masses.

If it is indeed true that the beginning and the end of all knowledge is practical activity, then one may well ask oneself how it can be that during our era of high technology and advanced scientific knowledge the practical lives of human beings can still be so blind and so indecisive. How does such an obvious contrast between a science proud of its triumphs and the humiliation and uncertainty of human lives come about? If all power originates in action, where do life's weaknesses and uncertainties – and its triviality – come from? How can practical, everyday life form the basis of human thought, power and splendour, when it is apparently so impoverished, so lowly, so blind, that we still feel the need to dress it up in illusions, decorations, lavish costumes, or at the very least in weird and bizarre disguises, before we can accept it?

The analysis of the organic and ideological confusion of our era offers an initial answer to these questions. And admittedly this diversity contributes to the richness of our consciousness and our culture. Still we must grasp it, define it, categorize its elements, for what we have inherited from past and superseded eras is precisely a shapeless and *irrational* mass of notions and feelings, a 'rich' but hitherto inextricable muddle.

Only a vast inventory of the elements of our culture – in other words of our consciousness of life – will enable us to see clearly.

This endeavour cannot be undertaken – it cannot even be conceived – with any method other than the Marxist dialectic. It can have meaning only in and through dialectical materialism. The philosophers, theologians, sociologists and literary hacks all *accept* the ideas and feelings that are passed on to them, and on that level. Their criticisms are abstract and timeless. They are unable to situate the elements of our consciousness in historical time, by linking them to successive social formations, to fashions and ways of life. They can describe, but they cannot understand, much less judge and criticize effectively. Only Marxist *social* criticism is capable of uncovering the genesis of 'representations' and feelings; it reveals their conditions, their practical functions, the way they work, and analyses the relative proportions of appearance and reality – the amount of 'play-acting' and the amount of 'human' – that they have contained in the past and that they contain today. It can make links between each 'representation', each symbol, each myth, each concept, and a specific human era.

It can trace the interactions of the social 'milieux' and in this way understand our composite and heterogeneous consciousness of life.

'Consciousness of life' – can those words be right? Are we conscious of our own lives? The words which spring to our lips, the ideas and images at our disposal, are they of a kind to allow us a *true* consciousness of our lives? ... No! Our lives are still unrealized, and our consciousness is false. It is not only our consciousness which is false: it is only false because our lives are still alienated. False representations bring with them a false consciousness of what an unrealized life is; in other words they do not bring an awareness of the non-realization (of the degree of non-realization) of human life: they present it as either realized (which leads to vulgar or moral satisfaction) or unrealizable (which leads to anguish or the desire for a different life).

More precisely, nowadays, *we do not know how we live.* And at the end of our lives, we scarcely know how we have lived them. And how bitter this unhappy consciousness is ...

While we are trying to live, at the moment we are living, religion, morality, literature and familiar words impose upon us an official image of ourselves. The individual's 'private' consciousness is complemented by a 'public' consciousness; they interact and support one another. The 'private' consciousness refers across to the 'public' consciousness and vice versa; the one is meaningless without the other.[5] The one is as real — and as unreal — as the other. For the 'private' individual, the public consciousness contains the most basic social elements that individualism can adapt to; and at the same time it is laden with deceptive words, mystifying ideas and images. In the 'public' consciousness the 'private' consciousness finds justifications, ready-made explanations, compensations. Individual life oscillates between the one and the other. The famous dialogue between the 'I' and Ego is simply that between the private and the public in the same individual. And in this divided, riven, torn consciousness the questions posed by one fragment are answered by the other. Together, the fragments take on the appearance of a self-sufficient whole. When the private man is secretly worried, his public consciousness assures him that there is no need to be, that everything is fine, that really he is happy — or, conversely, that owing to totally external circumstances, nothing can be done, that he will be unhappy throughout eternity. It eliminates the very need to ask questions. The private man never really asks himself 'how he lives', for he thinks he knows it in advance: he thinks that he owns life like just one more possession; he believes that happiness can be held in the hand, the pounds, shillings and pence of that great capital asset, life.

The critique of everyday life will propose the undertaking of a vast survey, to be called: *How we live.*

(a) We could begin this survey by attempting to reconstruct the real life of a number of individuals (comparing their real lives with their consciousness of them, their interpretations of them), using a variety of research techniques.

How were these 'private' individuals formed? Under what influences? How did they choose their path in life, their profession? How did they get married? How and why did they have children? How and why did they act in such and such a situation in their lives? ...

A survey of this kind would be fairly difficult to carry out (although some newspapers and reviews have already collected and published confidential information of the most intimate kind, if only for publicity purposes), but it would shed much unexpected light upon individual lives in our age. It would be fascinating to compare the results with religious, moral, political and philosophical ideas which are still in circulation – and especially with the individualism which is even more widespread in behaviour than it is in theory.

Methodically carried out, this survey would at long last supplant the ramblings of philosophers or novelists (including those who get emotional about 'beings' and harshly lucid about 'existence') with solidly established 'human truths'. In all likelihood it would help to shift our centres of interest, revealing the part played by alienation, fictions, chance and fate in the real life and death of men.

The documentation we have collected so far (some of which will be published in the *Critique of Everyday Life*) demonstrates the existence in today's social life of some largely unknown sectors – and all the more so inasmuch as the dominant ideologies suggest 'ideas' which appear to explain and schematize them.[6]

(b) This survey should not be limited to a certain number of individual lives taken in their totality, but should examine the details of everyday life as minutely as possible – for example, a day in the life of an individual, any day, no matter how trivial.

A trivial day in our lives – what do we make of it? It is likely that the survey would reveal that taken socially (examined in the light of the hidden social side of individual triviality) this trivial day would have nothing trivial about it at all. During a day at work or a holiday, we each enter into relations with a certain number of social 'things' whose nature we do not understand, but which we support by our active participation; without realizing it we are caught up in a certain number of social mechanisms.

One question we can ask ourselves, for example, is how the average man in his ordinary, day-to-day life, relates to the large corporations. Where does he encounter them? How does he perceive them and imagine them? Theory reveals a complex structure here – in what ways does he move within it? And how does this structure appear to him from morning till night?

(c) Taken more broadly and more generally, this survey of everyday life would become a survey of French life and specifically French forms of life – as compared with the specific forms of other nations.

How have the different 'milieux' of the French nation organized their everyday life?

How do these different social groups use their money, how do they organize their budget?[7] How do they spend their time, what are their leisure activities? In what forms do they act out their sociability, their solitude, their family life, their love life, their culture?

Going on the as-yet incomplete documentation we have collected, it would appear that genuine revelations may be expected.

The survey would reveal how the Frenchman has long been one of the most *exploited* members of the capitalist universe, and how the bourgeoisie which has exploited him has been one of the shrewdest – alternating between deceit and brutality, and always very 'modern', very much in touch with all the tactics of the class struggle (particularly and precisely when it indiscriminately uses either the nation or the individual to deny that the struggle exists ...).

Using precise cases and examples, the survey would demonstrate how this deceitful pressure results in the debasement both of the social structure (agriculture or industry) and of individual, everyday life.

It would thus contribute towards dispelling certain harmful myths (for example, the economic myth of France's 'natural' wealth – the cultural and spiritual myths of the inherent lucidity and spontaneous moderation of French thought ...) by demonstrating concretely *what is true* and *what is false* about them ...

It would also contribute towards the critique of a number of illusions which are particularly disastrous for France. Is it not surprising and fascinating that at the harshest, most oppressive moment of high capitalism so many of the French should have believed and should go on believing that they are free, and that in the name of their freedom a certain (and apparently large) number of them are still rushing headlong into slavery? What can be the meaning of the stubborn and persistent success of this mystification? What can examining the lives of 'private' individuals teach us about it, and what can it teach us about the real lives of these individuals?

In the name of freedom and individuality, we are told, the French have been 'abandoned' (just think of the situation of French youth!). This extraordinary observation was made by Drieu la Rochelle, and the conclusions he attempted to draw from it, were equally extraordinary; we know what became of him.[8] The fact is that the 'private' individual suffers from the kind of 'spiritual' abandonment which makes it easy for the whole gamut of phony 'spiritual' powers to tout their false solutions and vow to rid consciousness and life of their sickness . . .

It will probably never be possible to complete this picture of French life. But it would take but a few polls to counter the gloomy aspects of the situation, and to reveal the healthy, restorative side of our national life, its real possibilities and genuinely creative elements.

On a completely different level, the study of everyday life would dispel several literary and philosophical myths whose spuriousness is one decadent tendency among many. For example, the myth of *human solitude*. There is ample evidence to show that for the vast majority of human beings, immersed as they are in natural life or undifferentiated social life, being alone is a need, and something to be achieved. For the peasant, merged with the life of natural things, of animals, of the earth, of the village, as for the worker who lives with his family in cramped accommodation and who is even more unfamiliar with freedom to move around than he is with freedom to use his own time, there is no solitude in the 'deep' and 'metaphysical' meaning of the word. Peasants and the workers can be alone: by accident or by chance, through illness, through inability to express themselves, etc., but they are not truly solitary. On the contrary, a worker who lives with his wife and children in one or two rooms feels the need to reflect, to be alone with himself for a while in order to think or to read. He rarely experiences the joys of solitude. For him the need to be alone is already progress, something gained. It is the most 'private' individuals –

intellectuals, individualists, separated by abstraction and bourgeois scholasticism from any relationship or social life – who have invented solitude. Instead of seeing it as the time and the chance to develop a deeper awareness of human relations, they have transformed it – following the usual metaphysical pattern – into an absolute. And then they have used their poetry, their novels or their philosophy to moan and to wallow in self-pity. At the limits of the 'private' consciousness and in the human nothingness of their 'existence', they have rebelled – in vain – against the metaphysical alienation which their own attitude towards life helps to maintain ... For them, the fiction of solitude becomes reality. For them 'alone'!

(d) The critique of everyday life has a contribution to make to *the art of living*.

This art, as new, as unknown as happiness itself, has been pre-figured – in the context of an individualism and dilettantism which was limited even then and has been moribund every since – by several writers, including Stendhal.

It is a domain in which everything remains to be said. In the future the art of living will become a genuine art, based like all art upon the vital need to expand, and also on a certain number of techniques and areas of knowledge, but which will go beyond its own conditions in an attempt to see itself not just as a means but as an end. The art of living presupposes that the human being sees his own life – the development and intensification of his life – not as a means towards 'another' end, but as an end in itself. It presupposes that life as a whole – everyday life – should become a work of art and 'the joy that man gives to himself'.[9]

As with every genuine art, this will not be reducible to a few cheap formulas, a few gadgets to help us organize our time, our comfort, or our pleasure more efficiently. Recipes and techniques for increasing happiness and pleasure are part of the baggage of bourgeois wisdom – a shallow wisdom which will never bring satisfaction. The genuine art of living implies a human reality, both individual and social, in-comparably broader than this.

The art of living implies the end of alienation – and will contribute towards it.

From one point of view life strikes us like some immense anthill, swarming with obscure, blind, anonymous beings and actions – and from another we see it shining with the splendour and glamour which certain individuals and certain actions confer on it. We must not avoid the fact that the latter view is produced by the former, and 'expresses' it – that the contrast between the two is only momentary – and that up until now everyday life has been 'alienated' in such a way that its own reality has been torn from it, placed outside it and even turned against it.

In any event, this contrast cannot go on permanently deceiving us, its drama (with the condemnation of life as its theme) cannot be an absolute one. It is merely a passing contradiction, a problem ...

This problem, which is none other than the problem of man, can only be posed and then resolved by dialectical method. Should we admit for one moment that it is otherwise, and that the plebeian substance of day-to-day living and the higher moments of life are forever separated, and that the two cannot be grasped as a unity and made to become a part of life – then it will be the human that we are condemning.

5

Notes Written One Sunday in the French

Countryside

Some fairly precise documents exist which allow us to travel back in our minds to the origins of our civilization – not to prehistory nor to the so-called 'primitive' era, but to a more recent age, the dawn of Greek civilization, for example, or Roman, or medieval.

We can imagine villages and rural landscapes which scarcely differ from those we can see in modern Greece, Southern Italy or even in certain parts of the South of France. Let us conjure up this country life which in more ways than one has continued into the present day . . .

In Greece countryfolk had their festivals and religious ceremonies; the dates for these festivals were fixed by the country calendar. It seems that the religious season par excellence was winter, which in our rural areas is still the time for late-night gatherings. In the Classical period which followed the Archaic period, some of the most important festivals in Greece were still celebrated at the beginning of winter, or at the end: the Pyanespis, in autumn; the Anthesteria, when spring came; the Thalysis, a festival for the local goddess in which all the inhabitants of the village participated, lying on swaths of reeds and vine leaves and eating the θαγὺσιος, bread made from the new corn.

These country festivals consisted essentially of a large meal; the peasants feasted, lying on the ιστιϐάδες or swaths, and in specific places: near woods, mountains, springs, rivers.

Everyone brought a contribution to the communal meal. Each village constituted a community: a large family of people linked by blood, a way of life, and also by a practical discipline and a fairly strict collective organization of work (dates when tasks were performed, etc.). About the system of property we know nothing very precise or very

221

certain, but we can be sure that at the beginning it had not yet disassociated the peasant community.

The neighbouring villages in each canton came to the main festivals – as they do to this day in the fairs and 'votive festivals' still celebrated in French rural areas.

During the feasts there was much merry-making: dancing, masquerades in which boys and girls changed clothes or dressed up in animal skins or masks – simultaneous marriages for an entire new generation – races and other sports, beauty contests, mock tournaments; exchanging comical taunts and insults, neighbouring and rival communities, men and women, associated but competing guilds, would try to outdo each other. The festivities would end in scuffles and orgies.

Peasant celebrations tightened social links and at the same time gave rein to all the desires which had been pent up by collective discipline and the necessities of everyday work. In celebrating, each member of the community went beyond himself, so to speak, and in one fell swoop drew all that was energetic, pleasurable and possible from nature, food, social life and his own body and mind.

Festival differed from everyday life only in the explosion of forces which had been slowly accumulated in and via everyday life itself.

We must imagine rough peasants, full of joviality and vitality, and fairly poor. For these celebrations they make great 'sacrifices', in the practical sense of the word; in one day they devour all the provisions and stocks it has taken them months to accumulate. Generously, they welcome guests and strangers. It is the day of excess. Anything goes. This exuberance, this enormous orgy of eating and drinking – with no limits, no rules – is not without a deep sense of foreboding. Should a disaster happen, too harsh a winter or too dry a summer, a storm or an epidemic, then the community will regret this feast day when it devoured its own substance and denied its own conditions. How can the need for exaltation on both an individual and collective level, the need for a few hours of complete, intense living, be reconciled with foreboding and fear? Men know how weak they still are when confronted with nature! How can this contradiction be borne? Festival is a risk, a wager on the future. What is there to be won, and what to lose?

In those days when human beings lived so to speak on the level of nature and natural life, in its elemental violence, its uncomplicated freshness and also its ignorance, they imagined nature via their own preoccupations, fears and desires; conversely and simultaneously they still defined and understood their basic humanity through the phenomena of nature, animals and plants, the heavens or the bowels of the earth.

Already witches and magicians existed, with spells, rituals and gestures which were intended precisely to console weak humanity with the illusion of having direct power over nature – nature so familiar and yet so terrifying.

Rural communities associated nature specifically with human joyfulness. Nature was peopled with 'mysterious' powers, powers that were human and close, yet at the same time fantastic, distant and dangerous, distinct but at the same time merged in a recondite unity.[1] If festivals were successfully held, it was felt to be because nature and its powers had been good, favourable, regular, bringing rain and sunshine, heat and cold, the seasons and their allotted tasks, according to their expected, favourable cycle (birds, coming and going with the seasons, appeared as magic and prophetic signs of this order). Thus when the community gathered to carry out this simple action of eating and drinking, the event was attended by a sense of magnificence which intensified the feeling of joy. By celebrating, the community was welcoming Nature and was rejoicing in its gifts; more than this, it was associating Nature with the human community, binding the two together. The regular place given in the country calendar to festivals and specific tasks represented the regularity of human actions – their punctual accomplishment – and appeared to guarantee and assure the regularity of the seasons. Very soon, if not from the start, peasant festivals became eminently important; they represented not only joy, communion, participation in Dionysiac life, but also a cooperation with the natural order. Simultaneous marriages 'represented' the fertility of nature while at the same time ensuring it and fixing it firmly, as if to shape and tie down the future in advance (in this way certain polyvalent rituals had a magical aspect, a symbolic aspect and an aspect of play; in the primitive stages the latter was subordinated, but later it came to the fore, displacing the irrational aspects of the action; the seesaw, for example, was at one and the same time a game bringing the sexes together, a fertility ritual and a symbolic action . . .).

So the 'sacrifices' which everyone had to make for the festival – gifts, contributions from each family and each household – appeared as a down-payment for the future. To refuse to participate would have been to set oneself apart from the community – and to risk interrupting the normal, fertile course of nature and human life. It would have been to invite bad luck, starting with the magic curses of the people who collected the contributions. To this day in the French countryside, during certain festivals children or young people or poor people still exercise the last remaining privileges of the old peasant communities by going from house to house collecting (money, eggs, flour, sugar ...) for the feast; anyone who refuses is cursed ritually according to traditional formulas: drought for their land, sickness for their flocks ...

The Greek word: συμβάλλεσθαι, which gives us that word so characteristic of our religions and ideologies, 'symbol', means initially 'to pay one's share', hence: to participate in the magic action, in the effectiveness of the ritual.

It would be perfectly clear to the members of the rural community that the larger the gift, the more effective it would be; festivals were a way of assuring the future, and the more active the participation in them, the larger the amount of blessings in return, the greater the prestige, the influence, the power. Thus through their gifts to the community, the wealthy (once private property had become differentiated) could make their wealth accepted, and were able to consolidate it. The very fact that they gained social prestige enabled them to become even wealthier. Landowners became both powerful and blessed – and hated. They controlled the good fortune and the power of the community. At this point the object of study for the sociologist seems to shift: we move from the level of magic to the level of the 'social mystery' (i.e. religion); from man's relationship to nature to the formation of differentiated, divided human society, where all community is fictitious ...

So originally the human order and the natural order seemed interwoven, joined by a 'mysterious' link (but which for those simple peasants seemed the most immediate, the most natural thing in their world). If the peasant tradition was strict to the point of routine, it was only because all change threatens 'order'. Also, human activity tends to become codified practice, so that festivals, and even the gestures and speech of everyday life, became ritualized. Perhaps this sums up how magic developed, or even how it was born, and how solemn and sacred gestures became generalized, taking their elements from day-to-day life, but transposing them to the level of an imaginary effectiveness. In such conditions the festive meal became a sacred meal in a holy place, a cosmic and efficacious action. The union of the sexes also became a magical act which challenged nature in its entirety, which could be blessed or blighted, prefiguring problems or happiness to come. And the gift, the offering, the contribution to the celebration, became a 'sacrifice' in the mystic sense of the word: an insurance for the future, an exchange of favours with obscure forces, future benefits secured by means of present hardship.

The association of Nature with man means first and foremost the Earth. In the magic and the religions which have been part of the becoming of Western civilization, the Earth is represented humanly and sexually: Mother Earth, wounded and harrowed by the plough, and fertilized – like a woman – by man. Moreover, at once frightening and fruitful, the Earth receives the dead and grows fat with their corpses.

It would appear that the ancient peasant communities were fairly quick to achieve a relatively stable balance, which, as rural history (a recent science which is still in the process of formation) has demonstrated, had strict conditions and surprisingly subtle elements: a balance between pastures, forests and arable land; a balance between the animal and human populations; a balance in the organization of tasks between 'individual' activities and collective disciplines; a balance between the sharing-out of land and the structure of property. In our own history, in our Middle Ages, the sociological historian finds the same process once again, the same balance, which is shattered (as it seems to have been in Antiquity) by the formation of a rural aristocracy followed by a rural bourgeoisie. This natural and human balance, achieved and preserved by a peasant wisdom, by a set of techniques and a spontaneous skill which astounds the historian, appeared to be the supreme good, divine, marvellous, fragile. It was precisely in order to maintain this balance that the peasant community clung firmly to its own traditions and reinforced the role of magic and ritual.

To preserve this 'order', the peasant order – for every class, every social formation has its order and its idea of order – man cooperated with nature; he maintained and regulated its energies, both by his real work and by the (fictitious) effectiveness of his magic. But from the very moment they became prosperous, communities were faced with a serious danger. They needed children to renew the community generation by generation, children who would be initiated into its tasks and its secrets, receiving and passing on the communal heritage. Too many or too few births would endanger the balance: too many mouths to feed, or not enough arms to plough the land, and famine would engulf the community. By virtue of illusion which ethnographers discover in many places, the deep cause of which – in other words the *practical* cause – seems as far as our present knowledge can tell to be very simple and everywhere the same, and number of 'souls' was part of the 'order' as conceived by these peasants. Births and deaths were governed by the cosmic law, and remained regular so long as that law remained undisturbed. The number of human beings was determined by nature. Thus every birth was a reincarnation: a soul was taken from the group's available stock, and came back to life. 'Souls' were immortal, even if their existence beyond the living group remained shadowy and vague. (This notion of the soul 'overdetermines' even more ancient representations including perhaps that of the double, of that 'other' which is still a human being).

And it is the Earth 'who bears and fosters all living things and receives from men libation to quicken her seed anew'[2] who supplies the souls. Following one of their most ancient traditions, the Athenians of the Classical Era still scattered seeds on newly-closed tombs – just as we bring flowers. In the Earth, their temporary home – mother and tomb – the dead continued to participate in the order of things, in the regularity of the seasons and of human activities. Strange phantoms, they went on moving and living as they made their preparations to be born again. They were still part of the order; and they could disturb it. By dint of honours, of funereal rites – which guaranteed order and were a part of order – by dint of libations and sacrifices, the community sought the favour of its dead. And in these offerings, the fruits of the earth – wine, foliage, flowers, or wheatcakes – played an essential role.

The rural community was therefore also community with the dead, and festivals for the dead found a place amidst the festivals for the living. In man's state of weakness in the face of nature, disquiet appeared alongside joy, ever more defined, ever stronger, until it became anxiety, and anxiety too had its funeral festivals and its celebrations. And the wealthy, land-owning families, which were such a burden on the community, always tried to justify themselves by appealing to the past – to real or fictitious ancestors, heroes, dragon-killers, founders or pseudo-founders of cities, inventors of new techniques. Funeral festivals became the privileged festivals of dead kings and heroes. Dionysiac joy gave way to terror. Human life was torn apart as it embarked upon its harsh and inevitable journey into alienation.

Certainly, right from the start, festivals contrasted violently with everyday life, *but they were not separate from it.* They were like everyday life, but more intense; and the moments of that life – the practical community, food, the relation with nature – in other words, work – were reunited, amplified, magnified in the festival. Man, still immersed in an immediate natural life, lived, mimed, sang, danced his relation with nature and the cosmic order as his elementary and confused thoughts 'represented' it. On the same level as nature, man was also on the same level as himself, his thoughts, the forms of beauty, wisdom, madness, frenzy and tranquillity which were available to him. In his reality, he lived and achieved all his potential. Feeling no deep conflict with himself, he could give himself up – in that magnificent state of balance which was the peasant community – to his own spontaneous vitality. No aspect of himself, of his energy, his instinct, was left unused. Perhaps he was basic and elementary, but at least he lived without being fundamentally 'repressed'; and maybe he sometimes died appeased.

The 'pure' nature that some writers applaud is in fact this peasant life at a highly evolved stage, and in point of fact at only very rare moments and places in history has it achieved a successful, happy, balanced form. In most cases, the continuation of a nomadic, bellicose way of life, or poor soil, or a bad climate, or, furthermore, and especially, social crises and the rapid formation of brutally dominant castes, have dragged social life down dead ends, nearly always precipitating its decline.

The balance of the community was threatened on two fronts:

– in nature, by all manner of catastrophes, and even more by the fear produced when acts were no longer ritualized and performed in order to maintain and celebrate life, but merely for the sake of their sacred form and for the sake of the magical power that that form was supposed to exert;

227

– in social life, through ever more differentiation and inequality.

The simultaneous emergence of families isolated from the community, of 'private' property outside of the collective systems, and of the power which certain families and certain individuals wielded over the community, destroyed that community from within. The crisis of the community, its dislocation, the distress of most of its members, went hand in hand with technical progress and social differentiation. It is hard for us to imagine the astonishment with which the members of old communities must have greeted these social changes which were happening around them and which they were unable to comprehend. Let us not forget that by the gifts and 'sacrifices' they made in proportion to their wealth and influence, the chiefs became increasingly powerful while at the same time still appearing to be the embodiment of the community's own power. Those who were breaking up the community seemed to be strengthening its 'deep' reality; they were enslaving the community while appearing to be its servants – and in a sense they were serving it, in that they defended it, that they stood for technical progress, and that they alone had access to ideas, thought, wisdom, prudence, a sense of responsibility, of potentially rational foresight. The social process was now masked by its own conditions. How was it possible not to attribute it to 'mysterious' causes, external to everyday life: to original sins, supernatural punishments, an incomprehensible 'destiny'? The developing social mystery – the reality which escaped men's consciousness, although they were its authors and actors – was destined to become a religious mystery; and religion now superimposed itself upon magic, but without destroying it. Chiefs and kings contrived to receive the blessing of the communities they oppressed (i.e. the blessing of its gods); in a curious but perennial mixture of illusion and reality, they maintained both the cosmic order, by virtue of their magical functions, and the human order, by virtue of their political functions.

(But in these quiet little towns and villages which sit at the junctions of ancient tracks that have criss-crossed the French countryside for thousands of years, how does one become a public figure, someone respected, such as a town or regional councillor, or a member of parliament, nowadays? If there are no urban centres nearby and if the workers' parties have no influence, then even today it is only via the

Church, charitable organizations, the commune, sports societies or the fire department that a parvenu manages to become accepted and to consolidate his support and his influence. And this is achieved without any 'politics' – i.e. by the oldest of all political processes, which is just as unconscious now as it has been for centuries. It is taken for granted that unless there is some extraordinary accident such as a natural upheaval (a war or a crisis), the prosperity of public figures and the prosperity of the community go hand in hand; the one produces the other; everyone in the village or the canton benefits: through gifts, charitable donations, and because the important peasant or tradesman 'makes work' for the poor. These men are blessed – by the gods and by their fellow man. They have their own pew in church. People bless them in public but hate them in private. They are the object of a thousand repressed and 'private' grievances ...)

Therefore, in ancient rural communities, according to all the available documents, a certain human fulfilment was to be found – albeit mingled with disquiet and the seeds of all the agonies to come. That fulfilment has since disappeared. It has been lost in two senses. First, rituals and symbols and their interpretation as elaborated by the religious imagination have tended to dispossess human actions of their living substance in favour of 'meanings'. Secondly, social life has improved, but has changed its structure in the process; from being on a horizontal level, so to speak, on the level of natural life and the 'world', it has become pyramidal, with chiefs, kings, a State, ideas, abstractions, at its apex. Symbols have become more and more abstract; in its own way, like money, but on the political level, the State is also in a sense a *realized abstraction*, endowed with effective power which is ever more real. At first rituals conjured up the confused 'powers' of nature, the 'hidden side' of things and human beings, then mythical heroes, then increasingly elaborate gods; later, however, they came to centre on a 'spiritual' power, i.e. a realized abstraction, the God of the universal religions. At the same time, the theories justifying the power of political chiefs and kings have become more and more abstract. And at the same time too, century after century, genuine knowledge and thought, implying logical abstraction (science), have appeared to be progressing and advancing in line with ideologies – whereas these are two different and possibly incompatible levels of human consciousness.

The result for our rural areas has been a deprivation of everyday life on a vast scale, by religion, by abstraction, by the life of the 'mind', by distant and 'mysterious' political life ... Bit by bit everything which formerly contributed to the elementary splendour of everyday life, its innocent, native grandeur, has been stripped from it and made to appear as something beyond its own self. Progress has been *real, and in certain aspects immense*, but it has been dearly paid.

And yet it is still there, this innocent life, so very near, but impoverished and humiliated, both strong and pathetic, creative but threatened, producing the future but beset with foreboding about all the imponderables that future has in store.

It is still there, not unchanged, but degraded rather, humiliated, while in other respects, and proportionally, science and consciousness have progressed. Take for example an ordinary village in France ... The network of roads and paths, fences and hedgerows, encloses a land which is by no means unworkable, a docile, easy land which rises and falls almost imperceptibly as if with the breath of the distant mountains. Scattered farms and then, around the church and the graveyard, a few houses grouped together, the village. A green land; meadows, their brooks full with autumn rain.

The village still huddles closely around its dead. The living still bring their floral tributes to the dear departed; many people believe that it is the right thing to do to put cheap and nasty metal-and-glass mementoes on the graves; ritual has become hideously commercialized; the graceful tributes of fruits of the earth which sustained the life of the dead, linking them with the living and preparing for their return to life, have been replaced by a 'sacrifice' of money which is made once and for all – a way of settling one's conscience concerning the dead person, of making him permanently harmless. It is true that some people may think that what they inherit from the dead is somehow a settling of accounts, but they too can have pangs of conscience. Some visit the graves of the dead. ('I'm just off to say hello to my poor departed husband', said Mme X as she made her way jauntily to the graveyard where her spouse lay 'at rest'.) These are people who apparently believe that the dear departed are simultaneously and at one and the same time in heaven (or hell) and here, under these stones and this ground, under these artificial flowers. In this consecrated fold, they experience the feeling of a 'living' presence – instead of the terrifying reality, the horror of death. Their cold breast is flooded with a cruel, sweet emotion. Many of them believe in ghosts, in phantoms, in 'spirits'; yet instead of preparing the return of their dead to the light of day and the community with love, terror and respect, they simply relegate them to oblivion. Fresh corpses get visited; the others, the old ones, lie forgotten as in a communal grave. The myth of the community and its dead goes on, but demoted, weakened, deprived of warmth, linked to vague, abstract affirmations about 'souls' which can never be translated into tangible acts ...

The winter solstice is still an important date; but the great solar myth of the god who is reborn to fill the Earth with new and burning life has become just a sentimental, vaguely charming series of images – a little family portrait. What remains of ritual and myth? A date, a vague impression of birth, of hope, of grandiose drama – the idea of an all-powerful god who is nevertheless mysteriously destined to be born and to die; and then theological abstractions, sublimations relegated inaccessibly to the background; and then those childish but touching pictures – the animals, the manger, the Wise Men and their star, inseparably linked to the cosmic, human infant ...

Every time spring arrives, processions intended to confirm the regularity of the season and the fertility of the fields go round the village, winding drearily along through the paths between the fields. Drearily, plunged in an immense boredom which is like an ultimate sacrifice: people 'give up' the time, put up with the inconvenience. All the Dionysiac joy has gone out of this ritual, which is known arrogantly as 'Rogation Days'. It is a request for fine weather and a rich harvest. Actually, nobody believes that prayers can be really effective, but many still believe that not to attend or to stop the ritual completely would be bad luck. Prudently they take precautions. The negative side of the traditional ritual has completely annihilated the positive one, which was joy in human community.

In this same village, in the same springtime, pious hands still hang garlands on sacred trees and, occasionally, on the roadside crosses which have long dispossessed old Hecate of her domain ...

And when war comes, and drought, the peasants bemoan their fate, saying: 'Everything's gone haywire.' They see cosmic order and human order as inextricably linked, as in the original agrarian myth ... And they do not easily understand the specifically human means by which order (a coherent, rational order) can be re-established ...[3]

The mystical notion of 'sacrifice' lives on more or less everywhere; if anyone tried to forget it, there would be wars and social dramas to revitalize it. But age has not favoured it; and now sacrifices are only vaguely felt to be 'sacred'. Parents make 'sacrifices' to bring up their children; people also 'sacrifice' part of the present for the future, by saving from their earnings and 'investing' them, or by taking out 'insurance'. Meanwhile they continue preparing for the future by negotiating with the supernatural – donations, charity, offerings of personal suffering, of merits achieved in the eyes of men and gods – for a repayment proportional to the hardship involved ...[4]

There is one special little item which every well-off and god-fearing family budgets for: charity. By private gifts and public donations the god-fearing can relieve their consciences of any residual qualms they might feel, and can also justify themselves to other people. They are contributing to the permanence of their order, while at the same time reducing poor people's resentment – and making their lot a little easier. 'Sacrifice' has several meanings and several aims, some conscious, others unconscious, some selfish, others altruistic (and collectors and apologists for charity will quote one or other of these aims as circumstances demand ...).

It is well known that wars are a punishment for people's sinfulness, indolence and cruelty. And so is defeat. (This Christian mystique – originally a peasant mythology – was made official under the Vichy regime.) The poor should make sacrifices by working a lot, and the rich by giving a little. What are sacrifices? 'Spiritual' investments! Their worth is a function of the effort they cost, i.e. the amount of hardship people are prepared to put up with in their fear of the future. Unfortunately statistics concerning the amounts charities receive are never made public. What material they would provide for the study of everyday life across the classes and social groups! It is very possible that both in cash and in kind, the poor give more than the rich. Their uncertainties, their fears for the future – and their generosity too – are they not greater? Moreover, anyone who has nothing to give, or is unwilling to give, can always placate the mysterious powers by offering up their wishes, their sufferings, their hearts and their minds ...

The uncertainties peasants feel about nature become superimposed – as religion was superimposed upon magic – by the disquiet of several other social groups about human, economic and political circumstances. Ignorance of the laws of sociology, the inability to act without dependence on political lies and strategies, along with a sort of direct contamination from myths and rituals, fosters and perpetuates the idea of fate and predestination; masses of individuals (each believing himself to be free and lucid), entire groups react to human circumstances in the same way that countryfolk responded to the circumstances of nature; they accept wars and crises as inevitable, pleading with their gods to bring these calamities to an end, thanking or cursing the heavenly powers that be.

And in life itself, in everyday life, ancient gestures, rituals as old as time itself, continue unchanged – except for the fact that this life has been stripped of its beauty. Only the dust of words remains, dead gestures. Because rituals and feelings, prayers and magic spells, blessings, curses, have been detached from life, they have become abstract and 'inner', to use the terminology of self-justification. Convictions have become weaker, sacrifices shallower, less intense. People cope – badly – with a smaller outlay. Pleasures have become weaker and weaker. The only thing that has not diminished is the old disquiet, that feeling of weakness, that foreboding. But what was formerly a sense of disquiet has become worry, anguish. Religion, ethics, metaphysics – these are merely the 'spiritual' and 'inner' festivals of human anguish, ways of channelling the black waters of anxiety – and towards what abyss?

And if beauty has disappeared from everyday life, what of its great *mystical* heroes? No, the mystic hero is virtually extinct. Everything is calculated on a cut-price basis. A penny for heaven. A little bit more (but as little as possible!) to pacify the 'poor', whose real power is visibly on the increase ...

And yet, the more meaningless gestures become, the more solemn they are; and the more solemn they are, the more ludicrous, sparking off life's revenges: laughter and parody ...

And now let us go for a moment into the little village church, surrounded by its graveyard.

I hesitate on its humble, unadorned threshold, held back by a kind of apprehension. I know what I shall find: an empty, echoing space, with hidden recesses crammed with hundreds of objects, each uttering the silent cry that makes it a sign. What a strange power! I know that I cannot fail to understand their 'meanings', because they were explained to me years ago. It is impossible to close your eyes and your ears to these symbols: they occupy you, they preoccupy you immediately, insistent, insidious – and the more so for their simplicity. Already a feeling of disquiet, suppressed anger, mingled with the reluctant but tenacious memories of a childhood and adolescence shaped by Christianity ... And I know that this suppressed anger is another aspect of the power, the nascent fascination of the 'sacred' object. It is impossible to free myself from it. For me this space can never be just like any other space. But precisely because I feel this obscure emotion I can begin to understand its obscure causes. So I must not despair, the fight goes on ...

The country church is small and dark, despite its whitewashed walls. A sickly light filters through the grimy little panes of its narrow windows. Small, dark, mysterious, a bit like a cave. An ambiguous perfume – its familiar side: damp; its strange side: incense – hits the nostrils. The mystical, far-away splendour of the incense penetrates the ordinary smell of must and mould. Already I am inhaling the perfume of the Orient, I want to inhale it despite myself, to identify it. Unalloyed it would be overpowering, but here its mystical appeal is tainted with something mundane.

And now I can begin to make out the coloured or gilded objects and signs which surround the faithful and impose their presence upon them.

Around the vault, above the choir, a clumsy but inspired artist has painted a border festooned with stars (in silver and gold) on a blue background. This humble decoration on the vault is the church's way of offering undisputable proof that it sums up the cosmic order that the god who made the heavens is housed within it, but now time has almost erased it. (I forgot to check whether it is turned eastward towards Jerusalem and the sunrise.) And this lamp, shining dimly on the end of a wire hanging from the centre of the building's vaguely cross-shaped structure, what does it signify? Is it the light of the sun or the eternal light of the Spirit? Is it the mind of man which must remain ever-wakeful until the tragic final curtain?

Ah! Now here's something better, or more precise. In a relatively wide, deep recess (a chapel) two painted wooden statuettes face to face: St Blasius and St Roch. The region we are in has a long pastoral tradition. St Blasius and St Roch are the little patron saints of cattle and sheep. The inhabitants of P . . . have been crafty enough to obtain the protection of both saints simultaneously. At the back of the recess a rather sketchy painting (a fresco or a painting on wood? impossible to tell in the half-light) portrays the two saints in shepherd's smocks, their dogs at their feet, and carrying crooks which are drawn to look vaguely like bishop's crosiers. The damp has obliterated patches of sky, bits of meadow. Around the chapel, a low railing. Beyond the railing, coins, roughly-folded notes. Offerings, sacrifices. On their name days, the peasants burn a few bristles from the tails of diseased cows under their patron saints' noses.

In another, smaller recess, on a plinth, the statuette of a little patron saint of the family: St Anthony, who helps to find lost property. At his feet, a simple collection box. The saint's right toe is discoloured and worn down by the kisses of his supplicants.

But here, sovereign and placatory, on the right of the high altar, here is the Great Mother, who distanced herself from the Earth in the celestial mystery of a virginity made fruitful by God alone, the Father of all things. Eternal Virgin, yet at the same time the divine Mother of all men – and also known by such attractive names as The Gates of Heaven, The Morning Star, the Ivory Tower and the Consolation of the Afflicted. God is remote and terrible is the Father. The Virgin Mother is near. Absolute mother, absolute virgin, she conjures up mysteriously and poetically the feminine totality. Mother, she receives her children. Virgin, she reassures, for a virginity which has not been surrendered to anyone belongs to everyone. Great goddess in the process of formation (or revival), but reduced by a prudent theology to the rank of mediator, it is she who attracts the most wishes, the most support, the most prayers.

On the other side of the altar, Joseph holding a golden lily.

The lowly church presents the absolute, human Family, lit by the stars and the cosmos above and flanked by the two guardians of the regularity and the fertility of herds and flocks: the Mother whose infinite purity renders her universal – the earthly, fictitious husband, naïve and hesitant – the real, heavenly husband, the fearsome creative power that leads the drama – and her divine Son.

The heavenly family is visited by earthly families, who offer it their good luck and their misfortunes in homage. It gives them a magnified image of themselves. The heavenly and the earthly are joined: the human is still mingled with the heavenly.

And in the tabernacle, Power united with Goodness, fearsome despite the abstraction in which He has draped Himself (a circle of something white, light and dry, without taste or perfume): God, in a threatening offering! Should a sacrilege be committed (ah! the stories they tell in their pious conversations and their parish newspapers, of the host bleeding and speaking, of sudden deaths and unexpected conversions ...), should a sacrilege be committed, the world might collapse into nothingness! The firmament, that solid vault which supports the stars, might crumble. Fearful angels would trump forth the end of Time. For if God does not accomplish all that He is perfectly capable of as cosmic Father, vain, vindictive Creator, Lord of heaven, Master of good and evil, Throne of glory built upon azure, gold and banknotes, it is because He is also the Son, controlling Himself, checking His Justice and His Wrath, and showing Himself to be equally and at one and the same time very good, very mild, very brotherly towards the little human families which crawl along in this vale of tears.

If this church offers us the world and the human drama in résumé, it also gives us history. I can see Joan of Arc in her suit of armour; the Tricolour spreads its folds around her painted plaster breastplate; a plaque carries the names of the dead of the last war (the Great War, as the old men have long called it ...).

O Church, O Holy Church, when I finally managed to escape from your control I asked myself where your power came from. Now I can see through your sordid secrets, all the more obvious here for being without the beguiling adornments of art. How naïve people were to believe that they could get rid of you with a few sacrilegious protests. How holy men must have laughed at the 'freethinkers' (while pretending to be deeply shocked and making sure to retaliate at the earliest opportunity). Now I can see the fearful depths, the fearful reality of human alienation! O Holy Church, for centuries you have tapped and accumulated every illusion, every fiction, every vain hope, every frustration. You have garnered them in your houses like some precious harvest, and each generation, each era, each age of man adds something new to them. And now before my very eyes I see the terrors of human childhood, the worries of adolescence, the hopes and misgivings which greet adulthood, even the terrors and despair of old age, for it costs you nothing to say that the evening of the world is nigh and that Man is already old and will perish without realizing his potential! There are men who withdraw slightly from life so as to control it, using skills amassed by over more than twenty centuries of experience. And precisely because they have sacrificed themselves to the utmost, these men appear to be sacred; many of them believe they are sacred, and perhaps in a sense some of them are indeed sacred ... From the newborn babe's first breath to the dying man's last sigh they are there, ministering to questioning children, frightened virgins and tormented adolescents, to the anxieties of the destitute and even to the sufferings of the powerful; whenever man experiences a moment of weakness, there they are. For their old, ever-more-skilful tactics, for the 'spiritual' body of the Church, everything is grist to the mill – including doubts and heresies, and even attacks. The Church is nothing more and nothing less than the unlimited ability to absorb and accumulate the inhuman. Recently they have made their position more 'flexible', but I know that this is merely an attempt to absorb the enemy. Having condemned 'modernism' a dozen times, the Church now wants to be 'modern'. Her craftiest followers will say (they are already saying it) that she embodies man's progress towards the Divine, his centuries-old effort to transcend himself, and gradual divine revelation. But no – you are nothing more than man's alienation, the self torn asunder, a magic spell. I can read the message unadorned on the walls of this country church. They sum up your history, which is the history of human poverty! All your strategies are here in miniature, all the skills with which you have controlled and preserved the massive dehumanization which weighs men down, growing larger and larger like some living monster! You have served Roman emperors, feudal lords, absolute monarchs, a triumphant bourgeoisie. You were always on the side of the strongest (not without some craftily reticent manoeuvres to prove how independent and superior you were), but by appearing to stand up for the weak you ended up being the strongest of all. And now you have the gall to take up the cause of Man, promising to turn yesterday's slave into tomorrow's master! No. The trick is too obvious, and above all the task is too great. Until now the Holy Church has always been able to digest everything, but for the first time her mighty stomach may prove not strong enough. And she knows it. And she is afraid. And she wants to be everywhere, double-dealing, treble-dealing, winning on all the tables. But people can see it, and people know it. So what is to become of this accumulation of every conceivable myth and empty abstraction, of this extraordinary apparatus which combines the flaws of every State that ever was without even the virtue of some connection to the life of any one people or any one nation?

Sunday morning!

The bell has already rung twice, the first time slow and inoffensive, the second hurried, threatening, domineering. Away in the distant meadows, its reverberations have a melancholy sound; closer at hand, in the narrow streets of the apparently deserted village, it is something else again: it is the voice of the eternal father thundering down from the top of the belfry onto a barnyard of squat houses, scouring them, encircling every corner, every head, catching everyone by the ears, vibrating inside their skulls and their very bones. Come on, you childish, decrepit lot, get a move on!

The murmur of a threshing machine can be heard getting slowly louder, suddenly cutting out and then starting again. The godless are working on this holy day.

Through the open door and the clear window panes a soft, tawny sunlight redolent of October and the grape harvest floods the still-empty church; its beams dispel the Christian mystery which must have half-light; I can hear cockerels crowing, and the sound is astonishing.

Across the cold paving glides a black shape, the folds in its dress completely immobile. A widow! It's a widow! everything about her signals it. An unspeakably insipid, unspeakably dreary placidity fills her chubby face, settles at the bottom of her faded cheeks. Fat and stiff, she glides noiselessly. Surely nothing has ever disturbed this stagnating placidity. Surely she was born a widow. They say she is very good to the church; she comes to sweep it, tending to the decorations, replacing the dying flowers with armfuls of fresh ones; she is intoxicated with her own humility and self-effacement; she picks up the rubbish with her bare hands; she is the handmaiden of this holy house – but under her falsely pious modesty what pride lies hidden!

A sudden flight of sparrows and pigeons, a loud scuffling of chairs and benches; the clatter of clogs on the stone floor. Hands are dipped into the font and chests are hurriedly crossed. 'Religion' is about to attempt to 're-link' all this disparate human material into a community: old women enveloped in the black shroud of their *capulet,*[5] sly, impatient urchins, shopkeepers' daughters who have come to show off their Sunday dresses, one or two men. On one side, the guild of women. On the other, farther back, nearer the door, the men. They are the last to come and the first to leave. But nevertheless they come, they are there, holding their berets rolled up in their hands.

How many people here are genuine believers, not satisfied with gestures but ardently grasping their faith as an *object*? This young girl, perhaps, her whole body tensed and bent forward on her chair, gazing spellbound on the great Christ, his pink body stained with the blood of his wounds? There is something distraught about her eyes which contrasts with the peacefulness, the already unutterably bored peacefulness, of her face. Someone else cut out to be a widow, or an eternal virgin? With what sacrifices is she purchasing this peace of the true believer, innocently confident in an earthly and heavenly future, a little soul in the arms of the Father, a little lamb beneath the shepherd's crook? Contemptible, unfought-for peace; whatever deprivations and conflicts may exist, they are placidly ignored, disdained; childishness is prolonged, cultivated even – a premature annihilation; I recognize you, despicable peace of my childhood! But what torments it takes just to be free, just to destroy these ashes! They say that the true believer must always experience conflict, that faith is born of anguish. But what anguish? Yes, maybe the anguish which lies bogged down and rotting in its own peacefulness, where the deepest 'deprivations' are indistinguishable from mystical certainties! And yet surely they know that when it becomes clear that faith does not even exist, that it is an illusion, that there is nothing to have faith in, that there is only nothingness, then anguish is born in its place; and that once faith is gone it leaves the blood contaminated with nothingness. Then anyone who has been alienated and dehumanized by his childhood faith will begin a desperate quest for a pathway, a link with life; but his lost illusions still obsess him; his need for faith fills him with anguish, and he tries in vain to keep on believing. What a pack of lies: it is faith which produces anguish, like a painful scar, nothingness activated . . .

Mass begins, mundane, reduced to its bare essentials, with no grand organ, canon's kiss or plumed verger.

Basically, this Catholic Mass revives the oldest form of dramatic art, tragedy: an audience which participates in the action, a choir which responds to the protagonist, who conjures up the founder of the community, his life, his destiny and the inevitable catastrophe, the sacrifice and death of the hero. In the ceremony, the hero comes back to life and the participants identify with him; through him they can re-form a community which is both cosmic and human.

In a sense the Catholic model turns out to be richer, more complex than tragedy. What a poetic drama, where anyone watching who is not insensitive or immune is challenged, gripped if only by the style and flow of imagery – forced to participate, drawn on by the senses even into the realm of theological meanings! And here in this country church there is not even music, nor the magnificence and mystique of stained glass and sumptuous ceremony. What a combination – the art of fascination and the art of control! And until now there has been nothing to compare with its versatility. Mass for marriage, Mass for the dead, Mass for soldiers and Mass to bless the coming battle, High Mass in cathedrals (and one day I will describe a cathedral, in minute detail ...), Low Mass in suburban and village churches ... Yes, wherever something of man is born or dies, wherever there is some-thing vulnerable, like a child, like love, or something threatened, like a soldier, like a peasant, there will the divine tragedy be acted out. A bench and an upturned crate make as good a stage as the most extravagant marble altar.

On the other hand, the pathos is less than in high tragedy, and less perceptible. Despite the scope of the subject, the drama is far from perfect. Too many abstractions have had to be included, too many symbols piled one upon the other, too many gestures for their own sake. The fall in quality is inevitable! In the first place the foreign language,[6] while helping to reinforce the mystery, limits the number of dramatic effects available (it is true that the sermon in French comes just at the right time to compensate for this). The rhythm is slow. The audience is bored to tears by the respectful abstraction of it all. Religion will end in boredom; and to offer boredom to the Lord is hardly a living sacrifice. (Yet as I write these lines, I wonder if I'm not making a crude mistake. Magic has always gone hand in hand with emotion, hope and terror, and still does. But are there such things as religious 'emotions'? Probably no more so than there is a 'psychol-ogical state' – consciousness or thought without an object – that could be called 'faith'. These are ideological fictions. Surely religion, like theology, metaphysics, ceremonies, academic literature and official poets, has always been boring. This has never been a hindrance, because one of the aims of 'spiritual' discipline and asceticism has always been precisely to disguise and to transfigure this living boredom . . .)

The divine tragedy is overladen with riches. The journey the solemn words and gestures of the protagonist take us on is too long. Here too, as in the church itself, the listener, his suspicions aroused, discovers the secretions, the accumulated sediments of centuries. In a minute we shall be in a market stall in Alexandria, where some wily cabbalists are discussing mystical names and entities with a bearded Jew who has just arrived from Athens: *In initio erat Verbum* . . .[7] For the moment we are in the age of kings and princes. Armed with their pikes and with a great roar the infantry are setting off in a cloud of dust behind the war chariots, wheels bristling with sharp blades. And the High Priest invokes the divine Names: '*Deus, deus, Sabaoth* . . . Lord of Hosts! . . .' Did Judith murmur these words as she carried away Holofernes's head in her bag, his eyes closed in the voluptuousness of death? Yes, God was always on the side of the strongest, since victory proved whose side God was on, and defeat was explained as the wages of His Wrath. How childish, simple and profound divine mystification is! Lord of Hosts, Lord of Armies! But what armies, and armed with what arms? . . . But hush! We mustn't be flippant. Pay attention.

Introibo ad altare Dei, qui laetificat juventutem meam. What magnificent poetry. 'The God who makes my youth rejoice.' Really moving, really splendid, isn't it, this marriage of youth and eternity! Doesn't anyone here think about the young people who have been burdened, sickened, poisoned, by the philtre of the absolute, the venom of sin and the yearning for the dreary peace of innocence? What can these words mean to these people? Have they discovered how to avoid mental torture? Can I have been the last of the faithful?

I mustn't get annoyed. I merely want to understand 'their' secrets. *Et Verbum Caro factum est.* More abstractions, more symbols, but this time with the fascinating information that they are now merged with life. The Word, the mysterious, holy, magic Word of Words, is made flesh! Does that mean that speech takes the form of a tongue, or a mouth?

Maybe.

And now the priest turns towards the audience and begins making grander gestures. He is ageless, young rather than old; the son of a peasant, one can tell from his face; a slight figure in a tight black robe, but amplified by the alb and surplice; a long, pale countenance, bony and bluish with beard; a shy man, with little authority in the village. They say he has a weak chest, and that he's under his sister's thumb. But here he is another man; he becomes assured, imposing. Almost too much so: some of his gestures seem to be lifting some enormous but meaningless weight up towards heaven, and it's rather comical.

Now the moment for the holy meal has come. Time once more for the most venerable of these rituals. Will the bread and wine reanimate the faithful once again, restoring their oneness with nature and humanity? But how cold it all is, and how dried up! Where's the joy? Where are the overflowing cups and the huge, consecrated loaves of bread? Only the priest gets to eat and drink, consuming the principles of life in the form of the two basics, bread and wine. Then, to a couple of old women in black and the mystical young girl, he will hand out an insipid symbol of infinity . . .

So this is what the holy meal has been reduced to: torn away from community to be accomplished by those who mediate between us and the absolute – torn away from the life of the senses and from real festivity to become symbolic, abstract, distant. Transferred entirely to another plane – a spiritual and 'interior' plane, apparently. But where is the human community for these people in black I see filing back to their seats, their eyes half-closed, their hands clasped piously together, absorbed in the dreariness of what their mouths and their souls have just tasted? A caricature of a community! Profound? Inner? No! These dehumanized beings are self-absorbed from the moment they are born to the moment they die, and the only community they know is fictitious and abstract.

I remember a time when I hated them because I still loved them. My adolescence was drawing to a close – an adolescence which had lived through more than one season in hell. Hatching fiendish plans of revenge, I continued going to church and mixing with priests. Even the most terrible acts of violence seemed too tame, too simple. My friends made do with various small sacrilegious gestures which to me seemed meaningless (it was the time when Breton tied a crucifix to the lavatory chain in his toilet and thought he was exterminating Christianity). I thought about vaster – but no less naïve – ventures. I studied the history of the Church in the hope of ferreting out a vintage heresy I could resurrect, an indestructible, indigestible heresy with which to torpedo the Church. Jansen's? Too dry, too terribly eighteenth-century petty bourgeois, and as far as boredom goes, his *Augustinus* beats even the *Summa Theologiae*.[8] Only one heresy appealed to me. Everyone can see for themselves how far the Holy Ghost is absent from the Church; it appears only in the dubious shape of a pigeon, or as an excellent teacher of modern languages. So I started planning a revival of the cult of the Holy Ghost, making it as much a living presence as the other personalities in the Holy Trinity. I wanted to show that the incarnation of the Son was not enough to save the world (which is obvious), and to proclaim the imminent arrival and incarnation of the Holy Ghost. As a prophet of the Holy Ghost, I would have carried my ardent prediction into the very bosom of the Church, in the name of a neglected dogma. I would have paid anything – made any 'sacrifice' – in order to spread this heresy, and the best of it was that I didn't even believe in it! I wanted revenge so much, I would even have been willing to become a martyr.

One fine day, in an effort to think clearly which from this distance may seem facile, even comical, I understood that my whole satanic venture was just another way of *perpetuating mystical themes*; that by going in that direction I was simply a future prodigal son – a man in despair – one of the last believers – that I hadn't realized just how extraordinarily naïve the whole plan was (it wasn't as though the Church had never been attacked before!) ... and just how *clerical* my fiendish scheme really was!

So for a little while I adopted one of Nietzsche's great visionary theories. Dionysius – the living cosmos – is born and dies in order to be reborn. The Eternal Recurrence, the Great Year, the periodic Return of things, which so many wise men and philosophers have sensed are not and cannot be simply a dry, frigid theory. The universe, the Whole, is a god who becomes and accedes to consciousness within man; he is a Whole, but dismembered into fragments which also like him know suffering and joy. Through the torments of his cosmic journey, through the tortures of human consciousness, his eternal destiny moves on with each new cycle towards the joy of supreme consciousness, and at the same time towards the tragic catastrophe, the death of the planets and the stars, the new ice age or the gigantic atomic cataclysm. The god's destiny is accomplished; and because the god – creative energy – cannot end, he is reborn; he starts again. Spring of springtimes and everlasting joy. Sunrise, immense procession of resurrections, ascension of life, and also pain, immortal death of all forms and all past moments, winters and old age, cataclysms and massacres, a billion tragedies in the cosmic Tragedy ...

Since the sufferings of Dionysius could be identified with Christ on the cross, since all the symbols of art and religion must take on a new meaning in Dionysius, I dreamt of a total celebration, a Mass and a tragedy, intense and absolute, extraordinarily poetic and powerfully dramatic, which would rejoice in the tragic destiny of Nature, finite and infinite, divine and human, joyful and harrowing! ... Zarathustra would have been merely the prophet and the herald of this super-human Celebration, this offering and supreme sacrifice of man to the absolute! ...

Such are the difficulties we face when we try to liberate ourselves from mystiques, from our predilection for illusory greatness, for self-effacement, for the sacrifice of man ... The cruellest and most rigorous of self-examinations will always unearth some hidden radicle of alienation, of the perverse pleasure alienation of the self affords! ...

To conclude these notes, I would like to sum up briefly what dialectical method can bring to such chaos:

(a) *It allows us to* re-establish *order and reason in ideas*

Using Marxist method, every cultivated and truly 'modern' man will soon be able to look at the irksome and incomprehensible mumbo-jumbo of our towns and villages, our churches and our works of art, and read them out loud, like an open book.

(b) *Marxist method enables us to understand the 'secrets', the obscure aspects of the 'social mystery' and of history*

Thus Catholicism appears in its historical truth as a 'movement' rather than a doctrine, a vast movement, thoroughly skilled in the art of assimilation, which never creates anything new but in which nothing is ever lost, particularly the oldest and most tenacious myths, which for various reasons go on being accepted or being seen as acceptable by the vast majority (agrarian myths).

The mystifying skill of this 'movement' can be measured by the fact that it has been able to disguise itself as a rigid dogmatism. In fact it is exactly the opposite (like a crafty child who slides along while insisting he is sitting still). And this disguise is a cover for its press-gang tactics. Anyone who criticizes 'Catholic dogmatism' in the name of free-thinking and independent individuality is being ridiculously naïve.

This movement taps human weakness and helplessness; to be absolutely exact, it 'capitalizes' on them. Where does it get its universality from? From its ability to live with all the myths and rituals it has taken from the various social formations, to superimpose them and overdetermine them, and to churn them back in the guise of doctrinal 'rigour'.

This unstructured syncretism has been working unceasingly since the death of Christ up until the present day, and it is obviously the Church, in its role as a social and *political* organism, which props it up.

(c) *The problem of the Human cannot be resolved by inventing new rituals, be they spiritual or material, mystical or aesthetic, public or private*

That path (which is the one nearly all our philosophers and men of letters have followed) is the path of 'alienation'.

The Church has tapped and accumulated all human (or rather 'inhuman') alienation.

Its power comes from the fact that *it penetrates everyday life*. On the one hand it has created a dehumanized ceremonial, an official magnificence, an extra-national State, an abstract theory; on the other, it has produced an extremely subtle and precise psychological and moral technique.

In every act of one's immediate life, no matter how insignificant, religion can be present: in the 'internalized' form of a ritual or in the external form of the priest who listens, understands, advises, reprimands or 'pardons'.

Past religion and past moral doctrines (which deep down are always religious) tell us *what we must do* (according to them) in an everyday life which seems all the more derelict, uncertain and humiliated for the fact that the life of the mind, of knowledge, of art, of the State, is getting more and more vast, more 'elevated' and more ritualized.

We spend each day of our lives crawling along at ground level, while the 'superior' moments fly away into the far reaches of the stratosphere. Religion 'snowballs' as a result of all the practical helplessness of human beings, constituting an immense obstacle; it is there in life's most infinitesimal detail, knowing the weaknesses and provoking them, breathing in the positive substance of everyday life and *concentrating its negative aspects*. At each everyday event, at each emotive, disturbing moment when something begins or when something ends, religion will raise its head; it reassures, consoles, and above all supplies an attitude, a way to behave. It tells us what we must do (in its view – but until now no one has offered an alternative) when faced with death or birth. It provides a ceremonial; it relieves people not only of the embarrassment of not knowing what to do and what to say, but also of the fear and remorse their embarrassment produces (as though all misfortunes, past, present or future, were in any way their fault). It gives everyone the impression of doing something. The ritual gesture when a funeral procession goes by, words of insult, an 'A-Dieu' when we part, a wish, a propitious phrase of greeting or thanks – all such everyday attitudes still come down to us from magic and religion; they are really religious, or potentially so. And that is where in the end the secret of religion's strength lies.

In this way the illusion by which religion deceives us (that vain and ever-broken promise of community, of the power to act) tends to be born again with every action in our everyday lives. Exactly as, on another level, economic fetishism is reanimated every single time an individual, unaware of the social structure, uses a coin or a note to buy the product of human labour, transformed into a commodity.

(d) *The problem posed by Marxism is thus revealed in all its breadth*

We now know that Marxism wants to transform the 'world' (and no longer just to interpret it). But we need to understand fully what we mean by the term 'world'. It is not simply a matter of intensifying production, of cultivating new spaces, of industrializing agriculture, of building giant factories, of changing the State and then finishing once and for all with that monster, 'of all cold monsters the coldest'. These are merely means to an end.

And what is that end? It is the transformation of life in its smallest, most everyday detail. The world is man's future because man is the creator of his 'world'. And the problem is not simply to change the idea of man, to found the idea of the *total* man – nature and consciousness, instinct and lucidity, power over things and over his own products – and to place it at the apex of culture. The problem is not simply to achieve a dialectical unity of knowledge, to bring together the results of all the sciences in an organized and rational encyclopedic system. It is not simply to form a new type of men or to establish new general relations between men.

Those are still only means. The end, the aim, is to make thought – the power of man, the participation in and the consciousness of that power – intervene in life in its humblest detail.

More ambitious, more difficult, more remote than the means, the aim is to change life, lucidly to recreate everyday life. This is the exact opposite of the aim and the essence of religion.

By revealing its positive and negative duality, the critique of everyday life will help to pose and resolve the problem of life itself.

Human culture and consciousness incorporate every conquest, every past moment of history. In contrast, religion *accumulates* all man's helplessness. It offers a critique of life; it is itself that critique: a reactionary, destructive critique. Marxism, the consciousness of the new man and the new consciousness of the world, offers an effective, constructive critique of life. And Marxism alone! ...

6

What Is Possible

When the world the sun shines on is always new, how could everyday life be forever unchangeable, unchangeable in its boredom, its greyness, its repetition of the same actions?

Many who have lost faith in the human, and who get hypocritically emotional about the 'immemorial gestures' of peasants, mothers, or housewives, think it is ...

Everyday life is not unchangeable; it can decline, therefore it changes. And moreover the only genuine, profound human changes are those which cut into this substance and make their mark upon it.

It is fairly easy to demonstrate decline using one simple, important example, life in the country, because in many ways the traces of 'another life', a community life, are still more perceptible there than elsewhere.

A later instalment of the present study will endeavour to describe the decline of everyday life, on industrial housing estates, in so-called 'modern' everyday activity.

But for the moment we have to consider another factor, one which will make our investigation yet more complicated. Just as this decline proceeds to its ultimate consequences, *possibilities* become more apparent, more immediately perceptible, in this sphere than elsewhere.

Human life can decline and it can progress. Up until now it has followed this dual movement: on the one hand, and in one direction, decline; on the other hand, and in another direction, progress.

Life has 'got better', and we cannot entirely disagree with those optimists who insist obstinately that, favoured by some unspecified theological or metaphysical Providence, the human species is slowly advancing like a well-drilled army along a pre-ordained path from barbarism to civilization. They are not entirely wrong; and likewise the theory of 'decadence' is just as metaphysical – and just as dubious – as the optimism of the partisans of Progress, which it opposes. The abstract idea of 'decadence' in general conceals a very real decadence, present in the world today, albeit only momentarily: the decadence of the bourgeoisie.

And yet the optimistic idea of 'Progress' lacks flexibility and dialectical understanding. It fails to grasp the different aspects of human becoming. *Up until now* progress has carried within itself certain elements of regression. Spontaneous, objective, like a process of nature, this 'progress' has not been guided by a Reason. Thought has realized this at a very late stage; and it is only now that efficient Reason is making an attempt to penetrate it actively, to understand its laws and to transform it into a rational progress without negative repercussions.

Human life has progressed: material progress, 'moral' progress – but that is only part of the truth. The deprivation, the alienation of life is its other aspect.

In reply to the naïve theoreticians of complete, continuous progress we must demonstrate in particular the decline of everyday life since the community of Antiquity, and man's growing alienation. We must present a firm answer to the Robinson Crusoe-esque idyllists who denigrate the present and theorize the 'good old days', by demonstrating the progress that has been accomplished: in knowledge and in consciousness, in power over nature. Above all we must demonstrate the breadth and magnificence of the *possibilities* which are opening out for man; and which are so really possible, so near, so rationally achievable (once the *political* obstacles are shattered) that this proximity of what is possible can be taken for *one of the meanings* (painfully and frighteningly unconscious) of the famous 'modern disquiet', the anguish caused by 'existence' as it still is! ...

Now the simplest, most mundane events can show how economic and technical 'progress' has worked.

Several years ago a world-wide firm which was trying to extend the market and put a rival firm out of business decided to distribute paraffin lamps to Chinese peasants free of charge, while its rivals, less 'generous' or less shrewd, went on selling them. And now in several million poverty-stricken Chinese households artificial light (an immense progress) shines down on muddy floors and rotten matting – because even peasants who cannot afford to buy a lamp can afford to buy paraffin ... The 'progress' capitalism brings, like its 'generosity', is just a means to an end: profit.

To take an example from much nearer home: in France, in the Pyrenees, just a stone's throw from dams and powerful ultra-modern hydro-electric installations, there are many hamlets, thousands of houses where peasants live almost as 'primitive' a life as the Chinese. They have no electric light either. Elsewhere, more or less everywhere, in town and country alike, electric light illuminates the peeling plaster of slums and the sordid walls of hovels. (Although even in Paris there are still houses and flats without modern lighting.)

Mundane, without literary interest, and picked at random from an infinity of possible equally significant examples, these facts show that up until now 'progress' has affected existing social realities only secondarily, modifying them as little as possible, according to the strict dictates of capitalist profitability. The important thing is that human beings be profitable, not that their lives be changed. As far as is possible, capitalism respects the pre-existing shape and contours of people's lives. Only grudgingly, so to speak, does it bring about any change. Criticism of capitalism as a contradictory 'mode of production' which is dying as a result of its contradictions is strengthened by criticism of capitalism as the distributor of the wealth and 'progress' it has produced.

And so, constantly staring us in the face, mundane and therefore generally unnoticed – whereas in the future it will be seen as a characteristic and scandalous trait of our era, the era of the decadent bourgeoisie – is this fact: that *life is lagging behind what is possible*, that it is retarded. What incredible backwardness. This has up until now been constantly increasing; it parallels the growing disparity between the knowledge of the contemporary physicist and that of the 'average' man, or between that of the Marxist sociologist and that of the bourgeois politician.

Once pointed out, the contrast becomes staggeringly obvious, blinding; it is to be found everywhere, whichever way we turn, and never ceases to amaze.

Compare an 'average' house in one of our towns, not with an ostentatious and absurd palace, nor with some characteristically grotesque dwelling of the haute bourgeoisie, but rather with a 'modern' industrial installation – a power station, for example. Here we find hyper-precise technology, light, and a dazzling cleanliness; power methodically condensed into strictly contoured appliances. These machines are so amazing in the way they conceal their strength beneath an apparent immobility that more than one writer has used them to resuscitate the feeling of sanctity, of awe in the face of 'powerful', motionless fetishes. On the other hand, in the house where decent, 'average' people live out their everyday lives, all is petty, disorganized; dusty nooks and crannies; mean, pretentious furniture; petty-bourgeois knick-knacks; the strictly useless is accompanied by the absence of anything useful – and yet the cult of utility reigns; dark rooms; feather dusters, brooms, carpets which are shaken out of the window ...

Which is to say nothing of workers' lodgings and peasants' houses where the doorstep is a pool of liquid manure!

The power acquired thanks to technology and thought thus remains outside of life, above it, far away. And, if asked, very few of those affected by these simple facts would be able to account for them or for their consequences.

Likewise, compare an ordinary street, with its little shops, its rows of windows stretching drearily along like gravestones in a cemetery, with any monument screaming power and arrogance ...

In this country there is a striking, strident contrast between the appearance of things and the symbols of power.

In this quiet little town, there is nothing to make us think of war, of the tragic feeling of life, of the will to power.

Between the houses of the bourgeoisie, heavy, angular, with their ornamental structure, the breeze is heavy with a disturbing scent of lindens. In the nearby canal, thousands of frogs can be heard croaking interminably. Priests stroll by, little girls, prisoners, basset hounds. In a belfry daubed with green and gold, the bells are ringing. There must be a mistake somewhere in this picture ...

And at a bend in the road, that mistake becomes clear: a monument to some victory or other: a conglomeration of steel and stone, of predatory eagles and sharp swords, of taut muscles and stubborn faces ...[1]

That was how Pierre Courtade saw Germany just after the war. But the mistake in question was not specifically German. It was universal. A mistake that allowed human power to become the will of a few men to hold power. That allowed power to be placed outside of life, to be transposed to the level of State control – in a word, to be *alienated.* And it is not only in Germany that the contrast is so blatantly obvious between the painful or ridiculous situation of 'private' life (even among privileged people) and a power which only becomes 'public' in absurdly externalized forms and manifestations. Factories that are technological marvels (and 'private' properties!) are paralleled by monuments which *magically* concentrate not only the prestige of the State and the power of the rulers but also all the artificiality of empty celebrations, ceremonies and rituals – not to mention a host of mystical ideas, grandiose theories and 'official' abstractions; their only real purpose, however, is to proclaim, to express – and indeed to betray – the 'will to power'. The will to power? It is real power, stolen from the community (itself smashed and atomized into 'private' individuals) and turned into power over men, set up brutally above men, instead of being power over things. And it is precisely into things that it wishes to transform human beings, 'depriving' them of any real consciousness, and turning them into economic and political tools. As life drags on in all its weakness and humiliation, the will to power expresses itself in these cancerous monstrosities; to admire one of them is not only stupid and tasteless, it also amounts to acquiescence in a potential holocaust.

Everything great and splendid is founded on power and wealth. They are the basis of beauty. This is why the rebel and the anarchic protester who decries all of history and all the works of past centuries because he sees in them only the skills and the threat of domination is making a mistake. He sees alienated forms, but not the greatness within. The rebel can only see to the end of his own 'private' consciousness, which he levels against *everything* human, confusing the oppressors with the oppressed masses, who were nevertheless the basis and the meaning of history and past works. Castles, palaces, cathedrals, fortresses, all speak in their various ways of the greatness and the strength of the people who built them and against whom they were built. This real greatness shines through the fake grandeur of rulers and endows these buildings with a lasting 'beauty'. The bourgeoisie is alone in having given its buildings a single, over-obvious meaning, impoverished, deprived of reality: that meaning is abstract wealth and brutal domination; that is why it has succeeded in producing perfect ugliness and perfect vulgarity. The man who denigrates the past, and who nearly always denigrates the present and the possible as well, cannot understand this dialectic of art, this dual character of works and of history. He does not even sense it. Protesting against bourgeois stupidity and oppression, the anarchic individualist is enclosed in 'private' consciousness, itself a product of the bourgeois era, and no longer understands human power and the community upon which that power is founded. The historical forms of this community, from the village to the nation, escape him. He is, and only wants to be, a human atom (in the scientifically archaic sense of the word, where 'atom' meant the lowest isolatable reality). By following alienation to its very extremes he is merely playing into the hands of the bourgeoisie. Embryonic or unconscious, this kind of anarchism is very widespread. There is a kind of revolt, a kind of criticism of life, that implies and results in the acceptance of this life *as the only one possible*. As a direct consequence this attitude precludes any understanding of *what is humanly possible*.

Our towns may be read like a book (the comparison is not completely exact: a book signifies, whereas towns and rural areas 'are' what they signify). Towns show us the history of power and of human possibilities which, while becoming increasingly broad, have at the same time been increasingly taken over and controlled, until that point of total control, set up entirely above life and community, which is bourgeois control.

Rural areas tell us above all of the dislocation of primitive community, of poor technical progress, of the decline of a way of life which is much less different from that of ancient times than is generally believed. Towns tell us of the almost total decomposition of community, of the atomization of society into 'private' individuals as a result of the activities and way of life of a bourgeoisie which still dares claim that it represents 'the general interest'.

On the other hand, provided our purpose in deciphering them is neither the search for the superficially picturesque (after the fashion of a Jules Romains),[2] nor the search for would-be modern myths, then our towns will show us something quite different: the rebirth and reforming of community in factories and working-class neighbourhoods. There, other modes of everyday living, other needs, other requirements, are entering into conflict with the modalities of everyday life as imposed by the capitalist structure of society and life, and tending to re-establish a solidarity, an effective alliance between individuals and groups. How does this conflict manifest itself? Constantly beaten down, constantly born again, how is this solidarity expressed? How does it translate in concrete terms? This is exactly what the positive side of the *Critique of Everyday Life* should discover and describe.

It is not the academic literary hacks from the smart side of town, nor the 'populists' in search of ever-more-picturesque poverty to stimulate their descriptive whimsy, who can understand industrial housing estates and working-class neighbourhoods. Nor is it those false dreamers 'who leisurely imagine sublime anguishes, revel in lunacies, abysses and other evasions, while harsh reality is imprisoning the bodies, minds, days and nights of millions of men and women ...'.[3] Among the rare valid expressions of this reality are the *Poems by American Workers* translated in 1930 by Norbert Guterman and Pierre Morhange.[4] Listen to Martin Russak, a silk weaver:

> And so I was born, how strange, how strange,
> In the city of many tongues
> And came when a baby in arms and remain
> Rootless and restless in the city of silk ...[5]

> O Paterson, my home, my town, Paterson,
> With your church-spires and chimneys racing for heaven,
> With your statue of justice on your court-house dome
> Who has lost her sword and her scales and stands
> Blindfold and helpless in the smoky air, –
> When I lie on the cliffs at Garret Rock
> Eating a bag of lunch at noon,
> And considering you spread out below
> I could weep for myself and you, if only
> I did not know how to curse ...[6]

But Miriam Allen adds a moving message of combat to this curse:

> When you hear a bird singing, remember Sacco and Vanzetti
> When you see a wild flower growing, remember Sacco and Vanzetti ...[7]

and Ralph Cheyney adds a message of hope:

These little fingers soft as the fronds of a fern
must grow hard to grab an axe, pick, spade ...
In your dimpled hands and those of millions of other
working-class babies – white, black, yellow –
the future of the world rests.
Open your little mouth and bawl!
Clench those rosebud fists!
Suck hard so they'll grow strong
to smash the old world in which you were born ...[8]

Since these *Poems by American Workers* were published, American novelists have shown us the contradictions of that illustrious America and the poverty and slavery her real greatness implies.

While our own literature remained academic, abstract, psychological, *outside of everyday life* (to such a point that our most intelligent critics and novelists only noticed Faulkner and Dos Passos for their technical innovations!), American writers were accomplishing something we had not even been able to begin: the trial of so-called 'modern' life, the analysis of its contradictory aspects, poverty and wealth, weakness and power, blindness and lucidity, individuality and massiveness ...

A curious situation. In America, a country where the general crisis of capitalism has scarcely begun, and where imperialism is alive and well, writers have been able to open their eyes to what is nearest to them – everyday life – and to find themes in it which amaze us by their violence and originality. But in France, where the economic crisis has already turned into a political crisis, a crisis of the social structure and of culture, a crisis of life (it is becoming impossible for the French to go on living as before, or to even want to, although there are plenty who try to turn the clock back at every possible opportunity ...), writers are seeking the themes and the content of their books *far away*, in the unreal, the surreal, in abstraction, in pure technical virtuosity.

Instead of looking lucidly around them, they lose themselves in a distant vision (and it is taken as read that every young poet must live 'in ecstasy', 'out of his mind', intoxicated if only with words). In our country, with its tradition of struggle, there is not a single book to compare with Steinbeck's *In Dubious Battle*.

Considered as a symptom, what does the situation of French literature tell us? Could it be a proof of decadence or creative

255

impotence? Or does it indicate that for a people like us with an old culture everyday life has lost that spontaneity, that violence, that tangible, dramatic side which American writers have been able to uncover and make conscious?

Impotence? To a degree, yes. The comparison between American books and French books which have been inspired by them, is instructive. Monsieur Sartre's *Roads to Freedom* reveals an indisputable literary talent and above all a rather remarkable gift of *workmanship*; the content has not determined the form; the first wish of this over-intellectual, over-abstract novelist has been to master technique; his starting point is a formula, a procedure, and he even calls upon an entire metaphysics to help him out. Just as reading Faulkner forcefully engages our interest, awakening a thousand undefined emotions swarming beneath the everyday surface – cruelty, sexuality, surprise, worry, etc. – so reading Sartre is an increasingly cold, dry experience, overladen with falsely concrete details (noted down deliberately and consciously in order to be concrete!), without passion, without interest in life, without youth and without maturity, and quite simply boring.

Yes, a certain impotence. And above all a lack of vitality, an abstract attitude, a lack of direct and immediate interest in human beings and in the violence and drama of their lives. For in France, in spite of our relatively relaxed social mores, the lower classes – workers or peasants – would appear to enjoy their fair share of dramas, spontaneity, passions, elemental violence and humanity. Be that as it may, we do not know how to see them or to understand them. And it is the dreary, rigidly codified lives of the petty bourgeoisie and the middle classes which have imposed their style upon nearly all our literature. Class divisions, which are much more accentuated here than in America, stop our writers from watching the people live and from knowing how to watch them. For many years the rigid parameters and false freedom of petty-bourgeois life were thought to express eternal Reason, and to prove its validity. And when these parameters are threatened, petty-bourgeois anguish takes on metaphysical proportions for one and all. Only a few writers (Gide, Valéry Larbaud, Cocteau) have brought another element to our literature: facility, a free and easy air, cynicism, refined sophistication, the exquisite taste of the cultivated haute bourgeoisie; but no new way of looking at the world – Monsieur Gide's ridiculous claims notwithstanding.[9]

Petty-bourgeois individualism has reached the extreme limit of exhaustion, and that goes for the intellectual as well as the writer. In the 'human sand', each grain, which is so dreadfully similar to all the others (unless we look at it through a psychological microscope) thinks it is frightfully original, and even unique! *Individualism ends up as the impersonality of the individual.* It is the dialectical result of the 'private' consciousness and of its internal contradiction: the separation of the human being from the human. Nothing is easier to express literally than the abstract 'psychology' of this individuality, devoid of any content which might be difficult to express. Only a little knowledge of grammar is necessary. And there is plenty of that around! But unfortunately the tone of all these confidences and all these descriptions happens to be that of *impersonality*; therefore of boredom. The accusation that the Marxist dialectician levels at modern French literature as a whole is not that it expresses individuality, but rather that it expresses only false individuality, *a façade of individuality*, and abstraction. Nor is it by working in an element of 'anguish' that a young writer can give his descriptions or his story the direct, visual, physical, moving style, so much more individualized and varied, that one finds in Faulkner's characters and novels!

To see things properly, it is not enough simply to look. People who look at life – purely as witnesses, spectators – are not rare; and one of the strangest lessons to be learnt from our literature is that professional spectators, judges by vocation and witnesses by predestination, contemplate life with less understanding and grasp of its rich content than anyone else. There really is no substitute for participation!

And it is not that there is any shortage of subjects to write about. For example: in France the mixture of moral doctrines and politics has produced a species composed of some very varied types: the worthy-father type, the sexton type, the Pharisee type sweating with fear and guilty conscience, etc. Shared characteristics: immensely serious, generous or morally scrupulous to a fault, the kind of loyalty that fully expects its reward (in honours and influence, not to mention money), a few moral ideals linked to a very limited sense of immediate realities, and above all an excessive sensitivity (any attack on their ideals is taken as a personal affront!). Meeting places and social habitat of the species in question: certain political parties, which shall remain nameless.

This human species, so characteristic of our times, has not yet appeared in literature. And yet how picturesque, how comic it is! (There is nothing like the sight of an old lag from the dungeons of political idealism haranguing a critic (actually quite moderate), beating his breast with a combination of self-pity, terror at such sacrilege, and disappointment for not yet having received the honours and the positions his long martyrdom deserve, shouting: 'You young wretch, you are insulting an old Republican!' . . .)

Why this silence? Could it not be that a large proportion of our witnesses and judges – of our writers – are recruited from these same Pharisees of idealism?

And is this not the reason why our era has allowed itself to be literally dominated by Gidean cynicism – in spite of everything that might be said, and indeed has been said, against Gide?

Abstract culture places an almost opaque screen (if it were completely opaque the situation would be simpler) between the cultivated man and everyday life.

Abstract culture not only supplies him with words and ideas, but also with an attitude which forces him to seek the 'meaning' of his life and his consciousness outside of himself and his real relations with the world.

The exact nature of 'deprivation' and the relation between the 'private' consciousness and the 'public' consciousness changes as a function of social level. For the 'cultivated' man (one who has received what is traditionally called 'culture'), this relation undergoes a curious inversion. For him 'his' thought, 'his' culture, are a part of his most intimate self. He carries them with him in the silence of his office, in the even-more barren silence of his 'inner life'. He tends to forget that thought is human and not 'private'. He will readily talk about his 'social life' when he means his relations with family, friends and business partners, i.e. his 'private' life. This inversion of consciousness does not constitute an absolute error, for there is no such thing as an absolute error. In the course of his historical development, the individual has to take thought 'upon himself'. This is one of the meanings of the Cartesian 'Cogito'. In the context of individualism, of a highly fragmented division of labour, and of the division of society into classes, this absolutely necessary action, this 'assumption' of human thought, finds expression in an inversion of consciousness – a relative error, but one which has serious consequences. The 'cultivated' man forgets the social foundations of 'his' thought. When he looks for the secret of his behaviour and his situation in words and ideas that he has received from without, he imagines that he is looking 'deep into himself'. And at the very moment when he thinks the search for his own self is over, he is actually leaving himself, taking the path of alienation. Consequently his practical, everyday life, his *real* relations, he sees as external to him. The structure of his consciousness tends to annihilate any genuine consciousness of 'his' life. In individual life this error of structural origin is expressed by conflicts, by specific 'psychological' errors, by a shift of consciousness (so exacerbating what has up to now been the natural and inevitable tendency of consciousness to lag behind). Without resorting to any kind of psychoanalysis, we can use this error, to which all 'cultivated' consciousnesses within an individualist structure are prone, to explain a number of barely 'a-social' minor neuroses, accepted if not encouraged, which have until now been considered the bailiwick of psychoanalysis.

To attain a consciousness of life *in its movement* (its reality and its unfulfilled possibilities), but without losing anything of culture, our first task must be to break the limiting, narrow, erroneous form of this culture.

Intellectuals, 'cultivated' men, are convinced in advance (why?) that everyday life has only triviality to offer. In fact this belief plays an important role in so-called 'existential' philosophy, which condemns all non-metaphysical life to triviality and inauthenticity.

The study of everyday life shows clearly that people with secrets, with inner lives, with mysteries, lead mundane everyday lives.

Thus 'mysterious' young girls and women are mainly passive, with little reality; they hide behind the feminine mystery, which offers them a glamour and a means of control which they cannot find elsewhere. In literature, the case of Kierkegaard, who invented the 'category of the secret', is equally very significant (and not without its link with the myth of the 'mysterious' woman).

The myth of the triviality of everyday life is dispelled whenever *what seems to be mysterious turns out to be really trivial, and what seems exceptional is exposed as manifestly banal.*

It would be possible to interpret the works of Faulkner and above all of Kafka along these lines. But there is another, more moving question to be asked: what about urban life, the life of the people, the life on

259

industrial housing estates? Where, how and in what experiences can its essence be discovered?

When the first documents about the concentration camps in Germany arrived, they showed a horrible brutality: crematoria, living skeletons with crazy eyes, mass graves, corpses in gigantic heaps. News coverage, photos, then films, all the 'objective' accounts – but from outside the world of the concentration camps – stressed this first impression: they seemed to be revealing atrocities outside our experience, outside Western civilization and outside civilization itself.

Since then, the survivors have returned. And some of them have made the effort to speak of what they saw and endured. Even the most lucid of them have realized how extremely difficult it is to organize their recollections, to discover a guiding thread, to give their experience a measure of unity. Exhaustion has affected their memories; their sufferings have dulled their sensibilities; they are accustomed to horror, habit has trivialized it. But it is not simply that. Bit by bit, in the most interesting of these accounts, a conviction develops: the 'objective' reports have not fully explored the horror of the concentration camps; this horror is now an accepted fact that nobody can dare contradict; but it has a 'meaning'. Clear-minded observers ask the question: 'Why?' and fail to come up with a satisfactory answer. Were the concentration camps extermination camps? It would have been easier to shoot the detainees en masse. Were they work camps? The amount of work produced was insignificant. And so it seems that this unique 'experience', the strangest, the most immense experience of the war (between twenty and thirty million human beings were deported to the camps), has still not revealed its meaning.

The question 'Why?' was already being asked while the experience was being lived out, in the very heart of the world of the concentration camps. 'What characterizes German cruelty is a certain systematization of the absurd, a certain technique for driving men mad ...'[10] The universe of the absurd! As early as April 1945, a talented journalist offered the following striking vision of this universe:

> It was always the same. Nothing corresponded to anything. One of the characteristics of Hitlerian sadism is to rob things of their meaning, to plunge its victims live into a disorientating world ... From that point of view, the journey to the deportation camp was a masterpiece: an intermin-

able roll call which lasted an entire day, carefully packaged bundles which would never be sent on, disconcertingly polite SS officers who became increasingly harsh and brutal as the frontier approached ... Food distributed, but nothing to drink. They had been told to dress up warm, but at Neubourg they were stripped, completely in some carriages, partially in others ...[11]

Then, on arrival at the camp (Buchenwald), frozen with cold, exhausted with thirst, these naked men are ushered into a huge, well-heated hall. Many of them begin to feel more hopeful. Now they are moved to another hall festooned with electric shears; they are shaved by assistants in white coats, and taken to the showers. A veritable resurrection: hot showers, clean towels. Then, suddenly, they are beaten with sticks. Then something makes them laugh, uncontrollably; they are in fits of laughter:

Behind a counter there were several men who handed us shirts, trousers, hats. They were clothes taken from blokes who had been arrested all over Europe. What a scream ... Cossack trousers, Czech embroidered shirts, hats with feathers ... all of it too small or too big, creased, faded, stretched. When we saw each other we started laughing, and we couldn't stop ...[12]

Clean, disinfected, showered, these men are taken to filthy huts piled high with bunk beds, their restless, emaciated occupants crawling with vermin. The torture begins.

In a recent book, Pelagia Lewinska explains how she had to break with the *moral* way of thinking she had been used to until that point:

When they arrive the detainees are packed into a bare hall ... A young woman goes into labour. All her friends become concerned, they lay her out on the floor, a woman doctor – also a deportee – tries to take care of her ... But the expected stretcher fails to materialize; the women are surprised, but nevertheless find reasons from 'the other world' for the delay: shortage of staff, poor organization ... And yet someone has the bright idea of asking one of the detainees who was already there. Her answer stuns everyone: 'It's irrelevant ...'[13]

And according to Pelagia Lewinska, everyone began concentrating on one, dreadful question: 'What is Auschwitz?'

And Pelagia Lewinska is still asking herself the question: 'What is Auschwitz?'

The full meaning goes beyond the brute, objective facts. People who were there feel this. Their accounts are clearly marked by the effort to go back in time, back to the numbness, the suffering which killed their feelings and their power to remember, in order to recapture the things 'objective' reports have been unable to grasp. David Rousset has tried to define what he calls 'the universe of the concentration camp'.

> The camps are Ubuesque. Life at Buchenwald is lived under the sign of an outrageous humour, a tragic buffoonery ... [The universe of the concentration camp is] another world, a monstrous universe where human thought falters and ends up lost; a nightmarish Kafka-esque world where everything seems organized according to some implacable, rigid, rational mind; but which one? since everything here is unnatural, dehumanized, mad, manic ...[14]

Madame Lewinska has also evoked this contrast between an obvious absurdity and the hidden and yet rigid rationality which rules overall:

> The idea which governed the way the camp was organized had been well and consciously thought out ... They wanted to debase and humiliate the human dignity within us, to eradicate every trace of humanity from us, to make us feel horrified and disgusted with ourselves ... That was the aim, that was the idea ...[15] What at first seemed carelessness was in fact perversity. What had given the impression of disorder was premeditated, what appeared to be ignorance was subtlety. In organizing a concentration camp they had called upon all the German talent for meticulousness, all the absolute brutality of Hitlerism ...[16]

And as David Rousset writes:

> It is dark. Around five, the men start assembling. There is snow everywhere. The searchlights on the main gate are yelling through the storm like powerful, barbaric horns. 45,000 detainees move towards the parade ground. Every evening, without fail. The sick, the living, the dead. Curses are bitten back and silenced before the gods of the main gate. An emaciated people drag their feet in time to the music of an incongruous, ludicrous band. It is a universe apart. This intense life of the camps has its

laws and its raisons d'être. This people of concentrationists has motivations of its own which have little in common with the existence of a man in Paris or Toulouse, New York or Tbilisi. But the fact that this universe of the concentration camp exists is not unimportant for the meaning of the universe of ordinary people.[17]

A very striking assertion. But if the writer senses a link, he seems to find it rather difficult to define what it is. If the camps formed a universe completely apart, if the 'depths of the camps' afforded an absolutely unique experience, what can they reveal about the meaning of the human universe? He senses a link and cannot discover what it is because he believes (or so it seems) in the rather literary and idealized notion of distinct 'universes'.

The absurd and the rational coexist; absurdity of detail, of appearance, conceals and reveals an overall rationality. This rationality is rigid, cruel, inhuman. It is *scientific barbarity*! ... The 'why' is a torture, which only stops when habit finally kills rationality off (for it is still rationality which asks the questions and which affords the feeling of absurdity!).

These feelings may be pushed to crisis point in the 'universe of the concentration camp', but are they unknown to us men of Paris or Toulouse, New York or Tbilisi? Are they not precisely the most constant of all the feelings underlying everyday life, its very bedrock?

At every moment of lucidity we experience the torture of 'why'. It is the 'normal' state of childhood, which poetry and metaphysics prolong (and we know how much our poets rely on childhood!).

In moments of lucidity we sense the social mystery – all around us, in our most 'modern' towns. Why this? Why that? Habit and familiarity gradually dull our curiosity and bring, not peace, but a comforting indifference. And yet, how many times do we feel ourselves carried away by some enormous power, absurd and yet fearfully rational? In factories, government offices, courts of law, barracks, or simply in cities, an implacable mechanism is at work. And human Reason appears only as a terrifying, distant, dehumanized reason: scientific barbarity. If we are not so stupid as to believe that we have a hold over Reason simply because we utter the word, or that it can be invoked like some cheap goddess, then the only time we are aware of Reason within ourselves is when it raises its head to provoke a feeling of absurdity and to pose the generally unanswerable question: 'Why?' Hidden beneath what appears to be human reason lies an irrational reality; but lying even more deeply hidden beneath what appears to be absurd is a dehumanized Rationality. Where? All around us – though not so much in rural areas as in our 'modern' towns.

All or nearly all accounts of the 'universe of the concentration camp' are reminiscent of the strange universe of Kafka. It is an enlightening reference. Kafka's 'universe' is not and is not intended to be extraordinary, nor does it aspire to be a universe; it is everyday life – or Kafka's view of it – meticulously described and captured in its essence. How should we interpret *The Castle*? Is the hidden, malicious, punctilious, tedious power which drives K ... towards his fate in the village dominated by the Castle the power of bureaucracy? Of Reason? Of Providence or Divine Grace? How easy it is to pass from the social mystery to the theological one! It matters little whether it is the one or the other. The essential thing is that the everyday life of the 'modern' man in modern towns and on industrial housing estates (and above all the life of the ordinary man, the poor man, the worker like K ... in *The Castle*) is *tragically* controlled by unresolved contradictions and by the most painful contradiction of all: that between absurdity and Reason, both equally inhuman, both indivisibly united.

And if we are to understand the *everyday* universe of the modern man, surely we must abandon the illusions created by moral doctrines, together with the illusions – which form such a thick screen between consciousness and the real – of a beneficial Reason and a fully realized individuality. It seems that Madame Lewinska left her illusions behind without falling into another illusion, that of 'another world':

> I can only admire the skill with which the Germans had introduced the modern science of man into the way they organized life in the camp. Not only had they applied a system of conditions which killed people, but also, with great precision, they had used the science of psychology in order to disorganize the human soul, to destroy the human being morally ... Who were the women detained in Auschwitz? A motley crew, with every nationality, every faith, every social class, every kind of delinquent. Alongside a handful of political detainees, there were people arrested in street raids, in cafés, in trains, people dealing on the black market or haunting brothels ...[18]

Had this mass of detainees been swept together by chance? Nothing was left to chance at Auschwitz. The Germans made sure that no community could be formed in the camp ... They consciously created a jungle where brutal egoism, trickery, the lack of all deference towards anyone physically weaker, stifled any sense of human solidarity ...[19]

And here is probably the true vision of the concentration camp, the one which sums the experience up:

In this jungle which represented a condensed social image of the Third Reich, humanitarian scruples and thoughtfulness became a ridiculous weakness, while the bestial struggle to go on living was intended to produce a camp 'elite' in the image of the one that governed Germany. Men with a developed social sense, people with a certain cultural or ideological standard, had to perish crushed beneath a blind and primitive animality, paying the price for having subtler minds, for a generosity of spirit which in Hitler's book meant nothing but weakness and inferiority ...[20]

As if in a small State, a social organization was created which was based, and not at all fortuitously, on the Hitlerian theory of the people, the masters and the State.

At the base, a large grey mass of slaves working hard. At the apex the ruling class: white-collar women detainees, all-powerful, with the power of life and death over the majority; well-fed, well-housed, enjoying even the right to love (with the SS and the male detainees).[21]

And here is Auschwitz, *capitalist housing estate*:

If the material conditions of the camp improved it was the upper strata which benefited: the women who had all the wealth – what they had plundered from the slaves. The workers and agricultural labourers went on sleeping in the same huts, went on toiling, being beaten, and dying.[22]

That the concentration camps had other meanings – that they satisfied Hitlerian sadism, that they collected millions of potential hostages, etc. – is doubtless true. But the dominant, essential meaning seems to be this: if Fascism represents the most extreme form of capitalism, the concentration camp is the most extreme and paroxysmal form of a modern housing estate, or of an industrial town.

There are many intermediary stages between our towns and the concentration camps: miners' villages, temporary housing on construction sites, villages for immigrant workers ... Nevertheless, the link is clear.

And it is in the experience of the darkest tragedy – in the seemingly exceptional, at the pinnacle of absurdity, in the pathetic antagonism between man and a still-inhuman Reason – that the very essence of *our* everyday lives, of the most mundane of everyday lives, stands revealed. Will they understand, those who have never been able to see what is all around them? Will the cruel light of the concentration camps at last enable them to understand what towns and 'modern' life really are? And will they be able to understand that the *possibilities* of man and Reason can be transformed into the most monstrous of realities? ...

Up until now human possibilities have only been made available in a limited way, even though it is the 'masses' – the human community – who by their labour supply those possibilities with their material basis.

Through a lack of imagination derived from a lack of (dialectical) reason, most people (among the 'masses' themselves) do not think that things can ever really change. They are quite ready to believe that there will always be the same little shop – or a shop like it – in the same place; or that the same house, the same field, will remain where they are forever.

There are writers who have allowed their imagination to be stimulated by what is possible. They have dreamed; they have 'looked into the future'. And what have they seen? Fabulous palaces, buildings, entire cities devoted to pleasure, cosmic excursions. How many of them have tried to picture what would be in store for everyday life, if bit by bit it were to be raised to the level of what modern technology and science allows? If wealth and power were no longer outside of the community; if those cancerous monstrosities, art for art's sake, thought for thought's sake, power for the sake of power over men, were to disappear?

But should we in turn wish to 'look into the future' and form an image of what it will be, there is one childish error we must avoid: to base the man of the future on what we are now, simply granting him a greater quantity of mechanical means and appliances.

Also (and this is much more difficult and complex), we should acquire a sense of *qualitative* changes, of modifications in the quality of life – and above all of *another attitude of the human being towards himself.*

Our civilization, like every reality, has progressed in an uneven, spasmodic manner, complete with deviations, winding paths and sudden changes of direction.

The natural sciences were the first to progress. For a wide variety of reasons, certain sectors of knowledge and life lagged behind. The sciences of human reality (medicine, physiology and psychology – history – political economy and its applications, etc.) are still behind the natural sciences. As for practical, everyday life – a fundamental sector nevertheless – it is so backward that it can often appear unchanged or merely down-graded.

At certain privileged moments of lucidity or action, an increasingly large number of individuals are able to partake of science, of (technical) power over nature, of political power (organization, State, political life). Rarely, these individuals may succeed in thinking on the level of the Total Man – the level of the Possible. But aside from such privileged moments, even these individuals live almost every instant at a vastly inferior level. The contrast between the possible and the real, which is historical and social in character, is thus shifted (within) the most gifted individuals; it becomes the more-or-less conscious conflict between theory and practice, dream and reality; and this conflict results in disquiet and anguish, like any contradiction which remains unresolved or appears unresolvable.

As far as the majority of human beings are concerned, they only accede to the real and the possible by means of fragmented, monotonous labour, and no one individual can really grasp what the overall meaning and consequences of his labour might be. New forms of community appear tentatively – in action, in politics – but in our country, France, they have not yet been consolidated or made to enter into life, except in the case of the most advanced and lucid 'militants'. In their work as in their 'private' life and leisure activities, most people remain imprisoned within narrow, out-of-date frames of reference. Even if they are worried or discontented, even if they want to smash these social limits, they have no clear idea of the possibilities. They only enjoy derisory scraps and fragments of the power and the splendour they have themselves brought into being. This contradiction is an intolerable one, though it is familiar, and disguised, smothered beneath mountains of ideologies.

In terms of himself, and putting to one side the varieties of community which appear and disappear according to political circumstances, modern man finds himself ever more on his own and defenceless (by the expression 'modern man', we also mean today's children, today's adolescents). Moralists call this situation 'moral crisis', although it definitely concerns something other than moral issues. Deprived of the wisdom of Antiquity, which no longer has any meaning in a life so distanced from nature, modern man has not yet discovered a new wisdom, founded on power over nature (and over his own nature). Nobody has devised subtler techniques for him which would allow him to understand himself, to direct his passions, to control his life. The point has been made many times: we know more about what goes on in atoms or in the stars than in our own bodies and 'souls'. Everyday life thus still belongs to what Marxist theoreticians call the 'uncontrolled sector'. And this is what gives a final, sad meaning to the term 'private life'. The modern individual is 'deprived' not only of social reality and truth, but of power over himself.

So progress in the way life is organized cannot be limited to technical progress in external equipment, cannot be confined to an increase in the quantity of tools.

It will also be a qualitative progress: the individual will stop being a fiction, a myth of the bourgeois democracies – an empty, negative form – a pleasant illusion for each human grain of sand. He will cease being 'private' by becoming at the same time more social, more human – and more individual. We have shown how the forward march of human reality was progressing according to a dialectical process: greater *objectification* (the human being becoming more social, and realizing himself in a world of social, material and human objects) and deeper *subjectivization* (a more highly developed consciousness, reflecting on and conscious of power over all reality).

This dialectical progress supposes that the human individual will become the object (will take himself as the object) of certain infinitely delicate but efficacious techniques which will give him active power over himself qua content (and not simply as the empty form of individuality). Our pedagogy, our psychology, are but tentative sketches for these future techniques, which will make the subject into an object for itself (and therefore more real) and the social and biological object into a subject (consciousness, freedom, active power).

Although they are still very inadequate, and contaminated by the myth of the individual as *already-realized* – a given, a fact like any other biological or social fact – our developing pedagogy and psychology are already showing us that this power over our nature is possible. Here again, the way the real is lagging behind what is possible (not the fictions or the illusions, but what is really possible) is peculiarly characteristic of our times.

So it really is a question of man establishing a new attitude towards man, of a *qualitative* modification in life and culture. We already have the means to demonstrate that this fundamental modification is *possible*. We cannot begin even to imagine its inexhaustible consequences.

All we know is that the gigantic, shapeless movement, with its incoherent and complicated strategies and groundplans, that we have called 'human alienation', must eventually come to an end.

Alienation has stripped life of everything which blessed its primitive frailty with joy and wisdom. Science and power have been acquired, but at the cost of many sacrifices (so much so that the very idea of human sacrifice was an 'essential' stage in man's progress!). The human, stripped bare and projected outside of itself, was and remains at the mercy of forces which in fact come from the human and are nothing but human – but torn apart and dehumanized. This alienation was *economic* (the division of labour; 'private' property; the formation of economic fetishes: money, commodities, capital); *social* (the formation of classes); *political* (the formation of the State); *ideological* (religions, metaphysics, moral doctrines). It was also *philosophical*: primitive man, simple, living on the same level as nature, became divided up into subject and object, form and content, nature and power, reality and possibility, truth and illusion, community and individuality, body and consciousness ('soul', 'mind'). Via these ideological illusions, philosophy has given confused expression to this situation of man: division and supersession, dialectical process, subjectivity and objectivity progressively attained. With its speculative (metaphysical) vocabulary, philosophy is itself part of human alienation. But man has developed only through alienation: the history of truth cannot be separated from the history of errors. So it is that, in so far as it can be separated from an extra-human metaphysics, philosophy must not be condemned in toto, since now it has begun 'superseding' itself and is providing the means to denounce alienation and to indict dehumanization. With its help the problem can be formulated in all its scope: *it poses the question of the total man in its totality*, taking into account the entire range of our knowledge (physics, biology, economy, history ...). It asserts that the total problem of man (the problem of the total man) is posed and is resolved on the level of everyday life – by a new consciousness of that life, by the transformation of that life. And so philosophy is evolving into a new whole: the theory of knowledge, logic and methodology, social criticism of ideas, criticism of life. Philosophy is no longer speculative, separated from action and life, abstract, contemplative. And yet it is still philosophy: the search for, the discovery of a 'conception of the world', of a *living totality*. By superseding itself, philosophy has achieved a widening, a deepening of philosophy.

But henceforth neither philosophy nor the philosopher can be satisfied with themselves alone, closing their horizons and considering their work done.

Thought, even at its most genuine, is still no more than an exceptional moment. The mass of everyday moments (for the 'philosopher' and the 'scientist', as for everyone else) are only indirectly involved in these flashes of inspiration, these total visions. The metaphor which links thought to mountain tops and clouds is not a completely empty one. We may take it as proven that this metaphor does not express an eternal truth. But the problem remains: how can the 'masses' – whether masses of moments or masses of human beings – 'participate' in a total vision?

Mystics and metaphysicians used to acknowledge that everything in life revolved around exceptional moments. In their view, life found expression and was concentrated in them. These moments were festivals: festivals of the mind or the heart, public or intimate festivals. In order to attack and mortally wound mysticism, it was necessary to show that in fact festivals had lost their meaning, the power they had in the days when all their magnificence came from life, and when life drew its magnificence from festivals. Up until now the principle of Festival has stood for a divorce from life. Whether a festival for the inner or for the outer man, it has involved an increasing proportion of play-acting. Is this life's fate? And are we – the human masses, a mere accumulation of moments in time, fog-bound marshy plains, 'enormous, stupid' crowds – are we fated to contemplate and adore the pinnacles above us, raising ourselves to their level occasionally, only to find ourselves subsequently cast down from the highest points to the lowest depths?

Dialectical materialism negates this destiny, as it negates every 'destiny' which weighs down upon action from without. It negates it –and demonstrates this negation. On this precise point, from this point of view, we are witnessing the 'essence' of Marxism – one of its essential aspects.

Dialectical method applies its criticism to its own efforts as well. The 'vision' of the world it strives for, a vision it first glimpses at certain 'moments' of thought – the total conception of the world, the possiblility of the *total man* – will only make sense once it stops being a 'vision' and a 'conception': once it penetrates life and transforms it. This 'philosophy' wants to be serious without taking itself seriously.

The truly human man will not be a man of a few dazzling moments, a drunken man, a man who feeds upon himself. There have been and will always be visionaries, geniuses or heroes who have their 'moments', moments which may be extraordinarily important and effective. But man will appropriate nature, and will make the world 'the joy man gives himself',[23] for the days, for the centuries yet to come.

The programme we have sketched for a critique of everyday life can be summed up as follows:

(a) It will involve a methodical confrontation of so-called 'modern' life on the one hand, with the past, and on the other – and above all – with *the possible*, so that the points or sectors where a 'decadence' or a withdrawal from life have occurred – the points of backwardness in terms of what is possible – the points where new forms are appearing, rich in possibilities – can be determined.

(b) Studied from this point of view, human reality appears as an opposition and 'contrast' between a certain number of terms: everyday life and festival – mass moments and exceptional moments – triviality and splendour – seriousness and play – reality and dreams, etc.

The critique of everyday life involves an investigation of the exact relations between these terms. It implies criticism of the trivial by the exceptional – *but at the same time* criticism of the exceptional by the trivial, of the 'elite' by the mass – of festival, dreams, art and poetry, by reality.

(c) Equally, the critique of everyday life implies a confrontation of effective human reality with its 'expressions': moral doctrines, psychology, philosophy, religion, literature.

From this point of view, religion is nothing but a direct, immediate, negative, destructive, incessant and skilful criticism of life – skilful enough even to give itself the appearance of not being what it really is.

Philosophy was an *indirect* criticism of life by an external (metaphysical) 'truth'. It is now appropriate to examine the philosophy of the past from this perspective – and that is the task facing 'today's' philosopher. To study philosophy as an indirect criticism of life is to perceive (everyday) life as a direct critique of philosophy.

(d) The relations between groups and individuals in everyday life interact in a manner which in part escapes the specialized sciences. By a process of abstraction these sciences infer certain relations, certain essential aspects, from the extraordinary complexities of human reality. But have they completed this task? It seems that once the relations identified by history, political economy or biology have been extracted from human reality, a kind of enormous, shapeless, ill-defined mass remains. This is the murky background from which known relations and superior activities (scientific, political, aesthetic) are picked out.

It is this 'human raw material' that the study of everyday life takes as its proper object. It studies it both in itself and in its relation with the differentiated, superior forms that it underpins. In this way it will help to grasp the 'total content' of consciousness; this will be its contribution towards the attempt to achieve unity, totality – the realization of the total man.

Going beyond the emotional attempts by philanthropists and sentimental (petty-bourgeois) humanists to 'magnify' humble gestures, and beyond that allegedly superior irony which has systematically devalued life, seeing it merely as back-stage activity or comic relief in a tragedy, the critique of everyday life – critical and positive – must clear the way for a genuine humanism, for a humanism which believes in the human because it knows it.

Toulouse, August–December 1945

VOLUME II

◆

Foundations for a Sociology
of the Everyday

Translator's Note

This translation is for the people of Amara, who taught me how everyday life can be an art and a festival.

Itzuli dudan liburu hau Amaratarrei eskaintzen diet. Gora gu eta gutarrak.

Except when preceded by (*Trans.*), footnotes are from the original. When titles appear in French, the quoted material is my own translation.

Preface

The Moment of Radical Critique

Michel Trebitsch

How have the analysts, even master-thinkers, of the early twenty-first century managed to neglect a book as brilliant as the second volume of the *Critique of Everyday Life*? Assuming one has sufficient historical sense to discount the inevitable scoria of the vocabulary of the period – in other words, the ubiquitous Marxist terminology – it must in all honesty be acknowledged that we are dealing with one of the major works of the turn of the 1960s. Henri Lefebvre was then on top intellectual form – productive, creative, publishing some of his most accomplished works and dozens of articles in the space of a few years. The unqualified private college teacher of the inter-war period had, in the meantime, become a researcher and, soon afterwards, a recognized if unconventional academic. The Communist intellectual in search of legitimacy with those he always called the 'official Marxists' made a resounding break with 'the Party' at this point, making him one of the main figures of the contestation that prepared and prefigured the events of May 1968.[1]

The gap separating the first and second volumes of the *Critique of Everyday Life* – from 1947 to 1961 – is long enough, but not as long as that between the second and third (1961–81). However, it was marked by various extremely powerful, predominantly political upheavals against the backdrop of the *trente glorieuses*, which meant that everything changed at the beginning of the 1960s not only for Henri Lefebvre, but as regards the whole ideological and cultural climate. The 1947 book, it may be remembered, derived in large part from the pre-war period and could only have emerged in the short-lived context of the Liberation, just before the doors of the 'iron curtain' closed shut and the Zhdanovite ice age set in.[2] Between that date and 1961, nothing less than the trauma of 1956 occurred – the invasion of Hungary, Khrushchev's report and, for Henri Lefebvre, the start of a fairly slow process of detaching himself from Communism in the name of 'revising Marxism'.

The key book of a key moment, this volume is presented in a rather remarkable form explaining precisely these basic changes and, in addition, its author's lucid, even precocious, consciousness of them. Nearly a third of its 350 pages are in fact devoted to 'Clearing the ground', attempting, as Lefebvre indicates, a balance sheet of the transformations in everyday life over the intervening fifteen years. The first volume of *Critique of Everyday Life* already had 'Introduction' as its sub-title. These prefatory texts, or inventories, are at one with Henri Lefebvre's approach: the desire constantly to link the conceptual with the experiential; the autobiographical dimension of theoretical reflection; a relationship to 'experience', in Hannah Arendt's sense of the word. As Lefebvre formulates it with the utmost clarity in his 'axiomatic' chapter, knowledge of society is impossible without a critique of this society. This is the thread that will guide our reading: the essential link, forged during the 1950s, between the political whirlwinds generated by the rift of 1956 and the overall development of the field of the social sciences, especially sociology and its ideological function. What is so interesting about this book is that we have before us a mature work, firm and rigorous in its expression, resolute in its theoretical ambition, and with few equivalents in the rest of Lefebvre's output. It can be read as a veritable 'discourse on method' in sociology – in particular, because it aspires to restore a properly philosophical rigour to the latter. And it determined a scholarly stance in Henri Lefebvre which, lifting him out of intellectual marginality, gives all its force to the core of the project: the development of a *radical critique* of what exists that serves to clarify his trajectory during subsequent years. For what is in play, beyond the second volume of *Critique of Everyday Life* and the case of Henri Lefebvre, is a longer intellectual history, which could even be extended to Pierre Bourdieu, whose first major works appeared in the very same years. Here, however, we shall confine ourselves to the 1960s, taking the 'critique of everyday life' as a central element in a history of the 'ideas of May' which, in as much as it remains dependent on the effects of fashion and *a posteriori* reconstructions, remains to be written.

If posterity has retained any image of him from the 1960s, it is that of Lefebvre the political agitator; and here we shall indeed be examining the impact of his oeuvre, in particular its influence on the ideas of May '68, of which *Critique of Everyday Life* (the second as well as – retroactively – the first volume) forms a major component. But a condition of this is that we take the book as a highly theoretical endeavour, unlike the more polemical works of the period; that we recognize in it a surprising contemporaneity in its reading of the social, or what Lefebvre himself defined as the 'social text' – landscapes, cities, streets; that we carefully read his attempt to develop the formal implements and specific categories – his terms – of a critical sociology. One will retain, for example, the twenty or so pages on the 'idea of structure', where we find one of the best definitions of structuralism, and also one of the most virulent attacks on it at the very moment when the debate was at its height.[3] But in fact, much more broadly, the sociology that Lefebvre attempted to construct was defined with reference to the two currents dominant at the time: 'quantitative' sociology, which he criticized for sticking to enumerations and classifications that cannot exhaust reality; and, equally, 'participatory' sociology, the sociology of surveys and questionnaires postulating a spontaneity of the social rejected by Lefebvre. It is not within my remit to analyse the content and concepts at stake in this sociological controversy, which runs through the book – especially since they are presented to readers clearly enough. On the other hand, that controversy makes it possible to grasp what is essential if we are to understand the intellectual history of the 1960s: the fundamental link between sociology and politics, between the institution of contemporary French sociology and attempts to renew revolutionary thought in a rupture with Stalinism. This is the movement, which began well before May 1968 and continued for part of the 1970s, I refer to by the notion of 'radical critique' – a phrase to be found in Lefebvre and others. It is this closely linked relation that I would like to track through the dual trajectory, professional and political, of our philosopher of the everyday.

The Centre d'études sociologiques

In retrospect, we may start with a commonplace about 1968, according to which sociology and sociologists, students and teachers, were essential driving forces behind the May events. 'An immature discipline without any openings, sociology launched the movement of May '68,' wrote Georges Pompidou in *Le Nœud gordien*; and the idea that sociology was a site of revolutionary thinking because it was a dominated discipline pervades Bourdieu and Passeron's *The Inheritors*, one of the cult books of the period.[4] Underlying this commonplace are several deeper questions about the development of the discipline after the war, and its role as analyst and catalyst of a certain number of debates about society, as well as about the personal trajectory of Lefebvre who, even though he was now integrated into the university system, remained marginalized with respect both to the royal discipline of philosophy and a party that rejected this particular form of 'bourgeois science'.

In 1948, following a brief spell at Radio Toulouse where Tristan Tzara had introduced him at the Liberation, and then a return – briefer still – to secondary-school teaching, Lefebvre found himself among the six researchers appointed to the Centre d'études sociologiques, a laboratory of the Centre national de la recherche scientifique founded in 1946 by Georges Gurvitch, whom Georges Friedmann was to succeed in 1949. We must say a word about Gurvitch, an unusual character, 'the outcast from the horde' as he characterized himself in an article on his intellectual itinerary published in 1966, just after his death.[5] A socialist revolutionary, Gurvitch was exiled from Russia in 1921, first to Prague and then, in 1924, to Paris, where he took his doctorate in philosophy, before succeeding Maurice Halbwachs at Strasbourg in 1935. Exiled once again during the war – to New York, where he worked with the New School for Social Research – he returned to introduce American sociology for the first time and then challenge it. His international openness and personal charisma have often been stressed, but, remaining a philosopher in his references and categories, he was never himself fully integrated into French sociology. And yet, connected to a whole network – Lucien Febvre's sixth section of the École pratique des hautes études and the Conservatoire national des arts et métiers where Georges Friedmann was appointed the same year (1946) – Gurvitch represented both the link and the rupture with the Durkheimian legacy, with the sociology of social facts; and it was around him that what has been called the 'second foundation of French sociology' developed after 1945.[6] Hitherto hard to distinguish from social psychology and philosophy, of which it formed one of the diplomas, sociology had only been represented by a few posts at Paris, Bordeaux and Strasbourg. A generation later, in the 1970s, the main actors in the history of French sociology had passed through this small Centre d'études sociologiques.

With Henri Lévy-Bruhl and Gabriel Le Bras around him, and assisted in the secretariat by the marvellous Yvonne Halbwachs, widow of Maurice, Gurvitch founded the Centre d'études sociologiques with some singular, curious figures, who were rather non-academic and possessed little academic capital (few were *agrégés*). Their recruitment was a matter of chance, of relations forged in the Resistance and political activity (Edgar Morin), while two of them came from Uriage (Henri Chombart de Lauwe and Joffre Dumazedier); and of an interest in the working class, which explains the early specialization in the sociology of work (Georges Friedmann), but also in urban sociology and even the sociology of religion. This is the heroic context in which we must situate the arrival in 1948 of Henri Lefebvre, who had known Friedmann since the 1920s and who rapidly became Yvonne Halbwachs' god. Lefebvre was never a Gurvitchian, but Gurvitch, engaged with the problem of revolutionary change and defender of a fairly complex vision of a 'dialectical' sociology – a sociology of the totality – could not but be appreciative of his post-war publications, particularly *Critique of Everyday Life*. About his entry into the CES we possess the testimony of a second-rate novel by Françoise d'Eaubonne, *Le Temps d'apprendre à vivre*, where he is depicted in the form of the Marxist philosopher Hervé Lefort, and where she describes the highly politicized atmosphere of the Centre, several of whose members, like Lefebvre or Morin, were Communists.[7]

Initially Lefebvre put considerable effort into the area of rural sociology, creating a rural sociology group in 1950 to which he invited the best French rural scholars (Daniel Halévy, Michel Cépède, Louis Chevalier, René Dumont), and embarking on area surveys – in particular, in the Tuscan countryside in 1950–51.[8] During the war he had worked on the Pyrenean valleys, going through the archives of pastoral communities and discovering in them a kind of 'primitive communism' that had permeated his composition of *Critique of Everyday Life*. From this research he derived his doctoral thesis on *Les Communautés paysannes pyrénéennes*, defended in June 1954 (his first academic qualification since his *diplôme d'études supérieures*, obtained thirty years earlier in 1924!).[9] His work was marked by a militant dimension, by his links with Italian agricultural unions and even his influence on the Jeunesse agricole chrétienne in France, but also because his empirical research was systematically coupled with theoretical publications, on ground rent and agrarian communities, culminating in a *Traité de sociologie rurale*, the manuscript of which seems to have been stolen, and which put him out of tune with the PCF, then at the height of its Lysenkoist phase. This political investment was, moreover, to cost him an 'affaire Lefebvre' with the directorate of the CNRS. In 1953, during the 'Journées nationales d'études des intellectuels communistes', in his report on the Cercle des sociologues communistes he had attacked the 'police sociology' of the bourgeoisie, which indexed the working class, and had set about Gurvitch and Friedmann by name.[10] The reaction of the CNRS was immediate (the Cold War was then in full swing): he was demoted back down to secondary schools. Lefebvre defended himself in a statement, 'Protestation de M. Henri Lefebvre contre la fin de son détachment au CNRS';[11] and a campaign organized by the researchers' union, led by Alain Touraine and Edgar Morin, led to his reinstatement and his being granted tenure as *maître de recherche* in October 1954.[12]

Arguments and the 'Revision of Marxism'

At this point in time Lefebvre was already fighting on two fronts: while, vis-à-vis bourgeois sociology, he sought to develop the idea of a Marxist sociology, as regards the Communist Party he had to explain that sociology served a purpose and could not be reduced to bourgeois science. In truth, the misunderstanding went back much further. With the first volume of *Critique of Everyday Life*, we left Henri

Lefebvre verging on the status of official Communist Party philosopher, particularly with his participation in the anti-Sartre offensive
(*L'Existentialisme*, 1947) and the publication of his short 'Que-sais je?'
text *Le Marxisme* (1948), which remains the best-selling text in the collection at Presses Universitaires de France and which, like his 1939
book *Dialectical Materialism*, was to serve as a reference for generations
of Marxist intellectuals. The idyll, it may be remembered, lasted two
years at most. By 1949, Lefebvre found himself back in the position
of marginal Communist he had occupied for thirty years, from his
adhesion in 1928 to his exclusion in 1958. As early as 1948, the party
paralysed his projects, pulped a work he had already written,
Méthodologie des sciences, and delayed his *Contribution à l'esthétique* until
1953. And he was challenged on several occasions in *La Nouvelle Critique* for his 'neo-Hegelianism' and his intolerable claim to preserve
the relative autonomy of philosophy from political imperatives.[13]
What actually interested Lefebvre was not proletarian science as
defended by Zhdanov from 1947 onwards, still less the relative or
absolute immiseration of the proletariat that formed a great debate of
the 1950s, and even less Lysenko. What interested him was analysing
the debasement of everyday life in the modern world, marked by the
subject's separation from itself and the objectification of the object
reduced to reification, to the object losing any aesthetic value, to the
poverty of the modern world.

Nevertheless, the process of breaking with the Communist Party
was rather strange and poses the question, formulated by Edgar
Morin in the half-tone portrait he drew of Lefebvre in his 1958 *Autocritique*: 'Ah! Why did this butterfly crawl like a caterpillar for years?'
Why did Lefebvre remain in the PCF so long? asks Morin, while suggesting that he paid for 'his small margin of dialectical autonomy
with total political subservience'.[14] In fact, in contrast to the successive waves of intellectuals who were excluded from the party or
withdrew from it from 1948 onwards, Lefebvre did not make a mark
in any of the major crises – the Prague coup, the condemnation of
Titoism, the Kravtchenko affair, the Rajk trial, the Doctors' plot; or
even when faced with the earthquake of 1956 – the Twentieth Congress of the CPSU and then, in October, the Soviet intervention in
Hungary – when he had knowledge of Khrushchev's report very
early on, as early as February, during a trip to the GDR at the invita-

tion of the Berlin Academy of Sciences.[15] This was because his problem was more theoretical than directly political. In this sense, the first shock dates back to 1955, on the occasion of a lecture on Lukács to the Hungarian Institute of Paris when Lefebvre, while polemicizing with Raymond Aron (*The Opium of the Intellectuals*) and Merleau-Ponty (*Adventures of the Dialectic*), rejected the Zhdanovite thesis of 'proletarian science'. Attacked in the Communist press, he copped a warning from the party leadership, which prevented publication of his lecture.[16]

The key question for Lefebvre, as for a number of intellectuals at the time, was the crisis of orthodoxy and the revision of Marxism. The main anchorage point of this challenge was to be the journal *Arguments*, founded in 1956 and wound up by its editors in 1962, in which the prime movers were Edgar Morin, Jean Duvignaud and Kostas Axelos.[17] A 'research bulletin' rather than the organ of a group, this journal gathered together thinkers excluded from the PCF and a number of people from the socialist left who wanted to renovate socialism. Before and after the Twentieth Congress, the initiative of these revolutionary intellectuals was to seek to renew Marxism by all available means. Lefebvre himself only published two articles in it, and following his exclusion from the Communist Party – one in 1959, 'Justice et vérité', on Nietzsche (no. 15); the other in 1962, 'La signification de la Commune' (no. 27). A loose grouping round *Arguments* sought to rethink French society, particularly after de Gaulle's victory, which posed some new problems; to rethink modern civilization, the reign of bureaucracy, technique, the 'new working class' (Serge Mallet), 'fragmented work' (Georges Friedmann); to rethink international relations by posing the question of the Third World. In the name of a methodological position that consisted in trying to reason (the meaning of *Raggionamenti*, the title of the Italian journal that worked with them), to pose questions and not to try to offer an interpretative line on Marxism, they pondered a key word – 'alienation' – rediscovered via the young Marx and Lukács. Lucien Goldmann's *Hidden God*, Pierre Naville's thesis *De l'aliénation à la jouissance*, Roland Barthes's *Mythologies* – all these works from 1956–57, which coincided with the evolution of *Annales* towards the 'longue durée', shifted examination towards the everyday and modernity. Lefebvre's contribution to the question in this period was to be his long introduction to the second edition of *Critique of Everyday Life* (1958), in which he sought to examine what had changed between 1947 and 1958 in the modern world, and where he refocused on the question of alienation. In addition, *Arguments* opened itself to foreign currents (the Frankfurt School, Lukács, Marcuse, Kolakowski). Alongside the various movements attempting to revise Marxism in France, we should in fact introduce a series of international dimensions, whether the shock of Algeria, or Cuba, or Yugoslav self-management, and later that of the Chinese Cultural Revolution. However, the main point here is to clarify the parallel between debates on the 'revision of Marxism' and debates on the function of sociology. Just as *Arguments* served, in Rémy Rieffel's phrase, as a political 'decompression chamber' for the exit from Stalinism, so the Centre d'études sociologiques and the *Cahiers internationaux de sociologie*, founded by Gurvitch, served as a scientific and cultural 'decompression chamber'.[18] It was in part the same authors who confronted each other in both – Morin, Duvignaud, Balandier, Touraine, Naville – so that it is legitimate to define an axis extending from sociological research to the journals and magazines that relayed these questions to a wider public (*Esprit*, *Le Nouvel Observateur*), and the recurrent themes of surveys and colloquia clearly prefiguring many of the concerns of 1968: fashion, needs, social classes, urbanization, technical society and civilization, tradition and continuity, the sociology of change, prediction in sociology, the critique of modernity.

For this dual debate assumed a public character. Lefebvre's opposition to the party line had long been internal, notably within the oppositional cell of the Centre d'études sociologiques. But it soon extended to the 'fractional' groups *L'Étincelle* (Victor Leduc, Jean-Pierre Vernant, Hélène Parmelin, Maurice Caveing, Maxime Rodinson) in 1957 and, above all, *Voies nouvelles* in April 1958, where he published several articles – in particular, a set on 'Marxisme et théorie de l'information' in the first two issues that attracted a lot of attention.[19] This was the context in which Lefebvre published an article that was key in everything that happened thereafter, 'Le marxisme et la pensée française', which drew up a disastrous balance sheet of the theoretical regression of Stalinist dogmatism. Published in the Polish journal *Tworczosc* at the end of 1956, released in June 1957 in *France-Observateur* and in July-August in *Les Temps modernes*, the article earnt him exclusion from the editorial committee of *La Nouvelle Critique* along with various others.[20] This analysis was resumed and extended at the beginning of 1958 in *Problèmes actuels du marxisme*, published by Presses Universitaires de France.[21] At the same time, he participated, together with the *Temps modernes* circle and the Mendésist left (Bourdet, Martinet) around the Club de la gauche, in a number of discussions on the 'new left' and the 'new working class' that led to the foundation of the PSA and then the PSU, which Lefebvre never joined. He was to be criticized for all this. But it was on political grounds that a procedure to exclude him was initiated in June 1958. He was criticized for his prolonged 'activity of breaking away' through publications in the 'bourgeois press' (*L'Express*, *France-Observateur*, the *NRF*, *Les Temps modernes*), his revisionist works (*Problèmes actuels du marxisme*) and his 'blatant fractional activity' in participating in the Club de la gauche and oppositional publications (*Voies nouvelles*).[22] Pronounced for a year, the exclusion would in fact prove definitive: he would never return, despite the lines thrown him at the beginning of the 1980s by a party only too happy, in times of famine, to have a last intellectual to digest.

This exclusion calls for three observations. The first is the violence of the attacks the PCF unleashed against him, launching against the quarry its intellectuals – Gilbert Mury, Guy Besse, André Gisselbrecht, Lucien Sève, Jean Kanapa – and making him a privileged target at its Fifteenth Congress (1959). The virulence was commensurate with the 'extreme patience' of the PCF, to adopt a phrase of Lucien Sève from 1960.[23] This was because the loss of Henri Lefebvre was, as David Caute indicates in his classic *Communism and the French Intellectuals*, a heavy blow for the party.[24] But it was also the case – second observation – that, whatever the official grounds, the virulence and vulgarity of these attacks were directed at an intellectual, not a political figure. Henri Lefebvre is a unique example of an intellectual, a philosopher, excluded for his ideas: Althusser was not excluded and, as for Garaudy, it was the politburo member who was ousted.

If the political break was obviously fundamental in allowing Lefebvre to develop his thinking in total freedom, there was no real theoretical discontinuity in his desire to construct a living Marxism, freed from dogmatism and committed to the analysis of contemporary phenomena. Certainly, he responded to his exclusion by publishing an initial analysis, 'L'exclu s'inclut', in *Les Temps modernes* as early as July 1958. Above all, as if it represented a veritable liberation for him, he threw himself into the composition of *La Somme et le reste* – that strange narrative of a 'philosophical adventure' which remains for many his major work.[25]

From revolutionary Romanticism to the Situationists

'Having entered a Romantic, Lefebvre left a Romantic', wrote Maurice Blanchot in the fine portrait ('Slow Funeral') he drew of him in *L'Amitié*. If he stayed, it is because he believed it possible, thanks to the position he occupied, to maintain an opening, even if it sometimes meant playing a double game: 'a philosopher's head is a hard head, even unbreakable'.[26] In the interim, Lefebvre published another article in the *NRF*, drawing less fire from 'party intellectuals', which was different in scope and destined to have a different echo in the coming decade. This article, 'Vers un romantisme révolutionnaire', taken up and reworked on several occasions, notably in the *Introduction to Modernity* in 1962, ushered in his phase of 'radical critique', making it possible for him to quit the Communist Party 'from the left'.[27] In this text, Lefebvre revived the 1925 ideal of a revolution that could only succeed if it extended not merely to the economic infrastructure, but to mentalities and culture; that set out – hence the notion of revolutionary Romanticism – from the critique of modernity which was for him at the heart of nineteenth-century Romanticism, from a refusal of the modern world. This Romanticism must be oriented towards the production of oeuvres and the production of man himself – what Lefebvre, like many people in the Stalinist era, called 'the new man'. This text seems to me be essential for understanding the process of rupture and the various developments in which he was engaged from 1956 to 1958.

But first, in order to appreciate his sensational entry into radical critique properly, we must resituate Henri Lefebvre in the context of the scholarly legitimacy he acquired at the turn of the 1960s. Contrary to retrospective reconstructions, we may note that sociology was now no longer quite what it had been in 1945–46, when he joined the CES.[28] As early as 1946, Gurvitch had launched the *Cahiers internationaux de sociologie*, the first such journal since the disappearance of the *Annales de sociologie*. Under the direction of Friedmann, the CES, installed in 1951 with the Ecole pratique des hautes études on the rue de Varenne, had already been transformed into a genuine laboratory, conducting area surveys, forming research groups, while Gurvitch, appointed to the Sorbonne, launched the 'Bibliothèque de sociologie contemporaine' at Presses Universitaires de France, and directed the French version of a big *Traité de sociologie* long regarded as authoritative. The Gurvitch era was succeeded by the era of Stoetzel. Jean Stoetzel, a Sorbonne professor at the same time as Raymond Aron, became director of the CES in 1956; appointments to it now speeded up. In the academy, a key turning-point occurred with the creation in 1958 of a degree in sociology, which thus became an academic discipline in its own right. The same year, Gurvitch founded the Association internationale des sociologues de langue française. Relying on a system of publications, with Éditions Anthropos augmenting Presses Universitaires de France, and multiplying through the foundation of several journals alongside the *Cahiers*, particularly the *Revue française de sociologie* (1960), these were the years of major colloquia and public visibility for the discipline.[29] The turning-point represented by Stoetzel, who had staked out his position as early as 1946 in a kind of manifesto ('L'esprit de la sociologie contemporaine'), was still more profound on the methodological and ideological level. In demanding an empirical and even neo-positivist sociology, primarily preoccupied with quantitative techniques and indifferent to theory, Stoetzel consciously and explicitly established the discipline in the framework of the 'dominant ideology' and, more specifically, as a site of intellectual elaboration of major reforms implemented at the beginning of the Fifth Republic as regards technological modernization, planning, and national and regional development (DATAR). If this development cannot quite be reduced to a victory of 'American sociology', it did at least mark a crucial reorientation and explains the reaction of Henri Lefebvre and several other Marxist sociologists (Edgar Morin, Pierre Naville), who at just this moment were embarked upon the enterprise of revising Marxism and who proposed, in various forms, a much more militant vision of sociology.

For Lefebvre, this was expressed by the abandonment of rural sociology, an area in which he was replaced by Henri Mendras, who would direct his research towards the 'second French revolution': the end of the peasantry and France's entry into modernity. In the account of research in the CES in 1959, published in the first issue of the *Revue française de sociologie* (1960), Lefebvre's themes were as follows: 1) 'Research on needs in the framework of the family (How mothers see the needs of children. Sociology of everyday life. Theory of needs. Research into needs in the family framework). 2) The birth of a city (Lacq and Mourenx). 3) Monographs on villages'. We are at the pivotal point of an evolution that was going to lead towards urban sociology and, more broadly, a sociology of daily life. Thus, in 1960 Lefebvre created a 'Research group on everyday life' at the CES. It was at this point – the production of Volume II of *Critique of Everyday Life* – that he was to quit research for university teaching. Elected as a professor, in October 1961 he was appointed by the liberal philosopher Georges Gusdorf to the sociology chair in the faculty at Strasbourg, formerly held by Gurvitch, where he would remain until his election to Nanterre in 1965. Developing an academic practice that was self-directed in character, particularly with the creation of an autonomous department of applied sociology, his reputation with the bourgeoisie of Strasbourg rapidly became inflammatory and his courses would mainly attract those students most disposed to protest.

This is the manifold context in which the passing but striking encounter between Henri Lefebvre and the Situationist group must be placed.[30] The influence was to be fertile and mutual – for Lefebvre, who revived the strategy of rupture of the 1920s avant-gardes; and for the Situationists who, prior to heaping abuse on him, drew much of their theoretical inspiration from his work. Founded in 1957 around Guy Debord, Raoul Vaneigem, Asger Jorn and Constant, the Situationist International was itself the inheritor of several movements like the Lettrist International of Isidore Isou and above all COBRA (Copenhagen, Brussels, Amsterdam), created in 1948 and dissolved in 1951, with which Lefebvre maintained relations, as is indicated by his correspondence with the Belgian poet Dotremont, or his influence on Constant (Neuwenhuys), who was to draw upon the *Critique of Everyday Life* for his initial urban projects in the *New Babylon*. But it was indeed the article 'Vers un romantisme révolutionnaire' that prompted Lefebvre's encounter with Debord. As early as the first issue of *Internationale Situationniste*, the 'Thèses sur la révolution culturelle' were explicitly constructed with reference to that article: 'Lefebvre offers us a track for critique of the contemporary world, but he does not propose a political project for making the revolution.' From the outset, as we can see, the relations between Lefebvre and the Situationists were complicated and critical; they were not of the order of filiation or affiliation and, as the Situationist International made clear during their rupture, he was never a member of the movement. But it was with the thought of Henri Lefebvre that the Situationists were fundamentally in dialogue; and there was even a phase of shared existence, trips, stays in Lefebvre's house in the Pyrenees, genuine collaboration, since Lefebvre involved Debord in the work of his research group on everyday life within the CES.[31]

For a start, both parties had in common the idea that everyday life is governed in the modern world by the reign of scarcity, not by the wealth of the consumer society; that everyday life has become disconnected from historicity amidst industrialization and accumulation; that it has been debased into uniform, repetitive everydayness by its separation from the great cosmic, natural and vital cycles; that the individual is herself divided (this is Deleuze's 'capitalism and schizophrenia'), separated from herself and the world in the modern world. Such alienation can be expressed in terms of poverty. Guy Debord came to give a talk to the research group on everyday life in 1961, in which he launched the saying 'everyday life is literally "colonized"'.[32] This was a saying with a prosperous future ahead of it: expressly quoted by Lefebvre in the second volume of *Critique of Everyday Life*, it was to be met with again in 1967 in the manifesto *On the Poverty of Student Life*, and would even reach as far as Habermas in 1981, in his *Theory of Communicative Action*, which contains a whole chapter on the colonization of the everyday.

It was in response to this poverty and alienation that the Situationists developed a theory of revolution, even 'cultural revolution', in terms of 'revolutions in individual everyday life', which is at the root of the theory of situations. In their most theoretical text, 'Théorie des moments et construction des situations', they in fact defined themselves with reference to the 'theory of moments' developed by

290

Lefebvre in *La Somme et le reste* and then in *Critique of Everyday Life.*[33] Spatio-temporal, 'constructed situations' are said to supersede moments as so many procedures for rupture, acceleration, subversion with respect to daily life – particularly the Situationist *dérive*, close to the Surrealist *promenade*, which consists in passing so rapidly from one district to another that an effect of acceleration and fluidity, breaking with the everyday, is created. The main site of experimentation is the city, but also as an object of experimental town planning, an anti-Le Corbusier city, constructed to counter uniformity, based on an architecture of the labyrinth, of complexity, which makes it possible not to take reality for such. But there is a divergence between Lefebvre and the Situationists over what utopia consists in: abstract utopia or concrete utopia. Is experimenting with a different kind of city a concrete utopia that already forms part of the revolution? Or does it remain at the level of architectural designs?[34]

It was here that the tensions were to crystallize. The Situationists were to be stymied by the eternal problem of avant-gardes since the Surrealists: the difficulty, even impossibility, of articulating cultural revolution and political revolution. As early as the first issue of *Internationale situationniste*, and again in no. 3 ('Sur le dépérissement de l'art', December 1959), the Situationists had criticized Lefebvre, and indeed Goldmann, both defined as 'representatives of independent revolutionary thinking', for having nothing to offer on the organization of a political force. But it was Lefebvre's relations with the 'new left', particularly with what they dubbed 'Argumentist dung', that led to the rupture. The Situationists could not accept the revision of the 1957 text 'Vers un nouveau romantisme?', taken up again by Lefebvre in 1962 in *Introduction to Modernity*, where he related Situationism to this new Romanticism and reduced the group to a youth movement.[35] Above all, at the same time Lefebvre published an article on 'La signification de la Commune' in the last issue of *Arguments*, foreshadowing his 1965 book *La Proclamation de la Commune.*[36] These few pages had been requested by him from Debord and Vaneigem, who defined the Commune as 'the greatest festival of the nineteenth century'. This was the key theme of the revolution as festival, which would dominate the whole of May '68. But in 1962 it was the occasion for the violent break with Lefebvre, consigned to 'the dustbin of history' and accused of being a plagiarist, a renegade, a 'Versaillais of culture'.[37]

Starting from there, we could, notwithstanding the sensational rupture, expatiate on the basically fairly direct influence of Henri Lefebvre, appointed in the interim to Nanterre in 1965, on Situationist texts that would serve as a theoretical reference-point for May '68 – especially Guy Debord's *The Society of the Spectacle* and Raoul Vaneigem's *The Revolution of Everyday Life*, both of which were published in 1967. Did the *radical critique* characteristic of Henri Lefebvre's position at the time, and which aligns him with the current of *critical theory* in unorthodox Marxism, have an immediate impact on a movement that accorded more importance to 'cultural revolution', the seizure of symbolic power and 'seizing speech', than reversing economic and social 'infrastructures' and capturing state power? Rather than responding to that question, by way of conclusion I should like to take a different tack, starting from recent works on Michel de Certeau and the comparison that might be sketched between the author of *Critique of Everyday Life* and the author of *The Practice of Everyday Life*.[38] The works of Henri Lefebvre on everyday life were 'a fundamental source' for de Certeau, as he signalled in the general introduction to his book.[39] Unquestionably, the two part company on numerous points – notably, the historical apprehension of daily life, which is relocated by the philosopher in a history of modernity, whereas the historian confines himself to a 'phenomenology of social micro-behaviour pitched at the level of the *longue durée*'. But they coincide, particularly with respect to Marcuse and his pessimistic definition of the 'consumer society', in a reading of consumption not as sheer passivity within mechanisms of domination, but as a form of production, production of a different kind that comes to disrupt the established order – the 'anti-discipline' that is at the heart of de Certeau's thinking, as of Michel Foucault's. In *On the Edge of the Cliff*, Roger Chartier has provided a fine analysis of this central hypothesis of *The Practice of Everyday Life*: 'To a rationalized, expansionist and at the same time centralized, clamorous, and spectacular production corresponds *another* production, called "consumption." The latter is devious, it is dispersed, but it insinuates itself everywhere, silently and almost invisibly, because it does not manifest itself through its own products, but rather through its *ways of using* the products imposed by a dominant economic order.'[40] And it is above all here that we detect a proximity, even a direct influence of Lefebvre on de Certeau, on the basis of some fundamental ideas in de Certeau about 'tactics and strategies'. The terms, which are quite explicit and analysed at length, are to be found in Lefebvre, as a development of the Marxist concept of *praxis*, in Volume II of *Critique of Everyday Life*, which de Certeau read very closely. In it Lefebvre precisely defines the critique of everyday life as a 'theory of tactics and strategies', tactics referring to the everyday, to stagnant and trivial reality, and strategy to the domain of action and decision-making.[41] We can even go somewhat further: if *invention* in de Certeau is not that far removed from *critique* in Lefebvre, here is to be found the genealogy of the very idea of a science of daily life, which has been so essential in the recent renewal of the social sciences. 'Insofar as the science of man exists, it finds its material in the "trivial", the everyday', Lefebvre asserted as early as 1947, with reference to Marc Bloch.[42] This attention in Lefebvre to familiar gestures, to what he elsewhere calls 'the minor magic in everyday life', even treated in terms of survivals, certainly does not make him the grandfather of 'micro-storia', but definitely does open up the path to a contemporary reflection on the complexity of the 'forms of experience' and the role of an anthropological approach to the critique of modernity.

CNRS, Paris, June 2002
Translated by Gregory Elliott

1

Clearing the Ground

1

Is it enough to launch ideas and to hazard hypotheses, when some may be fruitful, and others sterile? No. If we are to advance knowledge, it is essential that we deploy a set of concepts which has inner coherence. For the scientist and philosopher alike, coherence is a basic requirement. However, should this requirement go beyond certain limits, which in fact are hard to define, it becomes system for system's sake, and restricts intellectual scope and theoretical inventiveness. There may also be the danger that changes which may be occurring in the field of study itself will be overlooked. For this reason, research in all scientific fields, and particularly in the social sciences, is governed by a twofold imperative: first to guarantee that the thought and concepts employed be coherent, and second to take into account whatever new and probably unforeseen insights may be emerging in the area being studied and in the conceptual apparatus being used. This twofold imperative is not always easy to satisfy, and in an age such as ours when so many things are changing, but not all and not all in equal measure, it is difficult to steer a firm course between systematic thinking and essayism.[1]

This difficulty is apparent in a large number of contemporary works. In some, the reader is aware that coherence is given prominence. The author isolates a theme and examines it in depth, or tries to examine its implications and consequences without ever going beyond those specific limits. He theorizes in order to produce a lucid piece of work (or at least apparently lucid), thus seeking to impose a logical order on the enormous confusion of ideas and the immense disorder of facts. The success of certain ideas (that of 'structure' for example) and the influence which certain works have had may be attributed to this concern. Such strict thematization may guarantee unity and cohesion, but does it not also run the risk of overlooking some of the realities and innovations, in particular those elements which are not easily thematized and conceptualized using standard, accepted concepts, and are thus intractable to logical coherence?

On the other hand, there are other more essayistic works which try to capture the complexity and the rapid, multiple transformations of the modern world – and it is quite right that they should do so. However, their authors are facing different dangers: that of over-estimating change at the expense of what is stagnating or regressing, and that of composing a rhapsodic and discontinuous work with no inner connections between its various parts. Such works make no attempt to find either a thread to guide them through the labyrinthine complexities of the modern world, or a precise definition or evaluation of what these complexities are.

2

The object of our study is everyday life, with the idea, or rather the project (the programme), of transforming it. So, what has happened so far? In the last fifteen years everyday life has undergone extensive transformations, and this has prompted us to ask whether in fact our aim has not been achieved, in remarkable and unexpected ways, by social practice itself. We have also had to ask ourselves whether the everyday as we had previously defined it[2] has not been absorbed by technology, historicity or the modalities of history, or finally, by politics and the vicissitudes of political life. These are questions which have also troubled many of those who originally supported the idea, the aim and the author himself. We still need to find an answer to them, since our previous answer has been overtaken by circumstances. It would be pointless to pretend that these obstacles strewn in our path have not obstructed the way forward.

However, it will not require lengthy thought or extensive documentation to observe that although the everyday has indeed been modified, and in a contradictory way, it has not disappeared. It has not been absorbed by culture, by history, by politics, or by technology. The situation of the everyday per se has become increasingly serious. It is true that technology is penetrating it much more than it did twenty years ago, and it is impossible to ignore the importance of domestic science, for example; but we also know that technology and domestic science have not eliminated the most trivial aspects of everyday life; by reducing the time spent doing tedious chores technology raises very clearly the problem of available free time. Rather than transforming the everyday into a higher creative activity, it has created a vacuum. Another example is the way very few people's lives have been changed by air travel, and even then only in minor ways. Will interplanetary travel prove to be the same? Probably. At some time in the future – although it is difficult to say when – such journeys will be the preserve of a technical, social and political 'elite'. It is easy to imagine that one day 'mankind' will have travelled beyond the sun, while on earth actual men, peasants for example, will still be hoeing the land, transporting things on donkeys and mules, and perhaps living in hunger. *Uneven development* remains the prime law of the modern world, and there is much to learn and to be said about it. The distance – the gulf – between the everyday and technology is mirrored by the gulf between investment in the arms industry or interplanetary exploration and investment in the construction of new housing estates.

Only days of revolution, those days 'which are equivalent to twenty ordinary years' (Lenin), allow everyday life to pursue history and perhaps briefly to catch up with it. Such days occur when people will not and cannot go on living as they did before: the everyday as it has been established is no longer enough, and it affords them no satisfaction. And so they shatter the boundaries of everyday life, bringing life as it is lived into the domain of history. The conjuncture is momentary. They separate once more, or at least in our experience of so-called 'modern' life and society they do. The major stirrings and creative drives of revolutionary events have a totalizing impact. For a brief moment they bring the elements of totality together, after which these elements separate out once more. The results of history differ from the goals pursued and the aims envisaged, which is something we will call 'historical drift'. Certain elements of totality assert themselves and become quasi-autonomous: arts, technology, politics, sciences. The everyday withdraws into itself. These complex relations can be understood either from a historical and political perspective, or from the perspective of the everyday. Here we have chosen the latter. This is not to say that the former is faulty or bad, merely that it can sometimes lead to a dead end. Sometimes the political theorist will recommend that situations mature slowly until such time as the lived and the historical coincide again; patience has revolutionary virtues. At other times, the very same theorist of political history will recommend quickening the pace, on the assumption that humanity only sets itself problems it is able to resolve, and as historical moments happen only briefly and infrequently, anyone who lets them pass by will pay dearly for his lack of impatience and imagination . . .

Finally, it is irrefutable that public (political) life has penetrated private life, and vice versa. Today private life is saturated with items of general, social and political information. Equally, public and political life has become 'personalized', as they say. As we shall demonstrate, this interaction has resulted in an indisputable 'reprivatization' of practical and social life and a withdrawal into a family existence, in other words into a 'private' everyday.[3]

Of course, we shall return to these themes, and this is only an initial reply to those sociologists, historians and politicians who have denied and who continue to deny the importance of the problems of the everyday in the modern world, some going so far as to deny that it even exists. When we look closely, we can see that this denial constitutes an astonishing paradox, and we need to discover what it means and what the reasons for it are. Meanwhile, let us emphasize yet again the efforts which literature, cinema and even some specialists in the social sciences have made to get closer to the 'lived', to eliminate the arbitrary transpositions of the everyday, to grasp 'what is extraordinary within the ordinary', and 'the significance of the insignificant'. Questions of the value of this or that novel or film[4] or aesthetic theory apart, all this proves the validity of a critical study of everyday life.

3

In the Introduction to Volume I of *Critique of Everyday Life* we presented a programme of empirical and theoretical research, beginning with the elaboration of a *theory of needs*.

In the event, and for reasons we will explain forthwith, this programme has proved difficult to achieve. We will be quite open about these reasons, since in our view they compromise neither the concept of the everyday, nor the programme itself. Quite the reverse: they consolidate them, since they foreground the real and complex problems to which they are linked.

Established and slightly shop-worn concepts are easy to work with. Empirical study of social reality requires more patience. It is not more difficult per se. The real difficulty begins when concepts which are new and as yet not fully clarified come into confrontation with a mass of empirical documentation, and our thinking is prepared neither to give up those concepts in return for innumerable observations, nor to give up facts in return for a conceptual abstraction. As its programme implies, analytic and critical study of everyday life is particularly suited to the bringing together of facts and concepts. This does not mean that it presents a preordained highway along which to travel. On the contrary, it must blaze its own trail between philosophical reflections and fragmented and specialized research.

Working with general concepts, we can define man as a 'being of need' and construct a theory based on need and the world of need.

We can show how through need, want and the consciousness of want, man and his consciousness leave nature, childhood and a whole magical fairyland behind, though not without nostalgia and regrets. It is through privation that consciousness realizes that it has been hurled into life and the world, forced to create its own world in a distance relative to the (natural) being it was initially given and relative to itself, compelled forever both to recreate and to surmount that distance. The god-like amazement of seeing the world for the first time and the marvel of first smiles are not enough. If he is to work and to create, man must experience want. Without the experience of need and want, without actual or potential privation and destitution, there can be no being – consciousness, and freedom will never spring forth. In the land of its birth – 'nature' and the unconscious – being remains a prisoner. It is in and through need that freedom is born and finds ways of acting, and if it is to modify the real, there is a fissure in its hard surface which it must discover and penetrate. Finally, need defined as want is the starting point from which man begins to explore a world of possibilities, creating them, choosing between them and making them real. He enters the domain of history. His consciousness can never come to an end. The consciousness of individuals opens on to social consciousness and vice versa, and the multiplicity of human consciousnesses opens on to the world.

This set of propositions is based on classic texts, and notably on a large number of texts by Marx, some of which are very well known, others less so.[5] The result of a theoretical development of this kind (and it could be a lengthy one) would not be without interest; but it is philosophy in its accepted, classic sense: a philosophy of want and need, unilateral and abstract like all philosophy. It turns need into a 'world'.

While not forgetting it, we will leave this conceptual development behind us; let us look towards what is called the 'concrete' (wrongly so: the concrete is also present in philosophical abstraction). In the press, in (visual or written) advertising, in household budgets and accounts or just simply in language, it is easy to observe that an immense number of needs are being expressed. These needs are precise, as are the goods[6] (objects) which are proposed or imposed in order to satisfy them. We are no longer considering need in general, but rather the need for this or for that, and thus defined in relation to 'this' or to 'that' (the object, the product, the goods: its absence or the enjoyment of its possession). Let us note that the apparently clear concept of satisfaction and of the fulfilment of a need – the need for *this* or for *that* – is in reality very obscure. Being in its entirety feels the pressures of need, whether it be satisfied or not. Will we simply describe, classify and 'typecast' these needs, and nothing more? That is how economists who specialize in consumer studies, or purely empirical sociologists, approach the matter. For us, the real problem is how to transfer from *need in general* (as a form of existence, as a manifestation of being) to the *need for this or for that* (in other words to a desire which is both individual and social, and as it manifests itself in everyday life). This theoretical transfer may not be impossible, but it is prodigiously complex. We will have to bring together an analytic presentation of needs and a dialectical determination of desires. If we are to arrive at a theory of the situations (concrete, of course) of social man, we must not lose track of the generic or general concept of man as 'being of need' when confronting the mass of contemporary facts.

We may be anticipating and taking the bloom off the part of our book which will be explicitly devoted to this question, but this does not worry us. Here as much as elsewhere we do not intend to avoid repetitions, or to take up the same theme, or to cast different lights on the same subject, or to treat different subjects using the same concept. What does social experience provide? *Desires*, transient and many-faceted desires, together with their 'motivations'. In spite of the indecisive character of this last concept, or rather because of it, we are led to something diffuse, obscure and real. To overestimate the 'motivations' of desires and desires themselves is to fall into subjectivism, psychologism and classic idealism. To disregard them is to fall into simplified and vulgar materialism and determinism, in which we forget man's obscure depths and his development. There are innumerable desires, some with often strange motivations. There are few fundamental needs: hunger and thirst, sex, play perhaps,[7] maybe the simple need to expend accumulated energy. Theorists do not agree either on the quality or the quantity of 'elementary' needs, or on the possibility of reducing them to a single, initial, primordial fundamental need: libido, *Trieb*, drive, will for being or will for power, etc. How can we pass from need or needs to desires? In other words: *what happens between them* in the *transition* from the one to the other?

Need is determined biologically and physiologically. It is 'generic': it belongs to the human species. Desire is at the same time both individual and social; in other words it is recognized – or excluded – by a society. Need is determined quantitively: a human organism needs so many calories, so many hours of sleep, etc. An industry needs so much energy and so many raw materials, so many machines. Desire however is qualified or qualitative. But these observations are too simple. Need is also spontaneity and vitality, and also depth and relationship to depth. So sexual need seems generically linked to reproduction; in the individual it cannot be separated from an organ and the way it functions, from a certain determined quantity of organic material, sperm or ova. At the same time, it is not only the drama of the relations between one individual and another (or the other) individual which is sketched out and foreshadowed through this need, it is not only the drama of the link between individual and species, it is universality which is being offered or withdrawn. These are the problems (or as philosophers put it, the problematic) of love. The biological and organic fact now appears like an initial and unique nucleus of being, now like a group (family) specificity, now like a general principle relative to the problems of the species, now like a proposed universality. We cannot limit ourselves to the organic or biological fact; as such, it is as abstract as the absolute idea of Love per se . . .

On the other hand, it is still too simple to see desire as qualitative and need as quantitative – the one psychological and sociological (or psycho-social), the other biological and physiological. There are needs which are social, objective and quantifiable: needs for so many sources of energy, so many houses or schools, etc. Economists and sociologists know these needs well. On the sociological level (to use the still-unclarified term 'level'), need and desire are still separate one from the other. A single human reality appears with two faces, one brutally objective – social need (for this or for that), the other subtly subjective – desire (for this or for that or for something else by means of this or that, or even for nothing or for the infinite or for pure surprise), with motivations which give meaning to the desired object and to desire itself.

There are many mediations between need and desire. In fact, there is everything: society in its entirety (productive activities and the modes of consumption), culture, the past and history, language, norms, commands and prohibitions, the hierarchy of values and preferences. Desire only becomes desire when it is assumed by the individual via his conflicts in a conscious amd accepted way, and when it is consciously confronted with 'goods' (the object) and the enjoyment afforded by them. It only truly becomes desire when it becomes a vital and spiritual power, accepted and used by the individual, and when his life is metamorphosed into a creative consciousness, creating and created: by becoming need once more. Initially, need is nature; it becomes a creative activity and comes to an end in the works creativity produces.

Now this is an immense journey, fraught with obstacles and pitfalls, empty spaces and gaping holes. The definition we have given of desire seems to be necessary, in that it condenses experience. And yet, if we accept it, it points to a limit, a kind of horizon. One may ask oneself whether there has ever been a true desire or even a true desire truly fulfilled. Kant, that theorist of the virtuous action, used to ask himself whether there had ever been a virtuous action which could conform to his concept. At every step of the immense journey, how many potential failures, deviations, regressions, mistakes correctable or beyond repair! But self-regulatory systems, such as feedbacks, do exist, which may be fragile and yet are real in the context of determined contexts and structures; an overall balance is established between differing needs, between satisfactions and dissatisfactions, as between offers and demands. Conversely, self-regulation does not appear to exist psychically. Always relative and forever in question, the balance of desires must be fought for time and time again. In the fabric of the everyday, the pathological and the abnormal are a constant menace to us.

Dreams, with their discontinuities, their surprising 'suspenses' and their obvious absurdities, sum up the transition from need to desire. They re-enact the journey from the certainty of need to the uncertainty of desire. Dramatically, they condense an enormous dramatic, social and individual history, marked out by symbols. It is not only the failures and the possibility of failure which they display, but also the illusory solution to potential failure which makes a different, more serious failure inevitable: nostalgia for the cosy warmth of the lost homeland, the journey back to an original state without problems, repetitions, refuge in symbols, and escape into a past of natural being in order to evade the problems of the being which is as yet unattained. In a spontaneous 'digest' of the drama of desire, dreams signal gaps and deviations, and in doing so make them more serious. If dreams re-enact the tremulous birth of desire, then should not desire act like dreams, going beyond the critical surface which separates sleeping and waking, images and the everyday, and create itself in an external form?

We are beginning to perceive an infinitely complex dialectical movement, which for the time being we will sum up with several propositions:

a) Desire is profoundly different from need. It can even go so far as to struggle against it, until it frees itself.

b) Initially, however, there is no desire without a need as its nucleus, its point of departure, its 'base' or 'foundation'. A desire without need can only be purely artificial, an extreme case which even the most subtly refined moral or aesthetic values or artificial modes of behaviour find difficult to create.

c) Sooner or later desire turns back towards need in order to regain it and to regain itself. By reinvesting itself within it, it rediscovers spontaneity and vitality. It is a return journey which crosses through the objectivity, impersonality and indifference of social need, as it is conventionally understood.

This dialectical movement permeates the everyday. It gives it life. The everyday is the space in which dialectical movement advances or comes to a halt, in an unpredictable blend of opaqueness and transparency, of clear-sightedness and blindness, of determinability and transience.

Therefore there is a transfer from need to desire which crosses the social and society in its entirety. This transfer is sometimes continuous, sometimes interrupted. Between myself and me, or if you like, between 'I' and 'me', or rather between 'me' and 'I' caught up in everyday life, there is everything. First and foremost there is language, which allows a consciousness of desire to be achieved and then inserted into praxis.

But this vision is still too simple. The transition from need to desire and the vital return of desire back to need, in order to reabsorb itself within it, this transition which the complexities of the journey have already impeded, is also obstructed by extraneous interventions. We live in a determined society (bourgeois or capitalist rather than socialist society, since that is different and in any case too badly understood for us to undertake a study of its everyday life). In 'consumer society', which is allegedly based upon mass consumption and massive production for needs, the manufacturers of consumer goods do all they can to manufacture consumers. To a large extent they succeed.

The consumer does not desire. He submits. He has 'strangely' motivated 'behaviour patterns'. He obeys the suggestions and the orders given to him by advertising, sales agencies or the demands of social prestige (not to mention worries about solvency, which are far from negligible). The circuit from need to desire and from desire to need is constantly being interrupted or distorted. These 'orders' from outside become subtly abstract fragments or absurdly concrete 'motivations'. Desires no longer correspond to genuine needs; they are artificial. Need no longer metamorphoses into desire. The process becomes complicated, or disintegrates. And yet it does not disappear; it continues its journey from the vital to the social, from want to fullness, from privation to pleasure, even if its nature is misunderstood or unrecognized. However, the 'system of needs', which Hegel considered to be the cement of social life, no longer seems coherent. It has been dissociated or shattered. As Guy Debord[8] so energetically put it, everyday life has literally been 'colonized'. It has been brought to an extreme point of alienation, in other words profound dissatisfaction, in the name of the latest technology and of 'consumer society'. Now this technology could make a different everyday reality *possible*. However, these very same causes have uniform effects, equalizing social needs and bringing 'desires' in line with one another; they replace previous highly diversified 'lifestyles' by everyday ways of living which are analogous, if not identical.

Therefore there can be no knowledge of the everyday without knowledge of society in its entirety. There can be no knowledge of everyday life, or of society, or of the situation of the former within the latter, or of their interactions, without a radical critique of the one and of the other, of the one by the other, and vice versa. For this knowledge, negative concepts (distance and omission, dissatisfaction, frustration or, more generally, alienation) are as indispensable as the positive ideas in use in the fragmented sciences.

4

Volume I of *Critique of Everyday Life* also promised a schematic of the situation of women in modern society. Two types of consideration prompted this intention. First, 'women' in general bear all the weight of everyday life; they are subjected to it much more than 'men', in spite of very significant differences according to social classes and groups. Their situation sums up what the everyday is. Second, this situation is an indicator and a measurement of the degree to which the human is achieved (or not) in a determined social practice, at a certain level of economic and social development, and at a certain degree of culture and civilization.

Now over the last ten years, this theme ('the situation of women' or 'the feminine condition') has subsided into literary and journalistic banality. It has given rise to polemics which have been as vague as they have been violent, and to very specialized monographs on points of interest but of minimal importance.

The salient feature of these polemics is that they were directly linked to political questions and to some quite astonishing political positions.[9] Like all polemics, they have their share of bad faith. Obligatory options, in other words choices, bias, partisan attitudes, party attitudes – all these make for an inextricable confusion. Everyone excels when it comes to pointing out other people's weak points. So, with statistics and texts at their fingertips, their partisans have no difficulty in showing the extent to which our society persists in disadvantaging women. And, with statistics and texts at their fingertips, the opponents of this neofeminism have no difficulty in showing that we are being threatened by a kind of modern matriarchy or gynaecocracy.

When polemics start off on the wrong foot, it is difficult to intervene without taking sides. This debate was a confrontation between misogynists and gynaecomaniacs. What was the point in intervening? Critique of everyday life has time on its side; it requires patience; it would be rather more in favour of people who wait for situations to mature (but it avoids those who let these situations atrophy, and who are human beings of another sort).

First and foremost the study of feminine reality implies the intervention of concepts which are still underdeveloped, for example the concept of *ambiguity*. If we say it is underdeveloped, it is because confused intuitions about obscure situations are often mistaken for concepts. If the object of the concept of ambiguity appears to be confused and unclear, the concept itself needs to be all the more clear and explicit.[10] In this day and age, who would deny that in 'being' or 'existence' or in 'life' or in 'praxis' there is much that is unclear and obscure? If the concept of unclearness and of obscurity remains

unclear and obscure, in other words if there is no concept, irrationalism triumphs. If the concept of unclearness and obscurity can be
clarified, then a (relative) rationalism will impose itself.

Study of the women's press, and above all of the so-called 'romantic' press, reveals a feminine world of singular ambiguity. That it
wishes to promote women socially is obvious, yet vague, and it does
not go beyond certain characteristics (themselves ambiguous) of the
vaguely defined social group they comprise. In the 'feminine world'
the analyst notices innumerable times the resurgence of myths, of
cosmological or anthropological symbolisms, which, from the perspective of modern science and technology, are all outdated. These
resurgences are analogous to something taking place on an apparently higher level than that of the 'romantic' press. If we have seen
the rebirth of myths in literature, art and culture, the criticism which
attacked these myths needed to be subtler than before; we have seen
the appearance of symbolisms, notably in cinema, at a time when old
symbols were being discredited and antisymbolism was intensifying
its campaign under the banner of realism or neoclassicism.

The analyst ponders these contradictory phenomena. He looks at
these publications which sell in their millions and asks himself what
link they establish between the everyday and the imaginary. On one
hand he tries to isolate themes (good luck and bad luck, chance
and destiny, happiness and fate) and their combinations, transferred to
the context of cosmological reference: the stars and their conjunctures.
On the other, he tries to capture the affective tonality maintained in
these readings. He discovers an ambiguous mixture of very practical
texts and of texts about the imaginary. His impression is that often the
practical texts (such as recipes, menus, dress patterns) read like
dreams, and that conversely the imaginary texts read in a practical
fashion, in a perpetual toing and froing from one to the other, in a
never-ending equivocation which reproduces itself indefinitely.

It is not easy to define what this ambiguity means. Is it a symptom
of the weakness and childishness persisting in a large number of
women? Is it a victory on the part of obscurantism and superstition?
Is it proof that this social group, 'women', is badly integrated in the
society in which we live? Is it a sign of resistance to the primacy of
technology and the rationalist ideology in industrial society? Or on
the contrary is it a confused protest against the shortcomings of

307

technology or a confused but profound perception of the role randomness plays? These questions need to be addressed.

It could be maintained that these facts and symptoms would disappear within a truly rational society in which the integration of women had been perfectly achieved, and where they would work normally in conditions which would resolve their specific problems. One may also think that this 'feminine world', with its mythologies and cosmologies (horoscopes, systems of correspondences and interpretations) demonstrates the permanence of a need or a deep desire to deny the triviality of the everyday by opening it up to the marvellous and to a kind of poetry, sometimes clumsy, sometimes subtle, which art and literature rediscover in their way but without being able to invest it in the everyday. This desire for another dimension of the everyday and the social may address itself to old-fashioned representations, but this does not make it any the less legitimate. It is like a serious game, an aestheticism for people deprived of art.

More concretely, the analysis of texts specifically directed towards women and their preoccupations reveals the permanence of *cyclic time scales* of biological and cosmic origin at the heart of the (intermittent or continuous) linear time scales imposed by technology and industrial labour. Now the link between the everyday and cyclic patterns and time scales, the time of day and night, week and month, season and year, is obvious. Furthermore, women's physiological and social lives place them at the junction between the controlled sector and the uncontrolled sector, which explains the role ideas such as good luck, bad luck or destiny play in their consciousness. All this reveals the link between the 'feminine world' and everyday life in a much clearer light. This link will be seen to be more profound than the (indispensable) studies of budget-time, women's work within and outside the home, etc., would have us believe.

Once more we see ourselves directed away from specific facts towards society in its entirety, and the analysis of totality. The study in isolation of the 'feminine condition' conceals more than one trap. Although it starts from characteristics which are indisputable, such a study runs the risk of recreating a metaphysical entity and an occult quality – the feminine, femininity – or conversely of dissolving these characteristics by considering important everyday problems to be minor ones. In order to avoid both these risks, we will not study the 'feminine condition' as a discrete unit, but instead we will divide it up across the whole range of our critique of everyday life. Thus the initial programme is restructured. While we will maintain the project for a *theory of needs*, we will abandon the theme of the feminine condition as a discrete and separate entity.

5

The obstacles confronting critical research into everyday life would be of little more than anecdotal interest if they did not afford us a theoretical experience. Here we are in the domain of movement, a domain which is at the same time extremely 'structured'. As we have just seen, it has been necessary to reconsider the concept of everyday life, to intensify it, to modify it, and to situate it in society as a whole. Research was focused on a huge pile of empirical facts (such as the appearance of new needs) and on a huge pile of documents (such as the 'women's press' and its themes). At the same time, a difficult conceptualization – to use the jargon of the social sciences – had to be undertaken.

Research in the domain of scientifically necessary abstractions (*concepts*) has adopted a threefold aspect. We have had to challenge a certain number of ideas and methodological tools, which had already been accepted but which were not yet fully developed, by confronting them with facts. An example would be the idea of *level*, which we will examine in a special section in chapter 2 in order to demonstrate how everyday life is one *level* of social reality. We have also had to introduce concepts which are new, but which correspond to a certain stage of knowledge and which therefore tie up with preoccupations and areas of research other than those relating to everyday life. An example would be the concept of the (*whole or total*) *semantic field*, which we will examine in chapter 4. By extension, we have had to *make concepts dialectical*, whether or not they are already known and accepted. Finally, it has been necessary to try to introduce some order into the immense theoretical and practical confusion which seems to be an aspect of modernity in general and the social sciences in particular, and which cannot be overlooked. This confusion stems from the proliferation of hypotheses, the considerable number of studies carried out, and their extremely uneven quality. When attempting to introduce some order and clarity, we must avoid simplification and artificial coherence. We have already pointed out this danger. It will confront us again in relation to ideas which are indispensable, but which if used or misused in an oversimplified way will allow us to substitute seductive and superficial coherences for the complexity of the facts. Some examples of this would be the ideas of *structure* and of *totality*, to which we will also devote some methodological considerations.

6

Among all these obstacles, one in particular is worth attention, namely politico-ideological controversies which, though inevitable and indispensable, have vitiated the atmosphere for research.

The social science sector is too involved in certain important interests not to be damaged in this way. The ensuing debates can be extremely lively, and perhaps this is to be welcomed. All in all, it is preferable to stagnation and indifference. The worst thing is that the one does not always exclude the other, and sometimes stagnation and indifference go hand in hand with virulent polemics, which are irrelevant to the actual issue.

No knowledge in any domain can move forward without controversy (and this is particularly true for political economy, sociology and history). Behind ideas there are men, and these men have their interests and their passions. Behind men there are other, vaster interests, those of groups, classes and nations. Only someone naive – or an academic – would insist that there should be a climate of affability and cosy tranquillity in the social sciences. But beyond a certain limit, it becomes almost impossible to work.

So in the last few years, how have these controversies changed? In the following way. It used to be agreed as a fact of civilization and the acquisition of culture that discussions degenerated when their arguments were used *ad hominem*. Now for some time many discussions, if not all (when they are carried out in public rather than by way of gossip or whispers), have rushed headlong and shamelessly beyond the pale. They begin with what used to be the conclusion. They become personal. They try to discredit, to disqualify, to dishonour. They try to show that the person they are arguing with is not 'valid'. They belittle him. In doing so, and without being aware of it, they are belittling themselves; the discussion itself is belittled, and they pretend not to notice.

If bourgeois thought, and we include liberalism in this, is trying to occupy a kind of artificially serene high ground, where it would be exempted from those genuine discussions which go right down to the 'foundations', then current dogmatism, and above all Marxist dogmatism, is just as guilty of breaking with the rules of dialogue. As a result the atmosphere is unlikely to improve overnight. Under the influence of Stalinism, controversies have become political operations deploying the techniques of propaganda. If you wish merely to 'neutralize' your opponent, you are being nice to him. More often than not, you will try your hardest to 'eliminate' him. As is always the case, these procedures of ideological warfare have gone well beyond the limited circle in which they originated. Bad manners have spread like wildfire. The good manners of liberalism are rather out-of-date, and have offered a feeble and timorous resistance.

The result is a generalized terrorism which would merit a study all of its own and which is part of a fairly serious and virtually ubiquitous contradiction between the creation of a new democracy and the undermining of the very foundations of this democracy. If minds, ideas and concepts manage not to be 'neutralized', then they are 'eliminated'. In the ideological jungle, terrorism rules. Everyone uses the same arsenal: intimidation, threats, repression. Terrorism paralyses. Be they liberals or not, those who 'resist' will suffer; ideas become stale and lifeless; men become tired and grow old. All the better for dogmatism and tyranny, or whatever you want to call them. Force and power have won. The procedures of the intellectual mandarinate and the techniques of intellectual gangsterism complement each other, though it is not the same men who use them.[11]

7

Putting this to one side, let us recapitulate the objections and aims of those who reject the idea of 'everyday life', or who deny that it has any interest. The arguments have been presented sometimes verbally,[12] sometimes in written form. We will sum them up without quoting names or texts. We will begin with the least 'intimidating' ones (by which we mean those who least use the authoritarian method).

Common-sense objections (Common sense is the trivial reflection of a fragmented practice, and should not be confused with good sense, which is nearer to analytic understanding and Cartesian reason.)

'To begin with, everyday life does not exist as a generality. There are as many everyday lives as there are places, people and ways of life. Everyday life is not the same in Timbuktu, in Paris, in Teheran, in New York, in Buenos Aires, in Moscow, in 1900, in 1960. In fact, what do the words mean? Whatever is repeated on a daily basis? The action of opening or shutting doors, of eating and drinking? Only organic functions correspond to your definition. Utterly without interest.

Everyday life in art? In politics? That must mean the everyday life of the artist, of the politician, what they eat, what they drink, how good or bad their digestion is. As far as art or politics is concerned, utterly unimportant. You are just a vulgar materialist . . .'

Reply

'Do you really think you have understood what the words *critique of everyday life* actually mean? Is it a question of describing, comparing and discovering what might be identical or analogous in Teheran, in Paris, in Timbuktu or in Moscow? Such an aim would indeed be restricted to the basic and the physiological. The aim of a critique of everyday life is quite different. It is a question of discovering what must and can change and be transformed in people's lives, in Timbuktu, in Paris, in New York or in Moscow. It is a question of stating critically how people live or how badly they live, or how they do not live at all. Would you go so far as to say that everyday life cannot change? If so, you destroy your own argument, because you have already admitted that it can. Critique implies possibilities, and possibilities as yet unfulfilled. It is the task of critique to demonstrate what these possibilities and this lack of fulfilment are. Do you think that basic physiological demands – organic functions, as you call them – are external to social life, to culture, to civilization, and are thus unchangeable, or relatively so? Such a postulate would be highly debatable and highly dangerous. Moreover, the term "everyday" has misled you. You take it literally rather than seeing its deeper meaning. Do you think that the repetitions which take place each week and each season are not part of everyday life? Frequently, and not for the last time, we have taken rhythms and cyclic time scales to be one of the contents of the everyday, with all that they organize and command, even when they are broken and fragmented by linear time scales. This is something which supersedes "the everyday" in its strictest sense. And another thing: do you think that art is external and superior to real life, and that what the artist creates is on a transcendental plane? Similarly, do you think that politics and the state are above everyday life and external to society? Critique of everyday life encompasses a critique of art by the everyday and a critique of the everyday by art. It encompasses a critique of the political realms by everyday social practice and vice versa. In a similar sense, it includes a critique of sleep and dreams by wakefulness (and vice versa), and a critique of the real by the imaginary and by what is possible, and vice versa. This is to say that it begins by establishing dialectical links, reciprocities and implications rather than an unrelated hierarchy, as you do. Finally, please note that what you say about the diversity of everyday lives is less and less true. Technological or industrial civilization tends to narrow the gaps between lifestyles (we are not talking about living standards) in the world as a whole. Having said that, your argument has a point and raises a question. Would everyday life be merely the humble and sordid side of life in general, and of social practice? To repeat the answer we have already given: *yes* and *no*. Yes, it is the humble and sordid side, but not only that. Simultaneously it is also the time and the place where the human either fulfils itself or fails, since it is a place and a time which fragmented, specialized and divided activity cannot completely grasp, no matter how great and worthy that activity may be . . .'

Objections from historians

'Everyday life is an aspect of history, an interesting one, maybe, but minor. To study it in itself and for itself entails certain dangers. Like it or not, aren't you falling back on the anecdotal, on something external to events and their deep-seated reasons and causes? Over the last few years there have been volumes and even entire series dedicated to everyday life in such and such a society, at such and such an epoch. Sometimes these are the work of serious historians. But do you honestly believe that they do not bypass history, that they are not merely marginal or anecdotal? Except when they deal with archaic societies, and are written by ethnographers, they add nothing to what we already know . . .'

Reply

'Agreed on one major point: history is a fundamental science. The human being is historical and its historicity is inherent to it: it produces and is produced, it creates its world and creates itself. Having said that, let us not simplify the process of historical becoming, and let us avoid historicism. Everything is historical, agreed, but not equally so. History as a science does not exhaust the human. It neither eliminates nor absorbs political economy, sociology or psychology. Remember what we sometimes refer to as historical drift, in other words the gap between intentions, actions and results. There can be no history without a critique of history itself. Above all remember the issue of uneven development. In the links between mankind (human groups) and nature, is that not a significant factor? And there is not only history, but culture too, and civilization . . . The more we distance ourselves from our "Promethean" society, and the more we look back towards archaic societies, the less the everyday life we are able to reconstruct is distinguishable from culture and historicity (in so far as there was history and historicity in such societies). In archaic groups, difference seems to disappear. Could their everyday be defined as the secular as opposed to the sacred? But the former haunted the latter, since even the humblest functional object was not just a product, and even less a thing, but a work of culture and art. Whether it was perfect or only half-finished, it was the bearer of multiple symbols and meanings! Let us not idealize this past. Let us not lapse into ethnographical romanticism. For us, here, the question is the modern everyday. We observe that history has had the following result: the separation from what is historical per se of that other aspect of history and of the human which we call the everyday. Today, in our society, everyday life and culture, everyday life and historical event, are dissociated (but without losing their solidarity completely). Marx was the first to perceive this characteristic of the period. Read the *Critique of Hegel's Philosophy of the State* again, where Marx points out the modern rift between private and public life which did not exist in antiquity or in the Middle Ages.

> The abstraction of the *state as such* was not born until the modern world because the abstraction of private life was not created until modern times . . . The abstract reflected antithesis of this is to be found only in the modern world. The Middle Ages were an age of *real* dualism; the modern world is the age of *abstract* dualism.[13]

We could study literary history, and in particular the history of the novel, in this light. We would see how the narrative of the novel distances itself from the epic and the tragic, just as the everyday it describes becomes distant from historical action and cultural totality. In fact it is true that at certain moments institutions, culture, ideologies and the most important results of history are forcefully brought into the everyday life over which they formerly towered; there they find themselves accused, judged and condemned: grouped together, people declare that these institutions, these ideas, these forms of state and culture, these "representations" are no longer acceptable and no longer represent them. Then, united in groups, in classes, in peoples, men are no longer prepared to live as before, and are no longer able to do so. They reject whatever "represented", maintained and chained them to their previous everyday life. These are the great moments of history: the stirrings of revolution. At this point, the everyday and the historical come together and even coincide, but in the active and violently negative critique which history makes of the everyday. After which, the wave subsides and spreads out in a backward surge. What other moments are there when the distance between what history makes possible and what it has achieved becomes so great, like the distance between what men have wanted, what has resulted, and what they have lived? History is necessary, but by itself it is inadequate. According to Marx, this historicity is nothing more than a summary of the prehistory of mankind, and indeed the men it tries to define become aware of alternative forms of knowledge and critique.

To sum up, the historian wishes to challenge the critique of everyday life in the name of science: but critique of everyday life will in turn challenge and accuse history in so far as it is a mere series of faits accomplis, in so far as it is history which has reduced the everyday to the state in which we find it!'

Objections from philosophers

'Be careful! There are particular sciences and there is philosophy. Each social science has its own domain, its vocabulary, its specific concepts and operational techniques. As for philosophy, it has its own concepts, terminology and intentions. It seeks either to attain being, or to totalize knowledge, or to bring something or other which has hitherto eluded it into language, in other words into consciousness and knowledge, or finally, to construct a total and totally coherent discourse. Does your critique of everyday life fall within any particular social science? It would seem not, even though now and then one glimpses a taste for sociology, and even unilateral sociologism. Does it come under philosphy? No, you have said so yourself. Rather it would claim to supersede philosophy by dismantling it and filching some of its categories. In a word, if we admit and accept that these disciplines correspond to precise theoretical procedures and to a certain general structure of human knowledge and consciousness, then it does not fit into any one of them. Moreover, what you call everyday life is simply what has been lived, and inauthentically lived: Heidegger's "ontic", external to the ontological; this is precisely what the philosopher must avoid if he is to unveil the authentic and to reveal the truth of being. Instead of lifting them, you are going to make these veils more opaque, and without contributing to the accumulation of positive learning and knowledge of the real.'

Reply

'The general question of philosophy has been debated time and time again, and at this point we will return to it only briefly. Because of its failure to supersede itself by fulfilling itself – or by fulfilling the aims and aspirations of philosophers by superseding abstract philosophical thought – philosophy finds itself in a difficult situation. It goes on seesawing between system and experiment, between state ideology and anarchizing critique. Today, if we must provisionally redefine it, our definition would differ from yours: it is an attempt to bring the greatest possible quantity of present-day human experience, the experience of our so-called "modern" era, along with the practical experience of love, political action or knowledge, into a set of reflections and concepts. This will bring us out of systematic tradition and the generally accepted tautology which turns philosophical discourse into a philosophy of discourse. In this effort to experience a totality (and the limits of discourse itself) philosophy includes a critique of philosophy, and this involves critique of everyday life on more than one account. To begin with, it is a mode of the "lived" which we have no right to overlook or to parenthesize in the name of higher or supposedly higher experiences. On the other hand, after the great hopes fostered by revolution, is not the situation of the everyday a specific experience, even a political one? What did Marx mean when he maintained that it would soon be time to stop interpreting the world and to begin transforming it? Did he mean simply the outside world? Here and now, we say no. For Marx, to transform the world was also and above all to transform the human world: everyday life. When they interpreted the world, philosophies brought plans for its transformation. Were we to fulfil philosophy, were we to change the process of the philosophical becoming of the world into the process of the world-becoming of philosophy, would that not be to metamorphose everyday life? We will therefore go so far as to argue that critique of everyday life – radical critique aimed at attaining the radical metamorphosis of everyday life – is alone in taking up the authentic Marxist project again and in continuing it: to supersede philosophy and to fulfil it. As far as the problem you pose is concerned, namely that of "relevance" in relation to a specific fragmented science, we will return to it shortly, and more than once. You formulate the problem in a very narrow way, thus vetoing anything which fails to fit into your self-imposed framework. In any event that is merely a secondary problem. It is true that critique of everyday life raises the question of authenticity, but it does so in its own particular way. Everyday life per se is neither the authentic nor the inauthentic. Instead it could be seen to define the milieu and the moment in time where they come into conflict, where authenticity justifies itself and must show its credentials. To take some examples from everyday life, neither love nor the relations between parents and children, say, are stamped in advance with inauthenticity. Doesn't all love want to embody itself in the everyday? Isn't that its wish? If you judge otherwise, it is because you are defining the authentic as exceptional and in the end as solitude, failure and death. It is to counter this excessive and speculative hypothesis that critique of everyday life launches its challenge: "Either man will be in the everyday or he will not be at all. He will live his everyday life by superseding the everyday life he lives today, or else he will no longer be. As long as everyday life has not radically changed, the world will be the same as ever. It is up to radical critique to bring those changes to the world! . . ."

As for the "lived" and *Lebenswelt,* the entry of such terms into philosophical thought marks a date or rather a turning point. Henceforth, philosophy must choose. It can stay within its habitual context and preserve its traditional categories, i.e., pure research into being by means of meditation: ontology. In this case it lapses into dogmatism, into the pure and impotent description of what exists, or into irrationalism. Conversely it can metamorphose into a critique of everyday life which uses the old ideas, above all the idea of alienation, but in a new way (which is difficult and problematic, and as yet to be determined). The option is not apparent everywhere, and is not always clear. The paths cross. Although the idea of inauthenticity is confused, it is a critical idea which we can use when we need to, modifying it and giving it practical meaning and content.

When philosophy tries to use the term the "lived" in a way which encompasses a determinable experience it immediately gets closer to becoming critical analysis of everyday life. Where does the intersubjectivity Maurice Merleau-Ponty talks about in his latest book[14] express itself, and where can it be grasped? The reply leaves no grounds for doubt, in our mind at least. All that remains is to add the negative dimension, that of radical critique.

Perhaps we will dare to go even farther and to say:

The time has come to summon up that elusive and pregnant reality, the everyday, and to bring it forth into language. The content of so much discourse has been based upon the everyday, but without being explicit or overt. Let us bring it openly and coherently into language and discourse, while not forgetting that language and discourse have their limits. Is that not a specifically philosophical procedure, or what, according to you yourself, used to be an essential procedure of philosophy? This is how Freud proceeded with sexuality, Marx with praxis, labour and production relations, Hegel with dialectical movements, Aristotle with language, logos and logic, and others with political life, the state, history, etc. With an action such as this as starting point, other creations which supersede it will become possible . . . Would this be too ambitious?

Objections from the fragmented sciences

'The social sciences – economics, history, sociology, psychology – are at an empirical and positive stage, that of specialization. They have left empirical and philosophical generalities behind once and for all. The scholar must define as narrow a *field* as possible. Then he must explore it, get close to it, and as soon as he can quantify it, he must treat it in a precise way. Thus such a scholar will no longer accept the concept of "everyday life" any more than he will any other general, totalized concept. This is all the more reason for him to reject a "critique" which cannot distinguish the value of positive facts, since by essence it denies facts in the name of a value. The scholar wants to be purely empirical and purely positive.'

Reply

'Specialists have every right, except the right to condemn critical thought to silence in the name of a conception of the real which they rarely explain and which is not relevant to anything. The "positivity" of this realness derives from critical thought, which begins by establishing that the negative and the possible are just as "real" as the positive real. The conception of a reality which would be the personal property of the specialist dealing with it produces a curious attitude: a paternalism, not to say an imperialism. Nothing gives these specialists the right to observe everyday life from aloft and from afar simply because they do not deem it worthy of being a specialism.

319

In any case, it would be easy to demonstrate that their specialisms often overlap into everyday life: they cut into it technically. Too many specialists regard their "field" as private property. As far as their "realness" is concerned, they have a curious way of dealing with it, which consists in thickening it, giving it consistency, making it so stiff it stands up by itself. As housewives say when they whip cream or make mayonnaise: they thicken it. Once it has "thickened", this realness is no longer a small field; it is a domain, a region, and if it has been whipped up by an expert hand it even becomes a little "world". Next, once his right of ownership has been established and he holds the deeds in his hand, the specialist can relax completely, enjoying his field and thinking about who he will bequeath it to. He can also think about extending it by appropriating more land. He becomes a touch imperialistic. Once the specialist becomes an unwitting technocrat, this is how his alienating and alienated, reifying and reified attitude functions. However, the best possible reply would be to integrate a "conceptual development" with a coherent set of empirical research programmes. We think that study (critique) of everyday life lends itself particularly to such a confrontation between facts and concepts. It goes without saying that concepts which originated in philosophy but which are no longer part of any philosophical system (alienation, totality, cycle, repetition, the process of dialectical becoming, etc.) must be tested by facts. If they survive this test, they will take their place among those concepts which allow us to dominate the plethora of facts and to go beyond the scope of fragmented research; in other words, they will become scientific concepts. As we know, an orientation of this kind is not without its difficulties. How are we to demolish an edifice as sturdy as philosophy? If a construction is coherent, how are we to extract separate concepts from it? And then, how are we to confront these concepts with facts in order to make them concrete? According to what criteria are we to ascertain that they have become experimental and that they have graduated from speculative philosophy to scientific knowledge?

These difficulties are at the heart of our research. They are its specific problems. In any event, critique of everyday life (in so far as it is knowledge as well as critique) consists of a twofold rejection of fragmented specialization and of the elevation of any specific science into the sum total of the other fragmented sciences (and is thus a rejection of sociologism, historicism and psychologism). There is a precise point on which we can reassure the specialists. Critique of everyday life is not intended to be a new specialism, or a particular branch of sociology. What it is undertaking is a total critique of totality. The most specialized and most technical research programmes are legitimate only if they satisfy the following conditions: that they do not change into a technocratic dictatorship within the social sciences (and elsewhere) and that the specialists admit the "positivity" of several negative and critical concepts which do not introduce value judgements external to the facts but which are clearly necessary for those facts to be understood.

We find that once the specialist has "set" the real to a compact consistency, giving the illusion of concrete perfection, it is often more apparent than real. The world of appearances lends itself to such treatment. The dialectic of what is real and what is apparent is well known. There is no pure appearance, no phenomenon which could only be a phenomenon without something behind it. The "real" displays itself by means of phenomena, thus by means of appearances: what is essential is made manifest. Thus every appearance and every phenomenon contains a certain reality. They reveal and they conceal this reality. To reach the essential, knowledge must both grasp it and push it to one side. Let us add here and now that these concepts of dialectical logic and methodology must be made relative. Appearance from one point of view is reality from another point of view. Thus, for the sociologist, up to a certain point, the psychological is appearance, and vice versa.

In critical analysis of everyday life, today's "consumer society" represents such a world of appearances. It hides a deeper reality: the manufacture of consumers by those who hold the means of production and who produce for profit. Consequently their perception of what needs are is governed by the profits to be gained from them. At the same time, this appearance contains and reveals a certain reality: the elimination of traditional "lifestyles", the levelling of needs, and the narrowing of the gaps between needs and lifestyles (and as we have said before, this does not mean the equalizing of standards of living).'

Objections from culturalists and structuralists

'How right you are to criticize the fragmented knowledge provided by specialized techniques and to wish to integrate them into a corpus of knowledge! But come on, at least be coherent! Follow your thinking through to its logical conclusion. What is a corpus of knowledge without organization, without an inner structure, without systematization? So, if a coherent structure such as this is to correspond to reality, surely general concepts, forms and structures must already be inherent in that reality. All knowledge relates to a totality. The idea of totality belongs at the centre of the real and at the centre of knowledge. This idea alone can guarantee that the two correspond. Moreover, in this day and age this ancient philosophical idea is becoming more precise. The ideas of structure, form, signification, culture and world-view make it more concrete; when they separate it from specifically philosophical systematizations, they give it the capacity to explore the real. If these ideas are profound enough to permit inexhaustible explanations, they are exhaustible in terms of the historical, economic and sociological humanness they encompass. From the moment it ceases to refer to a totality, critique of everyday life has no object . . .'

Reply

'The present prestige of the concept of *structure* arises largely from a general confusion. How could a concept which brings order and classification to all this chaos not be welcome? However, this coherence should not obscure movement. If the logical application of the concept of structure disguises the "destructurings" and "restructurings" which are in operation – the changes and action of the negative – then that too must be submitted to radical critique. Once the theoreticians of a science have discovered a fruitful concept, after a relatively extended period of time they often lose their scientific circumspection. They too forget that, inevitably, every concept and every technique has its limits, and so they proceed like the philosophers of the past did, and like specialists and technicians are doing today. They extrapolate from a strictly determined investigation. They transform the fruitful concept into an absolute, an ontological principle. They too become dogmatic. Thus an implement for knowledge, which is valid in certain conditions and in a determined sphere, is turned into a fetish. Over the last few years we have seen how the importance of certain otherwise valid concepts, such as structure, signification and totality, has been exaggerated to the point of fetishism. This fact is all the more remarkable in that certain minds which have strayed along the path of fetishism and dogmatism have in the past been often brilliant and worthy opponents of other fetishisms and dogmatisms. In this way we pass from the methodologically legitimate use of "structure" to a dogmatic structuralism, from the valid use of "culture" to a culturalism. More particularly, as soon as the theoretician believes he has grasped the idea of *totality*, it lays itself open to dogmatic misuse. At that point, he will either integrate you into his totality, or he will reject you.

The excuse of these theoreticians is that only by employing concepts can their limits be determined. How can one tell in advance whether a certain use is legitimate or not? Experience shows us that use quickly becomes misuse. Ideas have boundaries. We must do everything in our power to find out where these boundaries lie, and if we are to map them out we must cross them. Extrapolations and exaggerations are inevitable. All in all, a dogmatism which presumes to mark boundaries, and to signal danger zones in advance, presents more dangers than speculative unilaterality. These are likely to lead to the same tempting deception: dogmatism and the ontological illusion.

Theoretically, every concept exhausts itself. Thus excesses, superfluities, extrapolation and fetishisms contain within themselves their own critique (which is not to say that dogmatisms are capable of autocritique!). In practical terms, "scientific milieux" are human groups, and behave like many other groups. They will only give up on an interest, a technique or an idea when it has become "*saturated*". This consideration leads us prematurely into the everyday life of science, into the sociology of the mandarinate and the sociology of boredom. Let us put it to one side. Conclusion: we must resign ourselves to seeing concepts used until they are exhausted, and consequently to witnessing the saturation of these milieux. Let us generalize with the following Hegelian aphorism: the moment a dogmatism triumphs is the moment its end is nigh.

Having said that, it is impossible to separate "life" (nature), everyday life and culture into a kind of theoretical triumvirate. Such a distinction would duplicate the old theory of the three elements of man: the body, the soul and the mind. But these are merely preliminary considerations, not really pertinent to our concerns and, when all's said and done, they are merely academic. Let us go to the heart of the matter. Yes, there are social structures which maintain and cement society "as it is" (by aligning it with things, which, as we know so well, are what they are) on different levels of existence and consciousness. The principal function of these social structures is to obscure the horizons of everyday life, making it appear as a mere series of real moments within the real, and nothing more.

Yes, there is a culture which plays its part in structures, and it is located alongside other superstructures with less dignified names. Its main function is to make everyday life (apparently) coherent, to establish its coherence with itself and with the so-called superior norms and models, to blend "existence", "the lived", "the everyday" together until they are indistinguishable, and until future possibilities are blocked off, and the metamorphosis of the everyday appears impossible.

To the age-old problem of philosophers: "How can what is *be*?", to Kant's problem: "How can we know what we know?", to the problem of more recent thinkers: "How can what is born be born", we add another, simpler but just as serious: "How can men live as they are living, and how can they accept it?" Put another way, why does not every one of us imitate the man (the bourgeois) Kierkegaard talks about, who without warning feels he is suffocating and begins shouting: "Give me something possible! Give me something possible!"? This is an incontestable cultural fact, and demonstrates the effect structures have.

Voluntarily or not, when structure and culture are fetishized there is a risk that, although they are provisional and questionable, they will be turned into absolutes.

Our avowed aim is on the contrary to dissolve these structures and to demonstrate their state of dissolution in the very procedures of their restrictive functions. It is also to demonstrate the advanced disintegration of a culture which is all the more "negative" because it wishes itself and calls itself "positive". Because it claims to create something real, it is all the more destructive of future possibilities.

However well-meaning their scientific intentions are, the purveyors of structuralism and culturalism have not thought their concepts through, and this is our bone of contention with them. We will employ these self-same concepts in our arguments against their apologists, and against others as well.

As for the idea of totality, the problem is even more complex, and we will need to consider it very closely.

The idea of everyday life is only meaningful within a totality, but we must perceive that totality dialectically. If totality (society as a whole, social structure, culture, etc.) is to correspond to anything at all, all it must do is admit and contain levels (or if you like, "degrees" or "stages"). Everyday life can be defined as a level of social practice within totality. Or, in less unattractive and more poetic words, as a somewhat neglected fragment of it.

This introduces an additional reason why it is essential to elucidate the constantly used but as yet unclarified concept of *level . . .*'

The 'class perspective' and its arguments

'The real life, the everyday life of the working class has nothing in common with that of the bourgeoisie. It is therefore impossible to conflate them in the same concept, or to study them under the same heading. That would be an idealist distortion: the point of view of a sociologist who ignores class contradictions. Moreover, if it is true that the world and life must be changed, why study the very thing which has to be changed, which has to be transformed? The hardships of proletarian life should only be considered in order to provoke shame and anger, in other words for propaganda reasons only . . .'

Reply

'The partisans of the "class perspective" often forget that the proletariat and the bourgeoisie make up the same society, which is much more complex than the representation of two conflicting forces, face to face and mutually exclusive. Even in the struggles and conflicts of class and their antagonisms, the wholeness of society does not disappear (which is what justifies terms such as "society", "world society", "society as a whole", etc., which otherwise would be meaningless). This is a truism which Stalin himself sometimes had to point out to those class-perspective dogmatists who were frequently guilty

325

of class subjectivism. To round this point off, let us add that "society" is not only French society (or American, or Russian, in other words one specific national society), it is also capitalist (or socialist) society, modern industrial (or technological) society. While accepting that they designate units or types which are larger than a country or a nation, we have yet to determine the exact meaning of these terms, and exactly what the links between them are.

In a specific society (French and capitalist for example), at a certain state of development of the productive forces, at a certain level of civilization, do the *needs* of the working class differ absolutely from the needs of the bourgeoisie? This study demonstrates that they do not. Indeed, these needs are similar, and as we have already said, this is the reality of the otherwise mystifying idea of "consumer society". Needs are related to the productive forces and their level of development. Even more significant would be the question that, if the proletariat differs from the bourgeoisie from this perspective, would it not be because of the liveliness, complexity and abundance of its needs and desires? Certainly, while there is a quantitative and qualitative disparity (of "standards of living") between the extent to which these needs and desires are satisfied, needs tend to equalize. Privation and frustration (with their corollary: protest activity) imply and reveal the growth of needs, if only in their initial stages. This idea is important. It could be that an eventual and certainly *possible* social transformation might come from the pressure brought by needs more than by absolute poverty, want and pauperization.

When the unremitting partisans of the "class perspective" presented the car, the refrigerator, the washing machine and the television set as examples of superfluous and parasitic consumption by social strata which themselves were parasitic, they made several mistakes (objectively and scientifically speaking). They failed to understand the growth of needs and the way they have been used – and diverted – in bourgeois society. They confused differing facts: political propaganda via the television, for example, and the generalized need for information and communication. They replaced knowledge by ideology and real problems by the illusion of dogmatic certainty. In a word, they were perpetuating a rather old-fashioned, almost mythic image of the working class: a mass united by poverty, destitution, toil, absence of pleasures and profound want, including the want of basic needs.

In the general theory of needs, we will demonstrate how the proletariat as such contains the total human phenomenon – need, work, pleasure[15] – and how it remains close to the fundamental spontaneity which is revealed in these three dimensions. Dogmatism has no right to reduce the working-class social and human being to a single dimension, labour (on the pretext of saving the working class from reformism and of preserving an abstractly revolutionary project).

In this light, the bourgeoisie presents a mutilated reality, in that all it wants is pure pleasure. It is stricken by alienation, different from but more profound than the alienation which mutilates groups within the working class. Through dissatisfactions and privations, the working class maintains and asserts human totality. In other words, it bears what is most burdensome in the everyday. All it has is its everyday life. And if its life is to be transformed, then everyday life must be transformed, or to put it another way, sooner or later the working class will transform itself and will transform "the world" by transforming everyday life. That is the truth within "the class perspective", a truth which is not apparent in the discourse of those who support it . . .'

The political argument

'Political revolution transforms the world. It starts by transforming everyday life, since it happens precisely when the members of a society no longer wish to go on living as they have lived hitherto. It is true that this initial transformation is not absolute: it continues during the construction of socialism and the gradual transition to communism. Historical circumstances can facilitate this transition or hinder it. In any event, after the revolution, everyday life in socialist countries has nothing in common with everyday life in capitalist countries, which are controlled and developed by the bourgeoisie. It takes on a different meaning. Political consciousness, the consciousness of man living in the future and for the future, is enough to change it completely. Any comparison would be meaningless, and can never be anything other than absurd. So that in itself to compare means to betray, to deny, to reject what is essential in favour of what is contingent.

Reply

'In the political or "party" perspective it is not difficult to detect the extension of the "class perspective" pushed to the absolute. The Marxist officials who support it confuse the ideological with the lived, and this confusion makes up part of their ideology. The error is twofold: to exaggerate the role of ideology is to compromise it by wrongly muddling it up with the praxis it produces or "reflects". There is no longer any distinction between what knowledge, ideology, theory and praxis really are. A philosophical blanket has been thrown over everything.

It is certain that in the countries of the "socialist camp", ideologies and, more generally, superstructures have changed in the wake of a political revolution. Therefore everyday life has changed for people living on the plane of superstructures: the political and administrative apparatus, the militants, the ideologues, the men of politics. One can see that as ideologues, statesmen and members of an apparatus, they set themselves up on a plane exterior and superior to the everyday. Since Marx, this analysis has formed part of the theory of the state, of ideologies and of superstructures.

In the socialist countries, profound and irreversible historical changes have taken place in terms of society as a whole. All well and good. Politically, the state has transformed itself, although without moving towards the withering away contemplated by Marx and by Lenin. Economically, the process of accumulation is accelerating, above all in heavy industry (production of the means of production). As far as technical progress is concerned, these countries are in the lead. However, in so far as we know anything about it, the experience of the socialist countries demonstrates that their everyday life is changing very slowly. Everyday life may well be the slowest thing to change, and as soon as it experiences any difficulties, it may even adopt the old forms again, falling back into time-worn ruts. It can be backward, and very much so, in terms of the processes operating at the economic base (the productive forces) and at the apex (the ideological and political superstructures). Between the two, on the intermediary level of social relations, the everyday drags itself along in the wake of change. More than that: it resists change. Individuals and groups, including the working class, withdraw into the everyday, or at least when comprehensive changes do not offer them a new, acceptable and desirable lifestyle. Can one blame them? The masses come together to make revolution because they are no longer willing to live as hitherto. If revolution fails to bring them the new life they hoped for (and which perhaps can be expressed in Utopian terms: revolution, communism), if the revolution only changes representations, these masses seek refuge in an everyday which is an extension of the previous one: private life, scant public or political life, family life, life based upon the close relations of neighbourhood and friendships. Could not these facts be responsible for one of the inner contradictions of the world socialist and communist movement? On one hand, an officialized ethic encourages this withdrawal, which makes it possible to distinguish between work and life beyond work, and thus to devote the maximum energy to productive labour. On the other hand, is it not sometimes necessary to shatter the stability of the everyday and the obscure resistance it puts up through the structures it re-establishes at times of important change?

Now let us go to the heart of the problem. Official Marxism is inspired by Marxist thought. In fact, it does retain a certain number of concepts and representations (in political economy, in general politics, in philosophy and in ideology). However, it has lost sight of the initial Marxist agenda. Moreover, the purpose of the general philosophy which has placed itself under the patronage of Marx is to conceal this oversight or omission. Its role is to entertain and to divert. In the name of philosophical materialism (historical and dialectical, the one hopelessly confused with the other), it makes no attempt to reinstate the initial Marxist project, improperly insisting instead upon the materiality of the outside world, on its exteriority and anteriority in relation to thought and consciousness. The test and criterion of this abuse is the theory of the withering away of the state, which was essential to Marx and Lenin, but was concealed during the Stalinist period.

What did Marx want? What did the initial Marxist project consist of? Let us reinstate it once again in all its authenticity. First and foremost Marx wanted to change everyday life. To change the world is above all to change the way everyday, real life is lived. In so far as the times he lived in allowed him to contemplate such hypotheses, Marx considered that the upheaval in external nature and the conquest of space as a result of technical development on a colossal scale would only happen after human life had been metamorphosed.

How did he imagine this would be? We know that he was careful not to construct the future along the lines of Utopian socialists such as Saint-Simon, Fourier or Owen (although their theories had inspired him). He was mindful of the role of the unforeseen and the new in historical development (and how right he was!). Nevertheless he suggested certain tendencies which must be prolonged or promoted if superior wholeness and totality is to be achieved, if divided man is to be superseded, and if "the world turned topsy-turvy" is to be set aright again.

In Marx there are two projects for the transformation of everyday life. They lie halfway between Utopia and practice, but they both imply a total revolutionary praxis.

The first project is of an *ethical* order. It stipulates that the reciprocity of the needs and desires of men (as individuals and groups) be recognized. It implies the knowledge and, even better, the transparency of the relations between the two. It implies the end of the "social mystery", in other words of everything which makes the relations between men opaque and elusive, and which conceals these relations from their consciousness and their actions.

It is clear that this project is an extension of Hegelian thought, but with one essential modification. It is no longer the state which embodies and fulfils the ethical idea. On the contrary it is private, everyday life which raises itself to the superior level of the ethical; it is as though one of the effects of the withering away of the state is that the state's very substance is assimilated by the domain which has been kept exterior to it, subordinated to it and reduced by it to an abstraction which is a reverse but symmetrical image of the state's own abstraction. Marx proved the state guilty of malpractice: by its very essence it perpetuates the social mystery, swathing "private" and "public" social relations in murky shadows, by the simple fact that it splits them, divides them and makes them abstract.

The second project is *aesthetic* in nature. It is committed to the notion of art as a higher creative activity, and a radical critique of art as an alienated activity (exceptional, allocated to exceptional individuals and producing exceptional works which are external and superior to everyday life). At one and the same time, art must fulfil itself, and then supersede itself. Ultimately it must disappear. The creative activity of art and the work of art foreshadow joy at its highest.[16] For Marx, enjoyment of the world is not limited to the consumption of material goods, no matter how refined, or to the consumption of cultural goods, no matter how subtle. It is much more than that. He does not imagine a world in which all men would be surrounded by works of art, not even a society where everyone would be painters, poets or musicians. Those would still only be transitional stages. He imagines a society in which everyone would rediscover the spontaneity of natural life and its initial creative drive, and perceive the world through the eyes of an artist, enjoy the sensuous through the eyes of a painter, the ears of a musician and the language of a poet. Once superseded, art would be reabsorbed into an everyday which has been metamorphosed by its fusion with what had hitherto been kept external to it.

All in all, according to the first model, in the realms of the state and of politics, and consequently in objective morality and the law, the social powers of men have been alienated. They must turn back to and reabsorb themselves in private life in order to metamorphose it. According to the second model, men's spiritual powers, which have been realized but alienated in art, must journey back to ordinary life and invest themselves in it by transforming it.

As it happens, the duality of these images of what is possible opens up a new problem, that of the supersession of this duality in an even more total metamorphosis of the everyday, which would be achieved by the intervention of a unifying praxis.

Utopia? Fantasy? Imagination? It's unimportant. If one is inspired by Marx, everything must be judged in relation to his project: reality, what is possible, what has been achieved, history, revolution.

In fact, Marx provided very practical bases for this "Utopian" project: the growth of the productive forces in a pleasure economy (geared towards the greatest satisfaction of the greatest number of social needs and individual desires, quantitatively increased and qualitatively refined), the withering away of the state, etc.

It is evident that world revolution has not exactly followed the path Marx predicted. Why should we not admit it? The power alien to human thoughts and intentions, which we must call "destiny" ("historical necessity" and at the same time "randomness", "chance", "historical drift" in terms of projects and actions) is alone responsible. There has been no revolution in the advanced industrialized countries. Capitalism has corralled it. Revolution has been forced to abandon everything which in the first few years still corresponded to the original project. It has been forced to devote itself to accumulation, to giving priority to heavy industry, to maintaining a powerful army with all the equipment this entails. Thus technological imperatives have moved to the foreground. In a remarkably uneven development, everyday life has lagged behind technology to an immense degree! Given all the random circumstances, this was inevitable and "necessary". We must recognize the work of historical necessity in so far as it has made reality deviate in relation to the project, and results in relation to intentions. Let us accept this discrepancy. We should evaluate it rather than deny that it exists. If knowledge does not gain from this, then ideology will.

Has Marx's programme lost its meaning and validity? No. It is still the only project which implies a true conception of what is humanly possible. Why? Because it is alone in not contemplating simply a transformation of ideas or representations – an ideology – but rather a total metamorphosis of everyday life, bringing to an end those divisions and contradictions which make "the real" and "the possible" lag behind in a period when *uneven development* has become the norm.

Up until now, one of the great paradoxes of the twentieth century has been that capitalist economy has apparently taken the form of a "pleasure economy". Like a caricature of itself, this economy sometimes goes so far as to become organized waste. Since it conceals the economy of power while organizing, controlling and pulverizing pleasure, it is a form of mystification. In fact, as regards quantity and quality, it is very restricted. In a contradictory way it arouses many needs and desires, some artificial, the rest unsatisfied. Satisfaction is characterized by accident and contingency. It is "a stroke of good fortune", a windfall, a happy piece of luck. In so far as the words mean anything, joy and happiness consist of a series of favourable encounters and chances. Freedom, so frequently exalted, is no more than the skill of making the most of luck and chance . . . This explains the importance of luck and chance both in the highest theoretical thinking and in the ideologies some extremely unsophisticated people adopt and "live" on a practical basis . . .

However, it is still true that the socialist countries have not even begun to develop the features of a genuine pleasure economy. Far from it! Supposing that the imperatives of accumulation become less urgent in the USSR, for how many more years will they predominate in China? This does not mean that everyday life in the USSR, or elsewhere, is not already taking on some new qualities. The satisfaction of needs has lost its accidental, contingent and risky character, at least in part. If this constitutes a new quality, it does not mean that other aspects are obscured. Only a concrete, on-the-spot analysis of everyday life, using all the possibilities open to investigation and eschewing all ideological preoccupations, would allow us to specify the differences on this level between socialist society and capitalist society.

Next we could compare the everyday lives and everyday-life relations with their ideological representations. In so far as we are able to make this comparison, on the bourgeois side money gives prestige and power, in other words every possible joy, while on the socialist side it is prestige and status, in other words power, which give a range of advantages, one of which is money or its equivalents. Does this reversal rectify the world turned topsy-turvy, the upside-down world Marx talks about? Hardly.

Meaning or signification can change while "reality" remains analogous and stable, or perhaps we should say, almost stable. This is doubtless true. But if radical critique denounces the snares of "significations", which change while real substance does not, if it rejects moralism and the operation which consists in mistaking moral appearance for concrete reality and reality for the manifestion of the moral, why should it spare the official ideology of socialism? The ideological presentation of the acceleration of the cumulative process and of the intensification of productive labour as the fulfilment of socialism or of communism is objectively inadmissable. Scientifically, socialism can only be defined as production subordinated to social needs (and not to political imperatives). That in the course of a strategic operation and at a decisive moment the politician should declare: "If you're not with us, you're against us", is inevitable. The logic of decision-making demands it. But while ideologues are forever imposing this implacable logic on concepts and thought, knowledge cannot accept it. It goes against its own laws. They say:

333

Give us a few more years breathing space. Socialism, in other words the colossal creative effort of the masses guided and directed by scientific ideology, will resolve all the problems simultaneously: the conquest of space, the development of the backward countries, the satisfaction of every need, genuine sexual equality in everyday life, the conditions for happiness and for the flowering of individuals, the unleashing of their creativity, of lifestyle and the art of living, and reasons for living.[17]

Very well, let them have this breathing space. We are patient. For a start. the fact that they are still asking us to be patient and to give them a breathing space means that they are asking for the possibility that "history" should continue without being interrupted by some gigantic catastrophe. Very good. How could we refuse to support such an idea? We live in hope, which is to say that we have returned to the Marxist project; we are reinstating it in all its authenticity; we are presenting it once again as the aim and meaning of history. And yet we feel anxious and we admit it. We already know that history does not always go the way we would wish. It creates; at one and the same time it brings the unforeseen (which knowledge discovers "after the event" to have been necessary, except when ideology disguises this necessity!) – and the irreversible. The past weighs heavy. Socialism will never be exactly what it would have been had history proceeded in another way. What does it need to put "history" right, to halt its drift? Who can we turn to? Who can we trust? In the willingness or the good intentions of leaders and of specialists in economics and politics? Marx warns us about falling into this naive trap, as old as the world itself. Only the growth of social needs, the subdued but constant pressure of the proletarian masses, can shift the process in this direction. Constant pressure, i.e., gradual effectiveness (to use careful and precise terminology). In short, we have no choice but to place our bets on democracy.

As for revolution in general, and on the conceptual plane on which we are operating here, we say of it what Rimbaud said of love: 'Revolution must be reinvented.' And we must not worry about tactics or political strategy, or even about being immediately effective. As in Marx's thought, revolution must be reinvented, starting from a conception of what is possible. In other words, it is a choice between the various possibilities, then returning once more to the present and to the real to grasp them and to judge them. First, and patiently, we have reinstated the initial Marxist agenda, a project which is both Utopian and practical, the idea of a total praxis which will resolve the contradictions by eliminating all alienating divisions. Second, in taking Marxism up again as radical critique of everyday life in this way, we are shedding light on precisely what revolution would change, if the real stopped lagging behind the possible. Third, we will continue measuring the gaps between the following terms: revolution and achievement, the real and the potential. Last, in so far as knowledge has strength, and gives more than just ethical patience and aesthetic irony, we will bring pressure to bear on the situation in an attempt to narrow these gaps. In Volume I of *Critique of Everyday Life* our aim was simply to give the everyday access to history and to political life. Today we must build a long-term policy on how to answer the demands for a radical transformation of everyday life.'

8

How can everyday life be defined? It surrounds us, it besieges us, on all sides and from all directions. We are inside it and outside it. No so-called 'elevated' activity can be reduced to it, nor can it be separated from it. Its activities are born, they grow and emerge; once they have left the nourishing earth of their native land, not one of them can be formed and fulfilled on its own account. In this earth they are born. If they emerge, it is because they have grown and prospered. It is at the heart of the everyday that projects become works of creativity.

Knowledge, science and scientific discovery sometimes consist of brief instants of discovery. Yet science has its everyday life: training, teaching, the climate in scientific circles, administrative questions, the way institutions operate, etc.

The professional soldier dedicates himself to heroism. The army prepares itself for war; that is its aim and its purpose. And yet moments of combat and opportunities to be heroic are thin on the ground. The army has its everyday life: life in barracks and more precisely life among the troops (otherwise known as the 'contingent'; lexical familiarity may veil what is ironic and dialectical about this, but here, as elsewhere, the 'contingent' is the 'necessary'!). This everyday life is not without its importance in relation to dreams of heroism and the fine moral ideal of the professional soldier. It is the springboard for sublime actions. Questions of rank, promotion and military honours are part of it. There is a saying that army life is made up of a lot of boredom and a couple of dangerous moments.

Let us consider the state and the practical operation of its managerial spheres. There is an everyday life of the state. It is not the same thing as the everyday (private) lives of public figures. It has a well-known name: bureaucracy. There is a political everyday, the everyday of parties, apparatus, relations between these bodies and the masses who elect them and whom they administer. To study the everyday life of the state would thus be to study *in vivo* and *in concreto* the functions and the functioning of bureaucratic apparatuses and their relation to social praxis. Emerging above this everyday life are important decisions and dramatic moments of decisive action.

Factories, trades unions, work and the relations between workers all have their own everyday life. And from that everyday life come strikes, or the introduction of new technologies, etc.

9

Should we define the everyday as the petty side of life, its humble and sordid element? As we have already said, yes and no. Yes, this small, humble and sordid side of all human existence has been part of the everyday since time began, and until there is a project and a policy to restore technical possibilities to the everyday in order to overturn it from top to bottom, it may well be so for a long time to come.

> Every day thousands upon thousands of women sweep up the dust which has gathered imperceptibly since the previous day. After every meal, too numerous to count, they wash the dishes and saucepans. For times too numerous to count, by hand or in the machine, they remove the dirt which has built up bit by bit on sheets and clothes; they stop up the holes the gentle rubbing of heels inevitably makes; they fill emptied cupboards and refrigerators with packets of pasta and kilos of fruit and vegetables . . . [*which explains the following definition of everyday life*:] The ensemble of activities which of necessity result from the general processes of development: evolution, growth and aging, of biological or

social protection or change, those processes which escape immediate notice and which are only perceptible in their consequences.[18]

This attempt at a definition, with the vivid description which accompanies it, sheds a remarkable light on one aspect of the everyday: the reverse side of all praxis. However, it prompts several reservations and criticisms. Like all definitions, it tends to immobilize what it is trying to define, presenting it as timeless and unchangeable. And as definitions frequently do, it takes one aspect or one part as the whole.

If things were like this, the study of everyday life would be easy and critique of it would be effortless. It would suffice to note down and emphasize trivial details from one day to the next, the daily gestures with their inevitable repetitions. And after that a simple project: work, family life, immediate relations (block of flats, neighbourhood or village, town), leisure. The impoverished eloquence of tape-recorded interviews would reveal the poverty and misfortunes of the everyday. Analysis of the content of these interviews, and in particular of their language, would quickly single out a certain number of themes: loneliness, monotony, insecurity, discussions on solutions and the absence of solutions, on the advantages and disadvantages of marriage, on professional occupations.[19] One could possibly examine these themes using the well-tried methods of sociology or combinative analysis. One might succeed in determining fairly precisely attitudes within or towards the everyday (attitudes of acceptance, but more often of rejection) in certain groups. As well as quantifying in this way, the inquiry would retain a certain number of privileged pieces of evidence. It could even go so far as to attempt some experiments (similar to the somewhat too successful experiment in which a study group simulated a serious car accident in order to observe the behaviour of the other drivers on the road!).

With the help of a little irony, this path could lead us a long way. One may conceive of a sociology of the reverse images of society and of its duplicates, sacred or cursed. A social group is characterized just as much by what it rejects as by what it consumes and assimilates. The more economically developed a country is, the more gets thrown away, and the faster it gets thrown away. People are wasteful. In New York, in the promised land of free enterprise, the dustbins are enormous, and the more visible they are the more inefficiently public services operate. In underdeveloped countries, nothing is thrown away. The smallest piece of paper or string, the smallest tin is of use, and even excrement is gathered. What we are outlining here is a sociology of the dustbin.

Cemeteries, for their part, present a splendid 'negative' of built-up areas, villages, towns large and small. In their mirror, they faithfully 'reflect' social structure, economic life, and ideologies. As such, they deserve to be studied sociologically as much as any other social phenomenon. Finally, the men society rejects are no less interesting than those whom society assimilates, and down-and-outs still have a lot to teach us.

The sociology of 'duplicates' would not limit itself to these tarnished mirrors. It would study more attractive reverse images, although not necesssarily less disappointing ones. For example, 'leisure clubs'[20] where in the effort to break with everyday life by escaping from it, a strange everyday life, equally alienating and alienated, is reconstructed in caricature.

If this were all there was, critique of everyday life would only bring the disappointing aspects of social praxis to the fore. It would emphasize the trivial and the repellant. It would paint a black picture of dissatisfaction. It would tend to concentrate on the sordid side of life, on suffering, on a rather old-fashioned populism. It would use the pseudo-realism of a Bernard Buffet or the stammering, desperate lyricism of a Samuel Beckett as a means of understanding social man. If this were the only path it followed, critique of everyday life would be barely distinguishable from a certain branch of existentialism which took it upon itself – and very skilfully – to underline the marginal elements of existence. To a philosophy like this, all analysis of everyday life would contribute would be scientific jargon and a stodgy sociological pretentiousness.

The hypothesis of our study is rather different. According to this hypothesis, which underpins the programme as a whole, it is in everyday life and starting from everyday life that genuine *creations* are achieved, those creations which produce the human and which men produce as part of the process of becoming human: works of creativity.

These superior activities are born from seeds contained in everyday practice. From the moment groups or individuals are able and obliged to plan ahead, to organize their time and to use whatever means they have at their disposal, reason is formed in social practice. As day follows trivial day, the eye learns how to see, the ear learns how to hear, the body learns how to keep to rhythms. But the essential lies elsewhere. What is most important is to note that feelings, ideas, lifestyles and pleasures are confirmed in the everyday. Even, and above all, when exceptional activities have created them, they have to turn back towards everyday life to verify and confirm the validity of that creation. Whatever is produced or constructed in the superior realms of social practice must demonstrate its reality in the everyday, whether it be art, philosophy or politics. At this level alone can it be authenticated. What does such and such an idea or creative work tell us? In what way and how far does it change our lives? It is everyday life which measures and embodies the changes which take place 'somewhere else', in the 'higher realms'. The human world is not defined simply by the historical, by culture, by totality or society as a whole, or by ideological and political superstructures. It is defined by this intermediate and mediating *level*: everyday life. In it, the most concrete of dialectical movements can be observed: need and desire, pleasure and absence of pleasure, satisfaction and privation (or frustration), fulfilments and empty spaces, work and non-work. The repetitive part, in the mechanical sense of the term, and the creative part of the everyday become embroiled in a permanently reactivated circuit in a way which only dialectical analysis can perceive.

In short, the everyday is not a synonym for *praxis*. If we look at it in its entirety, praxis is the equivalent of totality in action; it encompasses the base and the superstructures, as well as the interactions between them. This view of praxis may be rather too sweeping, but if we substitute it with something more restricted and determined, it will disintegrate into fragmented practices: technology, politics, etc. We will have to look at the category of *praxis* again. For us, the everyday is a *level*.

Critique of unfulfilment and alienation should not be reduced to a bleak picture of pain and despair. It implies an endless appeal to *what is possible* in order to judge the present and what has been accomplished. It examines the dialectical movements intrinsic to what is concrete in the human, i.e., to the everyday: the possible and the impossible, the random and the certain, the achieved and the potential. The real can only be grasped and appreciated via potentiality, and what has been achieved via what has not been achieved. But it is also a question of *determining* the possible and the potential and of knowing which yardstick to use. Vague images of the future and man's prospects are inadequate. These images allow for too many more-or-less technocratic or humanist interpretations. If we are to know and to judge, we must start with a precise criterion and a centre of reference: the everyday.

It is in this sense that in Volume I of *Critique of Everyday Life* we defined everyday life initially as the region where man appropriates not so much external nature but *his own nature* – as a zone of demarcation and junction between the *uncontrolled sector* and the *controlled sector* of life – and as a region where *goods* come into confrontation with needs which have more or less been transformed into desires.

This definition is not exhaustive, and needs to be more thorough. Let us go back to the definition we suggested previously. It raises several questions concerning the general processes of growth, development, maturation and decline. To what extent do these general processes (not only individual ones, but social and historical as well) go beyond the boundaries of the everyday? Do they abandon it? To what extent do they return to it?

This is a question which will have to be addressed.

10

Let us look at things from another perspective. Let us use our thought and imagination to exclude specialized activities from praxis. If this abstraction is successful, it will rid practical experience of discreet occupations like the use of such and such a technique or implement (but not, of course, in physical terms of effort, time consumed, rhythm or absence of rhythm). What are we left with?

Nothing (or virtually nothing), say the positivists, scientists, technologues and technocrats, structuralists, culturalists, etc.

Everything, say the metaphysicians, who would consider that this abstraction or analytic operation scarcely attains the 'ontic' and is still far removed from the 'ontological', i.e., it fails to grasp the foundation, being (or nothingness).

Something, we will say, which is not easy to define, precisely since this 'something' is not a thing, nor a precise activity with determined outlines. So what is it? A mixture of nature and culture, the historical and the lived, the individual and the social, the real and the unreal, a place of transitions, of meetings, interactions and conflicts, in short a *level* of reality.

In one sense there is nothing more simple and more obvious than everyday life. How do people live? The question may be difficult to answer, but that does not make it any the less clear. In another sense nothing could be more superficial: it is banality, triviality, *repetitiveness*. And in yet another sense nothing could be more profound. It is existence and the 'lived', revealed as they are before speculative thought has transcribed them: what must be changed and what is the hardest of all to change.

This proves the general methodological principle of *double determination*. In our opinion, this principle is essential to dialectical thought, which is not restricted simply to discovering links (differences, oppositions, polarities and reciprocal implications, conflicts and contradictions, etc.) between determinations. It discovers differences, dualities, oppositions and conflicts *within each determination* (by conceptualizing it, i.e., thinking of it within a concept).

11

Let us look from yet another perspective. Cyclic time scales submerged themselves immediately and directly in the rhythms of nature, in cosmic time scales. For a long time they held sway over human life: social man had not yet controlled nature, that is, he had not separated himself from it. His life was made up of a set of cycles and rhythms, from birth to death. The regular return of the hours, days, weeks, months, seasons and years gave rhythm to an existence which was organically linked to nature. We can go as far as the supreme cycle, the temporal system of the world, the Great Year conceived of by so many thinkers since Classical and Eastern philosophy (up to Nietzsche and Engels). Villages and cities also lived in accordance with these rhythms which did not control individual life alone. The alternation and rhythm of the generations had a profound effect upon collectivities (age groups, the preponderance of those who resisted death: old people, etc.).

The study of these time scales reveals several more precise characteristics. First, cyclic time properly speaking has no beginning and no end. Every cycle is born from another cycle and becomes absorbed in other circular movements. Cyclic time does not exclude repetitive action. The cycle is itself a repetition. However, in cyclic time, repetition is subordinated to a more 'total' body rhythm which governs the movements of the legs and the arms, for example. Second, these rhythms do not exclude enumeration and measurement; one number in particular is extremely privileged: *twelve* (with the submultiples and multiples of twelve: minutes, hours, months; the division of a circle into degrees; the notes of the tempered musical scale, etc.). Third, no genuine cycle returns exactly to its point of departure or reproduces itself exactly. No return is absolutely exact (a remarkable example: the way an octave is divided up, scales and the cycle of fifths in music). If it were otherwise, cycles would be vicious circles and the geometry of the circle would exhaust all that is physically real. Finally, cyclic and cosmic time has always been and remains the subject of magic and religious representations. It is noticeable that rational and of course industrial techniques have shattered cyclic time. Modern man detaches himself from it. He controls it. This control is first expressed by interruptions in the cycles. Cyclic time is replaced by a linear time which can always be reckoned along a trajectory or distance. Linear time is both continuous and discontinuous. Continuous: its beginning is absolute, and it grows indefinitely from an initial zero. Discontinuous: it fragments into partial time scales assigned to one thing or another according to a programme which is abstract in relation to time. It dissects indefinitely.[21] Techniques which fragment time also produce repetitive gestures. These do not and often cannot become part of a rhythm: the gestures of fragmented labour, actions which begin at any time and cease at any time.

However, cyclic time scales have not disappeared. Subordinated to linear time, broken into pieces and scattered, they live on. A very large part of biological and physiological life and a very large part of social life remain involved in cyclic time scales. Even if in a few very large cities (but not in France) public transport runs for 24 hours a day, even if a few very limited groups free themselves from the times conventionally allotted to customs such as resting, sleeping and eating, these customs remain deeply rooted. No matter how highly developed an industrial civilization may be, hunger, sleep and sex are still bound up with customs and traditions linked to cyclic time. And it would appear that emancipation from cyclic time always follows a difficult path, by way of antinature and lived abstraction. It is unnatural not to sleep at night, not to eat at specific hours, etc. How would the complete control of nature, i.e., the complete metamorphosis of everyday life, be expressed? By an arhythmic individual and social time (and also athematic, as in the example of contemporary electronic and concrete music, which shatters rhythmic time scales and traditional cycles) which would render any specific action impossible at any specific moment? By a transitory or durable group freely inventing its own rhythm? By the invention of new rhythms (of which the working day without breaks would be the blueprint)? That is the problem.

Critique of everyday life studies the persistence of rhythmic time scales within the linear time of modern industrial society. It studies the interactions between cyclic time (natural, in a sense irrational, and still concrete) *and linear time* (acquired, rational, and in a sense abstract and antinatural). *It examines the defects and disquiet this as yet unknown and poorly understood interaction produces. Finally, it considers what metamorphoses are possible in the everyday as a result of this interaction.*

In this context and in relation to this definition, we can see the everyday life of social groups in a more determined and three-dimensional way. For example, let us take a young farmer. His life is still governed by cyclic, cosmic and social time scales, especially if he is the son of a small landowning farmer in a rather backward region: days, weeks, seasons; seed times, cereal or grape harvests; youth, marriage, maturity, old age; births and funerals. He is aware of this set of cycles and of his place within it, no different from his place within the village (which still contains several features of farming communities) or the house (where the generations live side by side, among latent or violent conflicts). He can still feel more insecure in his links with nature than with society, i.e., markets, technology, urban life (unless the two impressions of insecurity are not brought together in a feeling of profound disquiet or panic). For him, the everyday appears as an organic whole which is in the process of disintegrating, but whose nucleus remains stable. Nothing separates childhood from adulthood, the family from the local community, work from leisure; nothing separates nature from social life and culture. When he is at school, he helps his parents in so far as his strength and the time at his disposal allow. As a child he has a precise and solid status which his village environment confers, a restrictive awareness of his social being which defines and limits him: 'As the son of so-and-so, he will become this and not that.' In spite of the symptoms of dissociation and the already backward character of this 'state', this young farmer still experiences a certain integration of the everyday with the cosmic on the one hand and with the community on the other. Threatening, fascinating, terrifying, the outside world is the city, it is technology, it is today's society in its entirety. A multiplicity of prohibitions still protect this young man and the nucleus of the everyday as he lives it from the ever more numerous and effective attacks from outside.

As for the young worker, he is both integrated within (modern industrial) society on a world scale and thrown to the mercy of deeper conflicts. From childhood on, what he experiences is dissociation and creative but painful contradiction. He very soon comes to know insecurity; his life feels dependent and disorganized, because rational forward planning is difficult in a working-class family (fear of unemployment or of the need to move, lack of ready money, inconvenient daily working hours, etc.). The opposition between school life and family life already presents a striking contrast; then comes the brutal transition from the life of a schoolboy to that of a worker. Life at work and life with the family offer a painful contrast. The young worker tends to assert himself in and via work; at the same time he is well aware that work imposes new dependencies upon him. It is only through a greater social dependence than before that he achieves a certain personal independence. However, he does achieve it: he will 'earn his living' by working; but soon he must take on new responsibilities, staying in or returning to the social norm, building a family and taking on a twofold dependency, both personal and social.[22] In factory life, the young worker sees himself caught up in fragmented linear time, the time of production and technology. In family life, he will rediscover cyclic, biological, physiological and social time scales.

The one enables him to resist and to compensate for the other, but the balance will be a difficult one, and certainly problematic.

12

Once we have outlined the definition of everyday life as a *level* (of social reality) we can consider the situation of individuals and groups in relation to this level. Conversely, it allows us to clarify the idea of level and the idea of the everyday as a level of reality.

Thus it is clear that in terms of the everyday, the situation of a housewife and a 'society woman', of a tool-maker and a mathematician, is not the same. The housewife is immersed in everyday life, submerged, swallowed up; she never escapes from it, except on the plane of unreality (dreams: fortunetellers, horoscopes, the romantic press, anecdotes and ceremonies on television, etc.). The 'society woman' gets out of it by artificial means: society life, fashion shows, snobbery, aestheticism or the pursuit of 'pure' pleasure. The mathematician gets out of it by way of an extremely specialized activity in which, as it happens, moments of creativity are few and far between. If he 'is' a mathematician and nothing but a mathematician, how insipid and unbearably obsessive he will be! The more highly qualified and technical an activity becomes, the more remote from everyday life the time it takes up becomes; and the more urgent the need becomes for a return to the everyday. For the housewife, the question is whether she can come to the surface and stay there. For the mathematician, the question is whether he can rediscover an everyday life in order to fulfil himself not only as a scholar (even if he is a genius), but also as a human being. And the 'society woman'? No questions, Your Honour.

Take this tool-maker. He has a 'good trade' (relatively speaking). Up to a certain point he likes what he does. He 'earns a good living'. But this prompts the question: *what life does he earn with his work?* The life of a tool-maker? Yes and no. Looking carefully, we would observe that his work may leave an impression on him, so that traces of it can be seen in his life outside the factory. And yet, if this man thinks only of his work, if his work and his position as a worker determine him when he is outside the factory, he is nothing more than an obsessive who has been mentally 'alienated', that is, unless he is a production activist who freely and voluntarily assumes responsibility for the alienation of labour in its entirety (which in one sense would disalienate him, but in another would alienate him more completely than anyone else!). More often than not this worker will have needs, desires or 'cravings', determined in part by the amount of energy he expends, his skill as a craftsman, his qualifications and his love of his work, but which cannot be deduced from them. These needs and cravings will be influenced by his past and his memory, his origins (a certain country, a certain province, a certain town). Generally he has a family, he has a certain way of living out the link between his work and his family life, and between the latter and the hours he devotes to leisure. What does he want? What are his preferences? What is he looking for in the games he plays, in the films he watches (unless he cannot stand playing games and going to the cinema)? Work is not enough either to determine this man's life in its entirety or to define what the everyday is to him. Nor can this everyday reality be defined by an arithmetical calculation: work + family life + leisure. He is one human being, the same everyday being who divides himself between these three sectors and undergoes these phases. He is the same and not completely the same. He keeps going through rifts and separations, in the divided (alienated) wholeness of his proletarian condition. Generally, because he is a proletarian and solidly based in the everyday, a man like this will not allow himself to be carried away by dissociation. Even if he has a variety of attitudes (in the factory, with his friends, with his trades union colleagues or in the café, with his family, playing games or at the cinema, on holiday, etc.) he does not have a variety of personalities, several 'me's. He maintains a sturdy wholeness, an individual wholeness, both in his everyday life, in the group (the working class) and in society as a whole. If we could watch him at work, we would doubtless perceive in his mannerisms and attitudes (towards his superiors, his peers and his inferiors) an echo of what he 'is' when he is not at work – and vice versa. This is because in that 'substance' or 'matter' which is neither substance nor matter as the terms are usually understood, i.e., in the everyday, every sector cross-refers to another.

What this provides is the representation of a kind of range or spectrum of situations, located between two poles which are not absolutely conflicting or separated: at one end, or rather *underneath*, men and women immersed in the everyday and submerged by it; at the other end, or rather *above*, men and women who have no sense of the everyday, detached, external, devoted to exceptional or artificial activities, integrated into groupings set up above society, 'society' people, 'pure' intellectuals, statesmen, etc.

On the lowest level, we can describe an everyday life of the people, but in the knowledge that to overemphasize it would be to become too absorbed in the sordid aspects of life. In the everyday experience of the people (or as it is usually understood, in the 'lower depths') cyclic time scales and rhythms predominate, but broken up, fragmented, eviscerated so to speak (but to an uneven degree according to social group). In the 'upper sphere' (as it is usually understood) linear time scales predominate, pointing in a single direction, but disconnected from one another.

In the 'lower depths', time and space are limited, and these limits must be endured; and yet individuals and groups have an environment; they find something compact and (relatively) solid around them and under their feet. It is a zone of sweaty, suffocating heat, of intimacy, where the temperature maintains an organic warmth. For those who have managed to escape from it, this zone is painful, even unbearable. Those who go on living within it do not really understand it, and cannot imagine any alternative to it.

In the 'upper sphere', space and time grow larger and wider: they open out indefinitely in the icy air of higher realms. Like rockets going up in a shower of sparks, activities run the risk of disintegrating and disappearing.

In the 'lower depths', people and relationships gravitate around symbols, the general meaning of which they do not understand, perceiving them only as given realities: the father and the mother, the sun, the earth, the elements. Each symbol acts as an affective and organic nucleus. It is not an innate archetype from the depths of time or being, nor is it a myth or some obscure existentialist matrix. It is a perceptible and perceived reality, the centre of a cycle and a socio-cosmic rhythm: the nucleus of family life, the centre of the activity of the group throughout the day, the week or the year.

In the 'upper sphere', people move and act amid formal and conventional abstractions, or more precisely, amid signs and signals.

They have become distanced from the vitality and spontaneity of symbols. In order to wield power over nature (for themselves, or more often than not for others) they live through antinature. Thus the quest for power contains its own weakness, and weakness contains a certain power.

In the 'lower depths', people are weak but tenacious, like life itself. In more empirical terms, i.e., in terms of a description of praxis, they live inside a narrow time scale, with no understanding of what time is, not because they are stupid, but because they are unaware and powerless. They do not understand time (because they are immersed in it). They have little or no family history or folklore. Their origins are lost in the fog; it is amazing when family memories go back even as far as to grandparents. Moreover, as regards the future, actual wages and the way they are paid restrict the rhythm of forward planning. With hire purchase, forward planning becomes essential, and in restricted circumstances such as these, most people find it overwhelmingly difficult to accustom themselves to the rational and abstract kind of time implied by money and credit. They lie awake thinking about it. All they want is to get it over with. This abstract and long-term linear time ends up disrupting their rhythms. As for work in the 'lower depths', everyone knows that it is both fragmented and not very specialized. In the margin of the 'lower depths' we find certain jobs which are generally reserved for women, not only 'in the house', but in businesses and offices: cleaning, basic non-technical repairs, an endless response to the permanent process of erosion, soiling, wearing out and aging which all that is used or has life must suffer. Like all work, it remains implicated in cycles (days, weeks, months). Although it is essential, it is not cumulative, and what links it has with accumulation are only indirect and by the back door, so to speak.

In the 'lower depths', cyclic time is taken up in satisfying basic needs and basic tasks which are themselves governed by cycles. Like time, relative social space ('effective scope', as the American sociologist Lazarsfeld puts it), namely housing and environment, is given over to basic concerns. Every day, every week, the same places, the same aims, the same itineraries. People have very few 'relationships' or 'know' few people outside this space. They are anonymous within their own lives (which explains the passionate interest in the trivial news item, that 'poor man's tragedy'[23] in which destiny is revealed, symbols are reconstituted and anonymity is overcome in an effort to reach the great light of social day). This suffocating state of affairs has its compensation: the vitality and direct, immediate character of the 'lived', a sort of irrefutable concreteness.

In the 'upper sphere', there is much more adventure, more openings, more play; but people are always in danger of losing themselves, some in abstraction, others in artificiality, and others in pointless subtlety and refinement.

Thus, and gradually, we are establishing the everyday to be a level (in the way we talk of sea level and ground level).

13

More observations and objections from philosophers

'Well then, why not attempt a phenomenology of what is lived socially in the *Lebenswelt*, a description of space and social time in human, intersubjective experience? However, it's still not clear. Take me for example, I'm a philosopher and a teacher, and I give my philosophy lectures on a regular basis. Where in your opinion does the everyday start and finish for me? Isn't my activity entirely determined by something else, history of thought, say, the history of our society, institutions, the university, teaching syllabuses, etc.?'

Reply

'Let me take your questions one at a time. In the first place, the description we are trying to make here implies an analysis which is not really compatible with descriptive and purely phenomenological method. We are removing from *praxis* those activities which are apparently its most concrete and positive: the so-called higher activities. We are proceeding via abstraction, using analysis on the plane of the imaginary, because the operation requires a kind of imagination if it is to delve into the hidden life of visible and tangible human beings. The result may therefore *appear* abstract, fictitious and negative. What we are arguing here is that such an abstraction is legitimate and well

founded, because it reaches something which psychological or sociological evidence does not reveal or make immediately apparent. Our
thesis is that the negative is also positive, and that it is not a bad thing
to overcome the separation between the positive and the negative,
between description and imagination, between understanding and
analysis. In this way thought becomes dialectical by the very act of
thinking. Phenomenology, do I hear you say? Yes and no. In the first
place, no, for the reasons I have just given. And for other reasons.
How can we describe and understand anything if we make no attempt
to explain it? And no, because if we are revalidating the concept
(which is as negative as it is positive) we do so with a certain historicity. And no, because it is also a matter of changing things, and we
are *proposing* change by demonstrating what is capable of being
changed. Critique is inherent to our "monstration": critique of what
is "above" by what is "underneath" and critique of what is underneath by what is above.

And yet, to a certain extent, *yes*, it is phenomenology, because it
certainly is a question of the "lived". Yes, since whatever is total,
whatever is "mediated" and "*reflected*" through the multiplicity of
mediations, through culture and through language, must also turn
back to the unmediated in order to demonstrate itself, to offer itself
and become apparent. Objects, gestures, day-to-day words – they all
embody totality, in a real but fragmented way: on their *respective
levels*. They are partially beyond it, and yet they are a part of it. If
this were not so, there would be no mediation, no non-mediation,
nothing but permanent totality devoid of any real inner diffferences,
and all the more importantly, devoid of contradictions. To sum up –
using your vocabulary, Mr Philosopher – the total becomes a phenomenon. It expresses itself in fragmented actions, in gestures, in
objects, which are inconceivable without it, but which are not
defined according to it, since they have their own, specific reality: on
the level of the everyday. And now, my dear philosopher, allow me
to inform you that your activity – teaching philosophy – is both
everyday and non-everyday. In so far as it is an exceptional activity,
a mediation, a journey into the purely abstract and conceptual, philosophy is constructed above the everyday, even when it meditates on
life and the concrete. In so far as it is a social activity, integrated
within structured groups, with their models, their norms and their

social roles, such as the philosophy lecture, the lycée, the town, the university, it enters into the everyday. All the more so because you too "earn your living" by teaching philosophy. But what life do you earn? It cannot be reduced simply to philosophy itself, simply to the right to meditate! At least, for your sake, I hope not! In any case I think that like all human activities, yours can be examined on several *levels*: on the *biological and physiological* level (what you eat, the amount of calories you need to recoup your strength), on the *psychological* level (your personal relationships with the students you teach, for example), and on the *economic* level (your salary, your expenses, etc.). Taking the content of a single activity considered on various levels, and using a specific part of that content, thought can establish a virtually unlimited number of sets (of facts and concepts). If we abstract them out, what is left? The everyday "lived", doubly determined as the *residual deposit* and as the *product* of all the sets considered (and thus, in its way, a *total* phenomenon, that is, a level in totality, and on its own level, a totality.

14

Let us pause a moment to consider this new determination. Is the everyday a residual deposit? We must be clear about this. There is in effect a residual aspect to the everyday, since it can be defined by abstraction or by a series of abstractions. It could always become reduced and disappear. Let me give you an example. Take dreary and repetitive activities such as cleaning and repairing. To do away with the need for cleaning (by using materials which do not produce dirt, thus eradicating dust and smoke) would be to reduce the everyday and to lift it up methodically to the level where techniques operate. This would indeed be an objective: the metamorphosis of the everyday, which in our opinion implies a plan and a policy. However, this residual deposit is irreducible. Were we to suppress it would we not annihilate "being"? The study of everyday life does not focus solely on "survivals" in the sociological meaning of the term. One might just as well consider biological and physiological needs and desires as survivals from primitive man! Let us suppose that in the not-too-distant future human cells will be created artificially (which is perfectly

351

conceivable) and given consciousness. This man-made human being will still have vital rhythms, needs which are satisfied only to become needs once more, desires which may or may not be fulfilled, which come to an end and are born again. This "being" will obey certain laws of "being" which for a philosopher are related to the profound link between the non-finite and the finite, to the finiteness of the expressions of non-finite being. This created "being" will still contain an uncontrolled sector and a controlled sector, and thus it will also imply a problematic of everyday life, a perpetual confrontation between empowerment and powerlessness. It will experience an inner struggle to *appropriate* life, a struggle against whatever *disappropriates* it (whatever distorts it, degrades it or kills it). Can we say these are survivals? Yes and no. There can be no "survivals" without a real "base". To this vague idea of survival we would prefer the much more concrete idea of *uneven development*. In our history, the uneven development of sectors is also a consequence of history. Indeed, in uneven development the everyday defines itself as what *lags behind* history, but not as what *eludes* history, events, development and human power. In history, in development, the everyday is also *a product*.

The concept of the everyday can therefore not be defined as a kind of existential illusion: the illusion in which we (social man *hic et nunc*) appear and believe we can grasp what we are, in which we see ourselves from a certain perspective without knowing the reasons and the causes, without understanding history and ontological truth. Trapped at the centre of a kind of false consciousness or permanent bad faith, we try to evade them: in a word, it is inauthenticity. No. My dear philosopher, the level of *the everyday* is not the illusion of a false consciousness. "How do we live?" This question does not stem from ignorance, and moreover the problem cannot be resolved by knowledge and knowledge alone, nor by language or logos alone . . .'

15

This spectrum analysis, which places human reality between two poles, is not merely sociological. It also involves the psychological. In our opinion, the psychological is also a level. If it can be opened up to knowledge, it will present itself as a totality which encompasses historical and social determinations. Understood in the context of a wider field, it is as though the psychological were encompassed by the sociological.

The study of everyday life reaches layers deep inside the 'social individual', i.e., a non-isolated consciousness and a non-separated psyche.[24]

First layer: resistant, external, morphological, a kind of membrane through which the osmoses between 'the individual' and 'society' occur. The individual rejects uncomfortable questions. He evades problems. He confines himself to banalities, to the accepted norms of trivial communication and behaviour. He is at one and the same time shut inside himself and boringly social. The outside makes him feel extremely uncomfortable. It is the superficial context in which the individual 'adapts' to the different social 'circles' through which he travels in the successive phases of practical life. But this peripheral stratum is also where social (linear) time scales and the gestures of industrial and technological labour graft themselves, in so far as they have not been actively adopted by the individual and are not the consequence of a stronger interest, that is, in so far as they remain abstract. And yet, in one sense, this external sphere is also to a certain extent the most internal sphere of all. It makes decisions: it is here that decisions are made.

Second layer: a vague discomfort triggers violent reactions and revealing turns of phrase (often in an aggressive way): 'What a life! Why on earth do we put up with all this?'

Problems emerge, and questions, and the individual replies with fumbling and disjointed answers using the models, the norms, the values and the hierarchic attitudes and behaviour patterns of whatever groups he has chosen to identify with. And within these problems ready-formed choices emerge, more or less consciously (and which consequently, as will become clearer at a later stage, echo the opinions of these various groups, implying involvement in their activity and acceptance of their tactics and strategies).

Third layer: Finally a deeper sphere is revealed, an affective nucleus (with its own characteristic tonality). It is the sphere of non-adaption, of vague rejections and unrecognized voids, of hesitations and misunderstandings. When we reach this sphere, we discover the dramatic situation of the individual in society. Usually, however, all the drama is removed. Unbeknown to the individual himself, it is smothered by trivialities, emptied of all expressivity which might be compromising, and even more, of all lyricism and rhetoric. In this sphere of secrecy, the secret itself is smothered to the point of becoming unrecognizable, and it is generally a petty little secret, involving a deliberate or imposed choice and a mutilation. This is where the process of alienation and disalienation, of fulfilment and incompleteness, of (partial) satisfaction and (partial) dissatisfaction unfolds. This is the sphere from which spring the projects, the half-dreams, the little everyday miracles which horoscopes and predictions rework and embellish. It is also the sphere where what is possible and what is impossible for the individual confront each other. It is the most internal sphere, and yet, in one sense, it is the most external one, the sphere where the history of the individual reveals itself in the history of society.

It is essential to note that on every 'level', in every 'sphere' and in every 'layer' we discover social *representations* which are like representations of society: norms, models, values, collective and imperative forms of conduct, rules and forms of control, in short what is meant rather vaguely by the terms 'ideology', 'culture', 'knowledge', etc. A sharper analysis would require us to distinguish the different stages at which these external/internal elements are adopted, are assimilated and effectively function. The most profound and most effective stage is where *symbols* are active (perceived not as such, but rather as vital realities which consequently cannot be defined as 'representations').

What is the general function of these representational elements? For better or for worse, they guarantee the reciprocal adjustment of needs and desires, of desires and ideas, of cyclic time scales and linear time scales, in short, of the aspects and layers of the social individual. They are the equivalent of the regulations by which a (relative) stability is maintained within the social entity, but at the heart of the psyche. They normalize the individual and impose a minimum amount of cohesion and coherence in his everyday life. They compensate for privations, conceal frustrations, hinder demands and deviances. No spontaneous or mechanical self-regulation takes place in the consciousness. There is no feedback to guarantee balance. This role is played by *representations* at the heart of the conscious being, the social individual, and not by processes of stabilization. Thus, among the conflicts they conceal and to which they offer pseudo-solutions, critique of everyday life reveals the equivocal and ambiguous representations by which symbols are underpinned and encircled.

Rather optimistically, Hegel believed he had discovered *a system of needs* – a kind of substance of civil society – in the links between the individual and the social. What we have discovered are more like systems of *representations*. They are very relative and, despite their tenacity, rather fragile, but they guarantee the everyday an amount of stability even in its moments of disappointment and drama.

(These analytical considerations correspond to empirically observable facts, to 'cases' and 'situations' which can be classified, thus making space for a typology. As an example, we could take those people who assume tasks and responsibilities in order to disguise the emptiness and ennui of their everyday lives: who want a large family so as to give their lives a meaning; who 'have ambitions' far beyond their own existences and their immediate associates, etc.).

16

We are moving closer to a detailed and precise definition of everyday life. Now that we have situated it at its own level, and looking at it more closely, we can observe that it contains levels of its own, layers, degrees, stages. Reciprocity, interaction, the hierarchy of these levels and degrees, all depend in part (but only in part) on approach, point of view and perspective.

How can we talk about all this without resorting to verbal artifice, or to that indeterminism which destroys every structure, every regularity and every law? Because 'what is most external is also what is most internal' and vice versa. This statement formulates a law. 'Commonplaces' are to be found both in the peripheral layer of the individual and in his affective nucleus. He has a limited and subjective perception of the conditioned responses to stimuli by which society adapts him, willingly or by force, to external conditions – and a limited and subjective perception of the symbolisms which rise up from the depths within him. For him, conditioning and symbols, external or internal constraints, are all mixed up together. We, however, are drawing distinctions between the various layers and spheres.

First we perceive the struggle against time which takes place within time, as well as the conflict between the simultaneous 'temporalities' of the individual – social being *in our* (industrial) *society*. Lagging behind that society, the opposite of all that is magnificent and flourishing, everyday life consists of a set of basic 'functions' from which the so-called higher functions emerge. Thus it encompasses the *immediate and natural forms of necessity* (needs, cyclic time scales, affective and vital spontaneity) as well as the seeds of the activity by which those forms are controlled (abstraction, reason, linear time). Next it encompasses the region where objects and goods are continually *appropriated*, where desires are elaborated from needs, and where 'goods' and desires correspond. This is a zone of confrontation between the necessary and the random, the possible and the impossible, what has been appropriated and what has not, and empirical good luck and bad luck. In this zone, broadening what is possible is not an effortless task. With its regions of fulfilment and unfulfilment, of effective and possessed (appropriated) joys and lack of joys, it is the realm of the dialectic between 'alienation' and 'disalienation'.

Finally, we have discerned a third level or degree. On the one hand this third level can be considered to be unmediated and empirically given, and can be studied in terms of 'ideologies' and 'moral values'. On the other hand it can be considered as mediating between the individual and the social, and, within an individual consciousness, between the individual and his own self. It is a set of practices, representations, norms and techniques, established by society itself to regulate consciousness, to give it some 'order', to close the excessive gaps between the 'inside' and the 'outside', to guarantee an approximate synchronization between the elements of subjective life, and to organize and maintain compromises. This social control of individual possibilities is not absolutely imposed; it is accepted, half-imposed, half-voluntary, in a never-ending ambiguity; this same ambiguity allows the individual to play with the controls he imposes within himself, to make fun of them, to circumvent them, and to give himself rules and regulations in order to disobey them.

Here, on its chosen territory, critique finds its points of impact. It mounts an attack on gaps and imbalances (between temporalities, between the 'basic' and the 'superior', the historical and the private, the social and the individual). It points out the gaps, the vacuums and the distances yet to be covered and overcome. It criticizes the role of society and the roles society imposes, which bestow a pseudo-coherence, a simulated adaptation and an illusory balance to the whole. It attacks alienation in all its forms, in culture, ideology, the moral sphere, and in human life beyond culture, beyond ideology, beyond the moral sphere. Critique demands the dissolution and the revolutionary metamorphosis of the everyday, by reducing its disparities and time-lags. By demonstrating theoretically that the everyday is not an immutable substance, it has already begun to dissolve it. Finally, it demands a twofold movement within a unitary praxis: that the everyday catch up with what is possible and that the processes which have been distanced from it return and reinvest themselves within it.

This broadens the critical programme presented in the introductory Volume I of *Critique of Everyday Life* considerably. There we restricted ourselves to a generalized and as yet abstract critique of alienation in general. We also considered, but rather vaguely, a reciprocal critique of the 'positive' real by dreams (and vice versa), of the lived by the imaginary, by art and by the ethical (and vice versa), in short, critical analysis of the fictive (non-practical) transpositions and metamorphoses of the everyday, in particular by aestheticism, 'values', the cult of personality and personalities, and rituals and superstitions, etc.

Our plan is becoming broader in scope, and clearer.

17

Let us view our subject in another light. We will start with a 'classic' distinction in general philosophy and methodology, the distinction between *form* and *content*. A content can only manifest itself and be grasped within a form. What we perceive is always the unity of form and content, with the result that several doctrines have felt able to challenge the distinction between the two terms. The theories which reject this distinction also reject any kind of analytical method. In fact, analysis and analysis alone breaks this unity. It abstracts form and consequently determines it per se. Those who believe they can grasp forms per se, unmediated, are just as erroneous as those who challenge the concept of forms. As for content, the intellectual act of analysis determines and constructs it per se, by separating it from form.

In the context of this study, what do we mean by forms? We mean ideologies, institutions, culture, language, and constructed and structured activities (including art). Previously we used analysis to abstract these forms. What did we say was left? A sort of 'human matter', the everyday – a sort of 'human nature', but with the proviso that 'human matter' or 'human nature' can only exist dialectically, in the endless conflict between nature and man, between matter and the techniques which wield power over it. Thus we must define everyday life in two ways: as a residual deposit and as a product. If in one sense the everyday is residual, it also expresses itself as the product of forms: what has been acquired and won via these forms, their human investment.

Resuming this analysis, we will still see the everyday as doubly determined, but in another way: at one and the same time as *unformed*, and as *what forms contain*.

Bit by bit contemporary sociology has discovered the importance of the unformed and has reinstated spontaneity as a social phenomenon. The unformed spills over from forms. It evades them. It blurs the precision of their contours. By marking them with erasures and marginal areas, it makes them inexact. The everyday is 'that', a something which reveals the inability of forms (individually and as a whole) to grasp content, to integrate it and to exhaust it. It is also content, which can only be seized by analysis, whereas the unformed can only be seized immediately or intuitively by participating in spontaneous activity or by stimulating it.

To conform to an already established custom, and while stressing the incomplete character of any isolated illustration extrapolated from concepts, let us give an example. *Bureaucracy* tends to operate for and by itself. By establishing itself as a 'system', it becomes its own goal and its own end; at the same time, in a given society, it has real functions, which it executes more or less effectively. Thus it modifies the everyday, and this too is its goal and its aim. However, it never succeeds in 'organizing' the everyday completely; something always escapes it, as bureaucrats themselves ruefully admit. The everyday protests; it rebels in the name of innumerable particular cases and unforseen situations. Beyond the zone bureaucracy can reach, or, rather, in its margins, the unformed and the spontaneous live on. There is something tenaciously resistant within this organized or possibly overorganized sphere, which makes form adapt and modify. Form either fails or improves; and this is how it manages to go on living. The 'dysfunctions' studied by certain sociologists are remarkable in that they stimulate functions and functionaries alike. They set them a multiplicity of problems which prevent them from going round in circles, and from setting up a perfect form and a vicious circle. Thus, in so far as it is both unformed and a content, the everyday 'contains' an ongoing critique of bureaucratic form and its effectiveness. All that is required is to single this ongoing critique out . . .

In this way we can get a better grasp of the double dimension of the everyday: platitude and profoundness, banality and drama. In one respect everyday life is nothing but triviality or an accumulation of commonplaces. Only those 'lofty' activities which abstraction sets to one side possess breadth and elevation. In other words, they alone are profound. And yet it is in the everyday that human dramas ravel and unravel, or remain unravelled. It is 'there' that veritable profoundness shines through and the question of authenticity is posed, or, perhaps, the question of vulgarity and non-vulgarity. The everyday is neither the inauthentic per se, nor the authentically and positively 'real'. When a feeling or a passion avoids being tried and tested by the everyday, it demonstrates ipso facto its inauthenticity. Although the drama of love may well consist in it being 'smashed against everyday life', in the words of Maiakovsky, the boat must brave the current or stay at its moorings. This test obliges subjective feeling to transmute itself into willpower, in order to confront something for which it is not responsible. Taken in isolation, failure is just as lacking in authenticity. Sooner or later all feelings, passions and intentions come face to face with their own limits. They fail, making future endeavours impossible, but this in itself proves nothing. Only the history of feelings or willpower, only the events they incite or assume responsibility for, only their confrontation with what is 'real' within 'the real', demonstrate anything. In the narrative of every endeavour, what counts is the combination of failure and what has been won prior to failure, rather than failure per se. An event has unfolded; it has taken time; it has taken its time. Time occupied by the onward movement of an event – failure – on a winding path through the murky thickness of everyday life, that is what counts. Perhaps this is what creates the 'novelistic'. The quality of a failure is more significant than the fact of having failed. Therefore, if everything in the everyday ends in failure, since everything comes to an end, the meanings differ. Could not successes sometimes be the worst failures? And sometimes failure can give birth to its own meaning, to its investment in the everyday, to what can be learnt from the drama, and to what will survive it.

In the everyday, platitude and profundity do not coexist peacefully. They fight bitterly there. Sometimes profundity and beauty can be born from a poorly determined and unexpected combination: an encounter. Later on, this chance event seems deserved, perhaps even predetermined. Once profundity and beauty are lived (and not simply gazed at or seen as a spectacle) they become *moments*, combinations which marvellously overturn structures established in the everyday, replacing them by other structures, unforeseen ones, and fully authentic.

When we talk about 'society/individual', 'need/desire', 'appropriation/pleasure' as though they were units, we should take care never to be misled by the way the logic of coherent discourse uses these words. These units are always conflictual, and thus always dialectical and in movement. In the everyday, when the 'human being' confronts within itself the social and the individual through the test of problems and contradictions which have been more or less resolved, it becomes a 'person'. What does this mean? In our view, a cloud of possibilities, gradually vaporized by choices – by actions – until it is exhausted and comes to an end: until death finishes it off. It is not an untroubled scenario making its way towards a foreseen conclusion, but rather a drama, the drama of personalization in society, the drama of individualization. In this drama, death is the only conclusion we can foresee, because it is necessary, and it comes only in unforeseen circumstances which depend on the narrative in its entirety.

In the everyday, alienations, fetishisms and reifications (deriving from money and commodities) all have their various effects. At the same time, when (up to a certain point) everyday needs become desires, they come across goods and appropriate them. Therefore critical study of everyday life will reveal the following conflict: maximum alienation and relative disalienation. Not as goods and objects to appropriate, but as objects of property, things alienate and even reify human activities and living men.[25] But in the link between pleasure and objects as goods, the reification engendered by these very things tends to break up. It comes up against a hostile force. The theory of alienation and reification must take this dialectic into account if it is not to lapse into that speculative form of reification known as dogmatism. *There is a 'world' of objects*, but it is also a human world, an area of desires and goods, an area of possibilities, and not simply a 'world' of inert things.

In commonplace speech, the words 'good luck' and 'bad luck' make an arbitrary connection between the results of randomness in society and randomness in nature. They also confuse necessity which has been misunderstood or subjectively unrecognized with what is objectively random. Such-and-such an individual is unlucky because his health is poor or because there have been pitfalls in his career. Better hygiene, or a medical breakthrough, would have spared him his health problems, and improved social organization would give this individual a better chance, etc. However, we know only too well that the power social man wields over material nature and the power individual man wields over social reality are not the same thing. Far from it. Everyday life is also the realm of the confrontations and distances which the words 'good luck' and 'bad luck' summarize in a naive dialectic.

The realm of randomness and alienation can be reduced. But can it disappear? It would only disappear if technology were to gain complete power over material nature, and the random were eliminated from the social. Here, as ever, the 'residual deposit' cannot be deemed to be reducible. Its disappearance, which would give the non-finite a limit (as absolute learning gives a limit to the non-finiteness of relative knowledge), is not even desirable. In so far as we can conceive it, it would only come about through social overorganization and a terrifying intervention by information technology.

In the meantime, a social failure can signify positive qualities (independent thinking, critical intelligence, rebellion). A biological misfortune can have happy consequences: a child with defects in one area may compensate by possessing exceptional qualities in another.

In the psyche too, development is uneven. If we make a fetish of the total, it can be devastating for 'being', since we are underestimating the plurality of the sectors within the *configuration* which situates or rather constitutes everyday life. Now and again we will need to lay bare a certain nefarious pedagogic illusion, and in doing so we will be able to to highlight the part played by education and its importance in everyday life. This illusion is twofold: on the one hand, a fetishism of the partial, and thus of the fragmentary and the specialized, an acceptance of fragmentation and a dismissal of totality; on the other hand, a fetishism of the total, an equalizing of differences, a superficial encyclopedism, and a belief in the complete mastery of pedagogy and human knowledge over 'human nature'.

There is a middle way between the dismissal of totality and the fetishism of the total, and critique of everyday life can help to define it.

18

In years gone by, when cottage industry, trades and guilds were still very important, the social man *par excellence*, the worker, was formed in and by labour. In this sense, man as an individual being and man as a social being were formed along similar lines. It was a relatively simple situation. Essentially, attitudes and behaviour patterns 'outside work' derived more or less directly from work itself. The individual 'was' this or that: a miner, a carpenter, a stonemason, a teacher, etc. Everyday life was almost completely determined by profession. It created well-differentiated but more-or-less caricatured human types, such as Hegel's 'abstract animals' or the social species in Balzac's *Comédie humaine*.

We should note that this process has not entirely disappeared. Consequently there are many confusions. Uneven development intervenes here as well. What is no longer true in the 'modernized' sectors of industry remains true in a great many more-or-less backward sectors.

Nowadays, in the advanced industrial countries, this situation relative to work and 'outside work' tends to be reversed. There is a shift in the focus of interest. It is the attitude towards work which is formed in everyday life (including those leisure activities which have become a part of everyday life which do not involve getting away from it all – or apparently so – with breaks or holidays), and not vice versa.

To be more precise: in days gone by, work had a 'value' in the ethical as well as economic sense of the term. There were work 'values': the idea of work well done, and of the product as a personal creation and to a certain extent on a par with the object created by a craftsman or an artist, etc.

With the fragmentary division of labour (and with the mass influx of unskilled workers and machine operators in factories), this traditional ethic has crumbled away. Work has lost almost all its appeal, and all the more so because it is fairly easy to move from one job or company to another. What we are describing here is a certain period in 'industrial society', definable by certain characteristics and by certain types of machine, and very bleak it is too. So, for the worker, work and life outside work have sunk into the same lack of interest, a lack which is poorly disguised by entertainments which are as noisy as they are empty. In fact, our society has not completely emerged from this period (just as it has not completely emerged from the period which preceded it, given the way previous forms of techniques and organization persist at the very heart of the most modern forms . . .).

Recent techniques, such as automation, call for abilities and knowledge even in work which has become passive – almost absence of work (such as the control and supervision of machinery). Technicians, employees and operations coexist in an organization which wants to be *stable* because it is in its interest to be so. This produces new concerns, such as stable employment and therefore stable living conditions, or credit facilities giving workers access to durable consumer goods (housing, household equipment, cars, etc). Obviously, these economic and technical demands give rise to a deliberate policy and an ideology.

Therefore one can see stable employment becoming the predominant concern in the most advanced working class, at least for a period of time during which a (conscious or unconscious) option is taken and its results are forthcoming. For indeed there is a genuine option here, which, we may add, is not irreversible (or so it would seem). In any event, the focus of interest is displaced from work, which in this context we take to mean the use of a technique and a set of implements. It focuses on everyday life in general. It is in the everyday outside work that the attitude towards work is formed. Work is no longer considered as an end in itself, but as the means to an end. People 'earn their living'. And yet again we ask ourselves: 'What life do we earn when we earn our living?'

We shall see, or rather we shall emphasize once again, that the life earned is '*private life*', and nothing but '*private life*' . . .

19

In our initial project, we proposed that critique of everyday life would include an *autocritique* of the everyday. Its principal aim was to confront 'the real' and 'the lived' with their representations, interpretations and transpositions (in art, in the moral domain, and in ideology and politics). From this comparison would have come a reciprocal critique of 'the real' by the imaginary, of 'the lived' by its transpositions, and of what has been effectively acquired by abstraction. In a similar way, our agenda included the confrontation between *private life* (seeing the individual as distinct from the social, but without separating him from society) and *public life* (the life of the citizen, historical man, social groups and the political state), and reciprocal critique of these two fragments of totality.

We proposed a single solution: that private life should be granted access to collective, social and political life, and that it should be allowed to participate within it. In other words we proposed the bringing together of everyday man and historical man, and the participation of everyday man in the problematic of totality (society as a whole). In this way the political sphere of the state was raised to the rank of supreme authority. Essentially, our critique was directed towards 'private life' which we defined as an impoverished sector of praxis, a backward and underdeveloped region at the very heart of so-called 'modern', industrial and technological society, in the context of capitalism. We intended to devote several chapters to the scrutiny of the petty magic of everyday life (habitual gestures and rituals, proverbial expressions, horoscopes, witchcraft, diabolisms), intending to eradicate them by submitting them to practical reason. Certainly, we did not intend to merge the individual with the collective and the private with the sociopolitical, but rather to raise them to the level of the collective and the historical, and thus via political consciousness to the level of the political. A relatively simple theory of alienation and disalienation seemed to satisfy all these requirements. Before the great disalienation which political revolution would bring about, but preparing for it and proclaiming it, the opening up of everyday life to public life and its active participation in history and political action would disalienate everyday man and negate his 'privation'. Far from disappearing, the everyday would become enriched and organically linked to totality: to the total man.

These oversimplified hypotheses betrayed a certain naivety. And this is where certain modifications have transformed our initial project. Over the last few years important changes have become apparent within the configuration made up by private life, political life, history and technology. How could critique of everyday life leave them to one side? We have already alluded to these changes, indicating that while not destroying our agenda, they introduce new elements. We will now stress the importance of these elements, and devote some time to explaining what they are.

In the first place, the mid-twentieth-century man who belongs to an 'advanced' society and who is using Marxism as the theoretical means of understanding that society will find himself in the same position as Marx vis-à-vis *history*. He cannot accept or confirm the historical as a series of events and processes. If he is not a professional politician, and if he locates himself in the sphere of knowledge, he will refuse to award history its 'degree in philosophy'. The politician is involved in a strategy, and whatever he has to say he says in the context of this strategy. In terms of history and the historical past which weighs upon the present day, he must 'save face'. If not, he will put his strategy and, of course, his political career in jeopardy (because another and more effective politician would immediately be found to carry out the task). This divorce between knowledge and politics, and the inevitable renewal of a sociology of politics which defines politics as politics per se rather than as the supreme science, present some very disturbing features. Never mind. This is not the place to worry about them. In his time Marx submitted politics – events, processes. tactics and strategies – to a merciless critical analysis. Starting from an objective determination of the strengths and the possibilities, and assessing what had and had not been accomplished, in terms of these possibilities, he examined the decisions, the mistakes and the failures. He did not use simplified and schematized hypotheses to deal with the facts; he did not recognize a constant and coherent 'progress' in all domains, or a unilateral determinism, or an absolute necessity. Marx never considered the historical as a set of *faits accomplis* to be accepted and recorded globally. While disputing the absolute of history and politics (and notably Hegel's philosophy of history and of the state), he studied what we will call *drifts*. He drew many lessons from the discrepancy between intentions and results.

Today we must call history into question, even the history we have lived and to which we have contributed. This so-called history has not yet superseded the prehistory of mankind. From decisions and actions, *something else* suddenly appears, something other than what was intended and planned. Although we may accept that through the intervention of the revolutionary proletariat the gap between the plan and the result has been narrowed (although this is debatable), it has not yet disappeared. Far from it! Men make their own history, but not in the way they wish it to be. They do not do what they want to do: they do not want what they do. There is more to the 'world' than philosophy predicted.

So what can we suggest everyday life should do to bridge the gap between the lived and history? How can we persuade it that its model should be the political sphere, the sphere which intervenes in history in an attempt – in the best cases – to make it and to direct it consciously? The split between private life and political consciousness is self-perpetuating. The two forms of consciousness are juxtaposed when in fact they could coexist. But in many cases, private consciousness gains the upper hand over a political consciousness obscured and starved as a result of the rift between the two.

We have had to bring the theory of the *withering away of the state* back to centre stage. This essential Marxist theory has been obscured by contemporary history (and by the history of Marxism in particular). Is it a Utopia? Probably. In fact, nowhere in the modern world is there a state withering away to any convincing degree, and there is nothing in line with the process Marx considered the future of history would be.[26] If there is anything Utopian in the theory of the withering away of the state, it will make it even easier for us to demonstrate just how Utopian Marx's thought is, and to refute several erroneous assertions yet again, but with more effective arguments. Utopia, i.e., a theory of what is distantly possible, is not an 'eschatology', a theory that the process of becoming might be brought to an end. It is the very concrete and positive idea of a history which has at last been orientated, directed and mastered by knowledge and willpower. The day when the gap between aims and results is narrowed, and the end of destiny (in other words the end of prehistory) is nigh, the withering away of the state will be at hand.

The withering away of the state or the practical possibility of it is an objective precondition for the resolution and supersession of the rift between *private life* and *political life* (between consciousness and political consciousness). The *private* will only rise to the level of the *public* when the public ceases to place itself in inaccessible and mysterious realms, and goes back down to the private to merge itself in the everyday once more. This process of supersession also plays a part in determining concrete democracy. Democracy must move towards the withering away of the state and the supersession of the conflict between the 'private' and the 'public'. If it does not, it is moribund.

So how can we propose to the private consciousness of the everyday man of today that its practical aim should be to become recognized by political and historical man? In so far as this mutual recognition might possibly heal the rift between consciousness and praxis, it remains an abstract ideal: an idea, a 'Utopia'. In so far as this recognition can be reduced to a simple fact among other facts, it has already been accomplished. In propaganda, which epitomizes state action and reasons of state, ideology and political consciousness target private consciousness. The aim is not to fill in the chasm and to achieve fusion through supersession. Propaganda leaves everyday life, consciousness and private life intact. It takes them as objects and even as 'things'. It insinuates itself inside them in order to shape them. It does not lift them up to the level of the universal. It fights with other ideologies for their possession. Is this inevitable? Certainly. It is destiny we are dealing with, in other words historical necessity and chance which have been turned into strategic necessity and tactical calculation. Recognition has only been unilateral, and unity has been achieved by means of confusion. Hence a paradox

367

which will require further examination: the intensification of ideologies at a time when they are being discredited, and the (more or less deep or momentary) depoliticization of an everyday life which is prodigiously 'well informed' politically, at a time when pressing political problems demonstrate an urgency which nobody denies.

There is something else which acts equally as an innovation and a deterioration: the technical element. It forces us to formulate the fundamental demand of the everyday differently from the way we did in our initial project. It is no longer a question simply of carrying the private to the social via language, knowledge and concept – of raising the everyday up to the historical and then to the political. *Critique of everyday life requires a plan, in other words a policy which will raise the everyday to the level made possible by technology.*

20

We have already talked about the above idea, but it deserves and even demands further explanation, so let us clarify it. Although technology has gone very far and high above the everyday, and continues to do so, it has not abandoned this neglected sector to its own devices. Up to a certain point the everyday has ceased to be underdeveloped. *A technical vacuum,* long the characteristic of the everyday, has been partially filled in. Technology has introduced a host of household objects and gadgets. Thus small technical objects have become familiar (although many housewives still have no access to this 'familiarity' and persist in regarding technical knowledge, including that of small objects, as a masculine attribute). Indisputably, the uncontrolled sector has somewhat declined. Could it be that everyday life has become integrated within a 'technological milieu' or, to use our own terminology, within the controlled sector organized in accordance with industrial technology? Could 'industrial society' have given it a coherent and specific structure, thus separating it from contact with uncontrolled nature, or conversely allowing it to rejoin nature via the 'world' of technical objects and making it part of a set of dynamic balances, similar to the feedbacks, homeostases and scannings studied by specialists in autoregulations? Nothing allows us to confirm this. In fact, everything proves the opposite.[27]

368

With the introduction of the technical object within everyday life, the contrast between the aesthetic object (which may or may not be useful) and the strictly functional and utilitarian technical object has been revealed in a harsher light. Hitherto confined to being part of the décor of social life, the 'aesthetic/technical' or 'artistic/functional' dichotomy has entered into familiarity. The industrial aesthetic and the commendable efforts which have been made in the field of industrial design have not succeeded in conferring an aesthetic status on the technical object, nor a technical status on the aesthetic object. The 'world of objects' is marked by this dichotomy, which classifies them in two major categories. We cannot avoid the fact that extreme or moderate functionalism has failed time and time again to extrapolate a plastic art from the functional. The fact that aesthetic creation or production has become saturated with technology and abstract functionalism make these failures all the more astonishing.

Only partially technicized, everyday life has not created its own specific style or rhythm. Unconnected objects (vacuum cleaners, washing machines, radio or television sets, refrigerators, cars, etc.) determine a series of disjointed actions. Small technical actions intervene in the old rhythms rather like fragmented labour in productive activity in general. The equipment of everyday life finds itself more or less in the same situation as industrial mechanization in its early stages, in the period when specific tools had unique and exclusive functions. If these gestures increase effectiveness – productivity – they also split things up; they truncate, they make mincemeat of everyday life; they leave margins and empty spaces. They increase the proportion of passivity. Dialectically, progress consists of gaps and partial regressions. What is more, a reduction in the time devoted to productive actions and gestures which are now carried out by technical objects has raised the question of time itself, and already this is a very urgent problem. If we examine time as it is experienced by many of today's men and women, we will see that it is chock-a-block full and completely empty. On the horizon of the modern world dawns the black sun of boredom, and critique of everyday life has a sociology of boredom as part of its agenda.

Incorporation of the everyday within a concrete totality (the total or world man) via modern means of information and communication can be interpreted in a variety of ways. Is it correct to say that television gives the everyday a world-wide dimension? Yes it is. Television allows every household to look at the spectacle of the world, but it is precisely this mode of looking at the world as a spectacle which introduces non-participation and receptive passivity. The idea that the audiovisual as it was lived in archaic communities (in scenes of magic) could be reconstituted is laughable and frivolous. The mass media strip the magic of presence from what was the presence of magic: participation – real, active or potential. Sitting in his armchair, surrounded by his wife and children, the television viewer witnesses the universe. At the same time, day in and day out, news, signs and significations roll over him like a succession of waves, churned out and repeated and already indistinguishable by the simple fact that they are pure spectacle: they are overpowering, they are hypnotic. The 'news' submerges viewers in a monotonous sea of newness and topicality which blunts sensitivity and wears down the desire to know.[28] Certainly, people are becoming more cultivated. Vulgar encyclopedism is all the rage. The observer may well suspect that when communication becomes incorporated in private life to this degree it becomes non-communication.

Radio and television do not penetrate the everyday solely in terms of the viewer. They go looking for it at its source: personalized (but superficial) anecdotes, trivial incidents, familiar little family events. They set out from an implicit principle: 'Everything, in other words, anything at all, can become interesting and even enthralling, provided that it is *presented*, i.e., *present*.' The art of presenting the everyday by taking it from its context, emphasizing it, making it appear unusual or picturesque and overloading it with meaning, has become highly skilful. But even if the lives of the great and the good are 'presentified' in this way through the mediation of presenters, editors and producers, it is still never anything else but the everyday. And so communication passes from unmediated event (captured the instant it happens and where it happens) to unmediated reception, within the familiar context of the everyday. Concrete mediations – language, culture in the traditional sense, values and symbols – become blurred. They do not disappear. They are too useful. They are worn down, they deteriorate, and yet at the same time they hypertrophy. It is their mediating function which is worn away.

At the extreme, signs and significations which are nothing more than significations lose all meaning. At the extreme looms the shadow of what we will call 'the great pleonasm': the unmediated passing immediately into the unmediated and the everyday recorded just as it is in the everyday – the event grasped, pulverized and transmitted as rapidly as light and consciousness – the repetition of the identical in a wild whirling dance devoid of Dionysian rapture, since the 'news' never contains anything really new. If this extreme were reached, the closed circuit of communication and information would jeopardize the unmediated and the mediated alike. It would merge them in a monotonous and Babel-like confusion. The reign of the global would also be the reign of a gigantic tautology, which would kill all dramas after having exploited them shamelessly.

Of course, this extreme situation is still a long way away. It would be a closed circuit, a circuit from hell, a perfect circle in which the absence of communication and communication pushed to the point of paroxysm would meet and their identities would merge. But it will never come full circle. There will always be something new and unforeseen, if only in terms of sheer horror. There will be 'creations' which will stimulate informative energy and allow for a massive injection of new information. This extreme exists only in the mind's eye as a distant possibility, in the same way as the debasement of informational energy and the triumph of entropy are. And yet, this extreme allows us to imagine and determine certain aspects of 'the real'. The very least we can be sure of is that the mass media have not yet incorporated the everyday into a vaster, richer whole, such as spontaneity or culture. They have left it to its 'privation' while moving into this privation and taking it over. It is the generalization of *private life*. At one and the same time the mass media have unified and broadcast the everyday; they have disintegrated it by integrating it with 'world' current events in a way which is both too real and utterly superficial. What is more or less certain is that they are dissociating an acquired, traditional culture, the culture of books, from written discourse and Logos. We cannot say what the outcome of this destructuring process will be.

To conclude this point, let us say that we have many reservations about the terms we are employing: technological society, industrial society. Primacy of technology? Certainly, but technology does leave several essential sectors behind civilization, and outside it. Industrial society? Yes, but it is within this society that for the foreseeable future *uneven development* will go on producing all its effects.

21

Modified in this way by modern technology, the everyday has not disappeared. Although its problems may have changed, in a great many respects they have become worse. A prime example: new towns.

Here, the everyday reigns in what we might call the chemically pure state. The extreme example can be seen in practice. Here, everyday life is shrinking into private life. Every object has been calculated and technically realized to carry out a daily function at the lowest possible cost; it implies a series of actions, and brings them into being; these are actions which guarantee the bare essentials of existence, foreseeable and foreseen functional gestures which obey the peremptory suggestions of the Thing. When used, every thing must satisfy a need (not a desire, but a need: isolated, analysed, dissociated, and intended as such). And this integral functionalism could with some justification be seen as the best hypothesis: it is the best thing that could happen to people living in new towns and recent housing schemes; individual and social needs are too often overlooked, treated with contempt, repressed or frustrated.

Infinitely superior to the slums and workers' housing estates of the past, the flats and apartment buildings of today seem to offer the New Life in the Golden City. Propaganda shrieks it from the rooftops. And so we pass from exaggerated praise to exaggerated disparagement, from exaltation to despondency. Sociologically, the truth is that new towns reduce the everyday to its simplest terms while at the same time 'structuring' it heavily: the everyday in them is perfect and stripped bare in its privation, basic and deprived of basic spontaneity. It wanders around stagnantly and loses hope in the midst of its own emptiness, which nothing technical can ever fill, not even a television set or a car. Everyday life has lost a dimension: depth. Only triviality remains. Apartment buildings are often well-constructed 'machines for living in', and the housing estate is a machine for the

372

upkeep of life outside work. Every object is determined by its function and is reduced to being a signal; it orders one thing and forbids another; it demonstrates behaviour patterns; it conditions. Let us describe a new town and analyse it dialectically.[29] Every town planning scheme conceals a programme for everyday life. Explicitly or not, it refers to an overall conception of man, of life and of the world. In our new towns, the project or programme is all too apparent. Everyday life sees itself treated like packaging: a vast machine seizes the worker's time outside work and folds it in a wrapping as sterile as the protective cellophane round a commodity. People are separated from group to group (workers, craftsmen, technicians) and from each other, each in his box for living in, and this modernity organizes their repeated gestures. The same machinery whittles down the number of essential gestures. That most of these housing estates depend upon technically outstanding firms – automated – where work is almost entirely reduced to the control and upkeep of equipment makes the emptiness all the more blatant. Of course equipment does not function by itself; technical objects make up an ensemble which requires occasional attention. However, this can only come when the technical object issues a message, a *signal*. The town and the factory complement one another by both conforming to the technical object. An identical process makes work easy and passive, and life outside work fairly comfortable and boring. Thus everyday life at work and outside work become indistinguishable, governed as they are by systems of *signals*.

Controlled by signals, paradoxically dissociated, everyday time becomes both homogeneous and dispersed. Work time falls into line with family-life time and leisure time, if not vice versa. In the new housing estates, objects with aesthetic pretensions appear ridiculous, and indeed they are, because they have been added on in an intentional and clumsy manner; there is nothing surprising about them, except perhaps the surprise of uneasiness they afford. As for 'entertainment', that too belongs in this sorry scheme, unless it is rescued by the vigorous initiative of those concerned. Men come home from a day's work which has been almost as far removed from consciously creative activity as the spectacle of the world which they now view on the television screen from the passivity of their armchairs. Women (who work less frequently in the new estates than in the old towns, where there are more 'tertiary' jobs available for women) get their household chores out of the way, put the nagging task of minding the children to one side, and immerse themselves as soon as possible in the 'romantic press'. Yet all it needs is to visit the perfectly automated factory at Lacq, or to gaze at the hills above it, and then to go into the new town which shelters its workers, to observe a striking contrast. On one side, dazzling wonders, on the other the poverty of 'pure' everyday life. Let us take a flight of Utopian fancy. Let us suppose that just as much care and money had been devoted to Mourenx-Ville-Nouvelle as was to Lacq, and that these funds had been used wisely. What would the result have been for its inhabitants? How would the chasm have been filled? By means of what marvels of town planning, of variety, of games connected to culture and all that is serious in life? . . .

22

Admirably made by women for women (which does not mean it has no male readers), the women's press demonstrates by its quantity and quality an obvious wish to 'promote' women. At the same time it reveals the uncertainties and ambiguities of such a promotion. If women are still trying to assert themselves, it means that they have not yet achieved their goal. But what is that goal?

The women's press and specifically the 'romantic press' provide a sort of feminine ideology. Now every ideology is an implement for effective action. Therefore – consciously or unconsciously – this press is part of a strategy. What are its aims? Who makes use of this ideology? A women's lobby or the vast 'unformed' group of women in general? The critical reader is unable to understand. At first it seems that the aim is to sell feelings and dreams, or rather to help women 'assert' themselves. But the plethora of means for self-assertion or compensation exceeds so limited an objective. Could the aim be (political or non-political) power in general, or rather, and more vaguely, the will for power? Could it be ethical? Could these vast means be targeting 'ethical' recognition of the 'feminine being', as yet equally unachieved for women as for men and their ever-hazy consciousness? Could it be aesthetic? Or, in an immense confusion, could it be both at the same time? Finally, could it be some sort of grand game without any precise objective?

What is certain is that individually and collectively the 'modern woman' is involved in a long, bitter struggle for 'being', without really understanding and without even asking herself whether 'being' means social role, importance, power, pathos, mastery of the self, beauty, fecundity, mysticity, conformity or non-conformity. No thing, no possibility is excluded. So could it be all these things simultaneously, in a marvellous muddle which no philosophy, no option, no mutilating reasoning could clarify? Perhaps!

There is an opposite point of view. Whoever wants 'being' without knowing how to define it, without being able to define it and without even wanting to define it is just as incapable of defining 'non-being', and runs the risk of confusing the two. Without scruple and without measure, the women's press mixes the everyday up with the imaginary (so that the project of a mutual critique of the everyday by the fictitious and of the fictitious by the everyday has been both achieved and superseded – as a theoretical project – in the women's press).

What the so-called women's press creates and offers is a 'world', a feminine world. Temporary or lasting, the specific and complementary traits of a 'femininity' are literally made into a world in the women's press. It is a world where triviality does not exclude the extraordinary, where the physiological does not exclude high culture, where the practical does not exclude the ideal, and where these aspects never become disconnected. It is not a logical world, coherently abstract or abstractly coherent. It is not a full, concrete universe analogous to a great work of art. Coherent in its own way, incoherent in an original way (which is not apparent as such to the men and women who accept it), rich in surprises, inhabitable and densely inhabited, this feminine world has no closure. It opens itself up to be looked at and touched, even to males: it tempts them and it can captivate them, since it is not their world and there is no longer a virile world (supposing that virile virtues, together with masculine shortcomings, ever made up a 'world' or were able to assert themselves and to live according to this mode).

The feminine world is ambiguous and muddled. It does not even reflect a given feminine 'essence', an eternal feminine whose homologues would be found in the ephemeral and the instantaneous. This

375

world is a mishmash of the aesthetic, the ethical and the practical. It does not define an art or a moral domain, not even an art of living, but rather a moralism and an aestheticism, lipstick and powder for practical everyday reality which manage to conceal it or at least to make it look prettier from time to time. Nothing in this world or of this world is true, and everything is true, nothing is false and everything is false. Nothing is possible and everything is possible. Nothing is permitted and everything is permitted.

As far as men are concerned, this is a myth or a set of myths. In the eyes of society, it would be more of an ideology. In terms of women themselves, is it not a sort of Utopia? Everything happens as though the *image* (myth, ideology, Utopia, or what you will) of the *total woman* had replaced the image or the idea of the total man after the latter had collapsed. According to this interpretation, and we have no intention of glossing over its twofold irony, the feminine strategy – the strategy of 'women' as a vast, amorphous group or the strategy of their leaders – would have either a conscious or an unconscious goal: to form and impose the image of the total woman, a modern and practical version of the defunct 'total man'. After the demise of the latter, men themselves would accept the relay and the transfer, through powerlessness.

The illusion has changed. The image of the total man was political and revolutionary. It received its inheritance from a long and glorious past. It did not wish to separate virility from masculinity, virtue from skill and manual strength from mental strength; it did not claim to unite them easily. The state, history, wars and philosophy had influenced it, leaving traces and operating a hard process of selection. The image of the total woman is distinctly reformist and apolitical, confused and syncretic. It has the backing of this great force: newness, the effect of surprise, plus confusion and syncretism.

The total woman becomes everything because she does everything. She produces and directs consumption. She has children, she brings them up and educates them. She governs the family. She allows men to devote themselves to sterile games: politics, war, feelings, intellect. And yet artists create for her, woman, and about her.

The 'feminine world' the women's press offers us wishes to be total, so as to correspond to the total woman and to impose her image. It attains totality through confusion. And what a world it is!

Everything is found or reflected there, everything is recognizable, although not with the transparency desirable for a 'world'. Techniques and technology happily set up home with art and morality. Aestheticism and moralism bless these marriages, no better and no worse than any others. By using techniques, the feminine world has gathered together all 'worlds' past, present or future. It excludes nothing. In this it differs extraordinarily from that virile image which merely asserted its reality and inspirational values: work, courage, knowledge. Today philosophy is being distanced, and so, with all its demands, is the philosopher's lifestyle.

Recent and 'modern', still almost pristine, the feminine world has emerged from a series of tests which up until now it has avoided facing. It has even avoided the test of philosophy, for its birth coincides with the moment when the withering away of philosophy is at its height, and indeed philosophical discussion has become one of its most charming and interesting subjects. And so it takes in the most ancient myths and the most apparently worn-out symbolisms. In a mode of assertive triumphalism, images of the time when 'woman' was a slave reappear – the queen, the beast-divinity, the servant-mistress, the doubly martyred and oppressed mother-wife. Figures of fatal beauty, of Predestination, of absolute Good Luck and marvellous Damnation cohabit with the representation of free initiative and practical effectiveness. Courageous and virile heroes, moths and mayflies consumed by passion's ardent flame, seducers who fall victim to their own magic powers, Princes, Kings, Knights equal to their own destiny, all make up the retinue of the total woman. The feminine world is woven of indecisive correspondences and uncertain analogies. Its life is nourished and maintained by confusion. It generalizes the individual and personalizes impersonal techniques, and cheaply too; all it needs is a perfume, a colour, or not even that: an intention, a signification. Cycles intertwine in a tepid and murky harmony, from the hours and the days to the seasons and to entire lives. In the distance hard, linear time passes by, the time of masculine efforts. Colours, perfumes, numbers reply to and correspond with the stars and their conjunctures. It truly is a world, a romantic cosmos stripped of risk and violence, where lyricism has become familiarity. Benign or malignant impulses shoot through it, and we can believe in them, and we can disbelieve in them while still believing in them.

Neither the most insignificant of magical gestures conjuring up misfortune, nor the most minuscule of superstitions fabricating the
illusion of good luck, stand in the way of grandiose representations of
human dramas, madness, passion and death, theatre and religion. On
the plane of fiction, anecdotes and trivial events take on gigantic
meanings. Conversely, tragic Images and Figures are reduced to the
dimensions of everyday crimes, which above all are crimes against
common sense.

This ambiguous world – this world of ambiguity – is also the world
of universal muddle, where people talk colloquially about the sublime
and use the same tone of voice when talking about the familiar. (And
actually this is quite correct, since tone of voice metamorphoses whatever one is talking about, and in any case the familiar really does
contain elements of the sublime, and vice versa). This world is neither
true nor false. It is a microcosm: small, but for those who inhabit it
immense and perhaps infinite. Ambiguity allows people to pass indiscriminately from anything to anything else. Cookery becomes a
fairyland and fantastic stories are like recipes in a magic cookery
book, flanked by articles on fashion and stories about the romantic
agonies of a famous star or an oriental princess. Mystification? Mythi-
fication? No. It is less than that, and more, better and worse: it is the
ambiguity of the everyday, exploited by an ambiguous consciousness
which above all is not consciousness of ambiguity.

Hence 'something' irritating and captivating, slightly inane and
very intelligent (sometimes). What? The everyday wrapped up and
hidden away, metamorphosed and revealed. This 'something' which
wishes to be total and in a sense *is* total appears in all its ludicrous
weakness and poverty through its veil of transparent images. This
pseudo-everyday is lived and perceived in the manner of an ambiguous consciousness (neither false nor true, half-false, half-true, thus
contradictory, but without consciousness of the contradictions, so
that these contradictions become blunted and weakened, and this
could serve as a definition of *ambiguity* as a category of everyday life).
It can easily be linked to the ever-changing important issues of
current affairs, fashion, art, politics and history. At the same time it
offers an escape from the genuine problems of art, politics, history,
and, in the end, of modern life. It is a perpetual alibi, always accessible and welcoming. The doors of this world are open wide; you can

walk right in. The seats are cheaper than at the cinema or the theatre. What matter if the quality of illusion and participation (or rather of non-participation) is not as high? What is important is that eventually these cosmetics make everyday life bearable, that boredom is diminished and worries are forgotten, that private life becomes open to wonder (in part knowingly simulated, like a kind of semi-astonishment). This confused world restores a sort of wholeness to disjointed gestures and interrupted rhythms. The 'lived' will be lived in the manner of the 'non-lived'; the possible and the impossible are mixed up together. By transposing it, fiction and half-sleeping, half-waking dreams will make an intolerable life livable by offering it meanings which will support it and deceive it without being deceitful. In this pseudo-world nothing is, and everything signifies. Like wan haloes, significations exploit without exploiting, mislead without misleading. The virile mind was never satisfied with significations. The impalpable coefficients of spirituality connected to things could never satisfy the philosopher. Man, the virile mind, wanted to be; he wanted being. Feminine in essence, and by its very 'presence' (if we can use that word, since it 'is' the opposite of presence and a parody of it: a substitute for being, in a state of collapse), signification bears witness to the downgrading of philosophy. Nevertheless, a vague question remains, amorphous and unanswered. Who are these multiple significations of things and actions intended for? Why are they never able to attain more consistency? Why are they incapable of being anything more than a moralistic or aesthetic intention?

These phenomena – and it is difficult to state with any certainty whether they are temporary or long-lasting – have some disconcerting aspects. Before the Second World War the women's press and 'romantic press' were scarcely out of the cradle, but in only a few years they became very powerful. They quickly gave a certain pitch to the press in general, to news journalism and even to the male-orientated press (which was henceforth isolated and quasi-specialized). The content of these publications altered very rapidly in accordance with general circumstances: it shifted from a relative immoralism after the Liberation to a concern with moral order, and from a humanism discreetly tinted with femininity to a religiosity openly tinged with mythology. The same topics reappear, but in different guises, so that their repetition soaks into the public only gradually. Quasi-permanent, symbolisms appeared in some surprising lights. In effect, ambiguity allows for almost inexhaustible variations on the same themes, each variation containing a few fresh details and, most importantly, a new tone. The same love story can suggest erotic emancipation or the need for a strict moral discipline, according to its 'tone'.[30] By studying this press historically we can measure out a variety of ingredients contained in this volatile mixture: the 'promotion of women' and its uncertainties, 'techniques for finding happiness', moral order, the vicissitudes and anguishes of modernity, etc.

The crowning achievement of the operation, if we can call it that, is to suggest and insinuate a moral order by means of anecdotes which pander to cynicism, immoralism, eroticism and a tasteless romantic sentimentality. A press with a vast circulation sells moral order wrapped up as immoralism, just like a government policy in apolitical wrappings, and ideology disguised as ideological detachment.

As we have already stressed, our study of the reality in question, namely the situation of women in 'modern' life, raises other problems, problems of society as a whole. Where does moral order originate? What does it correspond to in history, to what necessity, or lack of necessity? Does it correspond to something more general than the requirements of particular groups, and more humble than the requirements of ethics or philosophy? How does it come about that today, for the first time as far as we know, a 'moral order' is not being imposed by force, but seems accepted and even called for by the wishes of most, if not of everyone? As for 'techniques for finding happiness', what exactly do they consist of, and what are they aimed at? Is it the satisfaction of those basic, fragmented needs, comfort and wellbeing? Is it security, tranquillity, peace of mind through order and a new modality of clear conscience? And by what means – cooking, fashion, do-it-yourself, relaxation, sexual and emotional harmony, general or mental health, catharsis or relief of tensions, an end to the romanticism of passion and the sense of the tragic? How do those who promote and employ these techniques hope to avoid boredom? What link do these minor, everyday techniques have with technology, with art, with aesthetics and above all with aestheticism as a social phenomenon?

These questions lead us to the connection of modernized every-day life to modernity in general. Therefore they go beyond the confines of the 'promotion of women' taken in isolation. The more we consider the 'promotion of women' the more vague it appears, like the ambiguous base or 'foundation' of ambiguity itself. The elimination of age-old sufferings, such as pain in childbirth, has not suppressed the specific links between femininity and nature and its rhythms. The great hope that work would 'emancipate' women brought them many setbacks and disillusions. They soon discovered that work in factories or offices was scarcely less monotonous than housework, which in fact was being facilitated by new technology, and that they were in danger of being landed with both. Meanwhile, industry had introduced fragmented labour. The number of success-ful women writers is more an indication of the crisis and decline of certain genres (the novel, for example) than of the triumph of vital intuitions or of strongly original ideas. The violent feminine onslaughts in the domain of ideology are as much an expression of their lack of self-confidence as of their robustness. The press con-tains as many compensations, justifications and consolations as it does 'positive values'. The tactics and strategies it employs are sur-prising not so much for their brilliance, but rather for their powers of innuendo . . .

Beneath personal narratives and beyond their symptoms and expressions, we sense the strange and painful zone of the 'private Eros', a zone where failures and illusions, superstitions and false powers, the images and myths of powerlessness all converge.

23

Seen in this light, could we not say that of all new phenomena the 'reprivatization' of life is the strangest, and that to a certain extent it encompasses all the previous ones? To use a certain philosophical language which explains nothing and which would demonstrate the need for a deeper theoretical development of these concepts as well as of the facts themselves, the point of view of totality bears witness to a 'detotalization'.

Let us look at these facts more closely. They are paradoxical. The 'reprivatization' of everyday life, which both modified and confirmed the everyday in the modern world, started from 1950 onwards. It consisted of an escape from the nuclear threat and from the setbacks of history. It evaded civic tasks while at the same time suffering the mystifications of official public-mindedness. However, we cannot explain reprivatization by these historical conditions alone, nor as a simple reaction to certain setbacks. At the same time needs were being aroused, some new, some existing potentially as mass phenomena and only crystallized by advertising, by the mediation of which they were connected to their objects. What was most striking, and still is, was the isolated nature of these needs and of the way they were stimulated. Each one of them has its objects and its slogans. Therefore each has its own distinct satisfaction which does not become part of a coherent totality. The satisfaction of contingent needs by objects which are themselves external and contingent defines one of the characteristics of the new 'private life', where general economic and social necessity is expressed by a series of chances (needs experienced, needs satisfied). Once need becomes need for *this* or for *that* it loses its fundamental spontaneity, while failing to individualize desire. This does not make the process any the less irreversible. Options have been taken (for example, as regards the role and importance of the motor car!). *Growth of needs, alienation of desire* is how we expressed it previously. We can now formulate it more precisely: *the external necessity of needs and the randomness of satisfactions*, with private life continuing to be the arena of these disjointed needs and satisfactions, and the link which joins them together.

Sociologists have noted how the contemporary family has been reduced to its simplest expression: to its nucleus. They speak commonly and without irony of the (isolated) 'nuclear family'. Well, this nucleus is being consolidated.[31] This 'residual deposit' has not yet broken up. It manifests itself simultaneously as a residual deposit and as a product (which is something we have said about the everyday in general). The family has not splintered as was expected a few decades ago. 'Reprivatization' is none the less surprising for not deriving from a precise, foreseeable function. It demonstrates that maybe the social cannot be reduced to the functional, and that the 'residual' not only is able to persist, but can also grow stronger. In any case, specialists can argue endlessly about the functional and its links with the real and the structural. Could the private life and the family of today be 'suprafunctional'? In certain circumstances, would not shelter from external dangers and pressures define a 'function'? In fact, the emergence of needs and the consumption of goods in this day and age can be seen as being 'functional' in the 'institutionalized' framework of the family and of private life.

In any event, everyday, private or 'reprivatized' life and family life are these days intimately linked together. Although the everyday does not restrict itself to the internal life of the family group and to 'private life', it encompasses the things which affect them. Therefore it includes whatever escapes from other groups as such, something which should not make us forget that in its way private family life penetrates, emphasizes and colours everything which spills over into it – work, leisure activities, sociability, culture.

The difficulty here is that if we are to grasp all the contradictions of reality, we must not overlook a single one of its aspects. Let us recall Marx's very illuminating observation: 'The abstraction of the *state as such* was not born until the modern world because the abstraction of private life was not created until modern times.'[32] This formula allows us to place the everyday within modernity, and we will have cause to remind ourselves of it more than once. Indeed, the paradox of the situation is not the consolidation of family life reduced to the 'nuclear', nor the process of 'reprivatization'. What is surprising is the set of contradictions which accompany this process and which constitute it. 'Reprivatization' takes place while history is speeding up. It is not only linked to the setbacks, trials and dangers concealed within this headlong acceleration; it is also linked to technology. Well, beginning with radio and television, technology should have given private life access to social and political life, to history and to knowledge. But while life and consciousness are becoming 'globalized', consciousness and private life are withdrawing into themselves, and this produces some unexpected results. Predictable and expected, 'globalization' is being achieved in the mode of withdrawal. In his armchair, the private man – who has even stopped seeing himself as a citizen – witnesses the universe without having a hold over it and without really wanting to. He looks at the world. He becomes globalized, but as an eye, purely and simply. He 'learns' something. But what exactly does

A Critique of Everyday Life, Volume II

this learning consist of? It does not consist of genuine knowledge, nor
of power over the things seen, nor of real participation in events. It is
a new modality of looking: a social gaze which rests on the image of
things but which is reduced to powerlessness, the possession of a false
consciousness, quasi-knowledge and non-participation. Without
seeing that it is doing so, this gaze banishes real knowledge, real
power and real participation. It really is a *private* gaze, the gaze of the
private man who has become social, and despite the fact that it harbours the potential for interests, for enjoyments, and for a kind of
'mosaic' of culture.[33]

'Reprivatization' has its pleasant advantages; it creates a certain
taste and a certain skill in the use of everyday objects. At the same
time, its end product is submission to an impersonal, encyclopedic
and vulgarized culture; like the feminine press, it introduces moral
order through innuendo; it facilitates all the rigging and fixing that
goes on in mass information. It is the world as an entity passively perceived, and without effective participation, and processes unfold
within it which are visible but inaccessible: technology, space exploration, political strategies. Under the socialized gaze which substitutes
for the active consciousness of social practice, these processes vanish
into the distance at breakneck speed.

So the word 'private' has not lost its main meaning: privation.
Private life remains privation. The 'world' is there to plug up the
holes, fill in the cracks, paper over the gaps, camouflage the frustrations. Time is crammed full and life seems fit to burst. Or else it is
empty. 'Chock-a-block full and completely empty.'

At the same time as life was being 'reprivatized', power and wealth
were being personalized, and by the same means. Public and political
life became laden with images borrowed from private life. For a long
time, perhaps from the start, 'public' men and women – in other
words, powerful or famous people – were commonplaces. They
belonged (apparently) to everyone. This illusion was part of the way
politics operated. It was part of the essence of the state and of the
culture which had been established above society while appearing to
remain part of it. It was not incompatible with democracy as a political system. It was one of the more honourable and relatively profound
contradictions of a democracy which had been relatively successfully
established.

Using modern means, this illusion deploys itself in a vast representation of real and practical social life. We are spared no detail of the everyday lives of princes and queens, of stars and millionaires, since 'great men' and 'bosses' and even 'heroes' have an everyday life on a par with our own. We 'know' their bathrooms almost as well as we know our own, we 'know' their mansions almost as well as we know our own flat, we 'know' their bodies almost as well as we know our own. This 'knowledge', if we can call it that, is spread throughout the world by means of images, and helps to create the attraction or powerful influence these celebrities exert. They are slaves to this knowledge. They cannot do without it. They know this, and submit to the demands of the public and of publicity, even if it means that they too must find refuge elsewhere. In short, seen from this angle, grandeur and the sublime are restored to the everyday. The public becomes private and the private becomes public, but in appearance only, since power retains its properties and wealth its possibilities. The humblest citizen knows his prince. He has been able to see him close up, almost as if he could touch him; but once he accepts this illusion, he has stopped being a citizen. The humblest farm-hand 'knows' queens, princesses and filmstars. But if he really believes he has attained a 'knowledge' of something, he is being trapped by one of modernity's strangest and most disturbing alienations. The rift between the private and the public has been overcome in appearance only. The supersession of these two aspects of social practice is nothing more than an illusion.

The social appears more open and more transparent than ever before. The *socialization of society* has adopted new forms, more extensive than previous ones, and on a truly 'world' scale, but mystification, alienation and privation have also adopted a world dimension. However, it is curiously 'worldly minded', and turns the world into a caricature of itself.

The world carries on its business beneath a gaze which has become social. But what happens in people's homes, in the enclosure of their private lives and behind the wall that is their forehead? Viewed from outside, private life appears opaque. From the warm and damp intimacy within, it is what is outside which appears threatening, storm-tossed and opaque. Inside, we do not know what is happening outside, where events come from or what causes tensions.

The most petty side of the everyday becomes reassuring. There, in private life, we think we are sure of being loved or hated (or both at once), of being protected and smothered, of being taken care of and pushed towards morbid states of mind. We are given the assurance that however insignificant we may be, at least we exist. This is one nucleus of the everyday, and one of its polarities.

It is the place where significations rise and then fall away into insignificance. (Let us take a photo album. Every face and every scene contains an episode or sums up a period in someone's life; each image is loaded with significations. Very quickly, these faces and scenes fade away; they become forgotten, dying their own social death, and are dead for ever; dramas lose their cutting edge and things lose their halo of meaning . . .)

Thus 'reprivatization' is prolonging and replacing the individualism of the earlier period, by substituting the small family group in place of the individual. Our society harbours profound contradictions, which mark the necessary and inevitable 'socialization of society'. While not making it completely problematic, these contradictions do raise many problems. Groups are getting larger (cities, businesses, classes) while at the same time the differentiations at the heart of these groups are becoming more strongly asserted. Information is increasing while direct contacts are in decline. Relations are becoming more numerous while their intensity and authenticity are diminishing. Along with segregations come diversities, and with possibilities of initiative and freedom come stricter conditionings.

Withdrawal into the self is passive in relation to an overcomplex social reality which oscillates between innuendo and brutal explicitness, but it appears to be a solution of sorts. It is as difficult to assess as it is to understand. It cannot be said that 'reprivatization' has not been *actively chosen*. There has been an *option*, and a general one (social options, group choices, socially accepted and adopted proposals for choice). Nor can it be said that it has been chosen freely. However, the choice itself is imposed and the solution is indicated or countermanded. This constraint operates within a fairly narrow margin of freedom; the weight from outside and from the 'world' becomes increasingly oppressive for an intimacy which has been metamorphosed into a mass phenomenon.

Is this a lifestyle, or is it life unequivocally stripped of all style?

Although we would tend towards the second of these hypotheses, it is still too early to reach a decision; scrutiny of these hypotheses and this problem is part of the *sociology of boredom* . . .

Very oddly, 'reprivatization' threw critical study of the everyday off course. 'Reprivatization' confirmed the everyday, but in an unexpected way; it modified and reconstituted it more forcefully than before as 'privation' and as the domain of appearances. This unexpected consolidation threw the study of it off track, because it altered the subject and the way of seeing it, as well as the methods being employed.

We have left several of the most surprising historical conditions of 'reprivatization' to one side, for example the temporary or permanent loss of prestige of the collective. Seen as a historical phenomenon, this loss of prestige was itself motivated in many psychological and sociological ways: experience of the restrictive nature of the collective; an end to the illusion of a 'catharsis' for the individual and his troubles by means of the social; an end to the illusion of a happy equilibrium for the individual within the social; and the realization that economic and political organization and overorganization were absorbing private life without creating a lifestyle free of 'privation', etc. What is most astonishing in all of this is not that the collective had been resorted to, nor the fact that this failed. For a long period of time, people were hoping and waiting for a radical transformation of everyday life: a new life. Only the collective (or rather a certain representation of the collective) seemed capable of delivering this transformation. This was the meaning of the 'Utopian socialism' which was so closely linked to 'scientific socialism'. The history of socialism offers a twofold lesson: the fall of the collective as a transforming agent of everyday life, and the rise of technology and its problems. Given this twofold experience, and given that the idea of a revolutionary transformation of the everyday has almost vanished, the withdrawal into an everyday which has not been transformed but which has benefited from a small proportion of technical progress becomes perfectly understandable. No, what is most astonishing is perhaps the fact that this withdrawal has in no way stopped collective organization and overorganization continuing to operate on its own level: the state, important decisions, bureaucracy. 'Reprivatized' life has its own level, and the large institutions have theirs. These levels are juxtaposed or superimposed.

Consolidated around this nucleus, private life and the everyday provide an alibi for escaping from history, from failures, from risks and from threats, and this creates a gulf between 'the lived' and the domain of history,[34] which is a consequence of its setbacks and backward surges. But let us not be misled. To be reticent about history, to run away from the historical and from the problems of society as a whole (in other words, to run away from politics), is nevertheless one of the ways history is lived. The extra-historicity of modern everyday life is itself a modality of history and a demonstration of its inner conflicts. When the everyday consolidates itself as 'private life' it does not eliminate history, no more than what is determined eliminates the randomness it contains. 'No throw of the dice can eliminate chance.'[35] Hesitations, hiding places, escape routes, they all disguise many things and prevent nothing. Never did history pursue people to the extent it has since people have entrenched themselves against it and attempt to take part in events as spectators of images.

Nevertheless it remains true that not everything is equally historical, or equally 'cultural'.

Although in fact men do not escape history, or culture, or knowledge, and are fascinated by them precisely because of the growing gap between such external forces and their own lives, they nevertheless consolidate a level of reality which offers a kind of passive resistance to history and knowledge. In certain cases this resistance becomes active; and so, withdrawn within their own everyday reality, the members of a social group can oppose an enemy, an occupying power, a 'creator' of events or a political leader.

In our view, there is a sense to 'reprivatization'. It cannot be defined simply as the search for an alibi or a means of escape from history. In its reactions to the setbacks of revolution or the danger of planetary extermination, it is not simply burying its head in the sand. Clumsily but insistently, it is seeking an acceptable way forward: not an absolute barrier between the private and the public, between the individual and the social and the historical − nor a completely free passage which would abolish the characteristics of the former in favour of the latter, and which would be nothing more than a gaping void. Radical critique of 'reprivatization' does not stop us from understanding it; on the contrary, understanding it is just as important as explaining it.

Along with 'reprivatization' are various phenomena deriving from social links and relations: the reinstatement of certain affective tonalities (such as friendship and comradeship) and ill-defined values associated with groups linked by affinity or affiliation – a hesitant return to social spontaneity. Moreover, the 'world of objects' has assumed new importance, while at the same time it has become more diversified: familiar or unfamiliar technical items, useful or useless items, luxury items, aesthetic items, objects which impose certain behaviour patterns or which allow for initiative by appealing to the imagination, to emotions, to memory. To study this world of objects and how it is divided and classified would require a *logistics of everyday life*.

24

Is this a matter for philosophy or philosophical analysis? Yet again: *yes and no*. Yes, since critical analysis and presentation of the everyday use categories which originate in philosophy: appropriation, alienation, privation, power (of man over nature and over his own nature), need, desire, critical negativity, etc.

And yet, no. Before they can be used in the pursuit of concrete knowledge, these categories must be extricated from the systematizations within which philosophical thought has imprisoned them, and made to stand apart from any specifically philosophical system.

So what is the core issue? In our view, critical study of the everyday contributes towards a *dialectical anthropology* which is itself dependent upon (or coincidental with) a *dialectical humanism*.

The real core issue is to define mankind. Marxist dogmatism defined it by labour and for labour, as a producer. But active man creates the human world and, through the act of production, produces himself. He does not simply produce things, implements or goods; he also produces history and situations. He creates 'human nature': nature in himself and for himself, nature appropriated to man by means of his many conflicts. Marxist dogmatism determines man unilaterally, and foregrounds the outside world and the thing, and power over matter and material production. It has parenthesized man's nature and the inner appropriation of nature by the human. In its pedagogy, in its philosophy and in its propaganda, in its art and in its system of education, its conception of them is purely cursory.

All dogmatisms mutilate the human by determining it as something unilateral. They take away one or several of its dimensions. Our starting point is a totality, but differentiated according to dimension and level. Our starting point is a total human phenomenon: 'need–work–pleasure', 'speak–make–live'. The term 'phenomenon' shows the will to supersede philosophical ontology and not to presume to exhaust the human and the 'world' by defining them as essences.

Could the human be essentially cultural? Could it be defined by tools and technology, reason, Logos or language, by knowledge, by culture, by an analytic intellect which calculates and organizes? These definitions are just as acceptable and just as limited as definitions which use historicity, or practical reason which projects and realizes objectives by taking risks and options, and less rational definitions which use dreams, laughter, play, love or awareness of death.

'Man' is this, but other things (or other 'non-things') as well. He is a plurality of dimensions, a multiplicity of forms and structures. He is a shifting hierarchy of levels (which means that the usual concept of 'structure' must be modified and dynamized). Thus he is also the everyday, in so far as the everyday introduces an unevenly developed level into totality, which nevertheless transforms itself, and which above all *must* transform itself. In the words of Nietzsche, 'Man is the animal which is not yet defined.' We would add the everyday to the dimensions we have previously defined, and that everyday is something which urgently needs to be transformed, so that its theory cannot be separated from a revolutionary praxis which has been restored to all its former breadth, and from a vision of what is possible (and impossible).

Dialectical anthropology does not exclude culture but neither does it parenthesize nature in the name of culture (which would be a 'culturalism'). It studies the conflictual 'nature/culture' relation, particularly on the level where it manifests itself: in the everyday. It does not exclude the historical and does not place 'the lived' outside history. It studies the conflictual 'historicity/lived' relation, particularly on the level where it manifests itself: in everyday life. By concentrating on this humble territory, which forms and structures both inhabit, it hopes to avoid unilateralities and neofetishisms (of signification, of non-signification or of the thing without signification – of structure and of the spontaneous – of culture and anticulture, of totality and non-totality, for example).

This anthropology takes history into account but excludes 'historicism', which sees everything as being equally historical. It encompasses the study of political economy, but combines with a critique of political economy which rejects and refutes economism (the doctrine of economic determinism). Finally, it includes a *sociology*, in other words a conception of the social ensemble; but equally it includes a critique of *sociologism*, in other words of the attitude which privileges one set of facts and concepts in totality since it eliminates history and historicity, nature, and the problems raised by the links between them. In short, it eliminates a whole range of dialectical movements. Therefore, and not without paradox, we will offer both a dialectical sociology (or an attempt at one) and a critique of the foundations of sociology.

To put it another way, our guideline will be a critical study of what can and ought to change in human reality. By emphasizing one part (one level) of reality, and above all by referring to critique of this level of reality – to creative negation – we will attempt to grasp reality, but not to exhaust it.

25

As we continue in this direction towards our goal, we will soon come up against some run-of-the-mill methodological concerns. There are a certain number of formal and general concepts which we need to review in order to see precisely how we can use them: the concept of *level*, of *structure*, of *totality*, of *tactic* and *strategy*, and finally, of *model*. The latter is particularly important in that we will be proposing a model (or several models) of social reality: nothing more, nothing less.

26

Once we have clarified this conceptual equipment, we will introduce several specific concepts.

391

From the outset we will divide these specific concepts into two groups: categories of ambiguity and categories of non-ambiguity. The following concepts belong in the first of these groups: *ambiguity, misunderstanding, compromise, misjudgement* and *misuse, denial, agreement* and *contestation, connivance* and *complicity, disquiet, alibi*, etc.

We will rank the following concepts in the second group: *decision* and *opposition, dilemma* and *action logic, challenge* and *mistrust, refusal, choice, wager, risk, repetition* and *recognition, the possible* and *the impossible*, etc.

27

Finally, we will present a certain number of theoretical ideas and theories with the intention of interpreting the everyday within the context of society as a whole: the theory of the semantic field and of the social text; the theory of (cumulative and non-cumulative) processes; the theory of moments; the theory of the world of objects and of the logistics of things; the theory of doubles, of reverse images and of breaks, etc. We have already presented or outlined several of these theories in previous publications. Finally, we will need to return to the theory of alienation and the theory of praxis in order to clarify them dialectically.

28

In no respects is this lengthy conceptual development an end in itself, and nor is the knowledge it may produce. Concepts and knowledge are not ends, but means. Means for what?

To reply, and to bring this methodological summing up to an end, we would like to reiterate our principles as strongly as possible. *There can be no knowledge of society (as a whole) without critical knowledge of everyday life in its position – in its organization and its privation, in the organization of its privation – at the heart of this society and its history. There can be no knowledge of the everyday without critical knowledge of society (as a whole). Inseparable from practice or praxis, knowledge encompasses an agenda for transformation. To know the everyday is to want to transform it. Thought can only grasp it and define it by applying itself to a project or programme of radical transformation. To study everyday life and to use that study as the guideline for gaining knowledge of modernity is to search for whatever has the potential to be metamorphosed and to follow the decisive stages or moments of this potential metamorphosis through: it is to understand the real by seeing it in terms of what is possible, as an implication of what is possible. For 'man will be an everyday being or he will not be at all'.*

This lengthy conceptual development will allow us to tackle a determined and precise problematic: the theory of needs; the links between everyday life, the modern city and housing developments; the place and the future of art in the so-called modern world, etc. Then we will be able to look at some of the questions which have been treated in a methodologically flimsy way by certain recent authors. Thus in *The Affluent Society*[36] Galbraith points out the drawbacks of the 'consumer society' in America, where the most important social needs are left to badly managed public services; and then, starting from the opposite political postulate, we have Moravia, whose *A Month in the USSR* shows that whereas the public domain in the USSR is generally remarkably well managed, most private needs are overlooked or scorned. How can we explain this symmetrical breakdown in the two conflicting modes of production in the world today? And what does it mean?

One day we might even try to deal with questions such as: 'In conditions which in other respects are well defined, what is the social cost of an ordinary individual life? And in equally well-defined conditions, what would be the social cost of a fulfilled individual life, if such fulfilment had become the norm?'[37]

2

The Formal Implements

1 Axioms and axiomatization

We will not make a systematic attempt to construct a table of axioms, in other words a group of propositions which have formal properties: consistency (rigorous coherence without contradiction); independence (relatively methodical) of the statements proposed; sufficiency (completeness of the system); saturation; categoricity.

In our opinion it is possible to formulate axioms in the social sciences and especially in sociology, but impossible to build any particular science using deductive theories (in other words, to establish a closed system by 'saturating' that set of axioms). It goes without saying that it is imperative to make ample room for forms and formal systems, both as regards the methodology of the sciences and as regards the object of study itself. In social reality, forms have their own existence and effectiveness. This does not make systematizing and formalizing them an any the less erroneous and impossible enterprise. Research, conceptual development and theories are a matter for dialectical method, not deductive logic. For example, *counting*, which is used in mathematics with the utmost rigour, can be found in every discipline; however, rather than demonstrating the inexhaustible character of a continuum, the act of counting, of classifying and of exhausting a set of distinct units (an act which gives rise to operations and operators) does not constitute absolute intelligibility. Only mathematicians have been able to imagine that it does. The human mind and knowledge begin with small whole numbers; nevertheless we very soon imagine the infinitely large and the infinitely small, the continuous, the inexhaustible. For century after century the mathematician has made every effort to extend counting into large numbers (something done by machines nowadays); today his concern is continuousness, inexhaustible units, and order for its own sake within these units. The social sciences and the study of human data use counting, but already they are subordinating it to a more complex set of implements. All formal implements are subject to the conditions under which they are applied; all formal systems have their limits.

In the course of this study we have already come across some axioms – but without recognizing them as such. One in particular scarcely needs formulating: 'There can be no knowledge of society without critique of that society, of its representations (ideologies) and its accepted concepts.' Let us proceed by drawing up a provisional, non-restrictive list of the axioms it is appropriate to formulate as such.

Axiom of language: The sociologist speaks the same language as the men (individuals; members of a group) he is seeking to reach and whose way of life he wishes to understand.

Comments. This axiom lends itself to a trivial interpretation. It has been pointed out a thousand times that it is difficult to gain access to a group which speaks a different language than the scientist studying it. It is not only dialects, vocabularies, jargon and languages specific to determined groups (such as small farmers from a specific region of France, or workers in a specific trade and from a specific city) which set traps for the investigator.

Let us get beyond these banalities. The very way this axiom is formulated underlines a danger and a risk which we must confront empirically: its value as a regulator derives from its falseness on the immediately empirical level. No matter how simple the facts of the everyday may be, the investigator and the group he is investigating will *never* use exactly the same words in exactly the same way. Every dialogue is made up of two unequal participants: one wants to know, and speaks the language of someone who wants to know; the other remains hidden, even when he is perfectly willing to answer the questions. When the 'subject' of an inquiry, the interviewee, coincides with the 'object' of study and opens himself up unreservedly, we have someone abnormal on our hands, an exhibitionist, and there is all the more reason to mistrust what he tells us.

In sociology, most interviews (and the in-depth, undirected interview in particular) begin with a period of awkwardness, as investigators well know. Beginners would like to avoid or shorten this period; they do not realize how fruitful it is. That such awkwardness cannot be avoided, that uneasiness arises almost of necessity when a living contact is established, is something which techniques of group dynamics and psychotherapeutic interviews would confirm, were confirmation needed. In all cases, the dramatic content of the lived is concealed beneath evasive behaviour patterns. The interview starts with a sort of tacit challenge to the interviewee by the interviewer (to reach him, to grasp him, to know him) and to the interviewer by the interviewee (to put him off track, to elude him). The higher the stakes the greater the challenge and the deeper the uneasiness. While this uneasiness lasts, the investigator, unable to fight back a kind of mental vertigo, tries to clarify his representations and to refine his language. During this same period, the person being interviewed slowly agrees to receive or to release a portion of the 'real': an aspect of the hidden drama, the situation of his everyday reality. Any common language becomes apparent at the end of these dialogues, once the 'dialogue of the deaf' has been avoided. It is at the end, and not at the beginning, that the common language is to be found.

Sadly, the police interrogation, the psychological investigation, the dialogue between someone who wants to know and someone who resists being known, and the psychoanalytic interview, all have more than one point in common. The big difference is in the way the initial awkwardness is dealt with and modified, and in the degree of caution – which is simply a form of respect – with which it is made use of. Some interviewers try to influence their 'subject', who is also an 'object'. Others, more attentive and more circumspect, seek to know their subject while modifying him as little as possible. Such investigators will rank patience among the virtues which are a precondition of knowledge.

Subsidiary axiom: Signs and significations are not things. Expressions, symptoms and manifestations are not beings.

To achieve a common language in dialogue, the investigator (who, no matter how cautious and respectful, will always be an inquisitor) must avoid imposing his own language on this 'subject' who is also the 'object' of knowledge and the 'theme' of the investigation. When the 'subject' bends over backwards to accept the sociologist's terminology, his statements become unreliable. Evasion and defiance are more revealing and more valuable than the accommodating attitude beginners find so beguiling.

But there is a lesson to be learned from experiencing this awkwardness. We could call it: 'the sociologist's catharsis', or a major aspect of 'sociological culture'. A profound culture and a difficult 'catharsis' are essential for grasping the sheaf of givens which, though objective, in no way share the objectivity of things, and which represent nothing more than an approach by 'being' caught up in the drama of its everyday life. The significations of these givens are formulated in the very *act* of *dialogue*. What words other than action and dialogue could define this subtle, delicate and finely honed mixture of sympathetic friendliness and harshness, perhaps even cruelty, which alone is capable of bringing what is concealed by evasiveness and yet revealed by it out into the open? When crudely conducted, a sociological interview modifies the semeiology[1] it is trying to grasp and interpret, as radically as any police interrogation would. Knowledge and understanding between human beings, individuals and groups can only be reciprocal, in and via an exchange. The relation between the 'subject' and the 'object', between the investigator and the investigation as a common language is sought (i.e., a semeiology which will reveal the secret drama of the group and of the everyday individual in the everyday life of the group), is one which is learned and cultivated. The wish to learn and to understand should reveal 'being' rather than fixing it in its inevitable evasiveness, and that is the aim of this culture. The more finely honed it is, the less it will suppress, and the more it will be capable of overcoming the distances and obstacles set up by defiance and misunderstandings. It alone allows us to be genuinely concerned with human beings, in a way which justifies the wish for knowledge.

A culture such as this is conditional on certain qualities and talents, such as tact and speed. It requires training. And even more: that the investigator involve and compromise himself within the dialogue. Only via a return to his own everyday reality will he reach the everyday reality of the people he is interviewing. It is a detour he must take, and a disturbing one. He must purge himself not only of his ideological and theoretical prejudices, and of his limited vocabulary, but also of his value judgements, which perhaps constitute the biggest barrier of all.[2]

Inspired by qualitative or ordinal mathematics (groups theory, information theory) certain theoreticians in the social sciences would surely formulate another axiom: *All research consists of questions which can be answered by yes or by no.* For them, a question for which there is not a yes-or-no answer is simply badly expressed; it is a question which cannot be answered.

While taking care to make room for these theories, and for information theory in particular, we would challenge this axiom (which precisely would lead towards an integral axiomatization and to a purely logical cohesion of science). To exhaust reality, the number of questions which must be answered by yes or by no would be infinite. What is more, there are questions which demand replies other than 'yes' or 'no' and yet which bring knowledge. And perhaps this is the moment to stress the difference between *information* and *knowledge*. Those questions to which the interviewee replies and can only reply by yes or no provide information. The questions to which he cannot reply by yes or no bring knowledge. 'Are you happy?' After a moment's thought, nobody could answer with an absolute yes or no. Everyone will reply: 'Yes and no. In this respect, yes, in that respect, no. And in any case, what do you mean by happiness?' The person who does answer yes or no is informing us of a fact, that he is going through a phase of satisfaction or dissatisfaction, that he is being optimistic, that he is simplifying his opinion in order to communicate it, etc.

There is nothing worse than a questionnaire which is so well constructed that it believes it can exhaust its 'object'. It imposes clarity and the vocabulary of science upon the people it is seeking to reveal. Much more valuable in a dialogue are chance and game-playing, when the participants talk about this and that. In this case, meaning may spring from a chance encounter, similar to a reward or, to use the register of psychiatry, a 'gratification', although knowledge cannot consist of such fortuitous 'gratifications' alone.

A vocabulary which is clumsily and disrespectfully imposed leads us easily to a certain scepticism. Since the chosen terminology is unusable, would it not suffice to talk to people in any way we like, and to make contact through any subject at all, by skilfully using their own language? This is not valid either. Although game-playing may be worth more than inflexibility, and chance just as valuable as excessive rigour, cunning linguistic manoeuvres are just as ineffective as the use of crude and destructive terminological implements. The goal of research, which challenges the 'sociologist' per se, is to enable a dialogue to produce knowledge by means of mutual understanding.

Obliged to take the language of the individuals and the groups he seeks to understand into account, should the 'sociologist' eschew the language of his own group and of science? No. The language of science must be as precise as possible, and act as the common denominator between the symbolisms and modes of expression which research will discover across a range of different groups. What is more, there can be no science without terminology.

But where does terminology end? Where does jargon begin? Must the sociologist force himself to use nothing but familiar words, giving them a conceptualized meaning which differs slightly from their usual meaning? Would this be a way of establishing a common ground between the relatively incoherent or systematized semeiologies he is seeking to reveal and interpret?

The physicist and the mathematician do not have this problem. As specialists, they divorce themselves from everyday men. They are no longer concerned with the link between the terms and signs they employ and day-to-day vocabulary, or between their concepts and common sense (their everyday reality). The correspondence is apparent throughout the history of knowledge and science for whoever wishes to find it – the philosopher, for example. For the sciences of mankind, it is quite a different story. It must be possible to transfer from the day-to-day language of social praxis to scientific terminology at any time. If not, the terminology will lose contact with the first and final object of knowledge – praxis – and science will no longer come together with praxis to change itself into action. Jargon begins with the hiatus between practical language and scientific language. From that point on, well-integrated sets of facts and meanings may be constructed, but they will have one drawback: arbitrariness, linkage by jargon terms. Hence *the axiom of discourse* which we will formulate for use as follows: *In his memory and in his thinking, the sociologist of everyday life must maintain the linkage between day-to-day language and his own terminology, and the transition from one to the other. At every moment he must be able to translate the one into the other and to carry out all the necessary intermediary operations.*

In this way the sociology of the everyday is reinvesting specific knowledge with a philosophical requirement philosophers have too often neglected. Its science never becomes separated from *poetics*, in the sense given to the term by Diderot in the *Encyclopédie*: a set of rules which one applies to create a work in a given genre. *Poetics* here is the transformation of everyday life in and by praxis. It extends philosophy, it satisfies the requirements of philosophy, and it supersedes philosophy . . .

Axiom of strategies: Whether they are aware of it or not, social groups and individuals within groups have tactics and strategies (i.e., series of connected long-term or short-term decisions). Conversely and reciprocally, a set of individuals without a tactic and a strategy cannot be a social group.

Comments. We are giving a definition axiomatically. Tactics and strategies correspond to what in often vague and philosophical language are called projects, decisions, plans for action and for the future, or agendas.

In its particular manner, the immobility of groups (always more apparent than real, like the principle of rest and inertia in nature) provides a tactic and a strategy for survival. Survival in itself is a form of action.

Tactics and strategies do not exhaust the reality of social groups within themselves and in their conflictual relations with other groups. To formulate the theory in a way which would eliminate other aspects of reality (alienation, for example, or symbolisms) would be unjustifiable. Nevertheless, this axiom is extremely important. It eliminates the illusion of inertia and rest, and this is a point we would like to emphasize. The existence of a social group (with the individuals it encompasses) is permanently called into question, both in the short term and in the long term. It either knows this, is reluctant to know it, or does not know it. If it does not know it, the group (and the individuals) will sink into mindless stagnation. To put it another way, individuals can be differentiated by their degree of participation in the consciousness and action of the group; leaders are people who think up the tactic and, most importantly, the strategy, and who devote themselves to putting it into action. It is clear that everyday life within the group depends upon these constellations (the consciousness and participation of individuals, and the presence and activeness of leaders).

The axiom of strategies demonstrates a multidimensionality. The sociologist belongs to one group or to several, each with its own tactic and strategy. Science itself has its strategy, of which the scientist is more or less aware, and of which he is more or less the leader. In short, every group we may study will have its strategy and its tactic.

Once it comes under scrutiny, a group may seal itself hermetically in the face of any investigation, or it may welcome the sociologist with open arms. Consciously or unconsciously, both reactions form part of its strategy. If a stranger is given a warm-hearted reception, apparent or genuine, it is because he is expected to bring something with him, such as information or propaganda from outside the group. As for the sociologist, objectivity is frequently and superficially trivialized as being a form of passivity, and this he cannot accept. And yet, he does not want to be biased. Therefore he will have to confront these multiple dimensions: the tactic and strategy of the groups to which he is affiliated or from which he originated (class, nation, intelligentsia, etc.); the tactic and strategy for knowledge and for the insertion of his knowledge into praxis; the tactic and strategy of the group he is studying.

This confrontation will provide a limited, relative but heightened objectivity. During it the sociologist of the everyday will make a comparison between the revealing (signifying) elements of the various projects for action, including language, symbols, attitudes, opinions and behaviour patterns. During this comparison he will disengage himself from his own subjective elements, ridding himself of them by calling them into question. As far as possible, he will free himself from the social contexts upon which he depends. He will force himself to adopt the asceticism which is an integral part of scientific culture: to think on several planes and to organize and structure the transfer from one to the other in a coherent way.

Axiom of mediations: It will be to the advantage of the sociology of everyday life and of empirical research in general to avoid groups which are too small or too large. It is equally to the advantage of sociologists engaged in empirical research if they parenthesize concepts which are too narrow and too precise, in terms of how they can be understood and to the connotations they have.

Comments. This axiom stipulates a regulatory rule or hypothesis rather than a form or a formal definition. It has links with the previous axiom. The sociologist of the everyday will not lose sight of the fact that he is acting as a rational 'medium' or intermediary between groups in society as a whole. Despite the many mediations and communications which exist between them (including language), these groups are partially external and opaque to each other.

There are occasions when this rule needs to be flexible. For example, the study of interindividual relations within the restricted framework of family life, and the description of individual roles and their relation within this framework, would fall more within the purview of psychology or social psychology. However, (private) family life in an overall context – the bourgeoisie, farmers, the proletariat, French society, etc. – is within the purview of the sociology of everyday life as we have defined it. This does not mean to say that it does not exist within even larger groups, where standards of living and lifestyles, etc., can be determined by the relations within them.

If we consider a very large group, for example the working class in general, i.e., on a world scale, it is a reality which goes far beyond our investigative possibilities. It is a matter for sociology in general: beginning with the concept, it seeks to define the link between this concept as accepted and current praxis, and thus to grasp the current situation of the working class within a specific social entity. However, it will be very difficult to study so vast a reality empirically – in its everyday reality. As an overall entity, society itself is very difficult to grasp.

It is in our (scientific) interest to move among intermediate realities, employing modest concepts which are not too wide and not too narrow. It is in our interest to begin our investigation with those realities which act as mediations and *means*, and which consequently are neither too secret nor too publicly manifest: tactics and strategies in so far as they become manifest in action; symbols and signs in so far as they are practically effective; communication groups, villages, neighbourhoods, towns, businesses, trade unions, etc. The macrosociological and the microsociological, the whole and the restricted, none must escape scrutiny. However, the restricted, the local and the 'micro' have limits and an opaqueness which resist investigation. In the pursuit of the whole and the total, sooner or later thought will be brought to a halt by the political decision which determines them, by the options which have been taken or are in the process of being taken, and by the ethic or the aesthetic which is in the process of making (or breaking) itself – invention, creative activity, *poiesis*. Now knowledge can offer them its contribution and its arguments. It cannot presume to command them.

As a working hypothesis, we will elaborate certain propositions which are linked to the previous axiom: *The sociological unity of a group and the social consciousness which links the consciousnesses of its constituent individuals to it are never more than intermediary states, mediations or means to an end. Tactic and strategy determine this and are determined by it. In phases of extreme tension, turmoil and intense social activity, the existence of a group becomes historical. Its structures burst asunder. Its everyday life is suspended, shattered or changed. It coincides with the historical. In the phases of complete relaxation and stagnation, interindividual and psychic relations predominate; the group tends to fall apart and everyday life tends to show only its most banal and trivial side. Thus it is indeed the medium, intermediary, mediating phases which we are considering here as providing privileged testimony.*

Thus, setting out from the medium zones, our study would go in one direction towards the broader zones, and in another towards the narrower ones, not in order to separate them from each other, but to reach them.

Our study holds no presuppositions about the complexity and the contradictions on these (micro and macro) scales, and this is what distinguishes the previous rules and axioms from Cartesian thought, which uses the simple to assemble the complex.

These givens underline the prudent, limitative and relative character of a research programme which nevertheless opens a vast field of experiences and knowledge. Every statement acts equally as a safety barrier and as a positive heuristic rule.

2 The role of hypothesis

The role of hypothesis in the sciences in general has been examined many times. We feel it could be useful to return to it in order to clarify its role in the social sciences and in our own research.

Let us remind ourselves that in all dogmatisms the process of knowledge is bound up with systematized philosophical arrangements, thus devaluing the role of hypothesis and the invention of hypotheses.

Dogmatism quite correctly gives prominence to the presuppositions inherent in the way facts are perceived, as well as in scientific observation, in conceptual links between phenomena and in theoretical developments, but then it extrapolates. It tries to reduce these implications to general, and thus philosophical, *postulates*; this would allow it to police the use of hypotheses. However it is clear that hypotheses which are subordinated to a systematized philosophy (to an idealist or materialist ontology) lose the characteristics of hypothesis, and are imposed a priori as absolute truths. This is the way the materialists (contradicting dialectic) and the idealists (totally in agreement with themselves, which guarantees them the benefit of coherence) proceeded. When knowledge is regulated in this way, the first thing to be compromised is the invention of hypotheses. This leads to sterility.

On the other hand, a certain subjectivism (equally philosophical in inspiration), a certain relativism and a certain positivism have stressed the hypothetical character of every science. The use of hypothesis would make knowledge conjectural. In its way, this tendency extrapolates as well. The invention of hypotheses and the very requirement for hypotheses may originate either in the elusive complexity of the real, or in an a priori inherent to the human mind, such as determined categories or a general (logical and formal) principle of identity.

Going farther than previous methodological work,[3] and with the desire to make room for imagination in the knowledge of the human 'real', we will maintain here that the role of hypothesis is connected to the *complexity* of the phenomena under scrutiny and also to their *random* character (both aspects being interdependent).

We are not using the term *random* in a pejorative way to mean whatever knowledge is unable to grasp, in other words pure chance, a radical contingency or an indeterminism. The thesis of an absolute indeterminism both in nature and in historical and social reality, as opposed to the thesis of an absolute determinism, is certainly untenable. Here as elsewhere we are trying to clarify a way of thinking dialectically. There are determined biological, historical, economic, sociological *conditions* (which are taken over and modified by their own creative praxis), which constitute the 'real' in its accepted sense. There are *processes*, which contain the evolution and forward movements of the real. These conditions and processes point towards *possibilities*.

It is itself a necessary requirement that a choice, an option or a decision (a tactical and strategic commitment) be made regarding these possibilities. Free actions – collective or individual, short term or long term – do not escape determinism; they are based upon it; they have their inner determinisms; they unfold; they are born premature or they come to full term; they are enacted with varying degrees of awareness and effectiveness, sometimes blind, sometimes calculated; they modify their determined conditions and create new ones. They modify and reorientate processes but they do not eliminate them.

We rule out the idea of absolute necessity along with the idea of absolute chance and the purely fortuitous. Absolute necessity, i.e., determinism, belongs to ideology, not to knowledge. It excludes dialectical movement, relative chance and relative necessity, the relatively predictable and the relatively unpredictable. From this viewpoint, there is a certain unpredictability (and thus the advent of something genuinely new) which does not come simply from not knowing the causes and limits of knowledge. It also comes from chance per se, and also from freedom. We cannot calculate a priori what the limits to predictability are, but knowledge can never predict everything, nor can practical action prefigure and control everything. By using formal theories (games and decision theory, information theory) we can even *predict the unpredictable per se*.

Thus this notion of randomness is based on a few recent acquisitions to the field of knowledge, and notably on *information* theory. If we are careful not to confuse 'information' with 'knowledge', this will facilitate the inclusion of information within knowledge. The concept of randomness in information theory profoundly modifies the concept of statistical probability which derives from the natural sciences (statistical and quantic theories). It implies an exploration of the *field of possibilities* (whereas statistical probability infers predictions based on the past). Above all – and this is its principal interest in so far as this study is concerned – it implies the idea of a *widening of the field of possibilities*. To our mind this widening is essential if we are to understand the life of groups and individuals in 'modern' society. In a sense it characterizes it. It is what makes it imperative to have increasingly more finely honed and conscious *tactics* and *strategies*. It is what makes it essential to *opt* more and more frequently.

The widening of possibilities is accompanied by contradictory phenomena: pressures and constraints, models and norms, checks, gaps and imbalances. Moral or ideological pressures and constraints maintain a sort of static equilibrium within individual or collective consciousnesses which run the danger of being swamped by possibilities. Thus *realization* can lag behind *possibilities* to a vast extent. In the random field of what is possible, realization – subjected to objective and restrictive rules – is itself random. The real, i.e., *realization*, can only be understood through the possible and the random.

Let us go beyond formal methodology and illustrate this statement by a few examples, i.e., a few *hypotheses*.

a) An individual can imagine himself to be a nebula (a cloud) of virtualities (*possibilities*). This representation is not a carbon copy of quantic theories of matter, which speak of a cloud of *probabilities*. The process of his practical life consists of a sort of condensation of possibilities. From being a nebula or cloud of virtualities, he becomes a constellation of actions and powers (capacities). He realizes himself, more or less completely. Complete realization, the exhausting of possibilities, is immobility and death.

The same is true of groups. They too make their way through randomness: they take chances, they wager on their future, or they stagnate. They come into being, they manage to survive, or they die.

b) The entry of *women* into industrial production has not resulted in a massive increase in the number of women in the active (productive) population. It has allowed for a redistribution of female jobs: fewer women employed in domestic services and more employed in commercial services and office jobs, etc. Above all it gives women – to a certain extent, and according to social class and country of residence – the chance to *choose*. They can educate themselves, take up a profession, give it up as soon as they marry or have a baby, or go on working. Possibilities require options – not irrational options, but ones which are motivated and thought through. Thus the determined economic and social process (the entry of women into industrial production and more generally into active life) has not revolutionized the female condition, as it was expected to do. It has increased the number of possibilities and choices, and the degree to which women can be free, both as individuals and as a social group. This produces obvious paradoxes. In the working class, many women choose, more or less freely, not to work in factories or workshops. In the comfortably off classes, many women choose to work in offices and to take up professions.

Thus the ideas of determinism or of necessary process, and of possibilities and options, are not ruled out either for groups or for individuals. The same applies for the idea of chance and of regularity (or determined tendency). If a group is to establish what its relations are to be, hypotheses are inevitable. The way options are shared out within a group is not completely predictable. Any study of the situation of women today will contain hypotheses about the grouping under consideration, the contingencies and possibilities of choice, and the variables within projects of choice which help to explain frequencies.

This brings us to the idea of *social options*. Individuals are not alone in making choices. Very large or restricted groups alike point themselves consciously or unconsciously in an irreversible direction, and select a particular solution for their problems, either collectively or in the person of their leader. Any given solution was not imposed by an absolute necessity. Other routes were possible. Sometimes we (individuals and groups, the masses and their leaders) realize this too late. In any event, a bifurcation has been reached, possibilities have been separated, and one possibility has been adopted to the exclusion of the others. Thus in the so-called 'West' we have opted for a durable consumer item: the car. We have given it an important place in our everyday lives. Though it was taken in the past, today this option controls the development of industry, causes traffic problems, and makes it necessary for towns to be restructured, etc. The example of countries of the East makes it clear that this was a social option and a collective choice (not a necessity). This option is an integral part of a comprehensive society: economy, culture, lifestyle. It helps to compose and to typify it. Just like important political decisions, collective options introduce *discontinuity* into the historical and the social.

c) When dealing with a sociological problem, it is sometimes possible to use the following formula: 'let us suppose the problem has been resolved, and let the person answering be x . . .' Given a virtual population or the virtual rise in an existing population, we may find ourselves faced with a problem such as the following: 'If x is the possible structure of the town which contains this population, what properties should we attribute to this possible structure to enable the population to draw predictable advantages from it?' Then, we will try to find a representation for x, i.e., to *imagine* it in function of the desired result. Generally we will find variants x, x, x, each one of which we must examine and criticize. Thus we will use the method of imaginary variants. It is obvious that these variants can be relatively daring, according to the quality of the imagination constructing them. The examination of solutions and variants may often force us to reconsider the problem, its terms, and the notions which allowed it to be formulated.

This is how the sociology of everyday life can consider the problems of *urban development*. It can contribute to the search for optimum formulae. The problem is a practical one. We have a great many experiences at our disposal to help us resolve it: the experience of old towns (spontaneous, historical), which were relatively successful, and of new towns, which have been more or less a failure. We are working on a *virtual object*, which must be brought into being. How can we achieve this without the use of images? If we are to move from received experiences to the construction of the virtual object, there are a certain number of steps we must take: the formulation of a problematic, the elaboration of *hypotheses* and propositions about what is possible, the invention of images, etc.

Therefore we must bring hypothesis into general use. No hypothesis must be excluded a priori, no matter how arbitrary, risky, extreme or even dangerous it may be. By introducing both chance and imagination into knowledge of the social real, we are making room for chance in the way we invent hypotheses, and for a kind of free play in the process of gaining knowledge.

The sociologist's investigative abilities are linked to his capacity to invent hypotheses. Consciously or not, he explores what is possible by using images just as much as concepts. Therefore, in the specific culture which follows the 'catharsis' we spoke of earlier, there is a form of imagination which has its part to play. The role played by imagination and hypothesis will have consequences in terms of styles of thinking, and the sciences of human and social reality will use imagination more or less consciously and deliberately to find an original style.

If hypotheses which share the random character of the phenomena under scrutiny are used extensively, this is also due to the *problematic* character of these phenomena. This term no more means 'irrational', 'uncertain' or 'impossible to formulate' than the term 'random' means 'indeterminable'. On the contrary! Human groups have problems, real problems which make up part of their total reality. Possibilities are answers and solutions – more or less good, near or remote – to these problems. To get close to a group, or to the individuals within a group, and to understand it, is to determine what that group's problematic is, at a given moment and in a given situation or set of circumstances.

The 'problematic' cannot be confused with the 'absurd'. In real life, human problems arise with contradictions which demand and imply solutions, opening up possibilities. The problems men set themselves are not insoluble (if it were true that humanity only set itself insoluble problems, and that its problematic is indefinite and undetermined, all present and future humanism would collapse, and nihilism would take over in its stead), but nor do they have ready-made solutions. Therefore it is the problematic side of a human group which enables us to grasp its reality, its possibilities and the (tactical and strategic) way it can achieve them. In this way we avoid yet again the false dilemma of either pure empiricism and the collection of unconnected facts or philosophy, dogmatism and presuppositions. Finally, we are connecting the social sciences as a whole to a general but determined problematic of man; the problematic of everyday life and of its radical transformation. By formulating specific problems (the problems of groups) and trying to see how they connect with the general problematic, we will stimulate projects, hypotheses and possible solutions.

In its turn, the confrontation between these possible relations stimulates the invention of hypotheses about phenomena. So what we are doing here is looking not for a method for formulating 'sociological problems', but rather for a method for connecting each given and each partial reality to the more general problematic we are concerned with. In our opinion, the common expression 'sociological problem' contains an illusion. In one sense, all problems are sociological, since every sociological reality can only be grasped in relation to its problems. On the other hand, no problems are sociological, since problems can only be formulated in relation to a general problematic of historical and social man which goes beyond sociology as a specific and particular science.

Propositions concerning *what is possible* must be scrutinized, confronted and argued. When projects are confronted with 'real life' (with practice) it is imperative that the interested parties participate. It is impossible to impose a solution. Whoever decides for one particular solution (and consequently integrates it in his strategy) is obliged to examine the counterproposals. He must bear in mind that his solution may fail.

Therefore the hypothetical character of this process, and the way its method is linked to a determined general problematic, has profound connections with the *democratic* character of social life and the free scientific study of it.

So to the generally accepted types of hypotheses we will add a new one: the *strategic hypothesis*. Taking the most distant possibilities as its starting point, it returns to the present in an attempt to extend the force lines and the tendencies of the real towards this extreme point of what is possible. Its aim is to be more precise than the other hypotheses in the way it mediates between facts and concepts, and between givens and solutions to problems. It connects all the fragmented empirical facts with the concepts it is elaborating and constantly calling into question. It has the classic qualities and properties of hypothesis: it keeps in contact with the facts; it discovers new facts; it organizes the facts without forcibly systematizing them; it is verifiable. It is verified within praxis.

The hypothetical character of the procedure and of its object will become even more apparent when we examine the following extreme case: the creation of the object (the construction of a new town or the development of a new kind of town planning informed by the ideas provided by the sociology of everyday life). We are no longer talking about the usual kind of case, i.e., where the observer modifies what he is observing and is himself part of what can be observed. The extreme situation we are examining seems both more dramatic (because it involves more responsibility) and more capable of founding a broad practical rationality. This practical rationality would not exclude the so-called irrationality of images, emotions and feelings by ignoring or harrying them.

As we have said, the sociologist of everyday life has his strategy. Moreover, what he discovers and makes public can modify certain other strategies, namely those of the groups affected by the problems posed. This gives knowledge an entry into creative praxis. By emphasizing the role of hypothesis, randomness and newness, and by making the procedures and the object of knowledge more hypothetical, rather than invalidating this knowledge, we are confirming its rational and scientific character.

The importance attributed to hypothesis does not authorize us to fetishize it in favour of an 'approach' theory by which approaching facts and problems would be more interesting and far reaching than actually grasping them, which would immediately be suspect. Such a confession of powerlessness would be incompatible with the will to enrich research and to open it up to new perspectives.

The importance of hypothesis does not exempt us from the need to look for *proof* and to scrutinize it. A mass of facts can only prove anything in cases where reality is static, in a process of becoming which does not experience any serious accidents. In such cases, it is the logical coherence of the hypothesis and the way it harmonizes with a set of phenomena which provide the proof.

Much more interesting is the case of a dynamic reality, racked by problems and possibilities, where the convergence of several privileged testimonies proves more than any amount of empirical observations. The real proof is to be found on the level of the *practical* verification of a hypothesis. We are therefore talking about two distinct types of proof, one formal – coherence – and the other experimental – realization within praxis.

3 Transduction and transducers

The classic operations of reasoning can no longer suffice. Induction turned fact into law, the particular into the general, and the contingent into the necessary. To draw its conclusions, deduction went from the general to the singular, from affirmation to implication, and from the necessary to the necessary. To these rigorous operations we would add the notion of *transduction*, which builds a virtual object using information, and which uses givens to arrive at a solution. We can also say that transduction goes from the (given) real to the possible.

The theoreticians of information talk about 'psychological transducers' in order to designate the psychic modalities of this operation, revealed by their theory. In a similar way, we will introduce the idea of *sociological transducers* to designate the operation carried out unceasingly by social groups (and the individuals within those groups). They go from the present to the virtual and from the given to the possible in a never-ending prospective operation which the usual psychological ideas of achievement, prediction and uncertainty cannot exhaust.

Theoretical transductions and effective (practical) transducers derive from the same theory.[4]

4 The idea of level

The idea of *level* is rapidly becoming widespread. As well as being adopted by scientific terminology (the terminology of the social sciences and even of the natural sciences), it is also entering into day-to-day vocabulary. This empirical usage in no way clarifies its scientific usage. On the contrary. Essentially it derives from the hierarchic structuring of modern bureaucracy, which expresses itself in the following way: 'At managerial level, prefectorial level, ministerial level, cantonal level, departmental level, regional level, etc.' Levels of authority are also degrees in the hierarchy. In the army, they tend to use the term 'echelon', which is similar. Therefore there is a meaning behind the generalized usage of the word: the astonishing role played by hierarchy and bureaucracy in the structuring of society. Are its scientific meaning and this popular meaning the same? If they are, the word is clear but worrying. If we use it carelessly we will risk validating a certain practice and ideological representation of the social. If they are not, then it will require elucidation.

In truth, the scientific meaning of the word is rather obscure, for sometimes it is used subjectively (on the level of good sense, on the scientific level), sometimes very objectively (at subatomic level, at molecular level, at the level of gravitational field) and sometimes in a mixed way (at infraconscious level, at linguistic level, at supralinguistic level). I have collected these terms from a variety of scientific journals. If we read the recent *Entretiens* between Lévi-Strauss and Charbonnier, we will come across even more obscure turns of phrase, such as 'level of participation' and 'level of authenticity'.[5]

Earlier we located everyday life rather summarily as a *level* within praxis and society as a whole, and we added several observations. Scientifically speaking, the concept of *level* is no longer distinguishable from several other concepts, i.e., *stages* and *degrees* or *planes*, such as *sets, frames of reference, perspectives* or *aspects*. And yet these concepts are not identical. They all contribute towards expressing a complexity which is differentiated and yet structured within a whole (a totality). A *level* designates an aspect of reality, but it is not just the equivalent of a camera shot of that reality. It allows for it to be seen from a certain point of view or perspective; it guarantees it an objective content. In a reality where successive implications can be seen, it represents a degree or a stage, but with more consistency and 'reality' than symbols or models, for example.

Taken in its widest sense, the idea of *level* encompasses the idea of *differences between levels*. We could even say that the actual or possible difference between levels is the criterion by which levels are determined. Wherever there is a level there are several levels, and consequently gaps, (relatively) sudden transitions, and imbalances or potential imbalances between those levels. Therefore this idea excludes the idea of the *continuous field*, although it is not incompatible with the ideas of general context, globality or sets. Levels cannot be completely dissociated one from the other. Analysis may determine levels, but it does not produce them; they remain as units within a larger whole.

The schematic of a scale or of a formal hierarchy of degrees is much too static. Although by definition they are distinct and are located at different stages, *levels* can interact and become telescoped, with differing results according to what the encounters and circumstances are. As one level mediates another, so they act one upon the other. At one particular moment of becoming, in one particular set of circumstances, one level can dominate and incorporate the others. The idea of a structural set of precise and separate levels is untenable. It would invalidate a concept which is indispensable: rigid concepts do not capture the real in some vast, flexible net, they let it escape. Thus the level of the everyday and the level of the historical can interact. Level must not be thought of as being incompatible with the process of becoming and with mobility. Realities rise to the surface, emerge, and take on substance momentarily at a certain level. At the same time, the concept implies an internal determination, a relatively stable situation overall. The fact that we can speak of a 'level' makes it clear that everything is not in everything; there are not only differences, but also distinctions.

The concept of level makes the concept of *implication* sharper and more concrete. Each level is the result of an analysis which brings out the content of the other levels, and makes it more explicit. To use a turn of phrase we employed earlier, each one of them is therefore both *a residual deposit* and *a product*. But these propositions are not sufficient. Each level contains others, in a state of possibility. It analyses itself and makes itself more explicit. Thus every level is a 'level of levels', although the analyst does not have the right to suppose that they are limited or unlimited in number, or whether they are finite or non-finite. Each level implies others. When the analyst has singled out two distinct levels, he may be able to find others in between them. By analysis and experiment he should be able to discover *thresholds* leading from one to another; the threshold confirms the level. Finally, multiple 'realities' coexist on each individual level, implying and (mutually) implied, enveloping and enveloped, encompassing and encompassed, unmediated and mediated (unmediated in themselves, mediated in relation to other vaster or more restricted levels). Thus, in a succession of dichotomies, the logic of genera and species begins to take shape and ramify, through its contact with the 'concrete' it helps to define.

This representation may be approximative, but it has the merit of uniting mobility and structure. As it becomes more explicit it stands increasingly apart from frameworks of social origin, such as military and bureaucratic hierarchies. It can stretch out towards the universe, which henceforth we will not imagine as an architecturally rigid edifice, or as a flowing river, but as a colossal interaction of *levels*, from the subatomic to the galactic, from microcellular organisms to living species, from small social groups to the large sociocultural formations we call 'civilizations'.

To make the representation more precise, we can turn to *physics*.

Spectrum analysis of light and harmonic analysis of sound make distinctions and discontinuities apparent within what are apparently continuous phenomena. In a spectrum, there are both stationary (or relatively stable) and mobile transients, periodic global formants and partials. Spectrum analysis, and even more so harmonic analysis, can offer us a guideline for the analysis of overall or periodic social phenomena which are apparently continuous and homogeneous.

There are certain branches of modern mathematics which may help us to get a tighter grasp on this representation. Let us write a random series of numerals:

$$8 \quad 1 \quad 9 \quad 2 \quad 5 \quad 8$$

Between these numerals we can write more at random, and so on, and similarly we can add more in vertical columns, above or below the original numerals:

$$8 \quad 87493 \quad 162199 \quad 0753$$
$$7 \quad 2193 \quad 829772$$

The sequences of numerals do not constitute a number and yet each one of them is a set. It has a structure, but this structure is not rigid as in numbers and numerical sets. It can be called 'semirigorous'. The set forms a grid (or trellis) to which we may add as many columns or lines as we wish. Thus the set is neither finite nor non-finite (or rather, like the sequence of numerals and numbers, it is non-finite virtually, but always finite). This set is never completed, and we can always add new elements to it in between any of its elements.

Instead of vertical and horizontal rows of numerals, let us put straight lines (see next page). This makes the trellis more concrete, more determined and mobile.

Although we can start from any line or column to begin the trellis, its structure is not arbitrary; we can insert any horizontal or vertical straight line we have previously drawn. The beginning is arbitrary, and so is the end (when analysis stops). Therefore we can start the analysis of levels where we wish and where we can, and still come up with something determined. The construction of the trellis determines the squares or rectangles implied within one another, and which are

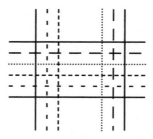

homologous or identical and spatially distinct. Thus the trellis (or lattice) represents *implications* of identical levels in distinct times and places. We will call these successive implications in the two possible directions – the broadest (macro) and the narrowest (micro) – *levels* with arbitrary starting points.

The broadest implication we can attain will always come within the scope of an even broader figure, and vice versa. The trellis makes us aware of the existence of *thresholds* and also of their mobility. It also makes us aware of the existence of differences between levels and their variability. There is nothing absolute about the split between them, and yet their relative variability is incontestable. Between any two implications there will always be an *interval* which is impossible to bridge.

To grasp the idea and how it may be used, we would do best to confront it with something concrete. So here are some examples of grids which present levels in their relative situations and their active reciprocities.

These examples by no means exhaust the fruitfulness of the idea and they only partially make what it means more explicit. In particular, they fail to make the distinction between *levels of reality*, *levels of abstraction* and *levels of meaning* completely clear. Nevertheless we can see a rule emerging: 'If the highest level of abstraction does not correspond to the deepest level of reality, the object of knowledge will become confused.'

The first table is a condensed version of material borrowed from various chapters of Robert Francès's book *Perception de la musique*. The other 'grids' deal with our own subject: everyday life and the analysis of it.

The schematic of levels has the disadvantages of all schematizations. The mobile network (trellis or 'lattice') of squares is by no means absolutely or definitely superior to any other representation. The problem of what is distinct (the problem of units, whether they are ultimate or signifying, or not, etc.) will crop up yet again.

In spite of its deficiencies, the schematic of levels has incontrovertible advantages. It demonstrates how a level which has been *chosen* as the starting point for analysing a set of phenomena defines a frame of reference. The level at which we begin restricts the horizon of our analysis. It will require other concepts on a corresponding level, it will stipulate the use of procedures permitting us to pass from one level to a neighbouring one, and it will forbid us to skip over levels, etc. Thus the schematic takes subjective or arbitrary elements of the analysis into account, while not insisting that the starting point must determine the object (which would lead to a hypersubjectivism, or to a pure probabilism, which would dissolve the object per se).

Levels of musical perception

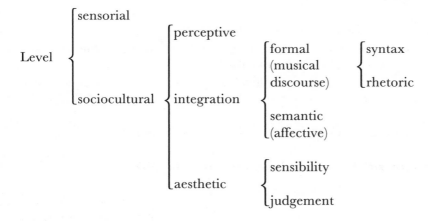

Note that:

a) Intensity, timbre and pitch in sound – melody, rhythm and harmony in musical composition – are not exactly *levels*, but elements, formants or 'dimensions';
b) the sensory level is a (necessary, non-sufficient) *condition*;
c) the perceptive level is the *foundation* (of the set, which the other levels return to);

417

d) There can be gaps, according to the people and the cases involved, and it is precisely these gaps which demonstrate the levels;

e) their hierarchy can change, as can the hierarchy of the dimensions, when one or other of them is emphasized.

f) there are still other levels which can be determined, for example levels of fullness of perception.

Level of analysis (in structural linguistics)

A) *Two levels of analysis* (and reality)

$$\begin{cases} \text{phonemes (non-signifying units,} \\ \text{objects of phonology)} \\ \\ \text{morphemes, words} \\ \text{(signifying units)} \end{cases}$$

(Liaison between the two levels: the principle of the *double articulation of language*)[6]

B) *Level 0*: the extralinguistic world, objects

    Level 1: speech as a system of signs and sets of words; language as a system of signs with rules for their use

    Level 2: a metalanguage, logical system of metasigns, referring back to the signs in level 1

(This is based on the work of various logicians and semanticists.)

Fragment of a grid of levels in everyday life

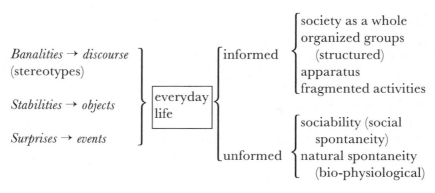

Another fragment of a grid of levels in everyday life

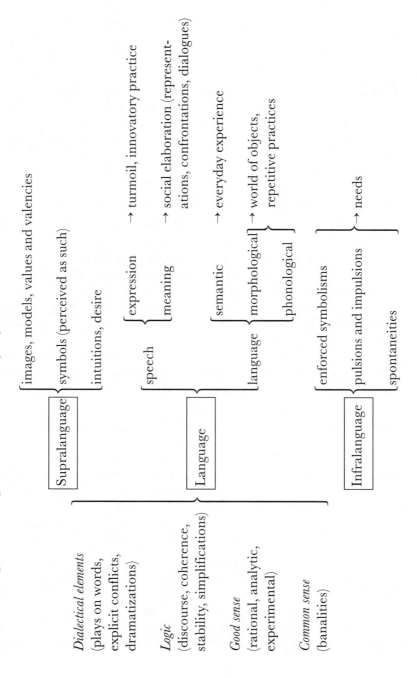

5 Continuity and discontinuity

The links between these two categories affect every area of knowledge. In this respect, considered per se, in the way they interact and in their links with objects and contents, and finally in terms of the operational techniques they bring into being, they should be granted prominence in any treatise on dialectical logic (which is a mediation or intermediary level between formal logic and the theory of concrete dialectical thought).

Here, however, we will merely offer a few methodological observations. Analytic reasoning, or understanding, which is an essential process of knowledge, examines continuity by using discontinuity (and vice versa). A straight line is the result of a cut made by thought in two- or three-dimensional space. To study it, I make a further cut; I select an arbitrary point of departure (point zero) on the line; I segment it; then I bring in an unlimited number of other cuts, which I can count (enumerate). I fragment it in enumerable sets of pieces, each with two ends. However, I know that this line still escapes me; every segment has the power of continuity, and enumeration cannot exhaust it.

On the other hand, if the study of a phenomenon – analysed in variables – gives me a series of discontinuous values, and consequently distinct points on a graphic representation, I join these points together by a curve; I look for the function best able to make this join. If necessary I extrapolate. Continuity will join the discontinuities together.

In this way, in so far as we can determine it, the unity of what is continuous and what is discontinuous is located first and foremost in pure abstract logic (where what is continuous is defined by what is discontinuous, and vice versa, the one referring to the other), and so on, concretely, dialectically, to infinity. Were it possible to grasp this unity concretely and to determine it fully, knowledge would come to an end, and the object, the universe itself, would be exhausted. We can only determine this dialectical unity by considering it to be inexhaustible. For knowledge such as ours, which proceeds by using categories and by applying concepts which have previously been developed with 'the real' as their starting point, 'reality' is not inaccessible or transcendental; and yet it can only be considered as a *limit to the* (asymptotic) *infiniteness* of finite knowledge. The infinite, which is the ultimate object of finite knowledge, manifests itself successively as an aspect of continuity (a mathematical example: the power of content in set theory) and of discontinuity (a mathematical example: a space with an infinite number of dimensions). On this point, it is surely bad dialectics to make the mistake of thinking that the *idea* of this unity constitutes effective knowledge, whereas in fact it merely indicates the vanishing point of our knowledge, which is only determined by the direction in which it is going. In our view this *idea* orientates knowledge, i.e., the use of concepts. It is less rigorous than an axiom but more demanding than a simple regulatory idea or aheuristic principle, as it is usually understood. Its content is more than an abstraction, and is less than concrete. It only becomes (apparent) knowledge when, as if by magic, an ontology changes it from being an idea or a distant and inaccessible horizon into a thing, a 'being' which has been possessed.

The result is a *relativization* of the knowledge obtained by the use of concepts. Inherent to dialectical thought, this relativism has always been fought by dogmatics, and above all by those who purport to be dialecticians. The 'grain of truth' (Lenin) contained in a statement or in a series of propositions is never anything more than a grain, and its truth only becomes apparent later on, when the grain has germinated and prospered, thanks to its own fertility. However, there is indeed 'a grain of truth', and we are not adopting an absolute relativism. Knowledge has points of impact and connections. To use a metaphor, it has anchorages.

We analyse the continuous using the discontinuous as our starting point, and vice versa. However, discontinuity enjoys a kind of privilege, which is malignant but at the same time benign (to use more metaphors). We set out from it, i.e., from the finite. The small whole number is still the springboard of science. Discontinuity constitutes the beginning and the stability of thought, the point from which its far-flung expeditions set out, and to which they return with their plunder. In praxis, there are distinct and stable *objects*, and analytic reason purports to know that these objects exist, and what they are, but then realizes that they are not particularly stable or distinct, and that it does not know what they are, which leads it to ask questions about their stability. These objects constitute the point at which knowledge applies itself, because this is what they are in everyday practice. Basically, to *produce* is to create well-defined implements and objects which are strengthened in the process of becoming. Knowledge always aspires to reduce its object to a *finite* number of answers to a finite number of questions, each question eliciting a *yes* or *no* (and thus logical) answer. Thus there is nothing immediately ontological about the privilege of discontinuity (even though it is connected to human finiteness and to what is *finite* in discontinuity). It derives from everyday practice and from the process which leads from ignorance to knowledge, from what is near to what is far away, from the unmediated to the mediated, from the small whole number to limitless sets, from solidity to randomness. Dialectical thought has not the right to compromise with vague propositions (there is continuity and discontinuity, and the two interact) by transforming them into absolute truths. It must establish a firmer grip on ideas and processes. Nor has it the right to identify the object of knowledge – marked by a certain relativity and a historicity of knowing – with an absolute objectivity to which it holds the key and with which it shares the privilege.

Dialectical reciprocity demands that thought should analyse the continuous by starting from the discontinuous, and vice versa. Concepts and categories do not coincide with reality. They illuminate it, and in doing so to a certain degree they 'reflect' it. As a result the application of categories such as *continuity* and *discontinuity* to a content (a set of phenomena or empirically verifiable facts) involves an element of contingency, subjectivity and relativism. In a sense, and up to a certain point, to illuminate something is to give it a certain *perspective*. However, one particular perspective implies another, and the confrontation of the two creates new problems; it brings forth the 'grain of truth' each one of them contains, and makes it grow. The objectivity of the object constructed according to each category is revealed; it takes on new shapes. Objectivity is heightened.

Georges Gurvitch believes that sociology establishes a perspective which sees human facts according to the category of *discontinuity*. It emphasizes distinctions and reveals irreducible diversities; it discovers types, genres and dichotomies. It traces the outlines of groups (such as classes and nations) and describes conflicts between structures. The historian, on the other hand, focuses on the same inexhaustibly diverse facts, but from the perspective of *continuity*. He emphasizes transitions and transfers; he thinks according to a pattern of continuous becoming, a single time, the time of history.

This ingenious and profound thesis strikes us as being acceptable, up to the point we indicated previously. In our opinion, the sociologist's perspective interacts with the historian's, and vice versa. Their mutual antagonism is intellectually fruitful, and the one must constantly take the other into account. The confrontation of their perspectives enables us to contemplate a unity between them. This is a path which leads us towards new truths. Could it be possible to alternate from the one to the other while leaving them mutually separate? Even if the difference between them proves insurmountable, and if the unity cannot be achieved and exhausted, it is nevertheless a process which must be attempted. Without it the sociologist's discoveries (of types and structures) and those of the historian (epochs, periods, processes and events) would become fixed unilaterally and would hinder the development of knowledge, i.e., of concepts and the dialectical movement of their effort to heighten objectivity.

So the sociologist reflects on the limits of history as a science, and tries to discover how it relates to his 'object'. We already know that sociology has formally recorded the unevenness of developments in history. We also know that it has observed historical 'drift': the gap between effective actions and intentions, and the results of events provoked by tactics and strategies. In this way sociology becomes a rational part of history, but in our view without having to relinquish the historicity of the human being. The relations it brings out differ from those discovered by the historian, but this does not eliminate the process of historical becoming.

Critique of everyday life emphasizes certain aspects of human experience, i.e., of *praxis*. It separates them out and classifies them according to type. The situation of the everyday in praxis and the level it occupies within it depend on society as a whole. In the monopolistic state capitalism which we know from experience, the gap between everyday life and the other aspects of praxis reaches a maximum; everyday life is subordinated to an extremely basic hierarchy of functions (such as norms, values, roles, models and apparatus) at the top of which come technology, bureaucracy and personal power. Sadly, it is *almost* the same in state socialism, which we only know from a distance; the difference – noticeable but not absolute – lies in the importance of politics and the understanding of politics in the social structures of state socialism. The idea of a *possible* transformation of the everyday and consequently of a radical critique of everyday life is the equivalent of opting for a decentralized socialism which would subordinate production to social needs which have been recognized and detected preferentially, thus placing knowledge and the recognition of other people, desires, creative freedom and the poetics inherent in social practice at the top of the hierarchy (of norms, values and models, etc.). Finally, we know that in archaic societies, the everyday was much less separate from culture, religion and ideologies than it is today.

Nevertheless, although we may emphasize differences, this is not to overlook homologies, analogies and above all transitional *processes*, in other words history and human historicity. In so far as it is sociological research, critique of everyday life will not be satisfied merely to emphasize and draw certain outlines for bringing what is empirically real into general social and rational contexts; it is concerned to discover where and upon what it can bring its influence to bear in order to transform everyday life. It sees itself as practice within praxis. It has a certain will, without which it would degenerate into poetic lamentation (like Rilke's, for example). It opts; it determines the stake and the risk; it gambles and wagers on history. In a sense the historicity of man can be defined by moments of great turmoil: revolutions. When these turmoils occur, the sociological and the historical, the everyday and the global, come together and fuse. Revolutions are total phenomena, essential events, or at least they are so in the modern world, the world where historicity asserts and confirms itself. After turmoil comes calm, drift, then divisions and gaps. We will come back to these processes, and when we do so we will give the category of *continuity* pride of place. It does not create them. It enables us to grasp them more effectively, while the (implied, reciprocal) rival category enables us to grasp the results of the process of becoming and of human actions.

Let us now consider another aspect of this question, namely the relations between the continuous and the discontinuous. Let A and B be two living or, better still, thinking and acting 'beings' (individuals or groups). A space separates them. If this space is impenetrable –

forests, uncharted mountains, seas – they must each go their own way, regardless of whether they want to meet or to avoid each other. If the space is completely penetrable and offers a continuous free field, A and B perceive one another, and walk forward either to fight or to love, or simply to get to know each other.

The most interesting cases are those where the intermediate space is neither completely penetrable nor completely impenetrable. There will be obstacles, and so there will be several paths A can follow to reach B and vice versa. These paths are distinct, yet they intersect, or merge. This is when discontinuity intervenes. A must choose a certain path. He sets out towards B (or towards where he thinks B is), and at each crossroads he must make a new choice. Every option obeys tactical considerations. A supposes that B is in a certain direction and that the path he chooses will lead him closer. If the series of choices is articulated according to coherent considerations, we say that A has a strategy, and so has B.

And so the theoretician can place A's and B's strategical choices in a matrix. Calculation comes into play. It reveals the mutual *chances* of the pair (they may be lovers or bitter enemies – what is important is that we know whether they want to meet or to run away from each other, or whether one wants to meet the other, and which of the two this is).[7]

Let us suppose A and B to be enemies. If the space is opaque and inpenetrable, neither has a vantage point, and they will have to trust to chance. The *alea* is complete. If they can see each other from a distance, they can challenge each other visually and run towards each other in a luminous, transparent space. The *agon* is complete. Therefore the *agon* and the *alea* represent two extreme cases and two characteristic polarities in the pure state. Between the two there stretches a vast mixed region where the *agon* and the *alea*, opaqueness and transparency, fear and daring, risk and chance combine in a variety of ways. In this vast region, *numbers* (small whole numbers, in the simple cases at least, the first numbers to be tackled by analysis) are in charge. The possibility of enumerating actions and events depends upon a certain number of choices, options and decisions, and how they are linked together. This enumeration must not lead our analysis to overlook the deeper dialectical movement: the relation between the *agon* and the *alea* – of the *continuous* (objectively, space;

subjectively, the will to strike the enemy) and the *discontinuous* (the coherent series of decisions).

To put it another way, distinctions (distinct units) must have a foundation. They cannot be taken as absolute, for this would be to overlook the fact that they are providing a momentary form or structure to something. After having made a distinction, analytic thinking makes connections. After having made connections, it makes further distinctions. Then, dialectical reason reconstructs the process of becoming and *tends* towards totality by heightening the object and objectivity.

The theory we are considering – the theory of tactics and strategies – is not limited to games, to warfare or to business relations. It is applicable to all temporal consecutions of distinct (discrete) units: sequences of regulated gestures, of words and utterances, of images, of symbols; dialogues with questions and answers, etc. As soon as a dialogue ceases to use the conversational register and rises above triviality, it has started to employ a tactic and a strategy. The same is true for regulated exchanges, be they nothing more than words or gifts exchanged between groups.

Be they extreme cases or mixed situations (with their context: love or intimacy, rivalry or alliance, the transparency or opaqueness of the distance in between), the *agon* and the *alea* appear in whatever becomes formalized or ritualized, or whatever unfolds in a distinct and successive manner, including liturgy, ceremonies, stage acting, and the set phrases of poetry or love.

During these processes (affective, subjective and spontaneous) *content* does not disappear; it survives in *continuousness*. However, it is the discontinuous which governs the form or rather the formalization which operates in the situation in vivo, in the relation between the protagonists: approach, challenge, meeting, confrontation.

Thus, in response to the concrete demand of a given situation, social modalities of *repetition* appear. These cannot be reduced to mere repetition of simple mechanical gestures, pure stereotypes, but rather are the repetition of the process and its development both subjectively and objectively. Analysis projects these periodicities like a spectrum, immediately distinguishing between them or between their 'formants' as they rise above triviality like the tides or waves of the sea.

To establish or re-establish the rights of the continuous as against those of the discontinuous (and vice versa) would be to agree that one had a privilege over the other. It is certain that nineteenth-century thought, inspired as it was by evolutionism and the philosophy of history, privileged *continuity* (although this statement is not valid for Marx and Marxism). Next the category of discontinuity was brought to the fore. This period produced a number of useful discoveries. Language is constructed with differences, incompatibilities, disjunctions and exclusions (short-term or long-term, on both the phonemic and the morphemic level). *Structuralism* takes these observations on, but develops them to a disproportionate degree. Here, as before, we accept the concept of structure, but in a limited way. What we are seeking is to follow the movement between continuity and discontinuity in depth, taking all the interactions and all the conflicts into consideration.

Seen from this angle, we can say that there are processes of becoming and development which are relatively continuous. We will need to highlight one particularly important type of process, the *cumulative process*. We will also show how processes, and especially cumulative processes, fall prey to discontinuities, obstacles, bottlenecks, halts, breaks, gaps and imbalances. However, a process per se never brings about decisions or events. Decisions belong to forces (for example, *social forces*) which come into being by means of a process, or as it is sometimes put, on its 'base' (for example, on the *base* of the *economic process*), but which cannot be reduced to that process. As regards events, it is men who produce them, men who formulate the tactics and strategies of social forces (or in the case of interindividual relations, of psychological forces) and put them into action.

We can discern three levels of analysis and reality: processes, forces and events. By passing from one to the other we will attain a greater complexity, more freedom, more randomness.

This is all to repeat propositions we have already presented, but more clearly and more intensely. All social groups from the 'micro' to the 'macro' scale have a conscious or unconscious, latent or formulated (openly demonstrated) tactic and strategy. So have individuals, in their unmediated or mediating relations. Why? Because, be we individuals or groups, we all have a relatively uncertain future which we must face up to, and for which we prepare in a relatively lucid way. We all have our problems, in which our existence is more-or-less completely involved. Complete societies and partial groupings interconnect, maintain each other, disappear or collapse. Lucidly or not, they know this.

There has never been a human 'substantiality', be it of a sociological, psychic, psychosociological, ideological, economic or political nature. The ontological category of 'substance' is disappearing from our horizon. The secrets of groups, their opacities and their ambiguities, which are what give the illusion of substance, are made up of anxieties or audacity with regard to *what is possible*, of entrenchments and offensives, of retreats and advances in relation to other groups, of courage or of weakness of will in response to problems. Human groupings see – or choose not to see – the results of 'conditions'. The spontaneity and vitality of these groups are reflected in representations (symbols, norms, models, images, etc.) or are formulated by means of ideological representations. However, it is individuals who reflect, who formulate opinions, and who define attitudes and crystallize patterns of behaviour. Individuals show the group to which they belong images of what is possible and what is impossible. They calculate and compute; they are spokesmen, deputies, 'elected' representatives: family heads, trades-union leaders, rural dignitaries, city administrators, party leaders, statesmen. There is no substance here, only men, actions, relations and (individual and collective) consciousnesses. In the beginning was action; in the end action is recognized (although the classic concept of act, action or experience does not exhaust the idea of *praxis*). Every human life is a progress or a process towards a possibility, the opening up or closing down of what is possible, a calculation and an option based upon random events and the intervention of 'other people'.

Beneath their ambiguities, critical study of everyday life will reveal the tactics and strategies of partial groups (such as women, young people, intellectuals, etc.) in society as a whole. Whether these tactics and strategies are manifest or concealed, it will be capable of detecting them and the ways they express themselves. The study of the everyday will grasp the relations between groupings which make their contacts opaque, or which make them mutually accessible, in spite of misunderstandings, tactical manoeuvres, disguises, strategic openings and adventures.

When groups become isolated, they degenerate; they cease to exist 'through action'. Continued existence in itself implies action and struggle, and therefore relations. The *agon* only disappears when groups and individuals go into decline. When they degenerate, groups break up into scattered elements, minigroups and individuals. The everyday lapses into triviality. As for the moments where strategy predominates, these are the great historical moments of revolutionary turmoil. Strategy gives a sense to groups and to their lives. 'Sense' – direction, orientation, expression, goal – is not some comfortable, speculative entity for a specialist, such as the philosopher, to elucidate philosophically. Sense is drama. It is constituted by strategy – the strategy of the group. The strategy of the group creates it.

Therefore the level of the everyday as a 'reality' would be the level of *tactics*, lying between the level where there are no more actions, where reality is stagnating and coagulating, and where triviality dominates, and the level of decision, drama, history, strategy and upheaval.

Once again we are repeating statements we made earlier, but from a different perspective. However, these statements must not be taken literally. In so far as the everyday is a reality which must be metamorphosed, challenged and made challengeable by critique, it can be observed on the level of *tactics*, of forces and their relations, and of stratagems and suspicions. Its transformation takes place on the level of events, strategies and historical moments. Therefore we will not allocate a statistical level to everyday life and our study of it. This would draw us down into triviality, or up towards factuality (in the stipulated sense).

Therefore we will try to discover how each group we examine responds to 'stimuli' (such as challenges, propositions and provocations, threats, claims and offensives) from some other group, and how it resolves tactical problems. Passing over to the level of strategy, we will try to see how groups tend to minimize the chances of maximal gain for their partners or adversaries – or conversely how they maximize their own minimal gain.[8] In a random series of an unlimited number of questions (with yes-or-no answers, and so of the kind which could figure in everyday conversation), it is the second of these strategies which produces the largest number of correct answers. On the other hand, the minimal strategy would determine a tactic of dissimulation, retreat, denial and misunderstanding, which would become apparent as such in the everyday.

Knowledge per se has its tactic: to know, to make known, to make the everyday known as an object of knowledge. It has its strategy: to bring about the dissolution of the everyday and to reduce it indefinitely – to provoke its metamorphosis by inferring the maximum number of options in this sense – by demonstrating the possibility of narrowing the gap between the everyday real and what is possible, by investing in what is (relatively) superior and by elevating what is (relatively) inferior. This strategy involves the use of philosophy while at the same time pushing it from its pedestal and realizing it as a vision of transparency in everyday human relations. This self-same strategy involves the struggle for the rights of science to be one of the elements of an overall (political) strategy.

We must distinguish between the theory of the *wager* (of Pascalian origin) and the theory of *strategies*. The individual can gamble and lay wagers. A group is never aware that it is gambling on its future, or that it is placing bets and running risks. It is to the 'distanced' observer on the outside that the activity of a group can appear like a wager. A group will only enter upon an action for gain, and with the certainty of winning. We call this certainty 'confidence'. It is the opposite of 'mistrust' and of the attitude of 'challenge' towards other groups. Only leaders can be aware of risks, i.e., the chances of failure and success, and usually they are careful to keep these to themselves; the 'confidence' groups have in their goals is also confidence in their leaders, something which the leaders themselves take every care not to jeopardize. Here ideology plays an ambiguous role: it fosters ambiguity. Both an illusion and a stimulant, ideology creates representations which belittle 'the other' and overexalt the self. Collective units gamble, but do not know they are gambling. A troop of soldiers which can see clearly that defeat is on the cards, i.e., that it is involved in a gamble, is already demoralized and half on the way to defeat. Only the chief receives exact information and transforms it into orders. He alone assesses the chances. He alone knows that he is gambling and that his wager is serious and at the heart of the drama. This is one of the most scabrous aspects of 'leadership' and of ideology. Raising morale by concealing the possibilities of failure effectively increases the chances of success. The chief assumes all responsibilities, for misinterpretations, misunderstandings, even for ideological lies and for the elimination of overperceptive individuals. In everyday life as well as at moments of crisis, the way men behave is frequently Machiavellian. What is more, the pursuit of any good and the fulfilment of any desire, no matter how incomplete, always incurs risks and dangers. Could bets and wagers be the prerogative of a few individuals who alone are capable of bearing the situation when they come face to face with randomness? This would hardly be encouraging for democracy, but, as Marx and Lenin have told us, democracy contradicts itself, it thrives on contradiction, and this self-destruction only comes to an end with politics, that supremely serious gamble, drama of dramas, destiny of destinies.

Critique derives not from theory, but from praxis. If we emphasize the tactics and strategies of groups, this is not to fetishize them. Only if we formalize them will they tend to become fetishes, since formalization would transform them into the objects of a higher science.

The traditional idea of destiny as elaborated by traditional (classic) culture contains and mixes together several contradictory elements which games and strategy theory helps to clarify somewhat. The idea of destiny, i.e., the tragic, contains the idea of the (inevitable) failure of every intention and every project. It contains the representation of a game which is weighted against the hero, who (inevitably) makes mistakes which lead to his downfall, while his opponent (god, determinism, mechanism) necessarily plays well. Finally there is the idea of an act which concludes in a way *other* than that which the participants expected and wished for. The tragic is nothing other than gambling, in all its breadth and seriousness.

In this sense, the everyday is both the residual deposit and the product of the tragic and of destiny. It is the tragic which has been smothered, undetected and unrecognized. It is destiny awaiting its hour and which the people it concerns await without knowing it, or more exactly without recognizing it. It is tactics and strategies which go their own way, without 'us' knowing it, since 'we' are caught up within it between the object and the subject: in an ambiguity which is never completely resolved, we are the object of the action and at the same time we are its subject. Therefore the everyday is also the non-tragic, the source of the tragic and its naked remains, and the empty place of Destiny, filled with an amorphous mixture of necessity, chance, freedom, dangers, assurances, risks and securities.[9]

Seen in this light, the everyday is on the one hand an *empirical modality for the organization of human life*, and on the other a mass of *representations which disguise this organization*, its contingency and its risks. Hence the impression given by everyday life as 'reality': inconsistency and solidity, fragility and cohesion, seriousness and futility, profound drama and the void behind an actor's empty mask.

Has not every distinct (individual and group) human unit been led or conducted to *somewhere it did not want to go*, and dragged to *somewhere other than it wished*? The experience of history and historicity weigh down on the present in a confused manner. Every human unit has a memory and a fund of information – good or bad – which are mixed together in the everyday. It cannot see everything and it cannot know everything, but it knows and sees something. If it cannot know its destiny as such (and the main protagonists are themselves ignorant of it because of all that is unforeseeable in the outcome of conflicts between strategies), every entity senses something which shows through or is revealed (or both at once) in the symbols, the sayings and proverbs, the images and the myths it uses. As well as concern for the future, as well as anxieties, symbols and memories, there is work, the pressing concerns of the moment, goods and satisfactions, ordinary pleasures, ordinary pastimes: the present moment or the actual (to avoid using the suspect word 'reality' with all its burden of fetishism). Present moments do not coincide exactly with the conditions or the results of data, and even less with possibilities. They are part of them; they are more than them; they are less than them.

Theory has revealed the importance and the penetration of *play* in everyday life and in social practice in general. Several distinct levels and dimensions of play are apparent. There are games of a spontaneous character, games with rules and games with tactics. Strategy can be a *serious game* although it may not be perceived as such. And there are others, such as games which are blindly unaware or ignorant of themselves (an extreme example: alienation through destiny and the tragic), objective games, which accept risk (an extreme example: adventures outside of an everyday context), and subjective games, with formal rules (an extreme example: frivolousness). These are various distinct and yet inseparable ways and stages of taking randomness into account, and to limit and control its freedom.

Thus play would be a (frequently disguised and misunderstood) dimension of everyday life and of praxis. It contains within itself several degrees or levels, several dimensions, according to how it relates directly and consciously to randomness per se. Could play be the starting point from which we could envisage the metamorphosis of the everyday?

6 Micro and macro

The distinction between the 'micro' and the 'macro' appears in most of the sciences, at the same time as the idea of level. It originated in mathematics, when Riemann conceived of large spaces with properties different from those of small-scale spaces. Subsequently physicists adopted it (i.e., the distinction between microphenomena and the macroscopic scale), followed next by sociologists, geographers and economists, etc.

In every field, and most especially in our area of research, the 'micro' and the 'macro' appear to be mutually irreducible. We say this warily, because it implies serious consequences: after having rejected Aristotelian epistemology, which changes the act (here, the act of the social group) into substance, we have rejected Cartesian epistemology, which uses the simple to construct the complex and deems that an exhaustive analysis leading to total synthesis is possible, on condition that the process is logically ordered.

In the everyday, on the microsociological level, unmediated relations are carried on between one person and another (via blood ties, or neighbourhood and socially contingent relations) which are complicated by ties of direct dependency and rivalry (i.e., husband/wife, father/children, employers/servants), and accompanied by rebellions which are just as direct. On the macrosociological level, these unmediated ties and subordinations are survivals which prolong archaic relations (of consanguinity and territoriality) or feudal relations (of subordination and vassalage). On this 'macro' level, such relations are mediated; they pass via 'the thing' – reified and reifying, alienating and alienated: commodities, money, language.

As a result the 'micro' level is ambiguous and the 'macro' level is abstract, and yet no sooner have we formulated this statement than we need to turn it on its head. If it is ambiguous, the 'micro' level is also the level where the question of authenticity has a meaning: the unmediated can become authentic, either in spontaneity or in truth; at least this is what we suppose and what we demand of it. If it is abstract, the 'macro' level is also heavily present. We need to emphasize this paradox. Because it is ambiguous, the 'micro' can be accused of being false. And yet only the 'micro' can become authentic, in other words transparent, through the mutual recognition of relations. The 'macro' which seems, and indeed is, so 'real' is also the realm of falsities and fetishes. And yet, if we are to validate and authenticate the 'micro', we must first transform the 'macro'.

Therefore there is a distance and a gap between the two levels. Any attempt to miniaturize social science by using the study of limited groups would soon come up against this obstacle. It is a barrier to analytic reason, which reduces the complex to the elementary and the compound to the simple. The 'micro' level is just as complex as the 'macro' level, but in a different way. As regards the reverse procedure, which would attempt to grasp the 'micro' via the 'macro', this leads to a sort of untenable and dangerous sociology which would define the everyday absolutely by the whole.

Gaps and differences between levels do not authorize us to dichotomize any one of them, and even less to 'scotomize' it.[10] Irreducibility is not the equivalent of separation. There is a multiplicity of relations, correspondences and homologies between the 'macro' level and the 'micro' level. Both levels 'reflect' the society which encompasses them and which they constitute. Thus, the correspondences between family (private) life and society as a whole are almost self-evident. Society as a whole acts, becomes apparent and intervenes through the ambiguity of direct ties which are simultaneously biological and social, or, perhaps we should say, because of that ambiguity. The contradictions and conflicts within families represent or reflect those of society as a whole (be it feudal, capitalist or socialist) and those of the classes (the bourgeoisie and the proletariat). What is more, in a sense, the unmediated character of direct relations is nothing but a mirage. These direct relations are also mediated: by language and by money, etc. On the level of these relations, the unmediated is as much of a reconstruction as it is a constituent. Perception of others also implies a network of mediations which determine it and limit it. The 'macro' level appears to be the level where the 'micro' is integrated within the whole, a process which leaves little room within its empty spaces for marginal, abnormal or 'deviant' elements. The 'macro' does not determine the 'micro'. It encompasses it; it controls it; it penetrates it and imposes regulations upon it, which are themselves at differing levels of depth and effectiveness: norms of conduct and behaviour patterns, models and roles, etc. Using and abusing the limits of the 'micro', the 'macro' brings all its weight to bear upon it.

Are these relations dialectical, in other words conflictive, polyvalent, mobile and multiformal? Doubtless they are. On one hand, the 'macro' makes every effort to contain, to absorb and reabsorb the 'micro' (but by means of the actions of privileged individuals, its leaders). It succeeds, but never totally. In spite of its ambiguities, or maybe because of them, the 'micro' puts up a resistance. The social and the cultural never reabsorb the biophysiological, the unmediated or the natural. The sector which is rationally controlled by praxis never eliminates the uncontrolled sector, the sector of spontaneity and passion. Once separated off, the 'macro' atrophies: mediations no longer have anything to mediate, and the means of communication no longer have anything to communicate. Isolated in turn, the 'micro' lapses into irrationality and meaninglessness.

When they are not governed by laws, spontaneity and immediacy lose direction. Conversely, without spontaneity, laws and norms resemble death. It is on the level of the 'micro' that life has rights, and spontaneity feeds into practice and culture; it is the living root of the social. However, it is on the level of the 'macro' that the decisions which eradicate ambiguities are taken, that the division of social labour is organized, and that norms and images are developed.

The existence of the 'micro' level implies and supposes *neighbourhood* (or *contingent*) *relations* in a social space. Distinct, but not separated, the sides and facets of microelements come into contact with each other. The fact that they are mutually distinctive should not disguise the homologies, correspondences and analogies. Families, villages, towns and businesses live side by side in social space and their 'internalities' interconnect. Considered from the point of view of the *continuous*, these relations in social space give rise to representations and mathematical formalizations (such as topologies, transformations and groups). From the point of view of the *discontinuous*, they also give rise to representations and formalizations (such as networks and graphs).

The *tree* offers a good representation of relations of neighbourhood and proximity within a larger unit. Small branches spring from larger ones, which in turn spring from the trunk; they grow in forks which produce distances but not separations. The leaves grow side by side at the end of the branches and only communicate via the branches and the trunk, i.e., via the tree as a whole.

Thus the interaction of distinct and inseparable units can be represented in images and forms which lend themselves to rigorous formalizations. This is a mode of thinking and investigation which makes use on the one hand of images and the imagination, and on the other of mathematical research.[11] Thus the tree is more than a physical reality transposed on to society; it is more than a symbol and something other than a symbol. It is a *formal instrument* with an original relation to the concrete. Is it a form or a structure? Let us leave that question to one side for the moment. The tree stretches out without losing its cohesion. As it grows it retains a particular and characteristic form. It presents a number of remarkable points – ramifications, bifurcations, disjunctions – which are also fragile points, points of fracture, changes of direction. It illustrates a dynamic and relative stability, a growth which is coherent, but always under threat. Would it resolve the problems of 'continuity/discontinuity' and 'the elementary/the total', in material nature and in society? In a sense, and up to a certain point, it doubtless would. In any event, it offers an illustration of social space and social time, and of relations of proximity and distance.[12] However, there are certain characteristics of society as a whole, such as alienation through money and commodities, which it does not represent. Nor does it demonstrate that (provisional) balances and self-regulations in social consciousness and society, and within determined social frameworks, are brought about not by mechanisms, but precisely by the intermediary of representations.

7 Indexes, criteria, variables

In these methodological considerations, we never separate the abstract from the concrete, or form from content. On the contrary: we use every occasion we can to demonstrate how the abstract already contains aspects of the concrete and how form is already an aspect of the real. However, if we do not separate them, this does not mean that we should conflate them, and to avoid this we will start from the most formal and the most abstract and progress towards the most concrete.

We must now point out the indexes, criteria and variables in this progression.

A social fact designating more and something other than itself: such could be the definition of an *index*. It has a meaning which is a content; it reveals, it indicates. Often, at first sight, an index is non-signifying; and therein lies one of the traps in the idea of 'signification'. An index refers to something hidden, or conversely, to something so obvious that the observer is unable to see it within the mass of evidence before him. Therefore the index is a sign, but is not intended as such, and consequently it is not arbitrary. It is part of the phenomena it reveals; it is linked to them as they are linked to one another, one expression among many others. It is as close to the symptom as it is to the sign. A symptom can be considerably far removed from the actual location of an illness or its causes; and yet the connection exists.

Therefore the index is only of use as a part, aspect or element of the phenomenon being considered. Its relation to this phenomenon is not generally clear, or easy to establish; some indexes are deceptive or disappointing. When an observer or experimenter first makes contact with a social group he begins by looking for certifiable indexes. At this level, only rational instinct is brought into play: the scientific culture which is sometimes called intuition. A social group presents a sort of face, an (open or concealed) presence, where indexes can be copious or scanty. Using indexes which are frequently secretive, the scientist makes things up; he uses his imagination. As Picasso is quoted as saying, 'First of all I find something, then I start to search for it.' This remark reinforces an old paradox; it brings to the fore certain characteristics of the dialectical movement of thought. An excessive concern for rigour and logical coherence makes thought inflexible; valid in

437

itself, this concern already presupposes the object without knowing it; it constrains thought to invest the object with the characteristics of formal rigour, which it assumes to be purely objective. This is to disregard the subjective aspect of formal rigour. It formalizes, it quantifies; or again, whenever it approaches a concrete object it grinds to a halt, unable to reach it.

Occasionally an index will reveal something other than was expected. Occasionally it resembles a clinical symptom. It indicates a crisis, tension or vitality, a failure or a decline. Sometimes what is most internal comes to the surface and reveals itself in what is most external, namely the index; what is most profound shows through in what is most superficial and fleeting. Conversely, research will sometimes show an index to be invalid.

The need to scrutinize the index in depth means it must be measured against *criteria*, some of which are general and formal, others specific. A good *index* shows itself to be relatively constant, within the limits of the observations or experiments being undertaken; it permits us to grasp a certain number of facts and to group them (by classification). No longer a mere appearance, it reveals the hidden reality; it translates it or it traduces it. In this way it supersedes itself to become a *criterion*. In fact the criterion is not external to the index; the index becomes a criterion when it becomes precise and heightened; at that stage the attentive observer or experimenter will distinguish it and separate it from its initial context, to apply it to other phenomena or other groups. The index becomes an analytic implement for penetrating and classifying. The *indexical criterion* changes into an objective criterion, which in turn joins forces with a set of criteria which are always *specific*. As for general criteria, they stipulate the use of specific indexes and criteria; they regulate the successive procedures and levels of this process: discovery and invention, the transfer from the fleeting index to the indexical criterion, the constitution of a coherent set of criteria characterizing a phenomenon.

An excellent illustration of these procedures would be the *criteria of underdevelopment* to be found in Lenin's *The Development of Capitalism in Russia*, and in his subsequent writings.

Let us consider the *criteria of underdevelopment* as Lenin has already defined them:

- the splintering of economic units;
- virtually autonomous local markets which are poorly integrated in a national market linked to the world market;
- low concentration both in industry and in agriculture;
- weak contradiction between the collective character of production and the individual (private) character of appropriation;
- forms of personal dependence in social relations;
- economically backward forms of productive relations with the predominance of agriculture and the slowing down of transfers of population;
- poor needs of association and archaic forms of association;
- weaknesses of the large groups (classes) occupying different situations in production;
- weakness of class antagonisms;
- traditional forms of moral life and social life, etc.

More recent authors have added further criteria to these economic and political ones: *demographic* (high birth and death rates); *technological* (poor per capita use of energy); *cultural* (high percentage of illiteracy); *sociological* (limited mobility, rigid structures along with poor overall integration, etc.).[13]

These new criteria modify and complete the set established by Lenin (which was limited to the economic aspects of the question), but they do not invalidate it. The general criterion of economic development and the criterion of social and political 'progress' is the reduction and disappearance of one or several specific indexical criteria of underdevelopment.

This set of criteria sheds a remarkable light on everyday life in a poorly developed society, i.e., a society *which must be transformed* by guided (planned) economic growth. Each criterion is like a spotlight, pinpointing a specific trait.

In accordance with our programme we will now complete the above list by adding the *criteria of the underdevelopment of everyday life in the developed countries*:

- the backwardness of 'services' essential to everyday life compared with production in general (production of the means of production or production of 'privately produced goods');[14]

439

- the manipulation of the consumer and of his needs by advertising and propaganda;
- the backwardness of techniques applicable to everyday life compared with production techniques, military techniques, and techniques for the exploitation of space;
- the splintering of local and territorial units (such as families, neighbourhoods and towns, etc.) and excessively powerful means of integration;
- an inextricable mixture of archaic forms of moral and social life and modern forms of communication and information;
- the backwardness of town planning as the form and context of everyday life compared with needs and technical possibilities, and compared with the social life in towns in the past;
- forms of personal dependence (consumer/producer, private/public, citizen/state, woman/man, etc.);
- a slowing down of possibilities;
- a reduction of possibilities involving spatial movements (so-called social mobility, tourism and travel);
- a relative erosion of certain sectors (such as cooking, housing and leisure, etc.) in various countries;
- a fragmentation of technology and an incoherence of the 'world of objects' and 'goods' in the everyday;
- illiteracy and 'cultural' backwardness in terms of the art of living and lifestyle, love and eroticism, sex and family planning;
- the abstract and mechanical character of the idea of happiness (reduced to the idea of comfort) . . .

This list of (indexical and specific) criteria is not intended to be restrictive. We would be happy to make the disappearance of one of these indexes a general criterion of progress, and the elimination of them all as a criterion of revolution . . .

As far as *variables* are concerned, at this stage we will merely point out the difference between the idea of *strategic variables* and the concept as it is usually understood. We would define the variable generally as an aspect or constituent element of a complex phenomenon, which possesses a relative independence, allowing it to vary separately, and by means of that variance to modify an overall phenomenon which is governed by a limited (i.e., countable) number of other parameters. The index should enable us to grasp a variable in its relative independence. The use of criteria should enable us to verify variables and their connections within a set which constitutes the phenomenon as a whole. Here the role of the index is analytic, and the role of the criterion is synthetic.

This classic idea supposes the existence of a *continuum* determined by parameters (thus possessing a certain number of dimensions). However, the strategic variable introduces discontinuity. It focuses on the future. It points to inevitable options, with all the (long-term negative and positive) consequences and risks choice implies. Of necessity there are several strategic variables, all mutually incompatible (and if they were not, there would be no options, no clear-cut decisions spelling out what is possible, committing the future and unfolding in a preplanned sequence: no tactic and no strategy). If they fail to determine their position in a specific conjuncture of their strategic variables, businesses, local groups and political parties will be unable to grasp what and where they are. Analysis of these strategic variables is interesting in two respects, theoretical and practical. What it uncovers will help us to get to know and to understand the problems facing the groupings and units, and consequently the changes in the offing. It will also allow us to act upon them, by modifying their strategic variables, options and shifts in direction.

Thus, by distinguishing between *structural* and *conjunctural* variables more precisely than before, we are introducing discontinuity. As it happens, this distinction is already known and accepted, but in a way which is frequently rather vague. In principle, structural variables affect the most stable part of the phenomenon under consideration, its centre or 'essence', its regulated nucleus, i.e., the part governed by laws encompassing in a general way the processes of internal balance and self-regulation, and thus of stabilization and structurization. Conversely, conjunctural variables are a matter of links and relations, accidents and interactions. In short, they are to do with the consequences of the process of becoming, and with the context beyond the whole phenomenon we are considering. By breaking structures up (by destructuring them), these consequences may modify the phenomenon; they may even change it completely. These conjunctural variables are sometimes subordinated, sometimes dominant and decisive; in the first case, the unit under scrutiny will be maintained and consolidated; in the second, its unity will be broken up and it will lose its wholeness as an entity or nucleus.

We will return to the relation between 'conjuncture' and 'structure' later. For the time being let us observe that we envisage a dialectical movement between the two terms: a conflict during which one controls the other or is controlled by it. The conjunctural is more than a mere sequence of events and contingencies; it is the pressure of the process of becoming on structures and their necessary inclusion in strategies. In a word, it is history, it is (relative) stability, the (relatively) defined, the (briefly) fixed, the diachronic; thus it is whatever the process of becoming will form, and then destroy.

From this angle we have established that one characteristic of the everyday is the fact that its strategic variables are misconstrued, disguised and *latent*, so to speak.

8 Dimensions

The concept of *dimension* comes from mathematics. Social scientists use it widely and somewhat arbitrarily. Sometimes they use it to formulate generalities (the human dimension or dimensions, the historical or the sociological dimension, etc.), and sometimes to calculate and list all the 'dimensions' of the phenomenon (its variables) they are researching.

In mathematics, the term has a precise meaning. A space has one, two, three, four . . . dimensions, or, when it satisfies certain well-determined conditions, an infinite number of dimensions. Dimension is defined very rigorously. Moreover, the mathematician knows that he can *conceive* of, but not *formulate*, a space with more than three dimensions (even though in science fiction four-dimensional space-time passes from the conceptual into the imaginary!). The correspondence of mathematical calculations with physical reality poses a certain number of problems, many of which have not yet been resolved – far from it.[15]

On the pretext of rejecting or limiting formalism, should we forbid the social scientist to take a distinct human unit and attribute 'degrees of freedom' to it, or to include some specific human event in a set of probabilities which have been calculated from hypotheses determining the field of possibilities and fixing the distribution of probabilities with x number of dimensions across the set as a whole? On the contrary. Nevertheless the social scientist must realize that these considerations remain within the formal domain and are a window on to the reality under scrutiny, rather than a means of exhausting it.

The question of 'dimensions' has been obscured by the veil of obfuscation which has shrouded and distorted dialectical thought. Never before has so much been said about dialectic and never before has it been so little understood. Before, thought was often spontaneously dialectical, and thus it was working in the dark. The passage from analytic understanding to dialectical reason was effected without any considered awareness, and yet there was more dialectical movement in thinking and in the way concepts were used[16] than there is today, when dialectic is the fashion among philosophers and elsewhere (above all 'elsewhere').

There appears to be a misunderstanding underlying this obfuscation, and it is important to clear it up. *Dialectic* and *dialogue* have points in common. Now dialogue, like dialectic, is in fashion, and with good reason. Who does not engage in dialogue, or does not try to? Who does not talk about dialogue? Who does not try to communicate, to communicate what they think, to enter into communication? Without developing the idea any further here, we would make the observation that this emphasis on dialogue comes with a profound doubt about its possibility; its means and mediations – and these include language and reason active within Logos – are brought into question and their limits are revealed. Is not language as opaque as it is transparent? Is it not a place of misunderstandings, misinterpretations and misrepresentations? Could not perfect and perfectly coherent discourse, total discourse – the discourse of the philosopher as it is traditionally perceived – be a metalanguage? Are there not several levels of communication and realization, with language being just one of these levels of experience, which is not self-sufficient and does not suffice in order to communicate, and even less in order to realize what has been said (and what has not been said) in praxis? In our view the privilege accorded to language in contemporary thought, and also in art, is the equivalent of a fetishism. Language is something other than a means of communication: something more and something less. The Word is not a 'being'. Taken as a simple means or considered as an absolute, language manifests itself as alienating and alienated; privileged, hypostacized (with or without communication and meaning), it changes into a thing. It reifies and becomes reified. This fetishism disguises real human relations, first that of communications, and second that of the realizing in everyday life (and in the 'lived') of what is said and what is meant.

Supposedly, dialogue unfolds between *two subjects* (any other terms are means and mediations without a specific reality). These two subjects are thought to determine each other grammatically and structurally: I and you, we and you. Quite simply, this model forgets that there are *never only two terms* (two subjects) involved. The third, the *other*, is always present. Why speak, why employ forms of communication and language in the act of utterance, if it is not to rid ourselves of an uneasiness, i.e., of hidden or recognized intentions, challenges and suspicions, so that the act of comprehending emerges from an incomprehension, which in fact is never completely eradicated? Living dialogue illuminates a misunderstanding, without which there would be nothing to say in any case, and which provides the 'matter' the subjects work on in a dialogue situation. This 'matter' is both the 'material' which is being expressed (hidden emotions, poorly revealed opinions, symbols) and the 'material' means of expressing them (the way words are used, intentions, intellectual operators, visible procedures, manifest patterns of behaviour).

This misunderstanding renders dialogue essential and yet difficult, possible but frequently doomed to failure. Where do its hidden roots lie? First, in language, in the words used and in the way they are used, in the symbols used and the intentions behind their use. And also in the systems of reference, which generally remain unclear. And also, and above all, in the *other*: the spectator (real or fictitious), the listener (present or virtual). Between 'you' and 'me', between 'we' and 'you', there is already another, 'he' and 'they', 'she' and 'they', 'they' and 'one'. Some people call this Other 'society', or the 'moral dimension' or 'values'. Believers call it God or the Devil, and psychoanalysts call it 'the Father'. It is close in language and distant in 'systems', 'frameworks', 'regulatory behaviour patterns' – and again, in the formal rules governing opposition and confrontation, the rules of tactics and strategies. As for philosophers, they have some very beautiful names for this included, excluded Third Party: transcendence, mind, thought, being, totality. All of these are correct: there can be no dialogue without a third party, there can be no relation between two without the other. But they are also all incorrect: none of the names is adequate.

Once it is restricted to two voices, a dialogue ceases; words are lacking, there is no common meeting ground. All that remain are cries and silence, cries which may express solitude and silence which may express a profound understanding, or its opposite. Into the two terms (with the second) I introduce the Third Party. It is part of the 'presence'; it takes part. Even in the most delicate conversation between lovers, it 'is' already there: the call of fear or of desire, fear of society (for its approval and consent), fear (or hope) of having a child, waiting for destiny, for passion. As for the monologue of challenge, adventure or desire, it is already a dialogue with a real or fictitious partner, and also a dialogue between the *agon* and the *alea*, which introduces death as a third term. The third term is always that which is possible, and it is this possibility that creates the common measure between the two terms or distinct subjects in 'the real' (the actual, what is present, presence), that both enables and compromises their mutual understanding by simultaneously creating misunderstanding and the possibility of eventual agreement.

How could there be art, poetry and theatre if dialogues in everyday life were limited to two voices? If this were the case, the words of two lovers, two allies or two rivals, two friends or two enemies talking to each other on the stage in front of the third party (us, the public), would scream of mendacity. If this were the case and if pure dialogue had any sense, 'them' and 'us' would take place in one world, and 'I' and 'you' in another; there would be neither society nor language; communication would not be a form of social practice. Or else communication would be a form without content: with nothing to say, without the barrier of opaqueness to overcome, without any misunderstanding to clarify. Or else communication would constitute its own content: speaking for speaking's sake, reflecting its own verbal reflection.

The Other and the Third Party are inherent in dialogue; they determine it and limit it. Forever invoked and forever discarded, evocative and evoked, the Third Party never completely enters into the actuality of the interview, in the presence and the present. It never exhausts itself. In itself, the Third Party is infinitely complex. It is infinite analysis – a hypothetical idea which must be handled with care, we should add. The characteristics of the Third Party are becoming more apparent; it is more, or it is less: more or less important, imminent, oppressive. Sometimes models dominate, sometimes symbols, sometimes one particular image or representation, and now and again 'something' more obscure. This imminence weighs down on the dialogue, directing it and regulating it. It is stronger than the minds which are exchanging words, i.e., it is something more than words alone, something more than 'being'. The Other always spills over from the act, i.e., from the reality of the dialogue. The lover, the poet, the actor – they all exhaust themselves in their effort to exhaust the possibilities of dialogue. They would like the act and the words, the real and the language they are using, to coincide; as if by magic they would like to make Logos effective and to tear it from its limits to make it coincide with life; but here too they are still acting: they resort to overdramatic gestures. If they were to achieve their aim, they would kill off their source of life: expressivity. All would be silence.

Through an initial and predictable misunderstanding, dialectic presents itself as dialogue: with *two* terms, two *dimensions*. Thus analytic understanding reduces dialectical movement to an opposition. In Hegel, however, whenever there are two terms or two voices – the master and the slave, for example – their conflict always contains a third term, born within and from that conflict, an active supersession: consciousness itself. The reduction of the dialectical relation to two dimensions is accompanied by a confusion between dialectical thought and logical thought, which has its own methods (disjunction, dichotomy, distinctions between genus and species, etc.). This confusion has sterilized dialectical thought, which has become unable to grasp movements concretely; on the other hand, it has been very fruitful for logical thought, which has superseded Aristotelianism and has created a multiplicity of operational techniques in which binary (two-term) oppositions and relations, including complementarity, interaction, reciprocity, etc., play a major role.

To eliminate this confusion, we will use the idea of *level*. We need to distinguish three levels: *formal logic* and *pure formalization* (including axiomatization); *two-dimensional dialectical logic* (including the operational techniques of complementarity, polarization, reciprocity and interaction); and *three-dimensional dialectical movements*. Analytical and logical thought may attack these movements in a variety of ways in order to reduce them to silence, but it never succeeds in exhausting them.

When we examine the breadth and depth of praxis by operating a *vertical* section (which cuts through and reveals the strata superimposed by time: the diachronic) and a *horizontal* section (which cuts through and reveals the actual: the synchronic, the structured), it will only afford us knowledge if we relate it to a third term: a process. Only a movement like this, a *growth* or a *development* for example, can make such operational procedures permissible, given the dangers of randomness and the damage that such sections can do. Only the third term can give meaning to analytical techniques which reduce destiny to two dimensions or a single one.

We can now sum up the question of dimensions:

a) *Dimension* ONE. This is the dimension of analytic understanding and formal logic. Analytic abstraction only comprises one aspect, one element, one variable. When applied to an object, formal logic leads to unilaterality. In what purports to be an in-depth exploration of the selected aspect, the tendency is almost always to privilege it, and to transform it into a mechanically dominant 'factor' or an ontological 'essence'. It is thus the favourite dimension of dogmatism; dogmatism sets up home there; it reduces everything (the totality) to a single dimension: to unilaterality, where supposed clarity is in fact a mutilation.

However, analysis of any comprehensive multidimensional phenomenon must break it up into 'formants'; this operation is essential. We are duty bound to make discrete studies of social time, social space, ecology, demography, norms, models, regulatory behaviour patterns, everyday life, etc. Nevertheless, certain methodological principles are imperative: to fight against unilaterality; to restore analysis in its entirety; to make distinctions without separating but also without muddling. Not to think that everything is in everything, and not to think that everything is external to everything. Not to overemphasize difference, and not to overemphasize unity; to handle analysis prudently and synthesis with suspicion . . .

447

b) *Dimension* TWO. Above all else, this is the dimension of dialectical logic, the realm of disjunctions, mutual exclusions, dichotomies, i.e., those operational techniques which enable us to define and to grasp polarized relations, reciprocities and interactions. In our opinion, the study of (relative) stabilities, structures, and (relative) constants should give priority to these two-term relations.[17] They allow us to grasp and to define (relative and momentary) balances and (provisional) self-regulations. They also explain why scientific knowledge makes use of binary arithmetic, matrixes and double-entry tables, grids, alternating (opening and closing) techniques, questions with yes-or-no answers, etc. This area is not purely formal; more exactly, the formal is also part of the real, up to a certain point. Dichotomies and oppositions on an abstract plane correspond to practical operations: bifurcations, shifts of direction, alternations, the presence or absence of a thing defined as a thing (as a stability). More broadly, there is a logic of action, of will, i.e., decision logic. There are options and choices. 'Either this or that.' As we know, language alone requires me to pronounce one phoneme as opposed to another, thus excluding the other by enunciating a different one in its place. To be effective we must make clear distinctions between possibilities and between relations (but this does not mean that there will not be waiting periods during which situations change and 'mature', or delays and temporizations, impatience, attempts at compromise, conciliation, synthesis, etc.). Decision logic has been developed by operational research and by games theory. Information theory has explained an aspect of social practice in communications which is formal, and at the same time real. At this level a *discontinuous* aspect of praxis becomes evident, which comprises calculations concerning discrete units (qualitative mathematics) and the concomitant operational techniques. This discontinuous aspect can be enumerated, and thus it can be exhausted. Every reality which is considered to be made up of a determinable number of discrete units can be exhausted in a finite number of questions with yes-or-no answers, and consequently in a finite number of signs or of words.

c) *Dimension* THREE. Tridimensionality is the level of dialectical movements, or more exactly the level where reality itself is grasped. Time and time again we have determined tridimensionalities in the knowledge of human reality: need–work–pleasure, do–say–live, the controlled sector – the uncontrolled sector – the mixed sector, etc., and we will have cause to do so again.

Nevertheless it would be incorrect to state that with tridimensionality knowledge fully grasps the 'continuous', the 'concrete' or the dialectical movement per se. Such a statement would fetishize tridimensionality and would be metaphysical or theological. What is more, the distinction between dimensions already implies analysis. Tridimensionality encompasses a formal framework: the three dimensions of space, the three dimensions of time (before, during, after), the three pronominal groups in the grammatical expression of social relations (I and you, we and you, they and them). This formal framework remains relatively constant and structural at the heart of a seemingly infinite mobility.

Human reality makes itself known tridimensionally. In the philosophical tradition, triplicity appears from the very start: body, soul, mind; sensibility, understanding, will, etc. These classic triplicities reverberate in every domain: feeling, perception, conceptualization; colour, intensity, saturation of perceptions of light; pitch, volume, timbre; rhythm, melody, harmony, etc.

In fact, action also has three dimensions. A decision cuts; it sections; it reduces a complex situation involving the past (which is irreversible and irremediable, but which has allowed for the gaining of a capability or an empowerment), with all its possibilities and impossibilities, to two dimensions, to the choice between two possibilities. The conflict between the controlled sector and the uncontrolled sector is constantly resolved by the acquisition of new knowledge and new empowerments, which moreover are always limited . . .

Grasped tridimensionally (thus by means of a certain form), dialectical movement extends beyond analysis; it cannot be calculated. It even eludes language, since the efforts made when people speak are nothing more than attempts to bridge the gap by inventing unexpected words and turns of phrase. Tridimensionality is not exhausted by finite knowledge. It forbids us to think that we can proceed only by asking questions which require yes-or-no answers. Sooner or later the moment comes when these questions and answers will lose all meaning, and when someone will reply: yes and no. Exhaustion is death, but before that it is defeat and failure, rupture and finiteness. In every domain, tridimensionality points to a determined movement, encompassing internal conflicts and proceeding by a succession of supersessions.

d) *Multidimensionality*. This becomes acceptable providing we refuse to fetishize tridimensionality. In a dialectical anthropology, man would be multidimensional, and we would be happy to grant games, for example, the theoretical dignity of a dimension. Each 'dimension' would correspond to a degree of freedom. However, if we accept this, we should be wary of substituting the constituent relations of a *presence* by a *representation*. We must not substitute the concrete space and time of praxis by a 'configurative space' analogous to the one physicists used in their formalisms. A configurative space is nothing more than an abstract representation of three-dimensional practical space.

e) *Infinity of dimensions*. Here we pose the problem of non-finite analysis. If totality or 'reality' – including possibility, and taken on all levels – proves itself to be limitless in complexity and in depth, then surely we must imitate the mathematician and introduce an infinity of dimensions. If 'the real' cannot be exhausted in a finite series of limited questions formulated in logical and precise terms, to which the interviewee can answer yes or no, and if in one way or another we must qualify it as being 'non-finite', surely we should take this into account in the representations we use.

The problem goes beyond our frame of reference. There is a law which knowledge still obeys: 'I must stop.' Sooner or later it comes to a halt before an obstacle which also acts as a support: an object. Praxis overcomes it; analysis dissolves it using other means. Knowledge and praxis perceive the non-finite as a possibility, a 'horizon of horizons'. We must not see it as actual infinity. We must make infinity relative.

9 The idea of structure

This idea was rapidly accepted by the sciences. Now it predominates. There is a widespread representation of reality as a structure, from which it follows that science is nothing more than the knowledge of structures and the truth of these structures.

Where does the idea originate? How could it have come into circulation so rapidly? Let us limit ourselves to a few initial explanations.

The idea of *structure* comes as much from the social sciences as it does from mathematics and physics; Marx used it before Sophus Lie who introduced it in mathematics in the study of transformation groups, and almost at the same time as Spencer in sociology. The term started to become widespread around 1930. It corresponds with a general preoccupation among scientific thinkers, which grew in opposition to the predominant concern of the previous period. This was continuist and evolutionist; its thought developed according to the scheme of a continuous process of becoming; it introduced the process of becoming into immobility. It studied forms and formations. The twentieth century has grown increasingly preoccupied with the discontinuous. Instead of introducing the process of becoming into what is stable, the question is asked as to how stability is possible at the heart of the process of becoming. Other aspects, the 'structuring' and 'structured' aspects of the real, become apparent. Driving analysis farther and in a different direction than hitherto, the search for structures reaches the discrete and stable elements of realities.

It is reasonable to think that these aspects – the process of becoming and stability, formation and structure – will lead to a more profoundly dialecticized knowledge, of which Marx's thought provides the model. It is equally reasonable to suppose that a certain stabilization of the world round about 1930 (with capitalism holding its ground, and socialism becoming frozen in the face of this persistence) played no small part in these 'structural' preoccupations, which facilitated and continue to facilitate certain discoveries, while preserving a certain unilaterality in comparison with a totalizing dialectical way of thinking.

The idea of *structure* has been highly elaborated, and has had many uses, but today it is rather shop-worn, and is becoming something of a blunt instrument. It is becoming confused. It is noticeable that the word has accrued a multiplicity of meanings and that when people use it they are never completely sure what they are talking about. Even the old and popularized distinction between *form* and *structure* has been lost sight of. In day-to-day language, a sphere and a circumference have a form; a polygon has a structure. Put more precisely, this means that there is a connection between form and continuity. Now what is continuous cannot be enumerated. On the other hand, when a totality is made up of discrete, distinct and discontinuous units, it has a structure; the discrete units make up a countable grouping, which can be exhausted in a finite series of questions answerable by yes or by no. It is extremely curious to see analytic thought pushed to extremes of sophistication and ending up with very fine differences and extreme distinctions, yet at the same time maintaining some very serious confusions. In this light, we are already seeing form and structure in opposition to each other. Grouped under the heading 'reality', the confusion between *form, structure* and *function* will soon reveal itself to be one of the weaknesses which impede knowledge of the everyday, the understanding of its problems and the imagining of its possible metamorphoses.

From numerous passionate discussions, symposiums and seminars on 'structure', three main conceptions emerge:

a) Structure is *what is intelligible*, it is *essence* in a thing or in a set of phenomena. Sometimes this 'essence' is represented philosophically as a sort of substance, and we have an Aristotelian epistemology. In this case it is an organic unity, as G. G. Granger demonstrates.[18] In this conception, form, function and structure become complete equivalents, since these terms are considered as being more or less the same as the existent 'whole' or totality.[19]

b) Structure is a construction, with reference to an object or a set of objects. By studying them we extrapolate a *system* of coherent relations, together with the transformations which enable us to pass from one system to another and to grasp their relations. Thus structure is located on a certain level above phenomena, but it allows us to grasp them in so far as they have an inner coherence and present combinations of finite and defined properties, i.e., probably in so far as they answer to certain functions (for example, marriage, to perpetuate society). In this conception, structure is therefore the formal representation of a group of relations which has been constructed with a view to studying a set of phenomena and a particular problem which concerns them. There is a confusion between *form* and *structure*, but it is no longer on the level of reality, but on the level of abstraction. Structure is the model, an unconscious or supraconscious representation in what exists.[20]

c) To conclude, a final conception places *structure* neither on the level of a substantial 'reality', nor on that of a constructed abstraction. It conceives of it as an intermediary and a mediation, and also as a relative constant at the heart of the real, as an unstable balance between opposing forces. Therefore structure is not self-sufficient. There are forces which carry it and support it from beneath, so to speak; other forces, higher units, maintain and control it from above. It is a temporary balance which can only be conceived of in reference to the other levels, to the forces and contexts. Isolated and taken per se, these considerations of balance bring us back to the initial conception of structure.

There are structures, and structures conceal forces which modify them in a perpetual movement (of destructuring and restructuring).

> Be it partial (the structure of a group) or total (of an entire society), every social structure is a precarious balance, which must be permanently re-established by ever-renewed efforts, between a multiplicity of hierarchies at the heart of a total social phenomenon with macro-sociological characteristics, of which it only represents a single sector or aspect . . . This balance between multiple hierarchies is strengthened and cemented by models, signs, symbols, social roles, values and ideas, in short by the cultural works which are specific to these structures.[21]

If we look back at Marx's thought in *Capital*, we will notice that he does not exclude any of these meanings and conceptions. In accordance with the programme he set himself in a well-known text, the Preface to *A Contribution to the Critique of Political Economy*,[22] Marx defines the production *relations* which make up the economic *structure* of society, the 'foundation' on which a legal and political super-structure is built, and to which the *forms* of social consciousness correspond. Here structure is the essence of a society, capitalist society, defined and determined by certain production relations. Structure and form are not synonymous. Legally elaborated and systematized property relations form part of the superstructures which carry out certain functions in a determined society. Social consciousness adopts 'forms' – of ideas, of ideologies, of civilization – which should be studied in terms of their formation in history. Structure *forms itself* in the course of a history. Knowledge of capitalist society implies knowledge of its history in so far as it is a 'socioeconomic formation'.

However, to study capitalist society in actuality supposes a series of analytic operations and abstractions (which grasp elements and which penetrate inside concrete totality). Not only does Marx begin from an abstraction in relation to real economic actions, exchange-value, but he also constructs an abstract capitalist society reduced to its essential forces and polarities: the proletariat and the bourgeoisie. Only then does he reintegrate all the aspects, all the intermediaries, all the elements he had momentarily left out of the concrete totality. Thus *Capital* constructs a model. Structure becomes an implement of analysis and dialectical synthesis. Finally, after a long analysis, this synthesis (which Marx left incomplete) reveals the forces which undermined the society in question from within, and led it to its downfall. Both negative and positive, these forces prepare for destructuring and destruction at the very centre of the structure, in its nucleus, at its heart. Structure is therefore never anything but a precarious balance between the opposing forces of momentary stability and revolution.

Thus we can recognize the three concepts of structure in Marx, but they are arranged hierarchically, and the third predominates. Marxist thought distinguishes (markedly, although not very clearly) between form, structure, function, system and totality.[23] All in all, is not structure the stabilizing factor, stability itself, by which a 'being' (an individual or a set of individuals, types, species, social groups, etc.) preserves itself until time bears it away? In short, is structure not its armature? Is not that the role of the skeleton, and of the shell?

In our opinion, the quite excessive emphasis on this concept in present-day structuralism overlooks everything structure contains which is dead or capable of dying. Certainly, in its way, structure has life. Let us take a skeleton, for example. It is born and develops within the individual and is his inner link with his species, its history and its struggle against its environment and within its environment. And yet, although it supports life, the skeleton itself is not alive. It is fixed, it survives the individual. When we examine the skeleton we will not find the living being; all we see is the anatomy, not the physiology. To privilege the skeleton is to proceed like a palaeontologist, a classifier who sees his studies as a convenient way of classification, and is more concerned with nomenclature (although this is essential) than with grasping what the human really is. It is a process in which death grasps the living. The human skeleton has a function, or several functions. For example, it facilitates the upright stance, and maintains it. It cannot achieve this without the help of the muscles or the circulatory system, etc. It is not synonymous with these functions, nor with any other determined function. The various functions (circulation, secretion, etc.) act upon each other, suppose each other and superimpose upon each other. Each makes up a partial fact, the cause and effect of a certain cohesion and self-regulation within the organic totality. The totality of these functions – life – is not synonymous with any of them and cannot be defined by any of them; as it is a totality, it is multifunctional or transformational. As for the form of the human body, it is a demonstration of life itself, i.e., the entire set of functions, the totality of functions and structures. It cannot be reduced to a series of distinct and discontinuous units, like the bones of the skeleton. It is nevertheless true that the skeleton becomes formed, and that, when normal, this form demonstrates a precarious but satisfying balance between the various physiological functions, producing the normal form of the living human organism.

We suspect intuitively that there are complex relations between these various terms (structure, function, form, as well as systems, totalities, coherences). We cannot separate them, but nor can we merge them; we cannot reduce them to each other, but nor can we isolate them. Could the way they interconnect be a matter for dialectical thought? What is certain is that the relation of these terms creates a problem. This problem disappears if we merge them, and even more so if we see them as being synonymous; as we shall see, this is what characterizes *structuralism*.

Before making our definition, let us consider the following image, which follows the concept very closely. I pick up an empty seashell on the beach; I examine it; I find it beautiful, fragile, perfect in its way, and it satisfies my mind like a materialized Idea. I see that it is endowed with a prodigiously delicate *structure*: symmetries, straight lines and curves, grooves and ridges, lobes or spirals, serrations, etc. It really is a structure where discontinuities stand out (in spite of the importance of continuous lines), notably in its symmetries and dissymmetries. I admire its delicate details; in each one I discover new details and new delicacy. I am lost in admiration. I decide to describe these structures carefully and to use them to learn about the living beings these shells once contained. An excellent method, since the shell is there, in my hand, stable, solid and precise. However, am I going to forget that it is nothing more than a piece of work and a 'product', and the product of a relation, the relation between a living being and its environment? If I find that living being in another shell similar to the one I have picked up, I will see that it is soft, sticky and (apparently) amorphous; taken out of its shell, how different the two are! And yet it is the shellfish which has secreted the shell; it has taken on the form of the shell; it has given itself that form. The living being and the living form make up the whole: the shell and the tiny, sticky animal I have separated with my knife. This mass of cells has functions – of which secreting its shell is at least one (or several) – and the shell has a function (or several). If I consider the shell in isolation, I emphasize the definite, fixed, and also mortal and dead, aspects of life. Part of the process of becoming and yet eluding it, the shell – a product or a work made by life – is not alive. Its description enables us to *classify* types and species, according to clear distinctions (logical ones: according to specific differences). And yet the shell is never anything other than a thing, the witness to a moment when life stopped, abandoned by death on the dead sands, exiled from the unflagging life of the sea, of the living space which goes on and on. It is perfect, it is beautiful, it illuminates life and the works of life, it illuminates beauty, but the light it sheds on the world is a cruel one. Why cannot life do without this framework which is more 'beautiful' than life itself, and which persists after it has passed away? So is there anything mortal in perfection and beauty?

With a question like this we bring dream and science, knowledge and art together in a shared borderland. But it goes too far in one direction. In its way, by privileging mobility and amorphousness, it romanticizes. Not for a single moment must we forget the extent to which the shell and the 'being' which secreted it are different. Not for a single moment must we forget the problem which this question helps to formulate in all its forcefulness. At the heart of the universal process of becoming which creates and which destroys, which asserts and negates, how and why do we observe (relative) stabilities, defined and relatively constant contours, regularities, forms which are born and survive, which produce and which reproduce, at the heart of innumerable interactions? Among the shapes of the continuous process of becoming – the circle and the spiral – how is it that there are discontinuous *structures* endowed with defined properties –

polygons, polyhedrons, groups, tree diagrams, networks? In the cosmic process of becoming, what is the secret of the Earth, that stable sphere betrothed to death? In the history of man, what is the secret of everyday life?

In the light this has shed upon our research, houses, neighbour-hoods and towns themselves – in a word, morphology – resemble the image of the seashell. The economist may perceive them in a different way, and link this morphology to other concepts, that of productive force, for example. He is right from his point of view, and this point of view is something to which we can refer, in that sometimes it can be considered of paramount importance. For us, morphological description enables us to classify; it sends us off in search of those living beings – hidden, (apparently) amorphous, sticky and soft perhaps – comprising the groups which have secreted these shells, it helps us to grasp them in their everyday reality. This every-day life is hidden; when the shellfish is alive, it closes up when we touch it. Dead or dying, it yawns wide open. But let us not overwork the image . . .

We have already partially linked everyday life to the idea of the amorphous or unformed. In a sense, it is part of the *astructural*, to use the expression employed by Georges Gurvitch in discussions and polemics against contemporary 'structuralism', with the precise aim of showing the limits of the concept of *structure*. For Georges Gurvitch, forms of sociability are astructural. Structures appear on the macro-sociological scale, but on that scale phenomena cannot be contained by structure, since they encompass non-structural elements.

However, it is not sufficient for us to identify the everyday with the astructural. A more detailed analysis is required. Whatever is apparently unformed can conceal a form or be part of one. Let us look at the seashell image again. The everyday differs from what the description of its external forms (its morphology) tells us, but cannot be separated from it. It must not be confused with a pure, unconditional spontaneity, a kind of absolute effervescence or primordial vitality, which is what the term 'unformed' conjures up. Could it be that it has no function? On the contrary, there is a multiplicity of functions which are carried out in the everyday and which play their part in defining it. If we are to get to know it, we must first distinguish between form, function and structure, and then look for their connections. If there are spontaneous, unformed and astructural elements in the everyday, there are also elements which are 'structured' by determined and fragmented activities, and by functions associated with society as a whole, and finally, there are elements which are organized by apparatus existing on the 'macro' scale in society as a whole. What is more, by using models to scrutinize what is apparently amorphous or unformed, we may discover forms or structures within them. Thus what appears most contingent and most accidental in the everyday can contain and translate – and sometimes traduce – group tactics and strategies. Analysis is never faced with an entirely irreducible residual deposit. In this sense we would accept some (but not all) of G. G. Granger's conclusions. In social phenomena, form and the formal intervene in the very depths of content (but without absorbing, reabsorbing or exhausting it). They bring logic with them (oppositions, disjunctions, polarizations) via the various effects of language or decisions. Therefore there are hidden structures which formal thought can grasp by reconstructing them according to diagrams or models.[24] What at first sight appears unstructurable can reveal structural determinants which are of paramount importance in the concrete process of becoming, namely strategies, options and choices. In short, the 'conjuncture/structure' relation is profoundly dialectical. Not only does structure refer us to conjuncture, with an implied reciprocity; not only should knowledge place itself now in the perspective of structure (of relative stability), now in the perspective of conjuncture (of the process of becoming); in a sense, structure is also conjunctural, and conjuncture contains structural elements. From the point of view of structure, conjuncture is made up of luck and interactions. From the point of view of conjuncture, structure itself is nothing more than a precarious and momentary success, a win or a loss in a complex gamble. Each term can be considered alternately as necessary and as accidental, as creating a free act and as prohibiting it, as failure and as good fortune. When a structure is broken up (by destructurization, which begins deep within structure), other structural elements appear, for which we may use the following terms: strategies, options, decisions, information, etc. Thus on every level, on every rung of society, the *event* is not irreducible. Even a revolution – that total phenomenon and creative turmoil – is prepared; strategies take it on board, or it overturns them; there is nothing unconditional about its origins. 'The lived' and the everyday can never be completely separated from totality. What appears to be conjunctural in the one can appear to be structural in the other; what looks like a simple event in the one looks like a strategy in the other. A notable example of this would be the confusion we have pointed out so many times between the *public* and the *private*, which caricatures their supersession in and by revolutionary praxis as predicted by Marx. This confusion has personalized and 'privatized' power and has made private life public by 'reprivatizing' it. On the level of society as a whole, this is a conjunctural situation which arises from the interaction of state-controlled powers with the new means modern technology has put at their disposal. On the level of the everyday, a multiplicity of events are dependent on this, as is the form they will assume. This is the way the social functions of information and communication work. The form they adopt and the social function have no relation of absolute necessity.

Once more we find ourselves with the 'conjuncture/structure' relation. We have by no means exhausted it in all the concrete situations in which it can be found. Conjuncture appears to us as a (non-finite and continuous) pressure on structure from the process of becoming, and as the virtual shattering of structure. Conversely, it also appears as a rigorously determined object, related to a logic (decision logic, strategy theory) or to a formal theory (information theory). Structure appears to us in turn as the solid, stable element, or as something fragile, constantly brought into question, constantly compromised, the precious and momentary result of the process of becoming and of history. It is the fulcrum of action and freedom, and thus of a disalienation, but from the moment it becomes fixed and made into a representation it becomes a force for alienation; but from that moment too, the process of becoming has already begun to dismantle it.

Let us try to push the analysis of the 'conjuncture/structure' relation a stage further by applying it to a specific case. 'The lived' in the everyday can and should be described using language. Now language does not have the privilege of expressing the lived comprehensively. Language is a conjunctural work, the work of a society, but it is heavily structured, and is a means of action and communication. At one and the same time it is more than a simple instrument at the service of a conscious will and a conscious purpose, and less than one. For these reasons alone it would be difficult to see language as the embodiment of universal Reason. It corresponds generally to a level of experience which has already been socialized and filtered, and specifically to what is lived (individually). It is not the equivalent of a Reason capable of grasping everything and of saying everything on the spot, nor of a social medium by which an individual consciousness might be able to express 'the lived'. Consequently the lived belongs to a broader 'living'; when formulated verbally it illuminates or focuses on a zone (a level) at the heart of living. In one sense the 'lived' is the work of an individual, the realization of a project in a 'living' constituted by social praxis, a general work by groupings in relation to one another. The 'lived/living' dialectical relation in which language intervenes as a mediation and a third term is partially beyond the scope of language, and thus beyond the scope of our logic and our analytic implements (which means we must make them keener). Why? Because language enters into this relation; rather than encompassing it, it is encompassed by it. Thus the 'lived/living' relation remains *unconscious* (except in the case of the mediation which assumes an exaggerated realness and which, in a spontaneously produced and constantly reproduced self-delusion, appears to coincide with the relation by absorbing its terms). We do not know how we live, and yet our consciousness can only be defined as consciousness of our lives and how we live them, and of our individual actions in social praxis. The term 'unconscious' refers no longer to a substance, but to a situation. It becomes relative and 'sociologized'. In this sense, *the unconscious is consciousness*. Conveyed by means of language, or rather linked immediately to language and coinciding in fact with 'what is said', it remains locked within itself, even when it falls silent when threatened by the 'other', since it consists not only of 'what is said' but also of 'what is not said'. It splits into two: 'the lived', what is experienced, the nucleus of that experience, and the 'living', the context and horizon of 'the lived'. From then on, consciousness seeks itself through the 'other', even though it is itself 'what is'. This paradoxical and permanently tense situation of a reality which coincides both with itself and with its mediation and its implement – language – and yet which hounds itself remorselessly, acts as a stimulation; it must forever 'become conscious' of living, of the 'other' and of itself.

Language must always open itself up; it must go farther and deeper in order to grasp something else, both in the luminous and sombre nucleus of 'the lived' and on the chiaroscuro horizon of 'living'. For the speaking, self-speaking consciousness, this search for 'something else' is the only way it can avoid succumbing to the alienation of taking what has been said as accepted (as its 'being'), and of considering the mediation to be the reality, and language to be a defined and defining entity. The result is that what is prior to what will be said and spoken is also subsequent to what was said (or not said). What is subsequent to what has been said and what has not been said is prior to what is going to be said. The 'prelinguistic' or 'unconscious' level is also 'supralinguistic' at the same time. The two levels, the infra and the supra, intersect. They are always relative one to the other, and the one defines the other, in an ever-repeated conjuncture.

Possibly there is a key which will enable us to grasp this highly complex relation: the grammatical structure of our statements. Practical statements formulate the lived, and pronouns provide these statements with a structure: *I, you* (sing.) *and he – we, you* (pl.) *and they – I and me – one and them.* The elements of this group enter into various configurations and constellations which are sometimes binary and disjunctive, sometimes three-dimensional. When brought together the terms are mutually inclusive and exclusive. In the I/you (sing.) relation, the third term 'he' is sometimes excluded or parenthesized (but is still there!) and sometimes explicitly present. The same can be said of the I/we relation. We can make a list of the possible oppositions and constellations:

- I/you (sing.)/(he) – (*he* parenthesized)
- I/you (sing.)/he – (*he* included)
- I/us/(he or they) – (*he* or *they* parenthesized)
- I/us/he or they – (*he* or *they* included)
- I/you (pl.)/(he or they)
- we/you (pl.)/(he or they or them)
- we/you (pl.)/he or they
- we/you (sing.)
- we/they
- one/I
- we/me, etc.

These constellations are finite in number. There are not even very many of them. Could they be similar to the well-known studies which determine and limit the number of situations in theatrical drama? It might be amusing to try to demonstrate this. However, the practical situations they become involved in are inexhaustibly changing, varied and mobile, and full of unexpected moments. Thus *structure* would be the finite (determined and logical) aspect of a movement whose infinite, mobile aspect would be *conjuncture*. Conjuncture is expressed in a structure, and structure signifies a conjuncture. However, when the conjuncture is modified the structure is transformed, and even shattered. Structure tends to maintain and to stabilize conjuncture. For this reason they have a dialectical relation in which neither term has an absolute pre-eminence, but in which a third term – the process of becoming – plays the primary role. Encounters, conflicts and possible reversals are of prime importance. The process of becoming does not burst forth from pure and unpredictable spontaneity. The form it adopts is that of the future, i.e., of projects and possibilities. Here too we can analyse conjecture: it conceals the tactics and strategies of the 'I's and the 'we's, the 'you's (sing.), the 'one's and the 'they's.

Let us note that each structural element contains all the others, potentially or in the present. In particular, the 'I' and the 'me' encompass 'we's and 'you's (pl.), 'you's (sing.) and 'them's. They cannot be isolated. They cannot be determined by themselves. Between and within 'I' and 'me' and the relation between them is language, society and the world. A particular structural element can become polarized or focused, and it can pass into language. It can become a nucleus or a focal point – or else, conversely, it can grow increasingly faint, blurred and obscure. In the latter case, the region which is emphasized (polarized or focused) changes place; it shifts elsewhere. If something loses weight and emphasis, this is not to say that it has stopped existing and being active.

When I emphasize my presence, my will or my thoughts by saying 'I', the 'we' (the interaction between individuals, or the social group of which 'I' am a part, along with its consciousness, its norms and its values – or again society as a whole with its regulatory representations and patterns of behaviour) becomes blurred; the social becomes 'unconscious'; it continues to be active; in my mind I can reproduce a social representation by endowing it with the warmth of a personal presence; without me even realizing it, my decision can be founded on a norm or a value, and I can believe in all honesty that something which has come from elsewhere really is my own. In this case the 'we' is the content and, more than that, it is the *law* of my consciousness and of its 'being', bearing in mind that we are not using these terms in any ontological, substantial or absolute way. The 'we', or rather the 'we's, are simultaneously internal and external to 'I' and 'me'; they determine them, but not in a crude, external way. And it is only at the heart of 'we' that 'I' can be distinguished from 'me', to the extent that the 'we' authorizes this split, making it possible and indeed inevitable. It only appears at certain stages of history, and in certain societies (such as ours!). The distinction between 'I', 'me' and 'we' operates in a specified 'us'. The 'I' takes the dominant voice; it illuminates certain fragments of the 'we' and focuses them. The 'me' encompasses the deep plurality of the 'we', or rather, of the 'we's.

But what happens if I speak out in the name of a group (family, friends, associations, etc.) or if I make an important decision justified by the norms and values of the group, and by the regulatory representations and patterns of behaviour of society as a whole? In this case, 'I' am speaking and 'I' am deciding; and yet, 'I' and 'me' become blurred. Whatever I am becomes unconscious. I can even misinterpret my feelings and my interests, and disregard what is closest to my heart by failing to recognize it. The 'we' becomes localized and focused. It becomes the centre and the nucleus of consciousness. 'I' and 'we' do not disappear. They still figure in the constellation. They remain active. It really is me who is speaking and making decisions, but only in so far as I am part of us. The 'I' and the 'me' lapse into relative unconsciousness.

The same thing happens when the 'I' succeeds in placing itself in the perspective of the 'you' during a dialogue. In this case the 'we' links the 'I' and the 'you' and takes front stage: preconscious but supraconscious at first, it becomes the focal point or centre of conscious activity, while the 'I' per se becomes 'unconscious'.

This dialectic of consciousness (i.e., of infraconsciousness and supraconsciousness, of the passage from relative unconsciousness to relative consciousness) corresponds to dialectical moments: 'the lived/living', 'conjuncture/structure', 'the everyday/totality'. It is clear that *signs* (words: I, you, he, etc.) play an important role. They are relative constants, crystallizations, nucleuses both of consciousness and of communication. Do they create what they signify? Yes and no. Taken absolutely, this idea is an extrapolation. Taken relatively, however, it is true. Language is a social fact, and plays a part in all social facts. It is a part of them. It is therefore the active element of every social phenomenon. It helps to bring it into being and to fix it. Realness and possibility, the project and its realization – they all pass through language. It enables works, but does not create them historically. In societies such as ours, where the individual manages to express himself (not without difficulty) because he manages to exist (not without difficulty), individuals have created their way of expression. Once it has been constituted, it becomes active. It creates individuals. Signs per se intervene. In this way the dialectical movements we mentioned above become interwoven with an even more complex movement: 'expressivity/signification', which unfolds at the heart of society as a whole.

Thus we are able to relativize unconsciousness, and to conceive of it socially by linking it to the idea, rather vague in itself, of 'the lived', i.e., in this context, the everyday. Given the importance of signs, we could connect the study of unconsciousness thus defined in the 'conjuncture/structure' relation for the conscious beings we are, to a general semantics and a general semeiology, but with the proviso that we do not assume that this way of studying language will have the privilege of delivering an essence.

Using this model, we will immediately be able to discern a concrete form of alienation in the everyday. Alienation does not only come from the norms and models we ourselves determine. It does not only come from the inventive patterns of behaviour and the fascinating images which distract us from ourselves. When it is born from a misunderstanding of the level on which consciousness is situated, it is the child of our own initiatives and our own actions. If I confuse 'I', 'me' and 'we' – if I merge them, if I overlook the distance between these levels – I introduce an alienation. 'I' thinks it is 'we', and even worse, 'them'. If I forget the gap between these terms, if I leave one of them in blind necessity by opting for another, if I disregard unperceived conflicts by accepting the set as cohesive, then 'consciousness' and 'unconsciousness' become blurred and their roles become reversed. 'Misconsciousness' triumphs. Now when social practice teaches us language it also teaches us how to pass from 'I' to 'we', and vice versa. It is a rather crude cultural apprenticeship, a structuring and structured verbal technique. In this context there is a risk that the terms 'structure' and 'technique' may lead us astray. They conjure up a sense of solidity. But in this context these techniques are random, and the social structures of consciousness which we are trying to delimit are both strangely vigorous and curiously fragile; effectively, on the individual scale, they are founded on words. Hence the constant possibility of a *misuse* of words and an *unawareness* of what they relate to.

In the preceding pages we have carefully distinguished the concepts (of form, function and structure) in order to grasp their connections more effectively. We can proceed in the same way for *system* and *structure*. The way the word 'system' and the word 'structure' are used is as vague as it is obscure. There is a tendency to make them synonymous, particularly when certain characteristics of structure are emphasized, such as coherence, inner logic, and the whole in which elements are distributed and maintained according to an immanent logic. The term 'system' used to be misleadingly clear, because it was used indiscriminately to mean 'the real' (the system of consanguinity, according to Morgan),[25] conceptual constructs ('legal systems', for example, or 'political systems') and pure abstractions ('philosophical systems'). In every case, the most important characteristic is balance and inner cohesion. And we need to know where this characteristic originates: from logic, from the real, or from both. If this question remains unanswered, the concept will be equivocal. This would perhaps explain the ambiguity of the idea of structure, which is understood sometimes as a construct (a model) and at other times as given (an essence), or as a mixture of these two polarities.

It would perhaps be feasible to keep the word 'system' (in the social sciences) for structures which reproduce their own elements with periodic regularity, thus imposing cyclic form on social time. This is a form (among others) of coherence and temporality, characterized by a circular process: the elements change, but their connections do not. Let us take one interesting case: *systems of agricultural cultivation*.[26] This has been the object of some significant work (more in Italy and Germany than in France), but it has been somewhat neglected, so that similar research has subsequently been greeted with a great deal of surprise. It is obvious that since land settlement and the growth of villages, peasant groups have had to take every element into account when organizing production: soil, climate, population, labour needs and resources, and techniques for plant cultivation, etc. Of course, in archaic peasant communities, this organization was not carried out according to our own rational and operational way of thinking. The indispensable balance was achieved by empirical trial and error, in the guise of representations and symbols, according to the order attributed to the cosmos and to the human community, and under the leadership of elders, chiefs and priests. Mistakes were very costly: famines, crises within the community. It is probable that mechanical self-regulation came too late, and that the prevention of mistakes and the prediction of errors was a matter of informed guesswork. In any event, balance was achieved in a situation of permanent change, which involved the reproduction of elements and their relations in a social practice as yet unaware of itself. The system of cultivation itself grouped a series of productive elements together in a coherent set: woodland (for gathering, breeding, wood); steppe, pasture (for livestock); arable land (for cereal production); gardens (for vegetables); orchards (for fruits), plus other less essential but in certain cases important elements (places for fishing, rivers, ponds, etc.). It is clear that these 'parameters' gave rise to defined conditions (notably by way of the techniques involved) which combined in ways which were sometimes viable, sometimes optimal, but sometimes destined to die out.

The balanced distribution of the various 'elements' establishes a system. The term becomes valid when we consider the balance and the necessary cohesion of the whole. When an agrarian system is well defined – notably by the implements and agricultural techniques it uses – it determines the landscape, and the structure of the village and its relation to the soil. It also determines a periodicity, i.e., a cyclic time scale made up of small cycles. The large cycles were biennial, triennial, quadrennial (in other words, at the end of two, three or four years or more, the same crops reappeared on the same land). The large cycle of crop rotation was made up of smaller cycles: years, seasons, months, weeks.

In a general context, the ways of adapting to a terrain were always flexible. Using wisdom and knowledge, experience and determination, human groupings have always used the land to enormous advantage (so much so that even brutal interventions by conquerors or landowners failed to shatter their representations of the cosmos and their sense of organic balance). There is nothing infallible about this wisdom; it is brought into effect to remedy mistakes which come in the wake of catastrophes, rather than as a sovereign cure for them. Therefore, given the diversity of concrete situations, the problem of classifying systems of cultivation is fairly difficult to resolve. Once again we are faced with indexes, criteria, typology and models. In spite of their unquestionably 'systematic' character, these systems do not coincide with other, more logical systems. For this reason agronomists and agricultural historians have suggested a great many typologies, using different indexes and criteria. Some – particularly in Germany – begin with the predominant element (woodland, pasture, ploughed land, fruit or vegetable cultivation) while not overlooking the dynamic aspect the system frequently adopts (for example, itinerant cultivation, or crop rotation and the burning of woodland, etc.). Others take a negative criterion: the extent of uncultivated terrain or of land left fallow. They draw a distinction between relatively discontinuous cultures and relatively continuous ones. Others base their classification upon the results of techniques; thus the famous agronomist Gasparin classed systems of cultivation into 'physical' (natural), 'androphysical' (a stable habitat, man's active intervention in nature, but with cultivation interrupted by fallowing) and 'androctic' (the increasing predominance of continuous cultivation and of techniques characterized above all by the contribution of independently produced fertilizers). One could even begin from a purely economic criterion (barter and the commercialization of products), from a purely technical one (the implements used), or from a purely quantitative evaluation (gross vegetable or animal product per unit of land or head of livestock).

Despite the rigorous character of these systems, a methodological problem remains, namely that of *type*. There is also the problem of the relation between historicity and structure. 'Systematicity' by no means eliminates the complexity of the facts. Moreover we should note that new techniques ('technical progress') do not always merely modify existing systems and structures. In many cases history proceeds by explosions, by sudden mutations which bring crises and dramas in their wake. Sometimes the leaders of a given society think they have achieved a definite equilibrium (as in the case of the average development of cereal cultivation from the eighteenth century up to the present day, which has been rationally managed). Sadly, modern techniques have purely and simply broken up the systems, the structures, the periodicities and the rhythms. Under favourable conditions (technical means and the amount of land available), freedom of initiative becomes such that nothing in nature stands in the way of options, choices and projects. Questions of profitability, yield, financial means, market, planning, tactics and strategy replace the old 'rhythms' imposed by the relations between man and nature. In this day and age, the ancient rhythms, cycles and regularities, all our ancestral representations of the cosmos and of human actions, are falling to pieces.

And yet, the old systems have not disappeared. They perpetuate themselves and carry on in a great many ways, not simply as survivals, but actively (unless one defines everything which is not the result of the latest techniques as survivals). Even in rural areas of the industrial countries, apart from regions where specialized cultivation has been developed using the most recent techniques (like the Corn Belt in the USA), we may observe many traces of ancient systems of cultivation. In so-called 'underdeveloped' regions and countries, they are in the majority. Nor have the corresponding representations disappeared, especially not those linked to cosmic cycles and rhythms. Doubtless their persistence is connected with other human phenomena, and these need to be studied.

What we have just said about agricultural systems could also be said *mutatis mutandis* of other systems. Relations of consanguinity have already been studied extensively, so let us leave them to one side. Instead we will look at musical systems. History reveals the existence of many musical systems (the segmentation of the sound continuum, scales, etc.), all of which are coherent. This characteristic – coherence – becomes conscious and predominant in the West during a rationalization which begins with the Greeks and reaches a peak in the eighteenth century. The system of tonality elaborated at that time is an integral part of a remarkable rationalization taking place in all areas and all relations. It truly is a system, with an ultimate logic (namely tonal harmony) which governs the other aspects of musical creation, song, the use of instruments and voices, and the rhythms and periodicities of repetitions of sounds and their combinations. From then on the system of tonality spills over into social life: popular songs and melodies obey the laws of tonality. Then we witness a twofold phenomenon, both sides of which are equally remarkable: the persistent echoes and revivals of archaic systems, and the shattering of all previous systems under the technical impetus of tonality.

These observations suggest a hypothesis (which in fact we have already formulated using other words, and which we have retained for further use). The system of tonality contains partial systems, which sometimes manifest themselves on a dual plane, that of aesthetics and that of day-to-day life (we do not consider songs to be external to everyday life; a symphony belongs to learned art, whereas a popular song is part of the dimension of the everyday and of the social which involves play, which is a dimension we are attempting to shed light on). These systems are remarkable for their coherence, even when this is obscured by everyday trivia; it is thanks to this coherence that they are able to go on surviving for so long, like the agricultural systems we can still observe in our own so-called 'under-developed' rural areas. In practice, these systems appear as vicious circles which emprison: A supposes B, which supposes C, which supposes A. How many times in our everyday lives do we hear the remark: 'It's just a vicious circle!' It is a characteristic of systems to be circular and cyclic, with periodicity and repetition. So what we are attempting is to make an inventory and a count of such partial systems: agricultural systems; logic and discourse in general, and the use of language; music, painting, and especially architecture, in so far as it enters into everyday life; links of consanguinity and relations; systems of ritual, gifts and barter; systems of signs, or semeiologies, in manners and dress, etc.

In one sense, the everyday is made up of such partial systems, juxtaposed without any rational links, and each with its own implications and consequences: temporality, rhythms, periodicity, recurrences and repetitions, specific works and symbolizations. These systems are distinct and disconnected. Some of them reproduce or prolong former dominant 'systems', such as agricultural systems or ceremonial systems for example. Most if not all are out of step with 'modern' techniques, which tend not only to reject them as anachronistic, but above all to dismember them. It will be our task to describe the remaining debris, which still retains visible traces of the vigorous structures which once supported it and are still legible within it.

Structuralism proceeds by privileging structure absolutely, and by absorbing within it the other terms we are considering, along with the relations they designate. Without admitting to do so, it substantifies it, presenting it as an essence and as something intelligible, thus acting as a belated marriage broker between Aristotelian ontology and a Platonism which dares not speak its name. Stability becomes both active and formal, the prototype and model for the real. In this way a certain elasticity or plasticity of structures, their inner contradictions, and the profound action of negation, i.e., of time, are marginalized.

The (relatively) permanent structures which 'succeed' after a period of time have survived the effects of time. They persist. But at the same time how can we suppose that during this same period certain structures (such as living species, social groups, patterns of behaviour and mental attitudes) have not disappeared, and perhaps in much larger numbers than the structures which have survived, either flourishing or impoverished? The negativity of time is at work. The gaps in our classifications are highly revealing and we cannot reduce the prehistory of life and mankind to a juxtaposition of biological and social fossils, like a display case of empty shells and pieces of bone. This hypothesis is impossible to ignore, that is, unless we confuse structuralism with a theological formalism. Following this line of enquiry, we discover chance not only in the inner combinations of structural elements, but externally in the way in which the combinations relate to the environment. If a given combination is relatively successful and permanent, this is not simply the result of its 'essence', its stability and its inner coherence. The secret of success is also to be found externally, in exchanges with nature, with other species and with other groups. However, sooner or later chance itself appears as necessary and determined, both in its elements and in the way they combine and 'succeed'. The inner coherence becomes clearly apparent when the other structures have been worn out or broken up, and have disappeared. It can also happen that coherent, and therefore stable, groups remain stagnant. As Hegel might have put it, we may measure their losses by the size of their winnings. And gambling is not entirely conscious or entirely unconscious; it leaves room for intelligence and stupidity, wisdom and madness. It would be possible to use these observations to draw up a schematic for a specific historicity and a sketch for a dramatic history which would leave room for rationality (including the rationality of numbers and of gambling).

If it is limited and delimited in this way, structuralism contains many truths. It has discovered a few. Moreover, we are not suggesting a conjuncturalism as an alternative doctrine to structuralism. By giving it a place and a part to play, we are not lapsing into eclecticism. What we are trying to do is to place unilateralities in a progressive dialectization of concepts. The preceding arguments confirm views we have already formulated. We accept the idea of structure, but in a limited way. What we say is: if the value of structures is exaggerated, the idea itself is compromised. (In a nutshell: 'structuralism versus structure'.) Despite its efforts to the contrary, pure structuralism loses touch with historicity and with social realities in all their diversity. Its favourite areas are to be found in archaic groups and survivals. It cannot cope with *processes* like the historical modalities of a process of becoming which smashes through obstacles. From our way of thinking, purely structuralist method (if indeed the words have any meaning) cannot tackle the problems of the modern world. Just like empiricism, it tends to exclude dialectical thought (although it does not succeed in so doing). By exaggerating the importance of stabilities, it also tends to reject the concept of alienation (including its extreme form: reification). It reifies actions and works precisely because it does not have a precise idea of what alienation and reification are. The structuralist school ratifies certain unfortunate consequences of the extreme division of labour in social practice and in knowledge. By separating them and then identifying them, it crystallizes and congeals them.[27]

We will continue to employ the methodological concept of *the model* by setting out precisely what its attributes and properties are:

a) It refines certain characteristics of the concept in general, and of conceptual elaboration or conceptualization. By summing up an experimental and practical given, the classic concept turned too much towards the past, and also towards the simple. The *model* is a more flexible tool, capable of exploring the complex and the random. With it, thought becomes 'propositional' in a new way: programmatic. However, if the 'model' refines the concept, it cannot dispense with it. It presupposes a conceptual elaboration.

b) Like the concept, the model is a scientific abstraction and a level of abstraction. It is always revisable, and cannot be taken either as a reality or entity immanent to the real beneath the appearances of phenomena (the ontological temptation, which structuralism finds hard to avoid), or as a norm or value (the normative temptation). The methodology of models forbids their fetishization.

c) The model is constructed in order to confront 'reality' (experience and practice). It is useful, not least because it helps us to appreciate the gap between itself and the facts, between the abstract and the concrete, between what has been certified and what is still possible. The model is useful: it is a working implement for knowledge. Only the concept has the dignity of knowing.

d) As far as a set of facts is concerned, there can be no question of a single model. If we are to grasp the actual and the possible, we must construct several models. The confrontation between these will be as interesting theoretically as the confrontation between one of them and the concrete element it represents. In this way diversity and discussion during the process of knowledge take on added value. No one model can be sufficient or pretend to be sufficient by bringing research to a halt. So we are faced with two alternatives: ontology or criticism, dogmatism or empiricism (or pure relativism).

e) The concept of the *model* also helps to refine the concept of hypothesis. Every model encompasses a hypothesis (in the broadest sense, theoretical or strategic). Every hypothesis concludes by constructing a model, which is the halfway stage between inventing the hypothesis and proving it. So the model assumes the qualities of hypothesis: provability, creativity. As Politzer said, it should enable us to move from philosophical luxury to the economy of philosophy, by separating the hypothesis out from speculation.

f) Because it must prove its creativity, the model must have an operating or operational character. However, this trait must not be fetishized. The operating techniques linked to a particular model must be examined with care and suspicion. Fetishization of this characteristic, which blows it up out of all proportion, is the feature of a certain well-defined ideology, namely technocratism. The operational model becomes the practical and theoretical property of a bureaucracy and a technocracy. This brings us back to the most disturbing aspect of structuralism. The fetishization of the concept of the 'model' is part of the strategy of the social group of technocrats.

In the pages which follow, we will construct and propose two models of everyday life in society as a whole: a model of needs and a model of communications.

3

The Specific Categories

1 The concept of totality

In the preceding chapters our examination of the formal tools (the intellectual implements) of the social sciences has led us time and time again towards concrete investigations about our object of study: everyday life. Now, in this inventory of the specific categories which this contact with the concrete has helped us to elaborate, we will sometimes find ourselves obliged to look back once more towards the formal. There can be nothing surprising about this. Surely that is what dialectical movement in thought is. We study specific categories and concepts in order to determine their relative importance and the limited spheres in which we may apply them. The specific does not preclude the formal, and the particular does not preclude the general. Overall we must have a precise and flexible set of mental tools at our disposal.

We cannot do without the concept of *totality*. When we are dealing with human reality, both theory and practice encompass a conception of totality (i.e., of society and mankind), implicitly or explicitly. Without this concept, there can be no frame of reference; no generality, and even more, no universality. Without it, knowledge itself ceases to have a 'structure'. It becomes scattered into fragmented studies which replicate exactly the division of social labour instead of controlling it and understanding it. In the best cases this is no more than the equivalent of a hypercritical self-destructive attitude (since the universal reappears with different names, and often dogmatically: globality, nihilism or postnihilism, culture, civilization, etc.). In less favourable cases the fragmented studies and disciplines dissolve into myriad isolated, empirical facts. In the final analysis, there is no longer any obstacle for thought to struggle with. That temporary barrier and limit to analysis, the real, has been removed. Thought has been engulfed and buried under a mass of facts which, to add insult to injury, it respects and sanctions. It no longer has a criterion or a hierarchy of facts and concepts; it no longer investigates the essential (because the essential is no more!). The very idea of knowledge as totality – as concrete universality – becomes blurred and disappears. For an empiricism without concepts, one fact is as good as another. When we try to particularize knowledge, we destroy it from within. The 'concrete' we have sought for so long eludes us. The hyperconcrete is as abstract as any other philosophical generality.

Over and beyond the methodological use of totality, we must also consider its practical use. Without an (illusory) representation or a (true) knowledge of social totality, without a participation in the social totality (an illusory or true *participation* – but the latter is preferable to the former!) in social totality, no specific group has any status or certainty. It feels it has no place. It lacks self-confidence in its own vitality. Its everyday experience breaks down into interindividual, socially contingent relations. As a result it has no confidence in its leaders, i.e., those of its members who enable it to face up to the future and who hold its strategy in their hands.

This highlights an aspect of democracy. Without the effective and well-founded (genuine) participation of citizens in totality, there can be no political democracy. In democracy, partial groups are forever confronting each other; each has its tactic and its strategy. Nevertheless they are participating in a totality which their confrontations and rivalries ('non-antagonistic conflicts', to use a widespread but rather vague formula) do not destroy. If there is no insistence upon totality, theory and practice accept the 'real' just as it is, and 'things' just as they are: fragmentary, divided and disconnected. Activities, and therefore individuals, become 'reified' like things, and, just like things, are separated one from the other. This insistence upon totality is nothing more than another aspect of the participation we mentioned above.

Without the concept of 'totality', how can we possibly formulate, or even conceive of one of the principal laws of social and human development? This is that law: once it has taken a definite shape in social practice, each human activity wants the universal. It aspires to universality. It wants to be total. It tends effectively towards totality. Therefore it comes into confrontation with other activities. In its quest for totality, it tries to make them its subordinates. It invents tactics and strategies. It makes itself real through *works*, and each work is the result of a momentary totalization through the predominance of a particular activity (aesthetic, juridical or legal, scientific, philosophical, even poetic, or through games, etc.) and consequently of a particular representation or tendency. Therefore, during this bitter struggle, each activity achieves a totalization of which it is the generative nucleus and the effective element. It is precisely in this way that it shows itself to be partial. Limits become apparent. The moment it becomes totalized is also the moment when its immanent failure is revealed. The structure contains within itself the seeds of its own negation: the beginning of destructuring. Achievement is the harbinger of its withering away, it announces it and provokes it. Totalization imposes doubt, collapse and disintegration. Every trial must be carried out, every hypothesis must be hazarded, every attempt at totalization must be put to the test before the irreducible residual deposit – the everyday – can claim its demands, its status and its dignity, before we can consider raising it to the level of totality, through a process of conscious metamorphosis . . .

What activities are we talking about? Religious representations and religion in general, which once aspired to universality and which compromised themselves in their struggle for control. Philosophy, which criticized religion and sought to supplant it, creating its own representations and concepts, but coming to grief as an absolute system. Science in general, which translated its ambitions and pretensions into scientism and technicism, thus demonstrating its own limits. Each particular science, and notably history, psychology and sociology, took turns in inventing totalizing hypotheses and 'structuring' representations. Political economy takes the human and reduces it to the status of a tool for production. The state, that coercive power, aspires to universality in a way which is apparent today on a world-wide scale. Finally art and culture produce aestheticism and culturalism.[1]

It seems to us that this conception of fragmentary totalities (each one of which empties itself of human reality after having sought to occupy that reality completely and in fact after having effectively contained and enriched it) does account for one aspect of history. On a vast scale – that of *Weltgeschichte*, world historicity – it makes the concept of *alienation* concrete. Each activity which creates representations shows itself to be both productive and alienating: productive at first, then alienating, as much for itself as in its efforts to absorb other representations or to exterminate them using a pseudo-critique which slips very easily into terror and violence. At their birth, many of the major works of culture and civilization could be characterized – in their structuration and inner balance – by the predominance of one representation which does not destroy the others, but which subordinates them. Works are determined by the hierarchy of all their elements, the result of an effort and a creative struggle, rather than by the fact that they may belong to a discrete and circumscribed domain such as religion (and the history of religion), philosophy (and the history of philosophy), or knowledge (and the history of knowledge), etc. From this perspective religion, philosophy, art and knowledge appear as *types* of works rather than as domains or regions. Works are linked to a typology which already possesses its own vocabulary. Each undertaking is an endeavour based upon a hypothesis. This hypothesis is not represented as such, but is presented as a truth, which, with the general backing of a group, one man tries to bring into language, and then to the absolute. No matter how close it gets to success, every endeavour is destined to fail in the end. Every endeavour is an attempt to realize mankind and its goals by determining them, i.e., by creating them. Every endeavour is an attempt to disalienate mankind and its goals by realizing them in a total work. Until such time as everyday life becomes the essential work of a praxis which has at last become conscious, every endeavour will lead to a new alienation.

With the dialectical movements of 'alienation/disalienation/new alienation' and the 'realization/fragmentary totalization/breaking of totality'; the concept of negativity gains fresh impetus. Every totalization which aspires to achieve totality collapses, but only after it has been explicit about what it considers its inherent virtualities to be. When it makes the illusory, outrageous and self-totalizing claim that it is a *world* on the human (and thus finite) scale, the negative

477

(limitation, finiteness) this 'world' has always borne within itself begins eating it away, refuting it, dismantling it, and finally brings it tumbling down. Only when a totality has been achieved does it become apparent that it is not a totality at all. Unlike those practical systems and structures which shatter, leaving their debris in the 'lived', these semi-fictitious, semi-concrete ideological worlds die slowly. With the occasional burst of energy, their death throes go on and on. Even as they wither away, they remain active. They have the prestige of having been achieved, the prestige of perfection. They are great works.

This schematic, which we have presented as a sort of world law (of the relation of the finite to the non-finite or of totality to elements), originates in philosophy. Hegel applied it, but incompletely, since on his own admission his own system and the state eluded him. Originating in philosophy, our schematic contains a fundamental critique of philosophy. We are replacing the philosophical idea of an achieved totality and a complete system with the concept of *totalization*. In our view, philosophies were attempts on the part of philosophers to carry a representation (i.e., something which was as much an interpretation of the 'world' as it was of the real life of mankind) to the absolute. Taking their hypotheses from real life, they have attempted to transform them into a 'world'; they have tried to metamorphose everyday life by 'worldifying' this or that, in a semi-fictitious, semi-real way. They have proposed an abstract way of living, a project, a semi-Utopia, a more or less delirious wisdom, while artists were offering works of art: an immediately habitable 'world' for the senses and emotions to live in.

In his critique of Hegelianism, Marx turns the Hegelian conception of the process of becoming against philosophy, a theoretical system, and against the state, a practical system. For philosophy, the process of *world becoming* is the law of the world and of the state; but philosophy or the state only become a 'world' by a process of supersession which comes when they wither away. Philosophy and the state were proclaimed to be 'worlds', while the real world – the everyday life of mankind – was left to one side beneath them. If philosophy and the state are to be part of the real world, if they are truly to become 'worlds' by summoning the real world up to the higher spheres whence they proclaimed themselves, they must die. This is the philosophical meaning of Marx's so-called philosophical writings. These have been called philosophical, but wrongly so, since they state that the death of philosophy is a necessity. It would be a creative death, a kind of battle, with all the pain a battle brings. World law decrees that all activities must end once their goal has been achieved and they have come full term, i.e., once they have reached their limits. In fact, Marx did not follow his thinking through to its conclusion. Just as Hegel exempted philosophical system, religion and the state from the law of the process of becoming (from the world law), Marx is reluctant to draw certain conclusions. In several texts he sometimes exempts art and the moral sphere from world law. He often accepts that when the economic, the political and their alienations come to an end they will be superseded by art, or by the realm of ethics. We do not wish to exempt art and the moral sphere from world law. The metamorphosis of the everyday demands that these ways of metamorphosing the everyday fictitiously must also wither away.

If Marxist thought since Marx has completely forgotten 'world law', if it is regressing (and with it philosophical thought in general) to system and to the fetishizing of politics and the state, there is all the more reason for us to get down to work again, and with renewed efforts. And so we are replacing philosophy with another form of investigation, which nevertheless contains and uses its concepts. We are aware of the theoretical experience of the last fifty years, and for this reason we say that the tenacious efforts of certain philosophers to maintain or revive philosophy have compromised it (in short: 'philosophism versus philosophy').

This theoretical experience demonstrates that the concept of *totality* has as many disadvantages as it has advantages. Without it, theoretical thought would be impossible. With it, theoretical thought risks losing itself in dogmatism. The idea of *totality* (or even of *totalization*) brings with it certain imperatives. Once put into place, it is in command. It demands *all* thought, *all* knowledge, *all* action. It directs knowledge; it orientates investigations and plans them. It tends towards immanent structure. It desires power. How can we conceive of totality if we do not share its point of view? Once it becomes dominant, the most general category tends to absorb particularities and specificities, and therefore to neglect differences and types. If I

479

conceive of the world, mankind and society on the basis of a broad and creative hypothesis, I subsequently verify my conception. With an inextricable mixture of good and bad consciousness, in bad faith or good, I tend to eliminate whatever does not fit in, whatever does not suit my purpose. After this, I start to develop arguments. I reject difficultly acquired partial knowledge for a superficial encyclopedism, which is all I need to crown my ontology. If there are any problems left, they are secondary ones. After I have found everything, i.e., the whole, even if I go on seeking I will find nothing. Once my totality is established, dogmatism is nigh. We are the whole, I am the whole. The total man belongs to us.

In *History and Class Consciousness*, Lukács wrote that 'The primacy of the category of totality is the bearer of the principle of revolution in science.'[2] This statement seems both true and false. It was true when Marxism was the only powerfully structured set of ideas at a time when the concerns of non-Marxist thinkers were completely fragmented. Since then, from the Marxist point of view, the dangers of this category have become apparent; as for the non-Marxists, they have adopted it. Structuralism and culturalism have taken the category up, and they have even turned it against Marxism. The former totalizes structure and enables it to absorb the other concepts and realities. The latter constructs a coherent whole, 'culture', using a variety of elements taken up from praxis: tools, implements, symbols, models, etc. It highlights their relations, and establishes a cultural totality. So Lukács's statement seems obsolete. We will subordinate the category of *totality* to that of *negativity* or dialectical negation, which strikes us as being more fundamental. What is more, we consider that the revolutionary principle is essentially critical (negative), and that today it applies more to everyday life than to knowledge in general or to society in general; this is our way of reintroducing science into praxis.

Today, methodologically speaking, the category of 'totality' plunges us into almost insurmountable difficulties. Are we *inside* a totality? Which one? Bourgeois society? Industrial society? Technological society? Society in transition (but to where)? How can we determine a totality *from inside*? In order to think of bourgeois society as a totality, Marx began by determining *what was possible* – socialism. He then turned back towards the real, seeing it in terms of the process of becoming, as a totality riven by inner contradictions and destined to be shattered by revolution in the near future. For us this process of thought is increasingly difficult to follow because, contrary to all expectations, capitalism has not been shattered under the pressure from the proletarian masses in the most capitalist countries, and equally because the very idea of socialism has become obscured by the way it has been put into practice. While we continue thinking along the lines of Marx's plan (from the possible to the real and from the real to the possible) we are not confident that it will help us to clarify the real and the possible which surround us. In any event, how could we validly determine a totality if we take up a position *outside* it, be it from this side or that? The recent concept of *signifying totality* aims to modernize the concept we are considering here. We have already pointed out how vague it is. For whom and by whom is the signification of the totality under consideration elaborated?

Consequently, in so far as it marginalizes the critical (negative) moment and has been handled in an ontological, normative and speculative manner, we are abandoning the category of *totality*. At the same time we are adopting it again, in a dynamic sense. We are dialecticizing it, on the one hand by introducing the concepts of *partial totality* and of *totalization*, and on the other by distinguishing between the *total* and the *universal* (the universal is thinkable in so far as it becomes created), but without separating them. If the will for totality remains an imperative in terms of theory, it is equally so in terms of practice (the demand for totality and for the supersession of scissions, divisions and dispersals). Without this initial option – the *will for totality* – there can be no action and no attempt to achieve knowledge. Without it, we accept whatever is empirically and frag-mentedly 'given', we accept a real which has been split into two and dichotomized; we ratify the social division of labour; we give our blessing to the analytic fragmentation of activities, functions, actions and gestures; we make the accepted '*thematizations*' and pseudo-worlds into laws, and we establish them as truths. In doing so, we are sanctioning separations.

Thus one initial act distinguished knowledge of social man and of praxis from the natural sciences: the will for totality. The mathematician, the physicist and the biologist can do without it (although no doubt it continues to be an implicit element of their research). In the

481

investigation of the human, this inaugural act – which aims to recapture a fragmented totality – is already total, or rather, totalizing. It has nothing to do with individual or individualist subjectivity. It implies a culture. It comprises a sensibility, a way of perception, an intellectual certainty, a *claim*, a movement of radical critique towards assertion and action. We see all this as part of the critique and the transformation of everyday life.

This initial act sets up a strategy. It is conceived within a strategy in which it plays a role and which contains complementary aims: to develop knowledge as an element of praxis, and to refuse to accept separations within praxis. In the name of this strategy, whoever exercises it will not be prepared to accept that knowledge is powerless, nor that those who possess knowledge should be conditioned, nor that the keys to knowledge should be surrendered into the hands of those who happen to be in power at any particular time. Moreover, their struggle is not against differences and diversities, but against pluralisms which beyond a certain point of affirmation split totality (for example: reformist and revolutionism; divisions in labour and the trade unions; the separation of the everyday and society as a whole with respect to immediate claims concerning the details and organization of practical life, and political claims concerning the state and social life as a whole, etc.).

Thus the idea of *totalization* is formulated not ontologically, but strategically, i.e., programmatically.

However, the 'bottleneck' which is hindering knowledge has still not been resolved. How can we avoid being trapped in a dilemma? Where do we start from, from the whole or from the parts? From the general, or from particularities? . . .

Would not the way out and the solution be to determine a *total phenomenon*, which would reveal a totality without granting it any theoretical or practical power, and without allowing it to be defined and controlled? To pass from phenomenon to essence is a speculative operation which leads to philosophism and ontology, and we must avoid it at all costs. We take the phenomenon as it is: a set of observations, i.e., of certified differences, which we link together without any ontological assumptions. Therefore, rather than having the wholeness of an 'essence' or a 'substance', the total phenomenon diversifies when scrutinized intellectually in terms of social practice. However, this diversification does not mean that it collapses into fragments. Thus it would open the way for dialectical reason, which is forever striving to reconstruct a whole from the differences and conflicts of its 'formants'.

In this way we have grasped a totality via aspects or 'formants', each of which is itself like an open or partial totality, so that nothing can be determined in isolation. But what should we call it? Man, or the human. Thus, using a process which is observable in praxis (and not simply in abstractions and theory), we will grasp a 'total human phenomenon' through its various determinations, each of which refers to the others. To put this another way, the aspects or formants of the total human phenomenon will constitute a theoretical structure; at the same time their practical relations and interactions will constitute the basis of a process of becoming and a historicity. Within this frame of reference we will observe active differences, relations and conflicts. By determining them we will be able to define historical and social particularities without assuming the supreme (and always illusory) power of capturing the universal and of exhausting 'being'.

We have already indicated what the initial dimension of the total human phenomenon is: need. Man is a being of need. He shares this fate with all living beings. It is only with human needs that man becomes human. In relation to nature, they are artificial, but they are the product of the process of human becoming. How does this happen, by what mediation and by what means? Labour. Other possible ways of specifying the relation of the human to the natural (culture, knowledge, etc.) presuppose that man has a certain power over nature, were it no more than an ability to detach himself from it. Therefore they imply labour; if we do not accept this mediation, then the arrival of man and his relation to nature are based on an ontology or a theology (the 'sudden appearance' or the 'abandonment' of man in nature). As well as being a mediation, labour is the second dimension. It has a reality of its own; taken simply as a concept it does not explain everything. This reality demands careful scrutiny; without that we will mistake it for an entity and not perceive it as a phenomenon and a set of relations. Labour characterizes social activity, with its conditions and attributes: tools, language, the (biological and social) division of labour, manufactured or consumed materials, formed and stabilized produce. If it is true that we find analogies with human labour in nature (such as hunting in groups, the work of the spider spinning its web or the bird building its nest), only man confers an existence of their own on the means and mediations between himself and nature: implements, materials, language, techniques, products and objects. If, at first, labour has the purpose of satisfying elementary and natural needs, it also contributes to their transformation. The needs of work and of the worker, the need to work and work as a need – these modify sensory activities, and even the sensory organs themselves. The 'human world' which is created in this way is composed as much of human bodies and their physiological activities as it is of the range of works, products, objects and goods. It has no precise limits; it excludes neither inert objects nor the obscure forces of nature: there is no frontier between the sector controlled by technology and labour and the uncontrolled sector. It is a vast, uncertain and highly populated region, the region of everyday life.

Once transformed, need becomes human and social need. But then the term 'need' is no longer appropriate. It is no longer adequate as a description of the real. It still evokes want. Now from one angle, once it becomes social, need becomes *capacity* and power. Man *is capable* of this or that action, creation or work in order to satisfy himself, or at least to try. The doors of what is possible begin to open. Although he has no alternative but to choose, and although society makes every effort to control his choices, it is always from the range of what is possible that the individual man will select them. On the other hand, once it has become individual, we call need *desire*, and it develops through controls, authorizations, inhibitions and possibilities. With acquired capacities and powers on the one hand, and the uncertainties of desire on the other, a dialectical movement is born, which fills everyday life.

As much as any other, and more, sexual need becomes modified and these modifications enable us to understand the others. It can be argued that it loses the characteristics of instinct and need, such is its attachment to symbols, images, rituals and ceremonies, i.e., forms which are external to nature. And yet it never manages to separate itself from sex per se, even in the wildest Platonic Utopias, even though it disrupts sex drastically (and not without damaging it), and metamorphoses it. The sexual act becomes a social act, and even the quintessential social act, in which an entire society recognizes itself, with all the orders and interdictions, the pressures and demands, the open possibilities and the closed ones. At the same time, the sexual act cannot be seen as one simple, coherent action; it is a microcosm with thousands of changing aspects. It crosses over disconnected areas: body and soul, spontaneity and culture, seriousness and games, covenants and challenges. The act of love between a man and a woman summarizes a society, and even in its clandestine and hidden aspects; but this is because it is consummated (lawfully or not) in secret, outside of that society. In a novel dialectical movement, *it is an extrasocial social act*. It is consummated in society and, if needs be, despite it and against it; and this is how and why it reflects society like a mirror. Hence its importance in the world of (aesthetic and ethical) expressivity. It is the most cultured of needs, the most refined of desires, with its social content which it supersedes in its search for the absolute, and yet it still plunges into the depths of nature, and into the profundities of dialectical contradiction.

Could need and labour be the two determinations of the total phenomenon we are seeking? Were we to reduce man to needs we would be forgetting the metamorphosis of need into power (and we use the word here not to mean power over things or over men, but the capacity to carry out determined activities at will). We would be guilty of overemphasizing the sordid side of life. We would be neglecting the important difference between *privation* (need which has become power, and the will to make demands) and *frustration* (need which has fallen back to the level of want, without hope of fulfilment), and this difference merits detailed examination. On the other hand, were we to define man by labour, we would be moving towards a fetishizing of productivity and the work ethic, or even regressing towards the archaic sanctification of craft and peasant labour. In short, we would be mutilating the human being by neglecting *pleasure*. Once need has become power and will, once it has been metamorphosed into desire, it demands pleasure, explicitly. Labour loses meaning and reality if it does not culminate in pleasure or open the way towards it: labour is social and collective; it is individual and interindividual power. Labour is indispensable if man is to *appropriate* nature, but pleasure alone makes this appropriation effective.

Three determinations, three 'formants', three dimensions: need, labour, pleasure. Each has its own reality; not one stands alone.

Without losing its own determination, each one refers to the other two, influencing and transforming them, and suffering the repercussions of this transformation. Thus we have a coherent triplicity, but in which the coherence – which is not without its contradictions and conflicts – does not result in immobility. So distinct are the three determinations that, in social practice and in history, they are allotted to different and even conflictual individuals and groups (classes). We observe the man of need (who is out of work), the man at work (who has few needs and little pleasure), and the man of pleasure (which does not mean that he achieves fulfilment). This lived unilaterality is unsatisfactory and it must not be transformed into representations, as is often the case; more exactly, every representation deriving from unilaterality must undergo radical critique; moreover, theoretical critique leads finally to practical critique. Those individuals and classes which demand pleasure pure and simple are doubly degraded: they are socially parasitic, and pleasure eludes and disappoints them. The worker whose life is devoid of pleasure and the glowing rewards it brings can only aspire to a dreary existence for which the work ethic is an inadequate reward. As for the man of pure want, if he is unable to grasp the lifeline of productive activity, he will rapidly relinquish all his humanity.

These many forms of alienation, privation and frustration, these voids and empty spaces, go hand in hand with large-scale conflicts and their innumerable ramifications.

The three dimensions are distinct, even disconnected, but they are nevertheless linked together and bring each other forth in an ascending spiral which crosses history and establishes man's historicity. We are speaking of a *spiral* here, and not a *circle*. When determinations fall outside one another they only do so relatively, momentarily and partially. And when they do so, the human will be mutilated in a manner which they imply and foreshadow, and which 'is' within them both virtually and actually. This certainly is a totality, but one perceived by the senses rather than by the mind. This human totality allows us to understand what constitutes the specificity of man compared to nature, from which he separates himself without detaching himself, and which he enters without discarding his artificialities.

In what way is this reality perceived by the senses? Could it be that without realizing it we have defined man's 'being', the universal, or have attempted to do so? Could we have elaborated an ontology, dressed up as an anthropology and a sociology? No. The totality we have defined does not purport to exhaust man's 'being', or to define it. It does not preclude other determinations and other dimensions, i.e., other degrees of freedom. On the contrary, it invokes them; it is a necessary and non-sufficient condition for them. It will be present in every human fact, on both the level of analysis and the level of reality, and will enable us to discover supplementary determinations. Moreover, it does not coincide with any one concrete observation (and for example it would be incorrect to identify the 'family life/professional activity/leisure' triple determination with the tridimensionality we have presented above!). Let us consider *play*. It springs from the depths of spontaneous living and natural activity: animals play games, and so do children. As an attribute of the human being, it does not coincide with any of the above-mentioned dimensions. Play is part of every human activity. In a sense life in its entirety is play: a risk, a game or match lost or won. From childhood onwards there is a need to play (and moreover want and privation themselves can be acted, simulated and disguised: in asceticism, and in privation which has been accepted in order to delay fulfilment or increase pleasure). Everything becomes a pretext for playing, even effort itself; serious games and work are often very similar. And so, the relations between play and pleasure are not easy to discern. If it is part of all activity, play soon relinquishes this ambiguous role and becomes distinct: it establishes itself as something separate; it adopts forms and rules; it becomes organized socially. It is impossible to imagine mankind without play activity, or society without underlying or manifest games. Could this therefore be a fourth dimension: human time joined to the three other spatial dimensions? Why not? But let us be careful. Let us avoid straying too far into the realm of paradox. But it is certainly rather surprising that it should be our era, the era of functionalism and technology, which has discovered *homo ludens*.

2 The idea of reality

This idea presents as many difficulties as the ideas we have already examined. The 'real'? It is the object and the objective of knowledge, the fulcrum of action. We reach out to it, we try to grasp it, either to observe it, or to transform it. The real demands realism. Is there anyone who does not want to be 'realistic', to be anchored in the real, to know it and to have a hold over it?

Sadly, those empiricists and positivists who merely want to observe it are frequently satisfied with small beer. Armed with their specialized techniques, they hunt down little facts. They discover a portion of reality, and the flimsier the observation, the narrower and more precise the comment they make; the more fragmented the fact itself is, the happier they are. The more realistic the realist is, the more blinkered he becomes. It is even worse when the philosopher defines the real in advance – philosophically – either as matter or as spirit. Taken per se, and fetishized, the idea of *reality* (even when adorned by adjectives such as 'concrete' or 'human') shrinks and shrivels. The real reveals its profundities to those who wish to penetrate it in order to transform it, and who attack it with determination, and a multiplicity of implements. But whoever wishes to transform the real has apparently lost touch with it. He is tendentious. What about objectivity? And why change the real rather than merely noting it down? In whose name and for what? To what end? For common sense, in day-to-day language, whoever wants to change the real is an 'idealist'. He sets out from an idea or an ideal.

Hegel has taught us that the real is more profound than existence or what can be seen to exist; would this profundity be metaphysical? Marx has taught us that there would be no knowledge (and no need to know anything) if the apparent and the essential coincided at the heart of the real, or if they were completely (metaphysically) separate. But if this is so, why are there so many appearances in the real? Why is there so much that is abstract in the concrete, and why are there so many forms in content? Why and how is the formal also concrete, and real? Sometimes the everyday appears to be the sole reality, the reality of realists, dense, weighty and solid. At other times it seems that its weight is artificial, that its denseness is insubstantial: unreality incarnate.

To dispel these obscurities, perhaps we need to clarify the terminology and to distinguish between the *actual* and the *real*, or again, between the *present* and the *real*. Maybe then it would be easier to link them together. In any event, we should certainly dialecticize the idea of 'reality'.

Let us begin by reintegrating the possible within the real. Usually a distinction is made between them – and quite rightly so – and then they are separated. The possible is seen as abstract and vague, while the real is seen as thick and weighty, as 'being' or 'existing'. But the possible enters the real. It appears there: it announces and invokes its presence within it, and then sets about destroying it and negating it. As for the real, it is a possibility which has been made effective or actualized. In one way or another, and regardless of what we imagine the link to be, we must conceive of a connection between the actual and the virtual, the potential and the possible. The actual and the virtual have a dialectical relation, even in the case of natural phenomena, but even more so in the case of human phenomena, where a consciousness of what is possible always intervenes. Human actions always define themselves as choices, as a means of access to what is possible and as an option between those various possibilities, regardless of whether the actions are individual or collective. Without possibility there can be no activity, no reality, unless it be the dead reality of things in isolation, which have a single possibility: to maintain themselves as they are. If we join the category of *possibility* to it – which, like the idea of totality and the idea of structure, is a philosophical legacy – the category of social and human *reality* can be retained. It becomes dialecticized. It continues to guarantee heightened objectivity to knowledge while avoiding superficial objectivism and illusively profound ontology. It eradicates a few false and insoluble problems, notably those which come as a result of the dissociation of fact and value, and of the real and the ideal. Why change the real? Because it does change, of necessity, and if knowledge begins with what is possible it can help to direct this change, and control it. The flat realism of the immediate strives desperately to prove how spacious it is. When it is dubbed 'materialism', its victory over an even more abstract and shrivelled-up idealism is an easy one.

We maintain that the possible demands a choice and an act, and therefore demands a yes-or-no answer. Given the 'real' with its problems (its contradictions) and the solutions proposed, sooner or later we decide unequivocally for one particular solution, and act accordingly. This is why an option involves a strategy and a series of options which amount to a series of bifurcations and disjunctions. Decisions have their logic, their mathematics and their calculus.

These calculations revolve around the 'possible/real' relation, in so far as it produces a form which, despite its formal character, is part of the real. However, this statement itself runs the danger of provoking a theoretical illusion: that of the superfluity of the formal. When dealing with possibilities per se, and with the coming forth of virtualities, we cannot answer the questions they pose by a yes or a no. Possibilities, i.e., solutions to problems, are discovered and invented; contradictions within the real are themselves heightened, or are evaded. It is a history, a dialectical process of becoming. Practical action itself differs from (mathematically) formalizable series and frequencies in the following way: the stake is constantly changing, and the goal becomes modified as do the number of players. Will-power makes what is initially impossible possible, while modifying both the means and the ends. Action does not transcend calculation and form: it encompasses them by superseding them. Quantitative or qualitative (ordinal) mathematics cannot grasp the 'real' completely. However, we do not know in advance exactly what it is that eludes them. Only the philosopher believes he can draw boundaries and demarcation lines. So the new mathematical implements enable us to perceive the human 'real' more effectively, and to penetrate it. But they do not exhaust it. It is in the everyday and its ambiguous depths that possibilities are born and the present lives out its relation with the future.

Is this a reason for replacing formal logic (which is binary: true or false, inclusion and exclusion, opposition, contrariness, etc.) by a logic with more than two valencies, three for example: the true, the false and the random (or the possible)? In our opinion, no. Decision logic justifies the old formal logic, and extends it. To choose is to exclude all the possibilities except one. To opt is to act so that the impossible becomes possible, and so that things which are possible become impossible. This implies a logical 'possible/impossible' relation subordinate to a deeper dialectical relation. Logic, which is the concrete form of a set of questions which are answered by yes or no, occupies a certain level. Consequently, this level must be that of games and strategy theory, of operational research and of information theory. Dialectical reason occupies another level, which encompasses the former. This relation (which is not always easy to grasp) is part of the 'real'.

Once it has been fetishized, the category of 'reality' has enormous disadvantages. It destroys specificities and differences. Under the umbrella of this concept, and with the misuse of the epithet 'concrete', the human real is considered to be on a par with nature, or the real of nature is considered to be on a par with the human real. Confusions are created, fodder for philosophical overindulgence. By dialecticizing the concept we can begin to answer questions about the *reality of consciousness*.

Consciousness does not appear to be 'real' in the way a substance or a thing is, nor does it appear 'unreal', like a reflection or an epiphenomenon, the accidental substitute for something else. Social consciousnesses are born, grow, wither away and die like individual consciousnesses do (and from which they cannot be separated). Social existence and consciousness (like every existence and every consciousness) have something *transitional* about them. They come into being and go towards something else or other than themselves. Every consciousness lights up or switches off, becomes transformed or stays the same (never for long, even when it is embodied in a work). It is born of a problem, when what has been accomplished – the 'real' in its narrow sense – has become inadequate. In this sense, it negates the 'real' concretely and specifically. It is born along with a possibility arising from the practical question the possible asks of the real, and vice versa. An appearance or an apparition, it changes itself into action, i.e., into 'reality', in so far as it resolves the problem posed. Therefore one of its conditions is the undermining of the 'reality' which has already been accomplished and structured. In the solidity and substantiality of a self-sufficient, self-satisfied 'real', consciousness falls to sleep. It 'is', and consequently it is no longer consciousness. We do not say, 'All consciousness is consciousness of something', but, 'All consciousness is consciousness of a possibility'; this is what gives it its acuity, its good luck and its misfortune. Without possibility there can be no consciousness, and what is more, no life. Presence implies what is possible in the present, and for the present; the future is an indispensable horizon and guiding light. Consciousness can never be at home in the real, in anything which has been stabilized or satisfied; and yet it seeks the real, or rather realization, as well as stability, and satisfaction.

Consciousness is born of problems, contradictions and conflicts, of options and choices which are both necessary and free. One must choose between various possibilities: that is what is necessary. One must take risks, wager on randomness and gamble: that is what is free. Thus consciousness presents itself as a specific 'reality', but not given, and not unmediated. Self-consciousness is born in the other, of the other and by the other. It 'is', and yet it is not. It 'is' action and relation, and not substance; it 'is' the confrontation between the consequences of problems, the demand for solutions, clarity of expectation, perspective and choice between possibilities (and impossibilities). It is born in action and action brings it into being. It is born in works, and works bring it forth. It is productive, it is self-productive; it resolves the problems embedded in what it creates. It is its own work, and yet it escapes as soon as that work is accomplished. It negates and it supersedes, but cannot be defined as absolute negativity alone.

Fully real in its way (but not like a 'region' which could be described separately from the 'real'), consciousness has necessary and non-sufficient conditions in other realities, whether they be biological and physiological, or economic and historical. It cannot be reduced to these 'real' conditions. As soon as we mould the idea of reality around any thing which has substance, we become trapped in a dilemma. Either consciousness eludes the category of 'reality', something caricatured in those theories which derealize it and reduce it to pure reflection, or to pure negativity; or else it conceives of itself as a thing which has substance and which segments into (historical, psychological or sociological) processes or into (individual or collective) states and representations.

We have already criticized and rejected several confusions, notably the confusion between 'reality' and 'structure'. There is another which is no less frequent, and just as dangerous for knowledge: the confusion between *function* and *reality*. Function is seen as the criterion of reality, biologically and socially speaking. According to a certain neo-Hegelianism which is as widespread as it is unaware of its origins, one of the philosopher's famous statements could be transcribed in the following way: 'Everything which is functional is real, everything real has a function.' Rationality and functionality are seen to coincide. Function would create reality (including the sensory object with a 'reality' that would apparently bring functions into play which would vary according to the culture and the civilization involved).

These formulations define a *functionalism*, a corollary of structuralism and of various realisms in contemporary thought. Functionalism decrees a rational balance and harmony between nature, culture, and society considered as a whole. It postulates a situation whereby, in itself and by itself, representations are completely aligned to actions, and what is real is completely aligned to what is true. For a functionalist sociologist, if something does not have a function it cannot exist. At the very most it can be seen as an offshoot of a real function. Families have functions. The working class has functions. Bureaucracy has functions (especially because it is mainly composed of 'functionaries'). As for the state, it obviously possesses many functions, by definition. In other words, functionalism eliminates critical thought. According to this criterion, since anything without a function is superfluous, it must disappear. Of what use is everyday life? What is its function? It has none. If we cannot suppress this regrettable residue, at least let us cast it aside. How easy it is to pass from observations to diktats, and from ontology to the normative. And how quickly doctrinaire functionalism brings a functionalist ethic and even a functionalist aesthetic in its wake.

Critique of functionalism has important implications for what we are talking about. The new towns have demonstrated the undoubted merits and the even more undoubted shortcomings of functionalism when it tries to create the framework and conditions for an everyday life. The errors and illusions of the doctrine can be grasped in action, in the work itself. Moreover, it is a question of a general tendency, linked to the importance of technicians and to the formation of a technocratic ideology in every present-day society. Like anyone who possesses a skill and who exercises a fragmented activity, the technician has a function in an overall unit. The technocrat oversees this unit, organizing its functions and supervising them. Therefore there is a link between integral functionalism and ideological and practical technocracy.

The idea of 'function' derives from several sciences and also from social practice. As far as mathematics is concerned, it seems possible to rationalize and formalize the functional completely; it can be analysed into variables and reconstituted in objective processes. As far as biology and physiology are concerned, they give the functional a kind of life-giving promotion. We are no longer dealing with abstract trajectories or units, but with organisms and organic totalities. So we can add the representation of utility, and of an indispensable system within an organism, to that of mathematical necessity and rigour. At the heart of every living and coherent entity, every part which is not the result of a destructive analysis of the whole and which maintains its integrality in the face of attacks from a relatively hostile 'environment' – in other words, every 'real' part – corresponds to a function and to an organ. From then on it seems impossible to dissociate function from organ and function from structure. Theoreticians may have rejected a certain simplistic organicism, but this has not led to a heightened critique of the concept of function. In so far as a society constitutes a whole and possesses a specific life, could it not be seen as a sum total, or a synthesis, or a totality of 'functions'?

This representation contains elements of truth and elements of error, and the latter predominate once the representation becomes systematized. Critical analysis discovers a mixture of fetishized determinism and of finalism, as well as an underlying tautology. Given what it is, an organism is made up of organs. Each organ perpetuates itself by acting upon the others and consequently by directing its own activity back upon itself. By definition, every organ perpetuates itself by 'functioning'. Thus every organ has more or less complex self-regulations (such as feedbacks, scannings and homeostases, to use the vocabulary of the cyberneticists who have helped to elaborate these concepts). The idea of self-regulation helps us to clarify the idea of 'function'. We imagine an organism to be a self-regulating ensemble composed of functional self-regulations which perpetuate both themselves and the organism. Thus, while changing, it maintains a stability and could be said to possess its own inner logic. This does not rule out chance or disorder, and so consequently it can become disrupted. Every self-regulation has its limits. The connections between partial self-regulations seem vague. A living organism is flexible because it is vulnerable. Complete adaptation would lead to lethargy and stagnation as surely as complete inadaptation would bring about its demise. So how can we know whether better results might not have been obtained with other adaptations or inadaptations, or other combinations of organs and functions? Perhaps a function is nothing more than a successful mistake, a non-functional element which has changed (since the conditions themselves have changed), or the result of a stroke of good luck. Today's dysfunction could be tomorrow's function. Functionalist finalism evades the issue; it is untenable.

Our objective conditions change and we change our conditions. If our consciousness can lag excessively behind these conditions, surely our body can too. The optimum would seem to be a halfway house between adaptation (indispensable but sterilizing) and maladaptation (creative, stimulating, but deadly). Exactly what is the relation between modern man and contemporary society, and the conditions they have created? How can we distinguish between the functional and the non-functional? At this point we would tend to argue that 'modern' man and society cannot go on neglecting everyday life and leaving it behind for much longer, and that its non-functionality will be transformed into supra-functionality. And perhaps this is one of those rare predictions one can make about the future without too much danger of getting it wrong.

It is quite amusing to observe the antics some highly intelligent, hyper-realistic and clear-thinking social scientists get up to in order to save functionalism. They cannot avoid admitting dysfunctions, and so surely they must accept 'survivals' or 'time lags'. This would add even more fuel to the argument against integral functionalism.[3] The dialectical trick (if we may call it that) is to absorb and resorb dysfunction within the functional by maintaining that dysfunction is the condition and inevitable reverse side of any function. When Merton looks at political bosses in American towns he finds they have many 'functions', including the function of attending to specific interests – the needs of their constituencies, or of the poor and the marginalized. The only means available to these wretched people is to exercise their civil rights by speaking to the local boss to obtain a few favours. In short, via its own 'dysfunctions', the political and bureaucratic machinery of American democracy can get its hands on something which might have eluded it: everyday life. It is true that the 'apparatus' and the 'machine' stifle news which might offer any encouragement. In doing so, they hinder communications, paralyse consciousness and society, and forbid any active criticism (not to mention a few other little irritants, such as gangs and rackets). Who cares? And this is the way the functional penetrates into the very heart of the everyday, absorbing it and integrating it into society as a whole.

Merton's realist and functionalist arguments are flawless. Why criticize 'dysfunctions'? Perhaps they fill in gaps in reality, albeit badly. Why consider them as symptoms of its deficiencies? Why use them to make a critique of the 'real'? One might just as well list the functions of the liver, and then complain because it is prone to illness, exclaiming: 'Ah! If only we didn't have livers!' To put it another way, social functionalism is not without its paradoxes. These highlight the disturbing side of the doctrine. Functionalism and 'integrationalism' make ready bedfellows. In society, as in a living body, the highest functions are probably the ones which exercise control and integration from above. The ideal kind of control and integration would leave no room for the unforeseen, the marginal or the 'deviant'. It would know how to predict randomness and to absorb it per se. Finally, the real and the rational would coincide in a social truth, that is unless the dysfunctions did not intervene to bring a little disorder and creative dissymmetry into all this well-established and well-controlled order. What an unexpected stroke of luck that would be!

The amusing thing is that this functional realism avoids philosophical generalities and is unaware of its own reactionary neo-Hegelianism.[4] It derives from the same radical critique: the real encompasses the movement which negates it, providing it is grasped in all its profundity. The actual comprises the possible and the negative operates within it. The real is the ephemeral and superficial side of reality ('existence'); it hides the deeper forces. 'That the rational is real is contradicted by the irrational reality which at every point shows itself to be the opposite of what it asserts, and to assert the opposite of what it is.'[5] This fully reinstates Marxist thought and method. It is not because we want to change it that the 'real' – the everyday – eludes us. We are not setting out from another reality external to the reality we are studying. We are setting out from its inner movement, and from what is possible. Then and only then can we grasp it and know it completely.

Biologically or socially speaking, could play have a function? In our opinion, it is impossible to answer this question by yes or no. In nature, since animals play games, it would appear to correspond to the need to get rid of excess energy, to an almost pure spontaneity, free from the pressures of the immediate 'environment' (which is not to say that it is undetermined and unregulated). Could we say that play is basically useless? No. It is practice for activities; it anticipates and prepares for practical situations, or presents them as potential risks and difficulties, in a diluted form. So it is useful, very much so, and perhaps the more 'useless' it appears the more useful it really is. It is useful because it is redundant, in that it owes itself to a redundancy of vital energy, implying the relief of elementary needs and functional requirements: hunger, thirst, fatigue.

In social life, play has a use. What is it? Relaxation and entertainment, yes, but more than that, it is rediscovered spontaneity, and even more, it is activity which is not subjected to the division of labour and the social hierarchies. At first sight, humanly and socially speaking, play seems to be a minor, marginal activity, sidelined and tolerated by the important functions of industrial society. Compared with the reality of practical life and the truth of representations, it seems to be an illusion, a lie, something phoney. On closer scrutiny, the reverse is true. Play recalls forgotten depths and summons them up to the light of day. By making them stay within the everyday, it encompasses art and many other things as well. It uses appearances and illusions which – for one marvellous moment – become more real than the real. And with play another reality is born, not a separate one, but one which is 'lived' in the everyday, alongside the functional. It may seem that we are regurgitating the old apology for the *acte gratuit*, but no. We are protesting against the loss of grace and gracefulness. Play is a lavish provider of presence and presences.

One can do without it. Austerity has no time for it and social order is afraid of it. Integral functionalism tries to eliminate it (as is so clearly demonstrated in the new towns and housing estates!). And this is one of the paradoxes we must highlight. For surely it was a dialectical movement within integral functionalism itself which gave rise to the study and the rehabilitation of games, at a time when 'industrial' and 'technological' society was at full throttle.[6] It could be that poetry and fiction are part of the same protest against the functional, in that they liberate a need for something marvellous, fantastic and even freakish.

Functionalism finds play hard to tolerate, because the territory it occupies cannot be defined in advance. It is a domain without limits, like that of (free) critical thought or of art (when it is truly free), which can and must appropriate matters which do not concern them from the point of view of social integration and the functional. Everything becomes play, in the theatre and in acting for example, including the most important matters and the most dramatic circumstances. Everything should be able to become a game, in the conscious simulation of tactics and strategies, in light-hearted imitation (and *homo ludens* has a host of tricks and dodges we will not mention to help him get involved in serious matters and to see them *sub specie ludis*). Games use many ancient magic, cosmic, religious and technical objects which formerly were important and serious, but they also provide a practical method for stripping anything too serious of its overimposing gravitas, and thus of its power, reducing it to the everyday by not allowing it to set up home above everyday life.

Did cathedrals have a use? Yes, and in many ways: a cathedral was a muster station in serious circumstances and a meeting place for ceremonies; it was a symbol of the community, of the medieval town and its territory; it was a politico-religious centre. Were they built functionally? No. Over and above their functions, they *presented* an image of the world and a summary of life according to a certain vision of the world and of life. The builders started from this symbolic representation (which was obsolete in itself, but vigorously spontaneous as far as they were concerned), endowing it with richness and embellishments, which are the attributes of spontaneity. Going beyond mere social function, they metamorphosed spontaneity into style. But then, through style and symbolisms, the cathedral became a monument which was always *present* in the town, active not only at exceptional moments, but also at the heart of the everyday.

Thus critique of functionalism leads us to new ideas. In the first place, the mechanisms of self-regulation in society are inadequate. Their balancing and 'structuring' mechanisms are always precarious. On the level of society as a whole, mechanisms are replaced by *representations*. The mechanisms for correcting imbalances are active on various important levels, but never on comprehensive or total ones. On the economic level, for example.[7] We can use the words 'function' and 'functionality' to qualify them, i.e., as processes operating through a kind of semi-awareness or even lack of awareness on the part of those who contribute to them. On the level of the state, of strategies and of society as a whole, functions are entrusted to 'apparatuses' which act by means of representations: ideologies. What is more, symbolisms introduced from elsewhere can prove very effective. Representations (ideologies) and symbols are passed off both as truths and as realities. Like symbolisms, the 'apparatuses' (which are constructed on the level of society as a whole, i.e., of the state and of political strategy) are redirected towards the everyday, grasping it in all its dereliction, and integrating it. In this way the highest level returns to the lowest (which does not stop the 'lowest' eluding it). Functionalism is itself a representation and an ideology, which consciously aims at exerting control and integration in conditions which are ipso facto given, accepted and recognized.

In the second place, we have highlighted the concept of 'polyfunctionality' and, more importantly, the concept of 'transfunctionality'. Certain 'realities' have several functions in social practice, towns for example (a place of everyday life, rest, family life, non-professional relations, neighbourhoods, etc.). After separating them analytically, functionalism projects them on the ground, and the result is a parody of 'reality', even though all the elements of the 'reality' are there (and even though, by its interest in the elements of the 'real', functionalism is in advance of those theories which ignore them, voluntarily or not). With functionalism, analytic understanding takes its labours to the bitter end, and at the same time goes to the bitter end of the social division of labour. It 'institutionalizes' the results, and there they are on the ground in the new towns, implacably 'real', inert and lifeless.

What would life be like for an organism which exercised the functions of each of its organs simultaneously and in isolation? What would our lives be like if – and the idea is horrendous – we had to use our consciousness and our hands to control the functions of our stomachs, our hearts, our livers or our kidneys? Functionalism leads to a dead end, the kind of false world nightmares are made of.

The multifunctional exists, and so does the transfunctional. By the latter term we mean whatever we cannot reply to by 'yes' or by 'no' when asked the question: 'Is that useful?' Play, for example, is transfunctional, and so is art, or the work of art, because they contain a play-generating 'yeast' (which does not exhaust them and which they do not exhaust). More generally still, what distinguishes a work from a *thing*, an *object* or a *product*? An inert thing (a pebble, a piece of wood) has no function, a product has at least one, and an object has several (for example, a chair, which helps me to do my job, to rest, to have a chat . . .). As for works, they are transfunctional; they have many uses, which they supersede.

Whether it is functional or not, an ornament – tolerated by functionalism as long as it remains ornamental – is a sorry caricature of the work of art. Whether it is durable or not, the transfunctional is a work. Play is momentary transfunctionality which consists of its own unfolding: the ephemeral work of an individual or several individuals, successful or not, perfect or not, marvellous or not. A town is durable transfunctionality. Brought off or botched, it is the work of a social group and of an overall society. Towns were no more than the vaguely conscious or even 'misconscious' work of everyday life. They must become a fully conscious *work*, with the purpose not of 'integrating' an everyday which has been cast aside at the lowest of levels, but of metamorphosing the everyday into a work, on the highest level the level of art and of freedom. Then, as social man nears a goal which today is Utopian (and consciously postulated as such), the everyday and the whole will be works which cannot be dissociated, and the real will no longer be split up into the 'real' and the 'true', in other words into 'true' versus 'false'.

3 Alienation

Since it was taken up again some thirty years ago, the idea of alienation has been studied many times. There would certainly be every reason to write an in-depth history of it. This history would allow us to resolve the following theoretical problem: 'The idea of alienation is a legacy of philosophy, and perhaps its essential patrimony. In what ways can we use it as an analytic implement to help us understand the modern world? In what ways does it introduce philosophy into the social sciences?' For the time being we will tackle the problem per se, rapidly and succinctly, without becoming waylaid by historical considerations.

Our first observation is that the way the idea is generally used seems quite clear: 'man' is alienated, torn from his self and changed into a thing, along with his freedom. However, at the same time, there is something vague about this. Too often alienation has been seen as a single unit and as an entity: the alienation of man. In fact, there are many alienations, and they take many forms. Too often 'disalienation' has been taken as an absolute, and as the end of alienation in general. In Marx's so-called philosophical thought, the alienation which Hegel presented speculatively becomes a historical fact. So does its disappearance. However (although we find many indications that his thought also moved in the opposite direction) Marx tended to push the many forms of alienation to one side so as to give it one specific definition in terms of the extreme case he chose to study: the transformation of man's *activities* and relations into *things* by the action of economic *fetishes*, such as money, commodities and capital. Reduced to economic alienation within and by capitalism, alienation would disappear completely and in one blow, through a historical but unique act: the revolutionary action of the proletariat. In this historical and revolutionary perspective, there remained something of the philosophical absolute from which it derived, in spite of Marx's critique of Hegelian philosophy and of philosophy in general.

Before we apply the idea of alienation to the social sciences and especially to critical study of everyday life, we feel we need to formulate several propositions. We have put these propositions (which are somewhat more than hypotheses and somewhat less than established truths) to the test during our research.

First proposition. We must particularize, 'historicize' and relativize the concept of alienation completely. To put this another way, alienation is only conceivable and determinable within a (social) frame of reference, and in relation to a whole which is both real and conceptual. Therefore absolute alienation and absolute disalienation are equally inconceivable. Real alienation can be thought of and determined only in terms of a possible disalienation. Conversely, disalienation can be thought of and determined only in terms of a complete alienation or of another possible alienation. Alienation is not a 'state', any more than disalienation is. Both are conceived of in movement.

Second proposition. Once relativized, the concept becomes dialectical. There is a perpetual dialectical movement: 'alienation–disalienation–new alienation'. Therefore an activity which is disalienating and disalienated in relation to what has gone before can lead to an even greater alienation. For example, to become part of a collectivity can 'disalienate' one from solitude, but this does not preclude new alienations which may come from the collectivity itself. Leisure activities 'disalienate' from the effects of fragmented labour; however, when they are entertainments and distractions, they contain their own alienations. One particular technique may 'disalienate' human activity from nature or from another, less effective technique, but it may bring a technological alienation which can be much deeper (such as fragmented labour, or the social imperatives of technology, etc.). The 'reprivatization' of everyday life disalienates from the state and from history. It alienates by bringing forth a deeper 'privation', that of private life established within an everyday context. Thus alienation and disalienation characterize concrete situations, taken in movement and not considered in a motionless way along fixed structural lines. More exactly, the 'alienation/disalienation' dialectical movement enables us to determine a structure within concrete, changing situations. Thus a disalienation can be alienating, and vice versa. Only by precise analysis will we be able to distinguish between the aspects of this movement, rather than muddling them up together.

Third proposition. The worst alienation is when the alienation itself is non-conscious (or unrecognized). Awareness of an alienation is already disalienation, but it can become changed into a yet deeper alienation (when failure, privation or frustration become fixed in the consciousness). So the option which brings one alienation to an end, by going towards a possibility, can create another mutilation and a different alienation.

Fourth proposition. The reification of activity (when activity and consciousness become 'things', and allow themselves to be taken over by 'things') is an extreme case of alienation. This situation constitutes a polarity and final frontier for alienation, but it does not exhaust the concept. Taken per se, reification disguises the many forms alienation adopts.

Alienation within and by the state (political alienation) must not be confused with economic alienation (by money and by commodities), although there are links between them. The alienation of the worker differs from the alienation of women and of children. The ruling class – the bourgeoisie – is alienated by artificial desires and phoney needs, whereas the proletariat is alienated by privations and frustrations.

The alienation of social groups, which stops them from fully 'appropriating' the conditions in which they exist and keeps them *below their possibilities*, differs from the alienation of the individual within the group or by the group (families, towns, nations, classes, etc.), which 'derealizes' the individual by subjecting him to external rules and norms. There is a technological alienation (which can be superseded, but not without bringing additional risks) and an alienation as a result of a low level of technology. There is an alienation through escapism, and a different one through non-escapism. We also need to be aware of alienation in respect of the other individual (subordination), alienation in respect of society as a whole (scissions, dualities), and alienation in respect of oneself (failures, privations, frustrations), etc. And so alienation is infinitely complex.

At this point we need to look for a criterion enabling us to orientate ourselves through all this complexity, and to give a precise and objective definition either of alienation or disalienation, or of the exact moment in the process of becoming, or of the essential character of the situation and the way it is developing. Using this criterion we would be able to perceive what alienates and what disalienates, what is alienated and what is disalienated.

It would seem that this criterion can only be situated within dialectical movement. It comprises dialectical movement per se. But since it is a matter of grasping this movement, can we really speak of criteria? The worst alienation of all, absolute alienation – in so far as that makes any sense – is when movement is blocked and is brought to a halt. Now this coming to a halt can seem beguiling, like a definitive solution to the problems posed, like a state of supreme satisfaction. There is nothing more comfortable than a 'state'. And this is how reification, an extreme case and a clearly determined 'state', both defines and disguises all alienations. As far as the movement itself is concerned, it can take the most disturbing forms, such as dissatisfaction, anxiety or crisis. Contradictions, which we tend to confuse with alienations, are creative. Contradictions give rise to problems, and thus to a set of possibilities and to the need to find a solution, and therefore to the need to make a choice. The solution may be optimal, mediocre, bad or phoney (i.e., illusory). A good solution resolves the initial problem by modifying the givens against which it is reacting and which it is transforming. When the movement stops the givens of the problem are frozen; even if it is not insoluble, it becomes so, in the name of a phoney solution, which is generally the result of a misunderstanding about the givens and an unawareness of what is possible. Thus the idea of the 'problem' and the 'problematic' no longer gets lost in the clouds, but nevertheless there is probably no general criterion which would enable us to reveal and classify problems in specific terms.

Let us give some examples, or use some of the examples we have already given, but in more precise detail. Innumerable human beings have been tortured by innumerable conflicts since abstract (rational) social processes became detached from the systems governing the immediate and direct relations between individual people. Such immediate relations prolong archaic relations before the advent of the major processes such as the formation of the state or the accumulation of capital, etc. In essence, processes develop well above the lowly realm of direct and immediate relations, which is situated in the everyday. However, the major processes and systems of relations are not completely external one to the other. Although there is a gap, they interact. As long as the Father was nothing more than the agent of biological life, of strength and direct authority, conflicts were probably frequent and brutal, but they were never insoluble. When the Father becomes the agent of the law and of the state within a family, conflicts are forced underground. No longer can a child avoid animosity towards the Father, who becomes an image and a model which bring together in a conflicting way the child's need for protection and wish for security, and its reliance on him as a mediator between the closed system of family life and society as a whole. At the same time, these contradictions stimulate the development of individual consciousness. Systems of 'private' relations are disalienating with regard to external pressures, and yet they make an even greater alienation possible, the alienation of the child by the Father (when the child identifies with the Father). The major social processes are disalienating with regard to the narrowness of systems of private relations; they offer horizons, open spaces and freedom. And yet, in so far as they are abstract imperatives, they are alienating. Movement and conflicts are creative per se. Contradictions are always preferable to the absence of contradictions.

Let us consider 'women'. The term itself seems to suggest a kind of alienation in which half of the human race is considered or considers itself to be like a different species. What is this alienation which subjects women, stopping them from fulfilling themselves, subordinating and degrading them, tearing them from their true selves and dividing them up the one against the other? Would the alienating power be love, or motherhood, or housework in everyday life?

It is as difficult to answer these questions as it is to deny that there is a general alienation which determines and damages the 'feminine condition'. The love which alienates – passionate love – is not thick on the ground, as they say; as for the love which disalienates – elective love – it is more frequent and more normal, and does not fetishize either the lover or his loved one, or their physical or spiritual relations. It disalienates with respect to loneliness, while imposing several obligations for the two elements of the couple. And what of motherhood? It means freedom from sterility and is alienating only when it is physically debilitating. As far as housework is concerned, sociologists observe that proletarian women do not dislike it as much as middle-class women say they do. The latter want to work 'outside the home', and preferably professionally. Proletarian wives do not find housework any more tedious and tiring than working in a factory. If they can, they choose housework. So can it be the drudgery of housework which alienates women? It appears that the alienation of women represents a heightened image of the general alienation of our own specific society; thus if we are to understand it we must scrutinize society as a whole. Furthermore, there are certain 'situations' to consider, such as the women for whom having a baby shatters their future, ruins their plans, and condemns them to poverty and failure; the mother is sacrificed on the altar of maternity.[8]

Could not certain very profound reasons for the alienation of women be found in representations and symbolisms, and thus on the level of society as a whole and of 'ideological superstructures'? In this case, these reasons would be as hidden as they are profound. They would intervene in the motivation of individual desires as much as or more than in the material conditions of activity (although the one does not exclude the other). Therefore we cannot define alienation in the everyday until we have revealed symbolisms, and described and analysed motivations. What is really interesting is that there are veritable treatises on female alienation which present it as inevitable and beautiful, which systematize it and raise it to the absolute and take it to the absurd. Thus in Gertrud von Le Fort's *La Femme éternelle*, to become someone else, through someone else and for someone else, be it man or god, to 'be' in turn Virginity, Spouse, Motherhood, to annihilate oneself to become the instrument of Providence, to appear as silence beside male voices, as fluidity at the feet of male rocks, to wear symbolic veils, to unveil, to offer oneself – such would be the destiny of Femininity . . .

Let us conclude with some less lachrymose examples. On many occasions we have pointed out the importance the car holds in our everyday life (or should we say, in our culture and in our civilization? We will keep such weighty words for later . . .). This importance is the result of a social option, taken without full knowledge or awareness of its reasons, and above all, of its consequences. This option has set a process in motion which is probably irreversible and which threatens to dominate a wide sector of the 'real', to disrupt towns, etc.

A car is an item of goods, an object whose use brings satisfactions and which has a functional utility. The relations forged between individuals and this object go far beyond mere use and sheer pleasure. There are many individuals who 'realize' themselves by driving their car. They deploy qualities which lie fallow elsewhere; daring, virility, mastery of self, energy, and even sexuality (or so they say) would all be part of this relationship with the car. It is laden with ideology. And then the pathetic comedy begins: conversations dominated by the car, anecdotes, stories about accidents, etc. It is plain to see that drivers identify with their cars, and become aggressive, coarse, brutal, and of course these qualities are not apparent only when they are driving, far from it. Where is the alienation located? In the usefulness of the goods and the pleasure it provides, or the manner in which pleasure is taken from it? In the attitude, which has become a pattern of behaviour? The answer is obvious. Thus here, contrary to the alienation of women (which refers us to society as a whole), we can grasp alienation, i.e., the alienating–alienated situation, on an unmediated level.

Sociologists in America have recently discovered a most exceptional man, not least because of his exceptional banality: the other-directed man, one of the other-directed people.[9] This remarkably trivial man possesses ultrasensitive psychological antennae via which he detects other people's opinions (principally important people's) and conforms to them. He is energetic in affirming his personal integrity. He chooses to integrate within the social group and society as a whole, because he believes in it and because he is morally sound. It is not imposed upon him. A man like this has principles. His judgements and his moral convictions are his own, and do not come from an external moral code or a religion controlled by an all-seeing, spiteful god, to whom the depths of his consciousness would be like an open book. So this new man has retained the mannerisms of the 'inner-directed man', but only as some kind of superficial joke. This social phenomenon is the product of the manipulation of individuals and consciousnesses by modern technology, along with the ever-increasing importance of bank accounts and credit, the growth of suburbs and new housing estates, the rising cost of setting up home (mortgage, furniture), and more generally, 'consumer society'. Sexual relations and marriage are the only sectors in which free competition persists. However, even here, it is the men who come closest to the current model who will get the bonus points in the sexual and matrimonial contest.

So this individual does whatever his group tells him to do, but without having to be told. He obeys the imperative representations and models of society as a whole, but from the bottom of his heart. Moral order is freely and democratically accepted. Only groups have an active reality; but groups and individuals are equally depersonalized, abstract and artificial.

And so recent American sociology gives us an excellent description of alienated man in an alienating society, at a time of monopolies, (monopolistic) state capitalism and bureaucratic overorganization. It does not use Marxist terminology, but it presumably is aware of the theory of alienation, even if it does not mention it. Is it surprising that, apart from a few short stories and novels which broach the theme, there is no equivalent critical analysis to inform us of the specific alienations in the socialist countries? Such is the fate of Marxist thought in the twentieth century . . .

The diversity of these situations shows the extent to which it is difficult to find a simple, objective, general criterion for alienation. This diversity equally shows that it is possible and indeed indispensable to elaborate a *typology* of alienation. We can determine *types* of alienated–alienating situations. Alienation in everyday life would appear in this typology and would constitute a part of these types (but not their entirety, because there are other alienations: the alienation of society in its entirety, political alienation, for example). New forms of alienation, unforeseen and unforeseeable only a few years ago, would also be included in this typology, for example technological alienation. As for 'reification', it would only be one of the types, the simplest, the clearest and the easiest to define. Perhaps this typology would re-employ the terms used by Hegel and Marx, while giving them a precise content, but without extrapolating a classification: *Entfremdung* (to become 'estranged' from oneself), *Entaüsserung* (to be torn from onself), *Verwirklichung* (to find in fulfilment the principle of one's decline and loss), *Verdinglichung* (becoming more thing-like), etc. Alienation in the (psychiatric or psychosomatic) philosophical sense could also be included in this typology, probably under a variety of names.

Fifth and final proposition about alienation. It is appropriate to make a clear distinction between the *other* and *otherness* (in order to make their connection, their dialectical unity and perhaps a dialectical movement from one to the other more clear).

Maybe this difference is one of the reasons for the problem facing us. Alienation is the result of a relation with 'otherness', and this relation makes us 'other', i.e., it changes us, tears us from our self and transforms an activity (be it conscious or not) into something else, or quite simply, into a thing. Now there are many thinkers who consider the relation with 'otherness' to be a creative one. This is profoundly true. No self-consciousness can close up upon itself. Man is a conscious being, conscious of what he is (of his being), but only in, by and through what he is not, otherness and action upon otherness, confrontation with otherness, want, privation, desire, work on external material, works (products or works in the strict sense of the term), and finally, what is possible. What a consciousness 'is' is hidden from it, and partially eludes it. This self-consciousness 'is' consciousness of not being the object of which it is conscious. Without consciousness of otherness, every consciousness will come to a halt, and become blocked (so that, in the theory of alienation, non-consciousness of otherness is precisely complete alienation, the immobility of alienation).

Consequently it is beyond doubt that 'otherness' is fundamental to human perception – and yet, that 'otherness' fascinates us per se, disturbing us and plunging us into the depths of uncertainty, and even more deeply into anguish. Where are the limits of otherness? There are none, neither in nature and in the 'world', nor in the depths of the body and of consciousness. These depths are bottomless; and 'I is otherness',[10] i.e., the separation between 'I' and 'me' is already complete. Therefore could otherness be the transcendental, the irreducible outside, given with the inside (self-consciousness) in an inexhaustible relation? In a hypothesis like this, alienation disappears; there is nothing to enable us to discern the tearing away from the self and the normative influence of 'otherness' as the transcendental, the 'world' or the thing 'in itself'.

The philosophical imbroglio seems inextricable. Indeed, it is. The concepts become tangled together in a Gordian knot. What makes 'being' and what makes 'the being' at the same time makes nothingness, and the nothingness of this 'being'. Transposed into an ontology which purports to describe the 'lived', everyday experience clouds over and the simplest differences become blurred.

Let us be bold. Let us cut through the Gordian knot by introducing a simple distinction taken from everyday life.

Let us use '*the other*' to mean whatever is near enough to us to enable us to be its accomplice. The other is something (possibly) friendly and accessible; the other offers itself to us, up to a certain point. When it looks at us, we do not feel at all uneasy, except perhaps for a fleeting moment. It is our fellow-man.

Otherness is distance, an inaccessibility which threatens us and drags us away. Ipso facto, otherness tears me from my self. It attracts me, it fascinates me.

Therefore there would normally be a dialectical movement, a never-ending passing from otherness to the other, and vice versa. The passing from otherness to the other is called knowing, gaining power over otherness and vanquishing it; what this means is that I approach otherness and bring it closer to me. It is a disalienation (which can entail risks of further alienations). To pass from the other to otherness is to discover something unknown; it is to discover something distant in what is near. What we knew and what we were familiar with moves away from us and makes us feel uneasy. It is an alienation which can also contain a certain disalienation. But should otherness come to dominate the other, should we lose contact, should we become tightly embroiled in mistakes, misunderstandings and misinterpretations, should we lose all control, then alienation will take over, i.e., otherness will tear us from our selves, otherness will make us lose both the other and our own selves. What is essential is the movement, the passing, the supersession. To come to a halt and become blocked is the greatest alienation of all.

In this sense, the concept of alienation could be brought closer to the 'lived'. The 'lived' could clarify the concept of alienation, and conversely, the concept of alienation could clarify the idea of the 'lived', which is still a vague one.

4 Lived and living

If we have included and continue to include the idea of the 'lived' among our specific categories, it is on one precondition: we must make it dialectical. If not, the 'lived' will remain on the level of a phenomenology, oscillating between a description of the immediate and a Platonist ontology of essences.

We have already used an image to determine the idea of the 'lived' dialectically. It is a focusing of practical consciousness, a centre of density and of heat, if not of light. This focusing or localization moves about. It changes level, with the gaps and imbalances these changes (which are differences in level) entail. Thus in no way can so-called personal or individual consciousness be a given centre, a fixed focus or a closed sphere. It – 'I' or 'me' – sees itself lit in a variety of ways. Sometimes it is the psychological or biological level which appears in close-up; at others it is the strangest motivations of the subtlest of desires. Sometimes it is interpersonal relations (the recognition by 'me' or by 'I' of a consciousness of otherness, or of the desire of another) which are brought into focus, sometimes it is the 'we'. At other times it glorifies norms, symbolisms, representations or general regulatory forms of conduct, on the level of 'they' or 'them', or 'one'.

Our individual and social consciousness is no less complex than the smallest fragment of material nature or the social totality itself (which consciousness reflects, or rather, *refracts*). To put this another way, it is infinitely complex, and yet at every moment there is a certain lighting, a focal point, a close-up, a creative determination. For all that, every dimension, every horizon and every level will always be present, and active.

We call this ensemble the 'living' (and we have described it using visual images, which are the subtlest kind of image in this imperfect language of ours). We will attempt to reconstitute the 'lived/living' dialectical movement, which encompasses the everyday and social consciousness. The traditional theory of consciousness, which congeals it by reducing it to the 'I' (thus to a congealed form of the lived) disregards this conflict. The 'living' has no precise frontiers, either on the dark side (nature and spontaneity), or on its social horizon. Always vaster, always virtual, it summons the 'lived' and provokes it. At the centre of this unstable, volcanic and tempestuous landscape, the 'lived' is like a nomad's tent. It is always what has been accomplished, or what 'is' in the process of being accomplished, and thus superseded, because it is always disappointing and in decline even while it is being realized.

Hence the inevitability of the conflicts between the 'lived' and the 'living', which make up the life of (individual and social) consciousness. They are to be found on various levels, and give rise to a great many tensions. Although they are not yet fully distinguishable from the images we have used, and despite their approximative character, these concepts enable us to represent consciousness as actuality and as a work. In one sense, the lived is what has been accomplished, it is therefore the real and the actual. And yet, with its multiplicity of virtualities, the breadth of its horizons and its low-key lighting, the 'living' is just as much of a presence, and thus an actuality. The 'lived' cannot be seen as the inert result of living, nor as its vague consciousness. The lived is the present, living is presence. The lived is also the work – be it alive or dead – created by living: it is whatever I do, whatever I know, in my own light and within my own horizons: it is the part of a 'living' which does not belong to me, since it is quintessentially social, but which I have been able to appropriate. Despite the close links between them, the lived and the everyday do not coincide exactly. 'Living' is not located outside of the everyday. In the everyday, moments of drama are stifled. Now *the lived is essentially dramatic*. However, we must make a distinction between its real drama and the dramatizations which it accrues. Just as there are always elements of sophistry and rhetoric in language, social living always becomes inflated. The dramas of individuals and the dramas of groups become magnified. In fact what happens is that real drama and artificial dramatizations reinforce each other in a mixture of serious mise-en-scène and natural theatricality. This is the case not only for art, but also for many 'demonstrations' of social life, which use symbols and representations widely in order to magnify the lived. Let us think of mourning, funerals, marriages or encounters. The incessant passing from the lived to the living and from the living to the lived is an aspect of the everyday.

5 The spontaneous

The category of the 'lived' permits us to rehabilitate the category of *spontaneity*, which has long been disparaged, thanks to the attitude both of rationalist and of transcendental philosophy. Neither culturalism nor structuralism can admit the spontaneous and the unformed.

However, the rehabilitation of the 'spontaneous' does not rob critique of its rights. Quite the opposite. Are we about to make an apology for the spontaneous which would fetishize it?[11] Certainly not. Spontaneity has no privileges in any domain, be it everyday life or politics. When it is lacking, 'something' fundamental is missing; there is a gap, like a sterile little vacuum in the tissue of life. However, spontaneity is not always creative every time, with every risk it takes. It makes mistakes, and it fails more frequently than rational prognostication and calculation. Neither the idea of it nor its reality offers a criterion for existence or for value. Authentic per se (but how can we know this?), it eludes control and integration. And yet it imitates and mimics itself. In the spontaneous, it is difficult to make out what are dramas, dramatizations, de-dramatizations or super-dramatizations (which procedures of social control and integration encourage, and then repress). In periods of intense ideological control, the spontaneous and the non-spontaneous become merged, as do the natural and the artificial. This means the members of a particular group discover ideologically saturated values, norms and symbols 'spontaneously'.

To put it another way, whether it be in our consciousness or in the outside world, we never attain pure nature or any unconditional 'being'. The spontaneous is already part of the social, although it is not the social per se. Everyday life gives it a place and a consistency, and is the level on which it expresses itself. The spontaneous is nothing more than an element of the social, on a certain level. As such, it exists. It is active, it grows, it withers away, and as such it dies, in everyday life.

6 The idea of ambiguity

Once we have rid it of any ontological preoccupations, this concept has a wide area of application.[12] Outside of critical periods (when anything problematic has more importance than acquired stability, when conjuncture dismantles structure, when strategy takes the ascendancy and when the need to choose becomes apparent and marks a moment of bifurcation in the process of social becoming), human groups live in the mode of ambiguity. As long as problems are not immediately pressing, or if they are yet to be posed, human groups can ignore them. This has an impact upon consciousness (and as always we use the term to mean a consciousness which is simultaneously individual and social, although at times the two aspects may well be in conflict). It is satisfied with an appearance of definitive stability; it swells up like a cyst, and becomes an untroubled reality and a 'being', rather than pursuing the possible and 'being' pursued by it. And so the dramas fade away, the tragedy of the whole is obscured by a comedy of little details. Because nothing vital is at stake, everything is acted out in a ponderous or flippant manner. The relations between individuals within groups, and the relations between groups themselves, become dedramatized. They oscillate between blinkered attitudes and hollow opinions: envy, jealousy, pacts and squabbles, ceremonies which serve to disguise mutual rivalry or admiration. Instead of passion there is an (illusory) impartiality and a (misleading) objectivity. Trivial representations suffice. Anything contentious is pushed to one side, although this does not neutralize it. People talk about such things as little as possible and the spread of banality goes unchecked. The realm of ambiguity is also the realm of everyday triviality. At every moment the elements of the lived and of the living seem on the point of splitting up and going their separate ways: groups within society, individuals within groups, patterns of behaviour within individuals.

It is not always easy to distinguish between the ambiguous and the ambivalent. At this stage we would tend to emphasize their differences, placing ambivalence within the purview of psychology. Ambiguity, however, is a sociological category, a lived situation which is constituted from contradictions which have been stifled, blunted and unnoticed (unrecognized) as such. In the case of ambivalence, it is within the consciousness of an active individual that the problem or conflict emerges; with his back to the wall, he has to choose (this or that, love or hate, subjection or freedom). Sometimes he will already have made his choice, but is unable to make it explicit or effective. Ambiguity, however, is a condition offered to an individual by a group. Faced with differences he finds difficult to explain, he adopts a kind of temporary and undisciplined indifference; one day, soon perhaps, he will have to opt; but the moment of choice has not yet arrived; he has still not reached the fork in the road. Ambiguity is a complex situation, but it lacks mindfulness, and is made up of several virtual polarities. Ambivalence comprises a conflict which develops between feelings, people or representations.

There is no shortage of cases or examples of ambiguity in everyday life. So much so that one could say that ambiguity is a characteristic of the everyday, and that the everyday is the sphere of application and content of ambiguity, taken as a category (i.e., a specific concept). The *family* has a biological and physiological reality; in the first instance it is located on the level of immediate person-to-person relations: husband and wife, children and parents. Does it possess social functions? This has been contested, and it has been seen as a 'residual deposit'; twenty or so years ago it was thought that industrial society and the proletarian revolution would dismantle the family and share out all its ancient functions across 'society'. But it would appear that, against all expectation, the family has been given new functions, provisionally or permanently, in consumption and in culture. Have these new functions restored the old ones? Has the family regained its educational function? This is open to doubt. What is not in doubt is that, throughout history, society as a whole has given the family a range of forms: the patriarchal family, the feudal family, the bourgeois family, the proletarian family, the socialist family. It is influenced by ideology and culture: we can talk of the Islamic family, the Christian family or the secularized family. Institutions intervene vigorously to prohibit cases of deviance, blatant survivals and transitions towards anything new: they impose a defined structure upon the family. At the same time, the family retains unmediated links which originate in the distant past, before the development of modern society, such as patriarchal links and feudal relations of subordination. In this complex interaction, it never becomes separated from its biophysiological 'formants', even when it has been elevated to the dignified status of a higher ethical or cultural value, with the concomitant representations and symbols. However, if its situation is de facto ambiguous, it also accrues defined motivations and recognizable attitudes. The 'modern' and the 'archaic' confront each other in the family, in a mutual recognition of differences which, once recognized, tend to be disregarded. Various symbolic representations or psychosociological motivations are used as theories of the family: emotions aroused by the immutability of human nature, by the maternal instinct, by virility in its role as protector of feminine vulnerability, etc. In its very basic principles, the family 'is' ambiguous. Hence the general ambiguity of everything which happens or which does not happen within it: love and rivalry, confidence and mistrust, suffocation and protection, use and abuse.

Together with the family, woman belongs to the category of ambiguity. As an informal social group, the only way 'women' can be understood and situated is as the embodiment of ambiguity. We have already mentioned the paradox that half the human race and organized society constitutes a group defined by gender, which is to a certain extent distinct, with its own aspirations, demands and strategies. Biologically creative, 'women' have always been ipso facto the natural mediators between social groups, generations, culture and nature, and individuals. They mediate – in other words, they generate conflicts and divisions even when carrying out the conciliatory role their 'functions' attribute to them! Biologically creative, and probably the creators of the first human realities at the dawn of history – agriculture, the village, the house and its basic equipment, the hearth, cooking utensils, furniture, fabrics – women have subsequently been demoted to carry out inferior tasks, making them relatively unproductive economically and relatively ineffective socially. And so they 'are' the illusory substance of the everyday, its unreliable depths, its terrain and its climate, and yet they are endowed with the attributes of the human race (intelligence and rationality) as well as with the specific qualities of the groups to which they belong. Nothing stops them intervening in the gamut of public or private situations, but everything forces them to use indirect methods if their interventions are to be effective. The consequence is a profound and permanent conflict which can never reach a climax, i.e., it can never become the kind of overt, explicit antagonism which would endanger society. So the conflict is contained in a state of ambiguity: a blunted, ever-rekindled, ever-stifled contradiction. There are times when 'women' as a social group are able to wipe away the traces of their historical defeats, and when, after exerting gradual but constant pressure, they finally gain the promotion they have so long waited for. At these moments ambiguity bursts asunder in contradictions: possibilities longed for and disappointingly fulfilled, the serious side and the frivolous side of 'femininity', 'femininity' per se and its harsh ethic, which women both desire and reject. From these moments on, the ambiguity of the past and of the present becomes explicit, whereas when it was in control it was 'unconscious' (unrecognized), hidden under representations and symbols which maintained and disguised it. From time immemorial and up to and including the present day, women have been the custodians of a treasure chest of norms and representations. How prosaic and tedious these norms and representations are, but also how tenacious in praxis, and how profound: everything involving the house, the 'home' and domesticity, and thus everyday life. At the same time, both symbolically and as conscious 'subjects', they embody the loftiest values of art, ethics and culture: love, passions and virtues, beauty, nobility, sacrifice, permanence. But these come into conflict with other supreme values: sensual delight, total pleasure, luxury and lust. These conflicts are profound but disguised, reduced to ambiguity and hidden beneath it, but nevertheless, and in spite of the mind-numbing nature of housework, women are less likely than men to be stultified by the specialization and fragmentation of labour. So superiority becomes inferiority, and inferiority contains the seeds of superiority (although they are reluctant to germinate). *Therefore, women symbolize everyday life in its entirety. They embody its situation, its conflicts and its possibilities. They are its active critique.*

We (i.e., in everyday or 'modern' life) are flooded by a generalized ambiguity, which perhaps explains why certain philosophers have used it to extrapolate a philosophy, changing what is a sociological category into an ontological one. Now this improper generalization finds itself challenged by an obstacle and one overriding objection: ambiguity prevents awareness of ambiguity. Sociologically, it is a category of unawareness and ignorance, or rather of misunderstanding and lack of knowledge, where appearances merge with the 'real'. As appearance and illusion on a massive scale, 'consumer society' has become stronger and stronger. Modern capitalism would appear to produce for social and individual needs; it therefore appears to correspond to Marx's definition of socialism (and this appearance in itself is enough to make our situation paradoxical). In fact, 'consumer society' manipulates needs; the masters of production are also the masters of consumption, and they also produce the demands for which and according to which they are supposed to be producing. Deliberately or not, they leave other equally valid needs and other equally objective demands to one side. It is not very often that a voice makes itself heard[13] to criticize this illusion which is not entirely an illusion, this appearance which is not absolutely an appearance, since needs – even if they are provoked and prefabricated – can not all be equally phoney and artificial. Ambiguity between individual and social needs and desires papers over unperceived contradictions, blunting them and coinciding with the three-dimensional 'realness' of the everyday. Only when there is this ambiguity can the illusion and the appearance be sustained.

From the moment we begin to scrutinize them, mass culture (together with mass consumption) and the effects of the mass media reveal an enormous ambiguity. Using highly sophisticated techniques, mass communications bring masterpieces of art and culture to everyone; they make history in its entirety, the 'world' itself, accessible to all. They bring the past and even the future into the present. By continually improving their manner of approach and their means of distribution, these techniques circulate what is most refined and most subtle in the works of mankind, those painstaking creations to which men devote their lives, and in which epochs and civilizations are embodied. Modern techniques make taste more sophisticated, raise the level of culture, instruct, educate, and bring an ency- clopaedic culture to the people. *At the same time*, they make their audience passive. They make them infantile. They 'present' the world in a particular mode, the mode of spectacle and the gaze, with all the ambiguity we have already noted and which we continue to emphasize: non-participation in a false presence. This distribution lives off the past, it cuts it up and wastes it. Producing images and representations, the techniques of the mass media create nothing and do not stimulate any creativity. They consume the precious goods accumulated over the centuries, exacerbating by their own actions this more general historical fact: history has forced many creative sources to dry up, and will go on doing so indefinitely.

The mass media shape taste and cloud judgement. They instruct and they condition. With their saturation of images, current affairs and 'news' devoid of anything new, they fascinate and they nauseate. They expand communications and they threaten coherence and thought, vocabulary and verbal expression, language itself. Will they reach the extreme point where the 'world of expression' is exhausted, where everyone will be a spectacle for everyone else, where the event will be broadcast while it is happening? We call this extreme point the Great Pleonasm, the Supreme Tautology, the Final Identification of the real with the known, surprise annihilated by the illusion of per- manent surprise – ambiguity annihilated by its own triumph. Here too ambiguity presupposes and produces appearances which disguise it; never to appear to be what it is – that too is an aspect of ambigu- ity. Everything takes place as though ambiguity were only apparent and manifest in the supersession which is destroying it.

Even more generally, the way the members of one group perceive or apprehend other groups and other human beings takes place first and foremost in the mode of ambiguity: amazement and curiosity, repugnance and rapacity, retreat and generosity, desire to assimilate and need to repel. It is a kind of 'apprehensiveness': grasping yet fearing, discovering a vague threat, seesawing between a reassuring present (the other 'is'; we can hold it, distance it and define ourselves in relation to it) and a disquieting future. All that we know about our possible relation with it is this one useless detail: it can harm us or it can help us. There comes a moment when we must make up our minds and make a decision: we must make a judgement and take a choice. Options are decisive. They shed light on all that is hidden in the twilight world of ambiguity. Ambiguity cannot last long. It is not permanent. It has a time limit.

Rightly or wrongly, and according to the circumstances and conjunctures, decisions begin with an assessment, which to a certain extent runs the risk of making a mistake in the present and of failing in the future. After assessing the situation (which hitherto was ambiguous, and thus impossible to judge) we go into action; we dive in headfirst; there are no more discussions. The best man of action is the one who chooses his moment well, who discusses the pros and the cons at length, but not for too long. He waits for the situation to be ripe, but not rotten. He takes his time, and avoids hasty judgements and interventions, but by no means does he drag his feet. He replaces the 'yes and no' of ambiguity and the suspension of judgement (the 'perhaps' or 'why not?', and the 'what's the point?' of caution and hesitation) with the dilemma of action. He answers a question either by yes or by no. He opts. His decision simplifies the complex situation and the ambiguity, and by the very act of simplifying them, transforms them. One sharp blow, and ambiguity collapses. And that is when ambiguity reveals itself to be what it is: uncontrolled complexity, confusion, opaqueness. Ambiguity leads us towards a decision which will negate it and reveal it, bringing it to an end and unmasking it. The sword of decision cleaves continuous time into a *before* and an *after*. True time – many-sided, continuous and discontinuous, way-marked by the forks in its paths, mapped out by decisions and options – is revealed.

So we see yet another dialectical movement emerging before our eyes: 'ambiguity/decision'. Once we have discovered it, we will no longer be able to fetishize ambiguity and to see the everyday and the ambiguous as being synonymous. We will no longer be able to behave as if this category – ambiguity – defined a situation of the human or within the human, irreducibly and irrevocably.

As an aspect of this movement, the act of decision itself becomes an object for theory and even for a particular science, a fragment of a general theory of praxis, similar to logic: 'praxiology'. This theory can no more be identified with critique of everyday life than it can with knowledge of praxis. It touches only one aspect of them. It completes the theory of ambiguity.

The essential point here is that the theory of ambiguity foreshadows and calls for the end of ambiguity itself. It gives rise to a general problem (together with its complement, decision theory). To study the everyday is to wish to change it. To change the everyday is to bring its confusions into the light of day and into language; it is to make its latent conflicts apparent, and thus to burst them asunder. It is therefore both theory and practice, critique and action. Critique of everyday life encompasses a decision and precipitates it, the most general and the most revolutionary of them all, the decision to render ambiguities unbearable, and to metamorphose what seems to be most unchangeable in mankind because it lacks precise contours.

7 Challenge and mistrust

If there is a category among today's social facts (i.e., a set of facts denoted and connoted by a category) which corresponds in our modern world to what Mauss described as the total social phenomenon, namely gifts in archaic societies, would it not be the notion of *challenge*? Today, challenge appears openly in all areas and at every level of social reality. It is becoming a recognized, explicit, conscious and almost everyday mode of social relations between individuals and groups (genders, ages, classes, peoples and nations, institutions and organized apparatuses, political regimes and modes of production).

In our resolve to make the scientific research in which we are engaged deliberately 'neutral', impartial and objective, we might well sometimes overlook these sociodramatic categories. In its beginnings sociology's favourite areas of study – and perhaps to an exaggerated extent – were the manifestations of challenge in archaic societies: potlatch,[14] ordeals and 'judgements of God', competitive forms of exchanges and gifts, ritual declarations of friendship or hostility. This tendency has been disowned, too much so. Let us reinstate the study of the social forms of challenge, while at the same time bringing it up to date and modernizing it.[15]

Once the importance of challenge in archaic or historical (Promethean) societies has been reassessed, its sociological study and its specifically historical study become complementary. The light shed on social practice is dramatically revealing. Thus the eighteenth century saw groups and classes with increasingly clear-cut contours throw themselves in the face of a multiplicity of challenges, in all areas, including culture, art and morality. ('We, of this particular group, are and will be more cultivated, more refined, more moral, more civilized and more reasonable than you, members of another group; or we will appear to be, which more or less boils down to the same thing.')

Challenge is part of tactics and strategies. It reveals them, while at the same time concealing them. Noisy, provocative, silent, there is a period of mutual challenge in every confrontation. Challenge is polyvalent. Thrown down on a certain level (economic, cultural, ideological, political, etc.), its presence comes to light and reverberates in other areas, and on other levels of praxis. It is a means of exerting pressure, and so it is an action rather than a declamatory and gratuitous mode of expression or an impersonal figure of speech in social reality. Challenge is a means of exerting pressure beyond the group, but its actions reverberate within it; it rallies elements which have been scattered, and regroups them; it puts an end to periods when collective life breaks down into individual preoccupations and trivialities. For this reason, it enters into the everyday and elevates it, by ridding it of part of its triviality. It gives it colour.

Seen in this light, the social groups reveal well-determined characteristics. The bourgeoisie has always lived in the mode of permanent challenge to its adversaries: feudalism to begin with, then the working class. It was able to include challenge as one of the apparently universal values, so that ideologically speaking it is more of a challenge to time than to men, whose lives are ephemeral. These values – reason, nationhood – belong to a class-consciousness which does not present itself as such. Every statement with the words 'reason' or 'nation' in it contained a challenge, but not expressed as such. The bourgeoisie sought to unite challenge with confidence, a most volatile mixture. Whenever it stops living on this particular mode, it becomes slack, unleashing fear, and even panic. Conversely, as a social group, technocrats avoid challenge, and provocation even more so; they work in silence, deep underground, and this distinguishes them from the other class fractions from which they derive or which they serve. The rowdy, provocative challenges hurled by intellectuals at general opinion (romanticism, surrealism, existentialism, for example) mark certain periods of culture, and certain other periods are marked by their silence. These differing attitudes can imply a confession of powerlessness, or a possibility of action. As regards the challenge of the proletariat to bourgeois society and to the bourgeoisie, it can be silent and mistrustful rather than provocative.

Critical periods, i.e., acute forms of confrontation and revolutionary moments, always seem to be preceded or followed by periods when tensions and challenges are less extreme. But challenge can be more far-reaching, and much more profound. It could be said that economic growth and the development of technology throw down a series of challenges – long suppressed – to the individual, to art and to the moral sphere, and to modern man in general.[16]

Could peaceful coexistence be an idyll, could there be fraternization without an ulterior motive, could there be mutual toleration with a pluralist ideology in both camps, in an unruffled juxtaposition of opposed regimes? Unthinkable! Interaction is a law. We must not confuse official declarations, which are often most perfidious when they are at their most diplomatic and skilful, with the dialectical movement of the real. Peaceful coexistence is a perpetual mutual challenge. Objectively, and in the mode of challenge, overt incompatibility makes way for a compatibility which is not without its own risks. With its component of randomness, a challenge replaces a threat. It is based on a situation – the possibility and fear of mass destruction – much more than on the will for anything. It comprises a volatile relation of forces within boundaries fraught with danger. We should not imagine it to follow any archaic model, like some kind of generalized 'potlatch' of nuclear or conventional arms; that would be too tidy and too simple. The challenge is many-sided, and will continue to be so: it is economic, political, military, cultural and technological. We are well aware of what its contents are: industrial growth, aid to underdeveloped countries (whose weight may well prove decisive) and unrestrained technical development.

And so challenge puts the solidity of existing structures permanently to the test, and at the same time it tries their ability to adapt to circumstances. When it is explicit, challenge resembles intimidation; when it is covert, it resembles tolerance and understanding, and therefore flexibility.

Can there be a challenge without mistrust, i.e., without fear? Not often. And if so, we would call it arrogance. When challenge became generalized it brought mistrust in its wake, and this fosters an immense and terrible uncertainty. We have learned a lot from the new concepts it has brought us: the ubiquity of randomness in the modern world, the importance of tactics and strategies in social 'reality', etc. Mistrust determines a specific alienation: it clouds things over, it creates panic and it stultifies; at the same time, it stimulates energies. The climate of challenge and mistrust is prodigiously uplifting, but it is as unbearable as it is stimulating. Mistrust also determines a disalienation, the vague anguish which comes when we are confronted with the innumerable questions randomness raises. 'Why this? Why that?' Perhaps when the need for security becomes less important it will lead to a mutation in social consciousness. With the current degree of anxiety and tension, the human mind becomes detached from nature. It demands that the tranquillity of nature and the restlessness of culture be superseded. Would this mutation open the way for a demand for a radical metamorphosis of the everyday? We can only hope so. If not, yet another failure will be added to the list, and it is already much too long as it is . . .

From the start of their coexistence, the two opposing 'regimes' or 'systems' have reacted one against the other, and in a very profound way. This is not the place to study this dialectical movement: the pressure of one 'system' upon another and the way the systems respond to that pressure, with all the repercussions and exaggerations which ensue. This interaction gets broader and more intense, with each side maintaining that it alone keeps all its promises (and even other people's promises, as someone notoriously once put it) and the ability to fulfil mankind's aspirations. In this interaction, *the image of the other* (the result of an unstable combination of information and propaganda) is already playing an ever-increasing and contradictory role. It is the image of challenge, an image we challenge and which we mistrust.

Thus a 'world' or 'planetary' unit is under way, contradictorily, dialectically, i.e., in a way which is both necessary and random, determined and aleatory. As we go beyond our own planet, and as the adventure of space opens up before us like a chasm, 'globality' enters into the dialectical movement of man and of history. But what will this globality be? We have no means of predicting it with any accuracy. The most we can do is to draw up a table of possibilities, chances and options. A highly complex interaction is unfolding before our eyes, and within us, on the mode of challenge. It is not mechanical, and is full of random elements. The way this challenge works is changing. At first it turned the bourgeoisie into wild beasts (fascists), and then – without making it any the less ferocious – it shook it from its lethargy, and, to a certain extent, from its stupidity; the bourgeoisie tries to rid itself of its old Malthusianism, to plan ahead, to 'harmonize' production and consumption; it succeeds to a certain extent, but without transforming the fundamental conditions and categories of bourgeois society, and without suppressing the class struggle or the proletariat. In the other camp, the capitalist challenge initially prevented the socialist state from withering away; it was one of the causes of Stalinism, perhaps the main one; then it shook socialism from its dogmatic slumbers, and it shook up state doctrinairism and crude centralized planning; and now socialism is at last beginning to take social needs into account.

We now know that, in their challenges and their contradictions, the two modes of production present some similarities and some curious homologies. Notably, on both sides, everyday life is neglected and abandoned to its backwardness, in the USA because of the inadequacies of the 'public services', and in the USSR because of the priority given to heavy industry. On one side, there is a dearth of statism, on the other there is too much of it. On both sides technological alienation has produced results which are in many respects comparable. The challenges of the two sociopolitical regimes concern the same category, the category of everyday life.

The regime which carries the day will be the one which produces the most wealth, the most means for action, the most freedom – in a word, the most possibilities. Will it triumph by the pleasure it offers mankind, or by power over it? Who can say?

This is why we have not taken any one idea (the idea of 'globality' for example) to guide us through the complexities of the modern world and its problems. One idea alone would not have enabled us to make predictions and to take options. To guide us through the labyrinthine world of challenge, we have chosen one humble and essential requirement: the transformation of the everyday through critical knowledge of it.

8 Social space, social time

There exist social time or social time scales which are distinct from biological, physiological and physical time scales. There is a social space which is distinct from geometric, biological, geographic and economic space. Everyday space differs from geometric space in that it has four dimensions, which are in a two-by-two opposition: 'right/left − high/low'. Similarly, everyday time has four dimensions which differ from dimensions as mathematicians and physicists would define them, namely the accomplished, the foreseen, the uncertain and the unforeseeable (or again: the past, the present, the short-term future and the long-term future).

The more deeply we analyse them, the more subtle and the more differentiated these ideas become. With respect to *social space*, we will distinguish between subjective aspects and objective aspects. Subjectively, social space is the environment of the group and of the individual within the group; it is the horizon at the centre of which they place themselves and in which they live. The extent of this horizon differs from group to group, according to their situation and their particular activities. Objectively, the idea of social space is not synonymous with the currently accepted idea of 'social mobility'. Taken in isolation, social mobility remains an abstraction; it implies networks and channels via which it is established, if indeed it constitutes a lasting phenomenon. Social space is made up of a relatively dense fabric of networks and channels. This fabric is an integral part of the everyday. We will study it later, in our model of communications, where we will try to see if we can give a precise meaning to the terms 'social distance' and 'social field'.

As for social time, let us emphasize once more the difference between cyclic time scales and linear time scales, and their relativeness. We know that the former have their origins or their foundations in nature; they are connected to profound, cosmic, vital rhythms.

The latter are connected to knowledge, reason and techniques; they correlate not with vital rhythms and processes, but rather with processes of economic and technological growth.

We will look closely at the results of the interactions between cyclic rhythms and linear (continuous or discontinuous) time scales in the everyday. Therefore we will be proposing a rhythmology or a socio-logical 'rhythmanalysis',[17] and we will attempt to distinguish between periodicities and to study their relations and superpositions, taking either mathematical harmonic analysis or physiological research as our model. Moreover, each group has its 'tempo', which is relatively fast or slow, and which varies between work and everyday life outside work. In this way we would hope to develop a theory of the multi-plicity of social time scales.[18]

9 Praxis

We now come to the simplest category, and the most difficult to eluci-date. It is the most abstract and the most concrete, since it applies both to the everyday and to the wholeness of society. It is the cate-gory of *social practice* or *praxis*.

Since Marx's early writings (which are also called philosophical), the idea of *praxis* has been distorted and impoverished. Before we try to reinstate the idea in its entirety we will look quickly at the restric-tive ways it has been interpreted.

Making[19] reduces social practice to individual operations of the artisan kind on a given material which is relatively pliable or resist-ant. During this operation, the producer or creator – part artisan, part artist – discovers himself. By means of the object, he recognizes his work and his own abilities. As he works, he forms his own abili-ties. This is as true for traditional potters and weavers as it is for painters. When they make something, they also make themselves.

At one and the same time, the idea of *making* is narrower and vaguer, more deceptively precise and more equivocal than the idea of *production*, which as yet is not broad enough to cover the idea of praxis completely. In spite of its apparent precision, the idea of 'making' is without contours. Is play a 'making'? If it is, the idea can be used to include whatever one wants. If not, it becomes restricted to productive work upon an object, work which is of a determined kind and, moreover, somewhat antiquated. As soon as we fail to stipulate the limits of the idea and the frame of reference in which we are using it, it can result in misuse, namely deceptive values. In modern industrial labour, the direct and unmediated contacts the operator has with his tools and his material are diminishing, and with automation they actually disappear. An analysis of praxis based upon this idea would be in danger of overlooking many facts. It lags behind reality, and the clarity which comes as a result of this lag is deceptive. We think of labour in the industrial era along artisan lines, and the labour of the present era − the era of automation − along the lines of 'classic' industry. Fragmented labour has altered the relation between work and life outside work, and automation has altered it even more. When he 'makes' something, the individual is no longer 'making' himself. He is 'made' in a complex totality of which 'making' is only one part and one aspect. For all that, on the scale of society, production and production relations remain determinants. Moreover, whenever there is a 'work', no matter how modest − and not a 'product' − the value bestowed on the individual act by the 'making' remains valid (including when it is in the caricatural form of a hobby, or do-it-yourself).

Here are some other reservations about the idea of 'making'. It does not help us to pose the problem of inventiveness in practice, nor does it help us solve it. It treats the technique as though it were the material, and tends to relegate both to the background, as general givens of all activities which make anything, without examining the implications and conditions or the consequences and results in themselves. In order to give more value to the agent's individual initiative and skill, it emphasizes the zone of indetermination (the margin of freedom) which the technique and the material put at his disposal. This does not help us to make a clear formulation of the problems of freedom, with all their implications, or of the problems of individuals and of the groups to which those individuals belong. And what happens to alienation in this schematic?

The narrowness of the way in which empiricism and pragmatism interpret the idea of 'practice' has been stressed so often and so vigorously that it is hardly worth reiterating. By only considering individual practical action and its result, by replacing breadth of theoretical vision (which they present as simple abstraction) by practicism and the vulgar practical mentality, by extolling success as the criterion and principle of judgement, Anglo-Saxon empiricism and pragmatism eliminate the drama, the profundity and the problems from individual life and from social life. They have proved attractive because they are simple, i.e., they simplify. They reveal the absence of a philosophical tradition, or more exactly the absence of an effective tradition which has penetrated culture. If they were able to spread their ideas it was thanks to the great crisis of philosophy, when the withering away, the supersession and the absence of philosophy all became merged in an inextricable confusion. The image of praxis they present is all the more false for being more 'realistic', more precise and more in line with the experience of fragmentation. They have even contaminated Marxist thought.

Against Anglo-Saxon pragmatism and its apologia to success, several philosophers – with little awareness of the situation or of the role they are playing – have made a virtue out of failure. They have rehabilitated drama and the tragic, but excessively so: only failure has any meaning, since success or victory simply demonstrates the platitude of the intentions and the goals which inspired them. So today the derisory sociological apologia to success is countered by the no-less-derisory idea that humanity only sets itself insoluble problems, that men play to lose, and that the magnitude of the aims and the profundity of the goals are measured by the extent to which they fail. We are now leaving this dilemma behind us.

Pragmatism disregards the fact that decisions are based on logic and that actions are dialectical. It disregards the theory of choices, possibilities and risks. It eliminates concrete problematics: conflicts, contradictions, openings. It thinks of praxis not as something concealing a complexity of movements, but as a cold, naked concept of the real, with the density of a stone. The atheoretical conception of human activity goes hand-in-hand with a functionalist conception of the real. Emphasizing one specific formant of activity – technology – the transition to a technocratic positivism which considers itself to be broad, deep and of course 'realistic' is easy.

An analogous restriction has occurred in dogmatic Marxist thought, in tandem with similar divisions. Using a different terminology, specific sides of praxis have been emphasized such as productive labour, the action of man on external nature, and matter as the object of the activity which precedes conscious activity. Ipso facto there is equally a tendency to give value to technology, productivity and success. We jump from productive labour, identified with praxis, to some other aspect (the planning of productive labour, political practice, the practice of the state or of the party) without worrying too much about piecing these multiple fragments back together again. Hence an ideological confusion which makes it possible to transfer the rather vague quality attributed to praxis in general to a determined (political) practice: the ability to achieve good results from an action, control over spontaneous or unwitting processes, technology, knowledge, and control over the forces of nature. This ideology does away with the need for a strictly political theory which would describe and analyse the means of state power and the sources of specifically political action: apparatuses, propaganda, methods of direction and command, techniques of distribution and constraint, in short, the penetration of globality and statism, and the marked separation between them, into the everyday.

In terms of its inability to analyse and its hostility to knowledge, so-called Marxist practicism is just as bad as pragmatism. Its idea of praxis is just as blinkered and just as obscurantist. It sidesteps the issue by presenting its own 'praxis' as an ideological (philosophical) representation rather than *reflecting* its truth in a critical fashion. Dogmatism has been able to present the total liberation of mankind and the blossoming of its freedom as having been accomplished, but it has done so within a framework which in fact makes this impossible: statism, the requirements of primitive accumulation, dissatisfaction, and the restriction of needs and pleasures. By dint of stressing specific aspects of praxis, or ideology (and notably matter and philosophical materialism), it has succeeded broadly in blurring and parenthesizing other aspects, and in excluding them from the idea of socialism: notably everything concerning everyday life.

After such a lengthy and effective obliteration, only by making a considerable effort will we be able to reinstate the idea of *praxis* in its entirety.

The action of social man on nature (the outside world) is only one aspect of praxis, but it is already a complex one, since when we analyse it we find a large number of formants: techniques (tools and knowledge), natural forces, resources and raw materials, the organization and division of labour (the *social* division and the *technical* division of labour are not the same thing, particularly in capitalist society), etc.

The relations between human beings – groups and individuals – are obviously part of praxis. Action upon nature (productive forces) implies social relations (production relations) and explains them, up to a point. Conversely, social relations cannot be established or conceived of outside action upon nature (productive forces). Social groups, and notably classes, are simultaneously productive forces and social forces. However, social relations and production relations are not the same thing, and praxis cannot be defined comprehensively either as a sum total or as an interaction: 'productive forces/production relations'. This representation fetishizes economy. It ends up as a simplistic productivism, as perfunctory as the functionalism we have already refuted: a productivism of material production. It forgets or refuses to listen to Marx's argument against Adam Smith's bourgeois productivism, which recent economists and sociologists have taken up again in the fight against vulgarized Marxism: all societies comprise and imply a non-material and yet practically creative production, namely the various 'services'. Now these services are woven into the texture of social relations, production relations and property relations. They make them more complex. They represent social needs *generally* and the *specific* social needs which have been accepted and controlled. They help to articulate production and consumption in the everyday (whether it be distribution, transport, health and medicine, education and training, leisure activities, advertising, specifically cultural works, etc.). Although simple and unmediated in appearance, everyday life reveals on analysis the presence of a range of effective representations, symbols, regulations, controls, models and norms (ideologies and 'superstructures') which intervene and mediate it. Conversely, these multiple mediations of everyday life take on an unmediated existence within it, albeit unevenly. Mediations of the everyday do not all intervene simultaneously.

Praxis reveals an extreme complexity on very varied *levels*: from the biophysiological level, which comprises relations with nature other than that of material production strictly speaking (as much within the family as in the village, the town or the nation), to the abstract and formal level of symbols, culture, representations and ideologies. The so-called 'superstructural' elements and formants react on the 'base'. This classic postulate of Marxist theory will be incomprehensible if we fail to perceive that there is a level in praxis which is relatively distinct and marked per se, the level of everyday life. Symbols and representations react first and foremost on unmediated relations, between which they intervene as mediations: the apparently direct relations between persons and things (goods) which are precisely what the everyday, as well as the apparently simple modalities of social consciousness, is made up of.

But praxis also reveals itself as a totality. We would maintain that the idea of totality derives from praxis. However, this totality never appears to be other than fragmentary, contradictory, and composed of levels, of contradictions on differing levels, and of partial totalities. How do we reach totality, i.e., society itself, from within? Precisely, via these partial totalities and levels which cross-refer to each other, and via these fragments which presuppose a whole and which necessitate the concept of a whole of which they are the evidence and the elements, but not the entirety. Fragmented in one sense but already total in another, every act of thought or social effectiveness refers to the totality via the other levels. It reveals a total praxis, and points the way towards it. Only by restoring this mobile and contradictory (dialectical) profundity to praxis will we be able to understand and reinstate certain of Marx's famous postulates. Social life, the life of society and of the individual, is in its essence social practice: praxis. Production produces man. So-called 'world history' or 'the history of the world' is nothing but the history of man producing himself, of man producing both the human world and the other man, the (alienated) man of otherness, and his self (his self-consciousness).

This is an ideal point at which to protest once more against the ideological operation which reduces praxis to production, and production itself to economic (material) production. Praxis encompasses both material production and 'spiritual' production, the production of means and the production of ends, of implements, of goods and of needs. To produce and to reproduce is not simply to cast a certain number of produced objects (implements of production or consumer goods) into distribution, exchange and consumption, or alternatively to invest or accumulate them. It is also to produce and to produce again the multiple *social relations* which enable production and the *appropriation* of goods (and which also limit or hinder them).

In this way, and in this way only, do we become aware of the coherence of a determined society (its structures), and of the incoherences which the coherent structure dominates and subjugates until such time as it disintegrates. To detach the productive forces from action on material nature, or more generally to single out certain categories from praxis by giving them a privileged status, to consider certain objects separately and to turn them into fetishes (commodities, for example, or money) – these are precisely the procedures which Marxist critique refutes. And this is how the foundation of all critical thought, including critique of religion, critique of philosophy and critique of everyday life, becomes manifest.

In production, it is not only products which are produced and reproduced, but also social groups and their relations and elements; members, goods and objects disappear while groups persist or crumble away, remaining active, playing their games and developing their tactics and strategies. Beneath an apparent immobility, analysis discovers a hidden mobility. Beneath this superficial mobility, it discovers stabilities, self-regulations, structures and factors of balance. Beneath the overall unity, it uncovers diversities, and beneath the multiplicity of appearances it finds a totality. Analysis must maintain these two sociological aspects (incessant change, the disappearance of elements, nascent conjunctures – the structuring of the whole, relative stability) and grasp them in the wholeness of a single history.

Praxis produces the human 'world', our world, the world of objects and goods, the world our senses perceive and which therefore seems a gift of nature to the organs and body of an individual. The expression 'outside world' is deceptive. It groups together *things* (e.g., a pebble), *objects* (e.g., a house), *products* (e.g., a pencil) and *works* (e.g., a painting). Through the mediation of language, the outside world 'is' also the inner world which reproduces the human world of objects, products and works by means of verbal structures. (Individual) consciousness 'reflects' a world which seems external and which social praxis has created. Up to a certain point (but this determination does not exhaust it) this consciousness can be defined as the place – the field – where significations and symbolisms left by praxis in the world of objects come together.

We must distinguish between repetitive praxis and inventive praxis. This distinction is essential if we are to make the idea of praxis more dialectically profound, and reinstate it in its entirety. Repetition plays a considerable role on every level. Sooner or later productive and technical actions end up as reiterated gestures, and this is an important if not essential aspect of labour. As for operations entrusted to material devices (such as tools and machines), they always involve many to-and-fro movements: oscillations, rotations, alternations. As Marx pointed out before our contemporary economists and sociologists did, products per se differ from works and natural objects by their capacity for unlimited production. We know that a large part of everyday life is made up of stereotyped and repeated actions. This repetitive praxis keeps the human world going, and helps to produce it over and over again. It underlies the human world and constitutes its stability. Is it intrinsically alienating? No. It will only alienate in definable conditions and situations: when 'something else' becomes possible.

However, we should not separate repetitive praxis from creative praxis. There are several types of repetition, and we will have cause to examine their differences at a later stage. The stereotyped, mechanical repetition of gestures and signals differs from the rhythmed and periodic starting and restarting which characterizes vital activities. Let us remember that in mathematics repetitions of formal operations (such as adding or subtracting an element from a set) – iteration and reiteration – are fundamental and prodigiously creative acts.

Therefore we can expect to find transitions and mediations between the repetitive and the creative. This is why we did not think it possible to define the everyday by the repetitive alone, but rather as the place where repetition and creativity meet and confront each other. Social praxis cannot be confined to supporting, maintaining and reproducing. In our arguments we have tried to demonstrate the relative character of structures, stabilities, constants and balances. Praxis is not confined to the everyday, nor is the everyday confined to a mechanical and unlimited recommencement of the same gestures and operations. Repetitive practice is necessary, but it is not enough per se. It never attains the definitive, automatic balance, a balance without contradictions. This would be the supreme alienation. It is the 'base' of the inventiveness which undermines and modifies it. Praxis is creative. On the frontiers of inventiveness, we sense the coming of acts which disrupt praxis and transform the everyday: revolutions, total phenomena which introduce a multiplicity of possibilities which the unfolding of history strives unsuccessfully to exhaust . . .

Other less garish and strident forms of creativity are much more humble. Creativity is not only produced outside the everyday, on the higher plane of representations and symbolisms. At first commencement and recommencement are indistinguishable, and their difference only becomes apparent after time, and as a consequence of it. We would go so far as to say that all inventiveness is born from the everyday, and is confirmed within it. Where and how is the act of creativity accomplished? We know that in terms of the norms and received frames of reference which govern higher activities it is often marginal, bizarre and deviant. Its creativity is only apparent later, in what follows. The inventive action is often similar to gambling: it comprises a wager and a risk of loss. The history of the sciences proves these assertions as much as the history of art and of political doctrines do. In our opinion, the most inventive people are individuals who are not isolated, but who have the backing of small groups. Certainly large-scale groups and society as a whole are essential in offering the necessary if inadequate conditions for inventive practice. Individuals in small groups achieve what praxis makes possible, on a comprehensive scale. Inventiveness makes its way from mediation to mediation through ponderous repetition, through the stimulations of conflicts and the enticements and interdictions of social values and controls. Could not inventiveness – or the seeds of inventiveness – be a product of the limited and daring praxis of small-scale groups: sects, secret societies, political parties, elective groups, laboratories, theatrical troupes, etc.?

Our analysis leads us to introduce a multiplicity of differences, levels and partial totalities into the idea of praxis, but without abandoning the idea itself. We will distinguish between the following:

a) *Total revolutionary praxis*, the praxis Marx dealt with in his so-called philosophical writings (which contain a radical critique of philosophy while perpetuating traditional philosophy). Total revolutionary praxis would overturn what exists from top to bottom. It would bring an end to alienation in one total historical act. It would reveal contradictions, and then it would resolve them. It would overcome scissions and separations, first and foremost those between *being* and *thinking* (consciousness), the *private* (the everyday) and the *public* (the state, politics), *need* and *desire*, and *nature* and *culture*, etc. It implies the supersession of philosophy and its fulfilment, as well as the withering away of the state.

Today the idea of total revolutionary praxis seems Utopian. And indeed it is. In so far as all philosophy has (directly or indirectly) presented some kind of half-aware Utopia, and in so far as Utopia stimulates action by achieving itself through a succession of approximations, we will retain the idea, and we will even foreground it. Whatever appears as a Utopia also appears as an Idea. The idea of *total praxis* is nothing other than the idea of *revolution*. When we introduced the idea of a metamorphosis of the everyday we stressed the twofold character of this programme: it is both Utopian and realist. Changing the world rather than interpreting it means not only changing the outside world but, above all, changing the everyday. This total praxis becomes possible as soon as it is thought, and because it is thought. However, given the real conditions (production relations, and the historical and political conjuncture), it is not possible. We return to Marx's idea of a dialectical unit comprising the supreme Utopia and the supremely real. Would not the idea of total revolution be as vital in determining the field of possibilities as the idea of absolute (achieved) knowledge is in determining the path of science and the sense of the relative?

b) *Partial revolutionary praxis.* The economic development of a country and the general growth of production (as opposed to an uneven and incoherent growth) represent a partial revolutionary praxis, a fragment of total praxis which can conceal it and even cheat it. It is not always easy to distinguish this partial revolutionary praxis from the reformist praxis which accepts and submits to the 'real' – i.e., production relations as given – rather than bringing pressure to bear on their contradictions, in order to transform them.

c) *Knowledge as practice* (in so far as it has its reason and its content in praxis) and conversely *practice as intervention and embodiment in knowledge.*

Knowledge is in no respect an abstract activity. It may have its theories and its concepts, and it can be host to the conflict between theory and practice (in their dialectical unity, i.e., a creative conflict), but nevertheless theoretical knowledge cannot be separated from praxis. It is an integral part of it.

Even the 'purest' knowledge uses techniques and implements, be they material or formal. It is therefore inseparable from the productive forces, from the social forms of the organization and the division of labour, and from the political forms which sanction and direct social forms of organization. Thus the foundation and, even more, the *content* of scientific objectivity are social (and thus relative, up to a certain point). To say that science is objective is to say that science is part of praxis. Sectors of knowledge can develop only if they serve the needs and the interests of a determined and relatively large social group (such as a class or a class fraction, a country, or a social and political regime), even if their theoretical foundations have been long established.[20]

d) *Political practice*, on the scale of society as a whole, but which is only one level of praxis at one particular stage of the process of becoming, which means that we have no right to fetishize it. 'Political practice' may have (momentarily) refuted Marx's ideas on total revolution, the withering away of the state and the end of political practice, but to present this as a definitive truth would be pure empiricism, and it would also 'ideologize' Marxism, which sought to be a radical critique of ideologies. At the same time, this attitude confirms that radical critique is a necessary aspect of Marxism. Ideology is part of political practice, but praxis contains the social truth of ideology, of politics and of the state.

e) *Repetitive practice*, an indispensable resource for the everyday. It is both irreducible (impossible to suppress) and reducible (in that it can be reduced indefinitely). It can be analysed according to different types of repetition (mechanical, periodic, cyclic, etc.).

f) *Inventive* (creative) *practice*, which derives from repetitive practice. We can already distinguish between practice which creates material works and practice which creates practice, i.e., which modifies human relations (including their ethical dimension).

g) *Specific practices*, uneven in terms of their technicality and of the extent to which they penetrate the uncontrolled sector. They belong to the skills and professions which act upon natural or human 'material': education, medicine, art, architecture, trades unions, farming, etc. In this category we will also include the social practice of small groups (elective or neighbourhood groupings, learned societies, theatrical troupes, and determined 'publics', etc.) which support and back an individual capable of inventiveness, until such point as he escapes them or they themselves reject him. On this level, and according to cases and situations, the historical can become what is most internalized (accepted) or most externalized (cast aside as unimportant).

These limited practices cross-refer to each other, and to the entirety of the set they constitute: existing practice as a whole. Via the groups we can grasp fragmented totality; passing as it does between practicism and speculation, this is perhaps the best route of access. However, this passing from the fragmentary to the total is not without its difficulties, as a careful reading of Marx's authoritative *Capital* will show.

h) When linked to the idea of praxis, analysis of the everyday reveals several formants. Not only do we find the various forms of repetition and the seeds of possible creativity, but we also find utilitarian and fetishist practice, which manipulates things on the level of analytic understanding (which disguises contradictions and dissociates dialectical movements into defined and isolated 'elements'). In the everyday we observe empirical thought at work, with its belief in commodities and money as things. Empirical consciousness takes things and objects from the everyday, and separates them from activity and social relations. It confuses products and creative works, things and objects, with no concern whatever for basic analytic distinctions (while proceeding according to the laws of logic and analytic understanding, which are also those of trivial discourse and day-to-day language). This empirical consciousness uses means as ends: goods, money, commodities, capital. It champions fetishism as a valid consciousness. This is the level on which it establishes itself: the reality and (apparently) unmediated positivity of accepted needs, representations and symbolisms. On this level, received representations, which are not recognized as the results of a history and as functions of an entire society, and are indeed unrecognizable as such, impose themselves unchecked. Inadequately aware of its link with totality, and based on the fragmentary division of labour and on class relations (themselves misunderstood, i.e., treated with suspicion and parenthesized), fragmentary practice is accepted as the real, in all its opaqueness and clarity.

It is precisely this 'realness', this 'positiveness', this 'practice' that critique of everyday life disturbs and dismantles (at least on the theoretical plane, the plane of concepts) by proclaiming *the possibility of its radical metamorphosis*. First of all, critique poses the problem: 'What is it that supports this realness and makes it appear as a solid and valid reality?' Therefore its first targets are the representations and symbols active within this apparent 'realness'.

10 Logos, logic, dialectic

Now it would be easy to illustrate the use of dialectical thought, and there are thousands of examples to choose from. Here are a few, and our selection is not without its irony.

France is the fatherland of eternal theoretical and practical reason, the country of Descartes and of Classicism, of the three unities, of the system of tonality in music (Rameau), and of the metric system, etc. The French system of road signs embodies and materializes pure reason for the senses of modern man, and provides a model for technicians the world over. France is the land of the hectometre.[21]

However, if our Frenchman is Cartesian, he also likes his life to be lively and volatile. He gets carried away by odd obsessions. France is also the fatherland of fashion, of ephemerality, of frivolity, fragrances and frills. It is the fatherland of femininity.

If we juxtapose these two aspects of the French genius, the resulting picture will be lacking something. We hope (in vain) that they will coexist peacefully; but the picture is in monochrome, the colours of drama are missing. It is the same when we make the euphoric suggestion that they can complement each other. On the other hand, to confront them as being logically incompatible would be to brand French culture as regrettably absurd, and our judgements would become increasingly disenchanted.

In truth, these two 'aspects' do indeed have their conflicts. They pose problems. On the one hand, they penetrate the most ordinary details of French everyday life, in the general context of modern life. On the other, they refer us back to history, to one particular history.

The fact that these specific characteristics penetrate everyday life (with their contradictions, and in spite of their contradictions) leads us to hope that they will endure. History tells us that probably they will disappear.

In so far as we know anything about it, the sixteenth century in France reveals an exuberance and a lust for life which was to be swallowed up by the Wars of Religion. Then came the century of classical rationality and the bourgeois bureaucratic state of absolute monarchy; the state made use of this rationality and imposed it, mutilating and alienating spontaneity. When it came to levelling out differences and originalities, state rationalism was as effective as state capitalism and administrative socialism! In the eighteenth century there was an attempt to reinstate our lost spontaneity; this attempt reached its critical point with the romantic rebellion, which was doomed to failure, as it was powerless to halt the effects of centralization, the predominance of the Parisian head on the provincial body, and many other phenomena.

In France today, the conflictual 'aspects' of the French genius coexist and affect different groups. Administration (which transforms rationalism into bureaucratic ideology) is the domain of rationality on the practical level, and the universities are its domain on the abstract (speculative) level. A section of the intelligentsia and the feminists represent the volatile aspect, sometimes in the form of rebellion, at others as a pure and simple caricature of spontaneity. The appropriation of these contradictory aspects by differing groups does not stop contradictions and conflicts from emerging, but it blunts them and plunges them into ambiguity. Because of this, the French everyday might be described as a volatile and ambiguous mixture of rationality and empiricism, of positivism and sentimentality. This does not stifle the demand for a supersession which would reinstate spontaneity without losing the clarity of reason, on the contrary, but it does give us reason to fear Americanization, that ideological commodity imported in the name of technical progress, 'consumer society' and the mass media. A socialization peddled by ideology and political models would be no better.

But there is more to be said about dialectical thought than these illustrations tell us. Let us return to another problem, a difficult one, and as yet not satisfactorily resolved: the relations between logic and dialectic. We have already stressed the distinction between *levels* of thought: *formal logic* (logic of similarity), *dialectical logic* (relations of difference, opposition, reciprocity, interaction and complementarity), *praxis* or *dialectical reason* (the exploration and the grasping – never completely – of real dialectical movements). Moreover we have granted logic its own level of reality: the study of relative stabilities, self-regulations, structures and momentary balances in a process of becoming at the heart of which structurings and the dismantling of structures (destructuring) succeed one another. It may be that we failed to stress sufficiently the relative, provisional and momentary character not only of concepts in knowledge, but also of stabilities in the real and in structures. If we are to get a clear understanding of the situation of the everyday within a comprehensively structured society, it is imperative that we return to this question.

Why is the problem so acute? Because post-Hegelian philosophy (including dialectical materialism) has too often taken Hegel's formulations about the emptiness of the categories of formal logic literally. Accordingly, logic is considered valid for 'domestic use' only, as Engels put it. This is to overlook the fact that there is nothing insignificant about everyday usage, and that the use of discourse – language – in everyday life precedes its use in knowledge and philosophy. And another little fact is frequently forgotten: mathematical science operates on the plane of formal rigour, i.e., logic, and dialectic is not an overt feature of it. Philosophical critique may discover some dialectical movements in mathematical thought (the finite/the non-finite, the continuous/the discontinuous, etc.), but nevertheless the rigorous techniques and operational procedures of mathematicians remain irreducibly logical and formal. So they are useful 'concretely'.

Certain people were led to imagine dialectical thought to be at one and the same time a subject ('dialectics'), a rejection (a pseudo-supersession), and a pure and simple reflection of the dialectical realities active in things, and which operate in the manner of things. This is to confuse dialectical contradiction with logical absurdity, because no distinction between logical contradiction and dialectical contradiction has been made. This presentation of philosophical thought as though it were higher philosophy degrades it and comes dangerously close to sophistry, but without any of the merits attributable to the critical thought of the Greek Sophists. In fact it did allow for a great deal of sophistry, and as an implement for analysing stabilities and dialectical movements it was worthless.

In this pseudo-philosophy, dogmatic sophistry consists of an appeal by the human to nature to 'found' historical and social dialectic by giving it a political (and therefore empirical) use, and then to legitimize it in this debased form. When the human is projected into nature without any prior critique, it is one particular way of acting within the human which is sanctioned, and not the human itself.

Galilean, Cartesian and Newtonian physics pushed geometry and mechanics to their farthest consequences. It was a science of trajectories, and gave very little houseroom to questions concerning the stability of mechanical systems. Once several general laws had been accepted, among which were the so-called 'universal' laws of gravity, stability was a logical conclusion. This science presented a single model of reality, *the planetary model*: at the centre, the sun, on the periphery, its retinue of satellite bodies, and a single force linking them together. This model constituted a defined, closed and stable physical system. Given gravitational forces, Newton's law and the tangential impulsions at the initial instant, it became increasingly difficult to calculate orbits, but the fact that they were stable was virtually assured. In passing, we should note that the planetary model appeared to be universal. For more than a century every effort was made to imagine human (psychological and sociological) reality according to this image: a central, primordial element, with subordinated elements gravitating around it.

When Bohr conceived of the differentiated atom of microphysics, he imagined it by analogy with the planetary model (the principle of correspondence): a nucleus, some electrons. However it quickly became apparent that the stability of the system conceived of in this way was no longer self-evident. The interaction of positive and negative electrical particles could not play exactly the same role as gravitational interaction; although the active forces were in proportion to the masses (electrical charges) and in inverse proportion to the square of the distance, negativity and repulsion came into play. The stabilization (self-regulation) of the system posed a problem. At the same time and correlatively, microphysics was moving from one model to another. It was abandoning the planetary model (on the microscopic scale) in favour of the *harmonic model*, which we will now explain. In this model, the atom is analogous to a vibrating spring or string (a linear oscillator). Like a string when it vibrates, it presents static states within a spectrum. Fixed at its two extremities, the vibrating string takes an infinite number of transitory positions between those two terminal limits. Within this infinite number, certain well-defined positions can be observed, which become consolidated, so to speak, during the vibrational movement, excluding other intermediate positions as they do so. Not only are these static states determined, but they are also determinable on the basis of numbers which are whole (harmonics), and therefore distinct and finite, although the number of harmonics remains unlimited. This relation between the finite and the non-finite gives rise to some precise calculations (Fourier's series and integrals, Freedholm's theorem, etc.). Where does this physical reality come from? From the remarkable fact that the initial impulse – the plucking of the taut string – exerts a *double* action: it displaces the string from its position of equilibrium and it also transmits a perturbation (a wave) along the length of the string, which seeks to regain its position of equilibrium. The law of perturbation must be calculated together with the law of the return to equilibrium. The first acts in relation to the distance on the string (frequency) and the second in relation to the square of the distance from the ends of the string to the position of equilibrium (amplitude). The force of gravity does not have this duality. It is a single force and the gravitational field is only influenced by the dynamic effects of a single force in opposition to the inertia of material masses. Therefore the harmonic model enables us to represent something which the planetary model could not: *dual* interactions (positive and negative, attraction and repulsion). Via this model we can turn our minds to representing a veritable *complex field*: spectrums, transitionals, static states, harmonics, the determinable relation between the finite and the non-finite (between the continuous and the discontinuous).

We should point out here that the concepts of equilibrium and of rest, immobility or inertia, are not the same as the concept of static state. This state stands out from transitionals, of which there are an infinite number, but there is nothing definitive about it. In a sense it is itself only a transitional; the string's final position – and its initial one

– defines the equilibrium at the beginning and at the end of the movement. However, there is another side to the question. When two sides of a set of scales are equally weighted they offer an equilibrium which the slightest addition of weight on one side will break for ever; the mechanical equilibrium disappears, because it has no capacity for righting itself or for self-regulation. Conversely, when a string vibrates it moves in a stable manner, and the movement itself creates a relatively stable form, although static states stand out from the continuous background provided by the transitionals; the force of the initial percussion or plucking and the actual place of impact modify the subsequent overall form and its distinct elements (harmonics) *relatively little*. Mathematically, in the case of fairly small oscillations, frequency does not depend upon the initial conditions of the movement, but is defined by the properties of the determined system per se.

Bohr used his planetary model to formulate his 'stability postulate', a mental process in which, precisely, stability was grasped as a problem. At around the same time, Planck published his famous hypothesis according to which an oscillator can only emit or absorb radiations in discrete and discontinuous quantities, measurable by whole numbers (energy particles: quanta, photons). This useful hypothesis also demonstrated the usefulness of the 'harmonic model'. We know that Planck's hypothesis contradicted Bohr's, but that eventually the two became merged. It was demonstrated that an atom (made up of a nucleus around which electrons with negative electric charges circulated) can only assume certain relatively stable configurations, and that when it shifts from one static state to another which has less energy, it loses a quantum or a whole number of energy quanta.

From then on, *double determinations* (continuous and discontinuous, positive and negative, finite and non-finite, etc.) come into play in microphysical material reality. Wave mechanics and quantum mechanics were to develop the harmonic model. The propagation of light waves allows for static states, relative stabilities, trajectories and discontinuities, in short, corpuscles. If continuous waves appear in corpuscular form, the corpuscles themselves will in turn become part of the vibrational movements (waves). The energy contained in the wave associated with a corpuscle spreads like that corpuscle. The 'wave/corpuscle' dichotomy and the 'continuous/discontinuous' dichotomy can no longer be separated from the idea that matter and the field occupied by physical (material) forces are dynamic.

And so it became possible to interpret these discoveries (which revolutionized physics) as a brilliant vindication of dialectical methodology and of dialectical materialism as a philosophy, and there were many who had no hesitation in doing so. The old geometric and mechanistic physics of continuous trajectories, simple fields, and discontinuous physical bodies posited without any concrete link with the surrounding continuousness, became old-fashioned. Although, on a rough estimate, this appeared to be quite correct, it was limited by its own logical character. If we are to grasp objective, material nature in all its profoundness, we need to make our concepts dialectical and to introduce dialectical ideas and movements. Is it not imperative to admit or to reaffirm a dialectic of nature?

And yet, is it really that simple? Are we not going rather too fast? Let us pause to think. How can the 'continuous/discontinuous' relation and the 'wave/corpuscle' relation be determined in microphysical reality? To begin with, determinations were posited as different and oppositional, and thus were seen as mutually exclusive. Then connections were discovered. These discoveries took place at the beginning of the era of classic physics: the study of optical phenomena (spectrums, rays, diffusion and diffraction) and of vibrating strings. From then on it became impossible to say that concepts and objects (fields and bodies considered as physical realities) can be grasped by thought and consciousness 'without reciprocal contact', which for Lenin and for Hegel is the essence of antidialectic. We can even say that the unity discovered between opposites or contraries modifies their relations and turns them into contradictions (dialectically). Thus we can talk about a dialectical movement of thought just as we can about the making of concepts and operational techniques dialectical. Moreover, these movements have a relation with objective reality, i.e., with movements in reality; this vibrating string, this tuning fork whose properties I am studying, 'exist'. They are fragments constructed from matter which existed before I did, which exist in front of me and outside of me; when I invent the formal implements which will allow me to define them and up to a certain point to demonstrate them, I am not creating their properties. In particular, the link between these properties and simple whole numbers and countable sets, static and distinct states, discrete units and relative stabilities, is an objective one.

And so can I cast caution to the winds and move from 'gnosiology' to cosmology and ontology by attributing nature with the dialectical movement I have just described? Can I make dialectical movement objective in knowledge without further process? This would be jumping the gun, and would pose problems which the philosophers of institutionalized dialectical materialism have failed to notice or have parenthesized. The scientists who revolutionized physics had no knowledge of dialectical thought and proceeded using experimentation on the one hand and formal rigour on the other. In so far as they had an 'ideology', it was a bourgeois one. But there is a more serious issue. Could the macrophysical material world be beyond dialectic? Could microphysics be governed by the dialectic of nature? The latter *is* dialectical and the former *is* non-dialectical, such is the effective conclusion of the official philosophy of nature, which serves it all up in a recklessly systematized mishmash of dialectical methodology and philosophic materialism. Now macrophysics is the world of our senses, of objects and of things, and of our social practice. *It is the world of the everyday.* According to this view, it would be perfectly stable, governed by logic and logic alone, like classic mechanics, and thus beyond dialectic! . . .

As it happens, the only way the science of physical reality can progress is by using the principle of correspondence (between levels of reality). If there is no longer any correspondence and analogy between the macrophysical level and the microphysical level, how can the latter be grasped? Only by reference to analogies and homologies can knowledge demonstrate differences. By granting it an absolute and abstract stability, the dialectic of nature not only makes the 'human world' of relative stabilities, discourse and logic incomprehensible, but also severs the correspondence between its different levels.

What exactly do we mean when we talk about a 'dialectic of nature' and of 'matter' on the microphysical level, the level of waves and corpuscles? Do we mean that there is a mobility, a movement of matter, a process of becoming? That is certainly true of classic mechanics and of trajectories. Do we mean that although they are distinct, the terms we use – matter and energy, wave and corpuscle, continuity and discontinuity, etc. – have a relation and a unity?

545

Although it is obvious that they do, what that relation is remains unclear. Are they identical? In that case we would seesaw between clarity and logical identicalness, and the absurdity of an absolute identicalness between terms which *a priori* are distinct and mutually relative. Are they contradictory, a set of contradictions? But that would imply the stability of a 'system' which becomes difficult to understand. It is true that stabilities are always provisional, and that they have critical moments. It is true that every structure collapses, or has the potential to do so. These considerations do not eliminate the very general and creative problem of stability and (relative) constants in the process of becoming. Moreover, the concepts of conflict, contradiction and antagonism do not exonerate us from the need experimentally to study critical moments and moments of rupture, the collapse of structures, and 'destructurations'.

So long and in so far as a 'system' remains stable (presenting static states, constancy and 'bodies'), can we talk about 'dialectic'? Only if we take great care. It is true that we do not really know what happens between the plucking of a string and its return to the stability of a static state (i.e., harmonics). To a certain extent and until further notice, transitions and transitionals cannot be calculated using mathematical implements. Equally, it is true that the string may snap. That is not our concern here. As long as our study highlights static states, constants, relative stabilities and the numbers which express them, we will remain on the level of logic, and we will not have the right to 'transcend' that level. All we can do is patiently to make the concepts dialectical, while avoiding the *philosophical* operation of creating an ontology: an 'in-itself' dialectic of nature. To do so would be to abandon our model; we would be turning our concepts into representation and turning provisional conclusions drawn from our model into absolutes. Stability (and this is almost a paradox) is much more related to discontinuity than it is to an 'existential' or 'ontological' continuity. Here, dialectical thought consists of a study of stabilities and structures which does not overlook the process of becoming, and of a study of the process of becoming which does not overlook stabilities. In short, it is a question of grasping structurations without omitting the process of becoming which dismantles them and which is already active within structuration per se. Thus our answer to the question about dialectic in nature will itself be dialectical, i.e., not 'yes' or 'no', but 'yes and no' (perhaps yes, perhaps no!). We will develop the harmonic model until we have exhausted it, and we will refuse to use philosophy to transcend it.

It is a truism that the achievements of contemporary physics have resulted in a promotion of logic and a dialectization of concepts, and thus in the consolidation of a dialectical logic as a level of thought.[22] The logical *formalization* of thought in mathematics and physics has become more profound in that it has been accompanied by a gradual *dialectization* of logic. But (unless we use a philosophical postulate which we must declare as such, and which greatly exceeds both the content and the form of knowledge) we have no right to go straight to the absolute by decreeing a dialectic of nature which our mind can immediately grasp. The official Marxist theory of *reflection* not only admits a dialectic of nature, but also supposes that our minds can seize it fully and exhaust it, since they 'reflect' it.

The concept of *complementarity* which comes to us from microphysics is in no way privileged. To grant it a special importance would be to set it up as a philosophy; we would soon be replacing the old determinist philosophy with a non-determinist metaphysics. The concept conceals the model and stops us finding the unknown elements which the harmonic model contains and to which it is a pointer (notably whatever happens between the initial disturbance and the static states in the transitionals). Thus the concept of complementarity is no more important or essential than those of reciprocity, interaction, contrariness or contradiction and antagonism. It does not account for the formation of stabilities (structuration), or for transitions, breaks or critical points. And yet, in so far as we can observe interactions between 'dual' properties, and relative stabilities, structures or forms deep within interactions, we can no more dispense with complementarity than we can with difference, contrariness, polarity, oppositeness and reciprocity of action, etc. With an extraordinary confusion between levels of thought and of reality, contemporary philosophers have believed in the dialectic of complementarity, while at the same time affirming the incompatibility of this concept with dialectical thought. With the same inextricable confusion, philosophers tried to remove stability from dialectic,[23] and then by some kind of miracle to extrapolate stability from antagonistic contradiction.

And so, when speaking about material nature, would we say: '*There are dialectical movements and processes, and there are stabilities which are based upon a refined logic'*? No matter how cautious this statement is, it cannot satisfy us completely. How can we separate logic from dialectic?

And could we distinguish between regional ontologies, by saying: '*There are regions for dialectic and for the process of becoming, and others for stability and logic. Similarly, nature is one region of being, and history or consciousness is another; dialectic may have a role to play in nature, at least in terms of region and species, but alienation never can. In history, consciousness and praxis, specific dialectic and alienation can both have a role to play'*? But how can we place these regions or regional ontologies in relation to each other? The idea of totality collapses. But totality is the inspiration behind our research, in which – above all and against all odds – we are striving to be systematic.

Would continuousness be the world's ontological background (or as someone who is 'listening in' on being might say, its background noise), against which objects, things, action, events and relative stabilities stand out? That is nothing more than a metaphysical thought; only in science fiction does an absolute 'continuum' in space and time, which is revealed only in so far as it is inaccessible, appear as a serious object of discourse. There are philosophers who draw their imagery from science fiction, but without really realizing that they are doing so.

Finally, could we say: '*The non-dialectical position is imperative for dialectic, that is its background and its foundation. When that position is present, dialectic enters into contradiction with itself. It posits and presupposes stableness in order to conquer and destroy it'*? This would be going back to Hegel, or even farther, to Fichte.[24]

Therefore we are finding the transition from methodology (or gnosiology) to an ontology extremely difficult to achieve. And yet, reliable sources – social practice, language – tell us that knowledge and method correspond to 'something'. This 'something' is revealed subsequently, in the history of knowledge. None of the schematics available to represent it in advance is satisfactory. In these conditions, there is only one way in, and only one way out: to abandon the system (momentarily, but probably for quite a long time), to abandon the comprehensive picture of the universe, and to abandon ontology – while making sure not to return to empiricism, positivism or simplified logicism.

Rather than exploring 'being', we must explore what is possible (and this includes the exploration of space, and the transformation of everyday life). Would not 'being' reveal itself in what is possible and by what is possible at the same time as it realizes itself historically? Is this not what the idea of total praxis implies? From this perspective, classic ontology would harbour a serious error, namely the wish to reach 'being' after the act, via the past and via what has been accomplished and made actual, in a metaphysical repetition, a new beginning or eternal return, a resurrection, a reminiscence. It tries to use thought to reduce the double determinations of the actual, and primarily by the rift between thought and reality. It ends up in a dilemma: it must either admit divine creation, or endow matter with a quality or property which already contains consciousness and spirit. Now these two affirmations are unacceptable. What right have we to attribute to the *non-finite* universe qualities and properties which only have a meaning in our *finite* world, at a fleeting moment of the development of mankind on Planet Earth?

Ontology is worn out. Let us use the exploration of what is possible and the development of knowledge to discover modalities of thought with which to replace it. Let us develop a metaphilosophy. In the meantime, let us make a careful distinction between the levels of reality and thought, while taking care not to merge whatever is linked together and not to separate whatever appears distinctive.

Will this detour (which is brief but at the same time lengthy) through the labyrinth of so-called philosophical questions be a digression from our subject: everyday life? No. It will enable us to draw up a series of propositions.

First, we must not overlook the constancies and (relative) stabilities of everyday life, but nor must we fetishize them. The everyday per se does not have the viscous consistency which is often attributed to it, nor the evanescent, fluid mobility which is a corollary of that representation. Stabilities are definitive in appearance only, and we must avoid confusing them with 'the real', the 'existential', 'being', 'substance' or 'human nature'. Once we penetrate a stability, its limits become apparent on all sides. We may think it is compact and durable. The critical thought inherent in knowledge dissolves this illusion.

Second, the solar–planetary model has long been presented as universal, and it still has an influence in the domain of the social sciences. Does it not underpin representations of hierarchies in the family and in the state? For our study of everyday man, we prefer to use the harmonic model, in so far as any physical model can be of help to us. Not only are we to trying make a kind of spectrum analysis of the everyday; we also consider that stabilities and periodicities emerge from a set of fleeting and profound phenomena: transitionals and transitions. Forms and structures, or static states, are born and prosper against a background of fleeting states which works select and consolidate. The actual and the potential are united in an intelligible way. Static states can extend towards limitlessness – towards formlessness. Whatever is fleeting and transitional receives forms and structures which deform or transform it but which do not abolish it. There is much that is unknown or unforeseen in these relations and connections, which are yet to be defined with any clarity. When we use this model we will often employ the terms 'formants' and 'partials' as used in harmonic analysis, rather than the word 'element', which is used in conventional analysis. However, we will not use them to hide 'dys-harmonies' and conflicts.

Third, we will say: 'In nature, history, society and knowledge there is a multiplicity of dialectical movements, each one distinct and specific.' Transposing the physical principle of the superposition of small movements and oscillations, we will go so far as to say: 'There are as many or more dialectical movements in social consciousness as there are waves on the surface of the sea.' We will never say: 'Dialectic wants . . . dialectic does . . .'. We will only employ the word 'dialectical', i.e., as an adjective, never as a noun. Moreover we will know that a dialectical movement of thought (or in thought) never coincides absolutely with a dialectical movement in nature, history or thought per se. This last proposition may seem paradoxical, but it means that thinking never exhausts the content of a concept or of a thought, and that there is a dialectical relation between all movements. Such a coincidence – which the vulgar representation of *reflection* postulates or suggests – would exhaust any objective dialectical movement by a thought or a concept, and would be 'exhausting' for human thought and for praxis. The identicalness of two dialectical movements is an *idea*, and can never be anything more than an idea, pointing to a convergence at infinity which is both necessary to postulate and impossible to attain. However, if there can never be an absolute coincidence of two dialectical movements for human thought (i.e., identicalness between an objective movement and a subjective movement of thought), nor can there ever be mutual externality. Dialectical thought grasps objective movements *partially* (fragmentarily, in approximative and provisional propositions), and in its own particular way (the way of knowledge – the process and the history of knowledge – through the specific contradictions of knowledge, which are not completely unconnected to the contradictions of society, history or nature, but which are resolved in another way). *The result is that a dialectical movement never takes place entirely within language.* Discourse can never express it adequately. Would not the idea of a total discourse also be an idea taken to the limit, to infinity? Discourse must make several approximative attempts before it can 'say' a dialectical movement, and even then it will never be exhaustive. The verbalization of praxis and the use of (day-to-day or sophisticated) concepts are both equally inadequate for the task. In short, just like concepts, language must use thought and knowledge effectively to make itself dialectical. Language is a work, the work of a society.

Discourse is an important if not essential fact of the everyday. It is controlled by logic (although in everyday life it never achieves the formal rigour which a logician's mind can draw from it). It is controlled by 'the world of objects', by concerns about stability, by effective stabilities, by questions which require yes-or-no answers. Dialectical movement reveals itself in the gaps and breaks in coherent discourse. At times the gaps and breaks or, so to speak, the holes within discourse, give rise to irrational obscurity or formlessness (the 'infralinguistic' level), and at others to the irruption of deeper movements (the 'supralinguistic' level). Thus we can define dialectical thought neither as incoherence nor as a higher coherence (discourse on discourse, or total discourse). Often it starts with play on words (including the most famous one of all, *aufheben*, to abolish and to construct, thus to supersede). It must stimulate discourse in some way, assaulting it even, in order to force it to say things which language would not put into words, and would even conceal. When Hegel brought dialectical movement in general to language, he achieved something unique, but he did not exhaust dialectical movements, nor did he make discourse absolutely and definitively dialectical.

And so we need to note a sort of unceasing dialectical movement between Logos (logic, discourse, the everyday) and dialectical thought per se. To elevate or bring a specific aspect of praxis (and the everyday itself) to language, to pass it into language, is an essential task for thought; it is a creative endeavour, and even a revolutionary act. To speak actions, events and objects – to put them into words – is the only means for conceiving of them (for developing concepts). However, language and discourse are not self-sufficient, and are always inadequate. The philosophical privilege granted to Logos by contemporary thought tells us much about the difficulties of philosophy: it is much more a position of retreat than an impregnable fortress. One level of experience and one part of the (everyday) real are passed off as being equals to totality. No doubt is cast either on the object of knowledge or on its reflection within the mind: they coincide, or almost. This implies a postulate: that the part is appropriate to the whole. But this implication is ignored. The mistake is so obvious that the philosophical and almost ontological privilege invested in the Word comes in tandem with a profound social crisis of language, expressivity and the 'world of expression'. It is as though praxis itself were refuting the appropriateness of the part to the whole, by destroying it! Language and discourse are valid only in so far as they are superseded by a tense and concerted effort, on all sides and in all directions: towards the everyday and towards the poetic, towards logical rigour and towards dialectic, towards the 'infra' level and towards the 'supra' level.

Therefore dialectical thought implies a permanent critique and autocritique of discursiveness, of logic, and of their categories. Let us repeat something we have said many times before. Dialectical contradiction is radically different from logical contradiction (or absurdity). It is reason on a higher level of intelligibility. Once grasped, it founds itself both as fact and as concept. Although it is inexhaustible, it is not irrational, arational or transrational. It develops on the conceptual plane where, in an ever-repeated process, concepts are rendered dialectical. As such, dialectical thought is clearly indispensable for all the sciences as well as for knowledge of praxis, but this does not confer any kind of a priori upon it. Dialectical thought avoids empiricism and it avoids rationalist construction. The moment of critique (the negative) is essential to it.

Therefore although language and discourse are facts of everyday life, a great effort will be needed to make them express the everyday. Language and discourse are part of everyday life, but this does not mean that we can put the everyday into words easily. To experience banality is not enough to tell us what banality actually is. Thought about the everyday tends to be limited to thought about everyday discourse (language). So it tends towards a simple semantics, a logic of the everyday, or simply a description of banality, whereas the aim should be to discover certain hidden movements: need/desire, private/public, natural/artificial, serious/frivolous, work/outside work, alienation/disalienation, etc. With their particularized movements, their specific contradictions and their interactions, these resonances and dissonances deep within the everyday are revealed only slowly and with difficulty.

Fourth, since we have not projected dialectical contradiction, logical identicalness, contrariness or complementarity on to being, nature or the absolute, we can discern *types* of contradiction. This is the kind of typology attempted by institutional Marxism, which distinguishes between contradiction and antagonism (in a way which purports to be linked rationally with practice, but which in fact comes straight from political empiricism).

Let us take the typology a stage further. First we distinguish an initial type, which is the contradiction to be found in concepts and representations, and which is resolved essentially by an effort of consciousness. Supersession always operates within a form or a structure of social consciousness. Principally, it modifies representations or concepts. Supersession takes place in and through language, by means either of a promotion (which delivers certain things into language) or of an invention (of words, images or symbols), but this does not mean that it becomes completely separated from practical action. This kind of invention of words, symbols and images – in short, of ideologies and representations – has its quota of effectiveness, and does not purely and simply 'reflect' accomplished facts with the aim of justifying them. It creates something: a unit within the whole. Since contradictions *between ideas* can be resolved in and through an effort of consciousness, this effort is itself an action. As soon as it resolves conflicts between representations in a *work*, it creates a unity. In this sense, any cultural, philosophic or aesthetic work is a highly complex social product, and quite distinct from material products. It does not simply reflect or express contradictions; it supersedes them and resolves them 'through ideas' or in and through a proposition, i.e., a unifying hypothesis. If this proposition brings forth new conflicts, we only notice this later, during a historical process. In itself, the *work* is a unit and a whole, and it also creates a unit and a whole: a specific unit made actual within the whole. Its content is indefinitely analysable, and thus inexhaustible. It contains the (provisional) unity of the non-finite and the finite.

We will distinguish between this first type of contradiction and those which, in the way they are represented, are insoluble by the effort of thought (knowledge) alone, but which are apparently *possible* to solve by means of creative praxis. The interested parties see the problems arising from the process of becoming, and in what these problems bring they see the actions which may modify them. By making the problems real, they resolve the conflict by establishing a higher unit. Then they must grasp profound dialectical movements which demand to be superseded: conjuncture and structure, problematic situation and categoric givens. In this case, no intellectual or cultural *work* – or no philosophical, aesthetic or ethical one – can offer or even suggest a solution.[25]

The distinction we have proposed is not exactly the same as the theoretical (methodological) difference between contrariness and contradiction, for it is well and truly a matter of *conflicts* between representations (ideologies, symbols, concepts). Moreover, no representation can remain purely 'representative', and all representations are represented in the real (practical) world. These conflicts stimulate the creation (production) of works and are momentarily resolved in a work. In 'real' life, every work is transformed more or less profoundly into a way of living and of acting.

Nor is the distinction the same as the political (practical) difference between reform and revolution. It is true that the second type of contradiction corresponds to the revolutionary situation. People can no longer go on living as before. They can no longer use representations to resolve their conflicts. So the question is one no longer of interpreting 'the world' – the human and natural real – in an (aesthetic, philosophical or moral) work, but of changing it. Therefore the change must be achieved within the context of the way of life and living conditions: in and through praxis. However, the changes which come about as a result of such situations do not always revolutionize ways of living. If they can affect 'real' life – ways of living and of acting – they can also express themselves in works and in simple changes of representation.

Finally there are the contradictions which at the moment are insoluble, i.e., whose resolution does not even appear *possible*. However, we cannot say for certain that such a situation will last for ever. Marx wrote that humanity only sets itself problems it can resolve, as though every problem already implied the burgeoning consciousness of solutions (possibilities). But surely this formulation is too optimistic. As for the pessimistic and nihilistic formula: 'Humanity only sets itself insoluble problems', it is untenable. The deepest contradictions are tenacious; the problems they pose can only be solved in the long term. Applying our thought to praxis, we will be able to distinguish between what is immediately possible and what is possible in the long term (but impossible for the present), and between the possible impossible and the absolutely (and ipso facto inconceivable) impossible. Therefore there is a profound analogy between the effort of an artist or a philosopher to express and resolve contradictions on the plane of 'ideas' (but in a 'real' work) and the general effort of individuals in social practice to formulate and resolve their problems. In the first case, the activity of creative consciousness produces a work which disalienates in relation to certain experienced contradictions but which produces another specific alienation (which may be ideological, philosophical or artistic, etc.). The work is a product, although not all products are works. In the second case, activity realizes individual possibilities; at first these are nebulous, but during his history the individual makes them actual in a generally limited series of choices; he becomes what he was; he produces and is what he becomes. His everyday life is a work of creativity. It is far from being a free and conscious work. It can sometimes transpire that the creative effort ends pathologically, in neurosis or psychosis. In its way, a pathological state is the creative work of an individual, elaborated, systematized, coherent and everyday, which resolves – badly – the inner contradictions of his consciousness (but without 'reflecting' the brutally objective, psychological or social external conditions which are shared equally by all the individuals of a class or an era). The pathological state is a lived work of creativity: a personal product, a bad solution to a conflict between what is possible and what is impossible. The pathological state disalienates in relation to the initial conflictive situation, but plunges the mentally alienated individual into a deeper alienation, by the fact that he imagines that the initial contradiction has been resolved by the creative work he is living through: the delirium, the pathological state itself.

One corollary of the typology of contradictions is a typology of negativities. In one case, negativity attacks representations; in another, it undermines situations; in a third, it challenges and dismantles the totality of what exists. The univocal and general negativity (the ontology) of Hegelianism – in its diluted version, contemporary existentialism – cannot satisfy us; it is of no use to concrete analysis (except perhaps in formulating the problem of analysis per se, which as we know implies general negativity, since if used without due caution it breaks, dissociates and isolates, taking differences to the point where they become separate and analogies to the point where they become merged). Beyond a certain limit, the negative becomes a fetish, a vision of nothingness; radical critique becomes hypercritique, and nihilism is established as a truth without that truth having been legitimized. Like dialectical movement, negativity or negation will always appear to us as particularized and specific: sometimes as a lack and a gap, sometimes as a (perceived or unperceived) absence, sometimes as a breakdown or a point of disintegration. We will see it at work in a variety of ways: challenges, disturbances, disintegration.

Should we attribute any 'functions' to negativity? Only with a great many reservations. For example, certain thinkers consider that terror has a sociological 'function', namely to drive the masses into an action of which it is the cause and the effect. Terror could be seen as the embodiment of the negative in political and historical action. Now on the other hand we could agree with Marx and Lenin that when the masses genuinely enter political life the need for violence and terror is reduced and even eliminated in favour of concrete democratization.

In any event, the ideas of specific negativity and supersession bring with them the radical rejection of one particularly tenacious fetishism which we will never stop criticizing, and that is the fetishism of 'the real' and 'the positive'. To present the negative in all its profundity, we shall use the precise concept we have used before: the concept of the *possible* (equally specified and concrete). Between the world which is chock-a-block full of realism and positivism, and the gaping world of pure negativity and nihilism, our aim is to discover the open world, the world of what is possible. We are not confusing this with indeterminateness, although it is not without chance and randomness.

11 Logic and characterology

We previously mentioned a dialectical movement within methodology itself. The formal already contains specificity (content and concreteness) and vice versa. Where specificity is concerned, it encompasses the formal because the formal also has realness, socially, in praxis. Thus the level of logical thought cannot be isolated and pushed to one side in an abstraction external to reality in general and to stabilities in particular (provisional balances, self-regulations, series of decisions and choices, etc.). Therefore when we pass from the abstract to the concrete, we must already be taking on 'the real' and recognizing it. The way we are going to apply this theoretical notion will seem paradoxical. In effect, to bring something which appears to be completely irreducible to logic – i.e., individual character – into logical patterns deemed to be inherent to the everyday real is almost attempting the impossible. Nevertheless we shall attempt to determine the logical frameworks of such a characterology.

It is easy to discover relations of opposition, of polarity, and even of complementarity between individualities. Every historical period offers types of individuality, the relations between which can only be understood by means of these formal concepts. Let us recall the feudal baron and the knight who devotes himself to defending the widow and the orphan, the faithful knight and the treacherous knight; the giant of art and knowledge in the times of da Vinci and Michelangelo, and the condottiere; Savonarola the mystic and the Machiavellian mind; the saint and the adventurer; the militant and the arriviste, etc. The opposition of these types does not exhaust their connections. Once we have analysed the way they are polarized, we must try to understand historically how such opposing types came into being simultaneously. The ways in which they relate would appear to be more complex than the ways in which they oppose and complement one another.

Correlation, complementarity and the division into opposites are transferred into the 'soul' and the individual consciousness. As Kierkegaard wrote in his Journals, it takes at least two men to make up a single one: Pantagruel and Panurge, Sancho Panza and Don Quixote, Leporello and Don Giovanni, *Jacques le fataliste* and his master, Faust and Mephistopheles (and the latter is a bit more than half of one man, and a bit less too!). Several great works have projected the parts (or formants) of the human soul into opposing and complementary individuals. As a result, every 'soul' seems to be made up of at least two individual souls. However, what is presented in art as a lively dialogue between two complementary individuals occurs in the 'lived' in the guise of a more or less profound conflict. The logical relation of opposition does not exhaust the real relations. Moreover, we have not yet reached the limits of the logical connections.

Let us leave history now and consider existing (bourgeois) society. In this society, the relation between the individual and the social exists. How could it not exist? The mutual exteriority of the individual and the social has never been anything more than a deceptive representation: even when the individual thinks he is separating himself from society, he remains a social being. And so the relation exists, but social reality is such that this real and incomplete relation lies hidden; for this reason it can be misunderstood. It is neither conscious nor unconscious in the sense that an occult or obscure substantial reality is. It is hidden beneath representations which render it effective and efficient: norms, attitudes, symbols, values. The present-day conformism which lies at the heart of everyday banality is happy to accept norms and models as though they were the true 'individual/society' relation, rather than an effective mediation of it. An essential element of the structure of this society and of the 'individual/society' relations within its frameworks is that there be a lack of knowledge of them. And if the real relation does become apparent, it is always in an incomplete and mutilated manner. Is this not what happens in the large economic and bureaucratized organizations within monopolistic state capitalism? The individual firmly believes in 'society', and sees himself as a member of it; but this society is nothing more than a limited company, in the capitalist sense.[26]

Because the 'individual/society' relation is not known or recognized as such, because it remains opaque and because certain of the socially imposed ways it is represented do not tally with the 'lived' (the individual within praxis), the individual tries to find out what this relation really is. His lack of knowledge gives rise to a fundamental uneasiness which is as stimulating as it is destructive, and this is the context in which he reconstructs the relation. But he does so using representations which have been developed for this very purpose. The 'individual/society' relation becomes the object of a variety of theorizations which employ elements borrowed on the one hand from the lived and from society as a whole, and on the other from institutions and ideologies. Ignored or misunderstood, the real relation becomes completely alienated and fossilized (reified) in a deceptive and limiting representation. Instead of participating fully and consciously in social praxis, the individual constructs himself on the basis of a particular form and a representation of that form. In his effort to rediscover the hidden relation he strays even farther from it and loses his powers (his possibilities). He becomes imprisoned within himself. This attitude by which he is formed as a conscious individual, and which will soon become a mere collection of behaviour patterns and stereotypes, implies some deceptively creative postulates: the 'individual/society' relation must and can be created – society has a coherence and a unity, since its inner contradictions are not of prime importance. Thus in all good conscience, good will and good faith, the individual will build his 'soul'. The basic materials of this 'soul' will be representations, and these will come up against other, previously accepted representations, which they will either challenge or reinforce. In all good conscience, the individual will believe that he is living to the full; his 'soul' will be his own creative work, and even a kind of cultural work in which creativity and representations are lived as everyday facts. In so far as they are stable realities, these 'souls' enter into a logical structure within dialectical movement. This determination interacts with the other economic and social determinations. It superimposes itself on them in a complex relation of resonance or dissonance. It does not supplant them and does not destroy them.

In the relation thus put together, i.e., constructed, let us observe three (logical) moments:

a *general, abstract, metaphysical:* the relation of the 'soul' with society in general, represented as a whole;

b *particular, positive, pragmatic:* since he perceives society as a given, the problem for the individual is to establish a determined relation with this given society, in given conditions;

c *singular, mystic, personal:* the representation which the individual has of himself as difference and in-difference, as irreducible originality and as personality.

Thus the active representation and the 'lived' which it represents enter into the logical pattern of classic syllogism: general/particular/singular. Each logical 'moment' implies another, and they all assume substance and reality independently of each other. Thus in the everyday reality of existing (bourgeois) society we find the general type, the particular type and the singular type, each one emphasizing a logical element or moment; what is more, at the heart of each class or type we rediscover all the other moments, in a subordinated or recessive state. For example, in the class (in the logical sense of the term), i.e., in the general type, we will recognize one general type (or subclass, or subtype), another particular one and another singular one. Thus we will have a formal combination: A.B.C.; A (a,b,c), B (a,b,c), C (a,b,c); A (aa, ab, ac . . .) with implied types, subtypes and sub-subtypes.

A. *The general type.* This is the highest class or type; he considers the relation with society consciously and takes it as a constant object of thought and meditation; however, his consciousness of the social remains abstract.

A.a. *The Utopian.* Utopianism poses the fundamental problem of the individual/society relation in such perfectly clear terms that the absurdity of formulating it abstractly by means of two mutually independent and external terms becomes blindingly obvious. The Utopian knows that the truth of praxis consists in a conscious oneness: the everyday/the whole, the individual/society, or even the individual/the human race. However he sees this truth as a pure ideal outside the real, something to be created *ex nihilo*. He cannot see that this oneness already exists, but in an incomplete way, mutilated, alienated, mainly because it lacks conscious expression. Thus the Utopian in the classic sense of the term wishes to create a new society and an entirely new life, with new men, individuals united in their desire to sign up to a new social contract. He thinks this is easy to achieve, since it relies merely on the consent of a certain number of minds similar to his own. He is not very aware of the practical conditions and problems. For him, the principle of the identicalness and oneness of the 'individual/society' relation remains general, logical and abstract, rather than being concrete and dialectical. Devoid of means, the pure aim becomes a false one. Mankind will fail, but the failure will be a noble one.

Subtypes: 'Idealists' in the commonplace sense; dreamers, reformers and founders of sects; leaders of literary or artistic movements, etc.

Sub-subtypes: the misunderstood, martyrs, minor poets . . .

A.b. *The man of action*. The opposite of the Utopian, and his complement, he gives priority to the real, realization and means. For him, the data of problems are solid ground. He uses them as a foothold. He has little concern for what may be in the distance. He accepts goals which come from beyond himself and his own thought. He spends little time mulling over the goals and a lot of time on the interests and on the solid means of action. In the case of the Utopian, only the ends counted, and without means, the true goal became a false one. In the case of the man who wants action for action's sake, good and genuine means become dubious if the goal for which they are used is an uncertain one. He thinks he is free, but he is the unconscious slave of real historical forces. If genuine freedom can be defined as knowledge and mastery of necessity, the freedom of the pure man of action can be defined as ignorance of his own enslavement. Among the humbler representatives of this type we find agents and hired men – among its more illustrious representatives are enlightened despots, and certain captains of industry and kings of finance. They can only 'succeed' by exploiting the stupidity of other people; their careers end tragically and they cannot understand what has happened to them.

Opposed subtypes: the activist and the militant; the organizer and organizational man; the politician; the boss; the male 'Rastignac' and the female one (a recent species).[27]

A.c. *The thinker.* He despises the Utopian because the Utopian is not a man of action. He despises the man of action because the man of action is not a Utopian. He is a thinker, therefore he thinks. He is particularly fond of problems of method. He tends to emphasize personality, which he understands to be the opposite of the social, but he tries to reconcile this opposition by being adaptable. In fact, the thinker is a subordinate of the Utopians in ideological terms, and a subordinate of the men of action in practical terms. Deluded by his own methodological or 'intellectual' efficiency, he effortlessly combines the inactivity of the former with the lack of awareness of the latter. He interprets the world, and thinks he has transformed it. He comes to believe that ideas act by themselves, or ends up adopting an ideology which justifies his real life.

Opposed and complementary subtypes: the systematic philosopher; the essayist; the eternally misunderstood; the resigned woman; the embittered cuckold, etc.

B. *The particular type.* The 'individual/social' relation ceases to be perceived as such. If there is any awareness of the social, it is as the postulate of a limited practical activity. Thus the relation is reduced to the particularity of the individual within a limited group. In the words of this individual, philosophers are not practical, and there is no social problem; everything is a mere question of force and adaption, whether by constraint or by consent.

B.a. *The civil servant (the bureaucrat).* With a bit of preferential treatment, a little savvy, a serious attitude and a couple of qualifications, all will be well. Remember the respect we owe to the hierarchy inside which we are on the up and up. Things being what they are, all we need do is to be virtuous in principle, i.e., to make virtue the principle of the state and to make decency the principle of bureaucracy.

Subtypes: the conformist; the specialist; the well-informed man who has his finger on the pulse of things; the pedant (the policeman of knowledge); the citizen; the matron or eternal mother; the member of the *Académie française*.

B.b. *The middleman or the bohemian.* The reverse and the complement of the bureaucrat, this ersatz civil servant tries to occupy every available hole in the social automatism to which he owes his appointment. Although this has no status, and comes to him from outside, he considers it to be the freest and most internalized act of his own personal initiative. Although his function is to act as a safety valve or conductor, he sees himself at the summit of the hierarchy. He despises bureaucracy for being too staid and too pragmatic, and thinks he is using it. In fact, by sweetening its brutal methods and by adapting it to local conditions, it is he who is being used by bureaucracy.

Opposed and complementary subtypes: people in 'public relations' and 'personnel management'; publicity agents; literary critics (benign ones); lawyers; well-meaning little priests; brokers; masters of ceremony; detectives, etc.

B.c. *The independent man.* He believes that conscientious work is the only road to success. 'After all, we need right-minded folk who do an honest day's work and who are not there merely for the show. Maybe us lot aren't famous, but at least we're our own men. The state, civil servants, thinkers and what they think, art, religion – what's it all for if not to be made use of and to make our lives that little bit more enjoyable . . .?' Such are the independent man's thoughts as he sets up his little business. A good husband and a good father, off he goes to war to get conveniently killed for his country. Is he the unknown soldier? He certainly is. On fixed days of the year he remembers that he is a citizen, and goes to vote. His life may revolve around himself and his relationships, but he has a clear conscience, for surely his way of life is essential not only to himself but also for the well-being and existence of society. 'If everyone thought only of themselves, and if God thought of everyone, what a wonderful world it would be.'

Opposed and complementary subtypes: the criminal; the scab; the professional double-dealer; the expert; the pure glance and the voyeur.

C. *The singular type.* In the previous two classes of types, the relation with the social existed, but in a mystified form and reconstructed misleadingly in a representation. So in A.a, the relation appears as goodwill, followed by an inability to make it real. In A.b, the relation is as sharply presented as it is in A.a, but in a negative form: the strength of this *positive* character comes from his *negative* completeness. This type of individual has sold his goodwill in exchange for success. He imagines that the structure of society is there to serve him, and that by exploiting it he has overcome the 'individual/society' division or the 'private/public' division to his personal advantage. In fact, although he is using society for his own ends and is controlling it for that purpose, he is allowing himself to become enslaved by the reactionary social forces of that society, without knowing how, and without even realizing it. In A.c, the relation degenerates somewhat more, both in practice and in its representation. Rather than being negative, it becomes indifferent. The individual puts himself 'above society'. This is why the philosopher finds it so easy to imagine that he has overcome the fundamental contradictions, in the Mind, or in his system.

In the B groups, we no longer find society as a whole, either as a practice or as a representation. The relation is between delimited spheres, and society as a whole disintegrates into particular groups. Every individual in these groups enters into contact with one or several 'circles' which he takes to be society as a whole. In this way the civil servant, or even the professional intellectual, believes in the generality of his experience, whereas in fact all he has experienced is a sum total of particularities and particular groups. The middleman imagines that he has a strategy for overcoming the fragmentation and the division of labour: to travel everywhere, to see the world. He thinks he has grasped the totality, whereas in fact he is fulfilling a function: he links people together. As for the independent type, he buries his head in the realness of a fragmented activity and thinks he has resolved the same problem.

In group C, we witness the complete degeneration of the 'individual/social' relation. Not only does it become blurred; it also dissolves and vanishes. The term 'society' disappears from consciousness; but the only way it can really disappear is as a result of a pathological state. Thus society appears to be completely disguised, and the return to generality is achieved by the invention of completely phoney representations. So logical structure does not stop alienation. This is two-sided, and consists of a weakening of any concrete link, and of a series of arbitrary representations (ethical, aesthetic, etc.). The individual man of type C sees himself facing the 'world' alone, and he tries to attain it without the mediation of the social, of history and of practice. An intuitive sense of a pure 'self' leads him from a lived, everyday situation into irrefutable fetishisms. Here, character per se disappears. Everything becomes attitude, role-play, theatricals, acted out on the theoretical stage of a vulgar empiricism.

C.a. *The fanatic.* A coarsely egotistical 'self' disguises itself under cosmic banners: god, nature, 'world'. This individual sees himself facing the universe, and his only relation is with the 'world'. Thus he believes himself to be universal, whereas in fact nobody could be more singular. He asserts himself hypocritically by using the 'world' as a sphere of influence and self-justification. This character, or rather this attitude, encompasses various stages and variants, from the cold-blooded calculator disguised as a Kindly Soul to the religious fanatic. This type is forceful and ferocious in equal measure.

Subtypes: the Lady; the pseudo-poet; the Kindly Souls.

C.b. *The oppositionist.* In C.a. there is a conscious emphasis on the 'world'. In C.b., the emphasis is expressly on the Self. C.a. says yes; C.b. says no. C.a. is a hypocrite; C.b. is a facile cynic. The type whose character is oppositional defines his 'self' as the contrary of someone or something, and often as the contrary of everything which is not him. He is 'pro everything anti, and anti everything pro'. He thinks he is more sharp-witted and human than the fanatic; and yet although his disposition is the complete opposite, he performs the same kind of social (i.e., antisocial) actions. Deep within his consciousness–unconsciousness he is often frustrated. Of all the types, this is probably the most unstable. Sometimes his relation with praxis sinks even lower, i.e., even farther from that of a genuine consciousness. Sometimes he finds a way out; he escapes from the prison of his own character. We can often detect traces of infantility in him, as well as many flagrant contradictions (for example, the superstitious atheist).

Subtypes: the ostentatious anarchist and the ostentatious anticleric; the hypercritic.

C.c. *The pompous idiot.* This one is well anchored in the everyday; he collects its most commonplace contents and inflates them crudely. He uses triviality to discover wisdom, a philosophy, a vision of the world. For example, he extracts proverbial sayings from their ironic context, their mutual oppositions and corrections, and turns them into eternal truths. There will always be rich people and there will always be poor people. Those people don't suffer as we do. Money can't buy you happiness. There will always be wars. You can't make an omelette without breaking eggs. We aren't choirboys. I'd rather be a happy pig than an unhappy Socrates. There's a nip in the air, etc. . . .

The pompous idiots are so stupid that they seem harmless. Because of their retarded and blinkered individualism, they are easy prey for demagogues. Through the inertia and mechanical nature of their stupidity, they go farther than others more treacherous or more intelligent than themselves in disintegrating the social and the human.

Subtypes: these are innumerable: the sententious sage; the sermonizer; the avid reader; the 'public-spirited' man, etc.[28]

12 The total field

Throughout this book we have challenged the right of the particular and fragmented sciences to encompass the whole. Not one of them can claim sole right of access to 'totality', but each is entitled to continue pushing its investigations farther and farther, without barrier or impediment. But they can only grasp partial totalities.

Moreover, we have accepted the idea of a 'field', while rejecting the idea of a 'continuous field'. Areas, sectors and regions cannot be in pure and simple juxtaposition. However, the concepts of level, unevenness, hiatus or gaps rule out the representation of an immense, coherently constructed set of sub-sets: the Whole. Gaps, holes, shadows and reflections, absences – these too form part of the total field. Therefore we reject the idea of a vast continuum which the fragmentary sciences can methodically and analytically carve into pieces. We also reject the idea of a sum total of areas. Each specificity constitutes an area, but the distinctions are relative, and we have no right to carry them to the absolute.

While we recognize the difficulties inherent in the concept of 'totality', we cannot do without it. However, only if our methodology is scrupulously prudent have we the right to use it. How can we develop a more-or-less coherent model to represent the entire range of knowledge and the situation of our own specific science within it?

Would levels and stages constitute a hierarchy, from a low level (the physical level of inert, material nature) to the highest level of all (the ethical and aesthetic level)? The representation of a hierarchy like this is still much too simple. What criterion should we use to classify these stages and levels, in order of importance? Every stage can break away from its initial position, overturning the entire set and taking prominence both in reality and in thought. For instance, demography can invade the social and influence the course of history, or even modify it. The historical (such as a war) can disrupt the economic, etc. The pattern of an ascending series of stages is too much like a clumsy metaphor – a ladder or a flight of steps – to be acceptable.

Should we group the areas and sectors into a circular pattern, with each area going from the centre to a section of the circumference? Should we imagine a circle made up of circles, a ring made up of rings? This would be more useful than the ladder pattern, by bringing us closer to one important truth: namely, that everything is in everything and everything is total – and yet nothing that is, is in anything other than itself. Within oneness, there are differences and disjunctions; both actively and potentially, there is multiplicity. Every human 'being' is physical, biological, economic, social or sociological, but unevenly, according to the aspects and the moments, sometimes this one more than that one, sometimes that one more than this one, but without ever losing unity completely. So it is not simply a question of lighting, or of perspectives, but of a 'reality' which must be understood.

Sadly, the circular pattern is as static as the linear one. If we try making it mobile (by using the figure or form of the spiral rather than the circle, for example) it will become quite imprecise.

And so, just as we have rejected ontologies and cosmologies, let us (provisionally) give up trying to construct a defined and definitive representation, while at the same time making sure not to regress into positivism. The 'total field' we have before us is as rugged as a mountain landscape and as tempestuous as the sea. We have maps to guide us, but they make us forget how diverse and magnificent it all is. They pinpoint regions and small areas in a way which ignores the fluidity of their borderlines. When each discipline tries to attain the universal (the total) it cannot but stir up conflicts, and yet imperialism is mortal. Each one must find a *modus vivendi* for itself and for the others, making pacts which grant self-determination to those who live in the neighbouring sectors. Tensions are fruitful; subservience is sterile.

The total field can only be grasped in a fragmentary way. We look for totality, we aim for it: it is an Idea (like the idea of absolute knowledge). You imagine you have a fragment of it in your hands, you hold it tight, you cherish it, and suddenly it assumes all reality and truth. You have the audacity to claim that what you are grasping is totality itself. Then immediately it breaks into pieces again, and all that remains in your hands is but a tiny fragment.

What we are faced with here is a precise methodological problem: the problem of *relevance*. Given a set of facts, on what level should we place it, and according to what criterion? What lighting and what techniques should we use to get to grips with it?

It is a very general question, but it is of particular interest to us, since in the confusion which typifies everyday life we are faced with physical elements, physiological elements, social elements, etc.

The rules we are about to lay down require us to take certain precautions. They have no ontological pretensions. They are not purely logical, nor are they purely empirical. They are an attempt to generalize a specific experiment. They refer to a praxis, the praxis of knowledge. They are similar to dialectical logic and are concerned with the connection between relevance and irrelevance. The intelligent reader will see why they differ from the (often profound but finally unsatisfactory) preoccupations of phenomenological philosophy. But let us be more explicit. We are making the concepts and the methodology dialectical, and this is where the difference lies.

a) Knowing that we must pronounce on relevance, we must take our time. First and foremost we must suspend judgement, and for a long time.

b) A decision about relevance is never fully acquired and definitive, like a decision in action; it can never answer questions by a yes or a no. Although it acts as a guide for research and investigation, and sometimes on a long-term basis (strategically), its involvement is never irreversible. Sooner or later, it must be challenged. No 'structuration' of the total field can impose itself as an eternal truth or as a logical statement.

c) The only sets which are easily classified are those which have been overelaborated, overconceptualized, and thus exhausted (grasped, counted, and so robbed of any element of surprise).

d) There is nothing more revealing and creative than mixed questions, marginal events, facts which apparently or really contradict acquired and accepted knowledge, and lateral concepts.

e) There is history, psychology, economics, etc. Historicism, sociologism, psychologism, economism are questionable, and every science comes in tandem with its own critique (which sooner or later becomes a critique of competence and relevance).

f) The obstacles in the path of knowledge – irreducibilities – are never definitive. In other words, we must not confuse 'essence' with 'nucleus'. The hard, dense nucleuses of facts and ideas, their nodes or nodal points, are also centres of interest and of problems, and thus of potentialities. Knowledge resolves them or disentangles them. We discover mediations in the apparently unmediated, and vice versa. Every level we observe presents us with several others to analyse. Again, because of this, relevance is never definitive, and neither is irrelevance.

g) Given a nucleus which seems irreducible (irrelevant), every method of attack is valid: classic analysis, arbitrary hypotheses, reduction and provisional parentheses, the full range of concepts.

h) And so relevance and irrelevance are aspects of a specific tactic and strategy, the tactic and strategy of science.

4

The Theory of the Semantic Field

1 The semantic field

The *semantic field* which we will now attempt to develop conceptually, only re-presents (makes present) a part of the total field for us. Language itself only re-presents a part of it. Thus the semantic field and language would be two levels of the overall experience we call praxis or the 'total field'. These levels would be linked together by implied mutual relations.

This conceptual development contains a critique of the fetishism of *signification* which is currently so dominant. We will try to show that together with, or in the margins of, the signifier, we will also find non-signifiers, and these can be effective and important. Maybe what is non-signifying now could be a potential signifier, waiting to be unearthed by the theoretician as he strolls through the semantic field like a sightseer. Admittedly this is possible, but then perhaps once it has become a signifier, the non-signifier may lose a reality and an effectiveness which its non-signification (its unknown or misunderstood signification) bestows upon it. Can the operation of tearing the non-signifier from its non-signification to bring it out into the light of formal and formalized signification be undertaken without modifying it? If we want to search the everyday for the non-signifiers which may be active within it we must catch them in the rough, in their unconscious or misunderstood situation, and not like water-creatures wrenched from the deep and left to die in the light of day.

For this reason we feel we must distinguish expression from signification, and keep the two concepts (the expressive and the signifying) simultaneously, studying their connections and their conflicts, in a word, making them dialectical.

At the same time we will continue the critique of another fetishism, a corollary of the previous one, that of language. Certainly, language is not simply a *means* or an instrument analogous to a hammer or a file. Its use is not simply to help communication between minds which to begin with were separately constituted. It is itself constituent. But between this and the idea that it is a privileged and sacred place, the realm of being or a modality of being, there is a chasm which some philosophers are reckless enough to cross. They are prey to the metaphysics and the ontology of the Word. If it is constituent, i.e., a time and place on the semantic field, language in our opinion is nevertheless a *mediation*, and thus a means and an implement, but not an irreducible nucleus or intelligible essence. We have already pointed out that this fetishist philosophy occurs in tandem with a crisis of language itself. What causes it and what are its effects? We will try to answer the question as quickly as possible. We will reinstate discursiveness in our own particular way, by understanding its current situation dialectically – as an awareness of Logos per se, implying a distance in relation to it, and the determination both of its level and its limits. And so our critique will be directed against the fetishizing of Logos and against the dissolution of language (or discourse). We will continue to 'bring' everyday life into language but in the context of the exploration of a semantic field which goes beyond discursiveness per se.

This theoretical hypothesis forbids us (as we already know) from adopting the *structuralism* derived from contemporary Saussurian linguistics. As we have already tried to demonstrate, structure is a formal implement and a scientific idea, and by hypertrophying and hypostasizing it, structuralism renders it sterile. For us, the arbitrariness of the sign must be seen in relation to the non-arbitrariness of the non-signifier and of expressivity. Structured by a series of disjunctions, implications, exclusions and inclusions on the phonemic as well as the morphemic level, coherent discourse belongs to a broader field. There are other regions in this field, including 'yes or no' questions and answers.

Next, once we have developed the idea of the 'semanteme', we will need to examine what the relation between critique of everyday life and a universal semantics is, by means of a series of particular semeiologies which are presently conceivable (i.e., the 'communications model').

2 Signals

In everyone's experience, two lights (red and green) are the prototype of the signal. Binary and disjunctive, they obey strictly logical laws, 'all/nothing', 'either/or'. They do not allow for intermediaries, transitions or evolution. They open a way forward, or they close it. They indicate a fork in the road or points on the railway line. They offer an option, and suppress another. A third term (the orange traffic light) can intervene to soften the harsh imperative of the signal. This third term complicates the signal and makes it less effective; it causes countless arguments.

The signal can only be directed at a single sense organ. It is either visual or auditory. In signals, ambiguity is unacceptable. Moreover, the signal has no relation to the command it signifies. It is completely arbitrary. Provided it has a distinct beginning and end, a bell will achieve the same results as an optical signal. Theoretically, a spray of perfume could be equally effective. Signals are entirely external to consciousness, and leave the active 'subject' externalized and passive, like an inert object at their command.

However the signal is not completely external to the human object/subject which it acts upon. It produces a well-defined effect, namely conditioning. I stop when the lights are red and keep going when they are green, and I don't give it a moment's thought. I have acquired a reflex action. The repetitions of the signal have conditioned me, and a good job too. Without this string of reflex actions of which traffic signals are a part, how could I drive my car? I have learnt them. They constitute a code. Once I have learnt them, it is as if the signals pass down from my hands through my body to my feet, according to a well-determined practice, in liaison with a determined technique or techniques.

Signals must be simple and obvious (clear and perfectly distinct), but they must also have a perfect stability. It is disconcerting when signals are altered; it causes serious disruption to what is a series of constituted and stable social actions, for example road or rail traffic. Constant and repetitive in essence, the signal is automatic, it is always there. It functions in accordance with a regulated frequency, without the intervention of any conscious volition, at least when it is in full working order. We should note that the signal does not give any information, or very little; it forbids or it permits; it includes or it excludes; 'one' does not always know why, and indeed 'one' does not need to know why. The perfect signal is perfectly impersonal, it repeats itself indefinitely, even when there is no one in front of it. It is defined by its redundancy, and it delivers no information. If it is well thought out and well used, it brings no surprises; it is always in the same place, always reiterating its imperious command or inter-diction, never beginning, never ending.

In the signal, signification coincides with the thing, i.e., the sign. Be it a red light or a green light, the given command (or interdiction) is entirely given by the thing. 'One' does not have to give a thought to what is being signified. *In and by means of the signal, signification is joined to and coincides with a thing which has been taken arbitrarily as a signal, but which itself has no signification.* Perfect rationality and perfect mean-inglessness come face to face. Should the signal signify another thing – or something else – for me, it will be because I am questioning it instead of obeying it; defying it, and thinking beyond what it 'is', in its entire presence or entire absence, I ask myself what someone to whom I have no access – precisely because they are not there and because I know nothing about them – has intended. 'Why have they put traffic lights at this crossroads?'

Although it functions in isolation like pure things do, the signal is not alone. It is always part of a defined (codified) *system*. For example, take the highway code, railway signals, or other, more esoteric systems, such as forestry or scouting, etc. When it is well thought out, a system can aspire to becoming very generalized, even to a 'world-wide' degree (road signals, or the Morse code, for example). Given that in practice there are so many situations, the pure objectiveness of the (crudely binary and disjunctive) signal within a system becomes diluted. Alongside signals per se, we see other elements appearing (words such as 'danger' or 'parking', and signs or symbols, like a skull, etc.), and this obscures the defined nature of the sign and of the system. These elements carry a certain amount of information (which

is minimal, entirely knowable in advance, and admitting of no uncertainty or dubious interpretation, or otherwise the system would
not work properly). A system like this must be closed, saturated,
coherent and rigorous. There may be a conflict between the requirements of practice and of rigorousness, but this should not blind us to
the (perfectly abstract and antinatural) 'nature' of the signal and of
systems of signals.

This is not the place to examine the case of highly complex
systems, which are already transitionals towards something else.
Doubtless we will have to consider them when we deal with the 'communications model'.[1]

3 Signs

The prototype of the sign is obviously the *word*, but it is not easy to
define it. The word has certain of the qualities of the signal, or rather
the signal has borrowed certain of the properties of the word. The
word can give commands. Used imperatively, it transmits an order; it
'signifies' a command. When I hear the word 'Halt!', I stop; but
according to the context, the word 'Leave!' evokes a more or less
powerful feeling of acceptance or rejection. Although there is no
power of words, certain words have power; this is nothing more than
a pole or a limit which would hardly suffice as a definition of the sign,
but which would be more appropriate for the signal.

The word is auditive but it is also visual. Ever since writing has
existed, reading has been closely implicated with listening, and con-
taminates it. So much so that in order to grasp language as a *form* (a
structure), linguists must first carry out the following operation,
which is both concrete and abstract: they must separate the language
chain from its environment and from its visual context, parenthesizing the latter. In fact, once they have accomplished this operation,
they are left with an abstraction: language as a verbal system. Once it
is reduced to being a purely verbal sign, the word *as sign* becomes
blurred and confused. Reading is a practical experience which children learn at an early stage, although they start learning aurally a
little sooner, and it is part of language as an implement for action and
understanding. Is it not very curious that today's audiovisual media

should be disrupting the practice of language after having played such an important role in constituting it, many centuries ago?

The elements in spoken (or written) language must be clear, easily distinguishable from each other, and understandable, demanding the least possible effort and avoiding the smallest possible chance of error. Thus they must be disjunctive (phonetically and semantically exclusive). However, the final element is never a simple signal. This final element, namely the phoneme, has no meaning (since it is a non-signifier), and does not appear per se in language. Contemporary structuralist linguistics has highlighted these phenomena.[2] Double articulation, which is made up of an internal difference, is what characterizes the linguistic sign, i.e., the word. Thus on analysis it presents two *levels*: the phoneme (in itself devoid of meaning) and the morpheme (which is a signifier). In practice, the former only appears as part of the latter, and the two can only be separated by analysis. This duality of levels means that in spite of their analogies, the sign cannot be reduced to the signal. The sign has a specificity which is demonstrated by its triple determination: the sign, the signifier and the signified. The signal does not have this triplicity. Although these three elements have a content, in terms both of the subject (movements of the pharynx, the glottis, the tongue) and of the object (things and objects designated with their connections, their relations of interaction, of presence and absence, of inclusions and exclusions), they tend towards pure form, becoming what Roland Barthes has called a 'tourniquet'. Thus content does not determine the use of words, their order and their connections, although it plays a part in the logical structure of the way they are used. Moreover, the formal order of signs leaves room for the unforeseen (randomness), and although their combinations are highly structured, since they are structured formally, they constantly provide something new, except in the commonplace discourse of platitude. So repetition makes way for inventiveness, but without actually disappearing (which presents some curious problems). This permanent renewal of possible discourse has its own laws (such as Estoup-Zipf's law on the frequency of the use of words). The order of signs allows for uncertainty, expectancy and surprise, and thus for play and imagination. The sentence has great elasticity, while the word itself has very little. The word must have a defined and conventionally fixed sense, otherwise the speakers will no longer understand each other. Thus every conversation oscillates between two poles. Around one of them, the chances of misunderstanding are reduced to a minimum, but the conversation will always be trivial. Around the other, the increase in chance and in the probability of misunderstandings increases the chances for inventiveness, discovery and mutual recognition, and for the obstacles to understanding being overcome. On the level of discourse, there is a considerable margin of uncertainty and freedom; on the level of signs (words, morphemes), this margin is very small. The role language plays in everyday life is a product of this duality, or double possibility. It oscillates between platitude and rhetoric, between banality and expressivity.

It follows that, with their formal rules of usage (syntax and grammar), signs (repertoire, vocabulary and lexis) form a coherent system, namely a system of language. The efficiency of this system makes it analogous to a system of signals: it gives commands; it organizes feelings and emotions as well as objects, because it contains an order and imposes it upon the chaos of fleeting moments; it enjoins because it joins and disjoins. It opens up possibilities, and then closes them down. Order in a language system determines the order of words and sentences; it is part of a more far-reaching order, in social practice. Imperious and imperative, language uses words to make us recognize feelings and actions. Ceaselessly, it eliminates ambiguities and misunderstandings, only to allow them to return once more, inevitably. In the tumult and vibrations of everyday life, it tends to create stabilities, static states which are determined in spite of their limitless resonances and their dampened harmonics. To speak is to act. When we use words and sentences (even when we are soliloquizing) we influence ourselves as much as the person to whom we are talking. What we are putting into words has been changed by the fact of being said, or rather of having been said. With its blindfold of misconceptions and misunderstandings torn away, what is being said is revealed in the light of discourse. It is discussed, it is clarified, it becomes impoverished and commonplace – and yet it is enriched by the fact of being present in social daylight. In any event, what has been said had to be said, so that what remains of it after its fleetingness and obscurities have been submitted to the test of language can be assessed. Discourse is an event and an act, and a prologue to action; it is a preparation for action; it forces us to act and to choose, unless we are speaking for speaking's sake, in which case the prologue to decision becomes an end in itself. To speak and to put oneself into words is both stimulating and destructive. Because discourses have continuity we are forced into their network and, as a consequence, into the network of the social actions they refract and specify: this action is permitted; that one is forbidden. But discourses are also discontinuous, and their discrete terms act like a sieve, straining the things which rise up from our inner depths. Logos is not simply a means of communication. It acts as a filter for the feelings and emotions which create it and which it regulates. For this reason, it really is a kind of being, a way of being.

When we bring what has not already been said into language, we are certainly winning a victory. In itself, the act creates something and opens up new possibilities; it is the prelude to unexpected creations, and may even be seen to constitute the essence of what is traditionally called 'philosophy'. When praxis permits an important sector to pass into language, or when its problems demand it, it is an important day for knowledge. And yet, how can there ever be an absolute victory without something being lost? What we are putting into words and what we have put into words is there now, facing us. Earlier it was something happening silently, spontaneously, joyfully, even harmoniously – or maybe something painful and muffled which is not happening at all. Once something has been spoken it will never be spontaneous again. We must think about it, and in the case of a requirement (a 'function'), we need to focus it patiently by trial and error until we can consciously carry it into effect. The 'spoken' is now abstract: presented on the plane of abstraction, on the level of language and the sign. As well as spontaneity and innocence, a little bit more nature or 'being' is lost. We all know that we must be prepared to risk losing everything if we want to win everything. But whatever the circumstances, risking and losing will always be risking and losing!

Thus the system of signs (of language and discourse) resembles a system of signals, but because the one is incomparably broader and more flexible than the other, the analogy will not help us to understand it. It is an open system, controlled by a coherence which is *almost* logical. This *almost* is supremely important. Formally, the non-signifying element in language (e.g., the sound, the syllable or the phoneme) is apparent, but is not recognized as such. Actually, however, in practical, social utterance, it is an important and conscious element, acting as interjection and exclamation: 'Oh! Ah!', etc. In this use of the non-signifier (which dogmatic structuralism finds rather difficult to deal with) expression is more important than signification. Now when it is actually spoken, and taken in its complete context – gestures, mimicry, grimaces – discourse is *expressive*. Inflections of the voice give constant support to the formal relations between the terms of discourse. In this way and in this way alone does it enter into the everyday, not as its loom, but as threads woven into its fabric.

4 The symbol

This has certain of the qualities or properties of the signal or the sign, but it differs from both. The symbol includes and excludes, by bringing the members of one particular group closer together, while excluding other individuals and groups. It makes orders or prohibitions, but in complex ways which are dramatically involving and which sometimes imply a conception of the world and of life. It reveals and conceals membership of a group, the reasons for its membership and the reasons of the group itself. It enters into a form, but this form develops concretely around the symbol, in rituals and ceremonies. The symbol initiates and it inhibits.

The symbol differs from the sign and even more so from the signal in that it appears inexhaustible. Effectively, it is. The signal takes place entirely within its own functioning, and is exhausted there; the sign (the word) is only valid in so far as it belongs in the series of signs and in their mutual interaction. Both as a fact and as a value without limits (even when it is not religious and sacred), the symbol is unassailable. It presents itself, it is a presence, it is present, rich with meaning, and as such is somewhat more than 're-presentation'. Does it express as much or more than it signifies? When Christians make the sign of the Cross, the evocation of the Cross itself is more important than the formal gesture; the believer traces the instrument of redemptive suffering on his own body; he sanctifies himself by deliberately identifying with the crucified god. If he is *signing* himself and *signifying* himself externally with a gesture which proves his membership and makes it manifest, he is also carrying out an internal *act* of faith and, more importantly, of participation. He is linking himself with the absolute Word, the Logos become flesh and put to death for him. When we examine it from outside, this gesture reveals a multiplicity of significations, but viewed from within, it is inexhaustible. Thus the gesture in itself has less reality and value than its symbolic content. It is much more of a symbol than a sign in the precise meaning of the term. It expresses, and this expressivity has primacy over what it signifies externally. When the sign is enough in itself, the form and the letter are more important than the 'spirit'. Sociologists and ethnographers have observed the oppositional and complementary properties of symbols (disjunction and inclusion in social practice) in factual terms. It has been left to philosophers to shed light on how symbols differ from discourse and representation. Discourse and representation distinguish between things and clarify them, whereas symbols are inexhaustible; they offer some kind of obscure and magical participation. Notably, in his *Aesthetics*, Hegel gives an analysis of the difference between symbolism, allegory, simile, metaphor and analogy. If I call someone 'a sly old fox' I am attributing the qualities of a fox (as I see them) to him. Obviously, I know that no human being 'is' a fox and I also know that there is no Platonic Idea of Slyness which would apply to foxes in the animal kingdom and to certain human individuals. However, these representations are too clear, and their very clearness betrays their logical incoherence. On an affective level, which takes me back to my childhood (stories and fables), to archaic times (myths) and also to the realm of the imagination (fantastic tales), I am saying that this man actually does share something in common with a fox – so much so that when I am with him I behave as though he really were a crafty, carnivorous animal, a danger to me and to my possessions, and I advise other people strongly (the people I talk to) to do the same. The symbol confers an effective, real and practical communality on two beings who are different both in appearance and in reality, but more so in the former than in the latter. It makes these two beings partly *identical*. It points to their mutual participation. When it refers to one, it evokes the other, and vice versa. Conversely, a simile would leave them mutually external and only brings them together by using comparatives such as 'like' or 'as'. As for analogy, which is elaborated as a kind of reasoning, it highlights differences. Or else it is subsumed by a symbolism, and directed by it.

Is it possible to list these symbols? Perhaps. Can we count them, or in other words, are they limited in number? Probably. Obviously, they include the sun, the stars and the 'signs' of the zodiac, as well as the sea and the mountains, the elements (water, fire, earth, air), spatial directions, the father, the mother, etc.

Taken in isolation, each one has its particular effectiveness and prestige. It immediately triggers off emotions, and even sensations. Surrounded by its own affective and imaginary retinue, it bursts its way into discourse like an exclamation: 'The earth! . . . The sun! . . . The night!' However, symbols do not exist in isolation. Could we say that they constitute systems? The term is only valid for representations which have been elaborated, and thus verbalized and formalized. Symbols come in groups. We will say that they constitute configurations or constellations: cosmic symbolisms, tragic symbolisms, religious symbolisms, etc. As well as being configurations they can be elaborated into symbolic systems. For example, astrology (as we know it nowadays in the press – daily, weekly or monthly – and above all in the women's press) has become an elaborate system for the psychological interpretation of everyday life, with fairly well-defined themes. This system has been superimposed upon some extremely ancient cosmic symbolisms, which have never lost their emotional effectiveness.

Where do symbols originate? From the depths of a collective or individual 'unconsciousness'? From mysterious archetypes, hidden emotional or existential matrixes? From the pristine discoveries of childhood or from the despair of old age and mortality? From archaic magic or from involuntary and spontaneous poetry? From flights of inspiration or from failures? From the 'world' or from mankind, or from the primitive and obscure relation between them? From power over nature or from powerlessness? From the first steps towards power? For the time being all this is of little importance. What is important as far as this project is concerned is that we emphasize the specificity of the symbol, its inexhaustibility for the mind which wishes to explore it, and its direct emotional (affective) effectiveness.

5 The image

Unlike the symbol, the image is an individual work, but is communicable. Unlike the sign, it does not belong in abstractness, any more than it does in sensuousness. Like the symbol, it appeals to affectivity; it is born in and emerges from a level of reality other than that occupied by signs and their connections. On one hand, it has certain of the powers of the symbol, arousing affective complicities and pacts directly, without using representations as such. It makes itself understood by setting emotion into movement, and by arousing it. It exerts an influence, and includes those who understand it within a group which is characterized by a certain tonality. And so to a certain extent it shares the selective and discriminatory power of signs. It is a form of consciousness, or a level, or a modality if you like, but not the emergence of an 'unconsciousness' which might resemble a storehouse of images. However, it is multiple; it appeals to all the senses, and it arouses obscure emotions by travelling back to ancient seasons and bygone ages of the individual, the group and the species. Thus it activates and actualizes a link between the present and the past, something the sign cannot do. In this respect it is an aspect of expressivity. Communicated and communicating, it is original and unique; it carries the hallmark of inventiveness, of spontaneous or cultivated poetry. It needs signs (today's words and graphic or typographic signs) to communicate, but it overloads these signs with its emotional (expressive) content, the origins of which are lost in the mists of time, together with symbolisms. Although it is alien to the (logical and formal) structure of discourse, it intervenes in discourse by propelling it forward and colouring it with its own emotional tonality. The threshold to this emotive content is always vague and hard to delimit. It works by insinuation and suggestion rather than by imposing itself, which is why it requires complicity and pacts; and yet it overcomes obstacles and barriers which hinder precise signification. It creates misunderstandings and dissensions, but it can also resolve them. Thanks to the image and the content which makes up a part of its influence, opaqueness becomes somewhat more transparent. Distances vanish as if by magic. Could this content be limitless? Possibly, although it may be an illusion inherent to imagination. If we speak of limitlessness, it is in the context of harmonics, where resonance goes on indefinitely, perceptible only to the sharpest of ears, although all perception is limited in such matters.

Therefore the image is the opposite of the signal and the sign. Whereas these address action and the present, the image turns towards the past, like the symbol. It rescues the past from darkness (from 'unconsciousness', to use another terminology) and dispersion, bringing it into the light of the present day. However, unlike the symbol, the image also goes towards the future. It strives to attain something not yet present and to 'presentify' or present it. So it is a prospector in the distant territory of what is possible and what is impossible. It prepares choices and indicates them. It arouses emotions, feelings and desires, in other words virtual actions, and compels imagination to wager on a future it foretells and anticipates, and which it helps to determine (through 'projects of choice'). Thus imagination could be seen as the function of what is possible (in so far as we can talk about 'function' in this context; troublesome but useful, demanding but free, this 'function' is something we could well do without).

From the point of view of reflective thought, there is a kind of incompatibility between retrospection and prospection. They are opposite attitudes or intentions. As for imagination, it knows how to use the past in order to invent the future. It projects what it has acquired through experience towards the future, and frequently starts from something extremely archaic to represent the farthest realms of the impossible/possible. This is not simply a reference to science fiction. We also have the brilliant Fourier in mind, whose vision of everyday life in future society was based upon archaic communal life, but enriched with everything that human development can offer, as Marx put it (and Marx owes much more to Fourier than is generally admitted).

The image is an act. In this respect it implies the will to be effective: sometimes to help make what is possible real or to represent the impossible, sometimes to prepare a project of choice, sometimes to captivate and touch another human being. In so far as it is a social act, the image is the image of an action which it deliberately projects towards the 'subject' – the human being it is addressing and whom it wants to influence. Touched and moved, this person responds to the effects of the image and projects it back towards its initiator. This double projection produces a result which is no longer a projection but a mutual presence, and even an emotional sameness. All communication involves images, and the deepest communication of all is achieved through images.

The image is only active when it is 'expressive'. It arouses what it expresses, and provokes it. The image has an inherently provocative character. When we use an image to provoke an emotion, we ourselves do not need to be moved. However, we cannot invent an image without having previously felt an emotion. As the concept of expressivity becomes more precise, it is turned on its head. On the level of the image, expression is active in its effect, as much and more than in its condition or cause. Whoever experiences this effect locates it in the image, which he qualifies as 'expressive', while for whoever employs it, its expressivity may well be far away in the past. The result is a permanent lag between the invention of images and their use, and between the situation of whoever employs them and whoever is influenced by their action. Thus mutual presence does not rule out misunderstandings and dramas, quite the reverse: it encompasses their possibility.

Although it is not up to us to give a theory of imagination (or of language for that matter), since it has been formulated elsewhere, we will summarize it.

The study of archaic magic and its repercussions demonstrates the emotional effectiveness of practices such as gestures, ceremonies and ritualized expressions, etc. The magician *evokes* people who have disappeared, who are absent; he evokes obscure powers; he *resurrects* the dead, and achieves the *repetition* or the renewal of the past. He can challenge what has been accomplished and act as though what is is not. He can influence the future by *bringing it into the present*. He changes his personality by *identifying* it with a wide variety of 'beings' – demons and gods, kings and genies – in a *participation*.

Now imagination and magic share the same categories. More precisely, the modalities of magic have become the modalities of imagination: to evoke, to resurrect, to identify. So we may maintain that, historically and sociologically, imagination is an extension of magic. However, a profound discontinuity divides them. The magician used his procedures (such as spells and dances) on his patient to produce emotional states which were both entirely illusory and entirely real (lived). The purpose of magic procedures was to create real states in a real collectivity (groups of initiates). When it is aimed at individuals, individual imagination produces images, not states of trance. The illusory character of the image is almost always perceived as such, although in the final analysis participation becomes complete again, and imagination joins forces with magic once more.

6 On several confusions

In order to locate the elements or formants of the semantic field as precisely as possible, we have made clear distinctions between them. We have emphasized their specificities.

However, rather than distinguishing between them, people tend to confuse them. Critical analysis reveals that several of today's most widespread theories are responsible for this.

There is absolutely no question of denying the importance of the work of the Pavlovian school, from Setchenov to Smolenski and Bykov. Some of the criticisms levelled against the scientific results of their research are unacceptable. It is irrefutable that Pavlov's work proved a total activity of the cortex in higher animals and in man (higher nervous activity), and not simply the existence of isolated reflexes. In any case, we can hardly expect physiologists to be sociologists and psychologists as well. However, what we can expect of them is not to refute the existence of other areas and levels of reality and analysis. Refusal to accept this may be partially and subjectively justified by the effort required to extrapolate all the consequences from an important discovery, but finally it will result in the dogmatism and subjectivism characteristic of schools (scientific clans), and their members run the risk of endlessly following up a line of research which will finally become exhausted. The Pavlovians simply forget that the relation of the human brain with the outside world cannot be reduced to the connections between the cortex and stimuli or signals. The human world is made up of objects, products and human works, not of things. It is also made up of other human beings and of the language which links them together. It comprises repetition and non-repetition, and the relations between the two are problematic. To a certain extent this human world which is given to the individual (who intervenes in it and can only assimilate it by being active within it) is the work of praxis. How odd it is that Pavlovism should have been adopted in the name of Marxist materialism, when it disregards the idea of 'praxis', which is the very foundation of Marxism! The 'conditioning' of the human infant in its relations with his father and mother (which are much too 'private', narrow and unmediated in the family of today and above all in the praxis of bourgeois society) has some specific and original features. It cannot be reduced to the acquisition of complicated reflex actions and a 'second system' of signalling, the verbal system. All the while it is learning, the child's relations with its parents are doubly ambiguous. They result from the powers of parents to teach and their powers to oppress. The Father is not given to the child as a simple, unmediated presence, good or bad, or simultaneously good and bad. The Father is not merely unmediated strength and authority, he is social authority: society as a whole, law, hierarchy, the state. Thus the Father is both reality and symbolism. God is known as 'our father', or 'eternal father'. The same applies to the Mother, although what she symbolizes is something more archaic and cosmic. Pavlovian theory eliminates the specificities of the symbol, in so far as it is directed towards creating and shaping basic affectivity. By conceiving of it purely as a second system of signalling, it also eliminates the specificity of the sign (which the structuralist school and the theory of double articulation have reinstated). It equates the symbol and the sign with the signal, which it thinks of in terms of physiology rather than sociology.

If the Pavlovian school proceeds by confusing and reducing specificities in a 'materialist' way, the procedures of the 'bourgeois' and non-'socialist' structuralist school are exactly analogous. It gives a privileged status to *signification*, which has the advantage of appearing to be socially real and yet at the same time immaterial and 'in the mind'. Signification can only be apparent to and for a 'mind', a 'subject'. Once this has been accepted, an inextricable confusion ensues. The significations perceived (in phenomenological terms, *made explicit*) by the reflective, thinking subject – the philosopher, the linguist, the sociologist – merge with the significations which are effectively and practically (socially) carried by signs. How are we to distinguish between them? There are no criteria. This has been a marvellous godsend to philosophical thinkers. What they had long since discovered elsewhere they can now observe in the facts; they make it explicit and separate it from signs, and receive it from significations like a kind of gift. Now the signal and the symbol have significations, but these are irreducible to the significations of simple signs, and they impose themselves upon their 'subjects' without the latter having to explain them. The privileged status these thinkers accord to signification simplifies reality. It suppresses the specificity of levels (of existence and analysis) just as much as when the signal is privileged. Their conception of a unitary field of significations (which ipso facto cannot be a genuine 'field') reveals what their attitude really is. By wishing to avoid the excessive realism and the reification inherent to 'processes', they go beyond the 'mental things' which are so familiar to psychologists and sociologists. At the same time the diversity of the real escapes them, and they feel no need to consider the processes and the differences between 'things': works, objects and products, symbolic works, or works laden with symbols which are aimed at emotiveness, or products which act like signals, etc.

More than thirty years ago, in his *Critique des fondements de la psychologie*, Georges Politzer introduced the concept of signification (in place of the concept of the unconscious), while at the same time protesting aginst the postulates of conventional signification in psychology. Taking the same stance, but developing it further, we would criticize the subjectivist philosophy which accepts the postulate that signification should have a privileged status; we reject the mixture of 'conventional signification' and 'real signification' which philosophers use as a phenomenological bran tub for whatever is convenient for them.

The idea of a 'symbolic function' perpetuates this confusion. It enables them to sidestep the difference between the *symbol* (objective content, emotional effectiveness, archaic origins) and the *sign* (intellectual effectiveness, formal, synchronic and non-dialectical reality). To say that the symbolic function intervenes every time a representation is substituted for a thing is to bring the signal, the sign and the symbol so close together that they become indistinguishable. It is also to forget that symbolism is not separate from the 'thing' (the father, the mother, the sun, the plain, etc.), but is joined to it in a mutual participation. On the other hand, when a signal functions, signification is at one and the same time entirely arbitrary and separate from the thing, and entirely identical to the thing. Therefore there is no univocal 'symbolic function' which would be applicable to all three cases.[3]

Signification is impoverished. Fixed, attached to the sign, established, repeated, codified, it 'is' and is active because it is fixed, stable and stabilized. Taken by itself it becomes disembodied: it is the desert of essence (Hegel) attached to words, to discourse, to Logos. *Expression* is far more creative, and creates in a different way. It lives in the voice, we would say, and in gestures, and in the face. Let us reinstate the living (dialectical) unity which structuralist analysis has shattered. This analysis has a threefold aim: to distinguish between levels and between formants, to reveal structures, and to rediscover a higher unity. Expression is speech. Signification is language as form. Speech carries words along in the flow and rhythms of the sentence; it is concealed beneath what in terms of form appears to be word frequency. When emotion and images intervene in living speech, they do not disturb the pure form of discourse, they bring it to life. Expressivity is a thing of flesh and blood; mobile, unexpected, it is for ever breaking through the barriers of signification, informing, communicating by means of acquired significations. When the individual expresses himself (through intonation or mime), he says much more than he puts into words. His activity is almost like a work of creativity: dramatized action, a theatre of mime.

Thus a dialectical movement becomes apparent in dialogue: 'expression/signification', i.e., a conflict between these two terms. Expression struggles to bear the dead weight and inertia of signification and to make use of it as a fulcrum. Signification fixes expression by immobilizing and reducing it; conventional, intentional, stereotyped, it deadens expression, which in turn forever reconstructs itself, breathing new life into signification.

From this conflict comes *sense* (the movement, orientation and direction of dialogue, and its ultimate goal). It is a term which is not immune from the generalized confusion we are at present living through. At times it refers to a direction, at others to a set (a system) of significations. While not eliminating the latter interpretation of the term, we would emphasize the former. Surely the sense of an act lies in its direction and orientation: the future which it is travelling towards, blindly or lucidly, in other words, *what is possible*. Expression is an act, and it takes on a sense in its oneness with established signi-fications and its conflict with them. Every social action which involves a generalized dialogue (of the self with the self, with another person nearby or far away) also has a sense. In the 'expression/signi-fication' dialectical movement, in which sense intervenes as a constantly renewed third term to resolve the first two, expression is forever striving to get the better of signification; to become unmedi-ated, direct, and directly (emotionally) transmitted. It is not always successful, even when it overloads discourse with exclamations, images and rhetoric. Signification goes on playing its stabilizing role of an inert weight, which expression must bear on its shoulders but without which it would dissolve and disappear into the void. On the other hand, signification is forever striving to kill expression and to kill itself with the banality and maximal frequency of trivial termi-nology. It can never succeed; success would mean its instant demise.

In some respects there is probably 'a sense' in the overvaluing of signification. Maybe it corresponds to a profound deterioration of expressivity and of the image per se (in terms of the imaginary as opposed to the brute force of the audiovisual). Expressivity is already fragile and weakened, and maybe this overvaluing points to a ten-dency to compromise it further by making it totally trivialized.

We will come up against these problems again when we examine communications theory (the 'communications model'). We will use these analyses to draw up a critical description of conversation – dis-cussions and dialogues – in the everyday.

7 The properties of the semantic field

Meanwhile, let us specify the properties of the semantic field, which is indissolubly constituted – and precisely by means of their differ-ences – by symbols, images, signs and signals.

While being careful not to take the analogy beyond certain limits (which need to be determined), we notice that the semantic field really does have the characteristics of a 'field'. It presents a continu-ity, and within this continuity, it has distinct and discontinuous elements, specific values and nucleuses. We can single out discrete units, but we can never completely separate them from the unit as a whole. Continuity and discontinuity are in a state of mutual relativity. At every point we observe a force: a vector. Once activated, these points become polarized, determining tensions, static states, momentary balances, and a temporary sharing out of the forces. At every point potentialities reveal themselves, and in doing so, they disappear. This produces stabilities (which, like the discontinuities, are relative against their background tension). The *dual* properties (expression and signification, emotivity and representivity) polarize the semantic field, maintaining the tensions and invigorating them. Generated by these tensions between the extreme polarities of symbols and signs, waves and vibrations run across it like electrical charges. However, the semantic field is more animated and more complex than physical realities, and the levels (of existence or reality) it presents are more varied and more discontinuous, with differences in level, gaps, and perhaps even holes.

Were we to reduce this complexity to a single one of its formants (such as the signal, the sign, the symbol or the image) it would slip through our fingers. What we would be faced with would be a simplified complexity: the 'field of significations', for example. Taken in its totality, the semantic field as we understand it has a structure, but this structure cannot be reduced to the structure of discourse, any more than it can to the formal connection between signs or to the relation between the sign, the signified and the signifier. It is a much more complex structure, which includes a limited number of variations: disturbances, instabilities and propagations. Although we have no wish to contest the importance of structural linguistics, we cannot use it as a model for structure. On the contrary, we want to carry the ideas of structure and stability beyond language, and to give them back their place in the process of becoming. Nor will we use the theories of gravity, electricity or magnetism as our model; in our opinion the theory we will use (and which we will considerably transpose) is broader and more comprehensive: it is the model of harmonics.

Thus defined, the entire semantic field is *open*. We cannot circumscribe or close it, any more than we can the horizon, even though every horizon is determined.

8 Consciousness and the semantic field

Can we say that (social and individual) consciousness is consciousness *of* the semantic field as a whole, or that it reflects it? No. It is not external to the semantic field. Could we say that it is active *on* the semantic field? Yes, but that is not enough. What we can say is that consciousness 'is' the semantic field, but only providing we purge the little word '*is*' of all substantialist content, and especially of all contamination by brute things. Thus consciousness 'is' not this and not that, but this and that taken as a whole. It 'is' in a specific manner: not a thing among things, nor the ideal or mental double of those things (reflected or not). 'Things' and objects are given to consciousness together with their connections and their significations, as an inextricable part of the semantic field as a whole.

Consciousness 'is' receptiveness on a particular (affective) level of the symbolic nucleuses. It 'is' put into the service of signs and of their formal connections. It 'is' receptiveness on a particular level of signals (the level of unmediated practical action). Finally, it 'is' the lived on the semantic field; it is constantly opening out to it, the semantic field is its basis, it coincides with it.

However, this description is only entirely valid for social consciousness. Although individual consciousness is included and implied within social consciousness, it only occupies a portion of it. So alongside levels of reality (of existence), we need to determine levels of experience and levels of analysis.

In the first place, the most solid aspect of the everyday, and the point of departure of individual consciousness and its sphere of activity, is only a portion of the semantic field: discourse, or even triviality in discourse; commonplaces, redundancy, intelligibility through familiarity. Symbols from everyday life intervene, but isolated, one at a time, and are rarely perceived as such. They are perceived as being within things, and not as a double of those things, and as something external to them which has come to reinforce them emotionally. The symbol is an integral part of familiarity. In the everyday, the Father as creative power, authority and law – the symbolic Father – merges with the father who is directly perceived and emotionally submitted to, a man with a particular voice, a particular face and particular behaviour patterns. Signals per se have much more importance in everyday life than symbols per se. This does not stop symbolisms from having a powerful influence, but this is 'unconscious'. The specific structure and dynamism of the semantic field produce the following imbalance, which is specific to the everyday: on one hand it is *determined by symbolisms which it fails to recognize as such, and which it lives as though they were realities;* on the other *it is orientated by signallings which it takes to be the essential elements which determine it.* The everyday takes its consciousness from signals and relegates symbolisms to 'unconsciousness', despite the fact that they are linked to the most profound vital rhythms such as day and night, the presence of the mother and the father, hunger and sexuality. Riven in two, this consciousness will always be superficial, the equivalent of a lack of consciousness. As for reflective consciousness, it distances itself from the semantic field in an attempt to control it. In the effort to see it in all its breadth, it loses contact with it. The danger is that it will select a fragment of it to use as a means of defining it. This is what theory does when it does not go hand in hand with permanent autocritique and does not consciously aim for the open totality of the field: it selects a fragment – a symbol or symbolism in general, discourse, signification, formal structure, or even the signal – and elevates it to the absolute.

Generally, the dialectical movements which are active on the semantic field as a whole (and which give it life) escape reflective consciousness. It observes them from afar, often as though they were anomalies, whereas in fact they are what characterizes the semantic field. In so far as it animates this mobile and diversified field, dialectical movement encompasses it and envelops it. There is no specific spot or place on the semantic field where it can be fixed. For this reason it is greater than the reflective and purely rigorous (logical) consciousness which attempts to articulate the diverse signs and their less-than-rigorous connections which are given in Logos and in discourse. And so we come back once more to what we have previously proposed, but in a different light. Discourse is (and is nothing more than) a level of experience on the semantic field as a whole. Composed of quasi-static states, it is particularly strong and stable. It opens itself comprehensively to this field, whether it be in the sphere of symbols and images or at the polarity of signals. As a level it is both a centre and an intermediary (a mediation).

As for the semantic field itself, it opens on to every sphere of praxis, with creative contradictions, repetition and inventiveness. Discourse and even the semantic field are made up of correlations, oppositions and contrasts. Dialectical movements encompass these terms and prevent them from succumbing to immobility. They breathe life into them, and for this reason, cannot be contained within them.

The first result of this is that the semantic field as a whole (or a 'totality') is a *concept* based on an experience or even on a level of experience which itself encompasses a diverse range of levels. This concept is not given per se in experience. There is no description, no phenomenology of the 'lived' which could grasp it. It is a theoretical concept, and thus forms part of a theory. A (phenomenological) description of it would take experience *partes extra partes*; it would shed light on small areas of it, appropriating them for its own devices and transforming them into private plots of land, rather than grasping the landscape and the horizon as an ensemble.

A further result is that any consciousness which has established itself firmly on the semantic field (or which thinks it has) cannot really be trusted. Just like an individual, society does not see itself as it 'is'. When we want to consult social consciousness, more often than not we come up against individual and 'private' groupings. Individual consciousness and even social consciousness can speak only of the parts of the semantic field on which they have set up home. They cannot bring total knowledge of it, but they do offer material for that knowledge. In particular, the contradictions of a society 'normally' elude consciousness, discourse and especially the everyday (except at moments of revolutionary crisis, or when revealed by in-depth critique).

If we are to grasp these contradictions we will need a theoretical knowledge which takes the semantic field into account but which understands it per se, and which consequently will grasp the praxis of which it is merely a level. Also we still need to mount an assault on the structures of discourse (in spite of the efforts of dialecticians from Heraclitus to Hegel and our contemporaries) in order to seize dialectical movements and 'bring them into language'. We must succeed in grasping whatever tries to slip through our fingers, not as essence (as unknowable) or as nature (irrational or ontological truth) but as it is, precisely because 'that' is what must be seized and what will reveal the process of becoming of knowledge and of the real. And if 'that' is inexhaustible, we will nevertheless succeed in grasping it if we persist in trying.

Thus dialectical thought will be necessary if we are to conceive of the semantic field, both as an entity (with its limits and its openings) and as a set of diverse elements. However, dialectical thought per se does not appear in or *on* the semantic field. And this is precisely how it *conceives* of it, from the vantage point of a higher level of reality (existence) and knowledge. If dialectical thought was available on the semantic field, there would be no more specificity, and differences would become blurred. The formal and the logical would be absorbed into dialectical movements, and would lose their own specific levels. Logos would be spontaneously and completely dialectical (which it is not).

And so we must think of the total semantic field using dialectical reason, rather than thinking of dialectical reason as something within that field. Dialectical contradiction is hidden from view, disguised between oppositions, 'contrasts' of the field, diversities and tensions. The semantic field is a level of experience and knowledge, but also comprises appearances, apparitions and manifestations of 'something' deeper. Being? Perhaps! But first of all praxis, and history. From within, the contradictions of the semantic field are sensed as powerful movements, producing the instabilities which run through it. From outside (relatively) they can be grasped and conceived of. Of necessity – and we cannot stress this hard enough – the same applies to each separate society and to society as a whole. Since the semantic field is located somewhere in between praxis and knowledge, and since it takes an enormous effort to raise consciousness to the conceptual level, only by painstaking analysis, or at a moment of intense crisis, will a society's contradictions be made fully apparent. Without these stipulations, *one* (i.e., social consciousness) will only be aware of certain partial and everyday effects of these contradictions: uneasiness, dissatisfactions, misunderstandings, disturbances. We can say for certain that socialist critique understands the contradictions of capitalism incomparably better than do the people who 'live' them and try to describe them 'from the inside'. But the opposite may probably be true!

9 The laws of the semantic field

The signal was born with industrialization. Sociological analysis sheds light on this proposition by dispelling some serious confusions, and in particular the confusion between the signal and physiological stimuli or signs in general. Before the advent of modern industry, a battle 'signal', a war cry or a raised banner was more of a symbol than a sign, expressive rather than signifying. The same would have been true of a distress 'signal', a beacon, a warning cry or an alarm bell. During the development of what is sometimes referred to in a rather confused way as 'industrial society' or 'technological society', there were more and more signals. At first they were limited to factories and railways, but soon they invaded everyday life in the form of traffic signals, and innumerable signals to permit or to prohibit. In 'industrial society', urban life becomes peopled by innumerable signallings. Each one programmes a routine, exactly like a calculator, regulating patterns of conduct and behaviour. We may well ask ourselves whether one day the entire set of signals will not constitute a sort of gigantic machine which will not need to be built, but which cyberneticists will simply formulate and put into action using existing connections and signallings. This colossal mechanism will already have regulated society and its everyday life. Perhaps it will give the men trapped within the prison of its machine a splendid impression of spontaneity and harmony. And this is what it will be: kindly towards the average socially adapted ('balanced') individual, pitiless towards the 'deviant'.

Not only are signals ever more numerous, not only are they becoming more dense, but bit by bit they are dismantling the semantic field. As the 'signalling' pole becomes more and more intense the magnetic power of signals is increased. They corrode symbols and lessen the tension between the poles of expression and signification to the advantage of the latter. The semantic field becomes simplified and unified, and dialectic is (superficially) replaced by logic. Hence *the law of displacement: in and because of modern industry in industrial and technological society, the field in its entirety is displaced towards the pole of the 'signal'.*

This law has a general significance, and we will try to explain it. To do this, we will come back to the symbol. The most profound symbols, the affective ones which we perceive directly in 'beings' and which seem to us to be inexhaustibly creative because they impose themselves upon us, have distant origins. We imagine that they are archaic, and indeed they are. On numerous occasions we have pointed out that the old sociological concept of 'survivals' is inadequate. Symbolisms duplicate the existence of 'beings' or of 'things' by reinforcing their immediate and fundamental presence. The Father represents robust affection, but he is also the Law, be it divine or human. The Sun is life and vitality per se. However, have these 'beings' and these 'things' always possessed a symbolic character? When the practical experience of human groups was constituted in an unmediated way, it was not duplicated by a symbolism, it imposed itself as a fact. Before the Father could appear as the incarnation of God or the State (of authority and law), religion and the state had to be constituted. The resonances and harmonics which reinforce fundamental reality make their appearance during the course of history. Symbolisms have no extratemporal or extrahistorical value. They too are established, formed and formulated. *They are the result of an initial displacement, an initial broadening of the semantic field.* For us, they are still linked to the fundamental rhythms and affective nucleuses which make up the immediacy of everyday life: night and day, 'private' relations, etc.

In all likelihood there were periods when symbolisms existed in a certain equilibrium with *signs* (such as written language and visual numbers). Would it not be true to say that these periods were particularly great and powerful aesthetically, and that they were the great periods of *expressivity*? Doubtless our present-day aesthetic perception of a whole range of archaic and ancient creative works is nothing more than a weakened version of symbolic perception as it was initially. We can also apply this proposition to medieval works of art. What does a cathedral mean to us? We may admire its elements and proportions, but what has that got to do with the way a thirteenth-century man would have grasped it as a set of cosmic, religious, political and human symbols?

For us there are still symbols in our everyday life, but at the same time they are no longer there. Everyday life immerses itself in them, but they elude it, because they elude us. We know them in diluted versions as allegories and metaphors, the stereotypes of good luck and bad luck, or petty superstitions. We have demonstrated how these symbols conceal dialectical movements which they keep to themselves. They are ambiguous. They suggest and they inhibit, they exclude and they include, they beckon and they reject, they reveal and they conceal, they act, they 'structure' and they disappear, they express and they dissimulate. What exactly? The life of a group, and its relation with nature and with other groups: what is or wants to be; what is not and does not want to be; a part of its secret.

In so far as we can know anything about them, the societies which were controlled by symbolisms were peasant societies solidly cemented by their cosmic rhythms and their human rhythms, and by their traditions, i.e., precisely by symbolisms. These appeared in stories of the kind we now call 'mythical tales', which specified in a very simple way the significance and the relations of the various symbols accepted by each particular society. What we must surely find paradoxical is that in societies such as these everyday life was not separate from symbolisms, and yet it did not merge with them. Our 'primitive man' knew perfectly well when he was dealing with a spring or a mountain as sacred powers, and when he was dealing with them as part of secular and practical life. The sacred and the secular, the everyday and the symbolic were not duplicates, but nor were they entangled together. Hence the astonishment of ethnographers (and of their readers) when confronted with such a 'mentality', and with the fact that primitive man makes excellent, practical use of objects which at the same time he endows with more-or-less occult properties.

What transpired when *signs* became more and more in evidence, and when men became aware of the use of signs as implements in their society? This took place not only with the invention and use of writing, but also with the advent of urban life, aesthetic and political life, and with the conscious use of discourse. The awakening of Greek thought and its history affords a wonderful example of this. It is here that Logos becomes aware of itself, i.e., that men (some of them specialists, grammarians and rhetors, others non-specialists, such as philosophers) become aware of Logos per se, and gain knowledge of it. It all becomes enormously confusing. Symbols and mythical tales are turned into discursive themes which have been liberated from their ancient constraints. The use of discourse comes in tandem with a marked scepticism about discourse. Alongside the philosophers of Logos we find the Sophists with their insoluble riddles. The signs which begin to proliferate (writing, written numbers, etc.) do not coexist peacefully with symbols, nor do they superimpose themselves upon them. The consequence is a twofold movement: a reorganization of symbolisms (which in their diluted version have been turned into objects for art and knowledge), and an appeal to symbolisms (as ethical or political models) as a means of orientation through all this great confusion. And so now, *signs masquerade as symbolisms, modifying and corroding them. A vast displacement of the whole semantic field takes place which both enriches it and overthrows it.*

We could suppose that henceforth the inner coherence of social consciousness (i.e., of the whole semantic field) and perhaps of society itself becomes a *work*. It is no longer accomplished with the rhythmic spontaneity of blissful unawareness. How does Greek thought re-establish a certain equilibrium in all this confusion? By the philosophy of Logos, of Plato or Aristotle? By tragedy? By an appeal to the sacred, in reaction against the dissolution of symbolisms and against the separation of the sacred and the secular, the everyday and the divine, which was already taking shape (and doubtless with great apprehension) in the irony of Socrates? Indeed, did the Greeks find a way out? Was not this great unheaval the harbinger of a very serious crisis in Greek society? This is neither the time nor the place to answer these questions. The fact that we use a historical example does not oblige us to theorize on the example per se; all we need is to be able to refer to history, i.e., to 'diachrony', in order to demonstrate the formation of a (synchronic) structure, namely the semantic field. What is more, reference to Greek thought may be extremely informative, but it has its limits; in our era, it is the signal – not the sign – which has the ascendancy. For obvious reasons, the Greeks never knew this child of technology.

With the period when signs come to prevail, symbols are hidden below signs masquerading as symbols. Modified, but still present and effective, they henceforth constitute a 'level'. Whereas signs intervene on the level of representations, symbols are active on another level of existence and consciousness: affectivity, spontaneity (if there is any left) and emotivity. We could talk about a social 'unconscious' inherent in everyday life, if the term did not bring with it a succession of

597

dubious representations. Misconscious is the term we prefer. There is misconsciousness of what constitutes the individual's affective nucleuses in his social group, and this misconsciousness is part of an uneasiness and an opaqueness which seem to be a prerequisite if those nucleuses are to be effective. The broader the semantic field, the more acute its inner tensions (the manifestations of dialectical movements). Levels cannot be quietly juxtaposed or superimposed, but neither can one level masquerade as another, or encompass it, without being disruptive. Dimly perceived as such, or not perceived at all, archaic symbolism is constantly intervening, creating confusions and tearing through the fabric of signs and of coherent discourse. It bursts forth dramatically, in cries, interjections and exclamations, in slips of the tongue – in short, in expressivity. Therefore there are literally holes and craters in the tumultuous volcanic landscape of the semantic field. Or else, chastened, modified, rationalized, in other words subjected to discourse and to the system of signs, symbolism slips into discourse through proverbs, sayings, fables, the old wisdom or the promise of a new wisdom. We will demonstrate how everyday communications presuppose all these elements.

Up until now we have concentrated on the most obscure and the most profound symbols and symbolisms, those which are linked to cosmic and vital rhythms and which are perpetuated (in liaison with these rhythms) in the profound affectivity of children and in the emotivity of adults. Religious symbolisms would seem to derive from a slow metamorphosis of primary or primitive symbolisms, a metamorphosis which maintains them during the growing predominance of signs, modifying and adapting them (more or less well) to dominant representations, i.e., to historical periods and social forces. Religion has managed to use these continual transformations and displacements of the semantic field to good advantage, or at least until now.

However, the laws of continuity which regulate it are not the only ones. Diachronically (historically), there are also discontinuities. *Every revolution destroys a set of symbols. Or else, in attempting to destroy them, it destroys itself.* It cannot but try to destroy them, because, as we now know, such symbols play a structural or 'structuring' role which is all the more effective for being hidden. As a consequence, every revolution makes enormous efforts to replace the old symbols it has destroyed with new ones (which are almost inevitably political). We can use these propositions not so much to define revolutionary activity as to characterize it, together with its successes, its failures and its limits. We know how violently the French Revolution 'desecrated' space, putting stipulations made by previous scientific knowledge about praxis and social consciousness into effect. It was in this naked, empty social space stripped bare of symbols that the everyday life of the bourgeoisie was to set up home. The same revolution would not withstand the pressures of time and the rhythms of (cosmic and social) time, which it was unable to rescue from the ancient symbolisms resurrected by religion: seasonal festivals, sacred numbers, cyclic organizations. Political symbols (such as the flag, etc.) could not replace and eliminate cosmic symbols. Henceforth, the symbolisms associated with lived (affective and emotional) time persisted, so to speak, beneath a social space which had been occupied first by signs, and then by signals. This confirmed the general tendency of the semantic field to structure itself in levels – with differences between levels, gaps, tensions and imbalances. The everyday life of bourgeois society was never to become established in a tranquil manner, although tranquillity was precisely what it was aiming for. Not only would it be forever shaken by insecurity, crises and wars, but the field upon which it was built was shifting, agitated, apparently stable on the surface, but undermined by forces from below.

Given an everyday life such as this it was useless trying to relegate symbolisms to the status of small gestures (goodbyes, farewells, handshakes, etc.), minor superstitions (touching wood, etc.) or dreams and folklore. Pointless! The bourgeois world – this world made bourgeois – of signs, significations and formalisms was to find itself caught between a rock and a hard place. On one hand, it was inevitable that there would be a resurgence of symbolisms, and that poets and philosophers would try to use them as a bulwark against the triviality of the 'world' of bourgeois significations. On the other, the signal was to attack and threaten the 'world' of signs and significations, in the name of industrial technology.

Furthermore, there were entire sectors of social practice which continued to be governed by symbolisms, although these were not without their conflicts. For example, symbols of femininity would conflict violently with the practical claims of women. And there was

one thing in bourgeois life which would never cease: the yearning for
the impossible event – a marvellous, omnipotent Word, which would
at last subordinate space to time, metamorphosing it and transmuting
the real into a limitless, immortal and magical timelessness . . .

For the time being we will put these contradictions to one side,
along with the way they developed in 'modernity' together with their
many aspects (romanticisms, Utopianisms, philosophies of the unconscious, imagination and dreams; the victory of abstract art and
threats to aesthetics in general, etc.).

Displacement now appears to be a general law. But it also becomes
more complicated, because there are some genuine transfers, such as
the reorganization of one level by another, and phenomena of
rupture. Finally, displacements provoke or reveal inverse phenomena: resurgences, returns, recollections.

10 The social text

For the time being we will present this idea without developing its
content. In effect, its significance will only become apparent in the
'communications model'. However it also has a place in the theory
of the semantic field. To be accurate, the 'social text' is an aspect of
the semantic field, and nothing more. It is how we each perceive the
semantic field in everyday life, in a non-conceptual or preconceptual
(affective and perceptive) manner.

It is the result of the combination of the above-mentioned formants, but in proportions which are infinitely varied: *signals*, which
teach us nothing, and make imperative commands using repetitions
which are always identical; *symbols*, which are hidden but which show
through from the depths of the social spectacle, transforming it into
something other than a spectacle. They bring influence to bear,
because they demand participation or challenge it, because they are
always a source of surprise, and because their reappearances are
always unforeseen; finally, *signs*, which only afford moderate surprises
and diversities, since to a certain extent they are predictable.

We all find ourselves constantly – on a daily basis – faced with a
social text. We leaf through it, we read it. It is via this text and our
reading of it that we communicate with the other, be it society as a

whole, or nature. At the same time, we are all part of a social text. We are not only readers; we are also read, deciphered and explained (or not). We are all there indissolubly as object and subject (*object primarily*, since the social text encompasses us and we must see ourselves thus encompassed; *then subject*, since we see ourselves within the text, and decipher and read it from inside, and never completely from outside).

Referring to information theory, we would say that *signals* constitute redundancy in the modern social text: banality and clarity, triviality and intelligibility. *Signs* bring information. *Symbols* can be compared to the 'noises' which interfere with the information which pours forth according to a known (codified and conventional) repertoire, surrounding it from all sides (background noises, empty sounds . . .).

Still with reference to information theory, we would say that at some times a social text is more legible than it is at others. When it is overloaded with symbolisms and overflowing with information, too rich or too rambling, it loses its legibility. When it is reduced to signals, it collapses into perfect banality. It is clear, understandable and boring, and repeats itself ad nauseam. It is the triumph of redundancy. A good social text which is legible and informative will surprise its 'subjects', but will not exceed their abilities; it will always teach them a great deal, but it will never overwhelm them; it is easily comprehensible, but never trivial. So we can measure the richness of the social text by the extent to which it can vary while remaining accessible: by the richness of newness and possibilities it offers to individuals.

Armed with these concepts, let us analyse a few forms of the social text as it is available to us all on a daily basis. The day-to-day reader is not aware of things which only analysis can reveal. The well-informed reader, however, realizes that he is looking at a part of structures: one level of existence and reality, bearing in mind that no one level can exhaust reality as a whole.

In *the village* everything remains symbolic and reveals the truth of symbolisms: archaic and powerful, attached to things, and equally attached to rhythms. The house, the field, the tree, the sky, the mountain or the sea are not simply what they are. Cosmic and vital rhythms envelop them, subtle resonances accompany them, every 'thing' is part of a song. Space and the land symbolize the community, and the church with its cemetery defines time and the world, life and death. Poignantly archaic, everyday life offers itself with complete simplicity: it is entirely humdrum and yet inseparable from its deeper resonances. Every gesture relates to 'something' fundamental, a need, a possession, an object, a presence or an absence, and has a symbolic meaning: picking up bread, cutting it, opening or closing the door of the dwelling, crossing the courtyard and the garden, going out into the countryside. In the village, everything is vigorously alive with the life of actions which are made all the stronger by the symbols they embody. And everything is outdated, old-fashioned, far away . . .

The landscape also offers a social text which is generally legible and often admirably composed, and in which mankind and nature come face to face: the symbols of the former, the signs of the latter.

If we look at *the city*, we will quickly notice how difficult it is to understand this masterly work created by social groups and by society as a whole. It bears the traces of struggles which stimulated the force of creativity, and yet this force tends to obliterate such traces. In the city, symbols have lost the ubiquity they have retained in the village. They become localized and condensed. This does not mean that their role is somehow diminished. Quite the contrary: everything which has prestige and influence, or aspires to having it, everything which organizes and controls this enormous mass of humanity, tends to link up with ancient symbolisms so as to exploit their age-old authority, or else to present new symbolisms in an attempt at self-justification. Symbolisms are condensed into monuments: churches, cathedrals, palaces, large public and private buildings are laden with symbols which merge with their decorations and aesthetic style. Monuments are the works which give a city its face and its rhythm of life. They are its memory and the representation of its past, the affective and active nucleuses of its present everyday life and the prefiguration of its future. We will call them 'suprafunctional' or 'transfunctional', but this is to say not that they have no function or that they transcend function, but rather that their functions are so diverse that no functionality can characterize them or exhaust their social function. On the other hand, in working-class neighbourhoods, in the districts near factories and in factories themselves, there are few monuments, if any. Symbols have disappeared (which means that everything symbolizes power and oppression, and in a hideous way). Nature has disappeared and culture is invisible. Here everything becomes a signal: the signal to start work and the gestures while working and the gestures which maintain the workforce.

Alongside its monuments and proletarian neighbourhoods, the city offers its informative text, rich in signs and significations. Here any analytic description should specify cities and typify them: the city of antiquity, majestically organizing movements which are still close to the old vital rhythms around a few monuments – the stadium, the temple, the agora, the forum, the theatre; the medieval city, with its prodigious vitality, where all elements intercommunicate, city and countryside, house and street, productive craft labour and barter . . . Let us make do with a quick word about the *street*, that phenomenon which epitomizes the modern city. It is in its streets that the life of the large industrial city is at its most original and authentic. It is the street which offers those possibilities and choices which are incomparably more numerous in the city than in the village or small town. We say they 'attract' or 'tempt' us, we call them bargains or fancies, whether we are talking about objects or people, encounters or enticements and adventures. As soon as the street loses this attraction, because it is empty or because the weight of traffic makes it unbearable, the city becomes transformed into a lunar landscape.

What this tells us is that in the society we are observing – the society we are reading – and of which we are a part, intermediaries have special privileges which are frequently excessive and detrimental to things which have or could have more reality. This proposition could be based on an economic analysis: the role of commodities and money, these intermediaries which are becoming increasingly powerful, these things which are becoming fetishes, these mediations which take on a determining role by dissimulating and overwhelming whatever they are linking together. We could read this proposition directly, here in the social text. We will find it on the level of good sense and everyday observation; and yet, there is something paradoxical about it. It means that all around us, the places through which we pass and where we meet – the street, the café or the station – are more important and truly more interesting than our homes and our houses, the places which they link. It is a living paradox, and if everyday familiarity makes us admit it, it does not allow us to see how absurd it is. In times gone by, in the city of antiquity or of medieval times, things were different. Traffic – people, commodities, vehicles – did not dominate. The means and the ends of communication, and indeed of everything, were subordinated to human beings. In this day and age, there is a situation which we are tempted to accept de facto, and even to emphasize: when the street stops being interesting, so does everyday life. Now the city is full to bursting with cars. It has been reduced to systems of signals. What will become of it?

Busy, active, its only link with nature the sky and the clouds or a few trees and flowers, the street represents the everyday in our social life. It embodies it almost completely, like a digest which is interesting because it is so condensed. And this is despite being external to individual and social existence, or because of it. A place of passage, of interaction, of movement and communication, it becomes, via an astonishing volte-face, the reflection of the things it links together, something with more life in it than those things themselves. It becomes the microcosm of modern life. If anything is hidden, it tears it out from its darkness. It makes it public. It robs it of its privacy and drags it on to the stage of a spontaneous theatre, where the actors improvise a play which has no script. The street takes whatever is happening somewhere else, in secret, and makes it public. It changes its shape, and inserts it into the social text.

Like the everyday, the street is constantly changing and always repeats itself. In the unceasing shifts of times of day, people, objects and light, it repeats itself, tirelessly. The street is a spectacle, almost nothing but a spectacle, but not completely a spectacle, because we are in it, walking, stopping and participating. If you hurry you will not see the spectacle, even if you are part of it. Almost an absolute spectacle, but not completely, it is an open book, or rather a newspaper: it has news, banalities, surprises, advertisements. Analogous and homologous, the street and the newspaper join forces in our everyday life. Simultaneously, they make it and they represent it. Changing but always identical, the street only offers a limited number of surprises. If anything sensational (really sensational), extravagant, absurd, offensive or sublime happens, it only vaguely interrupts the diversified monotony of the absolute quasi-spectacle. Symbols stroll by unnoticed. In this day and age, who takes the symbolisms of cathedrals with their devils and divine figures seriously, or sees any drama in them? The street confronts us with a social text which is generally good, dense and legible. All kinds of people mingle in it, becoming almost interchangeable. In times gone by, when class differences were less clear-cut than nowadays, when there were 'estates' and 'castes' rather than classes, these differences were expressed loudly and clearly. The street was expressive. Nowadays, these ostentatious differences have disappeared; they would make the crowds which throng the Champs-Elysées or the Grands Boulevards unbearably gaudy. However, social differences are still visible, signified by a number of indexes and signs noticeable only to the trained eye. This is to say that the street encompasses a multitude of semeiologies. Do faces express anything? A little, but not much. Clothes and body language signify. So the spectacle of the street stimulates our desire to see things and forms our way of seeing them. How many women there are who have unknowingly become part of subtle systems of signs, entering them from within, and using them to classify other women with one simple glance at their shoes, their stockings, their hair, their hands and fingernails, their jewellery and their general appearance! A detailed analysis of the social text would reveal these partial systems of signs and significations which interweave or criss-cross like the items in a newspaper.[4]

The 'world of objects' as they appear in the street is like a large, front-page news item, and yet it constitutes one of the most subtle and least defined systems of signs. In the street, commodities are on offer, but their commercial essence is concealed. They want to be nothing but loveliness, enchantment, pleasure and serenity.[5] In the large modern city, the street postulates and confirms the harmony between needs, desires and goods. Paradise lost is rediscovered in the form of a parody; at every step original unity is restored in caricature. Goods, things and objects are on display; they are offered to our gaze in order to attract and stir up our desires, proclaiming their principle with no apparent irony: 'To each object its desire, to each of us our desires, to each desire its goods and its pleasures. There are goods and desires for everyone, democratically, even for children, even for people who are not very rich, but there are a lot more – all of them – for people who are.' Infinitely near, because they correspond to a desire which is both genuine and phoney, and yet frighteningly inaccessible, like superbly presented women up for sale, objects lead

their sovereign life behind the shop windows. The street is an intermediary between human lives, and its commodities are exchange
values elevated to sovereign heights. Raised to its zenith, fetishism
attains a kind of splendour; and, in an astonishing subterfuge, things,
goods and objects join forces with symbolism again to become the
symbols of wealth and pleasure without limits and without end.
Certain streets have the same beauty as museums, weary and lifeless.
It is a closed circuit in which products – commodities – are changed
into desirable and desired goods. Here, in this involuntary work, the
street, the specific beauty of our society is accomplished. Through the
interplay of objects offered and refused, the street becomes a place of
dreams and imagination, but also of reality at its most implacable. In
the street men and women – particularly women – pay fool's court to
things. Queen-things, fairy-things, holding court behind the transparent windows which parody the transparency of human relations, they
have the magic power to transform their male and female courtiers
into things. Window-shopping has its magic and its religion: the perfected, all-powerful commodity. Sanctified, goods coincide with the
spectacle which they and their advertisements offer. Consumption
gleams in all its hallowed splendour. Through all the possible and
impossible physical delights, all the dreams, all the frustrations,
money claims its kingdom, its empire, its pontificate.

Far away, in the factories (the ones which produce these wonderful
objects, or those which produce the means for their production),
everything is functional or is intended as such; everything is a signal –
the repetitive gestures of labour and its technical organization. Far
away, on the working-class estates, everything is functional, everything is a signal – the repetitive gestures by which the labour force
keeps on going in its everyday life . . .

11 Dialogue, discussion, conversation

We will understand the use and misuse of discourse by analogy with
the social text. Most semanticists, linguists and language theorists do
the opposite; they use discourse to understand other forms of communication and other texts and contexts.

First and foremost, the language of conversation uses banalities.

We talk about neutral things, i.e., really about things and about people seen as things: the weather, the neighbours, friends, the high cost of living and the vagaries of politics, pecking order and wages, who's sleeping with whom and who's cheating on whom. In this discourse bulging with redundancies and commonplaces, dreary word follows dreary word. It is clear, understandable, repetitive. However this apparently useless exchange of trivia signifies something. It bears witness to a generalized need. Shy, awkward, sometimes coarse and sometimes discreet, it is the need to communicate and to exchange something other than mere things. What is more, through the banality which ravages this level of discourse like an unchecked epidemic, stereotypes of everyday life are visible, with the result that trivial discussions and banal conversations, with the family, in the café or elsewhere, can undergo a sudden shift of perspective, to become highly interesting and full of meaning. (For example: conversations about cars, traffic and road accidents between upper-class or 'comfortably off' men; conversations about technical matters; discussions between women about fashion, etc.). *In triviality, it is the dominant representations which are signified, along with their stereotypes.*

Sometimes an unexpected impulse shifts the direction of the discussion. We find ourselves talking about our own lives in terms which go beyond banality (not too far, except in the case of those innocent fools who confide in people without suspecting that inevitably the day will come when these confidences will be used against them. Nevertheless we talk about ourselves up to a point, using keywords, such as love and hate, father and mother, childhood and old age, 'home' and away, family, the world). Then come the long words and the important theories, metaphors and values (usually brought in unawares, by implication) which play in discourse the role played by monuments in the city: proverbs rich in wisdom, usually of the resigned variety, proper nouns affording sudden revelations, dramatizations and absolute principles, truths about life, folklore – sometimes domestic, sometimes social – which often comes from the depths of times long past. At this point, the dialogue becomes overloaded; it grinds painfully to a halt. It becomes a dialogue of the deaf, just as dialogues do when they are extremely trivial, but in this case because it is too rich, and has trespassed beyond the zone of average communication. To go any farther it would have to cross over into poetry or spontaneous lyricism. And it is usually on the threshold of truth, at the instant when communication is at its deepest, that dialogue stops. Sooner or later dialogue will start using symbols in order to guarantee mutual comprehension, and what are symbols if not deteriorated, shattered or buried nucleuses of sensibility, emotion or affectivity? On the lowest level, opaqueness provides a fulcrum, and we are as happy as sandboys among our ambiguities and misunderstandings. On the highest level, it is the emptiness of luminous and transparent space, reminding us of earth and its charnel house of dead symbols, or of an even emptier heaven with its population of inaccessible representations. Only poetry has the wings to soar there. Communication shifts between the silence below and the silence above.

It sets all the levels into motion, and challenges them. It implies and supposes them all: the coherence of discourse and the banality of coherent discourse; words acting like signals which trigger predictable responses; emotivity which introduces images and transmits unexpected impulses into discourse; the emergence of symbols; the emptiness and inadequacy of intended meanings, the gaps, the absences.

5

The Theory of Accumulative and Non-accumulative Processes

1 Critique of the idea of progress

Philosophical and sociological critique of this idea has become rudimentary and banal, since it is dictated by the most obvious and the most easily provable facts. An entirely optimistic idea that progress could spread simultaneously through every area (an idea which was linked to a simplistic evolutionism) has quite literally collapsed during the course of the twentieth century. After Hegel and Marx, the general theory of dialectical movement had stipulated that the process of becoming in all sectors (nature, history, knowledge) would surely be more chequered – discontinuous, conflictual, riven by partial or general regressions – than time as the naive evolutionist pattern represents it. Events have fully vindicated the pattern presented by dialectical thought, and more than anyone could have imagined.

2 Uneven development

We have already stressed the extreme theoretical generality of this concept, which was introduced into Hegelian and Marxist dialectical thought by Lenin. The idea of *uneven development* makes the general critique of the continuist (evolutionist) pattern of the process of becoming more precise, specific and particularized. In our opinion, the implications and consequences of the idea of uneven development and the law derived from it have not yet been exhausted, particularly as regards everyday life. We have already suggested the hypothesis of a period not only where the hoe or the swing plough would coexist alongside interplanetary rockets, and where small farmers would continue to work the land by hand and go hungry while an 'elite' of technicians and managers would be exploring outer space, but also where a backward everyday life would coexist with a highly developed technology, in a way which would be difficult to bear. The situation of everyday life strikes us (unfortunately) as being a prime example of the law of uneven development. But the proposition can be reversed: the law of uneven development points to the possibility of an almost limitless range of human (social) situations at the very heart of economic and technological development, from the rearguard to the front line of action, to use a military metaphor.

We know that the underdeveloped sectors do not remain quietly held back like a troop of soldiers dragging their heels far from the front line. The sectors which are destined to suffer uneven development, be it temporary or long-lasting, soon realize that they are being occupied and brutally exploited. They must regain their freedom or win it back by combat. They remain subjected.

Critique of everyday life generalizes this experience of the 'backward' or 'underdeveloped' nations and extends it to the everyday in the highly developed industrial countries. It lays down the principle that the great upheaval which calls on the consciousness of those nations engaged in the drama of uneven development to emancipate themselves should reverberate through 'modernity' via an upheaval of everyday life and a general upheaval in the name of everyday life, given that it is a backward sector which is exploited and oppressed by so-called 'modern' society.

We insist that this is not simply a metaphor, an allegory, or a mere simile or superficial analogy, but that the problem is fundamentally the same. The link between the situation of the everyday and that of the proletariat goes to the heart of the problem: the transformation of the world, i.e., of the everyday life of today, in 'modern' society, given its history and its structures.

It is a deplorable situation, which we have barely begun to describe, and which we must try to explain. But how did it come about?

3 Non-accumulative societies

Among the many debts the sciences of society owe to Marx, one extremely important discovery stands out, although he himself did not develop its consequences fully – far from it. There is a distinction between two major types of society: one is based economically on simple reproduction, the other on reproduction on an extended scale. To put it even more precisely, the analysis of capitalist society reveals it to contain a double process, one called 'simple reproduction', and the other, 'reproduction on an extended scale'. The second supposes the first, and the first continues a process within capitalism which was inherent in precapitalist societies.

A society should not only produce and reproduce the quantity of goods which allows its population to survive (to reproduce itself bio-logically, to bring up children and to maintain – more or less adequately – its non-productive members). This strictly economic interpretation of the patterns presented in *Capital* (Volume 3, Part 7) does not go deep enough. *Society must also reproduce the social relations between its members.* Thus 'praxis' as Marx describes it cannot be content merely to reconstitute a basis for consumption. It maintains production relations and the social division of labour. Social relations retain a (relative) stability while the members of a society are con-stantly changing; they are born and they die, and pass from one group to another (through marriage, notably) while maintaining their relations. The 'praxis' described in this way on the economic level is therefore not repetition in the same sense as industrial activity is. It repeats itself in cycles. Marx describes and analyses the process of simple reproduction as a *cyclic* process. The patterns of simple repro-duction express the distribution of human activities in a society based on a weak level of productive forces, but endowed with an inner cohesion (a 'structure'). Societies built on a (relatively) stable but stag-nant base are destined to be balanced in a static way. In this very stagnation they demonstrate an extraordinary ability to resist and to persist. The cohesion of primitive communities removes them from the historicity which could shatter them from without, and from the 'incidental' history which would destroy them from within. They can be conquered and subjected, but as long as the conqueror does not annihilate them, they carry on. Structure persists by recreating itself indefinitely, in a circular way. This pattern seems valid for all pre-capitalist societies based on agriculture and handicrafts. Marx did little more than outline this kind of generalization, but it is based on the theoretical and methodological propositions intrinsic to *Capital* and to his *Contribution to the Critique of Political Economy*. According to Marx, the study of capitalism sheds light on what preceded it and not vice versa, which is what evolutionism and the simplified theory of progress believed.

It is self-evident that the members of a particular society are not aware of the circular process and the internal self-regulation which make them tend towards a static equilibrium. However, we should not think they are somehow unaware or falsely aware of their own 'praxis'. The study of agrarian systems and the distribution of tasks in peasant communities reveals great practical wisdom, although this wisdom was never able to express and transmit itself conceptually.

It is also self-evident that the stability of these societies was constantly being threatened by aberrant phenomena such as excesses, defects or 'disturbances' (the 'hubris' of Greek thought). Governed by their Wise Men, the assemblies and councils of elders, and by priests, warlords and political chiefs, these societies employed various means to eliminate such perturbations along with their causes. Similarly, they eliminated any threat of surplus population.

On this point, Marx was happy merely to present a pattern of simple reproduction and to make a few general observations which we will return to shortly. He made no attempt to determine in what way the structures of these societies were analogous or differing, nor to grasp the underlying reasons for their stability on the base as we have just described it. Here as elsewhere, this economic 'base' allows us to know the skeleton of this society, but not how it really functioned (its 'physiology'). It offers us conditions for possibilities, and general conditions for societies which differ greatly from each other to construct themselves. In any case, this was not the task Marx had set himself in *Capital*. He left the job of studying precapitalist societies to others, notably to ethnographers. Everyone knows that in *The Origin of the Family: Private Property and the State*, Engels tried to fill this gap using the work of the first modern ethnographers.

There is one important idea which enables us to understand the real structures of precapitalist societies and the reasons for the stability which has helped them to survive into our own era. We have met it before. *In archaic societies, the fundamental processes are cyclic, and these cycles remain very close to cosmic cycles and the rhythms which come from nature.* The economic process of simple reproduction, which, as Marx demonstrated, is cyclic in character, is an almost unnoticeable component of the cycles and rhythms which predominate as an organizing factor in these agrarian societies: hours and days, seasons and years, generations, youth and old age. We find these societies surprising. They organize themselves in time and according to time more than in space, while significantly they have no historical time or 'temporality' comparable to our own society but, instead, a time scale made up of intertwined cycles. We have linked these social rhythms to the most ancient of symbolisms, and we have had no problem in demonstrating their continuation (we deliberately do not say their 'survivals') in our present-day villages, as shattered, buried or deteriorated nucleuses.

Could it be that these archaic, peasant and craft-based societies (but with embryonic commercial activity) had no history? To believe so would be a naive mistake and an absurdity. These societies have a history, a double one, but in their own particular manner which is different from our own 'historicity'. On the one hand, and from the outside, conquerors established vast political entities – empires – on a multitude of peasant communities, and often by the use of embryonic commercial activities (such as barter, exchanges, or the possibility of exacting tributes and taxes). In this political framework, states and dominant classes which foreshadowed feudalism or the bourgeoisie began to take shape. Immobile and almost immovable on their static and stagnating 'base', these empires lasted until such time as a weak tremor might lead to their sudden collapse. Empires like this have lasted until the present day – The Turkish Empire, for example. Notable among this type of political formation are the pre-Columbian American empires, the Roman Empire, the Byzantine Empire and the great Asiatic empires, each with its own specific characteristics within the general context we have defined above.

On the other hand, the archaic societies in question also had a complex internal history, precisely in so far as there were differences between them. By his pattern of simple reproduction, Marx drew attention to an important fact. These archaic societies had a political

613

economy, although the economic side of it was not predominant and determinant *stricto sensu*. Their political economy functioned blindly, spontaneously, almost automatically as the practice of economy in the precise sense of the term when we say that someone is *economical*: a distribution of tasks and products which is spontaneous to begin with, but which becomes increasingly conscious, in 'poor' societies controlled by governing groups which demand abstinence from the other groups, and sometimes from themselves. Marx criticized political economy and law as the knowledge and practice of non-abundance. Be that as it may, scarcity is a completely relative idea which cannot be taken to the absolute or be of any use as an explicative principle. A society without surplus product, in which labour allows for nothing more than the survival of its workers, will quickly disappear. In the archaic societies we are talking about, dominant groups, which were not yet classes in the exact, contemporary meaning of the term, were thus able to gain control of a certain surplus labour and surplus product. It is obvious that slavery and subsequently serfdom made it possible to increase surplus labour and to extort part of the surplus product all the more easily. These dominant groups seized the surplus social product and appropriated it to their needs and works. What is remarkable is that in most of these societies the 'masters' transformed the wealth they had levied into works, as if they felt they had to justify that levy to the people and account for it to the community, which had not yet been completely burst asunder. We use the term 'works' in its broadest sense: monuments, festivals, permanent or transitory works of art. As yet these masters justified their existence and their predominance not by using representations and ideologies, but by *symbols*, which they embodied physically in a multiplicity of works.

Only in this way can we understand how diverse these ancient societies were: violence and equilibrium, vitality and stability, poverty and splendour, shabbiness and beauty. In retrospect they offer us a diptych: on one panel, a realm of brutality and despotism, on the other, extraordinary creations in art, lifestyle, wisdom, culture and even philosophy (although the latter only emerges with conceptual thought and the awareness of discourse per se, which bring ancient wisdom to a close). Marxist thought contains the indications which enable us to approach the study of archaic or ancient societies in all their manifold aspects.[1] However, there is one particularly profound and well-known question raised by Marx, and which he himself did not resolve: how is it that the bourgeois and socialist cultures of today can be interested in works from distant periods, created in conditions which were very different from our own by groups (castes, embryonic classes) which established themselves using unbridled and limitless violence, and which used the meagre surplus social product to create all this sumptuousness? What can explain the lasting character of these works, these superstructures of defunct societies?

At this stage we will hazard a few conceptual elements for a theory. At the heart of archaic and ancient societies, everyday life was not separate from what was 'highest' and 'greatest' in culture and ideas. This is something we have already pointed out. 'Primitive' man, the archaic peasant and probably the citizen of ancient cities all knew full well how to distinguish between the sacred and the secular, the everyday and the sublime, while for us these two elements of their lives seem inextricably merged. This man may have believed that a given familiar object was possessed of an obscure power for good or for evil, but he still knew perfectly well how to put it to practical use; and he knew perfectly well when he was addressing that power and when he was not. Why? How? Because of the very nature of symbolism and of symbols, which enter the 'lived' and duplicate or reduplicate reality without becoming separate from it. Just as every object in these societies could easily become a work of art (all that was needed was a little effort and, far from being the exception, this effort was the rule. Absence of any art was the exception, and a sign of degeneracy), so everyday life could easily become a lifestyle. Every change in the men who commanded these societies and in the symbols which they used would have an influence on style in the everyday: it would be grandiose, sublime, sensual, sensuous, erotic or violent, according to the men and to the circumstances. From the very first peasant societies which saw the birth of meditation to the great empires and even to the Greek city states, almost every possible stylistic hypothesis was attempted.

Now if the analysis we are attempting here is at all correct, our own everyday life has a double character. On one hand, it has no style; in the context of a history which is moving ever farther away from the everyday, and of a globalized society which holds sway over it from the empyrean realms of the state, the utilitarian and the functional constitute not a style, but its opposite: the absence of style. On the other hand, there are some very ancient symbolisms which alone are able to restore some strength to gestures and actions which have been robbed of all meaning; although they have deteriorated and shattered, they still form effective nucleuses which, however destructive or inadequate, are still active. How could we not grasp the works of the past? They interest us, they fascinate us, and we call upon them desperately to give us a sense and a style. In the name of the vast emptiness which is everyday life, our everyday life, we look towards everything which could point to or perpetuate a plenitude. Any age, it does not matter which. It is not aesthetic sensibility or ideology which acts as mediator, but everyday life.[2] However our interest in the objects and ideas of distant societies labours under one serious misconception. We perceive them as art objects, whereas in fact this art was not something external to the everyday or, as is supposed, high above it and trying in vain to enter it, but a *style of life*. What we perceive as theories and philosophies were in fact ways of everyday living. This is why the more we return to these objects and ideas, the more they disturb us. We are well aware that we do not understand them. We look for their historic context (when there was no history analogous to ours), their social context (when there was no society analogous to ours) or their ideological context (when abstract ideological representations had not yet appeared, and concretely lived cosmic symbols and rhythms close to cosmic rhythms predominated).

4 The concept of the process of accumulation

Simple reproduction is and remains a necessary condition for all social life. From a certain date onwards (at the end of the Middle Ages in the European West) it gives way to another process, that of accumulation on an extended scale. Marx studied it schematically, restricting it to the economic point of view (and knowing full well that this level of reality does not encompass reality as a whole). In *Capital* he determines the reciprocal proportions of the different sectors of production which are essential for the effective development of reproduction on an extended scale, i.e., the accumulation of capital.[3] Marx did not specify the historical conditions and diverse conjunctures which allow or allowed for the insertion of the process of accumulation into stable structures governed by the previous type of process.

The process of accumulation profoundly modifies and overturns the previous process. It does not abolish it. It encompasses it, and introduces the fundamental contradiction between the social character of productive labour and the private ownership of the means of production. Despite this fundamental contradiction (which will develop into the polarized and antagonistic 'bourgeoisie/proletariat' class contradiction) society must remain coherent and internally cohesive. Antagonisms can lead to breaks; contradictions do not stop society from constituting a whole (a totality). Self-regulating mechanisms change, but they do not disappear.[4] And so cyclic movements are not abolished. A process resembling a rising spiral segmented by numerous accidents encompasses the circular process, which from then on maintains a periodicity. Society as a whole continues to reproduce its relations and conditions of existence, but the socio-economic proportions inherent to simple reproduction are modified by the proportions necessary for accumulation on an extended scale. On analysis we find that they are still present, as conditions for a dynamic equilibrium (rather as we find ancient mechanistic physics present within modern physics). If the society of economic growth did not go on reproducing its social relations, it would crumble away. But this would only happen gradually, and on a limited level: the level of the fragmented division of labour and of the conscious relations between separate individuals, and of the separation between 'private' and 'public', and between 'the everyday' and 'the world as a whole'. On the level of society as a whole, on the level of property and production relations (of class relations), social cohesion continues to grow ever more strong. The economic mechanisms of self-regulation in themselves are not enough to guarantee it, and as they only come into play on a certain level, the cohesion of the whole is guaranteed in another way, on the level of a certain consciousness: by representations, ideologies, models, values, and also by new works, and finally, by the use and misuse of ancient symbolisms.

This process of accumulation involves society as a whole, and the men who compose it, in a historicity: in *history* in the accepted sense of the term, and which Marx characterizes as natural history or the prehistory of man as a true human being. As we understand it, this history differs quite profoundly from the history affecting archaic societies. It has its specific characteristics: the process of accumulation controls it and determines its conjunctures. Unlike in ancient societies (although it was certainly important), the economic sphere becomes predominant and determining. This history is made by individuals and groups, but blindly. Trapped as they are in a deep and many-sided alienation, it is something they must endure. And so the accumulative economic process comes in tandem with a political and ideological history which is particularly linked to uneven economic development. The historical (political and social) experience of recent times makes it necessary for us to continue to develop Marxist theory beyond the point Marx himself left it. To begin with, let us present several propositions:

a) Marx conceived of socialism both as the end to the process of accumulation, and as its aim. Once this process had reached a high degree of productive investments (of productivity and production) in the highly industrialized countries, the revolutionary proletariat would take over its administration. It would not bring accumulation to an end, but would immediately orientate it towards the conscious transformation of the world.

Our reinstatement of the Marxist project has already shown that Marx was concerned not so much with transforming the outside world as with metamorphosing everyday life. The alienation of the everyday as a residual deposit and a product of all the partial alienations would disappear. This prediction has not been borne out. However, from the historical moment when growth and accumulation (the level of the productive forces) made what Marx predicted *possible*, there was a qualitative change. This was the moment we entered into 'modernity' and into the permanent crisis of modernity which is now permeating every sphere.

b) The socialism achieved as the result of a proletarian revolution in a poorly industrialized country seems to differ somewhat from the Marxist programme (but let us be prudent and optimistic: it is different until further notice). Socialism appears to be a social and political means for accelerating the process of accumulation in backward and 'underdeveloped' countries; it corresponds to the 'globalization' of the process, and not to the end of it. It consists not of enjoyment of what has been accomplished, but of an intensification of the accomplishment itself. The destructive character of the process, which determined European history for centuries, is becoming modified; in certain aspects it is becoming weaker, and in others more accentuated. It is remarkably obvious that the process of accumulation is speeding up. The factors of saturation and rupture which threatened it for centuries in Europe have been eliminated, but the ideological, cultural, political and 'human' consequences of this activity entirely devoted to accumulation remain with us in a permanent state of challenge and extraordinary tension. It is to this world-wide situation, which Marx did not predict, that we owe the intensification of old forms of (ideological and political) alienation, and the invention of new forms of alienation (technological alienation, and total alienation of the everyday).

c) The process of accumulation appears as the central axis or backbone of modern history. It is in relation to this process that historical situations are characterized and become specific. Let us indicate several of its types: when the process develops spontaneously, antedating the formation of the state (e.g., England, the United States, and France, in part), when the state accompanies and stimulates the process (e.g., France, in part, Germany, Italy, and Tsarist Russia), when the state organizes and accelerates the process (e.g., the Socialist states), and when the state antedates the process of accumulation (e.g., the underdeveloped countries which have recently won their independence). As a consequence there are remarkable historical differences in the role these states play, in how they are structured and in the way they function. This does not take other considerations into account, such as legal modalities and property relations within the state.

5 Generalization of the concept

This is not the place to study the patterns (in *Capital*) of how reproduction on an extended scale functioned, or to give a close analysis of the historicity and diversity of the historical situations during this process, or to describe the changing historical conditions of accumulation. We know that Marx did not present these conditions in their totality and diversity. He restricted himself to England and English capitalism (as a type or an extreme case: a spontaneous process which antedated the formation of the state and subsequently minimized its role). This initial gap has never been adequately filled, and has led to some serious misunderstandings. Some people in the Marxist movement have been too exclusive in attributing the simple requirements of industrialization to the ferocity of the bourgeoisie. We now know that no nation and no country can escape these torments, although the modalities and the nature of the devastation may differ.

We will restrict ourselves to a few comments which will allow us to present the concept of accumulative process (or growth by accumulation) on its most extended scale. As soon as the economic historian examines the conditions of primitive accumulation in Western Europe, he will observe that there was an increase in discoveries and technical progress during the Middle Ages. This was pointed out by Marx, who did not share the opinion of evolutionist and liberal historians about the 'Dark Ages'. Subsequently the work of technologists and historians has extended our knowledge on this subject. When we examine this early 'capitalization' of techniques, we discover the complexity of the historical conditions: the renewal of urban life, the recovery in commercial exchanges, the rediscovery of Greek science. The recovery of commercial exchanges was the result of improvements in agricultural techniques attributable to the arrival from the East of peoples who had hitherto been nomadic (progress in the use of horses, harnesses, ploughs, crop rotation, etc.). Technical progress in the Middle Ages was due to the fusion of several contributions, as much as it was to any special inventive capability. What did these contributions have in common? How can we explain the renewal of this inventive capability? It was a moment when thought was rediscovering the ability to be conceptual and abstract. Now only logic can determine a 'level' of experience and of reflective thought which will enable concepts, abstract (mathematical, physical and biological) knowledge and techniques to be accumulated effectively and transmitted more skilfully than with using examples or day-to-day discourse. Only logic defines a coherence on a level which is above and beyond nature, empiricism and spontaneous sociability. Using the rediscovery of Greek culture, and on an analogous economic base (commodity production, urban life, increased communications and exchanges), but without an unmediated or mechanical link between this 'base' and the acquisitions it facilitated, the Middle Ages were able to redefine *the form* which the process of accumulation would take. Then, after having been interrupted and slowed down for many centuries, the process gained impetus, producing a veritable discontinuity in the sixteenth century (which is inaccurately called the Renaissance).

And so our idea of the process of accumulation is now much broader. Knowledge is an accumulative process, and so is technology. Taken together they presuppose the elaboration of a form and are part of the conditions of a specific process: the accumulation of capital, i.e., of the means of production, which begins deep within the capitalist mode of production. At first we saw the process of accumulation as something uniform, but now we are beginning to see that it is composed of several related processes. It is a sheaf, a fasces. Once we have distinguished between them, its components themselves appear to be accumulative processes. *Rationality, for example, has an accumulative character.* Among these activities, which are partial processes within a comprehensive process, we may include knowledge, technology, production and productivity, i.e., economics, culture in the accepted sense of the word (linked to rationality and knowledge) and maybe political action, in so far as it operates from established legal and bureaucratic superstructures, which also 'snowball'.

Every process of accumulation can be represented schematically by an exponential curve (a^x or e^x, at the fastest growth: here this is a temporal function, a^t or e^t). This exponential growth can only be a *tendency*, or rather it is generally only a tendency. When of necessity the process involves factors which slow it down (more or less deep and lasting saturation), the exponential curve takes on a much more complicated form, called a 'logistic' curve.[5] In point of fact, we know that historical events and conjunctures can interrupt or break any process of an accumulative kind.

We can use this observation to draw up a schematic of history over the last five centuries or so. It is doubly determined by the economic process of accumulation, which is its axis, and the conjunctures and events which propel, slow down or interrupt it. The process constitutes the determination of a historical necessity; the historical situations which appear around this central axis introduce chance, contingency and initiatives by individuals and groups.

We could even use it to extrapolate a general periodization of history which would redefine their place and their role in political economy, sociology and history, as follows:

First period: non-accumulative societies. Predominance of agricultural production, localized crafts. Barter or commerce 'in the pores' of this society. Complete or almost excess consumption of production in terms of immediate needs. Slow or zero demographic growth, interrupted by regressions (plagues, famines, wars). Transformations by the governing groups of living wealth (abstractly capable of being invested) into dead wealth: treasure, monuments, works of art. Knowledge of a frequently remarkable kind, but not accumulated (the preserve of groups of initiates, and disappearing almost completely whenever the groups themselves disappeared). High standard of art. Authentic lifestyles. Marked contrasts between splendour and brutality. Predominance of cyclic forms of social processes and time scales. Predominance of custom, which held the community together.

Second period: Accumulative societies (or to be more poetic: Promethean societies). Initially poorly defined appearance of the process of accumulation (its various conditions come into being independently). Transitions. Silent, bitter struggle between this process (and the men driving it forward) and the grandiose, venerable and vulnerable world of the past. Ideological delusions introduced by this struggle (the 'Renaissance'). Unleashing of the process in an increasingly violent way. Revolutionary surges. World-wide extension. Substitution of cyclic time with linear time. Industrial production taking over from agriculture. Predominance of law rather than custom. Socialization of society.

A third period which would begin with the transformation of everyday life (following a deliberate and conscious policy) after a long and difficult transition. Do we need to add that 'modernity' represents this transition precisely, and that we are part of it . . .?

The term we have just used, i.e., the *'socialization of society'*, requires an explanation. In the pattern we have presented, the economic and the historical spheres match each other relatively easily. With the process of accumulation, history does not simply change direction. When it loses its cyclic character, it takes on a new sense, direction and meaning. This is not to say that it loses its violent and bloody character, but rather that something new appears. The economic sphere per se becomes the 'base' and the 'axis' of society and of its history. What is more, the constitutive links of the old society – links of consanguinity, links with the earth – become blurred or disappear within a vaster society. The process of accumulation shatters and subordinates whatever resists it: the limits of groupings, unmediated relations, pre-existing social structures. It does not entirely suppress them, since the family persists, and within the process nationhood comes into being. By submitting to the process of accumulation, groups originally formed by consanguinity and territory become its means, its implements and its context.

Society as a whole continues to consolidate and to form itself into a solid totality (or tries to). As a totality, its influence on its elements and members becomes increasingly profound: through the policies and effectiveness of state institutions, through culture, through ideology. In this way it submits them to the requirements of accumulation (acted out, of course, according to the aims, interests and perspectives of the dominant class). But *at the same time* we witness the appearance and consolidation of the individual and of private life, and of individualism as ideology. During the first historical period, the individual (in so far as we can talk of individuality) was always taken care of by a community. It protected him, but also it did not hesitate to sacrifice him ruthlessly. Then, during the period of accumulation, the individual acquires a certain practical and theoretical autonomy. He exists. But then society abandons him. Either he participates in accumulation, or he is on his own. He is on his own in so far as he exists as a 'private' person. Socially and legally, he has rights according to the law, and first and foremost the essential right to own property. This leads to a fundamental conflict between concrete reality and (legal and political) fictions, between theory and practice, between living and the law, between the hidden truth and the social appearance on display (represented). Officially, society respects the individual (a respect which 'representations' sanctify), but it is just as ready as it was in the past to turn against him. On the level of (national) society as a whole, the power of the state has all the necessary means at its disposal. In principle, in civilized society, the society of the process of accumulation, there is no more torture and there are no more massacres. Each individual can contribute to accumulation (of knowledge, of implements, of social capital, etc.). And yet 'needs must', and the requirements of accumulation outweigh all else.

This colossal and colossally contradictory process has a third aspect: it differentiates between groups and segregates them. From the seventeenth and eighteenth centuries onwards, across society as a whole, we see the emergence of sub-groups which hitherto had been ill defined and merged in what subsisted of the old community: children, young people, women, intellectuals, etc. Henceforth these large groups are seen as having their particularities, aspirations and claims. Differences such as these precede, announce and accompany the great polarization into classes: bourgeoisie, proletariat, middle classes. They make phenomena more complicated and are part of the 'socialization of society', with all its various aspects. The more effective accumulative society becomes as an integrating force, the more it loses control over its own elements. This society keeps its own inner contradictions alive and, surprisingly, it segregates as much as it unifies and individualizes. It emphasizes the particularities of these groups, and acts as mediator between the two aspects of singularity (the individual) and generality (unity and totality on the scale of society as a whole). Social segregation is based on the division of labour, but can be reduced to it, since it implies the intervention of analytic intelligence, which shatters, separates and dichotomizes. It is also not the same as reason, which is a function of accumulation, but reason makes use of it. Analytic intelligence probably reached its crisis with the advent of the bourgeoisie and of rationalist ideology, but it was not solely their preserve, since on the theoretical and ideological level it is an element of all accumulation and of the division of labour. Analytic intelligence applied itself actively and effectively, and the present-day social and human 'world' is to a large extent its handiwork. From then on analysis split up everything which could be split, until it almost ruined and (apparently) atomized the social totality. In our present-day society, everything which could be set apart, separated and 'autonomized' has been done so: aspects of labour, social functions, specialized activities, technology, the arts, the sciences, age groups, the sexes, classes, categories of urban inhabitants, and *of course, everyday life in relation to whatever is not everyday life*. So the 'socialization of society' conceals a dialectical movement: totality, or more exactly, totalization, individualization (or 'personalization' which had its abortive beginnings with individualism), and particularization, which becomes segregation at the hands of an extremely effective functional analysis of groupings and activities. This threefold movement encompasses a multitude of contradictions. It takes shape and emerges with the process of economic growth which 'conditions' it (which makes it possible). On one hand it depends upon accumulation, and on the other on representations, superstructures, and a socially and practically justified function: analytic intelligence.[6] What we have said so far only begins to explain and explore the consequences and implications of the concept of the process of accumulation. We will now draw a line under it, or otherwise it will deflect us from the task in hand. But we could take it further. For example we could ask ourselves whether the process of accumulation (with all its elements, which are themselves partial processes) bursts forth into the 'world' and nature like some sort of human miracle – a miracle laden with hopes and fears. Could it be born of a chance encounter between elements and factors which are mutually exclusive and with no connection other than this conjectural convergence, at a given moment in history? Or could it be the continuation of a deeper necessity?

We may suppose that, biologically and physiologically, life contains a *tendency* towards being accumulative which is immediately slowed and inhibited by opposing factors, such as saturations or obstacles. The growth of animal life is a prime example of this. Every species would flourish indefinitely if this expansion did not contain its own limits (its negation) within itself. In point of fact, every species is prey to other species. What is more, as it grows, every species modifies its own environment and destroys the species it in turn preys upon.[7]

As this process develops, the human brain (or rather the cortex) also seems to be an organ capable of 'capitalizing' experiences. It perpetuates and heightens the ability to which living 'substance' owes both its strength and its vulnerability: the ability to retain traces of the past while struggling to maintain itself within its environment at the heart of the present moment. The work of the Pavlovian school helps us to study the accumulative function of the brain and also to understand what hinders it. Men forget as much as they remember. The functioning of the cortex produces internal inhibitions and decelerations. The cortex is quickly 'saturated'; emotions disturb its accumulative but incomplete functioning. Self-regulations are never perfect and never allow for the complete 'capitalization' of what has been acquired. The same may be said of so-called psychological functions: memory per se, perception, intelligence.

And so it is as though a deeply rooted tendency within the process of accumulation, which in nature is frustrated by antagonistic 'factors', were emerging in man, in society, in history and in economy. Should we believe that in nature, cyclic rhythms originate in an embryonic accumulative process which returns to its point of departure? Should we go right back to the physical processes the growth of which is expressible by geometric progressions and logarithms? Such hypotheses go far beyond our aims and our competence.

6 Non-accumulative processes

The generalization we have just made of the concept of the accumulative process leads us to accept the existence of non-accumulative processes (not for the first time, but in a clearer light). They exist, as causes, effects, foundations or results.

Taken as a whole (the cortex, subcortical formations, the neurovegetative system), the human brain does not seem to function unilaterally, as one block. It comprises levels, differences in level, imbalances and conflicts. And much more than this, pathology seems inherent to human perfectibility, i.e., to its imperfections. Gaps, memory lapses and mistakes are part of how it functions. Men can make mistakes without going off track, and can then correct them. They can go astray, get lost, and then find themselves again. They can become alienated, and then disalienated. In the future there may be highly advanced machines which will duplicate logical, discursive and reflective thought. They may even surpass it in breadth and precision. Doubtless they will never have the power to forget. Forgetting is beneficial, in that it allows us to start again, but it is also harmful, in that it involves mechanical repetitions and gaps in accumulated experience. Will these machines duplicate affectivity and its disturbances, passion, laughter, boredom, fear of dying, alienation and disalienation? This is doubtful, unless we agree with the metaphysics of science fiction, which explores what is possible by using myths from the past.

Surely we must see *accumulative* functions in the activities of the brain (disjunctions which work on distinctions and differences, and 'capitalize' them), as well as *non-accumulative* ones. This idea could lead us to reconsider Pavlovian representations, which link a number of facts together, but then transform them into a system by a way of thinking which ignores dialectical method.[8] This hypothesis leads us to scrutinize nervous activity for levels, imbalances, differences and conflicts, while not breaking its incontestable unity.

Let us now move from the biological and physiological level to the psychological level in the total field we are hypothetically exploring. There is no justification for rejecting the thesis (which was robustly maintained by Marx and Engels) of a modification of human (sensory, perceptive, active) organs during the course of history and of the education of individuals. Surely it is impossible that labour should not have modified the eyes, the ears, the hands and the forms of sensory perception, all of which have their origins in nature. However, to what extent has it modified them? All we need is to look at the Lascaux and Altamira frescos to realize the naivety of the evolutionism which tries to assimilate the development of the body and its organs via labour with transformations of consciousness and reflective thought via abstraction and conceptualization. These age-old works of art reveal a sensory acuteness, a perceptive vivacity and a creative power of action and gesture which twentieth-century man finds astonishing; he is amazed, and wonders if Picasso's greatness is not due to his having rediscovered something of the freshness of our origins through the world of abstraction. Could we go so far as to maintain that the appropriation of external nature by the senses and the body is more active at the beginning of social and individual life, with primitive hunters, and with children? We certainly can. What does labour bring to this initial layer of perceptions? A great deal; first of all, abstractions and signs, and then signals. And yet, do not these great acquisitions come with partial regressions? When the abstraction of signs, and above all of signals, is superimposed on sensory perceptions, it constitutes a 'world' which is both external and abstract, the world of modernity which conditions individual gestures. Does this 'world' inhibit the freshness and vivacity of the senses? It certainly does, especially if it is true that in the modern world – with the perceptively efficient technology they represent – signals are characteristically accumulative. Hence, by contrast, the prestige of archaic objects, primitive arts, symbols, and the astonishment they provoke in men of the industrial era.

What we are suggesting about sensory perception can also apply to emotions and affectivity. They do not appear to be accumulative, which explains the way they crystallize around paradoxically durable symbols. As we already know, most of these symbols, if not all of them, come from the distant past of agrarian and craft-based societies. Their subsequent elaboration by philosophers, dramatists and poets helped to revive them, but without modifying them to any profound degree. With their origins deep within the direct and unmediated relations between men and nature, and between men themselves, they live on in islands of unmediated 'private' life which withstand the rising tide of relations mediated by commodities, money and technology. These symbols have become nucleuses of emotion and affectivity. When they are not used, exploited, consumed and devoured, they are attacked and concealed. When they crystallize (as the Father, the Mother, Woman, Virginity, Love, the Sun, the House, Water, Earth, Air, Fire, Hearth and Home) they degenerate, break up and scatter. They remain well outside the processes of accumulation.[9]

According to this criterion, we will classify human activities into two major types of process: *accumulative and non-accumulative*. Within this classification, we may discern genres or species: processes of accumulation which have been decelerated (saturated), liberated or accelerated, circular processes which have stabilized, and nucleuses which have degenerated or broken up, etc. This provides us with a starting point for an analysis of praxis and a representation of the process of human becoming. We have already drawn up a list of accumulative activities. Among non-accumulative activities we would include sensory perception, sensibility, sensuality, spontaneity, art in general, morality (subjective or deriving from custom, as distinct from objective morality which depends upon law and the state) and finally civilization in the broadest sense (as opposed to culture). The non-accumulative is also the non-rational. We use the term in its essentially relative sense, since there is no question of us positing an absolute (ontological) irrationality. We can also say that the accumulative would be related to space, while the non-accumulative would be related to time. However, there is no question of separating space from time.

Nor is there any question of separating the two types of process. They are permanently interactive, so that when we describe and analyse that interaction, we perceive various gaps, imbalances, differences and conflicts between levels. If our experience of 'modernity' is of a deep-rooted and ever-increasing malaise, our concepts will enable us to discover some of its causes and aspects, and perhaps to reveal the problem in its totality.

The problem in question is the problem of everyday life. Everyday life lies at the ill-defined, cutting edge where the accumulative and the non-accumulative intersect. On one hand, it must submit to the demands of accumulation, and suffer its effects and consequences. It exists on the level of the most pressing conditions and effects of the process of accumulation: cohesion, logic, language and, last but not least, signals. On the other hand it sees itself increasingly 'distanced' by the process, which becomes dissociated in the giddy heights of specializations and technology. In itself, it remains linked to rhythms, to cyclic time scales and to symbols.

This is merely putting what we have already said in another way. The everyday is situated at the boundary between the controlled sector (i.e., the sector controlled by knowledge) and the uncontrolled sector. This is ill-defined and dangerous border territory, particularly because its symbols give the illusory impression of controlling spontaneous nature, while the techniques which really do control it are increasingly hidden from view.

The malaise comes primarily from the extraordinary imbalance between the symbolic nucleuses and the acquisitions of abstract knowledge and technology, i.e., from the conflictual relation between the two processes. This imbalance itself has various aspects and various senses. The affective nucleuses are 'survivals' (in inverted commas; there can be no 'survivals' without a 'base' or 'foundation'). From a certain point of view, they seem more beautiful, more precious and more immediate than all the accumulations of experience and knowledge put together. From another rigorously equivalent and equally well-founded point of view, they are old-fashioned, ridiculous and backward. Similarly, from yet another point of view, the accumulative is the only 'truth' over and above 'the real'. It alone is important, great and creative, while the everyday knows itself to be negligible, superficial and non-essential. But another equally acceptable point of view would be that the everyday is the only thing which matters to mankind.

In themselves, symbols are only maintained by means of metaphorical language, words or the use of rather unusual words, literary or historical recollections, objects infused with meaning, and works of art. Their only 'bases' are their uncertain and 'private' social relations with nature, with the other and with the self. The vast tide of 'modernity' is sweeping these supports away. Economic backwardness and underdevelopment (villages, the mountains, the sea, picturesque tourist attractions, barren regions, etc.) feed these 'survivals' and maintain these nucleuses without breathing any new life into them. It is as though cyclic time scales have been ripped asunder by the linear time of the process of accumulation and have been left to hang in tatters within us and around us. And yet symbolisms, cyclic rhythms and the shattered or degenerate nucleuses continue to organize the everyday; they represent its stable centre and maintain the illusion of a pre-ordained harmony, if indeed we can still use that word.

The result is an incessant tension, and thus the possibility of sterile conflicts and pathological deviations, both in individual consciousness and in social consciousness. Reduced to silence amid all the verbiage and verbalisms, relegated to an obscurity which prompts us to speak of 'unconsciousness', private everyday life is built up around symbols which are constantly discredited by public life, economic and political praxis, signs, signals and significations. All that personal life has at its disposal to make itself into a conscious creative endeavour, and to give itself a conscious history, are these nucleuses buried within the deep secrecy of individual psychophysiological life: tastes and desires (amorous, erotic, affective, alimentary, etc.), or rather, the absence of tastes and desires. This is how public life, overtly subjected to accumulative processes, overwhelms private life, condemning it to powerlessness, unconsciousness and dissatisfaction. When it tries to become reconciled with private life, things are even worse: it invades it and absorbs it (cf. the mass media). In every case, everyday life is forsaken territory, an island of tears and tedium where man as the norm is normally cast away. The frontier between the controlled sector (controlled by knowledge and technology, and therefore by and in accumulation) and the uncontrolled sector is a no man's land where everyone lives more or less on the level of deteriorated and shattered spontaneity. The more people speak of adaptation, balance and harmony, the less real harmony, balance and adaptation there is. (And what do obsessions mean if not that even these conflicts are no longer creative?)

Within the individual, and at the heart of his consciousness and his ill-appropriated life, two processes are apparent: the rational and the irrational, the (relatively) conscious and the (relatively) unconscious. On one hand, if he cannot accumulate money, he accumulates experiences, and if he cannot accumulate capital, he accumulates knowledge. Even if they are fragmented, experience and knowledge join together to form a memory. On the other hand, there is something inside him which is ever more distant, ever more vulnerable, something he is consciously seeking, the childhood and the spontaneity which are as much a part of symbolisms as they are of memory. Is this not one of the secrets of the disturbed drama of modern life, this uneasy, private consciousness which is increasingly penetrated by the general process and is forced to conform to it, and yet which is becoming increasingly 'private' and trapped within the everyday? In fact, as soon as radical critique unmasks the situation in which consciousness and life are trapped, it seems intolerable, and we ask ourselves why the devastation is not even more destructive than it is.

7 The pedagogic and culturalist illusion

We must find a way out of this situation. How? By revolutionary praxis reconstructed in its totality. But what else? By following technology to its bitter end in order to reinvest it in an everyday life which has been metamorphosed, instead of merely observing the terrifying discrepancy between the two? By discovering new representations of time and imposing them (by persuasion) on time as we usually live it? By raising the everyday to the level of technology and by reinvesting technology in the everyday? By eradicating the old symbolisms and creating new ones, new images of life as a work of creativity?

But this is to jump the gun. Let us begin by closing off the false exits. In the modern world, pedagogic and cultural fictions have joined forces with the old legal, ideological and political fictions (the Citizen, everyone is equal before the law, etc.). The new fictions seize the baton when the old ones are too weak to stay in the race. What do they consist of? The attribution of the accumulative character to sensibility, emotivity and affectivity. Therefore it is considered possible to 'form' them in the same way as conceptual or technical knowledge through the accumulation of experiences, facts or representations, and despite all the failures of fiction both in the individual and on the scale of society as a whole.

It is obviously in the domain of art that this illusion and its consequences may be best observed. What is known about art grows in an accumulative way. The number of objects piled up in the universal museum and in the total library of books, records and films must increase exponentially. The viewer and the listener has increasingly easier and more frequent access to all works from all ages. It is assumed that when the various sources of knowledge are all bundled together in this way it will stimulate our powers of creativity, or even that technologies (and the last to be developed is always the best) will be a substitute for spontaneity. The two poles of activity – technological literacy and creative power – would merge. Not so. The welter of works, of knowledge and of technology comes in tandem with a gargantuan consumption which must surely be looting and devouring all the riches of ages which precisely did not accumulate, and which have left us their treasures in trust. The result is an astonishing sociological phenomenon: aestheticism (which is not caused and explained by its accumulative character alone) and its corollary, the permanent crisis of so-called modern art. In so far as there is such a thing as creativity, does it not come from a direct or indirect appeal to the symbolisms and the myths which supported it in times past, and from an effort to reinstate spontaneity in the face of the clutter of abstract culture and pedagogically cultivated consciousness? But nothing will spare symbolisms their inevitable dissolution. They too have already been relegated to the aberrant margins of culture: astrology and parascientific interpretations of science, science fiction, specific 'worlds' of women and of children, petty superstitions and ritualizations, and works of which it is impossible to say whether they are foretelling the future or falling into decrepitude at the very moment of their success.

The same is true of the moral sphere. Knowledge of morality, its history and its 'values' is expanding. Like discourse on aesthetics, discourse on morality and its 'values' is becoming increasingly facile. Ethics is the loser, and it will never be possible to extrapolate a practical lifestyle from moral knowledge.

And so the malaise of the everyday and of the 'privation' of private life is contaminating the higher spheres of art, ethics, creativity and the understanding between consciousnesses . . .

6

The Theory of Moments[1]

1 Typology of repetition

Previously we underlined the differences between several forms or types of repetition, which were mutually irreducible. Repetition of cycles and cyclic rhythms differs from repetition of mechanical gestures: the first of these types belongs to the non-accumulative processes, which have their own time scales, while the second belongs to the processes of accumulation, with their linear time scales, which are now continuous, now discontinuous. Repetition of behaviour patterns (conditionings) stimulated by signals cannot be assimilated to repetition of 'states', emotions or attitudes linked to symbols and emotional nucleuses. We must distinguish between repetition of situations (notably in pathological cases) and repetition postulated by certain systems (by Kierkegaard and Nietzsche, for example). If repetition, return or renewal of the same (or more or less the same) phenomenon should be understood according to each specific case and type, the same can be said of the relation between what is repeated and the newness which springs from repetition (for example, repetition of sounds and rhythms in music offers a perpetual movement which is perpetually reinvented).

Similarly, repetition of the *instant*, so frequently studied by philosophers (the *hic et nunc*, pure immediacy, the purely transitory in perception and the 'lived'), cannot be assimilated to repetition of the moment.

2 Moments and language

As regards the term 'moment', our first comment would be that it corresponds to the *sense* (expression + signification = direction) of a given word in general and common usage, or, if you prefer, to its lived *content*. Let us take the word 'love', which crops up so frequently in language. To what does it correspond? Is there a higher entity which is indicated by the word and which endows it with a general sense because it subordinates a set of situations and emotional or affective states? This classic Platonizing and rationalist theory is not tenable. And yet, if there is not a unified set of so-called 'love' situations and states, the word itself has no meaning. Could it be simply the abstract connotation of a range of states and situations with no concrete links between them? In this case, not only are there 'loves', as opposed to a few types of love, but an indefinite number of them, amorphous and multifarious. This equally classic, empiricist and sceptical theory is just as untenable. As we well know, it presents a challenge to language; it undermines and disintegrates it. Words are no more than arbitrary signs, and discourse is no more than a formal construction. But discourse is linked to praxis, a level of experience, and it has meaning because it has both a logical (disjunctive) form and an emotional and affective content, which it efficiently transmits. We understand it through its form and structure, but not only that. Communication presupposes all the levels, and all the tensions and conflicts between those levels; never complete, rarely real, it implies that the semantic field is neither opaque and solid like a stone, nor unstable like mist; it implies relative movements and relative stabilities. Why do the same words come back time and time again, with their images and symbols, and how do they make themselves understood? What is it that allows us to use the word 'love' in varying situations and conversations, and still be understood by the different people we are talking to? What is it that creates a certain alignment between the emotion expressed by one speaker and the emotion aroused in the other, just by the use of one word? When people are in love, or imagine they are, when they hate each other, or imagine they do, what is it that allows them to communicate what they are feeling or what they are not feeling, to recognize one another, to create misunderstandings and resolve them (up to a point), to rise above insinuation or silence, in short to avoid a dialogue of the deaf which would be no more than the sum total of two soliloquies (in which case language would be devoid of meaning, i.e., of effectiveness, and would inevitably waste away or would even have long since disappeared)? Through all the changes, 'something' remains. We would say that 'something' is the *moment*. Psychological terms (such as states, emotions, attitudes, behaviour patterns, etc.) do not adequately define it, since it implies a twofold recognition, of otherness – or rather, of the other – and of the self. This re-cognition, which joins forces in an original dramatic situation with what is known and what is unknown, explains and justifies the use of the word. It presupposes in turn the (confused or clear) perception of an analogy and a difference in lived time, i.e., a specific modality of repetition. 'Something' – which is certainly not a thing – is encountered once again. Both an illusion and a reality, lived time appears once more through all the veils and distances. It vanishes, and at the same time it makes itself known. No specifically sociological or historical determination can adequately define this temporality.

The theory of moments comes initially from an effort to give language significance and value, in the face of its critics (such as Bergson), and in spite of the undermining and disintegration of language which we are currently witnessing. It is the product of a violent protest against Bergsonism and the formless psychological continuum advocated by Bergsonian philosophy.[2] Its wish is to reinstate discontinuity, grasping it in the very fabric of the 'lived', and on the loom of continuity, which it presupposes (and consequently without making it abstract, and without merging it with the arbitrary and the purely formal – which is a reaction against exaggerated continuism, though not a supersession of it).

According to this process, we do not start from Logos (discourse and language), we come to it, time and time again. The theory does not postulate the value or the substantial reality of language. It does not take Logos as an axis of reference. On the contrary: it tries to reinstate language in all its power, by understanding (by knowing) certain conditions under which it can be fully exercised. Seeing it theoretically undermined by the attacks of some philosophers and poets, and practically (socially) undermined by signals, audio-visual imageries, jargons and by the isolation of minds incapable of communicating, it starts from an analysis of the conditions for communication. If it were too perfect, language would be of little use to communication, or rather, it would change it into a communion of angelic and disembodied minds (supposing that means anything). Everything would be instantly clear. Such magic transparency has not even the beauty of a dream. It implies a lack of depths, levels and planes, in life as it is lived. If it were too imperfect, language would fail to cope with differences; it would leave them to their own opaqueness. As it is, with its mobile complexity which is nevertheless 'structured' by constants, nucleuses and 'moments', language is of use to us. It is a good implement, and something more than just an implement . . .

More profoundly perhaps, the theory derives from a need to organize, programme and structure everyday life by transforming it according to its own tendencies and laws. It wishes to perceive the possibilities of everyday life and to give human beings a constitution by constituting their powers, if only as guidelines or suggestions.

This means that we are using the term 'moment' in a rather particular way, while still insisting on its day-to-day usage, and on the fact that certain words in common usage have a general, definable quality or property.

In day-to-day language, the word 'moment' and the word 'instant' are almost interchangeable. However, there is a distinction between them. When we say 'It was an enjoyable moment . . .', for example, it implies a certain length of time, a value, a nostalgia and the hope of reliving that moment or preserving it as a privileged lapse of time, embalmed in memory. It is not just any old instant, nor a simple ephemeral and transitory one.

In the Hegelian system, the term 'moment' receives special treatment.[3] It designates the major figures of consciousness; each of them (the consciousness of the master and that of the slave in their mutual relations, the stoicist or sceptical consciousness, the unhappy consciousness, etc.) is a *moment* in the dialectical ascent of self-consciousness. Even more essentially, *dialectical movement* marks the turning point of reality and of the concept: the fundamental intervention of the negative which leads to disalienation but also to renewed alienation, to supersession through negation of negation, but also to new stages in the process of becoming and to new figures of consciousness.

637

The Hegelian notion seems to have influenced day-to-day language. Did anyone talk about the 'historical moment' before Hegel? Definitely not.

Our use of the term will be more modest than Hegel's, but broader. We situate the 'moment' as a function of a history, the history of the individual. We consider that up to a certain point (very limited, and as yet, too limited) this history is his own creative undertaking, and that he recognizes himself within it, even if it is in a confused way. Moreover, the history of the individual in his everyday life cannot be separated from the social sphere. Narrow and limited though it is, it is part of other, broader works. However, the theory of moments parenthesizes these implications. Like all theories, it uses a justified abstraction to isolate its object. Moreover, it examines the 'moment' in general, and particular 'moments' in their relation with everyday life. Thus it does not presume to define them completely or exhaust them. There are other sciences and methods which could study these 'moments'.

The moment is a higher form of repetition, renewal and reappearance, and of the recognition of certain determinable relations with otherness (or the other) and with the self. Compared with this relatively privileged form of repetition, the others would be nothing more than raw materials, namely the succession of instants, gestures and behaviour, constant states which reappear after being interrupted or suspended, objects or works, and finally, symbols and affective stereotypes.

3 The constellation of moments

Among moments, we may include love, play, rest, knowledge, etc. We cannot draw up a complete list of them, because there is nothing to prevent the invention of new moments.

How and why should we classify any particular activity or 'state' as a moment? What should our indexes and criteria be?

a) *The moment is constituted by a choice which singles it out and separates it from a muddle or a confusion, i.e., from an initial ambiguity.* Natural and spontaneous (animal or human) life offers nothing but ambiguity. The same is true for the amorphous muddle we know as the everyday in all its triviality, where analysis discerns the detritus and the seeds of every possibility. Moments are there in embryonic form, but it is difficult to make them out with any clarity. And so it is in childhood and adolescence, in games and in work, in playing and in loving. If we are to particularize work, for example, be it of a material or intellectual nature, and if we are to specify the entire set of attitudes, behaviour patterns and gestures it groups together, we will need a very strict pedagogy and a great deal of effort. In a similar way, amorous playfulness – light-hearted chat, flirtation, teasing conversations, provocation – comes before love itself. Difficult to pick out in all this equivocal and muddled ambiguity, the one emerges very slowly from the other, and sometimes not at all. Until such time as we can distinguish between love and playfulness, there can be no love, or love can be no more. Love has its serious side. If it plays games, it dominates them. In this sense, love implies the project of love, of loving and of being loved. It chooses to constitute its moment. It begins with an attempt at a moment (and with the temptation of the moment, disturbing and frequently refused).

b) *The moment has a certain specific duration.* Relatively durable, it stands out from the continuum of transitories within the amorphous realm of the psyche. It wants to endure. It cannot endure (at least, not for very long). Yet this inner contradiction gives it its intensity, which reaches crisis point when the inevitability of its own demise becomes fully apparent. The manner of its duration means that it cannot be brought into harmony with continuous evolution, or with pure discontinuity (a sudden mutation or 'revolution'). It can only be defined as *involution.* Essentially *present* (an essential modality of *presence*), the moment has a beginning, a fulfilment and an end, a relatively well-defined start and finish. It has a history: its own . . .

And so 'love' is one particular love (the love of one man for one woman, or of one woman for one man). And it is also the succession of loves of one man or one woman, and a series of amorous passions in a broader history, the history of a family, of a group, of society (and finally, of the human being). The term 'moment' will be like a digest of all the analogies and differences involved.

c) *The moment has its memory.* For the individual and for groups, memory in love is not the same as memory in knowledge or in play. When we enter the moment we call upon a particularized memory (which does not exclude other memories completely, but relegates them to a background of 'misconsciousness' where they are disregarded). It is within this specific memory that the *re-cognition* of the moment and its implications are created.

d) *The moment has its content.* It draws it from conjunctures in more-or-less external circumstances, and incorporates it. All the content of moments comes from everyday life and yet every moment emerges from the everyday life in which it gathers its materials or the material it needs. The originality of the moment comes partly – and only partly – from its circumstantial content. Rather than tearing it, it weaves itself into the fabric of the everyday, and transforms it (partially and 'momentarily', like art, like the figure in a carpet). In this way it uses something it is not: something happening close by, something contingent and accidental. With its circumstantial contingencies, and while it lasts, the moment also has the *urgency of a command and a necessity.* So someone who makes up a game for children or for adults will use whatever he happens to have at hand (or on his lips: when there is nothing else available he will play with words).

e) *Equally, the moment has its form*: the rules of the game – the ceremonies of love, its figures and rituals, and its symbolism – the pace and principles of work for whoever is working, etc. This form imposes itself in time and in space. It creates a time and a space which are both objective (socially governed) and subjective (individual and interindividual). In this sense, the moment not only has a form; it 'is' this form and this order imposed on its 'content'.

f) *Every moment becomes an absolute.* It can establish itself as an absolute. It is even a duty for it to do so. Now we cannot conceive of the absolute, let alone live it. Therefore the moment proposes itself as the impossible. Here we are coming close to fundamental criteria. What love worthy of the name does not want to be unique and total, an impossible love? If someone has not wanted this, if he has not refused to compromise from the moment he fell in love, if he has not dreamed of the absolute, if he does not aspire to fulfil this dream (to be the first man to do so) and to achieve this fulfilment (to be the first man, the only one to do so) then he is not worthy to be called a lover. By analogy, play makes players and the player turns his game into an absolute: the aim, the meaning of life. He gambles everything which is not part of the game. It is a wager for random winnings – for the heady thrill of chance; his entire life becomes a stack of chips on the gambling table. Whoever wants knowledge sacrifices everything which is not knowledge in the pursuit of knowledge: everything becomes an object of knowledge and a means of knowing the object it is pursuing. The moment is passion and the inexorable destruction and self-destruction of that passion. The moment is an impossible possibility, aimed at, desired and chosen as such. Then what is impossible in the everyday becomes what is possible, even the rule of impossibility. And this is when the 'possible/impossible' dialectical movement begins, with all the consequences it entails.

g) Disalienating in relation to the triviality of everyday life – deep in which it is formed, but from which it emerges – and in relation to the fragmented activities it rises above, the moment becomes alienation. Precisely because it proclaims itself to be an absolute, it provokes and defines a determined alienation: the madness (not pathological, but often verging on delirium) of the lover, the gambler, the man of theory devoted to pure knowledge, the obsessive worker, etc. This specific alienation can be classified as one of a more general type, the alienation which threatens every activity within the very process of its accomplishment. In so far as it is alienating and alienated, the moment has its specific negativity. It is destined to fail, it runs headlong towards failure. Everything happens as if he – the man who has changed his passion into a 'world' – wanted to fail. Negativity operates at the heart of whatever tries to structure and constitute itself into a definitive whole, and to come to a halt. Inevitably, necessity and chance are destined to come together and to be superseded, and from that supersession the tragic is born. In our view, the link between the tragic and the everyday is profound; the tragic takes shape within the everyday, comes into being in the everyday, and always returns to the everyday: the tragic initial decision, which constitutes an absolute, and proclaims it, the tragedy of heartbreak, of alienation, of failure at the heart of fulfilment, of the return to the everyday to start the process all over again. This is how the contradiction between triviality and tragedy is determined, and we are bold enough to say that it can be overcome, and that the theory of moments gives a glimpse of its supersession . . .

We imagine so-called 'spiritual' life to be like a constellation, and this is a symbol we will deliberately use. In the light, or the half-light, of the everyday, the constellation of moments cannot be seen. But when something disturbing casts a shadow on the everyday, that constellation rises on the horizon. We each of us choose our star, freely, but with the impression of an irresistible inner necessity. No one is forced to choose. There is no astrological explanation for the constellation of moments: freedom has no horoscope. In this day and age, everyday life is lit by false suns: morality, the state, ideology. They bathe it in a phoney light, and even worse, they lower it to depths where possibilities cannot be perceived, and keep it there. Sadly, the stars of what is possible shine only at night. Sooner or later the everyday must dawn, and the suns must rise to their zenith (including the black sun of empty anguish). Until such time as mankind has transformed this light and this darkness, stars will shine only at night.

So-called 'spiritual' life offers several different absolutes: several paths towards totalization, several paths towards fulfilment, in other words, towards failure. This is how things are. And until things change, mankind can do nothing about it. If a man wants to be a man, this is how he will create himself, moving ahead as far as he can on one of these paths. Spiritually speaking, he is in a 'configurative space', with its given dimensions. However, this mathematical metaphor hides the truth: the freedom which dawns even in the inevitability of tragedy and the need for tragedy.

None of us can escape this drama, since absence of tragedy itself creates yet another dramatic situation: the desolation of everyday life, emptiness and ennui. And the moment? It is an individual and freely celebrated festival, a tragic festival, and therefore a genuine festival. The aim is not to let festivals die out or disappear beneath all that is prosaic in the world. It is to unite Festival with everyday life.

4 Definition of the moment

We will call 'Moment' *the attempt to achieve the total realization of a possibility*. Possibility offers itself; and it reveals itself. It is determined and consequently it is limited and partial. Therefore to wish to live it as a totality is to exhaust it as well as to fulfil it. The Moment wants to be freely total; it exhausts itself in the act of being lived. Every realization as a totality implies a constitutive action, an inaugural act.

Simultaneously, this act singles out a meaning, and creates that meaning. It sets up a structuring against the uncertain and transitory background of the everyday (and reveals it to be as such: uncertain and transitory, whereas before it appeared to be solidly and undoubtedly 'real').

Could this definition (which refuses to separate fact from value, with all the false problems that would create) be *philosophical*? Yes and no. Could it be an ontology? In one sense, yes, and yet the 'being' which is only revealed in what is possible does not correspond to the 'being' given behind the actual or within the actual as posited by classic ontology. The theory uses concepts and categories elaborated by philosophy, but outside of any system and any attempt at systematization. It uses them prudently, hypothetically, while consciously accepting a certain risk. It applies them to praxis: to everyday life, to individual man's relation with nature, society and self. The theory has no desire to be exclusive. In no respect does it rule out other theories or other perspectives. Ipso facto, it attempts to open an investigation which would no longer be strictly comparable with classic philosophy, but which would nevertheless continue it. It conceives of a kind of twofold critical and totalizing experience, and of a 'programmatic' which would not be reduced to a dogmatism or a pure problematic: the uniting of the Moment and the everyday, of poetry and all that is prosaic in the world, in short, of Festival and ordinary life, on a higher plane than anything which has hitherto been accomplished.

This theory does not fit into any philosophical category (and the same can be said of the theory of the semantic field). Could it be an *existentialism*? *Yes*, since it describes and analyses forms of existence, and *no*, since we could also say that it is 'essentialist'. It comprises a critique of existentialism and essentialism. We could say that moments are just as much 'essences' as they are attributes and modalities of 'being', or existential experiences. Furthermore we would be happier talking about 'powers' rather than 'essences', while making sure to remember that the theory has a practical goal: to transform these powers, these partial totalities which are destined to fail, into 'something' unforeseen and new, something genuinely total, which would overcome the 'triviality/tragedy' contradiction.

Similarly, the description of the 'lived' in the theory of moments could be baptized as 'phenomenological'. However, we have been very wary in our use of 'parenthesizing', so as to be sure to reinstate anything which we may have *momentarily* eliminated, and to avoid reducing the totality of the experience. Our descriptions and analysis were directed at praxis, and not at consciousness per se. We are dealing not with domains or regions, but with possibilities.

To conclude, let us say that we are determining a structure of possibilities and projects, while avoiding any structuralism by which actions could be predetermined.

In fact, in this day and age, there is a very widespread philosophism which sees philosophy everywhere and nowhere, and forces it into insignificance. We will have nothing to do with it, nor with the ontological presumption or the illusion of the most general (and the most 'nondescript') object.

If we must fit the theory of moments into some kind of classification, we will say that it has a contribution to make to an *anthropology*, but with two provisos: first that we do not confuse this anthropology with a culturalism (the cultural definition of man outside of nature and spontaneity), and second that we do not omit radical critique of all specializations, including anthropology. The latter obeys a general rule which we have already formulated axiomatically: in the domain of the social sciences, there can be no knowledge without a twofold critique, first of the reality which must be overcome, second of the knowledge already acquired, along with the conceptual implements necessary for the acquisition of further knowledge. And in the case of anthropology, surely the danger of making dogmatic statements (which would offer a limited and limiting definition of man) is greater than it is elsewhere, and surely its consequences would be much more serious.

In any event, all these considerations are only of marginal importance. What we need is a precise definition which will allow us to develop our analysis of moments.

5 An analytics of moments

So each moment can be characterized in the following ways: it is *perceived, situated and distanced*. And this just as much in relation to another moment as in relation to the everyday. However, the relation of the moment to the everyday cannot be determined by externality alone. The moment is born of the everyday and within the everyday. From here it draws its nourishment and its substance; and this is the only way it can deny the everyday. It is in the everyday that a possibility becomes apparent (be it play, work or love, etc.) in all its brute spontaneity and ambiguity. It is equally in the everyday that the inaugural decision is made by which the moment begins and opens out; this decision perceives a possibility, chooses it from among other possibilities, takes it in charge and becomes committed to it unreservedly. This choice is already a dramatic one: at the crucial point of decision, at the heart of the everyday, nothing is clear. How can we expect something which is blatantly relative and, even worse, ambiguous, to be absolute? What is possible and what is impossible are not yet part of the conflict; they are merged; there are no exact, predetermined limits which would enable a decision on what is possible and what is impossible. Once the choice has been made, we see that the 'subject' wishes something which is impossible in terms of the everyday; but the fact of making a decision changes what was a distant impossibility into an imminent possibility. For the passionate feeling which has now been aroused, what is impossible is precisely a criterion for possibility: it wants the impossible, it risks the possible to attain an impossible which at first seemed beyond the bounds of risk and chance. Effectively, when a decision is made it pushes back the boundaries of impossibility. In this sense, decision assumes the risk of failure completely, but it runs another risk for which it takes full and free responsibility (with the obscure but deep-rooted idea that by chance or by will-power it will avoid it), and that is the risk of terminal failure, when the moment's magnificent trajectory will be brought to an end. Decision refuses the initial failure, whereby the attempt is aborted and caricatured. So in the moment, the instant of greatest importance is the instant of failure. The drama is situated within that instant of failure: it is the emergence from the everyday or collapse on failing to emerge, it is a caricature or a tragedy, a successful festival or a dubious ceremony. In so far as it is inherent to the moment, to its goal, to its madness and its grandeur, failure must be considered as *terminus ad quem* and not as *terminus a quo*. If we are to understand and make a judgement, we must start not from the failure itself, but from the endeavour which leads to it. If there is a rise and a fall, a beginning and an end, the tragic is omnipresent in the genuine moment. Its fulfilment is its loss. Once again we are faced with the dialectical movement of 'totalization/negativity' or 'alienation/dis-alienation/realienation'.

The moment is not exactly the same as a 'situation'. The result of a decision and a choice – of an endeavour – the moment creates situations. Because it effectively links them together, in its capacity as a general term, it sums them up and condenses them. From then on they are no longer experienced in 'lived' banality, but are taken in charge at the heart of 'living'. We can attempt to define the relation between the moment and the 'situation' by starting with the difference between 'conjuncture' and 'structure'. The conjuncture is *almost* the situation, and the moment is *almost* the structure. However, in a conjuncture, there is less than the situation, and in the moment there is more than a structure. The conscious being 'in situation' is prey to an external conjuncture into which he must insert himself. As soon he attempts a moment, he is deliberately turning his situation into a risk: a series which from the start necessarily involves articulations in time and space, an order and a form imposed on the elements which have been taken from the conjuncture. And this is what properly and specifically constitutes the situation. Once more we are faced with the concept of the articulated, inner process of becoming, tending towards a specific end outside the general process of becoming, and constituted by a form which has been freely developed. It is a possibility which has been taken over and which will give a particularly intense and lived present moment. It will initially take a form which is as yet deprived of content (e.g., ceremony, ritual, rules of the game, principles of the activity, etc.). Decision gives this form its content, and this in turn creates a situation.

The moment commences and re-commences. It takes up the previous moment again (the *same* moment), reinvests its form and continues it after an interruption. This is the form in which it unfolds: ritual, ceremony and necessary succession. Thus moments lend themselves to formalisms (of love, of play, etc.), but if ever formalism triumphs, the moment will have disappeared. When the moment comes to an end, there is a break. In this sense, the theory of moments rejects both ambiguity and all philosophies of ambiguity, and formalisms and all ideologies of pure form (while reserving a place for them).

Like time, the moment reorganizes surrounding space: affective space – a space inhabited by symbols which have been retained and changed into adopted themes (by love, by play, by knowledge, etc.). The space of the moment, like time, is closed off by constitutive decisions. Anything which cannot be included is chased away.

Could *contemplation* be a moment? This can be argued for and against. There are a number of philosophical systems which imply that it is, or posit it as such. Perhaps all philosophy is an attempt to make contemplation a moment. If this is so, we could define philosophy as the deliberate structuring of the lived within contemplation, which it invests with value and factuality, spontaneity and culture. As we know only too well, a definition such as this renders philosophy unviable. Do moments die? Probably. If so, contemplation would be a dead moment.

As for the *look*, it is certainly not a moment. To constitute oneself as pure glance, to attempt the glance as a moment, to look with clear-sightedness (but at what? – at everyday life, and first and foremost the everyday life of other people), is obviously *tempting*. Since it is a practical and social fact, involving an important sensory organ and a form, looking seems capable of such an undertaking. Since the sex organ is capable of adventure, why not the eyes? Once the decision is taken, we become pure look, clear and clear-sighted: clairvoyant and voyeur. We draw strength and interest from the fact that we are outside what interests people in their everyday lives. This is doomed to fail from the outset, but this time the failure is not tragic, it is comic. The pure, disembodied glance which is so perceptive that it penetrates (or thinks it penetrates) the flesh of other people is one of the great comedies of our age. Penetrating and perceptive – subjectively – this glance is an objective feature of a world where everything becomes a spectacle for everyone, without any living participation. But the pure glance is unaware of this situation. Its own blindness condemns it. It seems that in contemporary philosophy there is a perpetual and ever-ambiguous seesawing between looking and knowing. Such an ambiguous mixture of effective knowledge and 'pure' glance seems unstable, untenable and unbearable. In the period when philosophy is withering away, could not philosophy be the Beautiful Soul of modern times?

With its various oscillations and compensations, this seesawing movement between looking and knowing caricatures ancient contemplation, which lived and died. Looking cannot hope to constitute or 'found' a moment. It destroys itself from the outset, and its possibility is sheer illusion.

We will not even ask whether fatherhood, motherhood, friendship, decency, etc., can constitute moments. These are virtues and qualities which can encourage endeavours and situations. As in the case of the pure glance, the endeavour collapses before it even starts, and sometimes even more ridiculously. And so there is not an unlimited or indefinite number of moments.

At the same time, we cannot wish the list of moments to be exhaustive. Were we able to complete it, we would be changing the theory into a system. Moments are mortal too, and as such, they are born, they live and they pass away. There is room not only for freedom, a limited freedom but a real one (which comes into being by structuring, destructuring or restructuring everyday life), but for inventiveness and discovery. In this day and age we are witnessing the formation of a moment: *rest*. With many ambiguities (non-work, leisure) and many ideologies and techniques (such as 'relaxation', or 'autogenic training'), modern man – because he needs to – is making an effort to live rest as a totality in itself, i.e., as a moment. Up until now, very little distinction used to be made between rest on the one hand and play and everyday life outside work on the other.

We can define *justice* both as a virtue and as an institution. We could see it as a moment if we were to restrict or broaden the concept to encompass what happens in the everyday and in individual consciousness (the consciousness of the social individual). The moment is constituted by the possibility of an act: in this case, the act of judgement. It is an action which never stops. We are always making judgements. And these judgements are always bad; we know they are, and we know that they are prejudiced and unsafe, and even that we have no right to make them in the first place. In practical terms, this act is thus both possible and impossible, and we try to live it as a totality. Since it takes its elements from everyday life, and since it tries to assess it, it does not accept it purely and simply for what it is.

And so a ritual is proclaimed, a ceremony, i.e., a form, and in extreme cases a formalism. Whoever judges, in other words, whoever wishes to judge, *summons* actions and events, from his own life and from the life of others (into which he enters to an unwarranted degree). His mind becomes ritualized, and it dons the regalia of the courtroom. The bill of indictment presents passions and past deeds to the court as proof in these criminal proceedings. Whoever is sitting in judgement has granted himself the power to do so. Self-appointed, he *summons* the witnesses. *He conducts the prosecution,* i.e., he investigates the circumstances and the motivation of actions (and usually loses track of them). He hears the evidence of the various witnesses. Finally, he *gives his verdict*; he passes judgement, but never does so without *appealing* to higher authorities (which do not exist, since he alone has decided to pass judgement).

It is easy to notice the similarity between the inner ceremony of the virtuous mind, and the highly externalized formalism of justice as an institution. And so the 'virtue or institution' dilemma is a false one, and the theory of moments resolves it.

The theory allows us to understand how and why justice becomes an *absolute* from the moment it is conceived. Whoever loves justice and wants justice – the Just Man – wants nothing but justice, and he judges everything according to justice. And yet he never manages to define it, let alone realize it. He determines justice according to what is just, and what is just according to justice. In this way he lapses into a specific alienation, the alienation of the moral consciousness which aspires to be absolute. To put it another way, justice as the goal of action (and philosophers fixed this goal for the worthiest actions of mankind) presupposes an action which goes far beyond that goal and which is inspired by other motives. Justice cannot be realized, or even begin to be realized, by its own powers alone. Its realization implies its suppression and its supersession.

Therefore the moment of justice has its alienation and its own negativity. It refers us to the Supreme Judge who would justify justice and realize it, who is always evoked and always absent. He maintains the powerful and beautiful image of the Last Judgement, which would also be the moment when the world is destroyed (*'pereat mundus, fiat justicia'*). Once we begin to judge, we never stop. How can we not judge? And yet: 'Judge not lest ye be judged.' Only the final, supreme judge, the ultimate authority, has the right to judge.

Like an ever-sought and ever-inaccessible absolute, the moment of justice obsesses our era. Hence the fixation with trials which is such a feature of contemporary art (in Kafka, Brecht, and quite a number of films, etc.).

We will return to the problem, but for the time being we will not include art or any activity which creates aesthetic works among moments. Provisionally, we will reserve the term for those activities which are undertaken in the lived and which do not produce an external object.

6 Moments and the everyday

We have still not isolated and defined this relation completely. Moments make a critique – by their actions – of everyday life, and the everyday makes a critique – by its factuality – of paroxysmal moments. We have not yet exhausted this reciprocity.

The moment cannot be defined by the everyday or within it, but nor can it be defined by what is exceptional and external to the every-day. It gives the everyday a certain shape, but taken per se and extrapolated from that context, this shape is empty. The moment imposes an order on the chaos of ambiguity, but taken per se this order is ineffectual and pointless. The moment does not appear simply anywhere, at just any time. It is a festival, it is a marvel, but it is not a miracle. It has its motives, and without those motives it will not inter-vene in the everyday. Festival only makes sense when its brilliance lights up the sad hinterland of everyday dullness, and when it uses up, in one single moment, all it has patiently and soberly accumulated.

And so the everyday cannot be reduced to 'empty moments', even though it is unable to grasp the exciting risks moments propose. Everyday life is a level within totality and for this reason it is denied totality, and it is unable to comprehend actions which unfold as totalities. They place themselves apart from everyday life; or rather, they try to live apart, and this is precisely how they miscarry, in all their splendour. Thus moments present themselves as duplicates of everyday life, magnified to tragic dimensions.[4] In this way – by critique – we can understand Lukács's well-known statements (about 'the anarchy and the chiaroscuro of everyday life') or Husserl's com-ments (on Heraclitian flux and the formlessness of the 'lived'), while nevertheless avoiding privileging art or philosophy. There are men who are not artists and not philosophers, but who nevertheless emerge above the everyday, in their own everyday lives, because they experience moments: love, work, play, etc.

All that spontaneous life can offer is muddle and confusion: knowledge, action, play or love. The man of culture tends to single out the elements or 'formants' from what is given as a mixture of spontaneous vitality, and to use them to constitute moments. Furthermore he tends to unify what is given to spontaneous consciousness as discrete elements (life and death, vitality and the tragedy of failure). Thus, according to the theory of moments, culture does not detach itself from nature, nor does it superimpose itself upon it. Culture selects, it makes distinctions (sometimes in an exaggerated way, separating and isolating the elements it wishes to use to such a degree that any further development becomes impossible), and then it unifies. It is in everyday life that this painstaking labour of selection and unification unfolds. Everyday life is the native soil in which the moment germinates and takes root.

Nature appears to us like a gigantic wastage of beings and forms, like a frenzy of creation and destruction. Outrageously playful, immeasurably tragic, its failures, monstrosities, abortions and successes are incalculable. (And who knows, perhaps successes are merely monstrosities which chance has smiled upon.)

Everyday life already imposes a certain order in all this chaos, a certain economy in all this profligacy. Compared with so-called 'higher' and specialized activities, and compared to moments, the everyday appears as ambiguous as it does trivial. And yet it is the spontaneity nobody can do without. And yet, compared with nature, it is already more ordered and more beautiful, and more economical with its means and its ends.

Unmediated and endured by those who live it, the everyday acts as mediator between nature and culture. The false light which bathes it grows dim and is outshone by the true clarity of critique. At the same time, its apparent solidity bursts asunder to reveal it as the point where nature and culture come together. Culture, which perpetuates this situation, is dismantled theoretically, and nature regains its strength, but far away from man and the human, which now must be redefined.

The theory of moments will allow us to follow the birth and formation of moments in the substance of the everyday in their various psychic and sociological denominations: attitudes, aptitudes, conventions, affective or abstract stereotypes, formal intentions, etc. Perhaps it will even permit us to illuminate the slow stages by which need becomes desire, deep below everyday life, and on its surface. But most importantly, it must be capable of opening a window on supersession, and of demonstrating how we may resolve the age-old conflict between the everyday and tragedy, and between triviality and Festival.

VOLUME III

◆

From Modernity to Modernism (Towards a Metaphilosophy of Daily Life)

Preface

Presentation: Twenty Years After

Michel Trebitsch

This book represents a leave-taking – in the first instance, for Henri Lefebvre himself – since it closes a long cycle, wholly unpremeditated at its inception, extending from volume one of *Critique of Everyday Life*, published in 1947, to the third volume, which dates from 1981. The philosopher, who had retired in 1973, died ten years later, at the age of 90. There is no better way of indicating that these three volumes span almost half a century of intellectual history – especially when we recall that Lefebvre's questions were inspired by theoretical lines of inquiry going back to the pre-war period and that to the trilogy we need to add one of the signature books of 1968, *Everyday Life in the Modern World* (not to mention a number of articles).[1]

The decades separating these works were full of historical upheavals: that is why this preface, in contrast to those to the previous volumes, will not merely offer a presentation or, rather, contextualization. Nothing could be less straightforward than jumping from the years around 1968, which postdate the second volume, to (in the French case) the arrival of the Left in power, which coincided with this work, not to mention the collapse of the Eastern bloc foreshadowed by events in Poland. But we must go further (and perhaps we should have done in the earlier prefaces) by considering not only the context – the reconstruction of the conditions of production of each of these texts in its own right – but also the effects they produced – that is to say, the conditions of their reception. Thus, as is well known, it was the first volume of *Critique of Everyday Life* that had the main impact on

COBRA and then on the Situationists; while the second volume (however densely theoretical, even abstract), which was contemporaneous with close relations with the Situationists, was construed by them as ratifying the summons to total revolution they thought they had deciphered in volume one and in those of Lefebvre's texts that they regarded as veritable manifestos, especially the article on 'revolutionary romanticism'. That is why it is worth returning to what was in fact at the heart of the reception of Lefebvre's conception of the everyday: the close relation between this conceptual endeavour and a component of *la pensée 68* – precisely what eludes the utterly one-sided analysis of Luc Ferry and Alain Renaut, obsessed as they are with anti-humanism.[2] Above all, we shall have to extend this examination by seeking to understand Lefebvre's evolution from the 'radical critique' of the 1960s to the more complex stance, albeit one still stamped by the need for critical radicalism, characteristic of the 1980s.

But this final preface also affords the requisite occasion for a more general appraisal. Not so much of the French variety of Marxism and its crisis in the second half of the twentieth century – a subject that has spawned a whole host of commentaries (not always of the highest quality) – as of the place of Lefebvre's own thought in the philosophical and ideological reconfiguration of the period, the position of his thinking in a landscape ranging from the French brand of phenomenology, and then existentialism, to the structuralism and deconstructionist theories of the years after 1968. The rather perfunctory observations I shall make will certainly not compensate for the surprising absence of Lefebvre in the (rather rare) histories of contemporary philosophy (one thinks, for example, of the works of Vincent Descombes or Christian Delacampagne).[3] Was Lefebvre too much of a sociologist and not enough of an officially recognized philosopher? Too much of a Marxist, but unaffiliated to respectable post-Althusserian orthodoxy? Without venturing an overly generic explanation, we shall try to read the partial oblivion that the work of Henri Lefebvre has fallen into as one of the symptoms of the end of an era of thinking that became apparent at the turn of the 1980s.

*

We must, however, do a little history. 1961–1981: twenty years separate this volume from the preceding one – years marked by profound historical changes. During them, Lefebvre reached the peak of his celebrity, first of all as one of the brains behind the radical critique of the 1960s, but also – in a complex relationship with institutions and institutional realities – as one of the pioneers in thinking about space and cities, especially during the 1970s, before various retreats and turns at the end of the decade tended to exclude and marginalize him. Thus, we could track his progress in an excursion through events which, on the one hand, continued to be borne along by the prosperity and growth of the *trente glorieuses*, while on the other they remained dominated by the idea of revolution, despite successive, cumulative setbacks.

Let us play with some symbols. Nineteen sixty-one, publication date of the second volume of *Critique of Everyday Life*, was the year of the Eichmann trial, the first man in space (Gagarin), and the Berlin Wall. From colour television to the RER (*réseau express régional*), from Concord to the Apollo mission to the Moon, there was an acceleration in technological breakthroughs, diffusing throughout the developed countries what came to be called the consumer society – the very thing Lefebvre analyzed and denounced while seeking, unsuccessfully, to define it in more complex fashion as a 'bureaucratic society of managed consumption'. Faced with this growth and its political, social and cultural effects, the great protest movement that dominated the decade had as its rallying cry the rejection of the Soviet model, whose crisis, official since 1956, crystallized with the fall of Khrushchev and the Brezhnev years. The search for alternative models, which tended to be rather martial in cast at the beginning of the 1960s (Vietnam, the Chinese Cultural Revolution, Che Guevara), and then became more democratic (Czech 'socialism with a human face', the brief Allende experiment in Chile, Eurocommunism and, in France, the Common Programme), in each instance ended in failure. This phase – still dominated by the idea that a revolutionary perspective was possible – was obviously symbolized by the shock of the events of May '68.

The phase of Lefebvre's greatest productivity and intellectual influence, and his attempt to conceive a model of radical critique that he would gradually distance himself from only at the end of the 1970s, was situated around 1968. Here we must go back over some points about this period that were dealt with rather hastily, particularly as regards the Situationists, in my preface to the second volume of *Critique of Everyday Life*. This provides an opportunity to fill in some gaps and correct some errors.[4] We should remember that after launching a 'research group on everyday life' at the CNRS in 1960, Lefebvre was made a professor at Strasbourg in 1961, where he remained until his appointment to the recently created faculty at Nanterre in 1965. At Strasbourg as at Nanterre, he inaugurated an academic practice that was unconventional for the time, encouraging students to work in self-directed groups, signing contracts with public institutions, and embarking on market studies, in particular in order to finance a number of young intellectuals. According to Eleonore Kofman and Elizabeth Lebas, having established contact through the New Left milieu in 1958 with the young Georges Perec, who at the time was doing his military service, Lefebvre employed him on various studies in Normandy and the Oise.[5] A friendship was born out of this and Perec subsequently stayed on several occasions at Navarrenx, Lefebvre's house in the Pyrenees, which is where he probably became fully committed to becoming a writer. Hence this was a significant encounter for both men, as Perec's biographer David Bellos has emphasized,[6] involving mutual influence, as demonstrated by recent work in the context of the seminar of the George Perec association at the University of Paris VII.[7] Thus, in his *Introduction to Modernity* (1962), Lefebvre draws a parallel between *Ligne générale*, a small avant-garde group Perec belonged to, and the Situationist group as one of the spearheads of a 'new romanticism' that was revolutionary in character. Above all, he refers to Perec's oeuvre, especially *Les Choses* (1965), several times in *Everyday Life in the Modern World*. As for Perec, the influence of *Critique of Everyday Life* and, more generally, of Lefebvre's thinking on alienation, on the cult of objects and commodities, on the banal, and on the 'infra-ordinary', finds numerous echoes not only in *Les Choses*, but also in *Un homme qui dort* (1967), and even *Espèces d'espaces* (1974) and *La Vie: mode d'emploi* (1978).

The proximity Lefebvre detected between Georges Perec and Guy Debord prompts us also to return to his relations with the Situationists. At the time of the publication of volume two of *Critique of Everyday Life*, relations were good, even if (as indicated in my previous preface) they were never straightforward, given that the Situationists were forever criticizing Lefebvre for his relations with the 'New Left' and the *Arguments* group and for lacking a revolutionary political project. To the bibliography I used at the time, in addition to the issues of *Internationale situationniste* and Lefebvre's autobiographical work *Le Temps de méprises* (1975), there have now been added not only a pile of studies of varying value, but Guy Debord's correspondence in particular, three volumes of which (covering 1957–60, 1960–64 and 1965–68) have been published to date.[8] This correspondence confirms and clarifies the very close links that briefly existed between them, while tending to relativize the consistency in their positions so adamantly asserted by the Situationists. As is well known, it was Lefebvre's article 'Vers un romantisme révolutionnaire', published in *NRF* in 1957, that attracted their attention in the first number of *Internationale situationniste* (June 1958). But it was apparently through Asger Jorn that Debord became aware of the theory of 'moments' as Lefebvre had just defined it in *La Somme et le reste* (letter from Debord to Jorn of 2 July 1959). The year 1960 would appear to mark the peak of their friendship, as indicated by the exchange of a considerable number of letters between Lefebvre and Debord from January to May. The major trips to Navarrenx, and the evenings of drunken debates in the tiny place where Debord lived with Michèle Bernstein, date from this time. In addition, it was Lefebvre, to whom Raoul Vaneigem had sent his manuscript *Fragments pour une poétique* (letter from Vaneigem to Lefebvre of 18 July 1960), who got Debord to read it, put the young Belgian in touch, and helped integrate him into the Situationist group. This ideological and political accord, marked by their joint signature of the 'Manifesto of the 121' and Debord's talk to the research group on everyday life in May 1961, would not survive beyond 1962. The Situationists reacted heatedly to the conclusions of *Introduction to Modernity* where the thinker they nicknamed 'Amédée', resuming and modifying his analysis of 'revolutionary romanticism', placed their activity in the category of youth revolt. Above all, there was the famous episode (I myself have already referred to it) when they accused Lefebvre of plagiarism over the pages on revolution as festival published in *Arguments* and foreshadowing his 1965 book, *Proclamation de la Commune*. The break was violent, sanctioned by the tract 'Aux poubelles de l'histoire' (21 February 1963); and the attacks on the '*Versaillais* of culture' would recur in the last three issues of *Internationale situationniste* (in 1966, 1967 and 1969). The additional information on this affair furnished by the publication of the correspondence is that Debord was initially prepared to restore relations, on condition of a public explanation at any rate (letter to Michèle Bernstein at the end of February 1963); but also that the political break was coupled with some rather ugly personal quarrels.[9] The conflict proved permanent, Debord treating Lefebvre as an 'old sponger' leading a filthy existence, whereas the latter would reply in kind in 1965 with his abusive letter to Asger Jorn, characterized as a 'dirty swine' for having referred to the Situationists' accusation of plagiarism.[10]

If there are good reasons for going back over the relations between Lefebvre and the Situationists – the recent publications I referred to – there are also bad ones: the massive wave of 'Debordmania' relayed, in particular, by prominent figures from the ex-avant-garde, which serves to conceal 'the era of the void' already diagnosed a good few years ago. In this respect, the form of Debord's published correspondence, especially coming from a major publisher such as Fayard, is (to say the least) surprising, because it flouts the basic rules in such matters: slim volumes with excessive margins, no means of knowing whether we are dealing with a complete or a selected correspondence, and no critical apparatus, except for a few ill-humoured 'notes'. Such publications in connection with Debord in particular, and now Vaneigem, are certainly not without interest. But they form part of a kind of deification, or at least heroization, utterly contrary to Situationist intentions. Whatever the heavily influential role played by the model of André Breton (infinitely more pontifical than his descendent, it is true), up until his suicide in 1994 Guy Debord lived through the troubled period from the 1960s to the 1990s without ever making the slightest concession to what allowed many other intellectuals among his contemporaries to set up shop and hawk their junk. This is why it is so shocking to see him instrumentalized in current commercial and editorial conditions. And hence it seems all the more important to recall, rather acrimoniously if needs be, this intellectual and even moral rectitude, on the one hand because of the problems of reception it poses – especially the diversions created by particular Anglo-American readings of 'French theory' – and on the other hand because it was in these terms, of joy and rigour, that the intellectual and personal relations between Debord and Lefebvre in the 1960s were played out. And it is also in these terms that we can decipher not only the influence of the latter on the former at this point in time, but also the more long-term impact of certain Situationist themes on Lefebvre.

*

This reminder of the relations between Lefebvre and the Situationists also has the function of reopening the debate on May '68 and the philosopher's actual place in it. Here we face a paradoxical situation: often presented at the time of the 'events' as a kind of *deus ex machina* of the student turbulence, particularly by his most conservative colleagues such as Didier Anzieu (Épistémon),[11] silence has since descended as to Lefebvre's role, so that the further removed we are from the years immediately following the 'events', the fewer references to Lefebvre we find, at any rate in the 'major' histories of May 1968.[12] As for his book written in the heat of the moment, like several other contemporary essays it long ago disappeared from the bibliographies and even more so from the histories, until its recent republication under a stupidly abridged title.[13] In truth, apart from the strange and brilliant essay by Greil Marcus on the 1960s, *Lipstick Traces*, where Lefebvre cuts a novelistic figure, it was not until Bernard Brillant's recent thesis that his role was recalled in a balanced fashion and his own ideas on 1968 analyzed in any detail.[14]

By the time of Lefebvre's move from Strasbourg to Nanterre in 1965, the break with the Situationists had been consummated. But that does not mean that this unusual sociologist, whose courses generally attracted the students most disposed to protest, and who enjoyed a nefarious reputation with the Strasbourg bourgeoisie, was not going to distil a certain line of questioning in the student milieu. Even so, it was after his departure that the Situationist scandals erupted at Strasbourg, making it a capital of the student revolt prior to 1968. These scandals initially involved the sociology department – in particular, in 1965–66, the cyberneticist Abraham Moles, whom Lefebvre had hired as his assistant and whom the Situationists treated as a 'conformist robot' devoting himself to 'programming young cadres'. After various uproars, they prevented him from delivering the inaugural lecture for his chair in psycho-sociology in October 1966. The second 'Strasbourg scandal', mentioned in *Internationale situationniste* and the local press, coincided with the Situationists' seizure of power in the local branch of the students' union UNEF. Accusing it of reformism, they decided to dissolve it and sell off its assets. The affair was taken to court and the assets sequestrated, provoking a reaction among teachers in the sociology department at Nanterre.[15] Meanwhile, the Situationists had despatched Mustapha Khayati to Strasbourg, where on behalf of the students he wrote a manifesto – read at the beginning of the new academic year – that was destined to have a certain resonance and which was rapidly diffused in a number of universities, *De la misère en milieu étudiant, considérée sous son aspect économique, politique, psychologique, sexuel, et notamment intellectuel, et de quelques moyens pour y remédier*, published in 1967.[16] Let us recall that the two principal Situationist texts – Guy Debord's *The Society of the Spectacle* and Raoul Vaneigem's *Traité de savoir vivre à l'usage des jeunes générations* – also date from 1967.

There is a paradox about Lefebvre in 1968, especially when compared with the current silence. While his contemporaries – or at least those of his colleagues most opposed to the student agitation – thought they had discovered in him the *deus ex machina* of the troubles at Nanterre, Lefebvre was rather invisible during the events, particular after the month of May, when the main action shifted to Paris. Yet even before 1968 his influence was undeniable. Appointed to Nanterre in 1965, he initially had the aura of an unusual professor. Head of the sociology department for a year, he was succeeded by Alain Touraine in 1967. Lefebvre surrounded himself with unconventional teachers (some of whom did not hold the *aggrégation*) – François Bourricaud, Michel Crozier, and then Henry Reymond, René Lourau, and Jean Baudrillard – whom he invited every Friday to eat together in his office with students. Without himself engaging in institutional pedagogy – the preserve of Georges Lapassade and René Lourau – he taught in a non-controlling, spontaneous sort of way, inviting Jean-Jacques Lebel, for example, for a lecture-demonstration on the 'happening' on 10 February 1967. Or, to take another example, without it being possible to speak of some discovery on his part, he gave a course on 'Sexuality and Society' in 1966–67, which coincided with the initial confrontations at the university halls of residence over the right of male students to enter the females' building. Thus, Lefebvre was the figurehead in what was unquestionably a troubled sociology department. There is no doubt that the sociologists, teachers and students alike, played a significant role in the 'events'. It has often been observed that the sociology students were particularly dynamic at Nanterre, including in the battered students' union. Moreover, it was a young, active Christian sociologist – Philippe Meyer – who launched the movement against selection; and there is no need to recall the role played by Dany Cohn-Bendit, who on several occasions was to acknowledge, alongside the influence of *Socialism or Barbarism* and various anarchist and Situationist texts, his debt to Lefebvre. This was a purely intellectual debt, for Lefebvre, free of any political affiliation, had no ex officio relationship with the Trotskyist, Maoist, anarchist and Situationist *groupuscules* that divided the campus between them in these years.

The unrest began at Nanterre in March 1967 with the occupation of the female hall of residence. But it was with the new academic year, in November, that the movement launched over the issue of the equivalence between the old and new second-year degrees adopted the struggle against selection as its key theme. The sociology teachers were soon calling for a strike and the celebrated disturbances began at the end of November with the occupation of buildings – including administrative buildings – by students, who thus broke with the traditional methods of student union struggle and more or less imposed their own negotiating structures (the Dean, Grappin, agreed to a dialogue). Accused by his colleagues of fomenting the revolt, Lefebvre was to play a role during the extraordinary faculty meeting convened on the 25th in the presence of a student delegation, which was to lead to the setting up of committees with equal staff/student representation.[17] In the meeting that was henceforth in permanent session at Nanterre, where *enragés* advancing provocative slogans ruled, Lefebvre was a significant presence, participating in staff-student meetings and the cultural turbulence in an ambiance of the happening and the festival that prefigured May – notably, for example, during the visit of the Living Theatre in December or, in March 1968, during the lecture by Mme Revault d'Allonnes on Reich's *Sexual Revolution*.[18] In January, Cohn-Bendit was threatened with suspension after the famous swimming pool episode (8 January) when he challenged the minister François Misoffe, whose official report on youth ignored the subject of sexuality. On 26 January, a demonstration of support, which denounced alleged 'blacklists' of students, turned into a riot and involved aggression against Dean Grappin. During the University Council and General Assembly of the Faculty convened on the 27th, Lefebvre, while condemning the violence, defended Cohn-Bendit and in turn denounced the 'blacklists'.[19] As is well known, the unrest, which did not let up, particularly in February in the halls of residence, led on 22 March to the occupation of the administrative building to protest against the arrest of students demonstrating against the Vietnam War and to the formation of the 22 March Movement. Moreover, the *enragés* did not let slip the opportunity to denounce the 'meta-Stalinist' Henri Lefebvre.[20] During February, Lefebvre left for Japan, where he made contact with the students of Zengakuren and had himself replaced at Nanterre by Edgar Morin. Grappin summoned a faculty meeting for 26 March and, despite the interventions of Touraine and Lefebvre, decided to close the faculty in April, on the eve of the Easter holiday. Given that the disturbances resumed in full force after the holidays, he once again requested closure of the faculty on 2 May. We know the sequel. The occupation shifted to the Sorbonne and was brought to a violent end by the police on 3 and 4 May, giving the signal for the sequence of major demonstrations and barricades from 6 May onwards. On Monday, 8 May, Cohn-Bendit and seven other Nanterre students were summoned before the disciplinary committee of Paris University, which, under the chairmanship of Robert Flacelière, director of the École normale supérieure, comprised the deans of the faculties. Four teachers – Lefebvre, Touraine, Guy Michaud, and Paul Ricoeur – came forward to defend the students. Thereafter, France entered into social crisis, as the major appeal, signed by Lefebvre and published by *Le Monde* on 9 May, observed. The following day – 10 May – symbolized it, marked as it was by events as disparate as Herbert Marcuse's lecture at UNESCO, the opening of US–Vietnamese negotiations, and the 'night of the barricades' that set the Latin Quarter ablaze. On 14 May, a meeting of teachers and students declared the Nanterre faculty 'free and autonomous' (according to Ricoeur, Lefebvre was responsible for the formula). By the end of May and in June, during the great strikes, Lefebvre was no longer visible: had Nanterre become inaccessible on account of the public transport strikes? But he was also scarcely to be seen at the Sorbonne or the Odéon, still less perched on a box at Billancourt. According to his own account, he took part in a highly charged evening on television on 13 May, with the leaders of the movement, but in a programme that was never broadcast for want of a 'representative of the working class'.[21]

Obviously, the question of May '68 is not limited to Lefebvre's role during the events. It also, and much more significantly, involves the reception of his ideas by the student audience – or, more precisely, audiences. And this is where we come back to an interpretation completely opposed to that of Ferry and Renaut. In his preface to the new edition of *Métaphilosophie* – the term that serves as a subtitle to this third volume of *Critique of Everyday Life* – Georges Labica remarks that the book, published in 1965, went completely unnoticed at a time when Althusser was publishing his two steamrollers, *For Marx* and *Reading Capital*.[22] However, with respect to Althusserian orthodoxy, which was imposed in terrorist fashion – rather like Bourdieu some decades later – we cannot (as Labica tends to) reduce Lefebvre to a culture of dissidence and heresy. Lefebvre himself vigorously opposed not only Althusser, but anything connected with structuralism, which he condemned irrevocably as a 'technocratic ideology'.[23] Responding to the Althusserian torrent was a multitude of Lefebvrian rivulets. This is what I mean by his various audiences. First of all, there was the quite wide audience for the little 'Que sais-je?' volume on Marxism dating from 1948, which persisted to his advantage with *The Sociology of Marx*, published by Presses Universitaires de France in the 'Sup' collection in 1966, and which immersed itself in Gallimard's 'Idées' collection, where Lefebvre published *Le Langage et la société* and *Everyday Life in the Modern World* in rapid succession. To these would need to be added the more diffuse influence of various journals – in particular, *Autogestion* and *L'Homme et la société*, in whose foundation Lefebvre participated in 1966. But there were other, unquestionably smaller audiences, such as the readers who, following the second volume of *Critique of Everyday Life*, set out to rediscover the revolutionary road in *La Proclamation de la Commune* (1965), by reviving the utopia of a total revolution that was simultaneously political revolution and spiritual revolt. Or again there was the audience – in fact, virtually the same one – brought together by issues of urbanism, which in 1968 took part with Lefebvre in experiments in self-management at the Institut d'urbanisme,[24] and in the activities of the group and journal

Utopie (1967–69), directed by Hubert Tonka, Jean Baudrillard and the architects of the Aérolande group.[25] In other words, while certainly highly diffuse and less doctrinal, was not the influence of the Nanterre sociologist, inspirer of journals and prolific author, equivalent to that of the philosopher cloistered in his ivory tower on the rue d'Ulm?

Even so, was Lefebvre one of the *maîtres-à-penser* of 1968? The question should, it seems to me, be posed differently, in terms that are largely opposed to the analysis developed by Alain Touraine in an interview published in the catalogue of an exhibition organized by the Bibliothèque de documentation internationale contemporaine – 'L'apparition d'une nouvelle sensibilité sur la scène politique' – which seems to me to represent a well-nigh caricatural instance of retrospective reconstruction.[26] In it, Touraine bases his explanations on a rudimentary and gratifying dichotomy between 'irresponsible teachers' and a few clear-sighted ones, present especially in sociology – a sociology marginalized by, and hostile towards, the more noble disciplines. This allows him to foreground his own role, which was indeed important, while suppressing all the contradictions – his initial caution, his ambiguous interaction with the academic and political authorities and the movement, and his then non-existent intellectual influence on students, at any rate until his on-the-spot book *The May Movement* (1968). Need it be said that he does not so much as mention the name of Henri Lefebvre? A link between the ideology of May '68 and what happened in sociology must indeed be made, in the sense that this discipline emerged as one of the crucibles of critical thinking – but without lapsing into a mythologization of the relationship between sociology and protest.[27] Because it was based upon a professional practice, the key theme was the critique of everyday life and the reading of modernity Lefebvre drew from it. For Lefebvre, fundamentally, modernity was not the domination of major economic forces, not even the advent of a state bureaucracy, but what had dehumanized and alienated man. In Lefebvre, the notion of *radical critique*, which lit up these years, and which is the converse of anti-humanism, referred to a notion – upheld ever since the avant-garde experience of the 1920s – of a revolution conceived in terms of totality. The fundamental revolutionary project, which revolved around the notions of festival, rupture in everyday life, and subversion, had the radical reformation of humanity as its ultimate objective. This is where Lefebvre coincided with, if not influenced, the 1968 protest movement and its aspiration to totality. Behind the notion of 'cultural revolution', seizing symbolic power, and wresting a voice – all of them phrases that seek to account for the 'enigma of '68' – Lefebvre detected a novel development that was incomprehensible and unacceptable to all orthodox thinking about revolution: while economic and social 'infrastructures' had not been overthrown, and the foundations of state power remained secure, the intellectual, moral and psychological 'superstructures' had collapsed. And he was not far from thinking that this was the key thing.

This is why, ultimately, if we wish to follow Lefebvre in his reflections on May '68, it is best to revert to his contemporaneous essay, *L'irruption de Nanterre au sommet*, which has been utterly neglected by most historians.[28] In it, Lefebvre proposes an initial classification, distinguishing between three tendencies in the ideology of May '68: those he dubbed 'archaic' – on the one hand the party of order that rejected subversion, and on the other dogmatists of the Althusserian variety; then the 'modernist' tendency – the main recuperator of the movement; and finally the 'possibilist' – more concerned with potentialities than reality, ready to go beyond reality and proclaim the primacy of imagination over reason. Doubtless it was to the final category that Lefebvre assigned himself. But the main interest of the book lies not in its judgement of the events of 1968, but in its analysis of the Nanterre phenomenon, treated in the same fashion as 'new towns' in earlier writings. The Nanterre faculty, opened in 1964, was presented by a number of observers at the time as a kind of focal point for grievances. 'Nanterre La Folie – University Complex': those who went to Nanterre in these years would not forget this signpost at the little station of La Folie, which, before the advent of the RER, linked the small faculty to the great city. At the time, it was not quite finished, the shanty towns had not completely disappeared, transport was inconvenient, and there was a single hall of residence on campus. Numerous were the first-hand analyses along the following lines: 'in this place they have concentrated all the possible contradictions required for an explosion'. In *L'irruption de Nanterre au sommet*, Lefebvre likewise starts out from the 'desolate landscape' of this 'Parisian faculty outside Paris', but does not confine himself to describing the contrast. 'The faculty was conceived in conformity with the mental categories of industrial production and productivity…. The buildings express the project and inscribe it on the ground. It is to be an enterprise, devoted to the production of averagely qualified intellectuals and "junior cadres" for this society'. Is the place cursed? On the contrary, it is a vacuum, 'the anomic, the extra-social social', absence; it is 'where unhappiness takes shape'. 'Far off, the city – past, present, future – takes on a *utopian* value for boys and girls installed in a *heterotopia* that generates tensions and mesmerizing images'. On site, a dual segregation – functional and social, industrial and urban – encloses culture in a ghetto, reduces the function of habitation to a basic minimum, maintains 'traditional separations – between boys and girls, between work, leisure and private life', and renders the least exercise of control and emblematic buildings – the estate, the administrative tower – *symbols* of repression. In other words, going beyond psycho-sociological analysis of rebellion against the father and authority, and the conflict between generations, through Nanterre Lefebvre proposed to read 'crisis that is far more profound, extending from everyday life to the institutions and state that hold everything together' (pp. 115–18).

It was in terms of spatial and urban issues that Lefebvre formulated the problem of 1968, not those of 'wresting a voice' (Michel de Certeau) or a 'breach' (Edgar Morin, Claude Lefort and Jean-Marc Coudray), because it was there – in the 'urban revolution' – that all the contradictions of modernity were operative. In any event, it was in the wake of '68 and during the ten years between 1965 and 1975 that Lefebvre achieved a peak of celebrity and intellectual influence, at the very moment when he was preparing to take retirement in 1973.[29] This decade marks the transition from radical critique to a more reserved stance, which nevertheless remains dominated by the search for a critical Marxism. It might be asked, and has been by various observers, whether despite (or with) the thunder clap of *The Gulag Archipelago*, the 1970s were not the golden age of a certain 'French Marxism' – precisely not structuralism and Althusserianism, but the Marxism of thinkers who were detached from Communism, from Lucien Goldmann to François Châtelet, from Kostas Axelos to Edgar Morin, Claude Lefort and Cornelius Castoriadis. These were the years when, pursuing a comprehensive line of thought already marked by the *Introduction to Modernity* (1962) and *Métaphilosophie* (1965), Lefebvre defended a general theoretical project (*La Fin de l'histoire*, 1970; *Le Manifeste différentialiste*, 1971), punctuated by a new all-out attack on structuralism (*Au-delà du structuralisme*, 1971; republished in part as *L'idéologie structuraliste* in 1975) and an ambitious reading of the 'statist mode of production' (*De l'État*, four volumes, 1976–78). However, this body of theoretical work was less well received than the works of the other non-dogmatic Marxists of the period. It was his thinking on towns and urban questions (*Le Droit à la ville*, 1968; *Du rural à l'urbain* and *La Révolution urbaine*, 1970; *La Pensée marxiste et la ville*, 1972), and especially that key work *The Production of Space* (1974), which earned Lefebvre recognition – strangely unconventional recognition, since it was bestowed less by philosophers and sociologists than by geographers, urbanists and architects. The 1970s were the years of *changer la vie, changer la ville*, both on the Left, with the Common Programme, and on the Right, with the new urban policy inaugurated under Giscard by Olivier Guichard. Thanks to his personal and social networks, and thanks to ministerial research assignments, from the 1960s urban research was in part organized around Lefebvre – for example, in the multi-disciplinary Centre de recherche d'urbanisme or the journal *Espaces et sociétés*, of which he was a co-founder together with Anatole Kopp, Manuel Castells, Serge Jonas and Raymond Ledrut, before breaking abruptly with it in large part on account of Castells' increasingly Althusserian positions. Amid much fanfare, Castells had taken up the 'urban question' in its relations with state capitalism, in particular in a provocative article, 'Y a-t-il une sociologie urbaine?', in 1968.[30]

It was also in this period, or in subsequent years, that Lefebvre's work enjoyed international diffusion via numerous translations. In Germany, in what was still a sort of pre-Habermasian phase and under the impact of the various alternative and autonomous movements thrown up by 1968, he was received as a French equivalent of Marcuse or of the philosophers of the Frankfurt School. This was the epoch which saw the development among historians (Lutz Niethammer) of the theme of a history 'from below', and among sociologists and philosophers of an 'ethnomethodological' reading, resulting in a theory of action. Two books were devoted to Lefebvre at the time, one of which – Thomas Kleinspehn's – deals directly with everyday life.[31] But it was at the end of the 1970s and the beginning of the 1980s that Lefebvre began to achieve legitimacy in the English-speaking world, because he was placed by various specialists in a much wider current, encompassing the whole of the heterodox Marxism that sought to think through its own crisis since the great breaks around 1956 – whether this body of thought was referred to as 'Western Marxism' (Perry Anderson), the 'New Left' (Arthur Hirsh), or 'Existential Marxism' (Mark Poster).[32]

*

At the beginning of the 1980s, with the appearance of the third volume of *Critique of Everyday Life*, completed at the very moment of the Left's electoral victory, Lefebvre found himself in a rather paradoxical position. On the one hand, he was, so to speak, still living under the impetus of the works that made him one of the representatives of the non-communist 'French Marxism' I have just mentioned. His latest work seemed to mark a return to philosophy. This was underlined by Olivier Corpet and Thierry Paquot – two of the leading figures in *Autogestion* with whom he was to break shortly afterwards – in one of the main articles on him published in the mainstream French press – an interview in *Le Monde* entitled 'Henri Lefebvre philosophe du quotidien':

> The first two volumes of *Critique of Everyday Life* seemed to be primarily sociological works. They contained a number of concrete analyses, accompanied by a theoretical inquiry into the instruments and categories required to develop a 'sociology of everydayness'. With this new volume, sub-titled 'For a meta-philosophy of the everyday', you appear to change your approach somewhat, moving towards more intensive abstraction, covering a wider field and more basic questions. So what register does your work, and specifically everything that relates to everyday life, pertain to?[33]

It is true that Lefebvre's main titles in the early 1980s marked, not without some Heideggerian echoes, renewed philosophical ambition: *Le Présence et l'absence, Une Pensée devenue monde, Qu'est-ce que penser?, Le Retour de la dialectique*.[34] This ambition could certainly be accounted for by his distance, since retirement, from the professional role of sociologist. But it is doubtless more readily attributable to his wish to resume what, as is indicated by this last volume of *Critique of Everyday Life*, he had defined in his work of 1965 as 'meta-philosophy'. What this had involved, at a time when radical critique was at its peak, was openly asserting that sociology could only perform a critical function if it formed part of a more ambitious examination, philosophical in kind. However, starting out from Marx, it also implied avoiding the alternative between the institutionalization of philosophy, preserving the figure of the sage, and the liquidation of philosophical speculation in the name of a posture that Lefebvre, targeting Althusser, charac-terized as positivist or scientist. Meta-philosophy was thus defined as a supersession of philosophy and this objective of transgression con-tinued to mark Lefebvre's thinking when he analyzed the prefix 'meta' in *Qu'est-ce que penser?*[35]

On the other hand, the 1981 work must be restored to its proper context – in particular, the Left's arrival in power. Amid the intellec-tual effervescence of the early Mitterrand years, Lefebvre had hopes of acquiring a position on key social issues where rapid changes were underway – towns, space and so on. Thus he played a role if not as expert, then as an adviser at least, for example, in connection with the Auroux labour legislation. Was not Michel Delebarre, minister for towns, reported to keep a copy of *Le Droit à la ville* on his ministerial desk, not hesitating to cite it?[36] But Lefebvre's thinking became par-tially inaudible – and not only on account of the ideological assault on Marxism. At the beginning of the 1980s, Lefebvre opted for a para-doxical reunion with a declining PCF, prompting many idiotic remarks. As Olivier Corpet rather disloyally put it in his 1991 obituary: 'Surprising, even saddening a number of his friends, from 1978 onwards Henri Lefebvre initiated what he wanted to be a "critical" reconciliation with the Communist Party'.[37] It was at this point that he published, with the short-lived Éditions Libres-Hallier, a book of interviews with the young Communist militant Catherine Régulier, *La Révolution n'est plus ce qu'elle était*.[38] The title is significant and in its way already signals the commentary on an aphorism of Adorno's that runs through all of Lefebvre's last writings: the moment for the realization of philosophy was missed. But for now, the rap-prochement with the PCF, which was all too eager to get its hands on a Marxist thinker in the straitened circumstances of the 1980s, found expression in numerous interviews in the Communist press. At the time of the book's release, following a PCF Congress that was presented as a significant turning-point, Lefebvre, in an interview entitled 'Not remaining a prisoner of the past', recalled that he had 'quit the party from the left', not seeking to conceal his bitterness and scars. The rapprochement was the product of a process of elimination among leftists – 'terribly dogmatic and divided into small groups' – and the 'more insidious [pressure] of social-democracy', which in his eyes was the vector of computerization and multi-nationalization under American influence.[39] Other articles followed, to the point where it might be said that the Communist press was virtually the only one to attend to Lefebvre in the 1980s, especially given that on several occasions he associated himself with appeals by intellectuals for a Communist vote. Readers were reminded of his oeuvre, in particular when the third volume of *Critique of Everyday Life* came out.[40] But his own interventions all revolved around a refusal to 'follow the pack' in regarding the decline of the PCF as irreversible, and the sociological and political necessity of its survival in order to preserve a radical pole capable of rallying new, alternative social movements, urban, ecological and pacifist.[41] For Lefebvre, this belated and ultimately limited reconciliation was wholly consistent with a stance that had always consisted in rejecting orthodoxy: faced with the prevailing consensus, he believed it possible to identify traces, albeit vestigial, of a counter-culture, a power to say no, in surviving Communist practice.

On this basis, his life came to an end. Driven out of his Parisian apartment – he, the thinker of 'habitation' – and not having retired (as was stupidly said) to his house in Navarrenx, it was after Lefebvre's death in 1991 that his thinking underwent a surprising, if limited, revival. Integrating him into some current of Marxism was no longer the issue. The renewal took two complementary forms. First there was a 'spatial turn', which naturally encompassed various aspects of the everyday. Even if Lefebvre had exerted some influence in the previous fifteen years, it was the English translation of *The Production of Space* in 1991 that marked an initial turning-point. It intersected with inquiries by geographers, sociologists, anthropologists – particularly from North America.[42] Mario Rui Martins, Kristin Ross and Stuart Elden, but especially Edward W. Soja, Fredric Jameson and Mark Gottdiener played a key role in introducing Lefebvre's thinking about space into the United States. Contrary to spatial metaphors à la Althusser or Bourdieu, they introduced two key ideas: the first was that everyday life is the equivalent of social space; the second – and doubtless more important – was that they presented Lefebvre as a precursor of postmodernism.[43] A characteristic phenomenon of 'French theory' was the re-export to France and re-acclimatization of a 'new look' Lefebvrianism, in the wake of this Anglo-American 'spatial turn'. First came the issue of *Annales de la recherche urbaine* in 1994, offering a balance-sheet of ten years on urban questions. While Manuel Castells did not even mention Lefebvre's name, a stimulating article by Isaac Joseph, 'Le droit à la ville, la ville à l'oeuvre. Deux paradigmes de la recherche', analyzed research developments alongside the evolution of urbanization during the *trente glorieuses*, comparing the notion of *droit à la ville* – the title of a work by Lefebvre published in 1968 – which he defined as one of the social rights and which still alluded to an urban utopia, and a book by Jean-Christophe Bailly, published in 1992, *La Ville à l'oeuvre*.[44] Likewise in 1994, virtually a complete number of *Espaces et sociétés*, which Lefebvre had helped establish, was devoted to him. Two articles in particular signalled the importation into France of the theme of postmodernity, discerning in it the epistemological openness and lack of dogmatism characteristic of Lefebvre's Marxism.[45] The same type of revival is evident in a recent number of the journal *Urbanisme*, significantly entitled 'Henri Lefebvre au présent', which is more testimonial than analytical in character, even if the aim is to detect a 'subterranean' Lefebvrian presence, including during the years of Marxism's retreat.[46]

*

The notion of a critique of everyday life was cardinal in Henri Lefebvre, especially when it intersected with the theme of space and towns. In addition to Thomas Kleinspehn's book of 1975, it has prompted a fairly large number of works, which vary in value.[47] Is not this final volume in the sequence stamped with a veritable nostalgia? 'Twenty Years After' is the appropriate title with which to summon up the exceptionally turbulent period, politically and intellectually, separating Lefebvre's last two volumes. It was completely dominated by the polysemic theme of 'crisis': not only the two oil shocks of 1973 and

1979, the failure of every revolutionary model, the death of Mao (1976), Sartre (1980) and Althusser, who strangled his wife (1980). There were also possibilities that had become impossibilities: 'At the end of the nineteenth century and the beginning of the twentieth, it was *possible* that the European working class would find itself strengthened, enter onto the political stage, make itself into a political subject and, by various means, become the dominant class'.[48] This was no longer possible. With the third volume of the *Critique of Everyday Life*, the hour of reckoning had struck ('Continuities', 'Discontinuities'). From the standpoint of Lefebvre's personal trajectory, more tragic perhaps is that at many points in this final volume we see that he too, while unable to abandon the organizing framework of Marxism, while unwilling to 'renounce Marx', had a clear sense that it was all up with a number of the notions, concepts or even realities around which a revolutionary system that also aspired to be a revolution in thought had been constructed. Lefebvre comes straight out with it: the notion of the people,[49] labour as the source of value, and the revolutionary project itself are at an end. This is how the dictum that the moment for the realization of philosophy has been missed is to be understood.

It is this general perspective that leads to the most tragic reality to be recorded: the end of an era in thought. Lefebvre's great contribution, on the dual basis of Marxism and the avant-garde experience, was unquestionably to have rendered the everyday, or more precisely the critique of the everyday, an essential field of sociological exploration and philosophical reflection on social change; and to have made it the theoretical basis of the demand to *changer la vie* that inspired the various movements around May 1968, as well as the thinking of the official Left, which adopted it for its own purposes and instrumentalized it. What volume three reveals is that Marxism, indispensable from the 1930s to the 1960s when it came to thinking about the contemporary world, had not succumbed only to the hammer-blows of the 'New Philosophers' ('Marx is dead'). Thinking about the everyday and the critique of everyday life no longer require Marxism: that, after all, is the lesson of Michel de Certeau.[50] If it is possible to reread Marx today, it is in an utterly different, non-synchronous intellectual configuration. In the mid-1990s, even before the Bourdieu wave, a crop of books on Marxism tried to broach it differently from the good old days when it was intellectually dominant. We had a glimpse of this, for example, at the international conference of the journal *Actuel Marx* on the results and prospects of Marxism in September 1995, or in May 1998 on the occasion of the 150th anniversary of the *Communist Manifesto*. Moreover, this renewed interest derives from intellectual universes that are often very different from Marxist thought in the classical sense of the term and is bound up, in France at least, with the renaissance in political philosophy under the influence of Cornelius Castoriadis and Claude Lefort in particular,[51] not to mention the flourishing in the Anglophone world of an 'analytical' Marxism that rejects Hegelian logic and endeavours to reconcile Marx with John Rawls. Has Marx become 'untimely' in the quasi-Nietzschean sense of the term?[52] At least he has not acquired the remote but venerable status of 'nine-teenth-century thinker' enjoyed by Guizot, Tocqueville, Renan or Taine. He still has some bite!

In the presentation of the issue of *Espaces and sociétés* devoted to him, the authors metaphorically evoke the 'ghost of Henri Lefebvre'. Jacques Derrida's attempt to flush out the 'spectres of Marx' is not conducted metaphorically.[53] Via the notion of spectre, he ponders the spirit of Marxism and contests the new dominant discourse that rejoices in its collapse. In this sense, the 'end of history' is a species of spiritualist gesture, intended to conjure the ghost of Marx. Marxism persists as a 'spirit', neither living nor dead; it haunts neo-capitalism on behalf of radical critique and a capacity for self-criticism. *La Fin de l'histoire* is a work by Lefebvre dating back to 1970 … 'The moment to realize philosophy was missed'. Is this not to state, in true philosoph-ical-poetical or poetical-philosophical style, and even though there is still something to play for, what François Furet had already announced in *Interpreting the French Revolution* in 1978 and which he sub-sequently analyzed at great length in *The Passing of an Illusion*: the end of the regime of revolutionary historicity, the end of the illusion that revolution is the only modality of historical change?[54]

Introduction

1

That changes have occurred in everyday life over recent years is scarcely open to dispute. How far have they gone? Have they worsened everyday life or qualitatively improved it? These are matters for discussion.

That new changes are in store, on the way, is incontestable. Whether, as is universally claimed, they will be radical (in other words, take things and people 'by the root'), is another question.

Nineteen eighty-one seems an appropriate moment to cast a retrospective glance over aspects of daily life during the twentieth century – in practice and 'reality', but also in knowledge, philosophy, literature and art.

Are we not faced with an alternative? Acceptance of daily life as it is (as it develops in and through its changes); or refusal of it, a refusal that can be either heroic and ascetic, or hedonistic and sensual, or revolutionary, or anarchistic – in other words, neo-Romantic, hence aesthetic?

Acceptance involves much more than consenting to trivial acts: buying and selling, consumption, various activities. It implies a 'consensus': acceptance of society, the mode of production – in a word, a (the) totality. In this way, people (who? each and every one of us) condemn themselves to not desiring, conceiving, or even imagining possibilities beyond this mode of production!

An assessment of the century in this respect will have to take account of technologies, but also of social relations and their various

677

expressions, political problems and history, daily life being in its way a historical product (possibly the 'product' closest to us, most accessible to our understanding).

Is it merely a question of analysing daily life as of 1981? Of determining what has and has not changed, forecasting what is going to be altered or consolidated in years to come? No. It also involves establishing whether the critical analysis of everyday life can serve as a guiding thread (an Ariadne's thread!) for knowledge of society as a whole and its inflection in a particular direction, in order to give it meaning. To put it another way, does (critical) study of daily life make it possible to resist the dual fascination – with 'reality' and with catastrophe – that seems to grip such thought as survives today?

2

Previously – in other words, a few decades ago – the term 'daily' referred to what was essential for day-to-day living or survival: 'Give us this day our daily bread'. Since then, its meaning and significance have altered. Broader and vaguer, the word 'daily' refers to the set of everyday acts, and especially the fact that they are interlinked, that they form a whole. Implicitly, it is accepted that daily life does not boil down to a sum of isolated acts: eating, drinking, dressing, sleeping, and so on, the sum total of consumer activities. Except when society is defined exclusively by consumption (something that is increasingly rare), there is an awareness that consideration of these isolated acts does not exhaust daily life, and that we must also attend to their context: the social relations within which they occur. Not only because each action taken separately results from a micro-decision, but because their sequence unfolds in a social space and time bound up with production. In other words, daily life, like language, contains manifest forms and deep structures that are implicit in its operations, yet concealed in and through them. In the shops we come across innumerable works devoted to everyday acts: housework, cookery, dressing, sleep, sexuality, and so on. We can even buy 'encyclopaedias' that attempt to assemble these particular aspects. But what is missing in such works is the whole, the sequence. Everyday acts are repeated (reproduced) by dint of this sequence and what it involves.

They are simultaneously individual, 'group' (family, colleagues and friends, etc.), and social. In ways that are poorly understood, the everyday is thus closely related to the modes of organization and existence of a (particular) society, which imposes relations between forms of work, leisure, 'private life', transport, public life. A constraining influence, the everyday imposes itself on all members of the relevant society, who, with some exceptions, have only minor variations on the norms at their disposal.

It is in this sense – broad, rather vague, and as yet not clarified – that daily life has recently entered consciousness and thought, allowing analysis to avoid mundanities about seemingly 'concrete' trifles concerning generations, sexes, incomes, 'household fittings', and so on: familiar details that might be taken for a 'scientific' description or 'phenomenology' of daily life.

In the past, philosophers excluded daily life from knowledge and wisdom. Essential and mundane, it was deemed unworthy of thought. Thought first of all established a distance (an *époché*) *vis-à-vis* daily life, the domain and abode of non-philosophers. Things have changed. In 1980, the Swiss Philosophy Society organized a European symposium on the subject of 'daily life and philosophy', during which it became clear that today philosophy can be defined by its relation to daily life, by its capacity to grasp it, to understand it, to integrate it into a conceptual whole aiming at totality and universality. Philosophy is thereby seeking to renew itself by overcoming speculative abstraction. And this has been the case since Marx, Husserl, Heidegger, Lukács, and various others. We shall see that 'pure' philosophers, having gripped daily life in their conceptual pliers, still propose to dispose of it by absorbing it, rather than accepting it as it is – or transforming it.

At the same time, the term 'daily' and the 'reality' to which it refers have made their way into newspapers and literature. An increasingly important section of the press revolves around daily life and its 'problems' (to such an extent that the term 'problem' has been trivialized and is becoming well-nigh intolerable). In literature from Joyce to Simenon and Japrisot (a deliberate and somewhat ironic association), novelists seek to capture daily life at ever closer range, in order to derive surprising effects from it. Not to mention American authors who systematically smuggle the extraordinary out of the ordinary (quotidian). Yet daily life is not counterposed in some *binary* opposition to the non-quotidian: the philosophical, the supernatural, the sacred, the artistic. A binary schema of that sort forgets a (the) third term – that is to say, power, government, the state-political. This involves, and even explains, other memory lapses.

3

Preoccupation with daily life has also made its way into what are called the social sciences: history as well as anthropology, sociology, psychology, and so on. Many specialists are discovering in daily life the 'concreteness', the 'reality' they were pursuing, but which, unfortunately, they divided up, in line with their methods, to carve out their 'field'. Some believe that the sciences of human reality converge on this concrete reality. Others, by contrast, reckon that a micro-sociology or micro-psychology is formed at the level of daily life in opposition to macro-sociology or macro-psychology, directed towards the totality. Concern with daily life can also enter knowledge under other rubrics, indirectly or illicitly: 'material civilization', 'habitus', 'praxemes', and so on. Some sociologists are taking up the theme of daily life: without referring to previous research, they call themselves 'new sociologists' after te manner of the 'new philosophers', and announce the advent of a sociology of daily life.[1]

In most of these studies, the critical – hence political – dimension is obscured to vanishing point. The pragmatic and positivist approach, which aims and claims to be scientific, involves endorsement. According to this method, positive knowledge precludes critical thinking. This is a symptomatic attitude. Of what? One records, one ratifies. Knowledge and acknowledgement go hand in hand, in tandem. The scientist – or, rather, the one who knows [*sachant*] – proceeds reflexively: he reflects on what he observes; he reflects it. According to this approach, positive knowledge does not step outside the *fait accompli*: the 'factual', the 'real'. Critical thinking is eclipsed and even eliminated, as is the invariably troubling issue of *possibilities* that are distinct from *reality*.

The theme of the mirror, so common in contemporary writing, perfectly encapsulates what it means: the inability of reflection to perceive anything other than the mirrored or reflected object; neglect of the utter difference between image and object; and finally, confusion between objects in the mirror and the image of the narcissistic 'subject' in front of its own mirror …

The 'real' and 'reality'? On the face of it, they do not shift; they are unchanging for thought and before it. In truth, if we may still put it thus, 'reality' is constantly moving, sliding, towards something else. For a long time, what philosophers and scientists understood by the term was something profound, secret, hidden: essence or substance, occult qualities, Ideas or things in themselves, transcendence. From this perspective, from Plato to Hegel, the philosopher promulgated the 'true reality', the 'real truth', or the 'deep meaning' – in short, the unity of the real and the true in, by and for the Logos.

What does the word 'real' mean today? It is the given, the sensible and practical, the actual, the perceptible surface. As for daily life, the general opinion is that it forms part of reality. But does it coincide with it? No, for it contains something more, something less, and something else: lived experience, fleeting subjectivity – emotions, affects, habits, and forms of behaviour. We may add that it also includes abstraction. Money and commodities possess an abstract dimension that forms part of everyday reality, which also contains images (a multiplicity of images, without thereby vanishing into the 'imaginary').

Surrealism unquestionably represented a milestone in the displacement of what is called the 'real', in its decentring and recentring. It was characterized by a flight from reality. Moreover, it was in reality that Surrealism discerned the imaginary, discovered the extraordinary and the supernatural. (In this context, see *Le Paysan de Paris* or *L'Amour fou*, with their descriptions of supernaturally charged real objects.) The simultaneous problems of classical idealism and philosophical realism induced a displacement that had been foreseen and heralded by poets. Since then, the 'real' has been represented and valued (or devalued) differently – all the more so since *abstraction* (to which the world of commodities, like that of techniques, belongs) is held, not unreasonably, to be more complex than the 'real', from which it cannot be separated.

Rather than deriving from a 'thing in itself', is not the 'real' usually a *product*, and occasionally a *work*? Sometimes it is the comparatively simple outcome either of knowledge and technical application, or of exchange or history; sometimes an object possessing boundless wealth, horizons, multiple meanings. Account must be taken of these contrasting aspects of 'reality'. Is this reality the opposite of appearances, décor, illusions? Does it not include them as such? Is there still a need for critical thinking to intervene? Unquestionably. All the more so since confusion between the poverty of the object and its wealth, between the product and the work, is common and even organized (by advertising). But at first sight it seems that critical thinking, having become sterile, serves no purpose. Hence its eclipse by a 'reality' that seems eloquent and self-evident.

The abuse of critical thinking, which has lapsed into hypercriticism, must also be acknowledged. For the time being, let us confine ourselves to the catchword of the protest movements: '*changer la vie*'. Originally subversive, it was circulated, trivialized, debased, defused, and touted indiscriminately. Thereafter, if something changed, it was not by virtue of this slogan, but for other reasons: struggles (by, among others, women) and/or techniques. We shall return to the debasement and recuperation that form part of this defeat, as well as to the transformation of daily life during the second half of this century.

A 'retrospective' would be in order here. It would bring out the continuities and discontinuities; what has stagnated and what has changed. This would make it possible to clarify the concept of daily life, deploying and restricting it, for it cannot claim to cover the periods under consideration. It goes without saying that such a project will figure here only in outline. What is more, an 'exposition' reconstructing what daily life consisted in at some particular date would be of aesthetic or anecdotal, rather than theoretical, interest. The important thing is to set out the main features of the transformation of daily life, illuminated in and by the present, with new 'problematics' extending old problems. I must insist straight away on various propositions connected with the facts, that is, the transformations: 'Knowledge of daily life is necessary but not sufficient or self-sufficient. For its objective and stake are not to ratify the existing state of affairs, but to move towards what is possible. Knowledge of daily life is not cumulative, conforming to the usual schema and project of the so-called social sciences, because it transforms itself along with its object ...'

A debate at once takes shape, introducing a subjective and even (why not?) emotional dimension into the proceedings.

4

Discourse of the optimist (he also calls himself a 'futurist' or 'futurologist', and is often accused of seeing only what is in front of him). Yes indeed, what changes! Go on, admit it: daily life has changed more over the last few decades than it has since the Gauls and Romans – and for the better. At the beginning of this century, and even up to its mid-point, there were few if any domestic appliances, few cleaning products and detergents. Women had to peel vegetables or do the washing by hand, item by item: what slavery! No fridges, only useless 'larders'. Obviously, there were few if any cars or telephones. Proxemics (do you know this highly scientific term?) remained immutable, distances fixed, communications slow and difficult. Compare the situation today: the amazing variety of tools, machines, techniques at the disposal of daily life, a variety that will increase with computer science and its extensions. Note the growing integration of family life and groups into the life of society and the world ... Isn't what you call daily life going to be absorbed into the intense sociability contained in, and diffused by, communication and information? Unless, with new light having been shed on it, this everyday life reveals novel wealth: the unsaid in what is said; the dramatization, at last unveiled, of human relations; the revelation as spectacle of what had been left in the dark ...

Discourse of the nostalgic (often dubbed 'devotee of the past', he recently had the bright idea of calling himself 'postmodern'). Thank you for reminding us of the blindingly obvious. Isn't it distorting your bedazzled vision? Go on, ask women if their everyday life has changed that much. Do you think a few objects and tools are enough to alter relations between the sexes and the division of labour between them? It is as if these machines you make so much of had made the women's movement possible, prompting them to formulate their demands – their problematic, as the philosophers say – but by no means to resolve it! The reign of the car, kingpin-object, pilot-object, has certainly influenced people and things. For the better? That is far from being proved: at the very least, the disadvantages match the advantages. But enough of these platitudes! In bygone days, there was no TV. But careful: rather than uniting people, can't the media, communications and information technology divide them? Doesn't it depend on the social and political use made of the new techniques? The integration of the private into the social? Do you believe that social life has greatly benefited, been much enriched, since the development of communications? Instead of getting excited, think. Look back a second, if you would, to appreciate what was abandoned *en route*. Paris in days gone by! The Ile-de-France and France of old! Then a building was like a house! The people inhabiting it – the best-off downstairs, the more modestly placed upstairs, and the 'domestics' under the eaves – knew each other, and liked or loathed each other. But they formed a small community within the larger community of the district, in a town that was itself perceived as one big, fine community. Paris, like Lyons or Lille or Toulouse, used to boast an industrious and cheerful populace. Singing was commonplace. Music ruled in towns without any need for DJs. The streets were vibrant. In squares and on boulevards, large circles of people gathered around singers accompanied by accordionists. People learnt the songs, bought the lyrics, and left humming the tune. What have you made of the people, apart from a demagogic theme? Is there still a people in Paris or the towns of France, a 'developed' country? There was unquestionably a certain narrowness in this everyday life: distant things, foreigners, the global horizon went unremarked. Gestures, social customs, rituals of courtesy and urbanity, the way in which women were addressed, the courteousness which concealed a slight disdain, the manner of greeting people – raising one's hat – all this remained traditional, and might seem antiquated. But what a sense of security! The individual felt supported as well as constrained. Relations between neighbours were strong; people helped each other. Events and formal occasions were celebrated collectively. Bread was still hallowed; values – like language the sediment of centuries, derived from long periods of penury and scarcity – had not disappeared. The slightest object could be considered precious, to be preserved or offered up. These rather narrow values simultaneously hemmed people in and protected them. There was no need for a sense of security imparted from on high or from without. Don't put words in my mouth: I'm fully aware that what goes by the name of social security represents progress. But you know as well as I do that it has served the state as a political means for changing an active, responsible populace into a population of welfare claimants, passive folk, who wait for the police when there is a crime or an accident, without stirring. Everyday life has lost the quality and vigour it once possessed, and dissipated, like the space that has been smashed to bits and then sold in pieces. What charms we have lost. In Paris, there were many enchanting places, not only Montmartre but on the heights – Belleville, Ménilmontant – and below, along the length of the Seine – for example, in the direction of the warehouses of Bercy ... As for the Ile-de-France, soon no-one will be able to recount its charm, which survived until the middle of the twentieth century ... But I could go on for ever: I'll stop ...

This debate runs through the century; its origins are more distant. Whether directly or indirectly, it is voiced in innumerable writings or speeches. Is there an answer to this pressing, insistent problematic? A solution? One of the aims of the present work is to avoid its alternatives by opening up a path which is neither that of nostalgia nor that of a futurology enthused by the 'scientific and technological revolution'. Such contradictions between ideas and conflicts in 'reality' can sometimes stimulate thought, and sometimes trap it in a dead end. The first important thing is not to stifle the debate but to follow it through, without imposing a prefabricated solution, be it an unconditional apologia for positive knowledge and technology, or historicism and obsessive recollection of the past.

5

The present work is the third in a series bearing the same title. The first volume appeared immediately after the Liberation in 1946, the second in 1961. These two volumes were complemented by a summary of courses given at the universities of Strasbourg and Paris X (Nanterre), published under the title of *Everyday Life in the Modern World* (1968), and various articles, including a manifesto of 'revolutionary Romanticism' (1957).

Two ways of studying daily life and its alterations might be envisaged: either a periodical publication or a series of works over time attempting regular updates. The first, doubtless preferable, was not feasible for material (editorial) reasons. The second, whatever its drawbacks, indicates a periodization (1946–1960–1968) corresponding to important changes in social practice, as well as socio-political representations and activity. Consequently, these works can today serve as markers, milestones, and even reference points for a balance sheet introducing a new critical analysis. Perhaps this will improve the chances of these works escaping the common fate of our epoch's enormous ideological output, doomed as it is to oblivion.

6

The first volume – entitled *Critique of Everyday Life: Introduction*, and setting out an initial project – was thus published in 1946 amid the optimism (hopes and illusions) of freedom restored. It formulated the concept of the everyday, bringing to developed language and conceptual clarity a practice that was named and yet not recognized – adjudged unworthy of knowledge. This 'elaboration' invented neither the word nor the thing, but overcame the divisions 'philosophy–non-philosophy', 'significant–insignificant', 'ignorance–knowledge'. This is how Marx proceeded with social labour and Freud with sex. The same is true of daily life as of labour: the concept reunites the partial aspects and activities in which limited descriptions and analyses lose themselves. Such a concept is simultaneously abstract and concrete. Daily life would appear to comprise particular cases, individual situations, or general banalities. Here we encounter one of the oldest problems of philosophy and methodology. *Conceptual* theorization resolves it: there is a knowledge of the quotidian. How was it defined at the time?

(a) In the first instance by a certain appropriation of time and space, the body, vital spontaneity and 'nature', an appropriation prone to dis-appropriation or ex-propriation (alienation), whose causes and reasons – historical, economic, political, and ideological – are discovered by knowledge. It none the less emerges that the everyday unfolds and is constituted in a space and time distinct from natural space and time, as well as mental space and time.

(b) With daily life, lived experience is taken and raised up to critical thinking. It is no longer disdained, regarded as an insignificant residue, produced by a necessary methodological reduction, ultimately destroyed. But nor is it overestimated, inflated, counterposed to what is rational. It assumes in theoretical thinking the place it occupies in social practice: there it is not everything, but it is not nothing either. On the other hand, lived experience and daily life do not coincide. Daily life does not exhaust lived experience, for there is lived experience outside it: above and/or below it. Nevertheless, the relation between the experiential and the conceptual is foregrounded. It contains a much larger issue: that of the relations between thought and life – a Faustian question that is scarcely resolved by apologias for life or for pure thought.

(c) *Vis-à-vis* more or less highly specialized, and hence fragmented, activities – thinking, circulating, dwelling, dressing, but also engaging in some particular piece of work – daily life is defined as both a *product* (the result of their conjunction) and a *residue*, when one abstracts from these activities. It receives the remnants, the remains of these 'higher' activities; it is their common measure, their fertile or barren soil, their resource, their common site or ground. This product-residue, result and common ground, can on no account be reduced to the arithmetical or mechanical sum total of these activities. On the contrary, daily life can be understood only if one considers the various activities in the totality encompassing them, that is to say, the mode of production. The latter is not viewed outside or above these multiple activities, but as being realized in and through them as well as in daily life. Daily life is thus the product of the mode of production (in the event, the capitalist mode of production, the case of 'socialism', which cannot be defined as a mode of production, being left to one side). The mode of production as producer and daily life as product illuminate one another.

(d) Daily life also results from conjunctions between cyclical processes and times and linear processes and times – that is, between two very different modalities of the repetitive. The body appears to be a bundle of cyclical rhythms; contrariwise, many regulated activities – a sequence of productive gestures, for example, or social procedures – are clearly linear. In present daily life, the rhythmical is overwhelmed, suppressed by the linear. But the rhythmical cannot disappear; the repetitive cannot be reduced to the results of a combinatory, a prefabricated, imposed linearity. Although such a tendency exists in the modern world, daily life cannot be conceived exclusively in accordance with functional linearity. Likewise, the qualitative cannot completely disappear into the quantitative, nor use into exchange, nor things into pure relations. Daily life includes both aspects, both modes of everyday repetition. (See, below, the paragraph on the 'elements of rhythmanalysis', developing a thesis that remained unexplained in Volume I of the *Critique*.)

(e) Daily life can also be conceived as an encounter and a confrontation between use (use-value) and exchange (exchange-value). Whatever the predominance of exchange-value and its importance in the mode of production, it does not end up eliminating use and use-value – even if it approximates to 'pure' abstraction and pure sign. Labour produces exchangeable goods, commodities; between their production and their consumption, they lead a unique existence that is more abstract than concrete. During this phase, the characteristics of exchange are prevalent: this is the reign of the commodity, its world. While it lasts, the object is *virtually* reduced to a *sign*. Then this mode of social existence is interrupted, and use-value recovers its prerogatives. As well as (social) labour producing exchange-values, we can also stress a certain non-labour (rest, holidays, private life, leisure) that plays a part in the use of products. The time of non-labour forms part of social time, as compensation for the time devoted to production (sold as productive capacity to those who possess the means of production). Like labour, non-labour, or rather the time of non-labour, forms part of the mode of production. It impels the economy – first because it is the time of consumption, and next because vast sectors generating products and surplus-value are constructed on the basis of this non-labour: tourism, the leisure industry, show business, 'culture' and the culture industry. Thus daily life encompasses these modalities of social time, the time of labour and of non-labour alike, the latter in particular being bound up with use. Furthermore, use and use-value are not immutable: they are mobile. For example, the use of space is not reducible to that of any object whatsoever, using and destroying it through consumption. Use of space involves a certain use of time:

transport, the relations between centres and their environs, the use of facilities. In short, there is no absolute priority of exchange, no vanishing of use into exchange, no reduction of use-value to the role of vehicle for exchange-value (all the more so in that in the era to which Volume I of the *Critique* belonged, 'values' in a broad sense, originating in scarcity, and hence use, were still very much with us).

(f) In daily life, what are called natural needs are socially moulded in a way that can transform them to the point of artificiality. In 1946, this social moulding existed, but was not yet very sophisticated and not yet labelled 'cultural'. From this point of view, daily life was defined as the site of a three-term dialectical motion: 'needs– desires–pleasures'. This dynamic was not separated from other elements: labour and non-labour, use and exchange, and so on. In 1946, work was still regarded as the concrete realization of human beings; it featured as one social need among others, and it was even declared that it would soon become the prime social need … under socialism. As everyone knows, and as we shall see later, what occurred was the opposite: compared with not working and leisure, work was discredited; its ethical value gradually faded. In 1946, this process had yet to begin. Work retained the prestige conferred on it by all social classes in the nineteenth century in a quasi-consensus.

(g) Here another aspect of daily life reveals itself: the set of relations of distance – proximity and vicinity or, contrariwise, remoteness – distantiations in time and space. This includes the relations of individuals and groups (families, workshops, corporations) to death in general and to their own deaths (photos, mementoes, commemorations and tombs), as well as the relations between bodies, the relations of the corporeal to the spatial and temporal. At the time of this book (1946), these relations still seemed to be established and solid, because they were traditional. They were soon to alter.

(h) Also at this time, the relations between religious, civic, local, etc., festivals and play on the one hand, and non-holidays, the serious business of life, and daily life on the other – these relations seemed reinvigorated. There was a distinction, but not a division; although it was distinct from daily life, the Festival – its preparation, its celebration, and the traces and memories it left behind – was never far off. Nor was the supernatural, or the extraordinary dimension of the ordinary. Rather than fragmenting it, the time of festivals doubled everyday time.

The complexity of daily life, as it emerges from the preceding summary, cannot be attributed to a linear process, whether historical, philosophical, economic or social. It results from many conjunctions. The realization of the social being known as 'human' found itself thwarted by distortions and alienations that were themselves attributable to a multiplicity of causes – the division of labour, social classes, ideologies and 'values', oppression and repression. But at the time under consideration, there was as yet no rupture between objects and people, their gestures, actions, situations and discourse. All these aspects of daily life were part not only of the mode of production, but of a totality called 'civilization' (a stronger term than 'culture', which was subsequently substituted for it). Fragmentation did not yet obtain; a certain unity persisted, despite wars and despite the disappearance of the major religious, historical and moral referents since the beginning of the century.

It was not yet over. As it manifested itself *at the time under consideration*, daily life harboured a hidden wealth in its apparent poverty. In it were to be found the norms and conventions that determined what is beautiful, true and good for society – in other words, the accepted ethics and aesthetics. Counterposing to them various absolute terms, classical philosophy believed it had invented absolute Truth, absolute Good, absolute Beauty, against which were ranged the False, the Evil and the Ugly. In the course of what are called modern times, the critique of philosophy, acting in concert with the 'human' sciences, has relativized these concepts. Every society, whether old or contemporary, has possessed and still (except in cases of decadence and rapid decay) possesses its norms and values. Nevertheless, dogmatism has not disappeared. On the contrary, it is as if relativism, scepticism and empiricism were creating a need for their opposite – a need for dogmas and absolute truths. Dogmatism is becoming a socio-political fact. The confrontation between dogma and doubt, norms and conventions, fidelity to the established order and rejection of it, occurs in daily life. If these norms are no longer strong enough to impose a representation of the true, the beautiful or the good, it is because the relevant society is decaying or fragmenting. The absence of norms and values demonstrates not that they are no longer important, but that they are disappearing in the course of a 'crisis', a 'mutation', or increasing stagnation.

As Nietzsche said on many occasions, the 'decadent' have chosen what was worst for them. How can this be? When and where was the choice made? Where and when did 'truths' and 'illusions' confront one another? When did the norms, values and conventions that make up a society appear? And how were they imposed? Where do we sense their absence? The dogmatic response is unacceptable: 'This is what you must think ...' The only response – poorly explained in the book I am recalling here, but already inherent in critical knowledge – is: *in daily life*. Rather than wishing to destroy existing values as ideological, the 'critique of everyday life' proposed to study their alterations in daily life and the emergence of daily life itself as both reality and value.

The determinations and definitions recalled above converge as aspects of daily life and its concept. Joined to it, closely bound up with the analysis, was a project. It proposed to set free the latent wealth, to bring out the implicit, unexplored content of daily life, valorizing it. It allowed that everyday mundanity, its time and space, contained things that were seemingly incompatible with it – play, the Festival, surprise – and hence the possibility of presenting this profundity and putting it into perspective. With a certain clumsiness of formulation, the project inherent in the conceptualization and theory presented itself thus.

How was this kind of project and book situated in a Marxist perspective, while not allowing itself to be imprisoned in a system? In the first place, it not only intended to complete the lexicon of 'Marxist' terminology by introducing the concept of daily life and various other concepts; above all, it proposed to open up Marxist thought to the realm of possibilities, rather than focusing it on the 'real' (economic) and the factual (historical). The same work also sought to transform the concept of 'revolution'. Revolution was not confined to economic transformations (relations of production), or political transformations (personnel and institutions), but (to merit the title) could and must extend as far as everyday life, as far as actual 'disalienation', creating a way of living, a style – in a word, a civilization. This precludes reducing society to the economic and the political, and modifies the all too famous controversy over 'base' and 'superstructure' by putting the emphasis on the *social*. Relations irreducible to the economic – relations of production and property – are involved in the 'social': namely, the relations between individuals and groups and the totality of those relations – daily life. The aim was to develop and enrich concepts which are employed by Marx, but are unacknowledged or impoverished: *praxis* (*social* practice), the relationship between the individual and the social, *civil society*, and even *mode of production*. In particular, *civil society* was arrived at by a different route from Gramsci: less historical, more contemporary. The much-debated relation between 'base' and 'superstructure' left scholasticism behind and was situated concretely, with daily life including 'superstructural' and 'infrastructural' elements. In short, that book attempted to pose various problems historically but without historicism, and philosophically but without philosophical illusions. As early as 1946, without shouting it from the rooftops, it thus attempted an updating of Marxism – an undertaking that failed for various reasons (historical and political).

To explain the incomprehension and disapproval the book met with, I must stress here some aspects of philosophical thought and 'Marxism' in France, and even in Europe.

Critical knowledge of daily life seems to be *punctual*, that is to say, bearing on various points: needs, activities, products, and so on. Hence a curious misunderstanding. The *punctual* became fashionable only much later, owing to the disappointing character of works about the whole and the totality, after some serious errors (for example, assessment of the 'Third World' as the future and model for the entire world). When this work was published, the whole and the totality were the predominant intellectual concerns (philosophical and scientific), but few people noticed that it arrived at a totality (the mode of production) via an 'element'– daily life – that supplied a path for approaching the whole concretely. That daily life provides a mediation between the particular and the universal, the local and the global, was scarcely understood. Studying daily life (its details) at a given moment bypasses the concept, simulates apprehension of the concrete, goes no further than what is immediate (clothing, housing, etc.), as opposed to grasping the concrete. The limits of this concept

– daily life – are, moreover, those of every concept: none vouchsafes mastery of what it grasps; it opens up a path to practice, but is not a substitute for it. Sometimes a particular concept (for example, art) is born with the end of its referent. Furthermore, knowledge must proceed with caution, restraint, respect. It must respect lived experience, rather than belabouring it as the domain of ignorance and error, rather than absorbing it into positive knowledge as vanquished ignorance. Feelings and emotions, play, festivals, the sacred itself – these are to be treated with tact. The situation is a delicate one: it involves understanding without believing, without endorsing, without taking statements literally. From the outset, the critique of everyday life imparted content to *alienation*, but did not define its status, whether philosophical or scientific or even metaphorical! Understanding lived experience, situating it, and restoring it to the dynamic constellation of concepts; 'explaining' it by stating what it *involves* – this was how the meaning of the work and project was expressed.

7

The originality of the project with respect to traditional philosophy has already been underscored. It regarded daily life neither as the non-philosophical, nor as raw material for some possible construction. It did not regard it as the thing from which philosophy distances itself in order to embark upon either a phenomenology of consciousness, or a logic, or ethics, or aesthetics. It sought to show that the confused character of lived experience, as of daily life, betokened not their poverty but their richness. The slightest object (still) had a direct or indirect relation with art, 'culture', civilization. The project aimed at a revived unity and totality – of the experiential, the philosophical and the political (something that existentialism aspired to a little later, but fell short of). If there was a magical dimension to daily life (rites, formulae, proverbs, traditions), that was also its complexity and its richness. Daily life was taken as an 'object' not in the sense of a static object or a pretext for building a 'model', but as the starting point for a form of action. It did not represent an inferior degree of intellectual or 'spiritual' life. Thus, it was not erected into an 'object' in the epistemological sense, and 'delimiting' it, constituting it as a 'field', was not the issue! All these clarifications are necessary to avoid – albeit belatedly – misunderstandings that were present some decades ago. With respect to philosophy, a metaphilosophical perspective was outlined. This problematic starts out from the exhaustion of the classical problematic – the 'subject–object' relation, or the 'real–ideal' and 'reality–knowledge' relations. Notwithstanding an arguably regrettable tendency to privilege sociology, from the outset the concept of *daily life* welcomed the contributions of economic, political, historical, etc., studies. This justified borrowing from philosophy, in a different inflection, the idea of *totality*, itself integrated into a process of *evolution*, that of the *mode of production* (in the process of being realized as indicated above). Daily life in the totality had nothing in common with the 'primitive', the 'pre-logical' or 'pre-scientific', the infantile. It had before it, around it, above and below it, other 'realities', networks, institutions, including techniques, positive knowledge, and especially the state. In the first volume, the penetration of techniques into daily life (still, at this time, close to 'spontaneity') was demonstrated, as was that of positive knowledge and political action. Even so, no concept – that of the state any more than that of technicity – possesses an ontological privilege with respect to it. They all have their limits. The problem of technique emerged, but was not yet formulated explicitly. Is it a factor which has become autonomous, and could wreak havoc on the world? Is it something destined to be mastered by a cast of technocrats – or by the working class? Must we repudiate enthusiasm for technology (which would later be all the rage, including among Marxists), or, on the contrary, accommodate it? These questions, which would emerge only subsequently, did not feature in the first volume.

It would be incorrect and dishonest to say that the critique of everyday life derives its philosophical positions from either Lukács or Heidegger; but it has not been unknown. It is true that Lukács introduced the theme of *Alltäglichkeit* ['everydayness'] as early as his first works, in *Soul and Form*. Was it he who inspired Heidegger to conceive the theses of *Being and Time* on abandonment and care in the *Alltäglichkeit*? Perhaps. But we should remember that these themes – the appraisal of everyday reality as trivial, given over to care and void of meaning, which directs philosophy to the true life, or authentic existence and authenticity – derive from Romanticism. And, more precisely, from German Romanticism: Hölderlin, Novalis, Hoffmann, and so on. Did not the philosophers, and Lukács in the first instance, turn the claims of the Romantic tradition back against it, supporting them with the modern critique of bourgeois society? After Lukács, Heidegger offered an ontological interpretation of this critique. For both philosophers, daily life, speculatively conceived, amounts to a chaos, a disorder of sensations and emotions, prior to the forms conferred on it by aesthetics, ethics, or logic – in other words, philosophy. Everydayness is a sort of primitiveness. At best, daily life is defined as spontaneity, flux, irruption, and hence as pre-logical. There is no doubt that Lukács demonstrates the presence in literature, and especially in the modern novel, of a protest against the triviality of daily life.[2] According to him, there is thus a tension between the 'problematic hero' and a social practice that has lost the 'immanence of meaning', and likewise becomes problematic in its triviality. Genuinely heroic, the 'subject' resists dissolution or is wrecked against the 'object', reality. In Lukács, however, the 'subject' seeks to rediscover the object. The philosopher never abandoned the philosophical fiction of unity regained – Hegelian reconciliation in supersession and the universal through art and revolution. As Adorno was to object, the negative and the moment of the negative never constitute a relation to the world of the 'subject' for Lukács, but an episode, a transient mood. He underestimated both the critique and the crisis.

As for Heidegger, the characteristic distantiation of being-with-others also implies that, in its *Alltäglichkeit*, *Dasein* finds itself in the grip of those others. It is not itself: others have divested it of its being. Moreover, the other is not someone defined. Anyone can represent it. It is neither this one nor that one; neither some nor all. It is neuter: the *'they'*, *das Man*.[3]

This phenomenology of the ontic thus involves a fundamental, absolute pessimism about the social and the practical. In this respect it is opposed to the Marxist tradition, for which alienation can be countered and overcome. An analogous pessimism is to be found in Sartre, above all in *Being and Nothingness*, a work inspired by a Cartesianized and psychologized Heideggerianism. The other is (only) the degradation of the 'subject', dereliction. For Marx, by contrast, *the other* is both alienation and disalienation (its possibility): alienation in class relations, disalienation in revolutionary potentialities.

Sartre's works contain the sketch of a critique of everyday life: the gaze of the other, bad faith, and the characteristics typical of the 'bastard'. But this critique of daily life remains incomplete, not referred to as such because it remains the prisoner of philosophy and its categories, and consequently condemned to pessimism tinged – but only just – with humanism.

La Conscience mystifiée (1936) already took a stand against the Lukácsian position and its rational optimism, together with the pessimism and nihilism foreshadowed in philosophy with the crisis of rationality. It sought to demonstrate that the anthropomorphism and anthropocentrism of reason were leading thought astray and condemning it to error, a travesty of errantry. It also sought to demonstrate the importance of critical, negative mediation in evolution, in consciousness and society: the moment of appearances and illusions seeking to become reality. This book went a long way in taking account of the negative. The vigour of this moment was displayed to such an extent that unity – of subject and object, the ideal and the real – receded to the horizon, and drew closer only in utopia, which for this reason was creative. Hegelian supersession? While it retains a sense and remains the goal, it can be achieved only through the severe ordeals of an evolution that has nothing linear or preformed about it.

8

A not insignificant point: critical knowledge of daily life does not require a special or perfect language, distinct from everyday discourse. On the other hand, as a familiar precept has it, we should use only such words as possess meaning – and one meaning only. Even when we are distinguishing between the spoken and the unspoken, the unconscious and the conscious, the unknown and the known in daily life – in short, detecting what is contained in the discourse of the everyday – there is no need to invent a different vocabulary, syntax, or paradigm from the one that is present in the discourse. Critical knowledge of daily life is expressed in everyday language and everyone's language: by making explicit what is implicit. This rules out 'proof', but does not preclude the element of play and risk inherent in any conversational discourse.

One postulate of the work (Volume I) that will have to be reconsidered, for it may be that the hypothesis is no longer correct and
requires modification, was this: people in general do not know how
they live, making the theory of daily life indispensable. This brings it
closer to the economic, and even the political! We must be clear as to
the meaning of this phrase. 'People' know their needs and their
wants through suffering and satisfaction; but they scarcely know how
to express them, and still less how to define them. Numerous documents indicate a poverty of vocabulary and clumsiness of expression,
but simultaneously the relevance of the testimony. Despite the abundance of information (from mid-century onwards), 'people' today
(1981) still possess only scant comparative data. Do they know what
they want? Yes, ever more clearly; they are less and less taken in. Do
they have a clear knowledge of their situation, their social relations?
No. An example: the more important space and place become, the
more the mass of people are ignorant of space, for everything conspires to detach them from it – the media, images, transport, general
abstraction. Socially, they understand only the rungs immediately
below and above them in the hierarchy. That hierarchy precisely has
the following function, among others: to obscure whatever would
make remote social strata and classes known to one another. Despite
innumerable images, or because of the very abundance of representations, the 'poor' can scarcely imagine the everyday life of the 'rich'.
They represent it to themselves in accordance with their own lives, as
made easier by money. When they are unveiled, power and wealth
astound them (as in Luigi Comencini's film *L'argent de la vieille*).
Wealth makes Olympians of the rich – inaccessible, outside daily life:
above it. There is thus a social 'un-conscious', as well as an 'imaginary'. How are they to be situated? At a deeper level? From the
outset, the critique of daily life responded thus: they are the *content of
representations*. The dominated represent to themselves the order they
belong to solely by means of symbols. To carry this content over into
theory is to explain what the symbols say (and dissimulate); it is to
explicate the content with words and concepts that escape ideology
as far as possible. Unlike psychoanalysis, bringing the (social) unconscious to light reintroduces not only the *relations of production*, but those
of *reproduction* (domination and power), as well as *representations* (of a
particular social class or stratum for itself, for other classes, for

697

society as a whole). This is the point at which to add that if class struggles, in all their complexity, have their significance and their impact on reality as well as representations, on daily life as well as what is exceptional, class compromises – whether historically proclaimed or not – are no less important. The reproduction of the relations of production and domination is at stake in periods of open struggle and compromise alike.

9

Also to be noted, after so many years, is the happy absence from this work of epistemological concerns. It contains none of what was soon going to obstruct the path of thought for years, to the point of impeding it. A question of generation? No: of orientation. This book was not aiming at a 'pure' or purified scientific knowledge. Knowledge is defined not by its epistemological 'purity', but by its critical import: thought is either critical or it is not (is only discourse). If the concept has limits, critical thinking does not accept them: it tackles what exists, including what is regarded as sacred, untouchable, definitive – the state, the party, the gods, the leader. May that which can resist do so!

Is the concept of 'daily life' operational or not? Yes, since it makes a critical analysis of the 'real' possible. No, for it produces nothing – nothing but a negative proposal as to what is possible: '*changer la vie*'.

From the outset, this orientation conflicted with the one that was soon to be adopted by an intelligentsia driven by the dominant ideology: structuralism and its annexes – epistemology and scientism (which claimed to put an end to ideology). 'Marxism', as they say, would itself capitulate in the face of technocratic ideologies, and divide into two tendencies, two contradictory forms, each with its own arguments: a radical, critical orientation, banking on the negative, which sometimes went as far as hypercriticism; and epistemology, neo-positivism, scientism – in a word, a dogmatism renewed in its vocabulary, but not its make-up.

From the start, the *Critique of Everyday Life* aimed to shatter Marxist orthodoxy and, more precisely, to put an end to the notion of an orthodoxy. In fact, at the time a boundless dogmatism reigned in 'Marxism', which is difficult to comprehend thirty years on. For the

698

dogmatists, absolute Truth pertained to the Party and hence to its leaders, repositories of this priceless treasure. The mere idea of *research* seemed ridiculous, since the Truth was there – already there. At most, those in high places could request – or, rather, command – documents and statistics to confirm established positions, to 'deliver blows' to enemies and 'crush' them. The result? Instead of a development of Marxist thought, through discussion and debate, innovative currents arose outside it. The obvious lacunae of official Marxism, which its 'representatives' did not even perceive, would be made good by philosophies in the usual sense, forming a system (or trying to form one) outside social practice and political action. Hence existentialism; and hence its success!

10

Nearly fifteen years passed. We are now in 1960. Changes – yes, lots of them. Not in the desired direction; on the contrary, in a quite different direction – or maybe inclining towards a loss of direction! The second volume of the *Critique of Everyday Life* sought to combine numerous observations as well as various selective critical studies in one theory. What occurred in the course of these fifteen years? First the apogee, then the decline, of Stalinism, and the failure of the critique of Stalinism inside the Communist movement, particularly in France. How did the contestation that emerged at the time differ from *critique*? In this: that it was intent on being immediately active, without operating through the mediation of what was already established (parties, doctrines, etc.). It also wanted to be radical. It took account of changes in the world and the onset of the crisis affecting the classical concept of *revolution*, substituting for it that of *subversion*.

11

The second volume of the *Critique* did not remain external to the movement. First of all, with official, institutional Marxism falling into discredit, unofficial Marxist thought found an increasingly large audience. In an unforeseen detour, a group such as *COBRA* – artists, writers, architects – which was very active in northern Europe, drew inspiration from the critique of daily life while carrying it further. The desire to transform everyday life made its way through ideologies, philosophies, metaphysical revivals. As early as 1953, the Dutch architect Constant, who inspired the Amsterdam 'provos', invented a new architecture of ambiance and situations, incorporating, as it were, the critique of daily life into space. It was via this detour that the transition was made from critique to contestation, a development involving students and new groups, among them the Situationists. What were the forces of protest directed against? Their objective depended on the groups and individuals. Some, especially among students and intellectuals, resented traditional morality, religion, Judaeo-Christianity. Others took as their target the 'thing', the object – that is to say, the commodity and its attendant ideology. Yet others attacked nationalism, the (in their eyes) neurotic attachment to Motherland and Paternalistic State. Many of them quite simply proposed to destroy capitalism, which they naively believed to be in a critical condition whenever they detected the slightest symptom of economic difficulties, when in fact, economically, the age was one of 'prosperity' and the onset of the 'scientific and technological revolution'. In short, the various forces of protest were not agreed either on the grounds and goals of the contestation, or on the line to pursue. But everyone was in agreement on one imperative: *changer la vie*. Were they demanding their 'share of the cake', of growth and the economic miracle? No. They rejected economic and political reality. They also rejected what was in the ascendant all around them: technocracy, with its dual fetishism of competence and performance; and an ideology that started proclaiming the end of ideology under the sway of knowledge and authority – so that these ideologues merely diffused their own ideologies more successfully (productivism, positivism, logical empiricism, structuralism, etc.). There was no lack of analogies between protest and contestation in France and Europe, and the Cultural Revolution in China: they were ten a penny. The same vigour – and the same failure. Was not this wave of contestation the provisional form of a comprehensive movement directed against fixed hierarchies, established apparatuses, enforced silence, and the ideologies of domination? In France as elsewhere, protesters rejected the productivist ideology that passed for 'pure' knowledge, as well as the reorganization of daily life around the couplet 'production-consumption' – a reorganization that gained ground and was to achieve a quasi-general consensus, except among the protesters. Rejecting, before the ecologists did so, growth, with its brutal implications – harsh technologies, the expansion of towns that remained such in name only – they counterposed the cult of pleasure to that of work. Against an economism void of values other than those of exchange, protest stood for reuniting the festival and daily life, for transforming daily life into a site of desire and pleasure. The protesters were protesting against the fact, simultaneously obvious and ignored, that delight and joy, pleasure and desire, desert a society that is content with satisfaction – that is to say, catalogued, created needs that procure some particular object and evaporate in it. They took radical critique to the extreme by opposing not working to work, which was being promoted as the supreme value. A paradox? Or a demand deriving from the high level of the productive forces and the possibility people sensed of abolishing work through automation of the productive process? In and through imponderables and ambiguities, sound and fury, the problematic of the modern world was taking shape. From 1957 or 1958 onwards, the protesters could legitimately describe themselves as revolutionaries, since they were demanding what the 'regime' and the 'system' (the mode of production) could not but refuse. They put their finger on some sensitive issues. Whether consciously or not, they demonstrated an essential emergent truth: production involves and encompasses reproduction – not only of labour-power and the means of production (classical theses), but of the social relations of domination as well. Thus, re-production took centre-stage. Production as such, and its study, fell to specialists, economists and technologists. As for official Marxism, it stuck to traditional claims about production. However, re-production, exposed by growth at the very heart of capitalist relations of production, could no longer figure as a secondary phenomenon, a simple result of production. Critical analysis of it involved reviving the concept of totality. Where and how was reproduction carried out? In and through the family? The state? The workplace, and it alone? The middle classes? Social practice? All these answers contained a grain of truth, but remained one-sided and incomplete as long as a new analysis of the everyday was lacking.

12

During the period under consideration (1946–61), daily life changed – not in the sense of displaying its latent wealth, but in the opposite direction: impoverishment, manipulation, passivity. Capitalism was in the process of conquering new sectors in these years: agriculture, previously precapitalist in large part; the historic town, which broke up through explosion and implosion; space as a whole, conquered by tourism and leisure; culture – that is to say, civilization reduced and subordinated to growth by the culture industry; finally, and especially, daily life.

The second volume of the *Critique of Everyday Life* contains a thesis that is possibly excessive, that is, hypercritical, but not meaningless. It was developed in co-operation with the oppositional avant-garde. According to this theory, daily life replaces the colonies. Incapable of maintaining the old imperialism, searching for new tools of domination, and having decided to bank on the home market, capitalist leaders treat daily life as they once treated the colonized territories: massive trading posts (supermarkets and shopping centres); absolute predominance of exchange over use; dual exploitation of the dominated in their capacity as producers and consumers. The book thus sought to show why and how daily life is insidiously *programmed* by the media, advertising, and the press. In great detail, and with many convincing arguments, people were having it explained to them how they should live in order to 'live well' and make the best of things; what they would choose and why; how they would use their time and space. These features marked society while wrecking the social. No particular feature – consumption as such, the spectacle and spectacularization, the abuse of images, the overwhelming abundance and redundancy of information – suffices to define this society; all of them are involved in daily life. The upshot is contradictory: undeniable satisfaction and a deep malaise. Rather than a qualitative appropriation of the body and a life of spontaneity, what transpires is a threatening and increasing expropriation by the outside, the quantitative and the repetitive, by disembodied images and alien voices, by the discursive and spectacular moulding of everything that happens. This was the case for 'people' in general, for society as a whole, the middle classes being the axis and support of these operations, their subject and object in so far as these terms still have a meaning. Various privileged products, which really are useful and agreeable – the car, the fridge, the radio, the television – are allocated the following mission: expropriating the body and compensating for this expropriation; replacing desire by fixed needs; replacing delight by programmed satisfaction. The 'real', displaced and situated in a new way in daily life, consequently wins out completely over the ideal. In fact, satisfactions cannot be regarded as negligible: subjective needs, produced for the consumption of objective products, are real; they are reality, which possesses a substance and coherence so often celebrated that it is erected into a criterion of truth.

This indictment, contained in the *Critique of Everyday Life* II, as well as *Everyday Life in the Modern World* and other articles from the same period, laid itself open to attack and was not without its faults. As far as production was concerned, the role of multinationals was hardly mentioned, whereas their intervention in daily life was already visible. Contrary to the Marxist schema predicting the formation and investment of large capital exclusively in what is called heavy industry (iron and steel, chemicals, etc.), many of the most powerful global enterprises established themselves in daily life in this period: detergents and cleaning products, drink and food, clothing. Some curious misunderstandings resulted: blue jeans, produced by these global enterprises – possibly in countries such as Hong Kong and Singapore, whose proletariat was super-exploited – were regarded by young people as a symbol of freedom, novelty and independence. This fashion supplied the critique of daily life with an excellent example of manipulation. A certain Americanism worked its way in – not so much through ideology as via daily life. Critical thinking captured this infiltration only with difficulty, though it detected it here and there.

Inadequately analysed, the production of needs – bureaucratically administered consumption – remained entangled with naturalism; as a result, the efficacy of the media by means of models and images was barely understood. The role and function of the middle classes in subtle changes in daily life, civil society, the state, and their relations, were glimpsed but not clarified. These works did not clearly show how and why programmed everydayness – that of the middle classes – is their reality, and is then transformed by them into 'cultural' models for 'lower' strata and classes. The analytical and critical examination of this manipulation lacked a foundation that would come only later: the theory of representations used by the manipulators, which includes critical examination of symbolisms, the social and individual imaginary, and 'culture'. As a result, the analysis of reproduction, as concealed not *under* but *in* production–consumption, remained incomplete.

13

After the Liberation, the 'people' still had a meaning in France. Peasants, artisans, workers – in short, all those who did not belong to the 'dominant' and 'propertied' classes – still had numerous links, not only in workplaces but also in houses, streets, districts and towns, regions. Over the next fifteen years, this unity began to break up not into clearly differentiated and opposed classes, but into layers and strata. In 1960, the people faded into a historical past, sometimes to be commemorated with a solemnity that allayed suspicion. The beautiful myth of the people as creator and repository of political and philosophical truth, which derived from the French Revolution, became blurred. Social unity fragmented. Although it was subject to the homogenizing instances of law, government and market, as well as the national identity stipulated and codified by the state, it crumbled none the less. This tendency – which was already apparent around 1960, and was destined to become preponderant, even appearing to be rationally self-evident – was not clearly perceived in the works under discussion. They still counted exclusively on positive knowledge: they accepted the hypothesis of the rational efficacy of knowledge, and were not as yet suspicious of what was being infiltrated under that rubric. They certainly wanted to oppose a sort of counter-knowledge to the official scientism, which is integrated into the institutions and integrates people into them, and hence to the relations of reproduction. But this counter-knowledge remained limited and largely ineffectual *vis-à-vis* a knowledge bound up, in one way or another, with power and possessions. It should, however, be added that this attempt at a counter-knowledge also contained a project of counter-power. This was intimately connected with the contestation as it mounted and became generalized during this period. But it was

704

not associated with its violent forms, such as the one which dispensed with any project, calling for immediate action, regardless of the consequences.

This project differed from the one presented in the first volume, because the latter had failed, become impossible. *Changer la vie?* Yes: but it was no longer conceivable or possible to liberate a sort of living core, to display the latent content of daily life. What had become of this core, this rich content? In 1960, they were in the process of disappearing, or had already disappeared. *Changer la vie?* A radical change was necessary, a revolution–subversion. The theory of revolution in and through daily life still sought to develop Marxist theses. It doggedly reminded people that social transformation cannot be confined to political forms and economic relations; that it runs the gravest risks of degeneration if it does not have the creation of a different everydayness as its goal and meaning.

The result, in this way of looking at things, is that subversion must work in tandem with revolution. Regrettably, what happened was that revolutionaries confined themselves to the politico-economic, whereas subversives distanced themselves from it. In short, these two aspects of the transformation of daily life were dissociated. Failure ensued. The critique of everyday life did not attain its goal, even if it was 'fashionable' for a time around 1968.

However that might be, here we must emphasize the *evolution* of the idea and project of *revolution* since its origin. At the outset, it was defined by Marx on the one hand by the *realization of philosophy*, and on the other by the unfettered growth of the productive forces. On the one hand, then, classical philosophy bequeathed to the forces of renewal, the creative capacities of the working class, its principal ideas – freedom, happiness, or quite simply the True, the Beautiful and the Good – for them to realize. On the other, this involved the end of the scarcity that is skilfully planned for the people, and the advent of abundance.

In the event, what happened? On the one hand, philosophy after Hegel and Marx gradually renounced the naive project of renewing the world through truth. The final blaze of this centuries-old project was Nietzsche's *Zarathustra*. Thereafter, philosophy stagnated and then withered away as it tirelessly wrote its own history. It drifted towards scholasticism (Marxist, Kantian-rationalist, or irrationalist). On the other hand, revolution could no longer be defined by growth, given that there was growth in the capitalist mode of production for which the state assumed responsibility; and that what is called the capitalist state succeeded in this task as well as (and sometimes better than) the 'socialist' state. Persisting with this definition, continuing to identify socialist revolution and growth, without even clearly distinguishing between quantitative growth and the qualitative development of society – did this not lead to a crisis of the idea of revolution? Did theory and practice not stand in need of redefinition? Clumsily perhaps, but stressing the main point, the critique of everyday life and related research sought to meet this exigency.

In these works, the study of daily life was carried out in accordance with dialectical procedures. Regarded and presenting itself as such, *positivity* – the programming of daily life – proved destructive of possibilities, even though it had many 'positive' reasons, of the strongest sort, for establishing itself in *reality*. As for negativity – that is, the critical element – it displayed an openness towards possibility. This dynamic internal to knowledge does not make it readily accessible. Around the middle of the twentieth century, it was still possible to capture the imaginary (the extraordinary, the supernatural, the magical, even the surreal, and hence the negativity) at the heart of daily life. A few years later, the imaginary came from without; it was imposed: photography, cinema, television, the world rendered a spectacle. It was now that the imaginary was discovered, and slowly but surely became fashionable. It was also discovered that the imaginary is sometimes identical with the logical (Lewis Carroll). Paradox: the imaginary kills imagination; the fetishism of the imaginary is constructed on the ruins of the imagination. This period of *dis-appropriation*, which provoked the radical protest movement, possessed an appearance that veiled its reality: the art of daily life or daily life regarded as an art and simultaneously 'positively' as a business. Its technical basis? Domestic appliances. A certain major brand launched a famous slogan at the time, which was as effective in advertising terms as it was mystificatory: 'X ... liberates women'. In fact, the positive advantages of this instrumentalization of daily life brought about a consciousness of enslavement. This paradox – another one – will surprise only those who are entrenched in *positivity*: quantified abstraction.

In short, it was under cover of practical innovations and undeniable technical progress that the forms of its own enslavement were insinuated into daily life, in conflict with those of liberation. Otherwise, these forms could not have been imposed. Daily life entered into the circuits of the market and managerial practice (the opposite of self-management), becoming a small business, a family subcontractor, subordinate to the dominant powers. This can extend to the 'self-management' of daily life.

14

The theory of a revolution in daily life was to have some unanticipated repercussions. Critical knowledge was going to spawn hypercriticism – at the extreme, sheer abstract negation of the existing order, rejection of the 'real' treated as a shadow theatre. It must be conceded and stated that this hypercriticism has had some disastrous results – for example, the extermination of humanism, philosophical support of human rights. On the pretext that humanism bore the marks of bourgeois liberalism and suspect ideologies, it was blithely trampled underfoot without anything being put in its place. On the road to hypercriticism, the ultra-leftist intelligentsia demolished all values, for excellent reasons, but in the process destroyed reasons for living. To employ an old metaphor, it sawed off the branch on which it was perched. This was suicidal behaviour. Moreover, the ideological representatives of this intelligentsia rarely took hypercriticism to its logical conclusion, that is, nihilism. Only a few writers – among them, Samuel Beckett – had the 'courage' to do that. Most of the intellectuals affected by hypercriticism accepted a compromise – living, or rather seeking to live, as if society was different from what it was; living outside this intolerable society, and yet within it. People made the best of the situation. In this little game, the so-called advanced intelligentsia gradually lost its credibility; by the same token, it compromised such effectiveness as critical thinking might still possess. This vague nihilism and incessant ambiguity produced a mindless voluntarism, in political action and everyday life alike.

The theoretical critique of work, adopted from Marx and Lafargue (*Le Droit à la paresse* – a text read and approved by Marx), *logically* entailed a rejection of work. Among the themes dealt with by Marx featured the triad, taken from Hegel, of 'need–labour–pleasure'. For certain tendencies, only the last term counted: the triad was dismembered in favour of hedonism. This is defensible when one notes that human beings today exercise only a tiny proportion of their potential for pleasure. In industrial societies, fascinated as they are by leisure, automation and information-processing, work is depreciated. This problematic cannot be overstressed; it accounts for some of the facts attributed to the 'crisis'. Around this time – between 1960 and 1980 – the old proletarian slogan – 'Those who don't work don't eat' – faded and vanished. However, the peremptory refusal of work ('Don't work!' 'Let it all hang out!') compromised a key demand by diverting it in the direction of absurdity. Obviously, this extremism could not speak to 'workers'; it could originate only in a certain middle class and an intelligentsia undeterred by paradoxes. What is more, if some people were saying: 'Don't work!', others – and sometimes the same people – were declaring: 'Stop consuming! Objects, get lost!'. There was, and is, a gulf between such slogans and critical analysis of the 'production–consumption' relation in daily life. Nevertheless, the stress laid on play, on the festival (naively regarded as immune to recuperation by existing society), provided a bridge; it made possible a compromise between the critique of everyday life and ultra-leftist extremism. The domain of the festival was extended: students spoke readily of 'violent festivals'; revolution itself assumed the appearance of a vast popular festival. Notwithstanding some profound disagreements, understanding and agreement were thus reached on various claims about what is possible. The general – and generally accepted – slogan *changer la vie* received a kind of complement, which made it more concrete: 'Make daily life a festival – make your body, time, consciousness and being something that resembles a work of art, something that is not content to give form to a lived experience, but transforms it.' Utopia? Once again, yes: utopia, impossibility. But for what is possible to come to pass, must we not desire the impossible? Thus developed, the theme and slogan *changer la vie* nevertheless remained incomplete, for the project specified nothing about space, the use of time, social relations. On the other hand, it explicitly involved an end to relations of *reproduction*.

15

During the same period, at the opposite pole, scientism was growing in vigour, if not in wisdom and beauty, with variants and implications that have already been indicated on numerous occasions: positivism, empiricism, epistemology, structuralism. The scientistic tendency rejected lived experience as a fact, alienation as a concept, and humanism as a project. Neo-positivism and its Marxist variant had no difficulty showing, or 'proving', that these concepts – alienation, the human – possessed no epistemological status. This seemed decisive to them; moreover, it was perfectly true. The stance of critical knowledge implies that such a problem is a pseudo-problem. These concepts have their reference point in practice and daily life, not in the pure knowledge baptized and consecrated by epistemology. If these concepts – social practice and daily life – lacked epistemological status, those who used them were untroubled by the fact. They declined to be dragged on to the terrain of epistemology, a terrain which seemed perfectly solid to the neo-scientists, but was in fact booby-trapped, mined, unstable. These theoreticians believed themselves to be liberated from all ideology by pure scientific knowledge, whereas they represented the ideology of scientificity or, if you prefer, scientificity become an ideology. Here we encounter one of the most curious paradoxes in an age full of them: the ideology of the end of ideologies. The error of these ideologues remains unforgivable: as from this date (1960 and subsequent years), rather than demanding an epistemological status for them, human rights should have been defended, illustrated, strengthened. Like the philosophers, epistemologists undermined these rights at their foundations, while also undermining those of thought. Indeed, what entity is more vague and more lacking in epistemological status than 'man'? Thought itself! Only mathematical logic, destined to be absorbed into machines, has a status of the kind that ideology strives to impose as primordial. Critical knowledge had no status!

In fact, two conceptions that did not feature in the categories of traditional philosophy were juxtaposed without ever confronting one another in debate – something that was always evaded by the dogmatists. Supporters of the one counted on positive knowledge, and exclusively on it; they defined life by the extension of such knowledge and its application. Even revolution occurred through the application of a positive knowledge contained in Marx and Lenin. Some of the most doctrinaire among them asserted that this knowledge extended from Thales to Lenin. In this tendency, lived experience is minimized; it is distrusted: to live is to know scientifically, and to make such knowledge the criterion of life. Lived experience – spontaneity – was held responsible for the problems and errors of consciousness, including those of political consciousness. Ultimately, lived experience disappeared: it was eliminated. It was reduced to the vacuum created by evicting certain elements from a vast combinatory constitutive of positive knowledge. Epistemological reduction, required for the construction of positive knowledge, focused, in the first instance, on this lived experience.

The opposite tendency, by contrast, counted on absolute spontaneity and on extolling lived experience, which was supposedly enough to transform daily life. Positive knowledge was mistrusted, in favour not so much of the irrational – an outmoded philosophical position – as of what springs up spontaneously, once the obstacles have been removed. Positive knowledge and power were among the obstacles. What this tendency sought to scale down was thus scientificity itself.

Is there room for a conception, an elaboration, which gives the conceptual and the experiential their due, which is not reductionist, but draws them both on to an expanding track, enriching them while critiquing them by one another? Submitting both to a creative activity comparable to that which produces works of art, without thereby aligning oneself with an aesthetic theory? One might suppose so. Meanwhile, confrontation between these hypotheses, tendencies and strategies did not occur. This was characteristic of intellectual life in France in the second half of the twentieth century: controversies were evaded. Instead of open discussions, there were allusions, indirect attacks, and sometimes insults. On one side, we witnessed the arrogance of the 'positivists'; on the other, the rage of the 'negativists', both of them employing *ad hominem* arguments. Similar contradictions ran through Marxism and Freudianism. Marx and Freud set out from a lived experience: social labour for the former; sexual libido for the latter. Both wanted to exalt this lived experience, in order to set it free: hence a revolutionary project on one side, and a project that was subversive in its fashion on the other. Up to now, both endeavours have ended in failure. Why? Among other reasons, it can be asserted that lived experience, thus marked out, has not escaped the sway of positive knowledge, the latter being formulated and codified in accordance with a systematization attributed to the founders.

Up to a certain point, the critique of everyday life followed the same path, with the same twists and turns. At the outset, it proposed to grasp and conceptualize the lived, while extolling it. Yet the very process of conceptualization is not without its drawbacks – among them, the domination of lived experience by the concept. It is clear that the problematic of positive knowledge cannot be avoided. Merely to communicate a project – whether in spoken or written form – it must be conceptualized. Even if the limits of conceptualization are carefully indicated, the process is not risk-free.

16

The Parisian penchant for cliques, clans and conspiracies was to aggravate the conflicts between partisans of *changer la vie* and varieties of scientistic dogmatism, without resolving them. The repositories of positive knowledge regarded themselves as highly superior to those who (as they saw it) were mere ignoramuses. Above all, they thought it would be possible to establish their propositions as definitive truths. Hence misunderstandings and disappointments. Hence also the splitting of Marxist thought into epistemological and critical stances. Hence, finally, manoeuvres on the philosophical and theoretical plane aiming to neutralize these opposed currents by means of one another, in order to dispose of any theory and leave the field free for empirically taken decisions. This brings us to around 1968, high point of contestation and critical thinking, as well as 'prosperity' and the economic miracle, that is to say, growth controlled by the state. In 1968, for the first time, and after various detours that we still do not clearly understand, critical thought again coincided with practice: the rapid rise of the movement, its no less rapid decline, accompanied by the separation of its constituent elements – thought and spontaneity, action and theory.

The critique of everyday life motivated the refusals and demands of the protesters by presenting a project. For the first time, theory was not focused on the past, on history and historical models; moreover, it was not content to propose an economic model. In and through counter-knowledge, it turned positive knowledge against itself, without abolishing it, but by opposing a knowledge of potentialities to ideologies of reality or models. It took its distance from classical positions in such a way as to open up different perspectives.

Another failure. A definitive one? We shall see. Pragmatists make success a criterion: what failed was bad and false. For his part, Nietzsche the anti-pragmatist understood that the decadent sometimes choose what is bad for them, propelling them along the path of decline. Unintended consequences and reverses have their perverse reasons. Moreover, for those who observe the radical labour of the negative, failures are not only failures: since Hegel and Marx, we have known that things also progress by the 'bad side'.

17

Let us jump forward to 1981. What is new? 'Everything,' declares the optimist with whom we are familiar, standard-bearer of realism and champion of modernism: 'Contestation is over. We are already in another era, post-industrial society, the information society ....' 'Nothing,' replies the nostalgic: 'The fundamental relations have not altered, only the discourse and rhetoric. Appearances notwithstanding, it is not the old constrictions that have been smashed to bits, but what remained natural and substantial in relations, proximity, warmth and any – what do you call the thing that has been made so much of since it ceased to exist? – any sociability!'

In 1981, problems are reconsidered and reformulated in terms of *crisis*. Hence many assessments depend upon the way in which this crisis is perceived and appraised. On this crucial point, however, there are significant disagreements, and the 'spectrum', as they say, of analyses and opinions is so wide that it is not easy to see how it remains a spectrum, since there are neither borders nor handle to control it. Some say: there is no crisis, simply a new division of labour on a world scale, as a result of technological progress; and, consequently, a displacement of the centres of production, wealth and power. If that threatens France, let it contrive to pull through with the minimum damage. Eurocentrism could not last for ever, nor could the historical privilege enjoyed by some countries (including ours) ... Others proclaim a total crisis: a crisis of everything that goes to make up a society, culture and values included. Hence a crisis of the Left as well as the Right. A terminal crisis, some go so far as to say, and, in the last analysis, an ineluctable one: catastrophe. A pessimistic conclusion, comes the rejoinder from the other side: the popular movement is fending off catastrophe, and will prevail. A simple economic crisis, declare a lot of realists, which is therefore bound to have political repercussions, good politics making possible the good economics that will lead us out of the crisis. Crisis of the capitalist economy or crisis of imperialism, say certain Marxists, who locate the epicentre of the global upheaval as follows: the relations between 'centre' and 'periphery' have shifted; there are new imperialisms which, although secondary, are active; on the other hand, various countries have embarked upon independent industrialization, and are discovering new roads. Even so, comes the response, the relations of hegemony, domination and dependency remain essentially the same ...

Among those who concede that the crisis is bringing about profound changes, simultaneously affecting labour and its organization, the way of life, modes of knowledge, the scale of recognized values, norms and conventions, many – whether conservatives or reformists – assert that the *enterprise* remains the site of these transformations. It thus supposedly escapes the crisis as a model, a solid, unchanging site amid the various changes. Some maintain that a privileged site of this sort – one that does not exclude productive labour, but incorporates it into a far larger space and time than the workplace and labour-time – is to be found in daily life, which does not escape the crisis but is transformed with it.

As for the crisis in general, a hypothesis is emerging which is rarely discussed, but has arguments in its favour. People always refer to the 'end of the crisis', a solution, a 'way out of the crisis'. They talk about containing or controlling it – which is what the word 'crisis', etymologically construed, suggests. The paradoxical hypothesis is that this 'crisis' cannot be reduced to a phase of instability between two stable periods: quite the reverse, it is becoming the mode of existence of modern societies on a world scale. Neither the thesis of a crisis of economy and society; nor that of a crisis of the bourgeoisie and the working class; nor that of a crisis of the middle classes as relatively stable supports of established institutions; nor the very widespread thesis of a critical period for institutions, values and culture – none of these accounts for the situation, does justice to its gravity or the extent of the problematic. Is not the phenomenon we continue to describe with a term that has become inadequate – crisis – more profound, more radical, than a mere difficult phase for the economy, politics, ethics and aesthetics? Might it not legitimately be thought that the 'crisis' will change these societies root and branch – in their 'anthropological matrix', their historical foundation, their economic 'base', and their superstructural apex? If this is the case, then the crisis is continuing the work of critical thinking, abandoned by thought. It (cor)responds in reality to those who did not want a considered, directed upheaval – something that was possible in 1968. Nothing will withstand this practical critique: the resistance of the existing order will sooner or later be swept aside, dissolved or shattered – even facile nostalgia and derisory optimism, which are complementary ideologies.

What are called modern societies will henceforth live under threat from within and without: threatened with ruin, decay, self-destruction; facing numerous challenges; exposed to unremitting attack. We must get used to the idea that a crisis of this order no longer has anything to do with 'crisis' in the classical sense; that constant invention is required to respond to such situations. Invent or perish! There is no definite or definitive solution, no model to emulate, only a road to open up and construct. This thesis goes beyond currently accepted theses, regarded as bold, on the 'serious crisis' or even 'total crisis'. It indicates the path that must be cut through the ruins. We must also get used to the paradoxical idea that this crisis is not some malady of society, but henceforth its normal, healthy state. A strong organism does not shrink back nervously, avoid risks and dangers, but on the contrary confronts them, acts and reacts accordingly. (It is true, however, that analogies between the social and the organic cannot be pushed beyond certain limits.)

Another, no less paradoxical implication: critical thinking tends to disappear or at least be marginalized, and possibly qualitatively transformed. The 'crisis' takes over the work of critical knowledge, continuation of ancient philosophy, the work that thought sought to accomplish, but which it could not see through to a conclusion. As a critical condition, the 'crisis' is critical thinking *in actu*. This thinking is superseded and realized; outflanked as knowledge, it becomes concrete.

What is left for it to do in its capacity as thought? First of all, to track the radical labour of the negative, the progress of the crisis through the world it engenders while tearing it apart. Possibly, what presents itself as positive (technology, etc.) will turn out to be negative; while the seemingly negative (the wrecking of institutions and values) will prove creative. The dissolution of traditional thinking and critical philosophy occurs on a dual basis: its failure and degeneration into hypercriticism; and the actively critical role of the crisis. This does not betoken the disappearance of dialectical thought and thinking *tout court*. Far from it! It means its renewal in and through a cultural revolution quite different from what has hitherto gone by that name. That said, there is no need to linger over the crisis of the theory of crises, of criticism, of Marxism as a critical theory or theory of crises, and so on.

This perspective does not involve a vision of apocalypse, a catastrophe; but it does not exclude them. The theory of permanent crisis thus replaces that of permanent revolution. The new state of the world, as of the thinking that strives to conceptualize it, could have unforeseen effects over and above such unintended consequences as can be anticipated.

By way of a preliminary question, we might also ask how we should characterize the existence of societies with respect to biological existence and cosmic energy. Is it a genuine problem? We will not know until the end of this study. An unduly famous formula has it that civilizations are mortal. Agreed: but the question posed here is rather different. Can societies survive without a trace of civilization – that is to say, style or, rather, grand style, high culture, and higher values – in a neo-barbarism? The most disturbing thing about organic life and nature is not merely death, but ageing. Everything is mortal: not only civilizations, but ideas, countries and peoples, classes themselves. Are they prey to the same fate as the living individual, reaching their term only through the slow, fatal loss of their vitality, their physical powers? Is daily life a site of decline? Or of attempts at sudden revival? Or sometimes the one and sometimes the other – a site of ambiguity, gambles and wagers?

If social life is subject not only to the organic law of evolution (birth, growth, decline and end) but also to the law of the dissipation of energy; if informational energy itself, and its transmission, are not exempt from entropy, then what are we to conclude as regards daily life? Is it not a site of dissipated energy, lost information, redundancy? This would amount to identifying in daily life an irreversible decline of the social, for which there is no possible cure. This is simply a hypothesis, examination of which we shall not evade. Possibly accepted and consented to in a vague sort of way, such a decline would render modern societies incapable of responding to increasingly numerous and urgent 'challenges', of understanding them, and even of formulating their problematic. From this viewpoint, daily life escapes the threat of obliteration only through its dullness, its ponderousness, its inertia, which make it unbearable.

How are we to dispel a state of confusion which grows from year to year, and certainly forms part of the world as it presents itself – that is to say, as we make it? Can the study of daily life still serve as a guiding thread through the complexities and sediments of modern society? A little later, we shall see that there is also a crisis of modernity. The situation, in the broadest sense of the term, will prove all the more difficult to grasp in that the *neo*, the *retro* and even the *archaeo*, which once, in the glory days of modernity, fought bitterly, are confused today. This also forms part of our world, and is an aspect we must stress right now. Around 1980, a rumour was doing the rounds that everything had changed, that we were entering a different era. The new philosophers, the new architecture, the New Left and New Right, even the *nouvelle cuisine*, sprang up simultaneously. There is indeed something new: but where and what? Illusion or reality? Potentialities, remote possibilities, or the consequences of decisions that have already been taken? There is indeed a neo-bourgeoisie, a new middle class, but they bear a close resemblance to the old ones, with fewer tics and added idiocies. The allegedly new is often only a revival that is unconscious of the fact. Sometimes people also wittingly revive religious, metaphysical and political themes, renovated like old palaces in historic cities: the new tacked on to the old. Some terminological innovations are enough to produce this effect. Fashion and culture have also become mixed up to the point of merging – an old phenomenon, but one that is increasing in scale. Anything that amounts to fashion is regarded as new. Clever advertising makes the neo contain the archaeo, and vice versa. Presentation and verbal packaging conceal the persistence and deterioration of the old in the allegedly new; they also conceal the fact that such exaltation of the archeo prevents the birth of what could spring from the genuinely new. By definition, fashion, even when it results from a cycle (the periodic return of forms), always passes for new. Otherwise, there would be no fashion! The cycle involves obliviousness of its own moments.

Thus, a closer analysis will be indispensable as regards modernity, the neo and the retro, seeking to define what persists under the illusion of the new; what is genuinely new; what is congealed in the old; what is regressing; and what is disappearing. No doubt this analysis will have to go into some points and areas more deeply, without abandoning a comprehensive perspective in the process. It is clear that sexuality and femininity in everyday life cannot be treated in the same way as techniques or the culture industry or the erosion of values.

To summarize: the object of this work is to resume critical analysis of daily life in the year 1981, referring to the previous analyses while trying to avoid their defects, and anticipating the future. The problem has changed. It derives not from a scarcity of material or ignorance of daily life but, on the contrary, from an abundance of material and a kind of excess of positive knowledge. The most cursory glance at publications of all sorts – on towns, on political life as well as private life – immediately informs us of these alterations. But what is their significance? Here our problematic emerges, and can be reformulated thus: is daily life a shelter from the changes, especially when they occur abruptly? Is it a fortress of resistance to great changes, or certain minor but significant changes? Or, contrariwise, is it the site of the main changes, whether passively or actively?

The upshot of these analyses, which remain incomplete, is that daily life cannot be defined as a 'sub-system' within a larger system. On the contrary: it is the 'base' from which the mode of production endeavours to constitute itself as a system, by programming this base. Thus, we are not dealing with the self-regulation of a closed totality. The programming of daily life has powerful means at its disposal: it contains an element of luck, but it also holds the initiative, has the impetus at the 'base' that makes the edifice totter. Whatever happens, alterations in daily life will remain the criterion of change. But that is to anticipate the conclusions of this work.

PART ONE

Continuities

1 End of Modernity?

Since the onset of what are called modern times, a standard question has involved the relations between tradition and novelty. It has prompted controversies like that of the Ancients and Moderns at the end of the seventeenth century; and continues to do so. It is not always clear what is at issue in these debates; sometimes that emerges only long after the quarrel – as with the concept of progress in the case of the Ancients and Moderns.

Today, another question is on the agenda: the end of modernity. This was noisily proclaimed as the 1980s approached. At the same time as an irruption of the new, people announced a reversion to tradition, but a reconsidered tradition – a tradition freed from ideology and authenticated by the test of time. The end of modernity heralded a great change, proclaimed from 'on high'.

It was unquestionably in architecture that the announcement caused the greatest stir. Common to technology, art, social practice and everyday life, the architectural is a domain that should not be underestimated or regarded as subsidiary. Developments in architecture always have a symptomatic significance initially, and a causal one subsequently. The Venice Biennale of 1980 was devoted to *postmodernity* in architecture – a slogan launched in the USA two or three years earlier. In what, according to its promoters, did it consist? In a return to monuments, a neo-monumentalism freed from the grip and imprint of political power, whereas monuments were, historically, expressions, tools and sites of the reigning powers. One ought (argued Ricardo Bofill) to go so far as to invert symbols.

So what is this modernity that has been wrecked during the current crisis, and renounced? Its reign dates from the early twentieth century, and ended around 1980. Portents of modernity can be detected earlier, but it did not flourish before the beginning of the twentieth century. Thus, around the 1900s, the 'modern style' made its appearance in France, promoting a kind of baroque: plant forms, curves and interlaces, a femininity indirectly suggested or directly expressed. Modern style soon succumbed to ridicule, and was replaced by modernity, which was more technical, more 'rigorous', sparer, distancing itself from the natural and not afraid to be sophisticated. The distinct lines of concrete replaced volutes. The amusing thing about this story is that the recent challenge to modernity is accompanied by a rehabilitation of modern style, which had in the interim come to be regarded as completely outmoded. It is pleasing. Symbolically represented by the exterior of the metro stations constructed at the turn of the century, it is admired in pride of place in New York's Metropolitan Museum and elsewhere.

Modernity begins with what might be called a silent catastrophe. Let us recall the key features of this singular event. Around 1910, the main reference systems of social practice in Europe disintegrated and even collapsed. What had seemed established for good during the *belle époque* of the bourgeoisie came to an end: in particular, space and time, their representation and reality indissociably linked. In scientific knowledge, the old Euclidean and Newtonian space gave way to Einsteinian relativity. But at the same time, as is evident from the painting of the period – Cézanne first of all, then analytical Cubism – perceptible space and perspective disintegrated. The line of horizon, optical meeting-point of parallel lines, disappeared from paintings. The gaze of the painter and the spectator skirts around objects, circles about them, catches the various aspects of the object simultaneously, rather than perceiving it from some privileged angle, be it a particular side of the object, or its surface or façade. At the same time, tonality in music was dissolved, and replaced by atonality, defined not by the 'dominant–tonic' pair but by the equivalence of all intervals. The classical unity of melody, harmony and rhythm in tonality disintegrated. At the same time, too, all coherent, developed systems broke up: philosophy, the city (the historical town), the family and the figure of the Father, history itself. Truth fell into disrepute. The crisis began with reference systems, that is to say, values and norms. Bizarrely, the First World War would soon foreshadow the end of Eurocentrism. Silent catastrophe prepared a noisy catastrophe: the safeguards had vanished.

What became of daily life in this unique mutation, which was not experienced or lived as such, and went unremarked by those acquainted with it (some of the most lucid of whom would later describe it – for example, Thomas Mann, Robert Musil, Hermann Hesse)? Daily life was consolidated as the site where the old reality and the old representations were preserved, bereft of reference points but surviving in practice. 'One' continued to live in Euclidean and Newtonian space, while knowledge moved in the space of relativity. Comparatively straightforward, Euclidean and Newtonian space still seemed absolute and intelligible because it was homogeneous and had nothing to do with time. As for time, it remained clock-time, and was itself homogeneous. People went on singing tonal melodies, with clear rhythms and harmonic accompaniment. They persisted with habitual perceptions and traditional representations, which were erected into eternal verities when in fact they derived from history, and had already been superseded in scientific knowledge. Daily life was certainly not immutable; even modernity was going to alter it. Yet it was affirmed as a site of continuity, exempt from the curious cultural revolution that set in train the collapse of European values constituted by the logos, active rationality, liberal humanism, philosophy, and classical art. Henceforth, thought and daily life, and thus theory and practice, parted company, taking different and divergent paths: audacity on one side, caution on the other.

From this upheaval emerged the three 'values' that were to make up modernity: technique, labour and language. The components of this triad would meet with different fates and follow distinct trajectories. Technique was gradually to become lord and master; like money and commodities under capitalism, it would take on an autonomous reality, escaping the grasp of thought, society, and even the state. It would spread as general power, simultaneously positive and negative, transforming reality and yet lethal (this includes nuclear technology). As for labour, it would become the rival of technique, privilege and supreme value under 'socialism' at the very moment when technology was discrediting it, because it promised – and doubtless enabled – the replacement of labour. Discourse? Language? They were to supply higher values – of stand-in and substitution – in Western societies. Hence the rise of linguistics and semantics, the incredible abuse of language games (from crosswords to puns and TV games), as well as discursive effects. In the West, and for the West, discourse was no longer a means of communication in the twentieth century, a generic and general tool of consciousness, but the way in which 'man' was installed in the world, and hence his relation to the world. The essence that had been abolished re-emerged in the place assigned to discourse. A particular discourse is 'valid' in and for itself, without reference to any other system than itself. Its apologists maintain that it is sufficient to the extent that it is necessary: it coheres as a function not of some truth or external reality, but of its own coherence. Meanwhile, opponents of this fetishization of discourse, and its unconditional valorization, maliciously observe that it involves the murder of language; language is dissolved along with what conferred meaning on it – that is to say, representations of the true and the real. 'One' – the impersonal speaker, now detached from the 'subject' – says anything, which is passed on to him via the '*one*'. The underlying, rarely stated project – 'Say everything! Voice what remains unsaid in what is said! Achieve uninterrupted speech!' – results not in speech that communicates, but in the dissolution of speaking and writing alike, by releasing uninhibited signification, itself separated from expression. Meaning lies dying. Rhetoric is unleashed. Freed from all ties, signifiers take flight. Thought disappears at the very moment thinkers believe they are thinking freely.

We cannot go into the concept of modernity and its critique in sufficient depth here to settle some rather serious questions. How should we assess what is called modern art, in its full range and diversity – painting, the novelistic literature often regarded as essential, but also music, architecture and sculpture – not forgetting poetry? And first of all, how is it to be situated? For Lukács, modernity and its idolatry accompanied the decline of the bourgeoisie, its decay as a class that was once in the ascendant and sufficiently bold to envisage the universalization of its concepts, values and norms. After Goethe and Balzac, creative potential within the framework of bourgeois society diminished, then disappeared. For the Marxist theoretician, the works of the decline bear its stamp. An increasingly sophisticated technology does not prevent art works or products being of no interest, especially when they claim to be 'interesting', and their only 'interest' is commercial. Let us cut short our evocation of this indictment. By contrast, for another renowned Marxist theoretician, Adorno, modern art possesses aesthetic significance and real value. Certainly, for Adorno, modern art works do not arise outside of their context, and cannot be compared with those of the Renaissance. They nevertheless secrete a profound meaning: they are the negative moments of their age, marking out the transformations of society and the world. Works of 'constructive deconstruction', they offer, if not the Truth, then at least truths about the unfolding process. They render it intelligible, precisely by virtue of those features which, for sectarian criticism, typify decadence: the systematic use of ugliness (from Baudelaire to Beckett), and its transformation into formal splendour through appropriate techniques; the absence of content and meaning, approximating to emptiness and nothingness, but only to skim them ("Twas brillig, and the slithy toves/Did gyre and gimble in the wabe'); or the use and abuse of imagery and discourse in Surrealism, in the return to rhetoric, and so on.

The debate between these two interpretations of modernity will remain inconclusive. It depends in part on the place allotted the negative in dialectical activity. Neither Marx nor Engels, and still less Lenin, accentuates the negative. No doubt Hegel went further than the dialecticians who succeeded him in stressing the profound 'labour of the negative'. If you believe that the negative consists solely in the other, reverse side of the positive; and, consequently, that it creates nothing, since it can only dissolve and decompose the positive to create space for what is to come, then Lukács's peremptory critique of modernity and modern art follows. If, on the other hand, you accept that the negative moment creates something new, that it summons and develops its seeds by dissolving what exists, then you will adopt Adorno's position ...

Today, this unresolved controversy is receding with modernity itself. Modernity appears as an ideology – that is to say, a series of more or less developed representations that concealed a practice. Modernity was promising. What did it promise? Happiness, the satisfaction of all needs. This *promesse de bonheur* – no longer through beauty, but by technical means – was to be realized in daily life. In fact, the ideology of modernity above all masked daily life as the site of continuity, by floating the illusion of a rupture with the previous epoch. Now that this illusion has been dispelled and modernity dismissed, discussions about its essence and significance have lost some of their interest. What survives of this period is the general slide from a concreteness derived from nature towards the abstract–concrete as the mode of social existence, something that extends to works of art. The predominance of abstraction in art goes together with the extension of the world of commodities and of the commodity as world, as well as the unlimited power of money and capital, which are simultaneously highly abstract and extremely concrete. The art work thus renounces its previous status: proximity to, and even imitation of, nature. It is detached and released from naturalism. This likewise goes together with the short-lived triumph of the most abstract signs – for example, banking and monetary dummy entries – over what remains of concrete reference systems.

The crisis has brought about the separation of modernity and modernism. If the career of modernity as ideology is over, modernism as technological practice is more than ever with us. For the time being, it has taken over from modernism as regards a possible real transformation of daily life. In short, modernity as ideology now appears as an episode in the development and realization of the capitalist mode of production. In contradictory fashion, this ideology provoked its own specific opposition: the heedless promise of novelty – immediately and at any price – has generated a return to the archaeo and the retro, the optimism of modernity becoming tinged with nihilism. From this great confusion emerges modernism: a clear field for the deployment of technology and the proclamation of the end of ideologies (the ideology of the end of ideology), and yet the advent of new myths to which we shall have to return, such as the myth of transparency in society, the state and political action.

How can we avoid the conclusion that the alternative – modernity or postmodernity – is false? Posed in this way, the question avoids the main thing: technological modernism, its import, its capacity for intervention in daily life; and the related problem, which is simultaneously theoretical and political, of controlling technology. Meanwhile, daily life goes on.

2 Constants

This refers to property, the family, morality, and so on. We hardly need remind ourselves that but a short while ago the family seemed very fragile, reduced to the couple, which was itself provisional, its unspecified mission ending with the increasingly early departure of children, and so forth. But now we are witnessing a consolidation of the family – not that this means a revival of the extended family, the large group of blood relations and collaterals. We shall return to this theme. The family is affirmed not only as a micro-centre of consumption and occupation of a small local space (a place), but as an affective group reinforced by a sense of solidarity, the moral complement of social security. This extends to a fraction of parental elders, without a clear distinction between its two components (blood relations and collaterals). Will it last? The increasing importance of the opposition 'insecurity–need for security' suggests that the decline of a grouping reinforced in daily life will occur only gradually, if at all. Added to this is 'home ownership', a mass phenomenon extending to the working class, and the result of a strategy long planned within the framework of the mode of production. It is sufficient to indicate this commonplace in passing.

Conservatism in daily life contrasts not only with revolution in and through daily life – a project that failed, leading to terrorism, hypercriticism and nihilism. It has causes other than those already mentioned – for example, the reference points that survived the collapse of the old systems. It also has some very strong social bases, such as the professions and the corporatist mentality, ownership and heritage in the traditional sense of the terms. Finally, and above all, a distant but decisive motive is the well-known fact that 'socialism' as we know it renders daily life impossible and unliveable. 'Socialism' seems to have assigned itself other goals and objectives – for example, the boundless growth of the productive forces, or the reinforcement of the state and its strategic power. While it is only too true that capitalism leads to the solitude of the individual or the family group in daily life – via the 'cottage', the car, the telephone and television, and tomorrow, no doubt, the home terminal and microprocessors – socialism obtains the same result by different routes: general mistrust and suspicion, the pressure of state ideology and internalized repression, the ethics and aesthetics of the pseudo-collectivity decreed by the state. Whatever political conclusion is to be drawn from this, it must be registered that in Poland in 1980 workers and the people in their entirety sought to take back control of their everyday life. The state wished to administer daily life, but, to say the very least, did not succeed in its aim. The new organization arose out of this failure. It declares itself self-managing at the level of daily life; and is intent on being such. According to the most clear-sighted Poles, 'Solidarity' is neither theology nor politics in the usual sense: it is 'ordinary life' emerging into the daylight, making demands, calling for help – sometimes incautiously, for it is on the brink of despair. Here, the left critique of the state is closely akin to the critique of everyday life: something we knew already.

That is how this society sinks into its 'crisis'. At the very moment when ideology, proclaiming the end of ideology, heralds the advent of the new, the older, the archaeo, resurfaces. To these – more or less veiled – economic, social and political contradictions, society adds contradictions between its norms and values. The malaise of civilization risks becoming intolerable – not so much for the elite as in daily life. New generations are already torn between the demand for satisfaction and disgust with those who are satisfied; between an expectation of unimagined happiness and a strong sense of being deceived, prompting them to outright rejection. Rejection of what? Of what is offered by way of either traditions or projects of renovation. People reject both repressive morality and any morality advocating sacrifice, whether in the name of religion or of some future revolution; both the work ethic and that of interest properly understood; both the values of altruism and those of calculated egotism. Sometimes people retreat into voluntarism in the name of constructive action, thereby running the risk of being flattened in daily life. This amounts to a failure to respond to the most urgent demands. A desire for uniformity and conformism then mounts like a wave, offering a glimpse of the possibility that one day everything – people and things – could sink into indifference and general equivalence. Unless, that is, a new wave of refusal and protest arises.

3 The World of Commodities

We are only too conscious of the fact that the world as currently established is not the product of revolution. Up until the middle of the century, it was hoped that the workers' movement would liberate all the peoples of the world from the capitalist and imperialist yoke, thus realizing 'humanity' on a global scale. But in their present form the world and planet derive, in the first instance, from the extension of the market and commodities to the entire earth, in an uneven process that has nevertheless swept aside all resistance. This does not mean that popular liberation movements have disappeared – far from it. But the world market exists; and it exerts very strong pressure on all countries.

So what is this commodity which defines the market, and has now conquered the globe or, more precisely, generated the global? The theory of the commodity is far from having been elucidated, still less universally accepted. As popularized in current interpretations of Marxism, this theory defines the product as an object, intended for exchange, which contains or crystallizes a greater or lesser share of average social labour, in conditions of average productivity in the society in question. This determines its exchange-value in currency (money). There is no need to query this thesis here by comparing it with other theoretical systems such as marginalism, and so on. It will suffice to register that it does not get us far: while it makes it possible to understand the economic and social status of the product, it does not enable us to understand the planetary extension of the market and the formation of the world market.

Lukács and various others took the analysis further by showing that, as a commodity, the object produced simultaneously contains and conceals the social relations that made its production possible. As a result, the commodity-fetish, accompanied by its ideology (fetishism in general, which takes the products derived from human activity for realities in themselves), ends up permeating social practice in the capitalist mode of production.

This theory involves the philosophical concept of alienation which, in line with Marx's own thinking, it extends to the economic. The thesis of alienation becomes that of reification. But this theory is also tied up with various implicit or explicit theses of Marx and Marxists as to the fragility of capitalism. Capitalism is supposedly held together only by the superstructural edifice, whose non-correspondence with the relations and forces of production is increasingly marked. Capital benefits from the fact that the relations of production are concealed at the stage of productive activity *under* – or, rather, *in* – products intended for exchange. According to this perspective, this does not render the institutional and ideological superstructures erected upon a fragile and already faltering base more robust. Crises, wars and revolutions will soon carry off this mode of production. One good shove by the working class – and the edifice will collapse!

Now, this does not correspond to what has actually transpired in the twentieth century – that is to say the solidity and flexibility of capitalism, and the skill of its leaders – for which we need a theoretical explanation. What accounts for the vigour of capitalism? The enduring strength of the states constructed by the bourgeoisie? The growth and technological progress in which the capitalist countries have held the initiative? Finally, and above all, how do we explain the formation of the world market and its power?

The theory of the commodity and of fetishism does not account for that market, of which we find only an incomplete study in Marx – one that is restricted to the world market prior to industrial capitalism, stretching historically from the sixteenth to the eighteenth century. In its extreme complexity (flows and currents), and extreme diversity (capital markets, raw material and energy markets, labour and technology markets, markets in finished goods and consumer durables, art markets, markets in symbols and signs, in information, etc. etc.), the current world market requires a different analysis from one that starts out from commodities and exchange. Otherwise, the whole theory collapses.

Take various quantities of different products: a of a product X (litres of wine, for example); b of a product Y (metres of cloth); c of a product Z (kilos of sugar); and so on. Here are these goods in front of me. I can use them (use-value); then they are no longer commodities. For them to be commodities – that is to say, for them to possess an exchange-value and be exchangeable against one another or with other products – it must be possible to write: $aX = bY = cZ = \ldots$ The series of products that have thus become exchange-values is limitless. But is there an end to this series, an ultimate 'good'? Yes: gold, guarantor of money, which is simultaneously found at the end of the chain, and alongside each term as money guaranteed by gold and defined relative to it. One can thus write: $aX = bY = cZ = \ldots = \omega$ (omega designating gold, located at the end of the infinite series). Or again: $aX(\omega) = bY(\omega) = cZ(\omega) \ldots$ Following Marx, gold is called the universal equivalent. In exchange, the materiality of the thing is momentarily erased by its form [*Formwechsel*]. Gold restores materiality to the formal. As a result, commodities are constituted as a non-finite, permanently open, and yet well-defined system of equivalents. The form of the commodity – which is simultaneously abstract and concrete, and whose content is goods and products – determines this system of equivalents. This poses the general question, which we cannot deal with here, of the practical mode of existence of socioeconomic forms.

Also to be noted is that in the unlimited series of exchangeable goods (objects and products), *three* goods enjoy a special role and a happy or unhappy privilege: sex, labour and information. In some respects they approximate to gold, in the sense that they are ubiquitous yet clearly situated. These activities, which are exceptional yet conform to the norm for exchangeable goods, the market and commodities, are carried on in daily life and obscure the system of equivalents to the extent of concealing it. Since Antiquity, sex has been sold and bought: prostitution – marriage. Recently, this business has entered directly into the circuits of exchange (sex shops, etc.). Moreover, sexual fantasy and imagery have widely penetrated the discourse of advertising and daily life; the sexual phenomenon in its own right has thus become the supreme commodity – the product that sells other products. The fate of labour is well known: in the modern age, since industrialization, labour features on the market – this was not the case with agricultural, artisanal, intellectual or spiritual activities, which escaped the harsh laws of exchange. The labour-commodity is special in that, by means of tools and machines, it produces all the other commodities (productive activity generating more market value than it is itself worth on the market – an obvious fact disclosed by Marx).

The latest of these privileged commodities is information. It has always existed, but only recently assumed the status of exchangeable product. The vast cycle and expansion of exchange, from primitive bartering onwards, seems to terminate with it. Exchange has conquered the world; or rather, shaped it. At the same time, an immaterial product has emerged from exchange that is abstract and concrete in its way: information. Is not information most deserving of the title of supreme commodity, commodity of commodities? Produced, it has material (technological) conditions; it requires investment and organized labour. It has a production cost. Once it is produced, it is bought and sold. But it is what makes possible all other exchanges: all the flows in which daily life is immersed. In a sense, it was always thus. But today, this strange, immaterial reality is produced in broad daylight. Information as such is as old as social life, in which information has always been transmitted and received. Specifically as a product, information is just starting out. In it, the logic of the commodity – that is to say, of equivalence – joins general logic, logic *tout court*, or consistency in discourse and statements. In fact – and this is extremely important – as a system of equivalents the commodity comprises a logic; it determines a language that modifies and unifies – globalizes – the languages of different societies. It is closely bound up with the general language of quantification. The fact that there is a commodity–world must be recognized and accepted. In its way, this world tends towards a sort of nothingness, through the abstraction of exchange, monetary signs, and the sign in general. But it never attains this limit. It is reinstated materially. Elements of a critical knowledge of it can be found in Marx, and elsewhere than in Marx – in contemporary social practice. It is in this way that the commodity can constitute and determine the global. As a real world, the world market cannot be conceptualized by a 'spiritual' activity pertaining to philosophy – that of Heidegger, for example, which nevertheless explored internationality as a horizon. Nor can it be conceived on the basis of empirical facts: the expansion of trade and the influx of increasingly sophisticated manufactured products. Such facts do not enable us to understand the possibility – the conditions of possibility – of the global. A straightforwardly economic or political theory of internationality underestimates phenomena that are planetary in scope. Only knowledge of the commodity as reality-producing gives us access to the global. This does not mean that it exhausts it – far from it. But it alone makes it possible to situate daily life in the global, and to assess the retroactive impact of international space on its own conditions, on the contradictions it contains.

One or two additional remarks. As a set or system of equivalents, the commodity has served as a model for other systems of equivalents: the contractual system, for example, based on a different form – reciprocity – as well as on the sequences and constraints determined by that form. Thus, modern society is constituted as a system of systems of equivalence. What is more, the state pronounces the general equivalence of these systems of equivalence; it guarantees and implements it. On the other hand, daily life is established thus: everything – the socio-economic-political whole – rests upon it. Ultimately, all moments would be equivalent in daily life. In that case, daily life would dissolve, as it were, like a bad dream. These limits – of daily life and of the sign – are never reached. The moments assert themselves. Each of them possesses a 'value' in the totality; in the absence of such a 'value', there would be no link between the moments of daily life. Yet they all logically tend towards equivalence. Within the system of systems of equivalence, a levelling occurs: not down to the lowest, and still less up to the 'highest' – the summit of society – but to an abstract social average. Assimilation, repetition, equivalence (calculable, predictable, and hence open to rational administration) – such are the characteristics daily life tends towards, characteristics which were already in evidence some years ago, but are becoming more pronounced. Everyday life managed like an enterprise within an enormous, technocratically administered system – such is the first and last word of the technocratic ethic: every moment anticipated, quantified in money terms, and programmed temporally and spatially.

Nevertheless, sexuality, labour and information retain a certain ambiguity and privilege in daily life. Intense instants – or, rather, moments – it is as if they are seeking to shatter the everydayness trapped in generalized exchange. On the one hand, they affix the chain of equivalents to lived experience and daily life. On the other, they detach and shatter it. In the 'micro', conflicts between these elements and the chains of equivalence are continually arising. Yet the 'macro', the pressure of the market and exchange, is forever limiting these conflicts and restoring order. At certain periods, people have looked to these moments to transform existence: to labour, in the name of socialism; to sexuality, in the name of freedom and pleasure, seeking to wrest it from the world of commodities; and finally, today, to information, to dominate and even dispel the world of material products and commodities. The failure of the first two endeavours, and the problems encountered by the third, indicate that there is no guarantee that we can open up a path in this direction. While it is definitely the case that sexuality and labour can, in their own ways (sexuality through erotic exhilaration and the joy of being in love; labour through strikes and rebellions), at least momentarily break the link between exchange-value and daily life, it may be that information-processing has arrived to complete the empire of commodities and the course of daily life. Unless, that is, it affords an opportunity and a conjuncture that are conducive to 'socialization' of a new type, one that would draw the totality on to other paths. Whence a problematic that has already been hinted at.

4 Identity

Among the factors of continuity, national identity – its acquisition and preservation in the course of the 'crisis' – must be accorded due importance. It corresponds, at the summit, to identity in daily life at the foot. Historically established on the basis of the home market and centralized state power, French identity was asserted and confirmed during revolutions and wars. Today, this formal identity, like the realities to which it corresponds – country, fatherland, nation, state – is under threat on all sides. These threats, which might lead to a loss of identity, are the object of numerous complaints. Is not the 'loss of identity' we hear so much about the (or a) contemporary form of alienation, without being named as such? The pressure of the international tends to break up national identity, by dissolving the sense of belonging to a political and cultural community. Likewise from below, if we may put it that way, with differentialist pressures: regions, towns, local communities. Compromised and even shaken, to a certain extent national identity is everywhere in search of itself and seeking to preserve itself. The tremors are inducing veritable panics. Is the groundswell of these terms – loss of identity, search for identity – at all levels, from the individual to the continental, an accident? No, it has a meaning. Where is Frenchness to be found? Is nationalism, whose pronounced return is becoming menacing, a recovery of lost identity or its ideological simulation? Whatever happens, the preservation of identity signifies the use and abuse of commemoration, the return of the historical as a system of reference, and pressure on daily life to prevent its 'destabilization' and preserve it as a locus of identity. This thus implies a tendency towards the reproduction of relations of domination in identity – a process that is not without its obscurities and uncertainties. Even so, we must distinguish in national identity between reality and ideology: the domestic market and the 'national' culture (in France, for example, the traditional rationalism whose national character is obscured amid the crisis – all the more so in that it is related to the European and Western logos, which is itself in crisis). This identity operates in the direction of non-development – in other words, of conservatism. It strengthens resistance to change, even as the urgent need for change in order to modernize national life is proclaimed elsewhere. Is it not weird that people so often refer to '*la France profonde*' in connection with backward corners, out-of-the-way villages, and small towns frozen in archaism? This Frenchness is obsolete, antiquated; yet it is exalted on television and in the press. Are not some harsh truths being masked under manipulative ideologies here? On the surface, France can be characterized thus: advanced ideologies and retarded structures, which are incredibly difficult to shift (constituent bodies and orders, frozen institutions, etc.). As for what is called '*la France profonde*', it is marked by ideologies that are as retarded as its structures.

We know that the major reference systems – the Town, History, the heavenly or terrestrial Father – have disappeared since the beginning of the century, releasing elements that were previously subordinate – among them, technology. Yet at the heart of daily life, tacit or explicit references persist that are more modest than the major systems of the past, but sufficiently solid and proximate to serve as reference points, if not safeguards. The private family, for example, which survives as a public service. This objective basis – mutual aid in a society that is, to say the least, difficult – does not preclude ties of affection; it keeps them in order. Various theoreticians of information and audiovisual techniques maintain that they do not alter the family reception of messages and images in the slightest – and never will. Simultaneously identified with and loathed as a prison, the restricted family survives, identical to itself and part of the general identity. The same goes for religion, a recourse in the face of anxiety, which is held in disrepute but nevertheless remains strong. Finally, and above all, the same goes for property, which is reassuringly solid – a bastion against all the world's onslaughts: it is valorized anew, with its train of institutions and rites, such as wills. These observations have nothing new or surprising about them, but must be included in any picture of what persists in the identity of daily life. Considered thus, private property is not confined to property in the means of production; it is not simply a means of participating in production and surplus-value. Individually or jointly owned flats (half the French population own their own homes), second homes – these serve not merely an economic function, but a function in terms of security, and hence of identity. Their purchase represents an investment: 'Invest in bricks and mortar'. At stake is certainly ownership and wealth, but also an ethical, and even aesthetic, value. The same goes for rural landownership, which maintains a long tradition – more so than the ownership of bricks and mortar. State and society, as they are, create anxiety, and compensate for it – that is to say, a demand for security that is closely bound up with the need for identity and continuity. The owner of a house is there for life, especially if he earned it by the sweat of his brow. He has his place in space. He dwells in the Same, and the 'other' cannot assail him or drag him out. He is installed in the identical, the repetitive, the equivalent. The permanence of property symbolizes, and at the same time realizes, the continuity of an ego. This ego unquestionably lives a better life in its own property than when it is exposed to anxiety in accommodation that might be lost from one day to the next. These commonplace details make up the mundane character and, consequently, the vigour of daily life. Like the personal objects that form the immediate environment around an individual or family group. To be attached to objects, to privilege them affectively, is today, as in the past, to create a shell or a bubble – that is to say, a protective layer against the assaults of a hostile world. This protection is simultaneously apparent and real, lived and valued as such. The more threatening the outside world becomes, the greater the importance and continuity of the interior – that which surrounds or protects subjective interiority. Disdained during the years of protest, things become 'goods' once again; the environment forms an integral and integrated part of the 'person', of their identity. Whether the objects constitute a system, whether they derive from a more or less rationalized and functional combinatory, is an important, but ultimately secondary, issue. Like the technicization and mechanization of familiar objects, studied by Siegfried Giedion in *La Mécanisation au pouvoir*. Far from imposing a new form on social relations, this mechanization, which involves personal existence in technology, strengthens the identity of daily life: it encloses it, rather than opening it. Take, for example, the mechanization of the bath.[1] Capitalist and bourgeois Europe made the transition from public baths, meeting-place and site of social life, to the bathroom, in which each member of the group is isolated. The mechanical function of 'cleanliness' was enhanced at the expense of bodily relaxation and restoration on the one hand, sociability on the other. Antiquity, by contrast, switched from the private bath to magnificently equipped public (thermal) baths.

This far-reaching dynamic of privatization and identification in the private sphere began a long time ago; it is being strengthened; it separates the private from the public, at the risk of causing a backlash – that is, the confusion of the private and the public. The latter, subordinate to political power and the state, can go and find the 'private' individual at home and draw him out of his shell like some edible snail. Isn't this what happens with certain objects, including the television set and the microprocessor? Public and publicity go together.

Domestic appliances have certainly altered daily life. By opening it out on to the world? Quite the reverse: they have aggravated its closure, by reinforcing repetitive everydayness and linear processes – the same gestures around the same objects. Let us note once again that 'household' appliances have not liberated women; they have made liberation movements possible by alleviating daily drudgery. Only then did specific demands regarding divorce, contraception, abortion, and freely chosen maternity emerge. Something new makes its appearance here. These aspirations, which have given rise to conflicting movements, were inconceivable when birth and death alike were the preserve of God the Father, Creator of Heaven and Earth. This remains the official teaching of the apostolic Roman Catholic Church, and is fiercely defended by it.

5 Everyday Discourse

Indeed, faith – shaken today, because it is prey to all sorts of contradictions – consists above all in this certainty: beginnings and ends,
creation and destruction, depend upon the Lord, his goodness and his
ire; they must therefore bear a sacred character. Men, and even more
so women, have only to accept this magical-metaphysical-mystical
dependency. Evolution pertains to the human; the event or advent
possesses a metaphysical significance and an ontological sense: it
derives from the eternal. This is conveyed by the solemnity of the
words attaching to these 'facts', which are not facts as such, because
they rupture the factual sequence. Faith of this sort once intervened
powerfully in daily life; it governed it. Has it disappeared? No, though
it is weaker. Hence a certain continuity, but also something different
that insinuates itself into the fabric of daily life: a more concrete
freedom, a secularization of the events that punctuate private lives –
births, marriages, deaths. This is a contradictory process. Many
people who do not practise religion and its rites, who have 'lost their
faith', continue to get married in church, have their children baptized,
evoke or invoke the divine in discourse. Religion persists through
several processes: rites and gestures, but also words, and the sacraliza-
tion and hence valorization of the crucial moments of existence. This
consecration of beginnings and ends paradoxically guarantees the
continuity of daily life. At the same time, it intensifies these moments,
dramatizes them, and imbues them with a kind of cosmic significance,
under the gaze of the 'hidden god'. Religion continues to impart
meaning to daily life – no doubt because it has yet to discover a different meaning.

Has everyday discourse changed much in half a century? Not
really. In some respects, it has been impoverished, reduced to 'basic
French'. In others, it has been enriched. We do not have a language
of daily life alongside the language of the commodity, or that of the
unconscious or science. Thus there are not several languages, but
various uses of the language, of each language. Nevertheless, new
words laden with meaning are making their appearance. So, the technocratic elite has its own vocabulary, which is gradually penetrating
ordinary language: *target* (an objective) or *niche* (an available space).
Other examples include the disturbing *position oneself*, or the curious

way out for 'mistaken'. New generations have their lexical innovations: *trip* and *flip*, straight out of the Anglo-Saxon countries, or 'having butterflies' to express nerves. This enrichment of vocabulary does not greatly alter everyday discourse, or its tendency to eliminate many terms of the best French as rather ridiculous archaisms. But this occurs together with the opposite tendency. Used by the middle classes, but also by popular strata, traditional sayings have been preserved. People still say: 'It never rains but it pours', 'what will be will be', 'he who laughs last laughs loudest', 'to put one's shoulder to the wheel', 'you've made your own bed, now you must lie on it' ... Proverbial wisdom has scarcely changed – which is sufficient to demonstrate the continuity of daily life. The semantics of proverbs must take account of a fact that is surprising, to say the least: it seems to indicate that practical situations are altering only very slowly, despite the enormous technical equipment surrounding and penetrating the everyday; despite the pressure of events and other pressures ...

Perhaps this is not the main thing. Lexicon and vocabulary do not determine the peculiar tonality of everyday discourse. Theoretically – philosophically – considered, this discourse is neither true nor false, although it is always presented as veridical. It is constantly organizing the conditions of existence of the group: the family, the office, the workshop, the firm, and so on. Even those who claim to be engaged in what is called plain speaking never say everything they have on their mind or in their heart. Can any social group bear to hear the truth about itself? When the truth emerges, the group risks splintering. The truth is always cruel: however 'spiteful' one considers the everyday nuisance who says what he sees and thinks, once the truth is out, it follows its own course. It most often emerges in daily life during 'scenes', for which it supplies the dramatic interest. For a 'scene' to occur, a discussion, initially muffled and toned down, must escalate, and a dispute or quarrel must loom – spirits with hands like glowing coal, fire in their eyes. The risk is that people will go to the heart of the matter and say what is best left unsaid, or what it is simply not done to say. The reality and truth of relations in daily life, including relations of force, then strike people all at once, and they are appalled not to have understood daily life once the event has finally transformed it. Without stating it, everyday discourse plays on the relation between truth (ineffable, even unknown) and non-truth. What is involved is a saying meagre enough to seem hypocritical, but not meagre enough not bring misanthropy to bear. It is a permanent wager. Daily life and its discourse are thus built on ambiguity, on a carefully arranged compromise. This not very historical compromise constitutes the mode of existence of the everyday – something that understandably displeases most adolescents. 'Scenes' and altercations cannot go on for ever; they exhaust themselves. People then revert to compromise, though the dispute and what is at issue in it will resurface in the near future. For there always is something at stake, even when it is not visible. Quarrels are always filled with unresolved – and often insoluble – problems: so much so that 'compromise' and 'ambiguity' mean 'adaptation and sociability by acceptance'. One must take people as one finds them ... This adage of everyday wisdom, and even political wisdom – adopted by Lenin – says precisely what it means. One remedy – or, rather, palliative – is humour, which has nothing in common with irony. The everyday gives rise to its own kind of humour: the humour of the office or workshop, family humour, and so on.

Humour is distinct from the bitter gibe as well as the sarcasm that figures in quarrels; and from the irony that evinces an unforgivable distance. Humour lightens daily life; it takes it lightly; it makes possible a discourse that can consent without capitulating. For humour accepts things: more precisely, it accepts the situation by veiling it, by sometimes covering it with a kind of affection, by remaining within it. It may be that despite humour, or in its absence, the situation degenerates, deteriorates in distressing or sickening fashion, especially when relations of dependency and domination are superimposed upon affective relations and specifically social (community) relations.

Dramatized, daily life explodes and its discourse shatters. Yet it lends itself to dramatization. Did not tragedy aesthetically elaborate what are commonly called domestic scenes – Agamemnon and Clytemnestra – or family disputes – King Lear's daughters, and so on – taking them to a climax? With one essential condition: that the scene is always played out between the powerful. Escalation starts with discourse and discussion, moves on to a dispute and a quarrel, and ends up in a bloody drama. The included middle – the fatal deed – then makes its appearance. Somewhere, there is always a rupture, a possible or actual murder. The everyday always contains comedy and drama, 'roles' that are more or less well played. Theatre pushes mundane drama to the point of Tragedy, and the comedies of daily life to the point of buffoonery. The everyday remains analogous to an improvised performance of a bad *commedia dell'arte* by ham actors. Sometimes a crime of passion, or a moral or political crime, is committed – after which it is buried, in everyday life as at the theatre.

Everyday discourse thus has a stable content, a core or foundation, which is bound up not (as the classical thesis has it) with an unchanging human nature, but with the fact that social relations have for a long time, if not always, been relations of force, authority and power, dependency, inequality in power and wealth. Such relations are tolerable only when they are masked. Stripped of all veils, they would be unbearable. Daily life and its ambiguity, simultaneously effect and cause, conceal these relations between parents and children, men and women, bosses and workers, governors and governed. For its part, critical knowledge removes the screens and unveils the meaning of metaphors. It demonstrates that what makes the functioning of societies possible is neither self-interest on its own, nor violence, nor the imaginary, but the (an) ethics inherent in discourse. At the heart of daily life and its speech we find ethical values, which are supports of social life in that they make it tolerable. Discourse and daily life cover the harshness and brutality of structural relations, the skeleton of society, with a weak but soft flesh. Are not the deep structures of speech and writing procedures – empirically discovered and established procedures – for preserving in one and the same present disparate elements, some of which derive from the past while others are merely potential? Take the sentence and the sequence of spoken or written sentences. This has its foundation in daily life as the reign of what is current – the preservation of its conditions – over past and future alike: the reign of the present, not of presence. Nothing in daily life dies. When someone passes on, people say: 'life goes on …'. It must indeed go on: the family, the workplace and the firm, the office, the entire society. Roles require continuity. Yet one occasionally wonders whether nothing in the everyday dies because everything is dead already: the repetitive buried under its own repetition, at once unknown and too well known, hidden beneath the surface of the wilted rhetoric of humdrum discourse. Is there an everyday life or an everyday death? Taken to a radical extreme, should not the critique of everyday life declare that life and death tend to merge in modern daily life? But we must know how not to go too far, how not to push critique as far as hypercriticism. Daily life is where 'we' must live; it is what has to be transformed.

The more daily life and its discourse bury life by eliminating death, the more they are consolidated in general ambiguity and compromise: between life and death, presence and absence, thought and non-thought; between the resolve to resolve and thinking that one might think, the creative and the repetitive, desire and non-desire, sublime heights and unfathomable depths. A compromise still obtains between self-loathing and self-love (the *amour-propre* of the Augustinians and Jansenists), between hatred and love both of what is close and of what is remote; and it always has obtained.

As they encounter more obstacles, barriers and blockages than ever in modernity, how is it that so many people have not realized that they were coming up against the boundaries of daily life, boundaries that are invisible, yet cannot be crossed because of the strength of daily life? They come up against these boundaries like insects against a window pane. And yet can people live informally, prepared for anything, in unrestricted, unorganized freedom? Is carrying chaos within oneself sufficient to give birth to a star? Does this not mean that daily life harbours the site, if not the content, of a creation which transforms it, and is to be accomplished? But possibility does not betoken reality.

Hence the strong need to break up daily life, to go off elsewhere, in deeds and not only in words: travel, tourism, caravanning, escapism, drugs and picking people up (the hippie movement), the disdainful attitudes of those who think the world is to be changed through contempt. Hence, also, the fascination evinced by endless discussion of the life of those commonly thought to transcend daily life: Olympians, stars, champions, millionaires, political leaders. And its opposite: readers and spectators then have the satisfaction of discovering that these people live like everyone else; that they suffer from identical illnesses and the same twists of fate. Everyday life is obsessed by what it perceives above it, and readily attributes non-everydayness to it. Through a familiar effect, this induces a new degeneration in daily life: at the extreme, the solitary who dreams of interaction, oneness, crowds. All this has been said many times, but usually from a moralistic standpoint – which is different from the attempt to situate such fascination, as well as its compensations, in daily life by demonstrating its ambiguity and wisdom, artificially complicated to the point of delirium.

While we must call upon fragmented disciplines and sciences such as psychology, history, sociology and so on, to elucidate everyday discourse, and replace it with a conceptual language that makes the transition from the experiential to the conceptual, it would not appear imperative to deconstruct this everyday discourse in order to construct an adequate text. What would that be? Written? Multidimensional? Would it bring to light representations that remain implicit? The underlying and the latent? The depth of lived experience? No doubt. But do we need to invent a jargon? And why invent words? The relation between everyday discourse and the discourse of a knowledge of daily life resembles the relation between the language of the theatre and ordinary language: the same, but different – the same, in another style.

These incursions into and excursions around everyday discourse do not exhaust it. Far from it. They have simply situated it. To proceed with the analysis of continuity in daily life, must we entertain the hypothesis of a latent discourse with psychoanalysts? Yes and no. Yes, in the sense that its elucidation involves making it explicit, unfolding or opening out what is found not below discourse, but in it – beginning with the language of commodities and the gradual extension of equivalents. No, in the sense that there are no grounds for positing a kind of mysterious substance – the unconscious – from which discourse issues while disclosing and veiling it. The everyday content of the discursive form is simultaneously and inseparably individual and social: the social is the content of the individual, invariably unrecognized as such; and vice versa. The elucidation of everyday discourse brings them out of one another and their mutual incomprehension. Providing, that is, it extends to everyday ethics and aesthetics, which exist, if only in the form of denotation – that is, simplistic metaphors and rhetoric: 'How ugly ... But isn't it dreadful! ... Now that – that's nice, that's beautiful. I like that ...'.

Should we adopt from sociology the hypothesis that there are representations which are specific to a society, and pass over into everyday discourse? Yes and no. Such representations exist, but they derive just as much from individuals and their inner depths as from society as such, in a process of constant interaction and conjunction. Contrary to what sociologists (the Durkheimian school) have imagined, representations are not external to individuals. Should we retain the idea of an evolutionary process, a formation, from history? Certainly, but not in the sense of a historical time: we are dealing with a simultaneously subjective and objective time – a subjective time created and measured by the outside in an unremitting confrontation. Finally, should we distrust psychology or draw inspiration from it? Both! Psychologists generally put their trust in psychic 'facts'. Yet everyday discourse and the daily life of discourse involve an ignorance of their own conditions. Nevertheless, these conditions are in them, appear in them: they simply need to be brought out.

Everyday discourse performs an important function: translating into ordinary language – that is to say, decoding in an accessible form – the sign systems and different codes employed in a society, from place signs to codes of courtesy and good manners, to the more or less secret codes of the bureaucracy. Unbeknown to itself, everyday discourse performs this continuous, indispensable labour. On the other hand, it is true that this discourse serves as a vehicle for representations; it consists in a flow of representations. Each word entails a succession of words, attached as 'connotations' to literal denotation. People are only too ready to believe that daily life uses only the denotative: a cat is a cat. In fact, connotations abound and overrun denotation, which does not mean that there is a codified rhetoric of daily life. But in a particular group or milieu, what is connoted is so heavily stressed that it is reduced to the rank of denotation. This is how evaluation, which is most often moral but sometimes aesthetic, works in daily life. What common sense regards as bad or ugly is thus expressed in demonstrative terms, which indicate the thing as if they were pointing to it: 'That's ghastly ...'.

Can we talk in terms of a *system* of representations that is inherent in daily life? This question has been examined elsewhere.[2] In brief, the answer is yes and no. Representations are displaced and substituted for one another. Accordingly, it is difficult to classify them into systems – all the more so since they contain multiple contradictions. They are neutralized or strengthened: in the latter eventuality, they sometimes conglomerate into cores, strong points. They involve more or less powerful values that strive to predominate and impose a certain coherence. In this way, they furnish materials and cases for philosophical and ideological systems, to which they sometimes approximate. Tendencies towards dogmatism are not foreign to daily existence. This is how practical and representative rationality functions in the modern world. If there is a system, it derives from either positive knowledge, or political power and its influence, or both; it would seem that systems derive not from representations as such, but from their methodical elaboration. Nevertheless, representations, as instruments of communication, can be practically elaborated in systems that are inscribed in 'reality' – for example, in architecture.

A kind of venerable Manichaeanism is still with us, and tends to crystallize into a system in daily life. The old paradigm 'friends and enemies – neighbour and stranger – pure and impure – light and darkness – good and evil ...' continues to govern much discourse and inspire much action. On many occasions, it has even been extended: socialism and Marxism are supposedly enemies, dark forces, impurity, evil and calamity.

Upon analysis, certain standard representations contained in discourse turn out to be highly complex, even paradoxical. In daily life, they are accepted without any difficulty. For example, death-in-life, with its opposite: living death. The dead survive in photographic documents; people recognize them; the absent becomes present once again, and people are moved. One should not speak ill of the dead. They are referred to in words that identify them with misfortune, not nothingness: 'My poor father ...'. A visit to the cemetery with flowers on All Saints' Day reawakens the dead by giving life to memory. As for death-in-life, a more explicit analysis might evoke dead gods who come back to life, the heroes and kings who reappear in history and the theatre. Everyone understands ghost stories. That is to say, death-in-life is the great presence–absence in the most elevated works and daily life alike. Is this not the figure, its strangeness softened by familiarity, which forms the link between everyday life and great works?

A string of relations between the living and the dead is thus woven into the heart of everyday life. The photograph and the mask keep these relations alive. The mask, the replica that clings to the skin, is closely related to the absolute other, the deceased. It reincarnates him, transforming the one who wears it into one of the living dead. Paradoxically, this produces a moment of festival, for death is overcome. This festival shatters daily life – or, rather, extends it by magnifying it – whereas the photograph and the image (the portrait) help to shore up its continuity.

Could we not say the same of representations as of power? The sovereign has always been regarded as immortal: son of the gods, his death immortalizes him. He is prince, king, emperor for life and beyond, because he is close to the Lord and the eternal Father. Thus, among the attributes of power was immortality, simulated by embalming and monumental tombs, and fostered on a daily basis by commemorative ceremonies. Everyone understands it within everyday life. The honesty and fidelity of 'subjects' are registered by the fact that they know themselves to be mortal. But they, too, can sometimes demand their share of immortality, through property and inheritance, mementoes, the cemetery and a plot in the cemetery. We know that in Egypt revolts were staged to democratize the immortality of the pharaohs. Modern cemeteries attest to an analogous democratization.

Despite the bizarre aspects running through it, everyday discourse is generally clear. Why? Because redundancy – that is to say, repetition – is the basis of intelligibility. Information theory teaches that redundancy is measured like information itself, since they are inverse quantities: $R = 1/1$. There is information only if there is no sheer repetition. However, pure information – a total surprise and an utter disordering of the elements of the code, or a highly unlikely combination – would be unintelligible. This occurs in screams, sobbing, which are ultimately inarticulate. Consequently, it is the mundanity of everyday discourse that makes for its intelligibility. It is maintained in redundancy: banalities and commonplaces.

Everyday discourse consists in spoken words; voices emit it. It is written badly. When literary discourse seems to approximate to it, it is in fact transcribed and transformed by being transposed. In everyday discourse, as opposed to literary writings, the denotative predominates. This does not contradict an earlier analysis: connotations feature in daily life only when they are reduced to the denotative, immediately linked as values and implicit evaluations to the words used and objects referred to. This impoverishes yet clarifies the discourse, giving it the appearance of a chain of signifiers such that it can be followed, recalled, even inverted. In daily life, time and discourse, everything, *seems* reversible, unlike historical time and natural time, as well as subjective duration. Daily life and its discourse tend to be installed in a space that has priority over temporality. A (seeming) simultaneity obtains. This sets traps for memory and thought alike. The equivalence 'intelligibility–redundancy' is not unimportant in establishing daily life, or in the domination of the linear over the cyclical, even though the latter persists in the alternation of day and night, hunger and satiation, going to sleep and waking up, and so on. Obviously, the intelligibility of daily life remains 'superficial'. Much more than that: it constitutes the surface skimmed by reflection, the fake mirror shattered by thought. The surface determines depth and height alike.

This predominance and equivalence assimilate daily life and its discourse to logic and logistics. Daily life requires us to be logical; otherwise, we are accused of inconsistency. Most of the statements made in this discourse contain a subject and a predicate linked by the copula. This copula, whose function and meaning pose so many problems for philosophers, poses none for interlocutors in daily life. 'The table is dirty', 'the soup is salty', 'the Hoover is bust', and so on. This logical lack of imagination seems to exclude any dialectic. Yet everyday discourse does not exclude provocations, challenges, argumentativeness, retorts, and consequently insolence, sophistry, even eristics, and so on. This reintroduces into it something that is not reducible to logic.

Symbols and metaphors abound and proliferate in commonplace remarks and informality: 'It's clear', 'it's not clear', 'he's doing me a favour', 'the chilliness of this reception', 'he parted on very cold terms', 'he made some warm remarks', and so on. These basic symbols are flattened out in the prose of everyday life, whereas nonquotidian discourses – of literature, the theatre or poetry – revive and amplify them. Daily life would be reduced to its reversible continuity were this one-dimensionality not continually interrupted, making way for dreams, daydreams, fantasies – everything that is called 'the imaginary' – but above all for the 'scenes' which, as we know, purge it through a rudimentary catharsis – rather as classical crises purged the economy of surplus factors.

745

In the course of their displacement and conflictual relations, repre-sentations collide and clash. They are thus put to the test in daily life. While one adman associates health with the representation of a pot of yoghurt, another, promoting for a different brand, will link the same image with 'velvety smoothness'. Who will decide between them? Consumers. Although they are manipulated, they still have a small margin of freedom: they will choose. 'Choosing' is represented in daily life as a value that manipulation does not destroy, but exalts. It might be that one of the two representations cited above succeeds, or fails. The same goes for political representations: rival candidates for power fight via the intermediary of their representations – in other words, their 'brand images' as developed by specialists in political marketing.

Manipulative and manipulated representations make it possible to disconnect in daily life what is linked and should remain so; and to confuse what should remain distinct. This effect derives from the fact that ordinary representations obscure what is represented, become mixed up or separated, depending on the intention of the manipula-tor. It has been possible closely to track the effects of such manipulation in urban questions: the way in which the fragmentation of the urban, breaks and ruptures, the separation of functions that were once performed in unitary fashion in historical space, have been made acceptable; or the way in which a confusion between the order of established power and the order of daily life has been perpetuated.

In daily life as a lottery, the actor-player budges only in wagering on his luck and bad luck: he will achieve some particular goal or result through mockery, courtesy, charm, irony, and so on. He always has an objective. But what is really at stake is only rarely represented – and then badly. During the action and discourse, it generally remains unseen: what is going to happen? What is going to emerge? Defeat or victory? Unless what is involved is a specific gamble, a settled bet. Then you place your stake on the table and the game commences. Daily life? It is now suspended, if not ruptured. The relation between play and daily life is a conflictual one. Yet the game does not succeed in vanquishing the everyday; it remains a moment.

6 On Vulgarity

Vulgarity is hard to define. But who can deny its 'reality', especially inasmuch as it consists in a certain way of being 'real' and understanding the 'real'? It is usually contrasted with *refinement*; yet this distinction belongs to the realms of vulgarity. Nothing is more vulgar than refinement and the desire to distinguish oneself (to *be* distinguished). An ethical-aesthetic value judgement, a sociological fact, vulgarity derives not from the popular character of gestures and words, but from the daily life secreted and ordained by the middle classes: a certain 'realism' about money, clothes, behaviour and gratification – a realism that is paraded and imposed – forms part of the 'vulgar'. Daily life is confined to what is; it dispenses with any horizon, any resonance; it congratulates itself on its limits and encloses itself in them. It flaunts needs, their objects and their satisfaction. This is its 'behaviour', a reflex and self-contented conditioning, a way of behaving, which extends to life in its entirety and taints it with its tonality – vulgarity. This casts suspicion on any rupture, prohibiting it, ruling out any alteration by identifying 'what is' with good sense and wisdom. Dull realism, which is vulgar and produces vulgarity, stifles even the sighs of the oppressed creature: dreams, appeals to what is different and other, the protests of those – women, children, deviants – who represent irreducible lived experience in daily life, demanding 'something different'. The extraordinary that pierces through the ordinary, the extra-quotidian that tends to break up daily life ('passions', demands that take the form of prohibitions and curses, interjections and exclamations, abuse and insults) – this vulgarity rejects, denying its existence, ridiculing it, reducing it to the extent of destroying it. Impervious, invulnerable, inaccessible, the vulgar being creates a shell around him, protecting him from all but the most commonplace suffering. From daily life vulgarity retains only the mundane. It is not exclusively attached to discourse, but to something more hidden and more essential. Does not satisfaction have a *cumulative* character? Not like positive knowledge, but in an analogous fashion? Satisfactions are added: as they are produced and reproduced, as they produce and reproduce their objects, needs generate the density of the vulgar. This does not mean that anxiety, imagination or distress wrest the 'subject' from vulgarity; someone who is 'frustrated' can remain vulgar in their concerns.

Vulgarity is not confined to daily life and those who focus on what is trivial in it. Certain 'reflections' that do their best to pass for thought are marred by vulgarity, and bear its stamp just as much as forms of behaviour rooted in habits. The vulgarity of self-satisfied knowledge bears some classic names, which apologias for scientificity and technicity cause people to forget: priggishness, pedantry, ponderousness. In times past, people used to call it 'Philistinism', and Schumann wrote his 'march against the Philistines'. The enormous and enduring success of psychoanalysis does not prevent reflection 'centred' on sexuality lapsing into vulgarity; there is something profoundly vulgar about the attention paid to 'sexual matters', 'sexual relations', sex in general or 'sexuality'. Today, after Nietzsche, a doctrine merits support only if it proposes a new (superior) type of man, society, civilization. Freud brought to language, concepts and theory a 'reality' that had hitherto been ignored, disdained, and even cursed (this is always worth recalling, to avoid misunderstandings). Freud's thought does not lapse into vulgarity; but it can lead to it. Here intellectual coarseness coincides with social crudity – the unhappy adolescents who are forever talking about sex, casting a shameful glance at the other sex and the sex of others. This 'reality' is not in any doubt; nor are the daily problems it poses (itself). But a 'reality', or rather 'realism', of this sort is inherent in vulgarity. Should not theorization of this 'reality' be understood *symptomatically*, as an indication of the malaise afflicting Western, Judaeo-Christian society? Capitalist and bourgeois society? Scientifico-technicist society? Symptom and symbol of a failure that extends far beyond sexuality, can psychoanalysis guarantee that an acceptable everydayness will be established on the language and positive knowledge of the 'unconscious'? Is it not precisely this implicit promise, which has never been fulfilled, this failed prophecy, that sets in train the decline of theory? Something from which vulgar Marxism is obviously not exempt ...

Are we according 'vulgarity' a philosophical status here, as Sartre attempted with his portrayal of the 'bastard' or the 'gaze of the other'? Not exactly. We are introducing into the theory of daily life what is generally regarded as a subjective judgement: vulgarity, boredom, malaise. The so-called social or human 'sciences' do not take account of such things. Thus, boredom does not exist for sociologists as a social fact. They are wrong! As for the move from malaise to ill-being philosophically conceived, that is a different operation.

Neither Marx and 'Marxist' thought, nor Freud, psychology and psychoanalysis, escaped the great illusion of the nineteenth century and part of the twentieth: the confusion between living and knowing – even its identification in the name of the Truth. From this deceptive viewpoint, to live is to know; to learn and know is to live. The lived and the conceived are identified. Confused with 'being', centred on the 'real', defining and consequently mastering it, knowledge has a simultaneously methodological, practical and ontological priority. According to the Cartesian precept, social, practical man becomes the master and possessor of Nature through labour and knowledge: the plenitude of his being is defined in this way, and realized. That's how it is for Marx. If I know what I feel and experience, if I access that in 'me' which eluded my 'knowledge' and pursued its course outside or without my consciousness, I create a satisfying, normal situation: assuagement and health. That's how it is for Freud. As if knowledge possessed the capacity not only to grasp the unknown 'object', be it nature or the unconscious, but to realize the 'subject'. The latter would thus be constituted by positive knowledge, lived as such.

A good deal of empty discussion stems from this attitude, which in practice slips into extreme vulgarity. There is a vulgarity peculiar to the specialist who knows what comes within his narrow competence, but is unaware of the world. There is also the vulgarity of the technocrat, who merely improves his customary performance, and is connected with other domains solely through utterly mundane commonplaces.

The attitude that likes to think itself rational, privileging the conceptual to the extent of hypostatizing it, induces a lively reaction, which remains face to face with the thing that motivates it: fetishism of the absurd, a cult of irrationality. Hence a loop and an imprisonment of thought.

Hence, equally, problems without answers and inconclusive debates, during which the debasement of theory into vulgarity continues. Take Marxists: do the superstructures merely reflect the base? If they reflect the base, how can they act, intervene, effectively? What is the base? Productive forces or social relations? Which relations? Take Freudians: does psychoanalysis possess concepts? What are they? Does psychoanalysis apply these concepts, or does the treatment of 'patients' follow a course in which concepts are of no practical relevance? Whence, if not from positive knowledge and the transference, derives the analyst's power over the patient, a power that is in theory beneficial? Does this process occur at the cognitive level, or within the affects? And so on.

So the fate of the philosophies of pure knowledge has not spared 'Marxism'. Revolution through positive knowledge, transmitted by the political party, brought by it to the working class *from without* (Lenin) – this revolution has miscarried. The result is a situation that would appear favourable to neither the theory, nor the political party, nor the working class; the latter cannot constitute itself as an *autonomous*, self-determining 'political subject' solely by means of positive knowledge (of the economic, of its own condition, etc.). Hence the painful *vulgarization* of Marxist thought. We have waited in vain for the 'working class' – which, according to Marx, had not yet attained the status of 'class' (for itself) – to assimilate the simplified knowledge that was offered it. This knowledge remains the preserve, even the (collective) property, of narrower groups than the 'class' – of an elite stratum of professionals, members of the 'political class', linked to the autonomization of political and state apparatuses. This situation is itself bound up with the autonomization of technicity.

The transformation of the social through and in positive knowledge ends up in its opposite, with positive knowledge promulgating its autonomy, thereby consolidating the existing order that is known and recognized as such. Need we recall here that the critique of everyday life proposed another way: starting out from actual experience, and elucidating it in order to transform it – as opposed to starting from the conceptual in order to impose it? And without disparaging or dispensing with the activity of knowledge ...

7 On Various Corruptions

The years following 1968 witnessed a renewal of daily life by sex and sexuality, which proved illusory and rapidly lapsed into vulgarity. This ideology, which did not think it was ideological, was 'scientifically' justified by psychoanalysis. In a crude reduction, the watchword of a new order – *changer la vie* – was narrowed down to sexual liberation, which itself took some crudely simplistic forms: for example, the negation of any difference between the sexes, the assimilation of the masculine and the feminine, undifferentiated, to the 'unisex'. In the event, it was in these years that the sexual entered completely into the world of the commodity, and sexuality became the supreme commodity.

The critique of everyday life in no way excluded sexuality, but it did not accept its vulgarization. The underlying project, doubtless incompletely formulated but inherent in the approach, involved the permeation of the sexual into everydayness, but not as commodity, as localized, functional sexuality. The sexual was to be transformed in the process of transforming daily life. It was thus a question of Eros, not organs, and of celestial Aphrodite, not the terrestrial Aphrodite, the Venus of the brothels. This in no way excluded pleasure, but included it in a larger project, in a higher quest (why deny it?). We should note that Herbert Marcuse's thinking has suffered vulgarization; he has been received not as a philosopher of creative Eros, but as the theoretician of a 'permissive' society without boundaries or values.

The 'specialization' of the sexual, which accompanies technological specialization and production for 'generalized' exchange, has serious, unnoticed consequences. The separation between social practice (referred to as 'culture', bound up with the abstract character of the whole society) and nature extends to a rupture between sexuality and reproduction. The goal and practical objective are legitimate: to allow lovers to experience pleasure without falling into the trap set for desire by 'nature'. Yet this attitude impacts upon the lot and social status of childhood. The couple tends to reject the child, the natural product of coupling. The special child becomes an object of specialism: there are now child professionals – educators, activity leaders, paediatricians, analysts and psychologists. A relation that was previously normal and normalizing between generations and degrees of maturation, between time and life – this old relation is strained and collapsing. Separation prevails and extends to family life; it eats away at unity and replaces what was once a matter of an open totality by fragmentation. Between excessive holism and mutilating disjunctions, this society has hitherto missed the road to renewal, inflecting it towards a remarkable touch of vulgarity: childhood and adolescence are asserted brutally; they are oppressed and they are praised to the skies; they are, for example, used as advertising and marketing devices. As for adults, who push children and adolescents away into autonomy, they become coarser as a result, for want of a lived relation with the future, which is socially and daily represented by differences between the generations.

For the time being, the transformation of daily life by poetic action and creative Eros has thus likewise failed in the face of the power of commodities, supported on one side by technicity and positive knowledge, and on the other by political power. Sex continues to sink into vulgarity; sexual misery persists despite the vast literature devoted to the 'vulgarization' of 'problems'. Must we therefore abandon the project – that is to say, the conception, going back to Plato, of desire that creates in beauty and involves self-transcendence, as opposed to being valorized as desire and the desire to desire? No – even if we must grant that it involves a distant horizon which is possibly unattainable, an ideal, a utopia even. There is no question of abandoning the thesis that the impossible orientates the possible, in life as in thought, so that during the long wait for transformation, freedom inevitably takes the form of transgression. While the bounds prohibiting transgression are reinforced, while various 'great walls' are raised at the frontiers on which the liberators fought, the fundamental thesis on the impossible and the possible still obtains. An elitist conception? No and yes. No, in the sense that it does not impute vulgarity to what is popular. Yes, in the sense that it differentiates between what has value and what does not; and between the habitable surface and the swampy depths, as well as the inaccessible heights.

8 Conservative Schemas

Received representations and commonly used words are insidious vehicles for a morality, an ethics and an aesthetics that are not declared to be such. Customs and social habits sometimes alter without those who are affected registering the fact. It may be that innovations, gradually accepted and virtually unnoticed, conduce to the inertia or corruption of daily life. Here is an exemplary instance, already signalled elsewhere, which is worth stressing given the gravity of its consequences: the substitution of the 'user', figure of daily life, for the political figure of the 'citizen'.

For a long time, representations of the user have been taking root in imagery and ideology, as well as everyday consciousness and practice. At the outset, this seemed to be the expression of a power of protest capable of acting in and on the everyday. It seemed subversive *vis-à-vis* the many services that are external to productive labour, and yet indispensable for the production and reproduction of social relations – *vis-à-vis* what constitutes the social organization of the everyday: transport and communications, urban living conditions and realities, health, and so on. From this standpoint, the user was going to become the essential component of a force as constructive as it was critical, a force that was restoring the use-value which had become so subordinate to exchange-value and exchange that it was nothing more than their prop. In this way, the priority of use over exchange, the commodity and the market was to be overwhelmingly restored in daily life, primarily in questions and problems related to space.

Was such a representation, raised to the status of a concept, 'false' from the outset? This position, unfailingly adopted by dogmatists and sectarians, discounts what actually happened – that is to say, a massive operation of recuperation, a skilful defusing, an appropriation carried out by state-political power over a fairly long period. The *fait accompli* is now with us: the citizen tends to fade in the face of the user. What, formerly, was the citizen for himself and for society, according to its political constitution? He bore a title that was not honorific or bureaucratic, but effective and even decisive: that of member of the political community. The idea of democracy and its functioning was inseparably bound up with the value and significance of this title: to the rights of the citizen (leaving aside here the historical and ideological justifications of citizenship, that is, the rights of 'man' in general). Now, the rights of the citizen have been devalued, taking with them human rights – and vice versa. Not only does the citizen become a mere inhabitant, but the inhabitant is reduced to a user, restricted to demanding the efficient operation of public services. The user figures in social practice as one party, invariably absent and represented, in contractual terms and conditions. He is transported, cared for, maintained, educated, and so on (by whom? The state? The local authority? The private firm in partnership with public bodies?). Obviously, services must function. The problem begins when the state claims to be a 'service state', not a political state. This allows the authorities to restrict the right to strike and to make strikes 'unpopular'. Individuals no longer perceive themselves politically; their relation with the state becomes looser; they feel *social* only passively when they take a bus or tube, when they switch on their TV, and so on – and this degrades the social. The rights of the citizen are diluted in political programmes and opinion polls, whereas the demands of users have an immediate, concrete, practical appearance, being directly a matter for organization and its techniques. In the everyday, relations with the state and the political are thus obscured, when in fact they are objectively intensified, since politicians use daily life as a base and a tool. The debasement of civic life occurs in the everyday, facilitating the task of those who manage everyday life from above by means of institutions and services.

Should the notion of users and the practice that corresponds to it be destroyed? No! But use must be connected up with citizenship, as opposed to separating the two.

Users become mere receptacles of 'culture' – that is to say, a mixture of ideology, representations and positive knowledge. The enormous culture industry supplies specific products, commodities to which users have a 'right', so that the output of this industrial sector no longer has the appearance of commodities but, rather, of objects valorized by them and destined exclusively for use. Like information! This is the consummation of the world of commodities, without objects and products being reduced exclusively to the function of signs and props of what is exchangeable. Use becomes mystificatory.

Are not this gradual appropriation and degradation of some significance in indifference towards the state and everything related to it? The state is of interest almost exclusively to professionals, specialists in 'political science', whereas everyone should feel 'concerned' and seek to understand the operation of 'apparatuses' that are not public services. This indifference leads to amazing leaps, to surprises that are themselves surprising, when the political is fully revealed: moments of international tension or simply struggles on a national scale. In the long term, this degradation threatens a political class constituted on the basis of the passivity of citizens who are no longer citizens. It is said that it affects workers less than the middle class. What is certain is that it is gradually working its way into habits and customs, into stereotypes. These set the tone of everyday discourse and practice, which tend to establish conservative schemas. It is said that the ideology – the ideal – of liberty and humanism is becoming blurred. Does this involve a loss of illusions, or a loss of social activity as well as political existence? The second estimate seems more accurate.

The programming of daily life is thus pursuing its course with remarkable continuity. The exceptions – the marginal, society's rejects – henceforth enter into computations and statistics. As we shall see later, the dual society, composed on the one hand of a hard core of techniques and high-tech products with related services, and on the other of marginal, even underground, circuits – this divided society is now among the prospects that are circulating. However that may be, there are now publications and information which ensure that everyone is aware of all that is to be done. Much more so than in 1960 (era of the publication of the second volume of the *Critique of Everyday Life*), everyone knows how to live in 1981. They know it thanks to a knowledge that does not originate with them, which they have assimilated, and which they apply to their own individual cases, managing their personal affairs – their everyday lives – in accordance with the models developed and diffused for them. They apply these models more or less methodically. In general, problems begin only when a choice has to be made. Too much choice! But the models invariably resemble one another so closely that choice is futile, and it is enough to pick at random: pot luck. Consequently, only those who refuse the models have problems.

Magazines and weeklies, particularly those directed at women and even those that defend the 'cause of women', work out complete daily schedules – buying and selling, shopping, menus, clothing. From morning to evening and evening to morning, everyday time is full to bursting: fulfilment, plenitude. With 'values' – femininity, virility, or seductiveness – but above all with the ultimate value: satisfaction. Being satisfied: this is the general model of being and living whose promoters and supporters do not appreciate the fact that it generates discontent. For the quest for satisfaction and the fact of *being satisfied* presuppose the fragmentation of 'being' into activities, intentions, needs, all of them well-defined, isolated, separable and separated from the Whole. Is this an art of living? A style? No. It is merely the result and the application to daily life of a management technique and a positive knowledge directed by market research. The economic prevails even in a domain that seemed to elude it: it governs lived experience. The leisure industry rounds off the culture industry by offering travel plans and tourism, which are bought like a wardrobe or an apartment you can move into immediately. *Discover* such and such a country, town, mountain, sea! People buy the 'discovery', the change of scene, the departure and escape, which prove disappointing because they no longer have anything in common with the wish (not desire) and the advertisement. In its turn, the tourist industry thus perfects that of organized leisure and culture, fragmented into exchangeable pieces like space. The extra-ordinary sells very well, but it is now no more than a sad mystification. In this way, the image of a pseudo-freedom takes shape, one that is practically organized and substituted for 'genuine freedom', which has remained abstract. Hence a continuity in the simulation of use, and in the simulation of not working by leisure.

Can such a burdensome rationality be accepted without offering some compensation? On its own, it tips over into the irrational. Philosophers maintain the thesis of a 'crisis' of the logos. This has a certain truth to it. But how and why would the European logos, rationality armed and always battle-ready, escape the total crisis? Yet the logos, which has become technicist rationality, has never had so much persuasive force, penetration, capacity. The inversion of the rational into the anti-rational is not performed reflexively, consciously, but affectively. Because they are disappointed, many people involved with techniques turn to the absurd, magic, occultism, underground ideologies and mysteries. The philosophical thesis of the logos in crisis neglects the paradoxical encounter of the rational and the irrational, which are one another's mirages, rather than mirrors. As for those who are affected, those who suffer the technological pressure, they are kept amused with promises. The entirely 'private' and yet completely liberated individual, cosy in his bubble among his appliances, would, as it were, become the equivalent of the world through boundless information. He would have the spectacle of transparency before him. How can we avoid reverting to myths to cast a chill shadow over this pitiless luminosity? How can we not have recourse to the imaginary, the resurgence of the historical past, the evocative fiction of other lives and different things? The more the 'real' asserts itself and closes before us, the more the present becomes imaginary, the more it is filled with barely credible fictions – tales, dreams, utopias – enriching what is actual with mere semblances.

To conclude this account of continuities, it is appropriate here to recall that an organizational – or disorganizational – schema which has been in place for a long time is currently more operational than ever. It has penetrated daily life, this penetration having been foreshadowed and prepared in other sectors and domains – positive knowledge, space, the state, and so on. Capital itself operates according to this mode or model: capital, which is the same everywhere, divided up in investments, organized in a hierarchy from the small to the large. Today, the everyday is subject to this schema, which simultaneously prescribes and imposes: (a) *homogeneity* – that is to say, the tendency towards the same, identity, equivalence, the repetitive and their order; (b) *fragmentation* – that is to say, the dispersion of time and space, labour and leisure alike, and ever more intensive specialization; (c) *hierarchization*, with hierarchical order equally being imposed on functions – more or less significant – and objects – cars, planes, clothes, publications, and so on.

This hierarchical order runs from the trivial to the exceptional, from the communal to the elite, from the ordinary to the luxurious, from the repetitive to the wonderful surprise ... Identified and formulated elsewhere,[3] this schema is implemented in practice with remarkable tenacity. It is implicit in Marx with respect to social labour, which is increasingly homogeneous, fragmented and hierarchically organized. Its generalization is typical of contemporary society, revolution in Marx's sense having neither swept away the capitalist mode of production, nor achieved its own objectives. The application of the schema to daily life makes the latter correspond with what has been realized in zones and activities that are more or less external to daily life, yet connected with it: the use of time, journeys, labour, and so on.

The following paradox was brought to light in the work cited above: Marx's thought prevails even in that which contradicts it, even in its failure. This failure of the Marxist project (whether temporary or lasting is of little importance here) comes within the province of Marx's thought, and confirms it. Is not the same true of the thesis, fiercely resisted by philosophers, which attributes crucial importance to the economic – a thesis, it is too often forgotten, that goes together in Marx with a no less fundamental critique of economics? The mode of production analysed by Marx has unfolded in a way that simultaneously confirms and contradicts his thought. The strategic estimates of the rulers were foreseen by Marx; he nevertheless believed in their rapid failure, in the imminent collapse of the mode of production. This is what has not happened. This mode of production has, in particular, created the developed world market, the 'scientific and technological revolution' (a substitute for social and political revolution), the world state system, a specific space, massive urbanization, a planetary division of labour and, finally, an everydayness. A homogeneous everyday time: the abstract measurement of time governs social practice. Fragmented everyday time: dispersed by abrupt discontinuities, fragments of cycles and rhythms ruptured by the linearity of measurement procedures, activities that are disconnected, albeit subject to a general plan decreed from above. Hierarchically organized everyday time: the unevenness of situations and moments, some regarded as highly significant and others as negligible, according to value judgements which lack justification, which are themselves in crisis.

It is not easy to grasp the paradox, which eludes all reductionist thinking, whereby the homogeneous covers and contains the fragmented, making room for a strict hierarchization. So here is a brief table of the 'factors' that intervene in daily life and realize the general schema in it:

(a) *Homogenizing factors*: Established law and order – Technological and bureaucratic rationality – The logic that claims to be unitary and is in fact applied to all domains – Space managed on a grand scale (motorways, etc.) – Clock-time, articulated repetitively – The media (not so much via their content as via their form, producing the uniform attitude of listeners or viewers, breeding passivity before the flow of information, images, discourse) – The search for consistency and cohesion in behaviour – Training for this behaviour on the model of the conditioned reflex – Stereotyped representations – The world of the commodity, intimately linked to that of contractual commitments – Linearly repetitive tasks (the same gestures, words, etc.) – Spaces filled with prohibitions – The segmentation of basic functions (eating, sleeping, dressing, reproducing, etc.) in standardized daily life, which goes hand in hand with the fragmentation of so-called higher functions (reading, writing, judging and appreciating, conceiving, managing, etc.), and their programmed distribution in time – The multiple inequalities in the formal equality of the law, inequalities that are precisely masked by homogeneity and dispersal – The epistemological fields and divisions implemented in and through positive knowledge – The bureaucracies and bureaucratic feudalisms, each acting in its own fiefdom – The importance of administrative divisions dividing up space between them – The disposition of space, a social product, into an infinitely divisible (optical-geometrical) visibility – The general and continuing tendency to administer everyday life as if it were a small firm – The tendency to appeal to a positive knowledge bound up with norms, and hence reductive of lived experience – The superimposition and mutual reinforcement of forms of alienation that act, so to speak, in concert, to the point of inducing pathological breakdowns – The domination of the abstract, which is concretely materialized socially in generalized exchange, extending to symbols that have degenerated and been reduced to signs – Fake encyclopaedism, accompanied by a proliferation of lexicons, dictionaries, and so on.

(b) *Factors of fragmentation* (within homogeneity): The many separations, segregations and disjunctions, such as private and public, conceptual and experiential, nature and technique, foreigners and fellow citizens, and so on – Spaces specialized to the extent of establishing ghettos – The division of labour – Fragmented space sold in parcels and lots – Splintered centrality, a theory which is spreading over urban reality in the name of decentralization, and will lead to definitive fragmentation – The dilution of the contrast between high (sacred) points and low points in everyday life, and a growing multiplicity of neutral, indifferent instants – Social separation and disconnection between protected workers (employment laws, unions, etc.) and the rest, who are less protected or completely unprotected, and so on.

(c) *Factors of hierarchization*: The multiform hierarchy of functions, labours, incomes, from the bottom (vanishing into the swamp of the rejects) to the top (disappearing into Olympian clouds), a hierarchy that extends to objects: cars, accommodation, jewellery, and so on – A hierarchy of locations, of 'properties', of the qualities recognized in individuals and groups – Society as a stratified, hierarchical morphology, with superimposed levels – The division of time by the media, broadcasting fragmentary representations rounded off by illusory totalizing visions – The hierarchy of knowledge, with the fundamental and the applied, the important and the unimportant, the essential and the anecdotal – Hierarchy in enterprises, workshops and offices (in the bureaucracy, despite – or rather in – the homogeneity of practice and in the ideology of 'competence–performance') – Degrees of 'participation' in power and decision-taking, from scraps of authority to sovereign power, and so on – Bureaucracy, in the service (not conflict-free) of technocracy, which has come to treat daily life and people in daily life as the raw material for its labour, as a mass to 'handle', as a people on benefit, but which nevertheless tends to get its 'subjects' to perform its own work of registration and enrolment, form-filling of all sorts ...

How are we to represent this society in a way that is simulaneously both rational and palpable (visual) as – albeit with a few upheavals – it takes shape? The metaphor of the pyramid, Hegelian in origin, supporting the various strata and classes from a wide base to a very narrow summit, is no longer representative. Why? A split has developed between, on the one hand, society's rejects and the people expelled outside of the main circuits (whole regions, the unemployed with no hope of work, youth, women, artisans overtaken by technology, small firms and businesses, etc.), and, on the other, people who are well-integrated into circuits and networks focused around so-called 'high-tech' production (nuclear energy, computer science, the arms industry, etc.). It is a well-known fact that parallel or secondary circuits, networks and channels are established among those 'outside the system': an underground economy that makes it possible for people to survive, without always avoiding degradation. At the extreme – counterpart of the comings and goings of the elite, who travel around in jets, and go from one luxury hotel to the next – we find the nomadism of poverty, wandering misery. And this on a world scale. We are equally aware that people who work in 'high-tech' industries do not fall outside the system, although not all workers enjoy this good fortune. Thus this cleavage divides the working class, part of which finds itself alongside the fortunate and the 'affluent' (terms that are abused so that they can be turned against those who do not count among the most destitute). The disadvantaged subsist at a lower level of everyday life, whereas the Olympians, at or close to the summit, are elevated above daily life. These Olympians engage in luxurious wanderings, high-altitude nomadism. They do not work in the trivial sense of the term, but are extremely busy: they chair, they organize (managers), they possess, and they administer. The classical terms *bourgeoisie* or *grande bourgeoisie* are no longer quite appropriate to these rulers of the international. The term 'Olympians' seems more fitting. It is nevertheless the case that a distinction must be introduced here. The rejects live at the level of *infra-daily life*; the Olympians in a *supra-daily life*. This makes daily life correspond to a sort of social mean. Is this not the life-world of the middle classes? This hypothesis will be expounded later; it is introduced here to explain the continuity in daily life despite the factors of change.

The preceding analyses have already defined a project and broad lines of action against the results, as well as the operational schemas, of the forces that remain dominant:

(a) *Differences against homogeneity*. We shall have to return to this concept of *difference* in order to refute its recuperation, wherein the right to difference includes and justifies social inequalities. 'As soon as it is experienced, perceived in everyday life and not merely imagined, diversity entails classifications, hierarchies, inequalities,' Alain de Benoist has written in his *Éléments*. However, the right to difference – between men and women, children and adults, countries, regions, ethnic groups – presupposes equality in difference. This can flourish only in a democratic society, which this right helps to define as it is added, along with various other rights, to the old human rights.

(b) *Unity against fragmentation and division*, the pursuit and realization of this unity not proceeding without problems and dialectical contradictions, since it is a concrete unity, not an abstract identity, that is to be conceived and realized.

(c) *Equality against hierarchy*, without levelling society, but strengthening the social as the level that mediates between the economic and the political, which are factors of inequality. This presupposes some radical (root-and-branch) changes.

This long struggle would involve a *dialectical* (not a logico-statistical) conception of:

(a) *centrality* in space and time (multiplicity of centres, mobility, dynamism);

(b) *subjectivity*: collective subjects (not only the workers in an enterprise, the inhabitants of a town or region, but the working class as autonomous), substituted for individual 'egos', and reconstructed in line with new concepts;

(c) *sociality*, as opposed not only to the individual but to the state, on the one hand, and hence to the political, regarded as reductionist; but also, on the other, to the economic, regarded as abstraction (exchange and commodity, money, division of labour, etc.).

PART TWO

Discontinuities

1 A First Glance at What Has Changed

Within the continuity, the inertia, of daily life, and its passivity, factors of change – even disruption – of the established order are becoming clear.

Technology makes the end of work possible (in the long run). What seemed abstractly utopian yesterday is now taking shape, is on the horizon: the wholesale automation of material production. As we have seen, devaluation of a seductive, prestigious image – modernity – goes together with an intensification of technological modernism and an expectation of novelty, in a kind of frantic fervour for a different society, the product of computer science, telematics, and so on. This society is to be reached via the scientific revolution pushed to the limit, carried through to its term. Cultural snobbery and enthusiasm for modernity have served their time: this myth is no longer required. Does not the new society, proclaiming the end of ideologies and myths, possess its own ideology and myths? Bit by bit, they are unearthed: the ideology of the end of ideology, of transparency and performance, and the myth of freedom realized by information technology, and so on. Thus, the separation between modernity and modernism undoubtedly already represents a change; it anticipates greater changes. Technological progress is occurring in leaps and bounds: some people (who? – a lot of people) anticipate that it will generate its effects *automatically*, since it involves automation. It is allowed to take its course. Is this an intellectual standpoint? The standpoint of the intelligentsia? Of a political party? No: it is the spontaneous orientation of social practice. Modernity is dated: industrial society, with the abstraction paradoxically produced by material production. By contrast, post-industrial society will be characterized by the production and exchange of non-material goods, which are nevertheless more concrete: information, services, and so on.

But *who* is going to carry this transformation through to a conclusion? *Who* is going to put an end to politics as fiction, politics as spectacle? For example: *who* today is in a position to direct computers towards calculating production costs not in money, but in social time and/or energy, so that exchange will no longer have to proceed via the mediation of the market, money and capital? Is it not the case that the existing economic and political powers intend to use recent techniques to maintain, or even perfect, their domination? The end of work? It is possible, but so is the opposite – the contradictory. *Who* is going to steer work towards its decline or end? Workers want to work; those who employ them and profit from their labour (through surplus-value which can, if you like, be called 'profit' – it does not matter) want to make them work. Men of good will and what are called the left-wing parties demand full employment. Is a reduction in labour-time sufficient to set in train the process of the end of labour? And what are we to make of the expansion of leisure, purchased by labour? Workers – the working class – find themselves caught between threatening technologies they scarcely understand, which have begun to wreak their havoc, and the conservatism that promises a more or less ameliorated status quo. In philosophical terms, what exists is the conditions of possibility, not the conditions of realization, which exceed the mode of production itself! The radical revolution – that of non-work – is foreshadowed in an obscure sort of way through aporias and utopias. It has not as yet been formulated clearly. What might daily life become from the viewpoint of not working? How can we inflect it in this direction? How are we to fill daily life or, more mundanely, occupy it in the event of a massive reduction in labour-time? What should we expect – an expansion of the everyday, or its decline? Up until now, the problem has been of interest only to science-fiction writers (e.g. Simak's *Demain les chiens*), and a few philosophers (we should not forget Lafargue's *Le Droit à la paresse*).

It must be clearly recognized that theoretical – that is to say, conceptual – thinking has only a remote connection with social and political practice here. Is this sufficient reason for abandoning it? For declaring it to be ideological or subjective? Or utopian in reactionary mode? No! Theory detects and states conditions of possibility. Nothing more and nothing less. The problematic formulated here corresponds, however, to Marx's most profound – most profoundly and paradoxically dialectical – thought: the working class can affirm itself only in its negation, unlike other historically superseded classes and the bourgeoisie. The self-determination whereby the working class attains the status of 'subject', transcending the condition of object, involves self-negation: the end of all classes, the end of the wage-earning class, and hence the end of work, the end of the working class itself. Utopia? Delirium? But here 'we' (all of us) are ready to get down to the task. The organization or establishment of a 'party of non-labour' cannot even be imagined. The business of a few utopians thus becomes a problem confronting everyone, a fundamental problematic, a vital issue. Smash the techniques and new machines, or use them and develop their potential? But what is going to happen in the course of this total crisis? For it is no longer a question of 'going slow' (André Breton and René Char), or of 'letting it all hang out' (1968), but of making the transition from work to the end of work, without catastrophe. Pending something different and better, the valorization of work – an important dimension of the consensus – is dissolving. Does the road to the withering away of work entail the despair of workers in the advanced countries, trapped in processes they endure rather than dominate, when control over conditions (self-management) has precisely been put on the century's agenda?

The reader will know that the total crisis, which is shaking the mode of production, set in at the beginning of the twentieth century with a silent catastrophe: the collapse of traditional reference points for – and by – thought; and a consequent collapse of values. Practice and daily life have preserved them. From this crisis emerged technology, labour and discourse – three aspects of the Western logos. This triad freed itself from subordination to a totality, with consequences that had not been foreseen by protagonists of such liberation, both in art (which declared itself to be 'art for art's sake', not without breathtaking abstraction) and in science (which also unfolded for its own sake, in collaboration with technology). In the triad 'technology–

labour–language and discourse', technology then freed itself from any control. All along this dangerous path, critical points were not wanting. The devaluation of labour and discourse in the face of technically applicable knowledge was not the least painful aspect of a process that tends to shatter the continuum. Does not the end of these values already register a rupture?

There are other aspects of this process, and different critical points. *Dwelling*, a social and yet poetic act, generating poetry and art work, fades in the face of housing, an economic function. The 'home', so clearly evoked and celebrated by Gaston Bachelard, likewise vanishes: the magic place of childhood, the home as womb and shell, with its loft and its cellar full of dreams. Confronted with functional housing, constructed according to technological dictates, inhabited by users in homogeneous, shattered space, it sinks and fades into the past. With this rupture – that is the substitution of functional housing for 'dwellings', of buildings for edifices and monuments – what are known as modern town planning and architecture abandoned the historic town, if only as example and model. Towns have undergone an 'implosion–explosion'. Crossing points and traffic have assumed greater importance than inhabited spaces. The façade and space on which the town imposed a style are becoming blurred. As the architects say, the volumetry, and the settlement it determines, impart a different style, ever more sharply marked by the opposition between stability and movement, fixed places and flows crossing through space. This produces some contradictory – even chaotic – results. Some people hold that we must forge ahead on this path, determined by technology. For others, nostalgia wins out over hopes for a future marked by incredible inventions. Continuities and discontinuities are thus interwoven in a confusion that is expressed in spatial disorder. Here we recognize the previously mentioned opposition between nostalgics and futurists. Is there another way, between a harsh, absurd 'reality' and compensations, unavailing protests, and the illusions of subjectivity, lyrical flights of regret? Such a road is all the more difficult to outline in that the culture industry knows how to capture the longings of souls, the attractive moods of consciousness waxing indignant and protesting, in order to transform them into profitable spectacles. Experience indicates that even the ludic and the tragic, regarded as irreducible and immune to recuperation, can be marketed up to a certain point. So that they are insufficient to open up another way – unless they take things to extremes: dangerous games, great risks, holocaust and sacrifice. There is often an element of play in daily life: everyone plays their role, their comic or tragic character, more or less well. Sometimes the ludic grows in intensity. Yet when an element of play mingles with exchange in practice – debate and bargaining, speculation – the operation of equivalents is scarcely troubled by it. On the contrary, this is how it operates and is masked: by establishing itself in daily life. Likewise with the ludic in discourse: puns and wordplay, language effects, even screams and inarticulate sobs. It does not prevent logic imposing coherence, sooner or later. Banking on the ludic to rupture daily life is probably a mug's game. For it is to mask the obduracy of the system of equivalents. And yet, at moments of intense risk, in passion and poetry, daily life shatters, and something different comes through with the work, whether act, speech or object.

In their obscure early stages, the commodity and the spread of commodities stimulated the imagination. It is difficult for us moderns to comprehend, but it is definitely the case – as confirmed by history and, better still, by reading texts and understanding art works – that the great imaginative creations followed an expansion of trade, which established contact between people, countries and towns that were oblivious of one another: think of Homer, the great Greek authors, *A Thousand and One Nights*, Shakespeare, and so on. The establishment of communication gave rise to more or less fantastic, untruthful narratives, and to legends and myths. Thereafter, the commercial mentality stifled creative capacity. At best, it yielded hedonism. As for technology, it is as unconducive to flights of spontaneity as to the imaginary. Contrariwise, the mass introduction of techniques into production and administration has generated astonishing creative capacity when it comes to perfected, sophisticated forms of exchange: credit, capital and technology transfers, currency manipulation. There thus develops a technological utopia with an ideology which justifies it, and responds in affirmative mode to negative, subversive ideologies, based on the critique of the existing order, which demand another life, an absolute difference, immediately. It none the less remains the case that the capacity to create – the imagination – first of all requires a simultaneously ideal and real, ideological and practical, break with what exists. This rupture can extend as far as neurosis, schizophrenia and paranoia.

Recent years have confirmed a surprising phenomenon, whose causes and import are obscure, but which seems in its way to mark a discontinuity. Up until the middle of the nineteenth century, the great artist was associated with excellent health, even if in our time a pernickety and slightly malevolent examination has identified symptoms of neurosis. Men of genius mastered angst: Michelangelo, Leonardo, later Diderot, and still later Stendhal and Balzac. Subsequently, the creator – artist or writer – was no longer content to oppose his subjectivity and problematic to real things, objects and people. He called himself into question and counterposed himself to a reality in which he could not put down roots or aspire to a status. He became a case, and it was from this unique case that he drew his inspiration. Can this semi-pathological state, neurosis and sometimes something even worse, be regarded as creative as such? Doubtless not. Yet the striving that seeks release from anxiety and delivery from angst by mastering it stimulates the creativity which contemporary ideology still seeks among so-called normal people. Classical subjectivity, capable of objectivity, gives way in the artist to a different condition: daily life has become so oppressive and repressive that dissolution (Rimbaud) is the sole means of escaping it. The artist can no longer make do with keeping his distance. As his neurosis gives him creative impetus, he cultivates it. This provokes a break, possibly a gulf, between daily life and creation, reality and the work, the state of the creator and therapeutic techniques, which are inevitably normalizing. These observations – or, rather, self-evident facts – confirm what was previously said about modernity and, above all, the action 'in the negative' of contemporary art. This negativity involves neither revolutionary proposals, nor a subversive project. Yet it is there, before 'us', in the works. Exasperation of the morbid is the one thing that allows the creator to rise above the everyday, if only to understand it and show it. Plenitude, whether of lived experience or of the ideal in the Platonic sense, loses its meaning. Hence another gulf – between production and creation – whereas cultural production, which has become a powerful industry, pretends either to deny this gulf, or to fill it. Kitsch, an industrial product, becomes positively comforting – an art of happiness in security – whereas the art work, born out of anguish that has or has not been mastered, disturbs.

The permanent, persistent things in the social landscape – which are relative, and hence in no sense vestigial, but retain their currency

– stem largely from the strategy of the authorities. Whereas a new world economic order is what is required (no-one is unaware of this fact), strategy prescribes a new division of labour on a world scale, maintaining and aggravating inequalities of growth and development. The rulers are opposed to any destabilization – a fashionable term that says what it means – and hence to any movement. If development occurs (even with the greatest power at our disposal, can we prevent it?), it occurs despite the dominant economic and political powers. They authorize technological innovations only after obtaining guarantees; and no doubt this is the form assumed today by the contradiction that Marx pointed out between the productive forces and social and political relations, as well as the 'law of value' considered on an international scale. These powers have disposed of – that is to say, destroyed or neutralized – attempts at direct democracy, for example in towns and local communities. Positioning itself at a global level, political power everywhere sets about obtaining by all possible means – pressure, repression, enticements and promises – the celebrated *consensus*, which assumes and creates stability. To revive and redeploy (another fashionable word) production and the productive apparatus would first of all require massive injections of technology, with consequences that are as formidable as they are unpredictable. Certainly, economic policy no longer consists in scrapping technology – something Lenin regarded as inevitable under monopoly capitalism – but in an adroitly balanced mix aimed at leaving the essential structures intact. Adopted or imposed, innovations are worked out in high places, in such a way as not adversely to affect the relations of domination, and even to strengthen them. Yet alterations occur that shake the system.

A hypothesis that has already been formulated concerns the dual character of the changes. Some, at the level of daily life, are imperceptible but cumulative. They are not merely minor events to be situated at the 'micro' level, simple isolated facts; they are added to, or superimposed upon, one another. Hence they end up generating irreversible, decisive alterations. A well-known historical case: the slow transformation of the Roman world into Christendom during centuries of transition long neglected by historians, but whose significance they are gradually discovering, with their efforts directed precisely towards reconstructing daily life during these times. Other changes occur at a macro level; they are abrupt, disruptive, not gradual, and are thus akin to a 'qualitative leap'. They come from on high, not from below: serious events, political decisions, mutations generally regarded as historic. So they occur at the macro level, but in the majority of cases this does not mean that understanding, a project, knowledge exist at this level. An equally well-known case: the French Revolution and its sequels.

Intermediate changes can also happen, deriving either from one of the above modalities and reacting upon the other, or from their interaction and conjunction. In other words, the duality under consideration should not be frozen; nor should the possibilities of change be fixed in models. A minor example: it would appear that today, within the framework of the current mode of production, the market is altering; there are more goods in demand and products for daily use, but in smaller quantities in each instance. So that it is necessary to envisage diversified production, and less mass production. From this perspective, enormous concentrations of machines, with an extreme division of labour and monotonous repetition of fragmented tasks, have supposedly served their time, work on the assembly line included. Digitally controlled machines, as well as computer and remote control of complex processes, could replace repetitive, dangerous operations (which, it is belatedly recognized, can stifle workers' capacity for invention and initiative). Such modifications of productive labour and the relation between men and machines would unquestionably entail recasting relations to labour, daily life and the world. But this process is only in its early stages – something that confirms several earlier remarks.

The crisis, so it is said, invariably ignoring or masking its profundity, affects daily life in surprising ways, at once crude and subtle, obvious and elusive, conservative and subversive, trivial and dramatic. A kind of crisis of consciousness and, above all, of confidence tends to weaken the relation between daily life and the major institutions that administer it. The consensus over the political and daily life alike, which political speeches ritually evoke on occasion, becomes increasingly blurred. Notwithstanding what specialists call 'dysfunctions' or 'perverse effects', the great institutional entities – justice, the Inland Revenue, the army, the academy, social security, the police, and so on – were generally regarded as broadly fulfilling their duties. The consensus that was indispensable for this had gradually faded in France with the Second World War, defeat and Vichy. Restored after the Liberation, severely shaken in 1968, it then regained some vigour and substance. Why? By dint of the growth to which all social classes and strata *consented*, each of them reckoning to be the beneficiary. However, the distribution of the fruits of growth remained extremely unequal; with the end of this relatively trouble-free growth, the bell tolled for the consensus over the established order, presaging the discrediting of those who banked on it 'democratically'. As long as rapid growth, which aimed to be exponential, lasted, 'progress' brought sizeable profits for some, and a certain comfort and improvement in living conditions for others. *We* were able to forecast needs because, in fact, *we* simultaneously produced these needs and the material goods designed to satisfy them.

Since the onset of crisis, the situation has tended to be turned upside down. The disadvantaged, the rejects, abandon the prospect offered them by the technological and scientific revolution – that is to say, unlimited growth. On all sides, people start blaming existing institutions, holding them responsible for all the illusions and depredations. There is more and more discrepancy between the institutional level and daily life. Without critical knowledge or formulated expression of the discontent that is materializing, what is established takes on a pejorative connotation, both factually and symbolically. Bureaucracy, a brutal and inefficient hierarchy, both cumbersome and tactless, is revealed to the public in all its horror; critical thinking is then at hand. Moreover, suspicion is directed at official institutions but is liable to be extended to other organizations – trade unions, for example. The links between individuals and groups, and between these and the nation (perceived and felt identity), loosen, in such a way that democracy as it is experienced, as national and political community, and the state as a set of institutions, become obscured and in need of profound transformation. Rather than being placed in remote entities, social trust, for all that it persists, is invested in what is proximate, in the local, which enjoys various assumptions in its favour: it occupies a well-defined place; it can be reached; one can act on it and on the people in charge of it; it supposedly eludes the manipulations and abuse of power, for it possesses its own capacity for organization, and the people in charge of it are sensible and sensitive. In short, it is close to daily life.

The symptoms of this new situation in daily life, and outside daily life, are multiplying – as if a rupture was brewing in social behaviour or, more precisely, in the behaviour of individuals *vis-à-vis* the social, which is impoverished, alienated, external. So it is that planning, which but a few years ago enjoyed enormous prestige, no longer elicits a consensus, still less enthusiasm. Planning by institutions is criticized, and not without reason, for impoverishing the social. For a certain period, neoliberalism, an official mystification, benefited from this mindset: a Western model, whose contours were very vague, was revalorized and identified with Freedom, while the standing of the socialist model, hypothetically identified with Soviet reality, fell.

In daily life, problems of an economic kind proliferate; they must be taken into account and taken on. This is the level at which people (people in the everyday) deal with managing the crisis. People at the base sense that what is involved is not a short critical phase but a long period, even though hopes of emerging from it shortly have not disappeared. Hence the shift in centres of interest, through a series of minute alterations that have produced a sizeable change in recent years: the importance of micro-decisions and micro-adaptations, and a lack of interest in the totality and theory. The result is that from 1975 onwards a 'reformist' game and stake replaced those of the contestation, without those concerned having a clear idea of where this attitude is leading them ... Rupture? At all events, a transition beyond contestation and conservatism alike. In their way, the interested parties are charting unknown territory. This goes together with the constitution of secondary circuits of substitution and replacement, external to the major established networks. It is as if, in order to avoid the traps, take advantage of the circumstances, and escape the adverse consequences, the people of daily life had anticipated the advent of the dual society: on the one hand, dominant, established circuits; on the other, external circuits, moonlighting, direct exchange and barter, more or less underground contacts. This sometimes creates the impression that 'subterranean' relations are not external to those established in the public light of day, but penetrate and possibly invigorate them.

Such an analysis accepts various typical features of the 'dual society', without endorsing the central thesis: the split between the two fragments of society. It would oppose any appropriation of the concept of difference by this thesis.[1]

The somewhat dislocated consensus leaves room, on the one hand, for constraint, should the state judge it appropriate; and on the other, for various currents, convergent or divergent. These currents of ideas and opinions – that is to say, of representations – are not unrelated to social classes and strata, but they do not coincide with them. A different 'classification' from classification in terms of classes is emerging, although it is not obvious that it is being consolidated structurally; the two classifications coexist, not without methodological and theoretical problems. The multiplicity of currents in opinion, and also in lifestyles, marks out the everyday, without abolishing its concept. Homogeneity does not disappear; it stands in for the vanishing consensus. Uncertainties, fears and scares, which are not dispelled by official security measures, prompt a sort of neorealism in behaviour: people (the people of daily life) start to respect power more than knowledge. When knowledge clashes with power, it loses all prestige in a confrontation that was once prestigious. Yet authority must still be combined with competence. It would seem that the quest for security at any price generates the opposite desire: a taste for risk revives among a section of young people – that is to say, a taste for living without guarantees. At the same time, the tendency to believe in progress, which seemed outmoded, is strengthened: in certain currents of opinion, the hope is that recent technologies will liberate society from established supervision and tyrannical protection. This hope is sometimes translated into a political aim: control of information from below and socialization of the social good that is information technology. What follows is a devaluation of ideologies, which has already been noted on several occasions. Marxism is not exempt from this: although ideology-critique was energetically pursued, and even inaugurated, by Marx, his theoretical thought is regarded as ideology, and sometimes as the prototype of the ideological. Contrariwise, technocratic ideology is not considered ideological, any more than religions, which are taken to provide models for everyday practice. Obviously, we are simply referring to social tendencies and trends here.

The erosion of institutional images is a subject for study (institutional analysis). These studies do not concern the critique of everyday life directly, yet they are of relevance to it in that they disclose modifications in practice, not merely in the discursive or the imaginary. It seems that a certain understanding of social facts is emerging among a wide public, which in no way excludes impoverishment of the *social*, reduced to 'community' and social security or security measures. Quite the reverse: they proceed in tandem. Naivety and credulity are slowly but surely disappearing: 'credibility' is demanded. People seek out the 'authentic', or tokens of it – which still leaves plenty of room for mystification and deception. It is none the less the case that mistrust on the part of the everyday person extends to all discourses. Have we not reached the point in everyday relations where we inter-pret gestures and facial expressions as much as we grasp the meaning of words? Interest in 'body language' increases with a certain revival of the body and of interest in the body, with the pursuit of its reap-propriation – above all, by and for women – at the expense of the image and the spectacle. The predominance of the visual – image, spectacle – over the corporeal is declining without disappearing – something that will slowly but surely alter the relation between daily life and space. Space is no longer defined exclusively in optical, geo-metrical and quantitative fashion. It is becoming – or once again becoming – a flesh-and-blood space, occupied by the body (by bodies). Judging from certain readily observable symptoms, daily life is tending to become, or once again become, multi-sensory; the quest and desire for a more actual presence are substituted for images as such. Hence a certain revival of the theatre and, on the other hand, the search for richer (three-dimensional) images.

Citizens – not to mention users – have a stronger and clearer sense of the relations of domination to the extent that authority as such impacts on them, the functioning of institutions no longer proceeding 'all by itself'. They detect manipulation through interpretations of 'facts' that are in themselves ambiguous. The conditions for a rupture and real change in life seem to be being created bit by bit, gradually. Yet who wants 'really' to change life, other than by discourse? Every-day existence at home, in the house (which in a majority of cases is no longer one), reflects office life or factory life; and vice versa. What is intolerable in the one reflects what is intolerable in the other. Taken together, they support one another and everyone, dominant and dom-inated alike, adapts to it.

At this point in the analysis, we can advance some hypotheses. This analysis detects symptoms of a gradual transformation, which is only just beginning. This does not preclude qualitative leaps as a result of global actions: decisions, events, catastrophes. At the political level, in this perspective, we are witnessing a transition from impersonal power – abstract power and sovereignty – to authority; and from the latter to influence – that is to say, a personalization of authority requiring direct contact with 'subjects'. There is also a transition from large established units towards smaller units, 'base cells' connected to local spaces (sites), which contains a risk of dislocation but tends to favour differences over homogenization. Will the crisis generate differentiation or fragmentation? For the time being, the question will remain without a definite answer, since that depends on both social practice and political practice, initiatives from below and decisions at the top. Furthermore, it may be that new contradictions will emerge, and that the crisis will induce both differentiation and fragmentation – that is to say, sites that are rich in relations and sites without relations, forms of solitude. Thus, we simultaneously observe a growing desire for corporeality, which always has something opaque about it, and a longing for transparency, which precludes any opacity in relations. Similarly, increasing interest attaches to results, which require strict individual or collective discipline, and at the same time to Freedom as well as freedoms. But the most significant thing today, when it comes to assessing factors of continuity and/or discontinuity, is to grasp the *importance* accorded to daily life. The dominated, the 'subjects', now represent themselves to themselves in accordance with everyday practice, not ideologies (which do not disappear for all that). In fact, today everyone banks on daily life: politicians as well as professional manipulators, advertisers and propagandists, and also 'subjects'. The level of the totality remains of decisive importance, since it is the level of decision-making. But it is perceived only in its relation to what are called local and limited – in reality, everyday – actions. Without denying it, this situates the theoretical and practical – that is political – importance of the whole, but registers the recent fact that the local, the proximate – that is to say, daily life – allows for action by those 'concerned' and seems to them to be the privileged site, the only site (and in this they are mistaken), in which they can be effective.

2 Recuperation

A question arises. The alterations now under way, which tend towards provoking rupture, encounter contrary – stabilizing and reductive – forces, which tend towards immobility under the pretext of equilibrium. How and why is it that the elements of mobility and renovation have not hitherto had more impact, to use the sociological terminology? How and why have they not broken through the barriers?

Recuperation is not something invented by intellectuals to explain the failure of subversive, innovatory ideas and projects. Its concept – for that is what it is – was fashioned to refer to a (social and political) practice. Moreover, in accordance with the famous Hegelian law, the concept appeared belatedly, when what it referred to had already occurred, been exhausted, and was even tending to fade.

The recuperative operations can be inventoried; they were deliberately targeted at what might have changed, in order to prevent change. The defeat of change can sometimes entail appreciable modifications, which nevertheless fall short of the possibilities and projects. A remarkable instance, to which reference has already been made, concerns the family. Until recently the family was the dominant figure in social relations, but the twentieth century saw it discredited and weakened; it is increasingly out of place in its social location: the junction between the public and the private. In the current mode of production, the enterprise is gradually replacing the family as dominant figure, for the family itself is assuming the shape of an enterprise. Even so, it still differs from the enterprise because of the affective as well as material investment required to educate children. Notwithstanding resistance, this tends to take pride of place; it becomes the crucial link in the transmission of capital, of material and spiritual (cultural) property. In this way, a model of the bourgeois family is constituted. Belatedly: prior to this, the bourgeoisie still followed the aristocratic model, which, in a manner of speaking, it imitated. Yet no sooner has it been constituted than the bourgeois, capitalist model, generated by the mode of production, tends to break down. Why? Because it is oppressive, even for those who benefit from it. It is attacked on all sides: by women's movements; by intellectuals ('Families, I hate you! ...'); by the proliferation of divorce; by the integration of women into economic activity; and perhaps above all by the control that women have won over the physiological process of fertility – a genuinely new power, or rather *counter-power*, and hence a factor of rupture. And yet, in the very process of this disruption, and in contradiction with it, the restricted family is consolidated. Much more than that: the popular (proletarian) family, previously larger than the bourgeois family and more open to the social, is modelling itself on the bourgeois family. Critical ideology – the rejection of institutions, the aforementioned disappearance of the consensus about institutions, the devaluation of the sacred conjugal bond and of the family as a privileged site – this 'advanced' ideology has not disappeared. It persists. But in social practice, the family, with its modern complement and model, the enterprise, remains functionally and structurally fundamental. Advanced ideology, backward structures! The laws in France reforming the situation of women and their legal status have strengthened the family. On the other hand, inequality between women and men – discrimination – eliminated to a certain extent from the family group, is maintained in the enterprise, workshop or office, and possibly even intensified. Whence the compensatory reference of these aspects of daily life to one another. Does this unquestionable recuperation of the familial derive from the state? From the strategy of the mode of production? From a spontaneous alteration in values and norms? Or from an unwitting return to traditions? It really doesn't matter. The phenomenon is with us: a case of alteration and recuperation.

There is no lack of subjects for recuperation: the urban question, difference, self-management, have been recuperated or are in the process of being recuperated. What does the process of recuperation consist in? In this: an idea or a project regarded as irredeemably revolutionary or subversive – that is to say, on the point of introducing a discontinuity – is normalized, reintegrated into the existing order, and even revives it. Shaken for a brief moment, the social relations of production and reproduction – that is to say, domination – are reinforced. Rather than analyzing the process – the diversion and circumvention of the initial project – the hypercritics, dogmatists and sectarians prefer to blame those who took the initiative and launched the idea. This is a theoretical and practical error. The fact that a project or concept has been 'recuperated' does not mean that it was not potentially active for a period of time. It means that 'people' (the opponents of the established order or disorder) did not know how, or were not able, to seize

777

the opportunity, the favourable conjuncture, and carry out the project. Conjunctures pass; opportunities disappear for good. Even before conquering the doctrine of historical evolution, the Greek philosophers were aware of that. Is this not how inventors, generally positioned on the Left, provide ideas for 'reactionaries', that is, the Right? Certainly. But attributing the failure or diversion to the person who suggested the idea is nevertheless a futile and dishonest polemical operation. Like blaming Marx for the borrowings and appropriations – by Keynes and so many others – that allowed capital to survive and win out. In this way, serious responsibilities are masked. Above all, a basic socio-political fact is veiled: for two centuries and more, invention has been the fruit of critical thinking, that is to say, of the Left. The established order has a great capacity for adaptation and integration; it assimilates what is opposed to it. It has demonstrated a surprising flexibility, an unsuspected capacity, which should taken into account, instead of attacking those who invent. Marx, to come back to him – is not in any way responsible for the degeneration and dubious use of Marxism. Another exemplary case is patriotism, a revolutionary invention that was appropriated over the course of the nineteenth century with national questions and their effects on social and political issues. Another example is planning, brainwave of Marxists and Marx himself, which obsessed statesmen the world over throughout the twentieth century. The sole exception is regionalism – for so long a rightist concept, adopted by the Left and even 'ultra-leftism', but one which the Right can still make its motto if left-wing decentralization misfires! Any misunderstanding on this crucial point leads to the loss of a tool for analysing the modern world critically. Hypercriticism has not made such analysis easier, or more profound, or more effective. It has become impossible to make any proposal without it immediately being accused of recuperation, in the name of a bolder project and especially a more radical negativism. This pseudo-radicalism has always confused moments and aspects within the process. First point: what can be recuperated is not, by the same token, recuperative. Second point, which must be stressed: there is nothing – no proposal, no project, no idea – which cannot be recuperated, that is to say, used by different social or political forces from those in whose name it was advanced. Third point: it is unjust as well as absurd to impute recuperation to those who initiate what is subsequently recuperated.

During the period in which contestation raged and blossomed, up to 1975 or thereabouts, recuperation became an official – in other words, political – activity. Private or joint research consultancies took charge of it. In the past, it occurred spontaneously, blindly, at the level of a fairly large group or social class. A reminder: patriotism, which was digested in the way an animal digests food by the right-wing bourgeoisie, its representatives and political supporters, and transformed into chauvinism. Nationalism made it possible for the dominant class to annex other classes or class fractions to itself by neutralizing opposition, before functioning as an 'ideological detona-tor' (to use Jean-Pierre Faye's expression, adopted by René Lourau)[2] – that is to say, exploding left-wing ideas and ideologies, and flying like an electric spark between two poles – Left and Right – which were suddenly assimilated, prompting novel political phenomena like national socialism. So recuperation has been going on for a very long time, but not in the manner of the years of protest. During this period, which was fairly brief, the tactic of the consultancies directed by technocrats was simple: assigning the protesters themselves the responsibility for studying delicate questions, thus obliging them to make daring ideas and projects assimilable. Once the idea or project had been 'studied' – that is to say, changed into knowledge and dis-course – the established order could take from it what suited it, both to disguise and to renew itself by discovering convenient solutions to real problems. Such operations assumed the priority of a certain positive knowledge, constituted as a corpus but still flexible – that of the technocrats. The latter were conscious of their own weaknesses: their dearth of inventive capacity – of 'creativity', to use their own terminology and mythology. With this shrewd move, the technocrats, who did possess powers of realization, stimulated their deficient imagination and compensated for it, while defusing dangerous theses. As a result, tendencies towards discontinuity, towards rupture, turned into factors for non-change. This fate was not reserved for Marxists, but even so they enjoyed a certain privilege. As the main target of these operations, Marxism was looked upon as the most fertile source once it had been appropriated. An exemplary case was the critique of everyday life, encapsulated as '*Changer la vie*'. This formula – which, to start off with, was disturbing and subversive, albeit vague – was then adopted and adapted on all sides, banalized, recuperated by advertising as well as various political parties, and ended up being blunted and flattened into 'quality of life'. This reduced it to signs of transformation and discourse on transformation, before it ended up in so-called concrete proposals concerning holiday periods and working hours. In lieu of changing life, the image of life was changed!

This prompts me to formulate as an axiom a proposition that I have already advanced: nothing is immune to recuperation. Let me end with the example of human rights. The fact that some dangerous forces, even imperialism, have sought to make use of them, and succeeded; the fact that they have supplied ideologies and tactics – these cannot justify abandoning or disavowing them, except out of sectarianism. On the contrary. We must understand the expression 'arena and stake of the struggle' in its strongest sense. Human rights? Through a hard-fought battle they must be wrested from those who seek to use and abuse them. It was a serious political error (a) to regard these rights as political tools permanently in the service of those who are dominant; (b) peremptorily to refute the ideology that has historically supplied their envelope, throwing the baby out with the bath-water; (c) not to give them a different foundation, extricating them from the old humanist ideology; (d) not to open them out by adding a multiplicity of rights, including the right to live in the city, the right to difference, and so on.

What happens when skilfully conducted recuperative operations succeed? Demands, aspirations, intentions are diverted and turned against the initial design. I must insist upon this paradox: confrontations and crises, including wars, as well as the more or less Marxist-inspired theory of these crises, have hitherto served the mode of production. They have allowed its representatives and leaders to introduce something new into the economico-socio-political order. From one recuperation to the next, the sovereign order and subordinate orders have acquired a capacity for integration that is achieved through opposition, demands, contestation. Recuperation has a most remarkable reduction effect – this observation applies not only to ideologies but to practice as well.

In recuperative operations, it is often difficult to distinguish the mix of strategic intention, ideology and practical spontaneity. Let us examine the case of the reoccupation of town centres by the middle classes and a neo-bourgeoisie – in short, by an 'elite'. For a period of time, it was possible that the deteriorating urban centres, which had been abandoned for the smart suburbs, would be taken back over and even reoccupied by the people. This movement could have become decisive and determinant in a strategy of urban revolutions. Latin America in particular was poised for an enormous revolutionary campaign: starting out from the shantytowns and seizing hold of the centres. Yet this movement has been temporarily broken by repression, violence and corruption, but also by recuperation. Neither workers, nor the unemployed, nor expropriated peasants have taken back control of the town centres.

3 Difference

This concept and its correlative, the right to difference, achieved theoretical formulation around 1968. Before this, obviously, a practice, aspirations and demands, attempts at a rational elaboration, existed. Round about this date, theoretical thinking arrived at difference via several convergent paths: (a) the *scientific route*: the concept of difference plays a major role both in mathematical set theory and in linguistics and related sciences; (b) the *philosophical route*, or general reflections on the human species and its possibilities, on anthropology and ethnic groups, on history, and so on; (c) the *methodological route*, the concept of difference featuring in reflections on logic, but also as an articulation between logic and dialectics; (d) the route of *protest*, in relations between sexes, generations, regions, and so on.

The formulation of the concept, and the right it involves, provided theoretical legitimation for some very diverse movements: the demands of immigrants, of women, regional movements, and so on. This theoretical formulation set itself against integration, whether by violence or, more insidiously, by 'acculturation' – a theme originating in American sociology, derived from such pseudo-concepts as 'cultural model'. The theory provided arguments against centralism and imperialisms. It sought to make a breach in ideology and practices subordinated to state power, and hence to the established mode of production. These practices proceed by the disintegration–integration of whatever resists them.

In the women's movements, difference theory sought to open up a way between two common errors: the one that regarded 'women' as a particular group, and even as a class embodying an essence – femininity; and the other that pushed 'women' to resemble men, to affect male behaviour. The way opened up by differentialist theory leads to demanding a status for women, as for the regions and countries concerned: *difference in equality*. It is self-evident that this equality in difference is not envisaged solely at the level of the individual or group, but on a world scale, between peoples and nations. This utterly transforms the old democratic concept of equality by releasing it from egalitarianism and general equivalence, and restoring a qualitative dimension to it. In this perspective, the right to difference must thus be added to human rights not only to complete them, but also to transform them. They no longer concern the entity 'man' but social and daily being, thus extending and deepening the orientation towards practice and concrete reality of the 'rights' proclaimed by the French Revolution, and originally restricted to property and opinion. In this way, we would leave behind the perennial abstract questions and no less abstract controversies about democracy, socialism and humanism. Today, rights can no longer be presented as a closed list of legal or moral principles, but as a series of practical maxims with the capacity to alter everyday life. This involves a project for society, or at least an important component of such a project. And the implication is that such a right and project are not proclaimed and demanded through discourse alone: they must be conquered; they are won in a political struggle.

The same conceptual and theoretical formulation has another meaning and another goal, indissociable from the one that has just been stated: to make Marxist thought more flexible, and to extend it. In Marx, but even more clearly in most of his successors, thinking is reduced to reflection on economic and political reality, on labour and workers, regarded as something 'real'. Thus, this thinking has become arid and scholastic. In considering only a uniform reality, it has assumed and retained a homogenizing appearance. This form of reflection is not on its guard against equivalence – and this despite appeals to the dialectic as well as historical development, and despite attempts to reintegrate national realities and historical specificities.

A case of unjustified mistrust? Misunderstanding? Incomprehension, or inability to tune into the world? 'Differentialist' research and analysis have found scarcely any echo either among official Marxists or among the others. No doubt they do not want to venture on to difficult terrain. This is the theoretically decisive point. Theses on differences cannot be separated from theoretical conceptions of the relation between *particularities* and *differences*, and the transition from the former to the latter.

Particularities are defined by nature and by the relation of the (social) human being to this nature. They consist in biological and physiological 'realities' that are given and determinate: ethnicity, sex, age. Being born white or black, small or large, with blue or dark eyes, is a particularity. So is being born in Africa or Asia. As for differences, they are defined only socially – that is to say, in specifically social relations. Unlike particularity, difference is not isolated: it takes its place in a whole. Particularities confront one another in struggles which run through history, and are simultaneously struggles between ethnic groups, peoples, and classes or class fractions. It is in the course of these struggles that differences are born out of particularities: they emerge, and this involves a certain knowledge and consciousness of *others* in and through conflictual relations – consequently entailing values that achieve relative acceptance. Spontaneous, natural particularities do not purely and simply disappear. Modified and transformed in the course of confrontations, they are integrated into these differences, which cannot be deemed exclusively cultural. The victory of a particularism abolishes difference and replaces it with a return to the natural, the original, affirmed and valorized as such. Could not the history of Greece, for example, be rewritten in this fashion? Starting with ethnic particularities, original groups and confrontations between them and with the 'barbarians', we have a first stage: the conquest of differences. Next there is a splendid period in which perceived and valued differences flourish. Finally, after the Median and Peloponnesian wars, we witness a return to particularisms and, consequently, decline. We could equally rewrite the history of modern democracies thus, with their oscillations between abstract generalities – permitting the coexistence of imperialism without and democracy within – and national particularisms.

The distinction between particularities and differences, and the dynamic it displays, form part of the theory. Neglecting it leads to confusions with serious consequences. To assert particularities as such under the guise of differences sanctions racism, sexism, separations and disjunctions. This is what differentialist theory, its methodology and concepts, precludes.

This theory and these concepts do not discredit class struggle in the name of difference and the right to difference. As if the bourgeoisie was within its 'rights' in affirming itself bourgeois! If we clearly distinguish between *particularities* and *differences*, the clash and confrontation of classes are born from historical particularities; they must produce a society in which, once 'workers' have grasped how they differ from others, they disappear as such with all their old particularities, the scars of alienated labour. This corresponds to Marx's strongest thinking, over and above vulgarizations of it.

This potential society will avoid the homogeneous – abstract and imposed identity – since, according to this schema, it will integrate what its history of confrontations has bequeathed. Equality in difference will be distinct from formal equality inasmuch as it is concrete. This confers a certain post-historical or trans-historical character on differences. And this assumes that history and evolution are not identified on principle, and that a social evolution beyond struggles to the death may be envisaged! This society is conceived neither as an ideal and a utopia, nor as an actual truth. The project of a plural society is also that of a democracy which unfolds its potentialities, rather than immobilizing them in struggles around state apparatuses. Why *plural*, not pluralist? Because the latter term is restricted to political positions and parties. The plural applies to daily life: to ways of living. Thus, on the horizon we find objectives directed against homogenizing powers, the state in that it erases differences and even particularities (rather than aiding their transformation into differences), as well as supra-national strategies and all *indifferent* operations. Taken to its ultimate conclusion, this theory thus introduces a new element into the debate. Assuming that the working class succeeds in conquering hegemony via the democratic route, it should not make its political goal the destruction pure and simple of the old dominant class – something that is regarded as essential in the classical conception of revolution. It should accept it with its acquisitions, in the name of difference, while obviously stripping it of its supremacy and the attributes that made it possible, therewith leading it towards the decline and end of all classes.

How and why has the theory of difference been ignored, neutralized, appropriated?

(a) *Politically*, self-evidently, this theory was intended for the Left – that is to say, the tendencies, organizations and parties with the orientation characterized thus, which is in principle innovatory and ultimately revolutionary. But these parties, inheritors of a strong Jacobin heritage which they did not recognize for what it was – that is to say, centralizing and somewhat phallocratic – have until recently failed to understand the right to difference, still less assimilate it. Perhaps they are fearful of its implications as regards women, regions and immigrants. Up until a few years ago, some politicians gave the nod (traditional terminology) to differentialist movements – regional movements, for example – with great caution, and mainly for reasons of popularity – in other words, to use such movements politically. Is this era going to end? We may hope so. Of the politicians said to be on the Left, some genuinely supported 'human rights', but in their legal, fixed form, as immutable, sacred rights, failing to see that the best way to defend them is actively to develop them (right to live in the city, right to difference, etc.). Others have adopted the defence of these rights reluctantly, following the Helsinki accords. Why? Because the critique of human rights and of formal democracy seemed to be part and parcel of Marxism. While numerous politicians rather grandly gave these 'immutable and sacred rights' a wide berth, making do with praising them from a distance, various ideologues worked no less arrogantly to destroy them, together with their legitimating ideology: humanism. Most of these ideologues were oblivious of the fact that the radical critique – too radical for once – of human rights and formal democracy, as well as their legitimating ideology, was already to be found in the Marxist tradition: refutation of supposed fraternity, of liberty for money, of fictional equality, of the political pseudo-community. Many Marxists have failed to understand that political strategy requires the realization of democracy by developing the rights that constitute its foundation. A positive struggle for the right to difference would have enhanced the effectiveness of struggles for and in democracy. When the 'Left' set about reflecting on differences – that is to say, on differential aspirations and demands – was it not already a little late? Had not the concept of difference already been diverted? Was it not already in the process of being captured and dragged to the right? On the other hand, the neoliberal ideology that has inspired political power for years had already done what was required to neutralize differential aspirations – for example, by baptizing the clear idea of decentralization and regional (territorial) self-management 'deconcentration', or (more ridiculously still) 'decongestion', of the state.

All in all, modifications in daily life in the direction of difference have hitherto remained the deed of a few groups of intellectuals, even though the influence of these groups is expanding and gradually prevailing (new household division of labour, at the micro level, that of daily life and private life, etc.).

(b) *Scientifically*, or rather, in accordance with the ideology of scientificity, an attempt has been made to substitute *distinction* for difference – and this in a rather underhand fashion, without discussion or debate, by mischievously confusing them (when in fact these concepts are opposed: the one implying relations, the other stressing that which separates). What is distinction? An abstract principle of classification and nomenclature on the one hand, and a principle of evaluation on the other. It is difficult to differentiate between these two aspects. The concept thus remains ambiguous as between logic and ethics (or aesthetics). The phenomenon theorized by it passes too readily from what is distinct to what is *distinguished*. In this way, it effects separations by accentuating social distances in the hierarchy. It is perfectly possible to detect and analyse distinctions, to make them an object of positive knowledge. Those who proceed thus will use them to 'classify', assuming that the operation has a strictly objective character when in fact it intervenes and modifies the object. One can easily employ distinction to 'classify' hierarchically organized populations sociologically, without troubling to define social 'classes', by appealing solely to the signs by which people distinguish themselves from one another. Here we recognize an old controversy in the social sciences, a methodological issue that seemed to have been superseded. There was a time when sociologists almost completely disposed of objective social relations, those of production and reproduction. They wanted to 'class' an individual in the bourgeoisie, among peasants, in the working or middle classes, only if she expressly declared herself bourgeois, petty-bourgeois, proletarian, and so on. Yet no-one who is blatantly a member of the bourgeoisie has ever been heard to declare: 'I am a bourgeois ...'. On the contrary. To such questions, the capitalist ingenuously replies: 'I work, I'm a worker!' – which is not untrue, or not completely so. Since the sociologists still refused to eschew subjectivism, it was necessary to refine the subjective criteria. In fact, those who distinguish classes according to the criterion of distinction always risk ordering social groups in relation to themselves, without explaining their link with their own group – the intellectuals – and the link between this group and society. To identify 'classes' with 'classification' defuses conflicts by eliminating the contradictions in the discourse of distinction and the distinguished. The two discourses – the discourses of those who distinguish and of those who are distinguished – are juxtaposed and sometimes combined. Thus we end up situating social groups exclusively by strata and layers, in a hierarchy acknowledged and sanctioned by ideology, taking little, if any, account of the major vertical and horizontal divisions with which the society under consideration is shot through.

Why does difference reconnect, as opposed to separating? Because it exists socially only as something perceived, and yet is perceived as such only in relations that are at once reciprocal and extensive. It situates differential elements, derived from particularities and history, in a whole where everyone has their place and which today extends to the global. Difference rallies by relativizing dissimilarities. Its concept makes it possible to let nothing slip and to lose nothing of the past, other than what evolution rejects – that is, exhausted and finished particularities. Distinction, in contrast, reduces the confrontations, aspects and elements of evolution to particularities that are preserved and asserted as such. In other words, the theory of distinction is centred on the real, what has been accomplished and the past, whereas difference is directed towards what is possible. The theory of distinction endeavours to bring the particular into the conceptual and into theoretical language, whereas difference tends towards the universal.

787

That said, it is only too true that present-day societies – in France, in Europe, in the Western world – may have missed out on difference. They tend to be founded on distinction – that is to say, on the ideology and practice of an important, influential section of the middle classes, with another section inclined towards protest, critical knowledge, and even contestation. In this sense, there is something novel in daily life: the emergence of distinctive criteria and characteristics at every level, and this without abolishing the general tendency to uniformity. Paradoxically, fragmentation does not preclude homogeneity.

It is only too true that the values and signs thus promoted as principles and criteria of distinction conduce to the disintegration of the social, its reduction. This emerges in Pierre Bourdieu's book on the subject, *Distinction*, which offers a remarkable description of the phenomenon, but without a critique of the process, which is treated 'positively', with the trained eye of the scientist. In sanctioning this process through the scientificity of his account, this scientistic sociologist not only ends up liquidating difference and differentialist thinking, but flattens social reality – that is to say, the reality of the social – by excluding several dimensions: the historical in the first instance, but also the values attached to the art works themselves and not the groups, values that are detached and killed by this sociological description. In defining these values exclusively by their social relation conceived as a factor of distinction, positive knowledge abolishes them. One-dimensionality *à la* Herbert Marcuse thus comes to pass in unforeseen ways, in knowledge and reality alike – and in France, too, not only in the USA. This flattening out is not confined to a work that is scientific in intent, but undoubtedly occurs in the reality described – that is to say, the middle classes, or a section of them at least. Such works perpetuate the most questionable aspects of positive knowledge in general, sociology in particular, and Marxism itself (sometimes reduced to a sociologism, sometimes to a historicism, sometimes to an economism or a philosophism). The reduction of the social to class interests and ideologies – albeit those of the middle classes, not the bourgeoisie – tends to destroy the social. What emerges from this reduction is a more or less static essentialism, or a more or less abstract voluntarism. Taken as a criterion, distinction generates an essence for certain strata, which is imputed to them, to which they are attached, and which is constituted with its distinctive conduct in the face of all opposition (in the face of the totality). It is also the case that ambitions or pretensions dressed up as 'distinction' with respect to supposedly inferior social layers can give rise to political aims that are enlisted in the rulers' game.

If someone prefers the *Carnaval de Vienne* and Schumann's music to the songs of Sylvie Vartan or Sheila, so the argument goes, it is in order to distinguish himself from the petty bourgeois who adore the latter – and also to cancel the distance by means of which the bourgeois elite distinguishes itself from other classes. Intrinsically, Schumann and his music are worth next to nothing. The aesthetic value of the music no longer enters into the equation: without saying so, obviously, the tendency is to eliminate it. What a reduction, what an impoverishment, compared with Adorno's remarks (to confine ourselves to one example) on the relation between the musical, the social and the ideological!

The accumulation of facts, data and even statistics proves what it is intended to prove, yet proves nothing. On the contrary: it tells against the 'realism' of a thesis that destroys potentiality in the name of positive knowledge. This thesis positively supports a mystification that sets out from the real, and uncritically sanctions it by abolishing what Hegel rightly considered to be as real as the accomplished facts, and more so – that is, the possible.

(c) *Strategically*. Here the New Right makes its appearance. Roughly, it says: 'The Left has made nothing of difference and differential demands. Left-wing politicians are basically Jacobins. They will not retreat from that even if they pretend to renounce the doctrine of centralization. If they loosen the reins with respect to differences – for example, as far as the regions are concerned – it is the better to ensure the privileges of the centre and state power. They have more chance of succeeding in this operation than the neoliberals, who failed miserably at it. The demands of the dominated, of countries and regions, young people, women themselves, have failed because they have received no more than lukewarm, mainly verbal, support from the Left. Let us learn the lessons of this failure. The socialist and communist Left is allowing theoretical concepts and instruments that were developed in its name, under its influence, and seemingly attached to it, to slip from its feeble grasp. What does it have to offer against homogeneity, the homogeneity of commodities sanctioned by the state? To this wretched, global, daily homogeneity of Western society as fashioned by the bourgeoisie, the boldest counterpose another homogeneity that is no less menacing and menaced, and which, moreover, can converge with it: the homogeneity of work and the worker. The Left envisages and proposes equality only in non-differentiation, in similarity, or rather in abstract identity itself defined by the state. If these left-wingers, politicians and thinkers, have hitherto failed in their endeavours, and will continue to do so, ceding to force of circumstance, is it not because there is some error in their reasoning, their calculations and speculative constructions? This is their error: they have failed to understand the meaning of the difference – that is to say, the *inequality* – between living species, peoples, groups and classes, and individuals. Differences are qualitative; or they are not differences. That differences exist means that there are superior and inferior types. Those who pronounce "difference" assert intellectual, moral and physical inequality between different people. Otherwise, difference boils down to generalities such as "man" and his various, equally abstract "rights" – as abstract as the entity to which they refer, in which all who reflect on the subject have ceased to believe. Only inequality, openly acknowledged and proclaimed, confers meaning, value and concrete significance on differences, which have hitherto been reduced to mere facts or extolled in utopian fashion by a destructive ideology. Inequality, which is always experienced but illusorily rejected, must be accepted precisely as difference. How can anyone deny that the children of the dominant classes and developed countries assimilate culture, science and knowledge better than the others? If one thinks in terms of "civilizations", rather than the levelling concept of "society", how can anyone deny that there are civilizations which are superior and others which are inferior, successful civilizations and failed civilizations? The egalitarian Left challenges this in vain, and condemns culture to decline. What a long way we have come since Marx naively but firmly identified the proletariat as the inheritor of philosophy! What the Left wants to impose could become law and norm only in the course of crises and struggles that would be ruinous for civilization. How distant is the golden age when revolutionaries dreamed of regenerating the old corrupted society in a bloodbath! Particularities, if we want to talk about them, are identified with genetic inheritance. Essential and not relative (relational), they must be carefully preserved. This thesis is based on the social sciences, and especially biology and sociobiology. As a new science, biology restores it centre-stage, with inevitable controversies that go back more than a century: "The chimerical equality socialism strives for is in total contradiction with the absolute inequality that everywhere obtains between individuals," the biologists Schmidt and Haeckel were already saying in 1877.'

Continuing his discourse, the representative of the New Right would say: 'We must go further and deeper than biology. Our new doctrine cannot make do with a foundation that is restricted to a single science. This position is insufficient to refute the Left by replying to the Marxist critique of capitalism and the bourgeoisie. That critique does not lack arguments or good motives, but today it may be regarded as outmoded. The Marxist Left was not wrong when it showed that the world of commodities extends to the planet, is constituted as internationality on the basis of Americanism and the commodity-order in the USA. Marxists were able to demonstrate the reductive and destructive capacity of this commodity-order with respect to all singularity, everything that resists homogeneity, the standardization and automation of social mechanisms. The Left was unaware, or did not want to see, that this tendency has been strengthened in the name of Marxism. Whether willingly or unwillingly allied to capitalism, Marxism proceeds in concert with it towards a system in which techno-economic rationality, resulting in the self-regulation of the system, becomes identical with madness, in a total, totalitarian mercantilism that destroys the life of peoples precisely by suppressing the right to difference – and to power! The complicity of socialism and capitalism is now established. That is where renewal starts out from. The automation of productive labour? You must be joking! We are heading for a gigantic self-regulated mechanism for organizing work more efficiently ...'[3]

At this point in the debate, the hypercritic inevitably intervenes. Let us give him the floor. He takes it and delivers his verdict: 'Just like the rights of man and the citizen, difference and the right to difference belong to the ideological inheritance of the middle classes, who today carry great social weight, out of all proportion to their political influence. Whence their attempt to end this discrepancy. In accordance with their position in contemporary society, they make contradictory use of this ideology. Either they criticize the political authorities, or they launch an attack on them with the aim of replacing them. They seek to distinguish themselves from one another, as layers and strata; and still more to distinguish themselves from the working class. Hence the cult of differences, hence the search for differences and distinctions in food, clothing, furniture, space – in short, everyday life. Differences? The proletariat has no time for them; it has nothing to do with these intellectual niceties; it could not care less about regions, about local or national differences. In so far as it is affected by this ideology, its (class) consciousness is confused, and this can lead it into dead ends. Self-management? It risks overshadowing, postponing, the self-determination, the autonomy, of the working class, and leading us towards a self-managed capitalism! Let us be clear! Let us eliminate these ambiguities! Whether on the Left or the Right, you are all making a fundamental error, an error of method and theory. What is important? Contradictions! Conflict! Not differences! ... Contradictions and conflict are blunted and attenuated by substituting differences for them. That is why liberalism yesterday and the Right today have recuperated supposed rights, including the right to difference. The bourgeoisie had to pay the price for what it calls the new deployment of its mode of production. It has paid to make the middle classes, intellectuals and technicians – classes secreted by it and kept for years on the fringes of power – partners in its system. Is it or is it not the case that the town centres and city life modelled by capital have just been occupied or reoccupied by the new middle class and the new bourgeoisie, whereas the people and the working class were not able to take control of them? The upshot, moreover, is that the people and the working class can neither take over the centre, nor achieve genuine decentralization – so that, pending a new order – that is, a genuinely revolutionary transformation – they can only endure the operational schema imposed on them from above: eviction as far away as possible from city centres, ghettos and segregation, with state and political control, and it alone, preventing society from splitting ...'

Answers (to the hypercritic as well as the representative of the New Right): 'Everything you have both said about self-management as well as rights, including the right to difference, is correct: it can be said, and already has been said. The right to difference does not preclude all ambiguity. It does not possess an implacable logic. Yes, self-managed capitalism is not inconceivable. Yes, human rights have served as a double-edged political weapon, sometimes for imperialism and sometimes for the struggle against imperialism. What does that mean? This is where we come to the main thing: the arena and stake of the struggle coincide. This is a fundamental formula, which is still barely understood. Moreover, the arena and the stake are expanding. The local, the regional, the national and the global are all part of the vast territory on which the political struggle is developing. You of the New Right reject 'rights' as negating what, for you, is difference. You set difference up against rights, whereas the introduction of difference into abstract rights modifies and transforms them. You, the hyper-critic, reject rights because, according to you, they are harmful – the naive, vain right to freedom of opinion, property rights that are all too real. You thus refuse what gives concrete expression to rights in democracy – that is to say, in the struggle for democracy. Rather than the rise of the middle classes, should we not accept that we are witnessing the onset of a crisis in society based on the ideological predominance of these composite, heterogeneous classes, under the hegemony of capital? You reject the concept of democracy, which you judge to be empty. You have your reasons. And yet critical reason demands another approach, enlarging the conception – classical on both sides, bourgeois and Marxist – of rights and struggles. Far from blunting their edge and rendering them empty, differential demands compound economic demands and conflicts, enhancing their strength. It is nevertheless true that the links between the differential and the conflictual change over time; the link is always conjunctural. Do you think a French-speaking worker in Montreal can bear to hear his English-speaking, Anglophile or Americanophile boss say: "Talk white!", without experiencing anger? The pressure of Anglo-American capitalism has been increasing in recent years, dispossessing the French Canadian worker of his "identity", this famous identity of which so much is made, and which is itself rich in hidden conflicts and contradictions. Hence the inevitable proclamation of difference – that is to say, of identity rediscovered and developed in and through difference. When national and linguistic – or, if you're fond of this term, "cultural" – oppression compounds economic and political domination, the latter becomes intolerable. Demands then become differential. It may be that the national takes priority over the social, and endeavours to subordinate it. Then, there is disjunction and separation; social demands have difficulty gaining access to consciousness, language and positive knowledge, action. In the course of this conflict, the national and the differential can smother the social. However, social demands have to go via the national, and retain it. They must pass through the differential phase, and retain something from this passage. The stress is forever shifting. It must be added that both of you, New Right and left-wing hypercriticism alike, confuse particularities and differences. Either you do not appreciate the transition from one to the other, with its problems, its conflicts, its relapses, its regressions; or you underestimate it. When the national takes precedence over the social, it is because it relapses into particularism, rather than raising itself up to difference. Finally – our last argument – both sides evince an extraordinary incomprehension of Nietzschean thought. You leftists and dogmatists end up saying that Nietzsche represents the landed aristocracy and its vestiges.[4] One might as well say – to take the texts of the very young Marx – that he represented the liberal petty bourgeoisie in Germany. As for you, men of the Right, you retain only the glorification of the will to power from Nietzsche, when we must also, and especially, see in him the inception of a critique of it. Thought, love and poetry commence where the will to power ceases, where it expires …'

4 The State and Daily Life

Let us now try to see the question of the state, which has already been glimpsed in certain aspects, in its complexity and totality. In fact, the question of the totality is posed here. From the analyses, an inversion of the common, daily accepted viewpoint has already emerged. The state and its administrative and political apparatuses *seem* to be the keystone of society; they appear to hold it in their powerful grip. This is not untrue, as regards either the representation or what it refers to.

Yet this representation is mystificatory. The state is now built upon daily life; its base is the everyday. The traditional Marxist thesis makes the relations of production and productive forces the 'base' of the ideological and political superstructures. Today – that is to say, now that the state ensures the administration of society, as opposed to letting social relations, the market and blind forces take their course – this thesis is reductionist and inadequate. In the course of major conflicts and events, the relations of domination and the reproduction of these relations have wrested priority over the relations of production that they involve and contain. In its way, daily life likewise involves and contains them. This is a curious inversion: daily life and people in daily life still perceive the institutional edifice above their heads. Similarly, the crowd of believers perceive the cathedral, caress its pillars with their eyes and hands, feel the soil under their feet. In daily life, these believers do not realize that they *are* the soil on which the edifice rests and bears down. With all their gestures, words and habits, they preserve and support the edifice. Neoliberal ideology has succeeded in maintaining this deceptive perspective, and has even reinforced it. Only a certain anarchist tradition has corrected it to some extent, but without succeeding in shaking the edifice. Since the *belle époque* of militant anarchism, which was coeval with the bourgeois *belle époque*, and despite the terrorism that prolongs the anarchist tradition, the edifice has been perfected from year to year, answering the terrorism of its opponents with state terrorism.

In so far as change has occurred, it has been for the worse. There is no need to discourse at length to prove the extension of state – that is, police – control. But be careful when it comes to the critique of the state today! The political situation obliges us to reconsider and reintroduce a distinction between *left critique* and *right critique* that seemed outdated. These two critical stances are often mixed up, in a dangerous confusion. The confusion is increased by the fact that for a long time hypercriticism has regarded as right-wing and reactionary any utterance about the state that did not include the demand for its imminent, even immediate, abolition. Furthermore, the difference between these critical attitudes was blurred by the fact that various political plans, tactically identifying themselves with national unity or democratic action, claimed to be situated beyond the division between Right and Left. This distinction is becoming current once more. What does the right-wing critique claim? It incriminates the bureaucratic cumbersomeness of the state apparatuses, their clumsy interventions, the enormous cost of these interventions, subventions and support for the various 'social rejects', and so on. As for the left-wing critique, it accuses statesmen of striving to reinforce the state, shattering the social by causing it to permeate society in its entirety, being repressive, using information tendentiously – ultimately, of treating the state as an end in itself, not as an instrument in the service of society. This dual indictment, inseparable from other ideological or strategic elements, cannot fail to shake the state at its foundation. The question of the state is transformed: it becomes – the state in question!

The contemporary state has three sides: managerial and administrative; security – the state as guardian, guaranteeing security, insuring and reassuring; finally, and above all, the lethal side – army and armaments, police and justice, repression and oppression. There is no point dwelling at length on the organization of the state here. It is sufficient to show that even in daily life an agonizing conflict sets in between security and risk, between fixed determinations decreed from on high (identity) and inevitable evolution. This contributes significantly to the malaise, the dissatisfaction that is mixed in with satisfaction. Simultaneously protector and oppressor, manager and arbiter, authoritarian and rational, liberator and identitarian, the contemporary state is piling up contradictions under official discourses of the utmost coherence. For years the state technocracy and techno-structure have long concealed the enormity of the bureaucracy and its arbitrariness under the ideology of competence and performance. Hence the critiques, but also the double-sidedness of those critiques. Hence also the vanishing of joy, pleasure and enjoyment in the clutches of the coldest of cold monsters. From what quarter will the deliverance we have been awaiting for so long come? The everyday is strictly dependent upon this situation: it unfolds, or rather stagnates, under this dominion, with functionalism and official formalism disguising the enterprises of the will to power. With what determination have statesmen for decades been cutting down anything that sticks out, destroying whatever does not conform to the established norms, striking at some particular social phenomenon – sex, drugs, idleness, and so on – in order thereby to target everything that threatens them. Thus is daily life normalized. Attempts at emancipation are sometimes repressed, sometimes skilfully recuperated and incorporated – these two aspects of the tactics of administrative apparatuses complementing one another. Need I remark in passing that what we are dealing with is administrative apparatuses, not ideological apparatuses, which are at most capable of erecting a smokescreen over real operations? Moreover, the state is capable only of a seeming preservation of national unity and identity, which it exploits shamelessly. In fact and in practice, the state apparatuses press towards rupture and fragmentation, a split society – the work of the state, concealed by it – forcibly maintained in the existing political framework.

Is it not clear, even obvious, that the critique of everyday lived experience must abandon the immediate, and be reconsidered in accordance with state activity and its enormous organizational capacities? It is not enough to blame capitalism, commodities and money, as well as 'bourgeois' society, for being dehumanizing and oppressive. It is no longer sufficient to invoke the transcendence of 'real life' or the 'true life'. It is no longer even necessary to establish the moral, mental or spiritual priority of the surreal, the ideal or the unreal over the real. Appeals to art can prove as disappointing as the appeal to truth against reality. Refutation of the commodity as a world, and of the global as a product of the market, still has a sense. Unfortunately, however, this sense also implies the non-sense of the refutation. For the essential thing today is the state, which increasingly elevates itself above its own conditions in the world of commodities (which simultaneously supports the state in general and tends to shatter each particular state, dissolving it into the global). The role of critical thinking consists here in demonstrating the mortal character of the state: it bears within it the conditions of its own death and, what is more, it leads to death. Once we have proved this, a choice, a bifurcation, seems unavoidable. Either we attempt to go beyond the level of the state, adopting as a practical and intellectual hypothesis its rupture or dissolution; or we seek to install ourselves in the actual, circumventing and diverting the pressure, if necessary using it to motivate micro-decisions. Is the latter option feasible? Unquestionably, if we accept that all the basic elements of the question have been clarified; that today there is nothing blind and opaque, as was once the case with the spread of the market, industry and technology.

But if it is true that changes in daily life occur by two routes, the local and the global, the micro and the macro, perhaps this option is unavailing?

People may think that the splendour of power and the splendour of the state have nothing to do with the humility of daily life. What a mistake that would be! Critical analysis begins with the disenchantment of the state and the sphere of power. They have nothing magical or sacramental about them. Charismatic? This metaphor, which is itself magical, is no longer meaningful in contemporary politics, where power is acquired through tactics and strategy, manoeuvres and campaigns, including advertising campaigns.

The state today is no longer content to 'discipline and punish'. It was the state of the *belle époque* that assumed an ethical function of normalization: weeding out the useless, eliminating the abnormal. Today, the state manages daily life directly or indirectly. Directly, through regulations and laws, more numerous prohibitions, and the tutelary action of institutions and administrations. Indirectly, through taxation, the apparatus of justice, steering the media, and so on. Since the *belle époque* of 'discipline and punish', a sort of inversion has occurred in the situation. Previously, what was not prohibited was permitted. Today, everything that is not permitted is prohibited. This inversion occurred from the de Gaulle era up to the Giscard era, and its consequences were perceived only after the event, and hence too late to oppose them – all the more so in that this extension of prohibition has been able to cloak itself in a pseudo-liberal ideology. It is self-evident that the state alone cannot ensure control over an entire society – that is to say, over groups and human beings whose numbers are often considerable. It thus functions by guaranteeing the imbrication and equivalence of various forms and 'sub-systems' – for example, teaching, medicine and the organization of health, the organization of time and space, and so on. It chiefly relies on the world of commodities, an active form in everyday life, as well as on the contractual system, another active form. A service state? So it is said; so it is claimed. In reality, what we have is a state controlling daily life because it helps to create it. And it even *moulds* it. It fashions it. This does not mean that each 'user' can easily pass from one to another of the sub-systems or forms linked by the state, and whose equivalence the state ensures.

What escapes the state? The derisory, minuscule decisions in which freedom is rediscovered and experienced: taking the bus to this or that stop; speaking or not speaking to a particular person; buying such and such an object; and so on. Starting from these micro-decisions, freedom seeks to gather momentum. While it is true that the state dispenses only with what is insignificant, it is nevertheless the case that the politico-bureaucratic-state edifice always contains cracks, chinks, spaces. On the one hand, administrative activity strains to plug these gaps, leaving less and less hope and possibility of what has been dubbed interstitial freedom. On the other hand, individuals seek to enlarge these cracks and pass through the interstices.

It is not certain that all the state's functions, old and/or new, archaic or historic, innate or acquired, are preserved as such, simply by being strengthened. Some functions fluctuate. We know, for example, that since the advent of so-called multinational firms, state management of the economic and the social has altered. It may be that what is called the national state will become the manager of outmoded national territories and relations of production for global enterprises. Some important decisions are taken at the level of the state – that is to say, at the national and global level, but outside of state institutions. Consultation and dialogue take place between personalities, meetings during which the 'private' – that is to say, the interests of national or international firms – and the 'public' – that is to say, the representatives of the various groups concerned – mingle and clash. State bodies and political leaders participate in decisions with the aim of maintaining the domestic market, strategic coherence, national unity, and the celebrated consensus – in short, the logic of the mode of production. Sparing unforeseen developments or innovations, one function seems set to be strengthened: the administration of daily life, as a general product at once of the economic, the political and the strategic, and even of ideology. So that everything we have hitherto observed risks being a mere joking matter in comparison with what lies in store: the state of total knowledge – the past, present and future of each member (individual or group) registered, described, prescribed by perfectly informed 'services', down to the smallest move, the smallest payment, the most insignificant of social and individual acts. If we let things take their course, this pessimistic science-fiction scenario will gradually become our familiar landscape, because it is convenient to have a technical device at home that seems to take the whole of everyday life in hand. One day it may well be that, sparing the unforeseen or some initiative, an army of bureaucrats, under the orders of a technico-political high command, will treat daily life not as an object or product, no longer as a semi-colony, but quite simply as a conquered country.

5 Space and Time

Before I examine information technology more closely, let me say a little about social time and space. In this domain, the changes were slow but profound. First of all, everything in terrestrial space has been explored, and nearly everything has been occupied and exploited. What remains unoccupied? The ocean depths. Once again, the major states are engaged in disturbing activities; some theoreticians of strategy have suggested that a global conflict could spring from rivalry over the resources of the oceans. As for forests, lakes, beaches, mountains, they have been well-nigh completely 'appropriated'. Is there any need for me to reiterate again that private property means disappropriation? The space of play, where the body rediscovers itself in rediscovering use, becomes an opportunity for profit, with the latter subjecting the potential for enjoyment to itself, and debasing it. Occupation by financial interests and private property signifies control – that is to say, the end of the freedom that is indispensable to full enjoyment. This occupation of special places and spaces has consequences for daily life. In fact, in the depths of despondency, monotony and boredom, the people of daily life have faith in unoccupied places and free time, in free activities – that is to say, play activities. The ludic can be recuperated; and has been to a significant extent. Yet it too remains the 'arena and stake' of a conflict, over a beach, access to the sea, grazing rights, and so on; and such conflicts can sometimes become acute.

In its multiplicity, time can be envisaged either qualitatively or quantitatively – as biological or physical time, as psychological duration, or finally as social time, leaving to one side sidereal time, historical time, and so on.

As natural time, it has a rhythmical character. Rhythm is an integral and determinant part of qualitative time. It also possesses a quantitative character: it is measured – frequency, intensity, energy expended, and so on. But rhythms are multiple and interfere with one another qualitatively: heartbeats, breathing, being awake and asleep by turns, being hungry and thirsty, and so on. The rhythms in question are only the most easily observable – some diurnal, others monthly, and so on. Although they are repetitive, rhythms and cycles always have an appearance of novelty: the dawn always seems to be the first one. Rhythm does not prevent the desire for, and pleasure of, discovery: hunger and thirst always seem novel. Is this a kind of gift of oblivion that protects the rhythmical from obsolescence, but without erasing all memory? In linear repetition, by contrast, the formal and material identity of each 'stroke' is recognized, generating lassitude, boredom and fatigue.

When Marxists have dealt with rhythms, they have considered them solely on the basis of labour. Indeed, originally the gestures and acts of collective labour were rhythmically organized, invariably accompanied by songs: the songs of oarsmen, haulers, harvesters, shepherds, sailors, and so on. A whole 'Marxist' aesthetic is based on the hypothesis of a transformation and artistic transposition of work rhythms becoming ends rather than means, and pleasures as opposed to punctuating productive activity. This thesis ignores a certain number of facts. In the first place, vital rhythms pre-exist organized social labour; hormonal secretions obey different cycles, making it possible to stress the differential character of rhythms. Secondly, the gestures of labour are organized rhythmically only in forms of work that predate industrial labour. The closer productive activity approximates to industrial production using machines, the more linear repetition becomes, losing its rhythmical character. Take, for example, a sequence of operations like hammer-blows to drive in nails, or the production of pieces by a milling machine, or assembling a car. If the sequence of hammer-blows sometimes takes on a kind of rhythm, it is because the worker is seeking to escape linear monotony. From the very beginning of industrial organization, there is a sudden mutual interference between rhythmical vital processes and linear operations. This foreshadows complex processes, and does not support the thesis of a direct transition from practical work rhythms to aesthetic rhythms in music, dance, architecture, and so on. The general problem here is the spatialization of temporal processes. In this respect, the work of art displays a victory of the rhythmical over the linear, integrating it without destroying it. Cyclical repetition and linear repetition meet and collide. Thus, in music the metronome supplies a linear tempo; but the linked series of intervals by octaves possesses a cyclical and rhythmical character. Likewise in daily life: the many rhythms and cycles of natural origin, which are transformed by social life, interfere with the linear processes and sequences of gestures and acts.

Rhythmanalysis, a new science that is in the process of being constituted, studies these highly complex processes. It may be that it will complement or supplant psychoanalysis. It situates itself at the juxtaposition of the physical, the physiological and the social, at the heart of daily life. Elements of rhythmanalysis could find a place here. This knowledge starts from empirical observations – for example, the sea's waves with their extraordinarily complex undulations and rhythms, or music as a unity of melody, harmony and rhythm. Compared with the existing sciences, it is multi- or interdisciplinary in character. It cannot but appeal to wave theories, to the principle of the superimposition of small movements, whereas larger wave movements create interferences. It equally calls upon a physiology of organs and their functioning, considered in time and not only in anatomical space – something that has limited physiology's perspectives for a long time. It would thus study all cyclical rhythms starting from their origin or foundation – nature – but taking account of their alterations through interference with linear processes. The important thing here is the progressive crushing of rhythms and cycles by linear repetition. It must be emphasized that only the linear is amenable to being fully quantified and homogenized. On a watch or a clock, the mechanical devices subject the cyclical – the hands that turn in sixty seconds or twelve hours – to the linearity of counting. In recent measuring devices, and even watches, the cyclical (the dial) tends to disappear. Fully quantified social time is indifferent to day and night, to the rhythms of impulses.

Critical analysis of daily life devotes a lot of space to the difference between the two types of repetitive processes and their conjunctions. It must give even more space to the complete quantification of social time on the basis of the measurement of labour-time and its productivity in industry. Starting from the organization of labour – divided and composite, measured and quantified – quantification has conquered society in its entirety, thereby contributing to the realization of the mode of production. It is likewise on the basis of this quantification that the everyday was constituted, almost completely eliminating the qualitative in time and space, treating it as a residue to be eliminated. The qualitative has *virtually* disappeared. But here, once again, this 'virtually' is very important. This is the sense in which daily life represents the generalization of industrial rationality, the spirit of enterprise, and capitalist management, adopted and imposed by the state and institutional summit. At the limit, absolute quantification, pure rationality, abstraction, would triumph. The 'virtually' means that this limit is unattainable, and that something else is always possible.

'What is urban space? What is a town? How are they composed at different levels – blocks of flats, buildings, monuments – in a word, the architectural and, at another level, the urbanistic?' We are beginning to think that these questions, which are seemingly empirical and a matter for positive knowledge, have a secret affinity with various philosophical questions: 'What is man? What is his relation to being? What is the relation between being and space? How do things stand with the man's being, his evolution, his ascent, or his nothingness?' If we knew how to define 'man', would we not be able to define the urban and the town? Unless it's the other way round, and we must first of all understand the town if we are to define this political animal who constructs cities, living in them or fleeing them. In that case, inquisitive thinking would investigate the urban in the first instance, rather than positive knowledge in isolation or power *in abstracto*. Perhaps the town holds the answer to some crucial questions that philosophers have ignored for years. Unless, vice versa, the mystery of the town betokens the absence of any answer. Do these enormous collections of things, men, women, works and symbols possess an as yet undeciphered meaning? Or do they have no meaning? However that may be, it is in towns and the urban that the everyday – ours – is instituted.

And here we confront a new paradox among so many others. The break-up of the historic town has been going on since the end of the nineteenth century and the beginning of the twentieth; it figures in the collapse of reference points already referred to. Yet one remarkable result of it has been to facilitate a novel analysis of the urban question. Here before our very eyes is the town, situated on the suburban outskirts; it is in pieces, fragments, parts, laid out alongside one another. In this fragmented city, the only thing to be done is to make an inventory of the elements of the whole, bearing in mind that some pieces may be missing here and there, and that the break-up might have distorted them. The elements that were combined into a strong unity by historic towns (a unity that fragmentation eliminates, and which consequently poses a problem) are perceived item by item. Thus, the activity of knowledge proceeds via the negative! Most specialists in urban questions, happy with such a godsend, make do with describing the fragments; they find the post-mortem analysis of the urban conducted by contemporary practice adequate. They refer to what they collect with terms that seem to contain impressive positive knowledge: housing conditions, the built environment, things mineral and vegetable, amenities, and so on. Yet these terms, far from containing knowledge of the urban, merely refer to functions separated by an anatomical operation, by separation of the historical elements of the urban into inert entities. But it is in this *framework* – a very precise term which encapsulates the rigidity or inertia of the result – that the people of daily life have to live.

Those who have not given up on critical analysis and theoretical thinking know that what they have before them is merely the spectre of the town. And this in the dual sense of the French word *spectre*: (a) an *analysis* comparable to that of white light by the prism which splits it up, revealing what is involved in the apparently simple clarity of the sun or light source; (b) a *ghost*, outliving what was once a vibrant urbanity and its unity.

Assembling and combining these separate elements does not restore the lost life of towns. Here, too, *le mort saisit le vif*! Like the humanity to which it offers shelter, the town is alienated. Moreover, spectral analysis is not exhaustive; the outskirts and suburbs exclude certain elements which are indispensable to the urban – for example, the memory and symbolisms that were once integrated into monuments. As is well known but frequently forgotten, any analysis risks killing its object for the sake of seeing and knowing what it contains. An effective analysis of towns in the real world of their break-up must now be subjected to a method whose watchword and procedure have already been set down: situating and restoring. But such an approach cannot be inaugurated and pursued without taking account of the everyday life of the relevant parties: inhabitants, city dwellers, citizens or, again, 'users'. What is outlined is a problematic. A new one? Not completely new, but one that is rarely articulated to its full extent.

The problematic of time and space far exceeds the present account. Research and discovery follow a path full of obstacles and pitfalls. For example, it may be that analysis finds itself faced with blindingly obvious facts – that is to say, faced with the causes of or reasons for certain observable effects, causes or reasons that have nothing occult about them, even though they need to be discovered; so familiar are they that they simply go unnoticed. This is how things proceed in the study of language, where everyone uses forms and structures without necessarily having a knowledge of them as such. Likewise with the study of everyday life and the urban, where what is most familiar is also the least known and the most difficult to make out.

Time as such is irreversible. It is impossible, inconceivable, to go in reverse. Complete repetition of the past can be demanded of the divinity by those who believe in his omnipotence (Kierkegaard). It can be conceived in the absolute, ontologically and metaphysically (the eternal return). Rerunning time is an initiative undertaken by thought, which reconstructs the past of the individual, the group or a particular society with difficulty. Inasmuch as it is reversible, space is distinguished from irreversible time, although space and time are intimately connected. But time is projected into space through measurement, by being homogenized, by appearing in things and products. The time of daily life is not only represented in clocks and watches; it is also represented in photographs and curios-souvenirs. These memory-objects, these palpable, immediate traces of the past, seem to say in daily life that the past is never past. Not explicitly but implicitly, it signifies the reversibility of time. In this fractured, fragmented time, we can return to the past, since it is there. More so than others, the kitsch object possesses these strange properties: a blending of memory, recollection, the imaginary, the real. The illusion of reversibility gives everyday time an air which might be taken for happiness, and does indeed possess a certain happy – or, at least, satisfied – air. Is it not pleasant to escape time, to break out of time – not into the timelessness of the great *oeuvre*, but within temporality itself? But one of the consequences is the elimination of tragedy and death.

People sometimes ask how and why this tragic age lacks a tragic consciousness, why it eliminates the tragic knowledge around which thinking revolves. Here is a partial answer: the appearance and illusion of the reversibility of everyday time, represented by objects that possess this meaning and this privilege. Eliminating the tragic is part of the tragedy of the age. This elimination does not go beyond appearances. Under the masquerade of kitsch, the tragic follows its course. If objects form a system – something we can accept in the case of functional objects, such as utensils and furniture – its meaning is to be found not in what it declares, but in what it dissimulates, which extends from the tragic to the mode of production via the malaise of daily life. The production of daily life, which is opposed to daily life as *oeuvre*, thus includes the production of everyday space and time, as well as the objects that fill up the everyday, the mass of objects intended to fill time and space. This mass is likewise simultaneously homogeneous and fragmented, and hierarchically organized. Regarding this schema – 'homogeneity–fragmentation–hierarchization' – the main point has been made. Since this organizational schema was discovered in connection with space, there is no point returning to it. By means of such organizational forms, operating in various sectors and domains, and even though these forms and schemas do not correspond to any determinate institution, daily life finds itself instituted. Strategy? Yes and no. No, because the result is obtained in accordance with the objective, and hence 'unconscious', modalities of the mode of production. But yes, because the orientation gives rise to multiple tactical operations directed towards an overall result.

Social space (like theatrical, pictorial or architectural space) can no longer seem like the discovery of a pre-existent, 'real' external space, any more than it can seem like the covering over of a natural space by an 'authentic' mental space. These philosophical schemas are no longer admissible. Social space manifests itself as the realization of a general practical schema. As a product, it is made in accordance with an operating instrument in the hands of a group of experts, technocrats who are themselves representative of particular interests but at the same time of a mode of production, conceived not as a completed reality or an abstract totality, but as a set of possibilities in the process of being realized. This theory accounts both for the specificity of the organizational schema (homogeneity–division–hierarchization), and for its historical appearance at a given moment in the evolution of the mode of production. At this moment, a representation of space – which is by no means innocent, since it involves and contains a strategy – is passed off as disinterested positive knowledge. It is projected objectively; it is effected materially, through practical means. There is thus no real space or authentic space, only spaces produced in accordance with certain schemas developed by some particular group within the general framework of a society (that is to say, a mode of production). This theory also accounts for the correspondence between the various spaces: the general space of society, architectural space, everyday space, the space of transport as well as that of furnishing, and so on.

The splintering of time and space in general homogeneity, and the crushing of natural rhythms and cycles by linearity, have consequences at other levels. This state of affairs creates a need for rhythms. The imposition of daily life as we have defined it thus goes together with rhythmical innovations in music and dance, innovations that accentuate rhythm and restore it to daily life. Is it any coincidence that the institution of this everydayness goes together with the enormous success of exotic or ecstatic rhythms, with the increasing role of music in social life, with the search for 'highs' and the extraordinary, in a transgression of all rules extending even to death trances? The festival, which in other respects has been recuperated and commercialized, is restored, together with features that had been done away with: rupture, transgression, ecstasy. In this way, daily life leads to retaliation; because it is becoming normal, rupture takes abnormal, even morbid, forms. We should not be astonished at this, let alone wax indignant over it. Among the Greeks, the Dionysian did not submit to the pure idea of beauty. The Bacchantes, roaming through the countryside, yelling, diabolical, tearing the living beings they came across to pieces, were not obliged to be 'beautiful'. Even then, it was not a matter of a rupture with daily life, but a return to cosmic forces ...

In and through music and dance, time becomes irreversible once again. The festival unfolds once more, headed towards its end, consuming what it draws its substance from: energy, desire, violence. At the heart of everyday positivity, the negative springs up in all its force.

6 Information Technology and Daily Life

For a long time, technological innovations in the domain of information (cybernetics) were principally applied to administration (administrative information processing). More recently, new technical progress and new economic processes have enabled – or, rather, dictated – their application to production. More precisely, the two applications are distinct and complementary. On the one hand, the processes of productive labour have changed, calling into question the old divisions of labour. On the other hand, computer scientists proclaim the generalization of their theoretical and practical knowledge to society as a whole. In contrast to the pessimism and nihilism, the apocalyptic prophesying that was still predominant among the intelligentsia only a little while ago, the optimistic prophecies of technicians and official circles have invaded the media and publishing.

This merits very serious consideration. Computer science and telematics are certainly going to alter social existence. They have already begun to do so. Communication has been an important – possibly essential – phenomenon in social practice since the beginning of history and prehistory. Will computer science, with its repercussions and related disciplines, go so far as to transform everyday life? To transform the social relations of production, reproduction and domination? That is the issue.

It is all the more significant and interesting in that the new technologies have arrived on time, if we may put it like that, in a kind of pleonasm. Grafting themselves on to it, they extend the process of 'formalization of daily life' referred to above. The increasing predominance of the abstract–concrete has already been analysed in its broad outline, without exhausting the theme (far from it). The abstract–concrete reigns in daily life, in place of the *concrete* (the human: each object and gesture having a meaning because they are practically bound up with a civilization) and the *abstract* (opposed to the concrete and distinct in the imaginary as well as ideology). How is this displacement to be characterized? We have seen how: by the world of exchange and commodities; by legality and the importance of impersonal, sovereign Law; by the value attributed to language and, more generally, to signs. These priorities have been readily recognized by positive knowledge, since it recognizes its own instruments in them. Even so, this recognition has given rise to interpretations and superfluous commentary, with all social acts, including buying and consuming, being construed as the 'effects of signs'. This vast process creates the conditions of possibility for a massive use of new technologies. Supporters of these technologies, their theoreticians – or, rather, their apologists – go so far as to claim that they will constitute a new *mode of production* – the one revolutionaries dreamt of, but to be ushered in by a peaceful, silent revolution. Essentially, this mode of production would consist in the production of immaterial goods, supplanting the production of material products, as well as the ever more complete predominance of services over other activities.

Sign effects? Now is the time to grasp them, define them and appreciate their significance as well as their limits. Contrary to Jean Baudrillard, the point at which the social signification of objects entered into their evaluation – that is to say, exchange-value – was not the appropriate moment for a definition and conclusion.[5] That was only one moment, one episode in a larger, ongoing process. Some theorizations characteristically extrapolate from a reality. They push the tendency inherent in this reality as far as it will go; this makes them worthy of note but, at the same time marks and dates them. In this fashion, we easily end up with a radical critique, but such a radicalism is absurd. Were each social act to respond to sign effects, it would sanction all the social relations conducive to this effect. The seemingly most insignificant objects would be the most active mediators. To eat a piece of bread would be to commune with all the labour and all the conditions of labour that went into the production of this foodstuff. Hence to accept them. Such a thesis is *true*, or at least correct, but it only serves to demonstrate unequivocally how a certain quest for truth can result in absurdity. Mirror effects! Language effects! Sign effects! So many effects that are exploited without searching for the real conditions of effects that are simultaneously both real and unreal. These conditions are discovered in the process that tends towards the abstract–concrete. This process never extends as far as pure abstraction, which would be equivalent to a vacuum and nothingness. It *nearly* gets there. But just as it is about to reach this extreme, the process is, as it were, put into reverse, reincarnated or reincorporated by daily life. Similarly, at the other extreme, it cannot vanish into the substantiality of the concrete and the real; it is returned to abstraction. May we not say the same to apologists for information technology? Nevertheless, it is certainly true that the advent of computer science, which is sweeping aside certain earlier ideologies, poses new problems that are planetary in scope. Must we choose between the terms of the alternative: computerization of society (from above), or socialization of information technology (from below)? Can this contradiction be resolved?

A new ideology is looming on the horizon, which is no less disturbing than those that discovered a pretext, a provenance, or a point of impact in use and exchange, the two modalities of value. A text that might already seem distant, but nevertheless stands out – the Nora–Minc Report (1978) – was presented as strictly objective and scientific. It contained political suggestions and warnings, which were formulated and justified. It signalled various dangers: the role of global enterprises like IBM; brutal state intervention in information. At the same time, this text offered a model of society. Technocratic utopia? Sociological forecast? Both. According to this perspective or prospectus, the information society was inevitably going to be divided into three levels or sectors: (a) the kingly, that is to say, sovereign (royal) powers – those of the state and the head of state – controlling information, but also the energy as well as the foreign affairs of the country, and hence relations with global enterprises and the market; (b) the community sector, reconstructing group existence, and hence the social, which had been obliterated and overwhelmed by the long predominance of an economy producing material goods, as well as by abuses of state power; and (c) the competitive sector or level, given over to competition between individuals, enabling their selection in a constant struggle for places and posts in the hierarchy.

All in all, this report proposed a triadic or ternary (three-level) model of society, whereas other authors (André Gorz, etc.) made do with a bi-partite division (the dual society). Unwittingly, the authors of these various texts introduced the 'homogeneity–fragmentation–hierarchy' schema into their conception of things, while spontaneously trying to limit its damage. For other authors, information technology will lead to a sort of cultural revolution, rather than a political and social mutation. Some go so far as to claim that the state will accept not being the exclusive or dominant actor in the social game, withdrawing in favour of other, well-informed actors; and, in this fashion, will even wither away. These models are based on the hypothesis of a society constructed exclusively on the basis of positive knowledge, therewith implying the death of lived experience, or at least its reduction to the sign effects of information technology.

We must therefore examine these theories closely, and discover whether it is possible to end up in the total administration of daily life through the totalizing action of information technology; the total transparency of the entire society with the end of opacity in lived experience; the reduction of the activity of knowing to information technology; and so on.

(a) *Against unitary theory*

With information technology, must we not very clearly distinguish the scientific theory first of all, the technological applications next, and finally the marketing of appliances, their entry into social practice and their introduction into everyday life?

Scientifically, information is a quantity. It is measured. It is defined by a *cost*: how many signs must be used to transmit a message or a series of messages? How many operations are required to discover in a mass of objects the one corresponding to certain features that have been identified in advance? And so on. This yields a probability and can be expressed by a logarithmic function: H (unit of information, the Hartley) $= \Sigma$ pi Log $2\frac{1}{pi}$, where pi refers to a probability of occurrence, that of an order of signs to the nth message. The quantity H is cancelled in a first borderline case, where all the messages are known in advance and are repeated purely and simply. Then redundancy, the inverse of H $(\frac{1}{H})$, is infinite. This same quantity – information – is maximal when there exist *n* messages that are completely different and, in addition, equally probable (H $=$ Log N). Then redundancy is minimal.

First comment: in the case of major redundancy, there is perfect intelligibility. It has already been noted that information theory demonstrates the identity of the intelligible and the redundant. This is of the utmost importance for understanding daily life and the role of repetition in the seeming clarity of the everyday. Redundancy eliminates the noise mixed up in the message; as for information, it involves surprise, and hence disorder. No differences would amount to dullness. By contrast, excessive difference kills meaning by preventing understanding – that is to say, decoding. Yet complete application of a code involves repetition in perfect intelligibility and, consequently, utter monotony.

A second, no less important comment: the mathematical formula above corresponds to that of energy and its dissipation – that is to say, to the theory of entropy. Information theory developed as thermodynamics. Since information comprises a disorder that involves a certain order, a dissipation (loss) of informational energy occurs through increased entropy. This seems to summon up a 'negative entropy' – that is to say, instants in which energy is revived and possibilities spring up – against the tendency to diminution. We glimpse a *dialectic* of information technology that envelops its *logic* – that is to say, identity, the repetitive, the redundant, the intelligible – by subjecting it to the clash between order and disorder. This aspect seems to have escaped the ideologues who graft their interpretations on to scientific theory and logic alone. Equally, we catch sight of a paradox of information ideology: basing a social order, and constructing a coherent model, on a theory that is in fact a theory of disorder. According to the proposed models, whence derive the sources of the disorder without which information technology cannot operate, albeit with a risk of dissipation?

The theory has no right to want and claim to be unitary – that is to say, to cover the whole field of information, practice included. In the transition from mathematical theory to technologies, we have a first discontinuity. Technological application requires the construction of apparatuses, some of them material (channels, transmitters, receivers), others abstract (conventions, codes and decodes, systems). Software is distinct from hardware. In the transition from technological development to social use, to the production and marketing of hardware, we have a further discontinuity.

The press, whether specialist or not, has for some years now been full of descriptions of technical innovations: microprocessors, optical fibres, networks, and so on. Consequently, it is pointless to dwell at length on equipment and techniques. It is sufficient to distinguish between three levels: science, with an implicit or explicit logic; technological applications – that is to say, hardware; and social practice in its various forms – the treatment of information, software and its extensions – which sets out a different problematic. Any theory that eliminates these discontinuities becomes ideology. Moreover, there is no question of some absolute separation shielding practice from certain implications of the theory – in particular, the entropy of informational energy and the dissipation of information. As for the extension of information theory to other domains (notably biology), the same comments apply. A theory based on information that aims to be general, on the model of classical philosophies, blithely crosses frontiers and borders that are in fact clearly marked out. It may be brilliant, but any such endeavour is bound to misfire.

(b) *Information is a product*

This product derives from a determinate productive activity, whose result is consumed and disappears in the act of consumption. The question: 'Does such a product abolish the difference between use-value and exchange-value? Does it inaugurate the reign of exchange in the pure state, without any material movement? Or, on the contrary, does it re-establish use-value?' – this question poses the issue of information as a commodity that is bought and sold. Before we examine it, there is another question. The confusion between producer and creator, between creation and production, has already entailed many illusions and done a great deal of harm, especially in the domains of art and aesthetics. Some people regard the production of information as creation, conferring on it a privilege that is not warranted by critical analysis.

Historically, communication in general and information in particular possessed an undeniable creative capacity. Bold navigators, explorers, discoverers, including plunderers and pirates, established connections between places and peoples that were oblivious of one another's existence. They did not 'transform' the world; they created it. Setting out from separate sites, they literally constructed the world by connecting them, constituting networks of maritime or terrestrial routes; they arrived at the world market. As we know, this world market has gone through two stages: the first predated industrial capitalism; the second came after it.

In this creative activity by means of communication, it was hard to distinguish violent pillaging and warlike enterprises of conquest from the peaceful exchange of goods – that is to say, products that were initially agricultural and artisanal, and subsequently industrial. The violence was only temporary; its enduring mark and effects are to be found in the networks. The result, however, was that exchange was a male preserve. Women were for a long time part of the goods, rather than agents in this creation, which initially unfolded at the level of inland seas – the Mediterranean and China seas – and then on an oceanic scale, before ending up as a planetary phenomenon. The violent, warlike form of relations came to terms with the logical form of exchange – the world of commodities – despite their opposite meanings; and possibly still does. Men stamped the world thereby created with their own imprint, even though reason – that of communication and exchange – was indifferent to violence, sex and location as such. Without their knowing it, through a mixture of struggles and logic, genetically and historically, warriors developed a relationship (to being? to the world? to nothingness?) in which bold, often brutal initiative, capable of the best and the worst, the supernatural and the humdrum, was allotted to them.

From navigation on seas and rivers, via railways and air transport, to the modern media, has the creative capacity of communication and information increased? There is no question that its productive capacity is growing. Yet it is as if production and creation varied inversely, the one declining while the other expands. Railways introduced more changes and novelties than motorways. This comes down to saying – a by now commonplace observation – that growth and development do not coincide. The product tends to predominate – not without environmental damage, as people say. Creation goes on declining and, in imperialism, production rediscovers its link with violence.

During this enormous lapse of time, extending from the first acts of exchange to modern industrialization and urbanization in a transnational framework, local life, rooted and confined to one spot, is preserved and affirmed in ignorance of the global, which is constituted elsewhere. The same applies to the everyday.

During this time, the creative capacity of communication and information is slowly but surely exhausted. With each new means of communication and information – for example, electricity (the 'electricity fairy!', 'electrification plus soviets!'), and then the telephone, radio, television – people anticipate miracles: the transfiguration of daily life. As if it could come from a means or medium. These means or media can only transmit what existed prior to the mediating oper-ation, or what occurs outside it. Today, communication *reflects* – nothing more, nothing less. What was the result of the multiplication of these means in ever more complex forms? Rather than a metamor-phosis of daily life, what occurred was, on the contrary, the installation of daily life as such, determined, isolated, and then pro-grammed. There ensued a privatization of the public and a publicizing of the private, in a constant exchange that mixes them without uniting them and separates them without discriminating between them; and this is still going on.

Should we deny all practical change as the media – that is, commu-nications and information – have multiplied? Certainly not. But that is not the point. The issue is different: 'What is the meaning of this multiplication, this abundance of goods which are no longer material, and claim to be substitutes for traditional spirituality? Does it not in fact risk resulting in the destruction of meaning by signs? Where is it leading, to what new order? But whence will this new order originate? From what and from whom?'

McLuhan's thesis about the creative role of communications can be upheld as far as the oldest forms of communication are concerned – for example, navigation, the phonetic alphabet and printing. When it comes to recent products – the telephone or the car – it evokes very strong reservations indeed. To claim that the creative capacity of communications and information increases with their abundance is (a) a postulate; (b) which is contradicted by the history of time, space and social practice; (c) which is equally contradicted by the principle of the dissipation of energy, whether we are talking about heavy energies or subtle energies like information energy. To justify this facilely opti-mistic and rationalist thesis today, one would have to demonstrate the springing up in the modern world of possibilities that tend towards their own realization. Yet what we actually observe is that the increas-ing intensity of communications harbours the reinforcement of daily life, its consolidation and confinement. It also harbours a mounting danger of catastrophe. Is it not demagogic to support this thesis today? Does it not involve negating the negative such as it appears and manifests itself in society?

Information is produced. It is consumed. Information technology confirms the outmoded character of the classical Marxist contrast between base and superstructure. Information is not – or not merely – a superstructure, since it is an – exchangeable – product of certain relations of production. What was regarded as superstructural, like space and time, forms part of production, because it is a product that is bought and sold.

Whence the question: 'Who produces information? How? For whom? And who consumes it?' This form of production is not exempt from the classical theses. On the contrary: it extends them. It involves labour and an organization of labour, production costs, an organic composition of capital, a surplus-value – that is to say, profits for those who are in charge of production. Nevertheless, it may be that the production and consumption of information deviates somewhat from certain classical rules or laws, disrupting them. Hardware, software, firmware – these do not have the same appearance. The processing of information differs from its production, yet forms part of it; the initial producer can inscribe it in its computerized activity – something IBM in particular does. As for databases, what precisely is their function and their place? To a certain extent, they are independent of information production, yet they are indispensable to it. Can they be counted on to operate in favour of a democratic management of information technology? Perhaps. But here another danger arises – the state monopoly of data, with the related risk of a global monopoly of information in a transnational system consolidated by this national monopoly. As a source of information, the database is, moreover, proximate to daily life. The consumption of information also occurs in the everyday. Enormous networks, channels, circuits thus start out from daily life, pass through various levels to the planetary (by means of satellites), and then return towards daily life. Whence problems which, some people maintain, have already been solved by technique or the economic and political powers; while others assert that solutions are still pending on account of their complexity, so that it is not too late to intervene.

Produced and consumed, information is sold and bought. It is therefore a commodity. Any commodity? No. It is not material; as we know, it possesses the peculiar characteristic of causing all other commodities to be bought and sold. This has always been the case – that is to say, since the existence of the exchange of marketable goods outside the gift and barter systems. It has always been necessary to know where a particular product is in order to go and find it, transport it, and finally hand it over in return for a determinable sum of money; and that knowledge derives from communication and information.

Information has always been as essential to exchange and markets as money and the quantification of products. Yet for many centuries, information as such did not appear on the market. Its appearance has a retroactive effect: it brings out the importance of information, as well as networks, channels and circuits, in the past. What is novel about the contemporary world is that there is a world market in information, which positively 'drives' the other markets, through advertising, propaganda, the transmission of positive knowledge, and so on. Is not information, the supreme commodity, also the ultimate commodity? Does it not complete the great cycle of the commodity, its extraordinary expansion – in short, the realization of the world of commodities in that of the mode of production, in the global? There are grounds for thinking so.

Far from ushering in a new mode of production, information technology perfects the existing mode of production – capitalism and its world market – which exerts such pressure on 'socialism' that the latter struggles to escape it. In this way, the extraordinary shift – already referred to – of the concrete towards the abstract, and their combination in the abstract–concrete, is rounded off. This way of looking at things makes sense of the enormous circuit that goes from daily life to daily life via the global. The complexity of the world market, which is part of information technology because the latter implies it and marks it out, needs no further emphasis (a market in finished products, but also instruments of production, techniques, capital, energy, labour, signs and symbols, art works and, finally, information, which envelops the totality and constitutes it as global). Complexity does not betoken coherence and cohesion. Although it is aimed for, coherence is not thereby realized. Information technology can neither resolve nor cancel contradictions: it can only express them – or disguise them. The power of the world market does not suppress all resistance – the resistance of a number of countries, particularly the socialist countries – or inequalities, or conflicts between strategies. Hence this market is not established, stable, coherent, even though it possesses an internal, highly potent logic – that of the commodity as a system of equivalents. It tends to homogenize the world, and at the same time to fragment it, since it reflects the diverse origins and provenance of products, including information. As we know, homogeneity no more abolishes fragmentation than aiming for coherence suppresses contradictions.

If is true that information technology presses the commodity to a conclusion, if it perfects and completes the world of commodities, what emerges from this is not something new. On the contrary: a world is coming to an end, in a slow but unyielding process. How can we get out of it? The crisis, as they say, is shaking the base and foundations as much as the superstructures. Hence the demand for something new, an inventive, radical opening: in particular, a different form of growth, intimately bound up with development.

(c) *The Information Ideology*

This ideology presents information in various ways that share the following feature: they do not advertise themselves as ideological, but as observations or positive knowledge. They also have this in common: they absolutize a feature of the 'real', rather than relativizing it and situating it. Here as elsewhere, the operation which constructs ideology, and differs from those that launch, transmit or seek to realize it in practice, consists in the following: an individual or collective *subject* that is more or less uncertain of itself manages to raise an aspect or element of reality or intelligence to the status of definitive truth via discourse. This what happened with the historical, the economic, the political, structure, language, the imaginary, and so on. This operation is reproduced today with information. Thus, the irruption of the supreme commodity has been presented as an adventure, or even as the great 'human adventure', giving this product a romantic halo. We cannot fail to notice that around us, in persistent modernism, other – more adventurous – adventures are indicated: the exploration and exploitation of oceans, genetic engineering and the results of biology, energy problems, and so on. The notion of adventure can be seductive. But in the case of information, and even in the various other instances, it does not withstand examination. How can we ignore the fact that the economic powers (firms) and political powers (states) reserve the ocean depths for themselves, disputing them; that they explore space for the purpose of appropriating it; and that the same is true of information? This ancient Odyssean image – the adventure – can be demagogically exploited. Does it have a meaning? Yes: it applies to the whole human race which, having become planetary and global, does not know where it is headed and risks going where it has no wish to go – that is to say, towards the abyss.

Not only does information ideology not present itself as ideology, but it proposes either to put an end to ideologies or to transfer the ideological function to information apparatuses, including the production and diffusion of positive knowledge, which was formerly the prerogative of schools and universities. The reduction of positive knowledge to information would have consequences: the end of critical and conceptual thinking, and hence the end of all thinking, or its departure to take refuge in illegality and violence. All the more so given that information apparatuses are in great danger of being administratively and institutionally controlled either by the national state, or by transnational forces which would use this supplementary means to consolidate their order. Not only would positive knowledge be reduced to recorded and memorized facts, but everything concerning the political and politics would go through the channels of official information. This would create the greatest difficulties for any action independent of established power, and possibly result in the disappearance of all counter-power. Contradictions at this level (i.e. between states and firms) offer a last chance in a world that aims for coherence and stability, but falls short of them. Information ideology masks the dangers and the opportunities alike. Politics itself would be replaced by the discourse and ideology of the 'competent' – that is to say, technicians who can produce information and technocrats who give them their orders. This tendency, which can already be observed, forms part of the crisis; it extends it, beyond ethical values and social norms, to political institutions and discourses. It might be thought that it favours the personalization of 'kingly' forms of power, as well as appeals for a new consensus around this personalized power. The paramount danger is this: the unchecked reinforcement of the state and its multiple capacities – in particular, that of seizing daily life in its organs of prehension and repressive comprehension.

Information ideology possesses the dubious merit of prophetically heralding the new society: post-industrial, post-capitalist and even post-socialist. Pre-industrial society was supposedly constituted regionally and territorially – that is to say, as is well known, around energy sources and raw materials. Industrial society proper was supposedly organized around the exploitation of energy forms freed from territorial constraints (electrical energy). As for post-industrial society, it is supposedly already being structured around information that is abstract, yet global and universal.[6]

This technological and technocratic utopia makes light of contradictions, old or new. It is true that recent technologies deploy and strengthen communication networks at the global level; and these thus tend to constitute a single network through the interconnection of national and regional networks, integrating multiple services. But at the same time, such globalization diversifies the network thereby constituted, which depends on sources, data banks, and so on.

Let us avoid making a Gothic novel, as well as a romance, out of information technology.[7] Information ideologues assert that society and the social are being transformed, and that a qualitative leap is about to occur. They also believe that information technology is necessary and sufficient to establish new norms and values. Which ones? The end of opacity and impenetrability – and hence transparency! If we credit these ideologues, the information society will finally realize the Truth. Not in the manner of the philosophers, as thought and abstract system, but as reality and practical system. No more secrecy! Anything that happens, anything that supervenes, will immediately reverberate in the totality with all its details. In short, a universal game of mirrors, finally materialized! An effect of signs, finally totalized! No more shadows, no more dark corners or recesses in this pristine practice. This would be tantamount to the realization of philosophy – not by the working class and revolution, as Marx believed, but through technology. Information, together with its extensions, would lead by the shortest route to a fully planned society, in which the centre would constantly receive messages from each base cell, with the result that culture and information, positively identified, possessing the same structure, would render each individual fully conscious. Of what? Of general constraints![8] Hence we are dealing not only – or not so much – with a technocratic utopia or ideology, but with a scientistic mythology – a paradox, what is more, with the myth of an electronic Agora and the disturbing project of a technological extension of the 'audit' intended for the internal control of workshops, but capable of being extended to political and police control of spaces much vaster than the enterprise …

These ideologues do not think that they are interpreting the techniques, but that they are estimating them objectively. They refuse to concede that they are presenting, or representing, a tendentious political project. To them, the project seems to follow logically from the technology. Is not technologizing the social and political, as opposed to socializing and politicizing technology, a choice and a decision? A political standpoint that presents itself as objective meaning? This line of questioning does not resolve the problem, but it does preclude accepting as a solution utterances that formulate the problem by distorting it, concealing the contradictions involved.

Those who flaunt the technicist perspective allow space and a function for base cells, for micro-societies and micro-decisions – in other words, for daily life. They simultaneously take it into account and abolish it. Information technology can reduce both knowledge and spontaneity. In this perspective, knowing no longer involves using concepts, but simply receiving and memorizing information. The concept is blurred – the concept of knowledge and knowledge by means of concepts. To all intents and purposes, concepts disappear in the face of the facts. Here we recognize a venerable philosophical debate being peremptorily resolved and terminated.

Yet information is lost. How is this dissipation to be resisted, if not by a project and an idea of knowledge? Take, for example, the affirmation of identity: it proclaims its persistence, its perseverance in being, its resistance to decline and difference alike. In this way, identity becomes abstract, fictive, unreal; in this way, it declines …

The paradoxes, aporias and problems of information ideology are proliferating. If we accept the distinction between activity that produces material goods and activity that produces non-material goods, we may conclude that the second sector is bound to grow more rapidly than the first. Yet it tends thereby to choke and even paralyse it. Some theoreticians – and not the least prominent – have reached the point of forecasting a crisis of information technology, in a society that is already in a critical condition, and from which the ideology in question promised an escape. It is argued that the capacity of useful labour, producing material goods, will decline once the energy dissipated in the production of material goods rises to half of the power that is available and consumed globally. Hence there is a threshold.[9] It is true that informational energy is a subtle energy, analogous to nervous energy in comparison with the heavy energy of the muscles. But is there no such thing as nervous fatigue? Exhaustion and a physiological threshold in organisms?

This conjures up the possibility of a confrontation between the socio-political and the physiological or organic. According to contemporary biology, relational characteristics – that is to say, relative to the *other*, not simply to an impersonal environment – polarize living organisms and define the organic. So that pleasure and desire enter into the genetic programme, together with the many indices and signs of sexuality: olfactory, auditory, visual. Is there not a conflictual, dynamic relationship between these three terms: the rational, the relational or positional, the informational – a relationship that cannot be reduced to quantification?

It is nevertheless the case that information ideologues take the sum of techniques, apparatuses and applications for a unitary, objective knowledge, for an activity capable of affecting the whole of reality. They make information the higher form of positive knowledge, destined to absorb the lower forms. Yet for theory and knowledge, information technology can today be regarded solely as an element and a moment of the activity of knowledge, as yet undeveloped. Substituted for knowledge, information deletes thought and reduces positive knowledge to that which is amassed, accumulated, memorized without gaps, outside of lived experience. The negative disappears in a perfect positivity. Information ideology – or, rather, idealism, dressed up as positive knowledge and even technological materialism on occasion – acts as a factor of dislocation in the activity of knowledge, in the political, and in daily life.

For centuries, progress in communications and information has unquestionably favoured central power and central political control; this forms part of the lowering of creative capacity to which reference has already been made. What is at stake in computerization is determined thus. The die is not cast, but the dice are rolling on a planetary cloth. In France there are imminent dangers. The machinery of information apparatuses tends to reproduce the characteristics of the French political apparatus; it is statist and centralized.[10]

(d) *Introversion*

Computerized daily life risks assuming a form that certain ideologues find interesting and seductive: the individual atom or family molecule inside a bubble where the messages sent and received intersect. Users, who have lost the dignity of citizens now that they figure socially only as parties to services, would thus lose the social itself, and sociability. This would no longer be the existential isolation of the old individualism, but a solitude all the more profound for being overwhelmed by messages. With all services at its disposal, ultimately, this individual atom or family molecule would no longer need to stir. Those analysts who have not renounced critical thinking have drawn attention to this danger. Some people have even looked to the state to ward it off. A pure dream: it is very difficult for state power not to favour a tendency that leaves the field open for it. What state and political authority can conceive of their own dissolution, and organize the conditions for it? State intervention inevitably drives 'users' to withdraw into their shells. Do not shells of this kind abandon individuals to anxiety, to an anguish bombarded by hubbub? Information ideologues hope that as long as the shell is filled with information, the individual will feel at home in it. Without any evidence, to say the least.

As for hopes for a reconstruction of a three-term unity – 'space–time–labour' – by means of information, they belong to abstract utopianism. Home-based, remote-controlled labour consummates the separation and fragmentation that are already under way. Rather than being surmounted, the schema 'homogeneity–fragmentation–hierarchization' will get worse. Once, private life eluded the social. The new privatization will be invaded by the outside while paradoxically losing all capacity for externalization.

People talk about a new society. Would it not be more accurate to fear a new state, founded on the political use of information, ruling over a population enclosed in bubbles it has inflated, and in such a way that each mouth believes its bubble comes out of it?

Control of information will come neither from excessive centralization, a unitary structure ruling over the whole of society; nor from excessive decentralization, issuing in fragmentation and formlessness. It requires a project for society, avoiding facile solutions the most likely of which, alas, can already be glimpsed: centralized power negotiating a compromise with global enterprises. Paradoxically, control of information involves an intensification of surprise effects and a reduction in redundancy, without succumbing to disorder. Yet such effects can come only from below – on condition, moreover, that the active base does not disrupt the network. In the relatively near future, it is possible to imagine everyone ordering what they want, or being able to pay for things, without having to step outside. Will women prefer to go to the market or into shops, rather than tapping away at home on a keyboard? Possibly yes, possibly no: it is a decision for those at the base.

So there are better things to do than disconnecting informational structures into a multiplicity of levels, nets, cells. This thesis, which remains technocratic, is well intentioned and has the merit of technically demonstrating the advantages of a differential organization of space and time. In the case of a crash or attack, differentiated networks can be substituted for one another. The differentiated structure foreseen by technicians does not extend to sanctioning the *autonomous* operation of partial centres; above all, it does not give the floor to those at the base. Hence it does not result in the introduction of *self-management* into information technology. These more flexible schemas foresee counter-powers, but only in order to 'balance' the real powers and decision-making centres without disturbing them. The question posed cannot be resolved solely by means of technique; it is *political*, and will remain so. In society as in art, technique is not an end but a means. A fundamental commonplace: everything depends on the way in which technique is used, who uses it, and for whom. Controlling information, if that is possible, requires accepting that the base – alveolus or cell – has an active life, an existence and a social form, and hence a capacity for self-determination. Here we re-encounter the general problematic of self-management, rendered somewhat more complex. The relations of self-managed units, enterprises or territories, are already in conflict with the market and the state. These conflictual relations interfere with the relations of these units to information technology. Will self-management be realized and actualized by acquiring a content and meaning in information technology? Or will technological and political pressures reduce self-management to a sham? That is the question. The coherence of human groups, such as the sociologist habitually defines them, is merely a fiction, except possibly in the case of a pressure group. In general, a social group has a concrete existence only if it seeks to control its conditions of existence, of living and surviving, and succeeds in so doing. This is how self-management is defined.

We have reached the stage of turning ideological definitions of information technology back round against them: information does not possess the quality, the capacity, of *conferring meaning* on that which does not possess it; or of restoring it to that which has lost it. On the contrary: information technology could well complete the destruction of meaning, by replacing value by signs, the totality by the combinatory, the living word by the message (in classical terms, the spirit by the letter). With the end of meaning, nothing would have meaning – information no more than anything else. (Would there still be anything else?) Where might a restoration, a rebounding, of meaning come from?

Information can no more create situations than it can create meaning. It can only transmit what is said about situations; it simulates or dissimulates situations, with their conflicts. From the standpoint of information itself, it is impossible not to call upon a source or resource, an eruption of surprises, a social negative entropy, violent or pacifying, innovative and creative. This capacity is discovered in the self-management, the self-determination, of effective centres of power, partially or utterly transgressing the order of power. Here alone, thought and the desire to shatter codes and create new codes coincide. Foundational violence? No, creative transgression, beyond transitions, means and averages, media, modes and models.

Daily life sometimes seems like the thing of substance that prevents forms from vanishing into pure abstraction, approximating nothingness; and sometimes like the place from which the content might arise that will transform forms, including the supreme form: information.

Only daily life can attach to the sites of production and consumption what unites them, and yet tends to become detached from them: information. Hence we are dealing not with a duality, a binary system, or bi-polarity, but with a triadic relationship: production–creation–information.

CONCLUSION

Results and Prospects

1 The Middle Classes

Marx forecast their dissolution, even their disappearance, with the polar system of proletariat and bourgeoisie and the essential contradiction between the two. This simplification bears a date; it marks a phase in Marx's thinking regarded dynamically, as intellectual activity and research, not as a finished theory and system. At the end of what is an unfinished work, *Capital*, Marx was obliged to reconsider the propositions he had previously advanced, in the light of a comprehensive analysis of the mode of production and society dominated by capital and the bourgeoisie. The surviving drafts indicate that Marx did not stick with a binary opposition, but reinstated the triadic character of his analysis; he included land, ground rent and agrarian questions in a three-term totality: land–capital–labour. He was likewise obliged to reinstate trade and the bureaucracy – that is to say, the functions of realization and distribution of surplus-value. In Marx, society as we perceive it appeared in all its complexity – minus, obviously, the modalities of social and political practice that Marx could not possibly have foreseen in his day (for example, the 'welfare state' with its networks of redistribution, income transfers, direct or disguised subsidies): practices that were grafted on to Keynesianism, a diversion of Marxism.

It is nevertheless the case that, on this important point, Hegel was right and Marx was wrong. For a historical period whose duration cannot be predicted, but whose end we can possibly sense today, the state has had its social basis in the middle classes, not in the working class. As a result, it has not withered away, as Marx forecast, but, rather, been consolidated. Sometimes it is erected on a pre-existing middle class; sometimes it produces or generates middle classes, bureaucracy and technocracy – and this often under the guise of democracy, even of the socialization of national life and society as a whole.

We can just as easily say *the* middle class as the middle class*es*. In fact, this socio-economic formation evinces a great diversity of standards of living, lifestyles, integration or non-integration into productive activities and institutions. The technostructure that forms part of the upper middle classes does not mix with the groups responsible for transmitting positive knowledge, or with lower-level technicians. For some years now, there has been a new middle class, comprising technicians and technocrats, without this entailing the disappearance of the old middle class composed of doctors, lawyers, and members of the liberal professions. However, there is a certain homogeneity to the layers situated between the summit and the base of society, allowing us to talk about the middle class.

The numerical expansion of these layers and this class occurs in tandem with economic growth in the capitalist mode of production, and also in socialism. This increase has been particularly marked in the United States. People have even wanted to base a new form of society on the middle classes: values, norms, lifestyles, ethics, aesthetics. Before embarking on a critique of this hypothesis, we should recall how fluid class boundaries are becoming. The most comfortably off section of the middle classes – senior managerial staff – is closely adjacent to the 'managers' and the *grande bourgeoisie*, whereas a gulf separates them from the *haute bourgeoisie*, or the directors of global enterprises. As for junior managerial staff – that is to say, junior technicians – this stratum is scarcely distinguishable from what Lenin pejoratively dubbed the 'labour aristocracy' (wrongly, since this layer or stratum would appear to be both robust and capable of political initiatives).

The numerical rise of the middle classes enables us to understand many facts and phenomena at all levels. In effect, we are faced with a society in which the middle classes are *ideologically predominant* under the *hegemony* of big capital. The result, in particular, is the consolidation of the state and the innovations bound up with it: the fact that, from a certain date onwards, the administrators of society have banked on the domestic market; the more or less successful attempts to incorporate the unions into existing institutions; the difficulties and divisions within the working class; the introduction of new techniques; and so on. People have questioned whether 'passive revolutions' in the Gramscian sense do not derive from the salience of the middle classes, which are indeed passive, objects of politics and not active subjects – which would avoid imputing responsibility to the passivity of the working class. The allegedly 'revolutionary' transfer to the state of activities that previously fell to the dominant class – in particular, supervision of the conditions of surplus-value, accumulation, in short, growth – assumes a support. The state that benefits from this transfer has been able to find such a support only among the middle classes. The thesis, widespread in the United States, of a cultural revolution via the agency of the middle classes does not stand up. Only the existence of the middle classes makes it possible for the welfare state to elevate itself above society; this state finds its resources, its personnel, its passive 'subjects', in its social base. Consequently, it can lay claim to the virtues appropriate to active 'subjects': competence, vigour, honest administration, and so on. That said, these strata and classes possess no creative capacity; they cannot institute either forms or values; consuming the products of the culture industry, they are incapable of creating a culture, still less a civilization worthy of the name; they mark out the road to decline. Whence some major malaises: they serve as an effective tool for barring the way to the working class, which they stifle even as the strategy of power is fragmenting it. They propose or impose *models* of all sorts, political as well as cultural. Mystificatory neoliberalism, which concealed wide-ranging economico-political operations, was enough to satisfy a significant section of the middle classes.

Can it last? No. To present this 'order' as definite or definitive, to believe that classes are being reabsorbed into strata, is sheer mystification. The middle classes possess no unifying principle, although they feature in the general homogeneity. They are divided. Some individuals and groups tend towards the Right, and sometimes towards right-wing extremism; others tend to the Left, even to ultra-leftism. Moreover, they have not been immune from attacks by the state-political power they helped to organize. In France, for example, this power has attempted to make it impossible for universities to intervene politically. But we do not have the space here for a closer study of these middle layers, or their relations with the state and society. It must suffice to consider them in the light of the everyday.

It is within the middle classes – in the middle of this middle – that modern daily life is constituted and established. This is where it becomes a model; starting from this site, it is diffused upwards and downwards. Formerly, modes and models derived from the aristocracy or the *grande bourgeoisie* in its *belle époque*. In the course of what are called modern times, the middle imposes its law. It goes without saying that this law has not been generalized, and that it cannot achieve equivalent universality to the historical compromise between a declining aristocracy and rising bourgeoisie in the eighteenth century. Various categories are exempt from the models (cultural and practical) generated within the middle class: the *haute bourgeoisie*, the establishment at a transnational level, the jet set that moves from palace to palace or lives on yachts – and, on the other hand, the 'lower class', which does not even have access to the everyday. So that we have had to distinguish infra- and supra-daily life from daily life itself. This situates it. The 'lower' and the 'upper' class are in a condition of 'survival', but not in the same way: sub-life for the former, hyper-life for the latter. As a model or mode of consumption (the term mode being construed in its twin sense of irresistible fad and way of being), but also as insertion and integration into the social, daily life thus has a highly determinate place of origin and formation. Together with its modalities: domestic appliances, the use of space and time, computer equipment, the car or cars. This set defines not a style of living but a lifestyle. The term 'style' refers to an aesthetic or ethical bearing in which the middle classes are precisely lacking. As for lifestyle, it is easily defined: it is the everyday itself. The predominance of the middle classes has repercussions in what is called culture – that is to say, ethics and aesthetics. Incapable of creating new values, the middle classes create the opposition between conformism and non-conformism. Ethics is confused with conformism, while aesthetics is inflected towards non-conformism.

Technological illusions, mystifications and utopias are attributable to the predominance of the middle classes in conditions of capitalist hegemony. Among them is the illusion that daily life being established in and through positive knowledge involves the death of lived experience: an insignificant fact. This illusion is exploited in all sorts of ways by power and information technology alike. How many people think themselves very human because they tell others how they should live, from menus to clothing, from housing to educating children! As if a society in which it is necessary to prescribe and describe the daily life that it institutes does not condemn itself solely by virtue of this fact. The myth of transparency and its ideology end thus: the substitution of a melancholy science for lived experience and a gay science; the administration of daily life according to models, modes and modalities that are mimetically connected.

These rather caustic observations do not entail rejection and condemnation of everything originating in the middle classes. Far from it. Such a rejection carries the mark of sectarianism. Women's movements originate among neither workers nor the bourgeoisie. Evidently reformist, their demands transform neither the everyday, nor the mode of production; they are, for example, content to improve the division of labour at the level of daily life.

The fact that the most comfortably off middle class seeks to reoccupy the centre of large towns does not militate against centrality and the renovation of the centres. It simply demonstrates that those concerned, being sensible folk, appreciate that everyday life is more pleasant in towns, for all their drawbacks, than in isolated outskirts. For a long time, who did not desire a country house or residence? The model and mode once again came from a section of the middle classes, the measures taken by the political authorities favouring their expansion. Disillusionment followed. Urban reconstruction – centres and monuments – can stimulate a new fashion. It is only a pity that workers abandoned positions they once occupied in certain major towns and cities without much resistance. In this respect, the case of Paris is exemplary. Who was responsible for the withdrawal? This is not the place to answer that question.

Thus, in the twentieth century, the middle classes provided the site where the everyday and its models took shape, but also protest and contestation, as well as rather naive attempts to transform and transfigure things that were becoming established: modes of fiction, of the supernatural, the surreal, the imaginary, modernism, and so on. Here too arose the mystification of a cultural revolution by the middle classes and their ways of life, destined in this novelistic fiction to

831

abolish classes by absorbing the various categories of workers. This fiction is becoming ideology in the United States, and could spread to Europe. The Marxist current of thought has not challenged it success-fully, for it continues to bank on the working class as if its existence as a class and a political subject were self-evident.

To talk about models and modes is also to talk about imitation. Mimesis rules, but a model is accepted only when people feel that it reflects what is most profound about them, and hence when it is 'freely' accepted.

The critique of daily life exposes this situation. It demonstrates that with the predominance of the middle classes everything becomes illusory certainty and problematic. The word 'problem' features in an incalculable number of expressions. And what a lot of researchers there are! And research! People search and search without finding anything very much. Rather than *oeuvres*, we have essays, attempts, cross-references, overtures. The word 'problem' is becoming intolera-ble, yet how is it to be avoided? How, getting through to the end of the night, can we cross the problem zone that is nothing but a symptom of total crisis?

Are the innovations in and through the middle classes being consoli-dated? This is a difficult question to answer. The modes and models of consumption? They quickly become obsolescent; a kind of febrile pseudo-dynamic, visible in advertising campaigns, carries them off: there are always new things, and better things, for doing the same thing.

The middle strata and classes lack substance. They are threatened with dislocation and disintegration. Their political parties cannot guarantee or restore their cohesion. The elitism to which they give rise contrasts with the profound stupidity of short-sighted people who believe they have sound judgement and good taste and are full of good sense, when in fact they possess only a meagre know-how, and the corollary of their distinction is vulgarity.

2 The Abstract–Concrete and the Fictitious–Real

A mode of social existence has gradually emerged, confirming other studies: the fictitious–real and the abstract–concrete. The mode of production involves and entails a mode of existence. The real? It exists; yet it no longer corresponds to the classical notion: something solid, being, independent of all subjectivity, all mental or social activity. This object is there. Its place depends on a choice, a decision. Its reality likewise, since it is the result of a production whose function, form, structure, and even material have been predetermined. Its social objectivity has nothing in common with the objectivity of the *things* of nature, which served as a model for philosophers. The reality of the product should be distinguished from the reality attributed to 'things', but it is difficult to differentiate it. Assigned a signification connected with a use, the produced object enters into multiple networks: it passes through the market, an intermediate but important stage. It is then that it is on the verge of being absorbed into language and signs, without this derealizing absorption being accomplished and 'realized'. The produced object thus crosses through abstraction, never vanishes into it, and yet never quits it. The abstract is not the duplicate of something concrete, but the abstract and the concrete are inseparable, and their unity makes up the everyday. Critical analysis of daily life is thus situated in a region that is difficult to grasp and express. The concrete existence of objects through the abstract assimilates them to abstract idealities that lead to practical, concrete actions: law, right, the accord between wills promoted to the title of contract, and so on. Thus, the abstract–concrete and the fictitious–real, in their ambiguity and duality, extend from simple products to major incarnations of positive knowledge, possessions and power; from humble babbling to higher brain activity, to the empire of signs and the information with which this empire ends. In the course of this enormous deployment, there is no rupture or discontinuity. From daily life to the state, the mode of existence does not alter fundamentally. Yet the various degrees of this deployment do not tally. They conceal one another. Daily life masks the state level while referring the reflective consciousness to it. Likewise, security measures, which are simultaneously fictitious and real, refer to menaces that are no less fictitious and no less real. Daily life conceals and contains the state, but the two taken together mask the tragic element they contain. In this way, daily life enters into the system of equivalents guaranteed by the state. But the identical, the repetitive and the redundant appear differently in daily life and in the state. The state promulgates identity – that of all 'subjects' in the general order – although it may mean subsequently contradicting this promulgation, and circumventing its own law. As for daily life, it endures identity, redundancy and repetition without understanding them.

Compared with the types and models derived either from philosophy or from science, this is a unique mode of existence. It is not a substantial or essential mode of existence. Hence the impression of escape, (bad) dream, even unreality conveyed by daily life, but also by the state-political, when thought attempts to define them. This is no longer the mode of existence of a relation between two terms, a relation that can be grasped – so that, according to positivism, there is no need to define the terms in themselves. Relations in daily life, as in the political and the economic, disclose the terms they connect; they declare them. Positivism and empiricism, which claim to make do with relations, overlook what is most important in the social. For its part, critical knowledge can only indicate an ambiguity, a contradiction that is masked and crystallized in a pseudo-knowledge, which is nevertheless 'realized' on the ground.

Over and above what philosophers thought to define as truth and falsity, there thus develops the real–unreal. The state itself sums up these paradoxes: fictitious but terribly real; abstract but ever so concrete. It is thus that it is the keystone and yet '*rests*' on this foundation, daily life.

This situation, which is intolerable and yet tolerated, doubtless accounts for another paradox: the return in strength of (and to) the Sacred. The Sacred seemingly escapes ambiguity. It gives the impression of strength, of true and authentically concrete *being*, whether we are dealing with the signs of the zodiac, the preaching of a foreign religion, or the traditions of the established church. The most venerable words acquire the appeal of genuine novelty; they emerge either through pathos or through ethos, above this gleaming or benighted unreality that we call the 'social' in contemporary society.

The preceding account is thus situated on the borders of philosophy and the social sciences. Philosophical categories – real and unreal, appearance and essence – are embodied in daily life, but extending beyond themselves to be integrated into elements derived from the various fragmented sciences. Daily life is not inscribed in one of the partial domains or fields. In order to deepen itself, its concept seizes what it needs, and what is its by right, anywhere and everywhere. The concept of daily life is, in its fashion, comprehensive; in the course of its deployment, it concerns and interrogates the totality. To seek to grasp and define daily life at its apparent level, the *micro* – micro-decisions, micro-effects – is to let it slip; to seek to grasp the macro without it is likewise to let the totality slip.

The conclusion of this work will be deliberately metaphilosophical, this term encompassing philosophy while carrying it beyond itself. In accordance with the philosophical approach, it turns towards what underlies daily life in time and space, towards the origin and history, towards the surpassed and superseded. But it also looks to what exceeds the actual, to the possible and the impossible. Philosophy has never gone so far as to demand or proclaim a project for society or a project for civilization. At the highpoint of research, the summit of philosophy, Hegel simply suggested a political model: the state founded on absolute knowledge. Philosophical utopia, like technocratic utopia, must be surmounted in the name of daily life.

(a) If revolution – in other words, the radical transformation of society – cannot have as its goal and end either faster growth or a mere change of political personnel, it can only have as its goal and end the transformation of daily life.

(b) As has already been established on many occasions, this implies not zero growth or reduced growth, but different growth – that is to say, *qualitative development*, and hence a greater complexity, not a simplification, of social relations.

(c) This equally implies a different way of living, extending to the creation of a new social space, a different social time; the creation of a different mode of existence of social relations and different situations, liberated from models that reproduce the existing order.

(d) This also assumes a different form of thought, to be defined later. Let me say straight away: to be defined while taking account of the negative. The project is thus not to know or recognize daily life, in order to accept or affirm it as such in the name of positive knowledge, but, on the contrary, to create it by controlling its ambiguity. Thus the project no longer consists in unfolding daily life to disclose what is concealed in it (first version of the *Critique*); or in an effort to transcend it (second version), but in a metamorphosis through action and works – hence through thought, poetry, love. Once we have obtained knowledge of it and defined it, we must leave it without hesitating before the risk we face: the risk of involvement. Daily life is simultaneously the arena and the total stake.

Contemporary society is sinking into hidden contradictions which form such a tight knot that people do not know which end to approach it from in order to unravel it. It is better to sever it.

Here is a contradiction indicated *en route*, which seems minor but has some serious implications. Modern society disposes of death. People no longer die; they disappear (Kostas Axelos). This society thus also disposes of tragedy, returning it to the spectacle or to aestheticism. Yet it is not enough for it to set the mortal power of the state over it; it runs on death. This other power creates the vacuums that techniques, production and satisfaction arrive to fill. It is enough in this context to recall the importance of arms in today's economy. It should also be remembered that the countries most devastated by the war – the defeated countries of Japan and Germany – are today at the forefront of progress, are comparatively rich and prosperous countries, with a strong currency, and so on. As is well known but rarely stated, wars and crises do their job; they perform the function of the negative, unnoticed as such; they purge the mode of production of its temporary surpluses, and prime a resumption of accumulation on a new technological basis. Destructive capacity creates the premises of prosperity. Thus moulded into a mockery of a full life, daily life itself enables the mode of production to function. It is true that the everyday offers much satisfaction and many amenities to those who live above the level of infra-daily life. That is precisely the trap. This tragic age repudiates the tragic. Moreover, there is no more reason to experience the feeling of tragedy than there is to ratify its elimination. In and through a knowledge of this age, a different form of thought is instituted. How? In the first instance, through knowledge of the negative powers driving this society, which aims and claims to be so positive – and is, moreover, in that it presupposes the positivity of what is operational and profitable. Thinking is born out of contradictions and consideration of the negative, but above all from the relations between the triads we have encountered *en route*, where daily life always figures in a larger whole – the mode of production. The thinking that clarifies daily life also discovers that it carries within it what it negates and what negates it. The negation daily life carries within it, and which it tries in vain to dispose of, is the tragic. In philosophical terminology and from a metaphilosophical viewpoint, it is the negative. A fundamental triad is thus disclosed: daily life–the ludic–the tragic.

Labour and non-labour, verbal language and non-verbal sign-systems (music, architecture, painting, etc.), are integrated into daily life. Daily life seeks to integrate the ludic and the tragic; it does not succeed. The most it can do is to detach some fragments, some scraps, of the ludic and the tragic.

Marx's thought now appears in a different light, casting him as a *thinker of the negative* (and not of the economic, the historical, or techniques), who has been widely misunderstood as a realist – a theoretician of positive reality and political realism. Workers, let us remember, have as their historical mission the negation of work. As has been indicated in the course of this text, when computer science makes it possible to alter work and, ultimately, to abolish it as manual labour, this problematic becomes topical once more. This is the negative mission, historical or trans-historical, of information technology; for the time being, no-one is proposing to see it through. The transformation of daily life can serve as a guiding thread. In daily life, work and non-work already confront one another according to conflictual relations whose analysis has been begun in outline in this and previous works. The end of work? Not yet. Its indication? No doubt, but with what conflicts and problems! Non-work includes not only leisure, but unemployment, absenteeism, the search for interesting or temporary work, festivals, various games. Daily life thus seems to be entirely taken up by and engaged in the positive; and yet we can see the negative at work in it. What are we to conclude from this? Is daily life, which seemed so solid at first, merely a kind of island floating in a swamp and ferment of technological and social forces?

This daily life trails along with it no more than fragments of the subject and subjectivity, which is endlessly fragmented within rational homogeneity. This dissolution was proclaimed by philosophy and

critical thinking. The subject and self-consciousness generated historically, during the era of bourgeois ascendancy, have long been in crisis.
Is this sufficient reason to abandon them? Just because philosophers
have manipulated the subject/object relation in every imaginable way
(from the tautology 'no subject without an object, and vice versa' to the
widest horizons of past or future subject–object identity), is that a
reason to shelve the problematic? No. The crisis, itself total, demands
a total response. Like everything else, the subject is to be reconstructed.
How? In the first instance, through action in the everyday pursuing a
course opposed to the operational schema of the existing order: that is
to say, by opposing difference to homogeneity, unity to fragmentation,
concrete equality to pitiless hierarchization, in a real struggle. This as
regards practice. In theoretical thought, the subject must be reconstructed in accordance with a new approach that foregrounds not the
positive, but the negative and all that it involves. Without shying away
or giving up, but looking it straight in the eye, the subject braves death,
conflict and struggle, including the struggle against time. To use a word
that remains philosophical, the subject regards the *other* in all senses of
the term. Philosophy used not to envisage all these senses: the remote
and the close, horizon and surroundings, ascendancy and decline, difference and indifference, but also debt, dues, contract – and generosity,
gifts, grace.

   Physical energy and biological life are already defined solely by possibilities and potentialities. The organism is torn from its habitat to
perform its vital functions. The living self, which is not yet a subject,
exists only for and by the other – not transcendental, metaphysical or
ontological, but concrete and practical: the prey, the sexual object
from reproduction by mating, progeny, above all from fertilization.
Just as it is difficult completely to separate so-called inert matter and
its forms from living matter, so it is difficult to demarcate between
living species and the human species. Continuity? To a certain extent,
yes. But there are also discontinuities. While it is true that human
action impacts back upon the *physis* it issues from, it is in order to
unfurl it in a second, infinitely rich and complex, nature – products
and works – but at the risk of destroying the first nature and severing
the increasingly frail nutritive bond that links the two (we might say,
with Spinoza: *natura naturans* and *natura naturandum*). Social practice
unfolds the life of the living being, but in another space and in

analogical fashion: sooner or later, it wrecks the attempts of groups to isolate themselves and of individuals to shut themselves off. Whence, probably, the incest taboo, exogamy, ritual and symbolic exchanges, and so on. Other-orientated people (Robert Jaulin) always prevail, though not without great suffering. Systemic, functional or structural reality cannot be established in a sustained equilibrium. Even a self-regulated system, closed off to evolution and emergent phenomena, disappears in the face of unforeseen aggression or through internal decline. In the more or less long term, self-sufficiency kills. In this way, the relational character of human beings becomes more pronounced via language, communication and exchange, and the displacement of Eros towards creation through prohibitions and conflicts. Is this how we make the transition from one logic to another, from the logic of life to that of social exchange? Should we not say instead that every logic is inscribed in a dialectical movement that envelops it and carries it beyond itself? Biological life and social life prefigure thought in the sense that they are constantly resumed, recover themselves for a new effort, so that the singularity of individuals and the impact of constraints prevent neither permanent creation and the irruption of possibilities, nor decline. The other is also novelty, emergence, history. The triads 'alterity–alteration–alienation' and 'procreation–production–creation' are dissociated only in the course of evolution – dramatically, in a way that is unforeseen by the actors and yet retrospectively foreseeable. Biological life, like social practice and individual thinking, always present a totality, but one that is constantly evolving, always going beyond (meta) itself, despite the simultaneously formal, functional and structural coherence required by practical existence. This is how coherent organicism and systemic logic sooner or later shatter, thereby opening up to directionality (direction and orientation). Thus is posed the problem of life, from organic spontaneity to social daily life. From this standpoint, there is an analogy between problematics at the different levels. Daily life, the organic body of modern society, summons up its *beyond* in time and space. The work that is now concluding has consistently adopted this (relatively) optimistic perspective, despite the introduction of tragic knowledge – or rather, precisely because of it!

Even so, various anxieties remain. The notion of an ascending life, of an evolution that passes through revolutions in order to progress towards more successful forms, prompts more than one objection and several questions that remain unanswered. How far does entropy extend? Do possibilities suddenly emerge, bursts of possibilities and spurts of energy that counter degradation in biological and social life? We can find arguments to support this hypothesis of a constant dissipation counteracted by irruptions all over the place. But for now, it is unproven. In the biological and historical spheres alike, does not time always bring decline and degeneration? Some regard ageing, and the terrible certainty that it will occur, as proof of the existence of an infinitely cruel, as well as ingenious and powerful god, of an infinity that is simultaneously diabolical and divine, but forever inventive in the ways of spitefulness. Death and even pain are one thing, but growing old? Life recedes slowly, implacably, while we are fully conscious. For consciousness ages only in becoming more refined, improving – unless, that is, it hits upon a way of concealing, through representation or stupidity, what is occurring within and without: the body's treachery, the source that runs dry, the light and heat that fade. Is not ageing the dereliction that some philosophers have described, but without referring to it as such, avoiding it by offering a metaphysical picture? But we do not know how far this ordeal extends. Do societies grow old too – and peoples, and nations, and civilizations or cultures? Are the symptoms interpreted as those of a 'crisis', which a skilful initiative would lead us out of, in fact symptoms of an irreversible decline? Of whom, and what? These questions will remain unanswered here.

But wait a moment. Thought has some privileges. Like all ordeals, those just described have their compensations, at least at an individual level. So why not when it comes to groups and peoples? Consciousness of time and thinking about time struggle *for life*, so to speak, against time. Dominating the process that starts from the outset, dominating ageing and anguish at the same time: this is the force of life to the second degree – thinking, not to be confused with reflection, which knows only how to attend to the first level. At the first level, spontaneity and youth, vitality, spring forth. They are free gifts. From whom? From that same cruel infinity we call *nature*. At the second level, which is not that of a rhetoric, a reflexive decoding or a discourse on the first, but a quite different force, the capacity to master the ordeal, to counter time and prevail, is created. This strength used to be called 'spiritual'; it is thought, which cannot be defined by discourse but as an act.

Today, no one is unaware of the fact that the elementary forms of life are steeped in immortality. The greater the differentiation that culminates in the human species, where everyone is unique, as is each situation, each thought and each love, ageing and death make themselves ever more cruelly felt. We are thus begining to think that the human species and, consequently, its social history spring from a decline in cosmic life, which possibly comes to a halt with humanity, a frontier in the void. A catastrophic, even nihilistic thesis, which is widely endorsed, whether consciously or not.

Objections: the bursts and spurts, the moments when a bundle of possibilities suddenly arises. There are bursts that inject energy into the *reality* of decline. And then, above all, there is the new arrival – the thinking that does not shy away from the horror of the world, the darkness, but looks it straight in the face, and thus passes over into a different kingdom, which is not the kingdom of darkness. This thinking asserts itself while wandering among illusions and lies, beyond truth as well as error. If a consciousness of ineluctability wins out, then we have nihilism and the confirmation of decline. Tragic knowledge does not betoken melancholy science. Quite the reverse. If there is a reconciliation, or at least a compromise, between first and second natures, it will occur not in the name of an anthropological or historical positive knowledge, but in and through daily life transformed from within by tragic knowledge. Sensed by Nietzsche, who drifted towards the 'over-human', this knowledge conceives the negative in all its strength, in order to turn it against itself and try to overcome it. Daily life has served as a refuge from the tragic, and still does: above all else, people seek, and find, security there. To traverse daily life under the lightning flash of tragic knowledge is already to transform it – through thought.

Epilogue

To finish this conclusion, which is in no sense definitive or conclusive, two remarks:

(a) By virtue of its situation in contemporary social practice, daily life functions as the non-tragic *par excellence*, as the anti-tragic. The seeming reversibility of everyday time, demonstrated in the course of this work, establishes a sort of bulwark against anguish. Like a fortress that has been painstakingly built over the centuries, but above all in 'modern' times, objects are piled up against death and consciousness of the end. The same goes for utensils as kitsch objects, for the interior of dwellings as the spatial and architectural organization of contemporary towns. What is described as a 'beautiful' *oeuvre* has a quite different significance and a quite different effect. The tragic is the non-everyday, the anti-everyday. So that the irruption of the tragic in daily life turns it upside down. It is thus possible to make out a dialectical dynamic between tragedy and daily life. The everyday tends to abolish what tragic words and actions brutally restore: acts of violence, crimes, wars, aggression. Whence an extremely serious interaction in the permanent separation and mutual penetration of tragedy and daily life. Tragedy as an *oeuvre* reconnects these aspects: it seeks both to transform daily life through poetry and to conquer death through the resurrection of the tragic character.

(b) The end of work promises to be a long and difficult process which is already permeating the everyday, and which will have very varied forms, improvements and regressions. This is distantly foreshadowed by the end of work as *value*: the *end* of work as a meaning and *end* 'in and for itself'.

Paris, November 1980–May 1981

842

Notes

Volume I: Introduction

Preface

1. Jean Kanapa, 'Henri Lefebvre ou la philosophie vivante', *La Pensée*, no. 15, November–December 1947.

2. 'Introduction à l'esthétique', *Arts de France*, nos. 19–20 and 21–2, 1947. Detailed bibliography in Rémi Hess, *Henri Lefebvre et l'aventure du siècle*, A.M. Métaillé, Paris 1988.

3. Jean Beaufret, 'A propos de l'existentialisme' (six articles), *Confluences*, 1945; Jean-Paul Sartre, 'A propos de l'existentialisme, mise au point', *Action*, no. 17, 29 December 1944; Henri Lefebvre, 'Existentialisme et marxisme: réponse à une mise au point', *Action*, no. 40, 8 June 1945. On this debate, see Mark Poster, *Existentialist Marxism in Postwar France*, Princeton University Press, Princeton, NJ, 1975.

4. *La Pensée*, no. 15, November–December 1947, p. 2.

5. Unpublished letter to Norbert Guterman, 4 September 1947 (Guterman Papers, Butler Library, Columbia University, New York). See also Hess, *Henri Lefebvre*, pp. 115–20.

6. Jean Bothorel, *Bernard Grasset. Vie et passions d'un editeur*, Grasset, Paris 1989, p. 409.

7. The most detailed account of the 'Nizan affair' is in Pascal Ory, *Nizan. Destin d'un révolté*, Ramsay, Paris 1980, pp. 237–60.

8. Pierre Hervé, *Lettre à Sartre et à quelques autres par la même occasion*, Table Ronde, Paris 1956, p. 124. Henri Lefebvre, 'Autocritique. Contribution à l'effort d'éclaircissement idéologique', *La Nouvelle Critique*, no. 4, March 1949, pp. 41–57; see also his 'Lettre sur Hegel', ibid., no. 22, January 1951.

9. Henri Lefebvre describes these episodes in *La Somme et le reste*, La Nef, Paris 1959, pp. 535–42 and pp. 555–8. I have a copy of *Méthodologie des sciences*.

10. (*Trans.*) 'Art is the highest joy that man can give himself'. See below p. 269, n. 33.

11. Michel Trebitsch, 'Philosophie et marxisme dans les années trente: le marxisme critique d'Henri Lefebvre', *Actes du colloque L'engagement des intellectuels dans la France des années trente*, CERAT, University of Quebec, Montreal 1990.

12. See below p. 270, n. 2.

13. Norbert Guterman and Henri Lefebvre, *La Conscience mystifiée*, Gallimard, Coll. 'Les Essais', Paris 1936. The 'Cinq essais de philosophie matérialiste' listed on the front page are respectively: *La Conscience mystifiée, La Conscience privée, Critique de la vie quotidienne, La Science des idéologies, Matérialisme et culture.*

14. Michel Trebitsch, 'Henri Lefebvre et la revue *Avant-Poste*: une analyse marxiste marginale du fascisme', *Lendemains*, no. 57, 1990.

15. *Avant-Poste*, no. 1, June 1933, pp. 1–9, and no. 2, August 1933, pp. 91–107.

16. *La Conscience mystifiée*, pp. 69–70.

17. Marx, *Early Writings*, trans. R. Livingstone and G. Benton, Penguin, Harmondsworth 1975, p. 379.

18. Guterman Papers, letter dated 17 February 1936.

19. Cf. Agnes Heller, *Everyday Life*, trans. G.L. Campbell, Routledge Chapman and Hall, London 1984.

20. Lukács, *History and Class Consciousness: Studies in Marxist Dialectics*, trans. R. Livingstone, Merlin Press, London 1971.

21. Adorno, *Negative Dialectics*, Seabury Press, New York 1973.

22. Henri Lefebvre, *De la modernité au modernisme (Pour une métaphilosophie du quotidien)*, l'Arche, Paris 1981, pp. 23–5. See also Henri Lefebvre, *Lukàcs 1955*, Aubier, Paris 1986.

23. Heidegger, *Being and Time*, Harper and Row, New York 1962.

24. (*Trans.*) The German *Man* can be rendered in English as 'they' or 'one'. For the problems of translating Heidegger's terminology into English, see George Steiner, *Heidegger*, Harvest Press 1978, pp. 25–71.

25. Lucien Goldmann, *Lukàcs and Heidegger*, Routledge and Kegan Paul, London 1977.

26. Lukács, *Introduction to Metaphysics*, Yale University Press, New Haven, Conn., 1959.

27. For the broader issues of this debate, see Perry Anderson, *Considerations on Western Marxism*, Verso, London 1976, and Martin Jay, *Marxism and Totality*, University of California Press, Berkeley and Los Angeles 1984.

28. Henri Lefebvre, *La Somme et le reste*, pp. 408–9.

29. Idem, 'Du culte de "l'esprit" au matérialisme dialectique', in Denis de Rougement, 'Cahiers de revendications. Onze témoignages', *Nouvelle Revue Française*, no. 232, 1 December 1932.

30. (*Trans.*) See below p. 127, in fact, the concluding pages of the first chapter.

31. Michel Trebitsch, 'Les mésaventures du groupe *Philosophies* (1924–1933)', *La Revue des revues*, no. 3, Spring 1987; and 'Le groupe *Philosophies* et les Surréalistes (1924–1925)', *Mélusine*, no. XI, 1990. See also the thesis by Bud Burkhard, 'Priests and Jesters: The Philosophies Circle and French Marxism between the Wars', PhD Georgetown University, Washington 1986, typescript.

32. See below p. 123.

33. *L'Esprit*, no. 2, 1927. Published in 1930, *Le Malheur de la conscience dans la philosophie de Hegel* was followed by *Vers le concret* (1932) and *Etudes kierkegaardiennes* (1938).

34. Michel Trebitsch, 'Le renouveau philosophique avorté des années trente. Entretien avec Henri Lefebvre', *Europe*, no. 683, March 1986. On the *Revue marxiste* 'affair', see *La Somme et le reste*, pp. 429–35.

35. In particular in *Philosophies* Henri Lefebvre published 'Fragments d'une philosophie de la conscience' (no. 4, 1924), 'Positions d'attaque et de défense du

nouveau mysticisme' (nos. 5–6, 1925); and in *L'Esprit*: 'La pensée et l'esprit' (no. 1, 1926), 'Reconnaissance de l'unique' and 'Notes pour le procès de la chrétienté' (no. 2, 1927).

36. 'Le même et l'autre' is the title of the introduction he wrote for the 1926 French translation of Schelling's *Of Human Freedom* (Open Court, Chicago 1936).

37. See below p. 216.

38. Ibid., p. 207.

39. Ibid., p. 132.

40. Cf. *La Somme et le reste*, pp. 251–66, and the analysis by Kurt Meyer, *Henri Lefebvre: ein romantischer Revolutionär*, Europa Verlag, Vienna 1973.

41. Hess, *Henri Lefebvre*, p. 114 and pp. 165–8. Cf. Henri Lefebvre, *La vallée de Campan. Etude de sociologie rurale*, PUF, Paris 1963.

42. See below p. 133.

43. In 1946: Georges Friedmann, *Problèmes humains du machinisme industriel*; in 1948: André Varagnac, *Civilisation traditionnelle et genre de vie* and Philippe Ariès, *Histoire des populations françaises et leurs attitudes devant la vie depuis le XVIIIe siècle*; and in 1949 alone: Georges Bataille, *La Part maudite*, Jean Fourastié, *Le Grand espoir de XXe siècle*, Georges Dumézil, *L'Héritage indo-européen à Rome*, Mircéa Eliade, *Le Mythe de d'éternel retour*, Fernand Braudel, *The Mediterranean*, Claude Lévi-Strauss, *The Elementary Structures of Kinship*.

44. Marcel Gauchet, 'Changement de paradigme dans les sciences sociales', in *Les idées en France, 1945–1988, une chronologie*, Gallimard, Paris 1989. On Lefebvre's attacks on 'bourgeois sociology', see his report for the Cercle de Sociologues, at the Journées nationales d'études des intellectuels communistes in *La Nouvelle Critique*, no. 45, April–May 1953.

45. Henri Lefebvre, *Everyday Life in the Modern World*, trans. S. Rabinowitch, Allen Lane, The Penguin Press, London 1971, p. 25.

46. Ibid., p. 24.

47. Henri Lefebvre, *La Proclamation de la Commune*, Gallimard, Paris 1965. See also: Richard Gombin, *Les origines du gauchisme*, Seuil, Paris 1971; *Internationale situationniste, 1958–1969*, facsimile reprint, Champ libre, Paris 1975. The influence on Jean Baudrillard, who was Lefebvre's assistant at Nanterre, is also undeniable (*La société de consommation*, Gallimard, Paris 1970).

48. See above all Thomas Kleinspehn, *Der Verdrängte Alltag: Henri Lefebvres marxistische Kritik des Alltagslebens*, Focus Verlag, Glessen 1975.

Foreword

1. Written in 1945, published by Editions Grasset, Paris 1947. The text is reissued here in its entirety, including certain passages which the author now considers out-of-date.

2. Lenin, 'What the Friends of the People Are', in *Collected Works*, vol. 1, Progress Publishers, Moscow 1963, p. 141.

3. Lenin, 'On the Question of Dialectics', in *Collected Works*, vol. 38, p. 360. Since the Twentieth Congress of the Soviet Communist Party it has become fashionable

among Marxists to make fun of quotations: 'the shortest way from one idea to another'. The men who started this fashion are precisely the ones who were unable to write a single line or say a single sentence without quoting Stalin. Nowadays they have found other ways of disguising their ignorance and the emptiness of their minds.

4. (*Trans.*) Not only were the ideas not 'ripe', but the Stalinist dogmatism of the French Communist Party had been and was a formidable obstacle to their development. Lefebvre felt this keenly, and during the decade between the two editions of the *Introduction* he was regarded with increasing suspicion by the Party directorate. The development of his critique of everyday life must be seen in the context of his growing malaise with the prevailing ideologies within the PCF. The Khrushchev report of 1956 was instrumental in permitting the open criticisms of Stalinism which appear in this Foreword, but in any event Lefebvre was disciplined and excluded from the Party shortly after its publication, making it one of the last things he wrote before his independence, which he inaugurated in 1959 with his remarkable autobiography *La Somme et le reste*.

5. (*Trans.*) Lefebvre's translations of the *1844 Manuscripts* were the first to appear in France (in the review *Avant-Poste*, 1933, and in *Morceaux choisis de Marx*, 1934, both in collaboration with Norbert Guterman), and the theory of alienation they propose was to afford one of the linchpins of his critique of everyday life. Marx uses various words to express the concept – *Entfremdung, Verfremdung, Entwirklichung, Verselbständigung, Entaüsserung, Vergängliching* – but it is Lefebvre's practice to translate them all by the single word 'alienation'. His particular contribution is to extend it from the domain of work into everyday life in general, and specifically – in this Foreword – into the realm of leisure activities. For problems relating to the translation of these terms from German into English, see the Glossary of Key Terms in Marx's *Early Writings*, Penguin, Harmondsworth 1975.

6. This argument was developed in my *Pour comprendre la pensée de Marx*, Bordas, Paris 1947. It is of course well known that various interpretations of Marx's early writings have been proposed by Gurvitch, Merleau-Ponty and Sartre. Some important recent works have helped to pose the question more clearly, notably Pierre Bigo's *Marxisme et humanisme*, PUF, Paris 1953, and Jean-Yves Calvez's *La Pensée de Karl Marx*, Seuil, Paris 1956.

7. Presented in the Preface to *Capital* as well as in Lenin's 'What the Friends of the People Are', something that Henri Chambre appears to neglect in his *Le Marxisme en Union Soviétique*, Seuil, Paris 1955, cf. pp. 48, 505, etc.

8. (*Trans.*) Léon Brunschvicg was a leading figure of the French philosophical establishment, and Lefebvre studied under him at the Sorbonne in 1920. In response to Brunschvicg's scientific culture and mathematical intellectualism, Lefebvre began for the first time to develop the desire for a concrete, total reality which was to lead him to Marx and to the critique of everyday life.

9. (*Trans.*) The group which was associated with A. Kojève just after the war, and which included Maurice Merleau-Ponty, Jean-Paul Sartre, Jean Hyppolite, le Père Fessard, etc.

10. It would be unfair, however, not to recall that Emmanuel Mounier and Georges Gurvitch indicated their approval.

11. (*Trans.*) Husserl's 'phenomenological reduction', namely the 'bracketing' or suspension of belief in objects.

12. Cf. for example Jacques Soustelle's book on *La Vie quotidienne des Aztèques*, Hachette, Paris 1955. (*Trans.*: A similar series of books was published in England and

the United States during the 1960s by Batsford and Putnam respectively.)

13. Cf. Lévi-Strauss, 'Diogène caché', *Les Temps Modernes*, no. 110, p. 203. Is Lévi-Strauss not going too far in this direction? Is this perhaps his way of compensating for the extreme intellectuality of his position?

14. *L'Express*, no. 5, March 1955. Unsigned.

15. Ermilov, *Dramaturgie de Tcheckhov*, Moscow 1948 (quoted in the French edition of Chekhov's plays, translated by Elsa Triolet, Editeurs français réunis, Paris 1954, p. 17).

16. Which cannot be separated from the extraordinary success of the 'Salon des Arts Ménagers' (*trans.*: Ideal Home Exhibition).

17. Cf. the sociological studies of Chombart de Lauwe, Andrée Michel, Lucien Brams, etc. There is a complex of economic phenomena, social facts and 'crises' of various kinds from which the housing crisis cannot be separated.

18. A distinction must be made between the deterioration of everyday life and impoverishment. They are related but different phenomena, and up to a point one can exist without the other.

19. Jean Duvignaud, 'Le mythe Chaplin', *Critique*, May 1954 (a survey of recent works on Chaplin). But Duvignaud lays too much emphasis on the defeated, tragic, 'down-and-out' aspect of Charlie Chaplin. In this connection it is worth noting a curious mythology that has developed in recent years, one which treats failure as an index of authenticity. This is a form (or ethic) worked up on the basis of a fact of everyday life, namely disappointment, to which has been added an important ideological dimension, namely the proof of authenticity. We shall need to come back later to the nature of this disappointment, its content and meaning. Embracing such a mythology could make Stalinists out of people with not the slightest inclination in that direction. For when history judges him, Stalin's one and only justification will be that he was victorious. Moreover, it is certain that if a new optimism is to be founded and if humanism is to be renewed, at least one victory without lies and violence must be demonstrated, at least one victory which is not smeared with blood and mire ...

20. The theory of the *reverse image* differs considerably from the magical theory of the *double* on which Edgar Morin bases his analysis of the cinema (cf. *Le Cinéma ou l'homme imaginaire*, Editions de Minuit, Paris 1956, notably pp. 31ff.). In the romantic press we find the *reverse image* of the everyday life of women, of their aspirations and their profound needs in contemporary society. But a book like Hemingway's *The Old Man and the Sea* also contains a reverse image – that of the toil, the illusions and the failures of individual and 'private' everyday life. He presents these in all their profound drama, while placing them in the very setting that they lack: the luminosity of the sea, the immensity of the horizon ...

21. (*Trans.*) Directed in 1953 by Herbert J. Biberman, and sponsored by the International Union of Mine, Mill and Smelter Workers, this film used Mexican-American miners to reconstruct a strike which had actually taken place. Many of the people involved in the production were persecuted by the Unamerican Activities Committee.

22. Too often 'realist' writers, authors or film directors do the opposite. Instead of extracting *the extraordinary from the ordinary*, they take the ordinary as it stands (the average actions of a man like any other man, the average events in a day like any other day) and are at great pains to make them interesting by putting them under a microscope like 'specimens', and insisting how very interesting they are. When in fact they have merely painted the grey in proletarian, peasant or petty-bourgeois life with

false colours. As Brecht said, such 'realists' merely repeat the obvious ad nauseam.

23. Brecht, 'The Street Scene', in *Brecht on Theatre*, ed. J. Willett, Methuen, London 1978, p. 126.

24. Brecht, 'The Life of Galileo', in *Plays*, vol. 1, trans. J. Willett, Methuen, London 1960, p. 231.

25. (*Trans.*) A reference to Sartre's *Being and Nothingness* (trans. H. Barnes, Methuen, London 1957, pp. 59ff.).

26. The chapter 'Having, Doing and Being' in Sartre's *Being and Nothingness* offers an indirect critique of everyday life, carried out in a speculative manner and aimed at solving the problem that 'there is nothing in consciousness which is not consciousness of being ... Nothing comes to me that I have not chosen.' This way of posing the question completely avoids the problem of concrete alienation. Cf. ibid., pp. 525ff. for the difficulties Sartre encounters when he tries to show that alienation is (after all) desired as such. (*Trans.*: In French the word 'privé' and its derivatives mean both 'private' and 'deprived', and Lefebvre ironizes on this throughout in a way which is inevitably blunted in translation.)

27. The 'ego', with its (apparently) well-defined outlines, is a fact of history. It appears in the eighteenth century (although of course its seeds were sown earlier, it was prefigured in various ways, etc.). It has a practical foundation in the internal contradiction of bourgeois life, where relations become more numerous while the individual himself becomes more isolated. Concomitant with it are ideologies and ethical attitudes. The impression of well-defined outlines comes from the influence of individual attitudes and ideologies upon lived experience. And yet, beyond these outlines (and the people concerned admit it themselves) there persists a zone of obscurity which is only gradually being explored.

28. Cf. *In Camera* (Sartre) or *Waiting for Godot* (Beckett), or the plays of Ionesco, Adamov, etc.

29. (*Trans.*) In French the word 'jeu' and its derivatives mean 'play', 'gambling' and 'acting', which permit ambiguities which are difficult to render in translation.

30. We are even sometimes unsure on the political level, despite the fact that – in principle – it is a level on which the element of chance is reduced to a minimum; and on the strategic level, where the aim is always to determine an outcome.

31. Here specialists will recognize analyses borrowed from operational logic (considered as a reflection of everyday life *as well*) and from decision theory. This theory takes an aspect of what seems to be the domain of the irrational (pure will, etc.) and makes it rational.

32. Action based on knowledge transforms necessity into freedom, certainly. But knowledge – even when directed towards an 'essence' – can only ever be approximate. That is why decisions always involve risk, while at the same time partaking of the absolute; and why they often imply a gamble or wager. Do they also perhaps involve art? For the classic Marxist theorists, politics becomes a science, but insurrection remains an art. (Cf. in particular Lenin and his commentary on Marx in 'Advice of an Onlooker', in *Selected Works*, Progress Publishers, Moscow 1967, pp. 426–7).

33. (*Trans.*) Transliteration of the Greek *koivov*, meaning 'common to all the people'.

34. Brecht, *Brecht on Theatre*, p. 37.

35. In the book referred to above, Edgar Morin studies some bad films (considered in the same way as 'good' films, as sociological data) and concludes that aesthetic emotions are of a magical nature. Here he is following Jean-Paul Sartre's analyses of the

imagination, and this leads him to make some superficial evaluations (cf. *Le Cinéma du l'homme imaginaire*, note, p. 160).

36. As Geneviève Serreau has pointed out in *Brecht*, Editions de l'Arche, Paris 1955, pp. 44, 82, etc.

37. (*Trans.*) In English in the original.

38. Cf. René Wintzen, *Introduction aux poèmes de Brecht*, Seghers, Paris 1954, p. 139.

39. Georg Buchner, *Danton's Death*, trans. J. Maxwell, Methuen, London 1968, p. 38.

40. (*Trans.*) Vailland was a personal friend of Lefebvre's, and a PCF member until the Khrushchev report and the invasion of Hungary led him to resign. His novel *The Law* (1957) was a great international success.

41. In his book *L'Expérience du drame*, Corréa, Paris 1953.

42. Club du Livre du Mois, Paris 1956.

43. (*Trans.*) The *pays du Tendre* was the allegorical region of amorous feelings invented in the seventeenth century by Mme de Scudéry.

44. *Beau Masque*, Gallimard, Paris 1954, p. 153.

45. 'Nothing is more graceful than a woman occupied in the small tasks of the kitchen', ibid., p. 148.

46. Irwin Shaw. *The Troubled Air* (1951), Hodder and Stoughton, London 1988, p. 75.

47. Ibid., p. 299. (*Trans.*: Set during the period of the Unamerican Activities Committee, Shaw's book gives a gripping account of the destructive effect of dogmatism on the left as well as the right, and one can understand Lefebvre's interest in it in 1958.)

48. Virginia Woolf, *A Room of One's Own*, Hogarth Press, London 1935, p. 131.

49. Autocritique: in the text below, first published in 1947, the reader will find a partially unjust assessment of Surrealism. The author was carried away by his polemic, and consequently his point of view was one-sided. The errors of Surrealism as a doctrine (pseudo-philosophical, with a pseudo-dialectic of the real and the dream, the physical and the image, the everyday and the marvellous) notwithstanding, it did express some of the aspirations of its time. As a doctrine, Surrealism ended up with some particular forms of alienation: with the *image-thing*, magic and the occult, semi-morbid states of mind. However, its scorn for the prosaic bourgeois world, its radical rebellion, did mean something. And the hypothesis that only the *excessive* image can come to grips with the profundity of the real world – a hypothesis which one can identify just as much with Picasso, Eluard and Tzara as with André Breton – needs to be taken seriously.

50. (*Trans.*) Made in 1931, Nikolai Ekk's celebrated film was about the rehabilitation of a group of juvenile delinquents in Russia.

51. Reserving the term *individuality* stricto sensu for forms of consciousness and activity which emerged in the eighteenth century.

52. Definition of leisure given by Joffre Dumazedier: 'An occupation to which the worker can devote himself of his own free will, outside of professional, familial and social needs and obligations, in order to relax, to be entertained or to become more cultivated' (Symposium on Leisure at the Centre d'études sociologiques, 10.1.54). Cf. also the article by the same author in the *Encyclopédie française* on 'la Civilisation quotidienne'.

53. Such exploitation was examined during a study week at Marly, from 28 March 1955 to 3 April 1955 (Publications du centre d'Education populaire de Marly [roneo]). (*Trans.*: This study week dealt specifically with the problems of youth activities with

special concern for leisure and cultural activities. Lefebvre's own contribution was a paper on the women's press. His interest in this area in the 1950s is touched upon in this Foreword, but left undeveloped. The paper itself, though short, is much more explicit, and presents a model and a method for cultural analysis which seems well ahead of its time.)

54. Replies to various surveys, notably those carried out by Joffre Dumazedier and his team.

55. Psycho-physiologically the sexual image abruptly 'refreshes' the unconditioned stimulus which is already linked to a number of conditional stimuli and inserted in 'stereotypes'. It links it to a new signal (for example the trademark on a poster). That these images are effective presupposes both conditioning (triviality) and the inadequacy of this conditioning, the absence of social fixation and human determination by 'instinct'. It presupposes the hidden demands imposed by the shift from habitual but unstable and uncontrolled conditioning to a new type of conditioning: i.e. dissatisfaction.

56. Genuine strangeness (a *valid* aesthetic category) can be seen in Melville, Gogol or Kafka. It must be properly distinguished from a strange (and mystifying) *tone* used to speak about trivial things in a trivial way. The reverse image can also produce valid literary procedures (*In Camera*, a dark, brilliant, *definitive* little play, and Jean-Paul Sartre's best). The case of the children's press is different from the 'case' of the romantic press and crime fiction. They have a common element: the break with – and transport out of – normality. However, the children's press and children's literature have their own set of themes. Less structured than, and differently structured to, the world of the adult, the child's world does not require the same kind of reverse image. In fact there is no world of the child. The child lives in society, and in his eyes the adult world is what is strange and marvellous – or odious. *Simply being a child makes him already a critic of adult everyday life,* but it is in this everyday life that he must search for his future and disentangle his own potential. In the works which are most successful from this point of view, a familiar animal (a dog, a duck, a mouse) supports a reverse image in which the trivial changes into fantasy and the fantastic, with an element of explicit criticism.

57. (*Trans.*) 'Sportsmen' and 'supporters' are in English in the original.

58. (*Trans.*) An independent Marxist sociologist who specialized in the world of work and leisure. Lefebvre and he were fellow students at the Sorbonne, but after Friedmann left the PCF in 1939, their relationship became increasingly acrimonious.

59. Georges Friedmann, *Où va le travail humain,* Gallimard, Paris 1950, p. 22.

60. Ibid., p. 242.

61. Ibid., p. 244.

62. Ibid., pp. 336–64.

63. Ibid., p. 268.

64. Ibid., p. 370.

65. Lenin, 'The Highest Stage of Capitalism', in *Selected Works*, vol. 1, Progress Publishers, Moscow 1967, p. 776.

66. Marx, *Capital*, vol. 3, trans. D. Fernbach, Penguin, Harmondsworth 1981, p. 959.

67. (*Trans.*) In English in the original.

68. Jean-Marie Domenach, 'La Yougoslavie et la relance du socialisme, *Esprit,* December 1956, pp. 812–13.

69. Unfortunately materialism is presented in far too many publications as the most depressing of platitudes. In fact it appears to reach the heights of platitude (so to

speak). If it were a completed system, or simply a weapon for the working-class struggle, why indeed would it have to be *interesting*? After all, when philosophy lost metaphysics, it might also be said to have lost its picturesqueness! ...

70. Let us reiterate that the *everyday* struggle in Russia to achieve properly observed labour norms and increased yield and productivity in factories and collective farms can also express itself in an *epic* style. This alone does not suffice as a definition of socialism. The Stalinist definition: 'to maintain the maximum satisfaction of material and cultural needs ...' does not get very far. For what is required is to show *what needs* are specific to socialist society, what needs characterize it, are born in it and from it. Khrushchev has already gone beyond this in his Report at the Twentieth Congress in his demand for an improvement in 'the qualitative structure of consumption'.

71. (*Trans.*) *Critique de la vie quotidienne 2: fondements d'une sociologie de la quotidienneté*, L'Arche, Paris 1961.

72. Let us be clear about this. Stalin was a Marxist; and even a great one, according to Khrushchev (on 1 January 1957). And yet it is impossible not to talk about a Stalinist *interpretation* of Marxism (or even of Leninism).

73. Lenin, 'Plan of Hegel's Dialectics', in *Collected Works*, vol. 38, p. 320.

74. Cf. *Introduction à la critique de l'économie politique* in Laura Lafargue's translation, Edition Giard, p. 342, and *La Pensée*, Colloque du 19 mai 1955, no. 66, p. 35, and also Emile Bottigelli, 'Faits et lois dans les sciences sociales', *La Nouvelle Critique*, January 1956.

75. It is easy to see how this interpretation differs from class and party subjectivism. Marx discovered the working class, its alienation, its 'negativity', its struggles, its historic mission, *and he took its side*, analysing bourgeois society, starting from all existing knowledge, *gaining knowledge* of it in its *totality*, with all its becoming, its aspects, its limits.

76. Marx, 'Economic and Philosophical Manuscripts', in *Early Writings*, Penguin, Harmondsworth 1975, pp. 322–30.

77. Ibid., p. 360.

78. Ibid., p. 369.

79. Ibid., p. 349.

80. Ibid., p. 358.

81. Ibid., p. 366.

82. Which is what some otherwise highly informed exponents or critics of Marxism appear to believe (cf. for example Calvez, *La Pensée de Karl Marx*, pp. 626ff.).

83. (*Trans.*) László Rajk was a minister in the Hungarian government from 1943 until 1949, when he was arrested as part of the Stalinist purges. He was executed after a 'show trial' which aroused an international outcry, and was posthumously rehabilitated in 1956. The Khrushchev report to the Twentieth Congress of the Soviet Communist Party has been called 'one of the most important documents of our century'. It caused disarray in the PCF, where it was denounced as a forgery. In *La Somme et le reste* (1959) Lefebvre describes how his friends in the Party were 'traumatized, morally and physically sickened' by it, while he himself remained unmoved. Obviously, the crimes of Stalinism came as no surprise to him.

84. Marx, 'Economic and Philosophical Manuscripts', p. 351.

85. (*Trans.*) The pages which follow draw extensively upon Hegel cf. note 86 below).

86. Cf. Norbert Guterman and Henri Lefebvre, *Morceaux choisis de Hegel*, Gallimard, Paris 1939, notably pp. 144ff.; also Jean Hyppolite, *Logique et existence*, PUF,

Paris 1953, notably pp. 91ff., and idem, *Etudes sur Marx et Hegel*, Rivière, Paris 1955, which poses several problems remarkably well, but which draws conclusions which we would disagree with. (*Trans.* Lefebvre's Introduction to the *Morceaux choisis* attempted to rehabilitate Hegel's reputation in France, arguing that the opposition between Fascism and Marxism rendered his work of great contemporary importance, since both had their roots in Hegel's philosophy.)

87. This is something Jean Wahl has seen perfectly in his *La Conscience malheureuse chez Hegel*, Reider, 1926. Cf. also Benjamin Fondane, *La Conscience malheureuse*, Denoël et Steele, Paris 1936, Georg Lukàcs, *Die Zeistörung der Vernunft* (The Destruction of Reason), Berlin 1954, and Löwith, *Von Hegel bis Nietzsche*, Europa Verlag, Zurich 1947.

88. This is what J.-Y. Calvez seems to be saying in *La Pensée de Karl Marx*, particularly in the section where he argues against Marx's analysis of the formation of capitalism at the heart of the feudal mode of production (pp. 610ff). It is an argument which paves the way not for mysticism but for a reinstatement of traditional theology.

89. Here we are faced once more with the difficulty of terminology pointed out above (cf. note 51). The individual *stricto sensu* did not appear before the eighteenth century, with the growing complexity of social relations.

90. In everyday life, *ready-made expressions*, frequently taken from eras long past and remote activities, play an important role (as 'throw down the gauntlet', 'fire a Parthian shaft', and so on). Such commonplaces are in fact strange places, where analysis discovers both archaic modes of behaviour and superseded models. The same remarks apply to the thousands of superstitions (touching wood, throwing spilt salt over one's shoulder), to interjections, whose magical character is often quite clear, to the rituals of politeness and etiquette, etc. In this sense, the collecting of archaisms and the study of their uses is a task for anthropology and sociology.

91. Any professional philosopher who reads this will recognize a variety of contemporary doctrines, despite the brevity and the particular slant they are given here. We are happy to leave the task of naming them and analysing them to him. It's a philosophical guessing game.

92. (*Trans.*) A reference to Rimbaud's 'Letter to Paul Demeny', *Collected Poems*, Penguin, Harmondsworth 1960, p. 10.

93. Cf. Descartes: 'I will always be more indebted to those to whose favour I owe the ability to enjoy my leisure without restriction, than to those who might offer me the most honourable employment on earth.'

94. (*Trans.*) Cf. above, n. 11.

95. In this sense and from this point of view phenomenology and existentialism can be defined as philosophies which have fallen to the level of the everyday (a symptom of the crisis of 'pure' philosophy), but which have retained the negative characteristics of traditional philosophy: devaluation of the everyday (of the factitious, of the instrumental, etc.) in favour of pure or tragic moments – criticism of life through anguish or death – artificial criteria of authenticity, etc.

96. (*Trans.*) Lefebvre's translation has 'philosophical' here instead of 'German'.

97. Marx, 'A Contribution to the Critique of Hegel's Philosophy of Right. Introduction', in *Early Writings*, p. 250.

98. Marx, 'On the Jewish Question', ibid., p. 234.

99. Ibid., p. 220.

100. Ibid., p. 233.

101. Cf. Stalin, *Anarchism and Socialism*.

102. In the capitalist economy, commodities exchanged must be consumed. It is a

matter of indifference to the capitalist whether the commodity produced corresponds to a genuine need or not, or whether it is effectively consumed, as long as it is paid for and the profit (surplus-value) is realized as money. It is even possible to stimulate false needs. The theory of a capitalist production determined by needs is therefore a mystification; however, like all mystifications, it contains an element of truth, without which it would be meaningless. Sooner or later need intervenes; and the commodity which does not correspond to a need disappears from the market.

103. Including the disappearance (loss? theft?) of several notebooks containing the draft of the second volume.

104. (*Trans.*) Inevitably the second volume differs in many respects from this proposed plan.

1 Brief Notes on some Well-Trodden Ground

1. (*Trans.*) Thinly veiled references to Gide's *Fruits of the Earth* (1897) and *The Immoralist* (1902).

2. (*Trans.*) In his translation of Baudelaire's *Intimate Journals*, Christopher Isherwood renders this as 'Squibs and Crackers'.

3. I shall deal with failure, defeat and the duality of the individual in *La Conscience privée*, where I shall study the history and structure of individuality. (*Trans.*: The book never appeared.)

4. (*Trans.*) Notably in *Le Génie du Christianisme* (1802), which contributed to the revival of religion in France in the aftermath of the Revolution.

5. (*Trans.*) Set in Scotland, 'L'Aigle du Casque' (*La Légende des siècles* 1, 1859) tells of the pursuit and slaughter of the youth Angus by the evil Tiphaine. The eagle in question comes to life from Tiphaine's helmet and exacts a bloody retribution. *La Légende des siècles* itself was written between 1859 and 1883, and is composed of a series of epic poems which set out to portray the history of humanity. As the title suggests, Hugo envisages history as legend or myth.

6. Baudelaire, 'The Painter of Modern Life', in *Selected Writings on Art and Artists*, trans. P.E. Charvet, Cambridge University Press, Cambridge 1981, p. 329. (*Trans.*: The essay examines the paintings and sketches of Constantin Guys.)

7. Ibid.

8. Ibid., p. 398.

9. Baudelaire, *Intimate Journals*, trans. Christopher Isherwood, Blackamore Press, London 1930, p. 36.

10. Ibid., p. 39.

11. Baudelaire possessed specific information about this dialectic, although it is difficult to say how he obtained it. Who is he referring to in the following lines: 'Portrait of the literary rabble. Doctor Estaminetus Crapulosus Pedantissimus ... His Hegelism'? (Ibid., p. 74.) He himself (Baudelaire) could write in the purest Hegelian spirit: 'What is the Fall? If it is unity become duality, it is God who has fallen. In other words, would not creation be the fall of God?' (Ibid., p. 75.) And a little further on: 'two contradictory ideas ... are identical ... this identity has always existed. This identity is history.' (Ibid., p. 98.)

12. Ibid., p. 49.
13. Ibid., p. 69.
14. Ibid., p. 99.
15. Ibid., p. 91.
16. Ibid., p. 42.
17. Ibid., p. 37.
18. Here it is appropriate to distinguish between the case made with such obstinate ill-humour by Julien Benda and our own. Benda proclaimed himself the censor of his age in the name of classical, eternal, unchanging Reason. His bill of indictment was based precariously on a misunderstanding: as Gaëtan Picon properly points out in *Confluences*, no. 6, the target for his attacks shifted back and forth between what may be called anti-intellectualism and what may be called anti-rationalism. He failed to understand fully the philosophical distinction between intelligence (the faculty for understanding and analysis) and reason (the faculty for unity and synthesis). Instead of carefully defining his terms, he relied on the common-sense and accepted opinions of 'the man in the street' for the meaning of the words he used. But, 'if we ask the man in the street what his views are on Proust, Valéry and Gide, he will reply that they are too intellectual' (Auguste Anglès, *Action*, 28 September 1945).

One can accuse all 'modernity' of not respecting the canon of traditional reason, but not of being anti-intellectual, quite the reverse.

And in any case, if traditional reason, embodied in Julien Benda, complains that it is being abandoned, then surely there is something complacent about its claim to be eternal. And should not traditional reason itself accept some responsibility? What we went in search of, however, was a new Reason capable of organizing the human world, of acting within time rather than claiming to be beyond it. And we found a new Reason, effective and concrete. As the reader will have realized, we are referring to Dialectical Reason.

We do not put 'modernity' in the dock on the grounds that it is irrational, but more generally because it is an attack on mankind in its very life and totality – an attack which, seen in another light, has helped to define the problem, to sharpen the sense that it is serious, and even to contribute some elements towards its solution. (*Trans.*: Benda was an ardent critic of most forms of modernism, and considered that it was the duty of the intellectual (the 'clerc') to defend against the erosion of universal values by the introduction of transitory concerns (such as politics) into literature. His most famous book was *La Trahison des clercs*, but Lefebvre himself was particularly influenced in his youth by *Belphégor* (1918). Writing about this in *La Somme et le reste*, he says: 'I could have become a Surrealist ... if it had not been for André Breton's insufferable personality – and for Julien Benda ... His very existence proves that the thesis of the "destruction of reason" is not valid for France, and that Lukács is exaggerating when he suggests that this destruction is characteristic of the philosophical history of capitalism, imperialism and the bourgeoisie. Moreover, Benda's dogmatism paved the way rather well for Marxist dogmatism ... Influenced by Benda, I began deliberately to do the things I didn't enjoy – like abandoning my first love, Schumann, and adopting his polar opposite, Bach ...')

19. Rimbaud, 'The Drunken Boat', in *Collected Poems*, Penguin, Harmondsworth 1960, p. 167.
20. 'Letter to Paul Demeny', ibid., p. 10.
21. 'Letter to Georges Izambard', ibid., p. 6.
22. Ibid.

23. (*Trans.*) Coined by Franz Roh in 1925 to qualify an aspect of German art, the term has of course been used subsequently for a wide range of authors.

24. André Breton, *Manifestos of Surrealism*, University of Michigan Press, Ann Arbor, 1977, p. 123. (*Trans.*: This use of the title 'Monsieur' is particularly contemptuous – a tonal device adopted by Lefebvre elsewhere in this book – and reveals the personal antipathy he felt for Breton. However, his relations with the Surrealist group as a whole had always been difficult. The Surrealists had been perceived as rivals by the *Philosophies* group which Lefebvre led between 1921 and 1929. An attempt to merge the two groups in 1925 was unsuccessful (ironically Lefebvre was instructed by his colleagues to tell the Surrealists that the *philosophes* would not be prepared to relinquish their belief in 'the Eternal'), and subsequent relations between them were acrimonious. In *La Somme et le reste* Lefebvre admits that under different circumstances he could have been a Surrealist, and in the Foreword to this *Introduction to the Critique of Everyday Life* he qualifies his antagonism. Cf. above, Foreword, n. 49. Nevertheless, Lefebvre continued to consider Surrealism as an extreme form of aesthetic individualism.)

25. Antonin Artaud, *Oeuvres complètes*, vol. 6, Gallimard, Paris 1966, p. 16.

26. Cf. Maurice Nadeau, *The History of Surrealism*, trans. R. Howard, Penguin, Harmondsworth 1978.

27. Ibid., p. 85.

28. André Breton, *Les pas perdus*, NRF, Paris 1924, p. 110.

29. On the subject of this *Pedantissimus*, his literary career and the principles of government he employed, we may relish *A Corpse* by Jacques Prévert, and reprinted in Nadeau's *History of Surrealism*, p. 301: 'When he was alive, he wrote to shorten his time, he said, to find men, and when he happened to find them, he was mortally afraid, and pretending an overpowering affection, lay in wait for the moment when he could cover them with filth.'

30. Breton, *Manifestos of Surrealism*, p. 26.

31. Ibid.

32. Ibid., p. 14.

33. Louis Aragon, *Paris Peasant*, trans. Simon Watson Taylor, Cape, London 1971, p. 24.

34. Ibid., p. 27.

35. Ibid., p. 28.

36. (*Trans.*) A reference to Eugène Sue's novel of criminality in nineteenth-century Paris (*Mysteries of Paris*, Dedalus, Sawtry, UK 1988). Marx examines it at length in *The Holy Family.*

37. Salvador Dali, quoted in *The History of Surrealism*, p. 200.

38. Ibid., p. 204. (*Trans.*: The object described is Giacometti's sculpture *L'Heure des traces.*)

39. Ibid., pp. 204–5.

40. André Breton, *Mad Love*, trans. Mary Ann Caws, University of Nebraska, Lincoln and London, 1987, pp. 15–16.

41. This law, the first of the laws which the critique of everyday life will formulate, has already been hinted at by some sociologists, but on the whole it has been disregarded. Thus Roger Caillois, for whom the 'sacred' is an external category of feeling, has simply failed to understand its fate.

Jean Effel's charming drawings of angels, saints and holy fathers in comic postures are much more 'profound' in this connection than much of what the professional sociologists have produced.

42. (*Trans.*) A reference to Apollinaire's poem 'L'Enchanteur pourrissant'.

43. *Intimate Journals*, p. 92.

44. (*Trans.*) Baudelaire's most famous presentation of this idea is in the sonnet 'Correspondences', in *Selected Poems*, trans. and introd. Joanna Richardson, Penguin, Harmondsworth 1975, p. 43.

45. M. Chestov, *Pouvoirs des clefs*, Pléiade, Paris 1928, p. 382.

46. Benjamin Fondane, *La Conscience malheureuse*, Denoël et Steele, Paris 1936, pp. 270–71.

47. (*Trans.*) Between 1945 and 1950 the PCF attempted to put on a united front to condemn Sartre's existentialism, which was perceived as being idealist, individualistic and anti-Communist, and as the Party's leading intellectual Lefebvre directed the attack, notably in *L'existentialisme* (1946). Some of the acrimony of this classic 'argument', which is well-documented in Mark Poster's *Existentialist Marxism in Postwar France*, is apparent in the references made to Sartre throughout the *Introduction*.

48. (*Trans.*) Garcin in *In Camera*.

49. (*Trans.*) Brilliant for the power and inventiveness of his novels (the most famous being *Journey to the End of the Night*), despicable – presumably – on account of his anti-semitism and his defection to the Nazis in 1944.

50. Jean Cassou, *Le Centre du monde*, Sagittaire, Paris 1945, p. 199.

51. Ibid., p. 238.

52. It is rather significant that Aragon's great novel *Aurélien* should also be a novel of defeat (the failure of a man and a woman, the failure of a love). Why failure? Through duality. Bérénice is in love with Aurélien, and her love is 'absolute': Aurélien is in love with Bérénice. As both of them are indecisive, idle beings, as 'relative' as it is possible to be, and led on by circumstances over which they have no control, they are unable either to fulfil or even to recognize their love. The most moving parts of the book are achieved through the intervention of a *magical* object: a strangely beautiful plaster mask ...

The author's social realism appears only marginally in the story. By an analogous contradiction, Marcenac's short story 'A Merveille' is a satire on the marvellous written in a wonder-struck manner.

2   The Knowledge of Everyday Life

1. (*Trans.*) Charles Maurras and Maurice Barrès were both writers with nationalist right-wing credentials. Maurras was a founder member of Action française.

2. Marc Bloch, *Caractères originaux de l'histoire rurale française*, Colin, Paris 1956, pp. 64–5.

3. (*Trans.*) Pierre Emmanuel's poetry is a complex mixture of Catholicism, Freudianism and myth, and attempts to continue the tradition of French Symbolism.

4. Now and again, even in the time of sublime history, someone would let the cat out of the bag. For example the naïve historian of Gascony, abbé Monlezun, who around 1850 gave a learned account of how the Church had accumulated its wealth in the Middle Ages: lords and kings spent rashly and became impoverished; but the Church 'managed the assets' of the poor prudently; and in its blessed hands, those assets bore fruit.

3 Marxism as Critical Knowledge of Everyday Life

1. Kant, 'Preface to First Edition', in *Critique of Pure Reason*, trans. N.K. Smith, Macmillan, London 1973, p. 9.

2. (*Trans.*) All the preceding quotations have been from Kierkegaard's *Journal*, in my translation from Lefebvre's unspecified French version.

3. (*Trans.*) This seventeenth-century theologian is most famous for his funeral orations. His *Discourse* gives a theological interpretation of history.

4. (*Trans.*) Cf. Chapter 1, p. 117, where it is categorized as the law of the 'transformation' of the irrational.

5. Cf. Norbert Guterman and Henri Lefebvre, *La Conscience mystifiée*, Gallimard, Coll. 'Les Essais', Paris 1936.

6. (*Trans.*) Cf. Foreword, n. 26 on the word 'privé'.

7. (*Trans.*) The first section of *The Human Comedy* is in fact subtitled 'Scenes from Private Life'.

8. Cf. Norbert Guterman and Henri Lefebvre, 'Individu et classe', *Avant-Poste*, no. 1, Paris 1933; also *La Conscience privée*, sequel to *La Conscience mystifiée*, in preparation (*Trans.*: but never published).

9. (*Trans.*) Charles Péguy was a poet and essayist who transferred his allegiance from socialism to a kind of idiosyncratic Catholicism. He was an ardent nationalist, and was closely associated with the cult of Joan of Arc. He died in 1914.

10. Marx, 'The Holy Family', in *Collected Works*, vol. 4, Lawrence and Wishart, London 1975, p. 42.

11. Ibid.

12. Ibid., p. 43.

13. Cf. Léon Blum's speech at the 1945 Socialist Congress, etc.

14. (*Trans.*) Cf. Proudhon's *Théorie de la propriété*, vol. 4.

15. Marx, 'The Holy Family', p. 42.

16. Marx, 'Economic and Philosophical Manuscripts', in *Early Writings*, Penguin, Harmondsworth 1975, p. 361.

17. Ibid.

18. Ibid., p. 377.

19. Ibid., p. 358.

20. Ibid., p. 359.

21. Ibid.

22. Ibid.

23. Ibid., p. 352.

24. Marx, *Capital* Volume 1, Penguin, Harmondsworth 1976, p. 310.

25. Marx, 'Economic and Philosophical Manuscripts', p. 324.

26. Marx, *The German Ideology*, Progress Publishers, Moscow 1968, p. 45.

27. Marx, 'On the Jewish Question', *Early Writings*, p. 183.

28. Ibid.

29. Marx, *Capital*, vol. 3, p. 959.

30. Marx, 'Economic and Philosophical Manuscripts', p. 351.

31. Ibid.

32. Ibid.

33. (*Trans.*) This 'quotation' – 'l'art est la plus haute joie que l'homme se donne à lui-même' – is Lefebvre's own formula, although he used it later as a preface to his

Contribution à l'esthétique (1954), attributed to Marx. This 'forgery' was included among the reasons given for his suspension from the FCP in 1958.

34. Ibid., pp. 351–2.
35. Ibid., p. 352.
36. Marx, *Capital,* vol. 3, p. 959.
37. Ibid.
38. Ibid.

4 The Development of Marxist Thought

1. (*Trans.*) This is a perennial problem for translators of Marx and Marxist literature, and is compounded when one is translating *from* a language other than German. I have used 'supersede' and its derivatives throughout. Cf. the Glossary in the Penguin edition of Marx's *Early Writings*.

2. The aim of several books which were written before this *Critique of Everyday Life* was to rediscover authentic Marxism, to bring these fundamental notions to light and readopt them. In our introduction to Marx, *Morceaux choisis*, Norbert Guterman and I drew attention to *economic fetishism* (a notion long neglected by Marxists) as well as to dialectical method. In *La Conscience mystifiée* we showed how the movement from appearance to reality (and vice versa) functions in the domain of ideas and represent-ations. We attempted to analyse this movement in our times, by showing how, on the basis of an existing 'mode of production', the bourgeoisie pushes towards mystification, while the proletariat and its representatives struggle towards demystification. In the second part of that book we presented the entire scope of the alienation of 'modern' man. Lastly, in *Dialectical Materialism*, I developed for the first time in modern philosophy the notion of the 'total man', linking it to the fundamental theses of Marxism, to dialectical logic and to the theories of alienation and of economic fetishism. Since these works are either out of print or were destroyed in 1940, it seemed worthwhile drawing attention here to the overall plan on which they were based. (*Trans. Dialectical Materialism* has been reprinted at least seven times, and has been translated into many languages. *La Conscience mystifiée* was reissued in 1979.)

3. (*Trans.*) Although Lefebvre has become better known as a theorist of urban space, his studies of rural communities were crucial to the development of his critique of everyday life. In 1948 he undertook research in rural sociology at the CNRS (Centre National de la Recherche Scientifique), and in 1954 he defended two doctoral theses on rural communities in the Pyrenees.

4. (*Trans.*) Lefebvre was to address this question in more detail fifteen years later in his *Introduction à la modernité* (1962).

5. Cf. an attempt to analyse this interaction in *La Conscience mystifiée*. Psychoanalysts have attempted to examine this situation of the so-called 'modern' man. The higher mental agency they describe, though without understanding its social nature – censorship, superego, etc. – corresponds to the 'public' consciousness. But their realistic conception of the unconscious limits the value of their analysis considerably. What we must discover in this mystifying notion is precisely the real content of our consciousness, merged with deprivation and the growing awareness of it, and repressed by the 'public' consciousness.

Kafka's novels also try to describe the life of men who move forward blindly towards their 'fate'. And yet by overemphasizing the tone of anguish, he misses the worst deception of all: the moral or social euphoria in which public consciousness attempts to keep the 'private' individual (unless it casts him down brutally, and without transition, into so deep a despair that he no longer even attempts to realize his 'destiny').

6. In particular, the life of women and the way their tasks are organized, etc., constitutes one of these little-known sectors which are explained officially by a mystifying moral scheme (sacrifice or dedication as a 'vocation' – or else a lack of moral sense with prostitution as a 'vocation' – these alternatives are what the average public consciousness proposes as explanations for the lives of individual women) . . .

7. The study of everyday life can supply socio-economic science with some extremely important documentary material. For example, it confirms the following fact, or rather law, established by Marx: class implies not only a *quantitative* difference (in salaries, wages and income), but also a *qualitative* one (in the distribution and use of income). Thus in Paris (quoting the prices for 1938) the boundary between poor-quality, unsanitary accommodation and bigger, better-lit, better-situated and equipped housing clearly lay between 4,000 and 5,000 francs rent a year. With a relatively small amount of money extra – but too much for the proletarian to afford – one could move from working-class or very petty-bourgeois accommodation to a 'middle-class' flat. Other examples: normally or even under black market situations, a shoddy suit would cost *x* francs, while a high-quality one costing one and a half times more, apart from being nicer to wear, would last three times as long. Labour-saving devices in bourgeois flats (refrigerators, washing machines, etc.) were also much more economical. Proletarian life is not defined simply by lack of money, but also by pointless but unavoidable expenditure and waste.

A law can be formulated: the richer one is, the cheaper one's life will be (relatively).

During an 'abnormal' period of black market or underproduction, well-off families with a farm or a smallholding are able to lay their hands on foodstuffs which are of better quality and much cheaper than those 'poor people' have to buy.

The boundaries between classes may not be rigorously defined, but they exist none the less, and in every area of everyday life: accommodation (space, surface area, ventilation, sunlight), food, clothing, use of leisure time, etc.

The well-off classes generally spend their income more wisely than the working classes or the peasants, who are always short of something and who are thus unable to use their money *rationally*. A relatively small increase in income results in a move up from one category into another because of the things it makes possible.

8. (*Trans.*) Drieu la Rochelle was a novelist and right-wing ideologue. He edited the *Nouvelle Revue Française* during the Occupation. He committed suicide in 1945.

9. (*Trans.*) Cf. Chapter 3, n. 33.

5   Notes Written One Sunday in the French Countryside

1. (*Trans.*) A reference to Baudelaire's sonnet 'Correspondences': 'In unity profound and recondite . . . Sounds, fragrances and colours correspond.' (*Selected Poems*, Penguin, Harmondsworth 1975, p. 43.)

2. Aeschylus, 'The Choephori', in *The Oresteian Trilogy*, trans. R. Fagels, Penguin, Harmondsworth, 1959.

3. In Romantic drama and in melodrama, great crimes, betrayals, parricides, all take place during violent storms (cf. the third act of *Trente ans ou la vie d'un joueur*). The next part of this work will include a sociological study of melodrama, its relation to life and the curious fact that at the beginning of the twentieth century a huge number of people stopped understanding melodrama; certain myths, certain moral postulates implied by melodrama and still 'lived out' during the Romantic era, suddenly disappeared from people's consciousness.

4. In a 'modern' ceremony which deserves a detailed ethnological analysis – the drawing of the *Loterie Nationale* – the mathematical chance by which fortunes are made used to be set off by children in care. (Did this practice become ritualized, and is it still maintained?) It exemplifies an 'apparent immorality' which conceals an underlying 'morality', and some characteristic myths. It seems that only the hands of children and paupers are 'pure' enough (pure in what way – unsullied by money?) to act as an instrument for the Goddess of Luck, to embody her momentarily, to observe the laws of absolute chance and to confer wealth unearned by labour without incurring some kind of divine wrath. In this ceremony dedicated to Money, poverty is there, not as a metaphor, but present in its cruellest form: poverty-stricken little orphans. Money, the capitalist Fetish, deigns to come down from its heavenly throne and move among those whom it has damned, and who are therefore in some sense dedicated to it. Apparently it was customary for the first-prize winners to donate part of their winnings to these children (the 'sacrifice'); thus the children's participation in the ceremony gave them a kind of 'right'. The winners, meanwhile, were in this way somehow excused for their excessive good luck, vouchsafed more luck for the future, and enabled to justify themselves vis-à-vis morality, the law and the last remnants of human community … This remarkable form of festival, ceremony and sacrifice makes the 'modern' meaning of these fairly clear; it also helps to situate our 'civilization', with its metaphysical and moral fictions.

5. (*Trans.*) A Pyrenean woman's hood.

6. (*Trans.*) In 1945 Latin was still the liturgical language of the Catholic church.

7. (*Trans.*) 'In the beginning was the word.'

8. (*Trans.*) Jansen's *Augustinus* (1640) develops a doctrine of almost Calvinistic severity, which denies free will. In *La Somme et le reste*, Lefebvre talks of the narrow, 'almost Jansenist' faith of his mother. During his studies under Brunschvicg at the Sorbonne, Lefebvre's *diplôme d'études supérieures* was on Jansen and Pascal. The *Summa Theologiae* is by Thomas Aquinas.

6   What Is Possible

1. Pierre Courtade, *Action*, July 1945.

2. (*Trans.*) Jules Romains founded the Unanimist group (1908) which tried to replace fin de siècle individualism with a vague communal spirit. His most famous work is the sequence of novels *Les hommes de bonne volonté*.

3. Pierre Morhange. (*Trans.*: The exact source is unspecified.)

4. (*Trans.*) The poems collected here had originally been published in the American Communist revue *New Masses*.

5. Martin Russak, 'The Candle', *New Masses*, November 1928.

6. Martin Russak, 'Paterson', ibid., June 1928.

7. Miriam Allen deFord, 'August 22, 1927', ibid., February 1929.

8. Ralph Cheyney, 'Bawl, Kid', ibid., July 1929.

9. (*Trans.*) Lefebvre was always very scornful about Gide, who had been a significant influence on many of his generation, but whom he considered to be over-intellectual, and a crypto-puritan. In *La Somme et le reste* he says that 'I could well have become a follower of Gide, just as I could have been a Surrealist ... [but] he failed to reach me because – his homosexuality apart – I had already lived through most of the tribulations he describes, but much more violently.'

10. (*Trans.*) The source given by Lefebvre for this quotation is *Confluences*, no.5, but this appears to be incorrect.

11. Pierre Courtade, *Action*, 25 April 1945.

12. Henri Meggle, *Récit d'un rescapé*. (*Trans.*: I was unable to trace this text.)

13. Pelagia Lewinska, *Vingt mois à Auschwitz*, Paris 1945, pp. 40–41.

14. David Rousset, *Revue internationale*, no. 1.

15. Lewinska, *Vingt mois à Auschwitz*, p. 61.

16. Ibid., p. 70.

17. Rousset, *Revue internationale*, no. 1.

18. Lewinska, *Vingt mois à Auschwitz*, p. 126.

19. Ibid., p. 129.

20. Ibid., p. 130.

21. Ibid., p. 135.

22. Ibid.

23. (*Trans.*) Cf. Chapter 3. n. 33.

Volume II: Foundations for a Sociology of the Everyday

Preface

1. The text of this preface draws on a talk on 'Henri Lefebvre et la critique radicale' presented to the working group on 'Les années 68', Institut d'histoire du temps présent, Centre national de la recherche scientifique, 17 March 1997 (see the group's *Lettre d'information*, no. 23, July 1997). This talk served as the basis of my contribution, 'Voyages autour de la révolution. Les circulations de la pensée critique de 1956 à 1968', in G. Dreyfus-Armand, R. Frank, M.-F. Lévy and M. Zancarini-Fournel, eds, *Les Années 68. Le temps de la contestation*, Complexe, Brussels 2000, pp. 69–87.

2. I take the liberty of referring readers to my introduction to the translation of the first volume, *Critique of Everyday Life*, trans. John Moore, Verso, London and New York 1991, pp. ix–xxviii.

3. See, for example, p. 176 below: '*Structuralism* proceeds by privileging structure absolutely, and by absorbing within it the other terms we are considering, along with the relations they designate. Without admitting to do so, it substantifies it, presenting it as an essence and as something intelligible, thus acting as a belated marriage broker between Aristotelian ontology and a Platonism which dares not speak its name. Stability becomes both active and formal, the prototype and model for the real.'

4. Georges Pompidou, *Le Nœud gordien*, Plon, Paris 1974. Very few works have tracked the relation between the development of sociology and the great ideological debates of the post-war period. See Michael Pollak and François Bédarida, eds, 'Mai 68 et les sciences sociales', *Cahier de l'IHTP*, no. 11, April 1989.

5. Georges Gurvitch, 'L'exclu de la horde', *L'Homme et la société*, no. 1, July/September 1966. Cf. especially Georges Balandier, *Georges Gurvitch, sa vie, son oeuvre*, Presses Universitaires de France, Paris 1972; Phillip Bosserman, 'Georges Gurvitch et les Durkheimiens en France, avant et après la Seconde Guerre mondiale', *Cahiers internationaux de sociologie*, vol. LXX, January/June 1981.

6. Terry Clark, *Prophets and Patrons: The French University and the Emergence*

of the Social Sciences, Harvard University Press, Cambridge, Mass. 1973; 'Reconstructions de la sociologie française (1945–1960)', *Revue française de sociologie*, vol. XXXII, no. 3, July/September 1991. See also Alain Drouard, 'Réflexions sur une chronologie: le développement des sciences sociales en France de 1945 à la fin des années soixante', *Revue française de sociologie*, vol. XXXIII, no. 1, January/March 1982; 'Les commencements des *Cahiers*. Une anthologie', *Cahiers internationaux de sociologie*, vol. 101, July–December 1966.

7. Françoise d'Eaubonne, *Le Temps d'apprendre à vivre*, Albin Michel, Paris 1960.

8. Henri Lefebvre, 'Les classes sociales dans la campagne. La Toscane et la Mezzadria classica', *Cahiers internationaux de sociologie*, no. 10, 1951. On what follows, see Rémi Hess, *Henri Lefebvre et l'aventure du siècle*, A. M. Métailié, Paris 1988, pp. 165–72.

9. His secondary thesis, *La Vallée de Campan*, was published in 1958 by Presses Universitaires de France in Gurvitch's collection.

10. See 'Rapport du cercle des sociologues', in 'Journées d'études des intellectuels communistes', *La Nouvelle Critique*, no. 45, April/May 1953, pp. 247–50.

11. BN Fol Ln 27 72054.

12. Hess, *Henri Lefebvre et l'aventure du siècle*, pp. 152–4.

13. See, in particular, Henri Lefebvre, 'Autocritique. Contribution à l'effort d'éclaircissement idéologique', *La Nouvelle Critique*, no. 4, March 1949, and 'Lettre sur Hegel', *La Nouvelle Critique*, no. 22, January 1951.

14. Edgar Morin, *Autocritique* (1958), coll. 'Politique', Seuil, Paris 1975, pp. 113–14.

15. Cf. Henri Lefebvre, *Le Temps des méprises*, Stock, Paris 1975, pp. 94–6.

16. Henri Lefebvre, *Lukács 1955*/Patrick Tort, *Être marxiste aujourd'hui*, Aubier, Paris 1986; see my contribution, pp. 21–4.

17. *Arguments* (1956–62), reprinted in 2 volumes, Privat, Toulouse 1983 (with prefaces by Edgar Morin, Kostas Axelos and Jean Duvignaud and presentations by Olivier Corpet and Mariateresa Padova).

18. See Rémy Rieffel, *Le Tribu des clercs. Les intellectuels sous la Ve République*, Calmann-Lévy/CNRS Éditions, Paris 1993.

19. See Dominique Desanti, *Les Staliniens*, Fayard, Paris 1975, p. 324; Victor Leduc, *Les Tribulations d'un idéologue*, Syros, Paris 1985, pp. 203–4.

20. Henri Lefebvre, 'Le marxisme et la pensée française', *Les Temps modernes*, nos 137–8, July/August 1957.

21. Henri Lefebvre, *Problèmes actuels du marxisme*, Presses Universitaires de France, Paris 1958 (fourth edn, coll. 'Initiation philosophique', 1970).

22. See *France Nouvelle*, 19 June 1958; *Le Monde*, 20 June 1958.

23. Lucien Sève, *La Différence*, Éditions sociales, Paris 1960. Attacks on

Lefebvre, including those of an *ad hominem* variety, were kept up from 1955 onwards, particularly in *Cahiers du communisme*.

24. See David Caute, *Communism and the French Intellectuals*, André Deutsch, London 1964.

25. Henri Lefebvre, 'L'exclu s'inclut', *Les Temps modernes*, no. 149, July 1958, pp. 226–37; *La Somme et le reste*, 2 vols, Le Nef de Paris, Paris 1959 (reprinted Méridiens-Klincksieck, Paris 1989).

26. Maurice Blanchot, *L'Amitié*, Éditions de Minuit, Paris 1962, chapter 8, pp. 98–108.

27. Henri Lefebvre, 'Vers un romantisme révolutionnaire', *NRF*, no. 59, October 1957; *Introduction to Modernity*, trans. John Moore, Verso, London and New York 1995.

28. See above n. 6, particularly 'Reconstructions de la sociologie française (1945–1960)', *Revue française de sociologie*, vol. XXXII, no. 3, July/September 1991.

29. Cf. 'Les cadres sociaux de sociologie', 1959; 'Signification et fonction des mythes dans la vie politique', 1962; 'Les classes sociales dans le monde d'aujourd'hui', 2 vols, 1965.

30. See *Internationale situationniste, 1958–1969*, facsimile reprint, Champ Libre, Paris 1975. For a bibliography, readers are referred to the numerous studies, of variable quality, which have appeared in the last two or three years.

31. See *Le Temps des méprises*, pp. 109–10.

32. *Internationale situationniste*, no. 6, August 1961.

33. *Internationale situationniste*, no. 4, June 1960.

34. This is the theme of 'a different city for a different existence' defended by Constant (*Internationale situationiste*, no. 3, December 1959), as of Lefebvre's analyses of the new town planning as 'experimental utopia' (*Revue française de sociologie*, July/September 1961), which were criticized by *Internationale situationniste* for reformism (no. 6, August 1961).

35. See Lefebvre, *Introduction to Modernity*; and cf. *Internationale situationniste*, no. 8, January 1963.

36. Henri Lefebvre, 'La signification de la Commune', *Arguments*, nos 27–8, 1962; *La Proclamation de la Commune*, Gallimard, Paris 1965.

37. Lefebvre was the target of a Situationist tract published in Februrary 1963, 'Aux poubelles de l'histoire'. *Internationale situationniste* was to return to this affair at length in its three last issues, even after May 1968 (no. 10, March 1966, no. 11, October 1967, and no. 12, September 1969), thus marking its pique at the rupture. Lefebvre himself would respond one last time in 1967, in *Positions contre les technocrates*, accusing the Situationists in their turn of having been unable to propose anything other than an abstract utopia.

38. I refer readers to my text 'Henri Lefebvre en regard de Michel de Certeau: Critique de la vie quotidienne', in Christian Delacroix, François Dosse, Patrick Garcia and Michel Trebitsch, eds, *Michel de Certeau. Chemins d'histoire*, Complexe, Brussels 2002.

39. Michel de Certeau, *The Practice of Everyday Life*, trans. Steven Rendall, University of California Press, Berkeley 1988, p. 205 n. 5.

40. Ibid., pp. xii–xiii. And cf. Roger Chartier, *On the Edge of the Cliff: History, Language, and Practices*, trans. Lydia G. Cochrane, Johns Hopkins University Press, Baltimore and London 1997.

41. See below, pp. 132–9.

42. Lefebvre, *Critique of Everyday Life*, vol. 1, p. 133.

1 Clearing the Ground

1. (*Trans.*) Specifically, the 'age such as ours' is the beginning of the 1960s, a time of particular political and cultural effervescence in France, with the Algerian troubles, the consolidation of Gaullism and the growing international prestige and influence of structuralism and the *nouvelle vague*. It was also a pivotal moment in Lefebvre's own career, since in 1961 he took up his post as lecturer in sociology at Strasbourg university, transferring to Nanterre in 1965. Many of the ideas in this book must have informed those lectures, which were so influential for what was to occur in 1968. In the quicksilver intellectual shifts and (sometimes bewildering) idiosyncrasies of his style, which is frequently nearer to speech than to conventional prose, the reader of this book may perhaps catch a glimpse of how exciting and charismatic these lectures must have been.

2. See *Critique of Everyday Life*, vol. I (Grasset, Paris 1947), trans. John Moore, Verso, London 1991.

3. See below, and Jean Lacroix, 'Le public et le privé', *Cahiers I.S.E.A.*, series M, no. 10, 1961.

4. For example, in 1961, *Les Petits Enfants du siècle* by Christiane Rochefort, and the film *Chronique d'un été*, directed by Jean Rouch and Edgar Morin. See also Lucien Goldmann's definition of the 'novel': 'It seems to us that the novel as a form is the transposition of everyday life in the individualistic society which was born of market production to the plane of literature . . .') *Médiations*, vol. 2, Editions Gonthier, Paris 1966, p. 149.

5. See Dionys Mascolo's *Le Communisme*, Gallimard, Paris 1953, which contains nearly all of them.

6. (*Trans.*) As the word for goods can be used in the singular in French –

un bien – it retains a sense of value and worth in the plural which it no longer has in modern English.

7. (*Trans.*) The word *jeu* has several meanings in French: play and games, gambling, and dramatic acting. Throughout the book Lefebvre plays on these ambiguities in a way which can only be paraphrased in translation.

8. *Internationale Situationniste*, no. 6, 1961, pp. 20–27. (*Trans.*) Debord's friendship with Lefebvre began in 1957 (he was thirty years his junior), and during the time they spent together, notably walking in the Pyrenees near Lefebvre's house in Navarrenx, their discussions about modernity, revolution and critique of everyday life were mutually influential. Debord edited the review from 1958 until its demise in 1969.

9. Let us remember the impassioned discussions on birth control and family planning, with all their practical and political consequences. The opposition to birth control by official Marxists and the Communist Party was very influential in the serious rifts which occurred during this period. This attitude is of great theoretical interest. In particular it shows that for the time being, in the Marxist movement and official communism, the idea of (technical) power of man over nature and the outside world has supplanted the Marxist idea of man's *appropriation* of nature and *of his own nature*.

10. Simone de Beauvoir must be congratulated for introducing this concept to philosophy and to the study of the situation of women. However, she did not clarify it. Before Simone de Beauvoir, women – and we mean women who read philosophers, and their entourage – refused to be 'things' or 'commodities'. Since her works have appeared, the same women call themselves 'subjects' who do not want to be treated as 'objects'. Sadly, the less charitable observer will note that many of them seem to want to have their cake and eat it too: they want to be objects (beautiful, well dressed, desirable, desired) and subjects (free, and recognized as such). Hence an additional ambiguity, which comes from the vocabulary of philosophy, and which has the advantage of being like a game. Furthermore, as one woman wittily put it: 'Of the two, the one most like an object is not always the one you think . . .'.

11. (*Trans.*) An attack on dogmatic communism. Lefebvre joined the PCF in 1928. However he became increasingly uneasy with its Stalinist policies, and his open criticisms, which came to a head with the Khrushchev report in 1956, led to his expulsion in 1957. Lefebvre's vehemence in this passage should be seen in this context.

12. Notably in the meetings of the Groupe d'études de sociologie de la vie quotidienne, (Centre d'Etudes sociologiques) and in various symposia.

13. Marx, 'Critique of Hegel's Doctrine of the State' in *Early Writings*, Penguin, Harmondsworth 1975, p. 90.

14. Maurice Merleau-Ponty, 'Philosophie et sociologie', *Signes*, Gallimard, Paris 1960, pp. 137–9.

15. See Henri Lefebvre, 'Psychologie des classes sociales', in Georges Gurvitch, ed., *Traité de sociologie*, vol. 2, PUF, Paris 1960, pp. 364–86.

16. (*Trans.*) A paraphrase of the controversial aphorism '*l'art est le plus haute joie que l'homme se donne à lui-même*', which Lefebvre attributed to Marx in *Contribution à l'esthétique* (1953), but which he later admitted was his own invention. This 'forgery' was one of the reasons given for his exclusion from the PFC in 1957. See above, note 11.

17. Cf. *Colloque de Royaumont*, 16–18 May 1961.

18. This is from a report sent by Christiane Peyre of the Centre national de la recherche scientifique (CNRS) to the Groupe d'études de sociologie de la vie quotidienne, Centre d'Etudes sociologiques, 1960–1. (*Trans.*) Lefebvre himself became a researcher at the CNRS in 1948, a post which he lost in 1953 because of his involvement in PCF activities. He was reinstated in 1954, and in 1960 he was appointed Director of Research.

19. Interviews such as these have been collected for the Groupe d'études by Nicole Haumont.

20. The term (*sociétés de loisirs*) was coined by Henri Raymond, who together with Nicole Haumont made a study of the Club Méditerranée.

21. See Michel Clouscard's studies of '*Les temps marginaux*' as reported to the Groupe d'études.

22. See the excellent film *Saturday Night and Sunday Morning*. (*Trans.*) Dir. Karel Reisz, GB 1960.

23. The expression (*le tragique du pauvre*) was coined by Georges Auclair in a report to the Groupe d'études.

24. These layers become apparent in genuinely 'undirected' interviews, especially when they are taped. The intervention of the tape recorder produces a greater 'distancing' than in the usual interview. The interviewee feels much less at ease and consequently, when the interview is well conducted, there are moments when, through the malaise, a deeper truth emerges.

25. On alienation and reification, see Lefebvre, *Dialectical Materialism*, trans. J. Sturrock, Jonathan Cape, London 1968.

26. Yugoslavia has retained the Marxist model, as we know, but not without difficulties and some bending of the rules.

27. We raised these problems in the Foreword to *Critique of Everyday Life*, vol. I, but without clarifying them.

28. Surveys of children living in several new housing developments where there are a large number of television sets have shown that boys and girls aged between 10 and 12 know an incredible number of technical details about things such as space rockets, but are ignoramuses about maths and

basic French grammar. The conclusion is that the 'civilization of the book' will disappear.

29. (*Trans.*) Lefebvre deals with this topic much more extensively in 'Notes on the New Town', the extraordinary Seventh Prelude of his *Introduction to Modernity* (trans. John Moore, Verso, London 1995, pp. 116–27), where he compares his own town of Navarrenx with the new town of Mourenx, built to house the workers at the oil refinery of Lacq, near Pau, and which he has in mind in this section.

30. This is what restricts the scope of a formal, structural and semeiological study of the romantic press and horoscopes, etc. Studies of this kind would look at themes, their combinations and their significations, but (here as elsewhere) would be unable to grasp their historicity, and therefore their *real meaning.* (*Trans.*) For the spelling of 'semeiological', see below chapter 2, note 1.

31. Summing up this point of view, Andrée Michel writes: 'Far from being a basic cell, to use an overworked phrase, or a natural grouping, to use a vulgarized definition which has been rife in France since Le Play, the family is nothing more than a resultant and a residual deposit; those functions which society has not yet shouldered are shouldered by the family . . .' (*Cahiers internationaux de sociologie*, no. 20). Therefore 'as an institution, the family does not antedate the group', which makes the consolidation of this 'residual deposit' even more surprising. We could quote various sociologists who would back up this interpretation: Gooda, *Die Struktur der Familie*, Cologne 1960; Pearsons, *Socialization and Interaction Process*, etc.

32. (*Trans.*) See above, footnote 13.

33. We borrow the expression from Abraham Moles. (*Trans.*) See *Information Theory and Esthetic Perception*, University of Illinois Press, Urbana and London 1966.

34. This is the gulf which Jean-Paul Sartre attempts to bridge in *Critique of Dialectical Reason.* (*Trans.*) Lefebvre had always been highly critical of Sartre. However, in his introduction to the *Critique*, Sartre tells us his method is based upon his reading of Lefebvre.

35. (*Trans.*) Lefebvre is quoting the title of Mallarmé's famous poem *Un coup de dés jamais n'abolira le hasard.*

36. J. Galbraith, *The Affluent Society*, Penguin, Harmondsworth 1958.

37. For a similar problem, see Alfred Sauvy, *Théorie générale de la population*, vol. 1, pp. 312–52, François Perroux in *L'Encyclopédie française*, vol. 20, and Abraham and Thédié in *Revue française de recherche opérationnelle*, no. 16, 1960. See also an interesting discussion in ibid., no. 19, 1961.

2 The Formal Implements

1. (*Trans.*) Throughout the book, Lefebvre chooses to employ *séméiologie* rather than the more conventional *sémiologie*, presumably to distance himself from that particular school of thought. I have observed this in my translation.

2. This is the theory of double maieutic which we developed elsewhere, but from a different perspective. (*Trans.*) The Socratic method of producing knowledge through questions and answers. See *Introduction to Modernity*, First Prelude, pp. 7–48.

3. The American sociologist Merton has made the distinction between the *working hypothesis* (which is empirical), and the *theoretical hypothesis* (which is developed conceptually). This distinction is valid in principle, but its view of 'the real' is limited. We will return to it when we examine that category.

4. See Mandelbrot, *Lecture de l'expérience*, PUF, Paris 1955, p. 43, on psychological transducers.

5. See Charbonnier, *Conversations with Claude Lévi-Strauss*, trans. J. and D. Weightman, Jonathan Cape, London 1969.

6. See A. Martinet, *Elements of General Linguistics*.

7. See Williams, *La Stratégie dans les actions humaines*, a remarkable popularization of the extremely technical work of von Neumann, de Luce and Raiffa, etc.

8. This is a reference to Bayes's theorem on strategies. See Claude Flament, 'Modèle stratégique d'influence sociale sur les jugements perceptifs', *Psychologie française*, April, 1959, a psychological rather than sociological study.

9. For a definition of the tragic, see Nietzsche, *The Birth of Tragedy* and Clément Rosset, *Le Philosophie tragique*, Paris, 1961.

10. (*Trans.*) A scotoma is a mental blind spot.

11. It would be impossible to deny the theoretical interest for the social sciences of these forms or structures which are initially apparent in material nature: circles and cycles, spirals, periodic phenomena, trees, networks. In the search for unity, this is a more useful direction than any systematized philosophy. In our view, however, they can only serve as *models*, which do not reduce the dualities of the representations (see below). A model is nothing more than a representation, and cannot exhaust the process of becoming.

12. Thus we will come across the *tree* figure in the theory of needs and the theory of social networks of communications, etc.

13. Alfred Sauvy, *Population*, no. 6, October 1961, p. 601, Marthelot, *Pays riches et pays de la faim, 39e semaine sociale de France*, 1952, and Henri Janne, *Colloque de 1956*, Institut Solvay, Brussels, etc.

14. The term is Galbraith's. It demonstrates how this production is only apparently directed towards needs. See Bernard Cazes, *Cahiers I.S.E.A*, series M, no. 10, p. 38.

15. The mathematical idea of *dimension* is not spatial. Thus the calculation of probabilities defines distributions in *one dimension* (the mathematical hope of a random variable) and in *two dimensions* (in the case of a random pair).

16. In Descartes, for example.

17. See 'Les dilemmes de la dialectique', *Médiations*, vol. 2.

18. 'Evènement et structures', *Cahiers I.S.E.A*, Series M, no. 6.

19. See Gestalt theory, or theory of forms, which had a great influence in all areas of the sciences of human reality. It is in the 'Gestaltist' tradition that we will find the best examples of this idea, whether the authors explained and admitted it or not.

20. See notably Claude Lévi-Strauss, *Structural Anthropology*, trans. C. Jacobson and B. Schoepf, Penguin Press, London 1968.

21. Georges Gurvitch, *Vocation actuelle de la sociologie*, 2nd edn, vol. 2, p. 441. See also *Cahiers internationaux de sociologie (CIS)*, no. 19, 1953, etc. (*Trans.*) Gurvitch was one of Lefebvre's staunchest friends, and it was through his interventions that he joined the CNRS in 1948. Between 1948 and 1965 Lefebvre published ten articles in the *CIS*, which Gurvitch edited.

22. (*Trans.*) Marx, *Early Writings*, pp. 424–8.

23. See the distinction between forms of family and systems of consanguinity in Engels, 'The Origin of the Family, Private Property and the State', in *Marx and Engels: Selected Works*, Lawrence and Wishart, London 1968, pp. 466–8. Quoting Marx, Engels demonstrates the *passivity of all systems* (political, juridical, philosophical) and how they lag behind the active forces and forms of development, and thus behind the theoretical and practical conflicts which ensue.

24. See G. G. Granger, *Pensée formelle et sciences de l'homme*. So it is not a question of 'latent structures' in the sense the term is used by American sociologists such as Lazarfeld and Guttmann.

25. See above, note 22.

26. (*Trans.*) When Lefebvre took up his post in the CNRS in 1948 (see chapter 1, note 18) his research topic was rural sociology. This had been one of his interests since the 1930s, but his active involvement in it dates from the war years, when his Resistance activities put him in contact with peasant communities in the valley of Campan in the French Pyrenees. This was to lead him in turn towards his theories on urbanism and the production of space which have since been so influential.

27. In our view the cleverly tempered idea of '*signifying structure*' does not avoid the shortcomings of structuralism in general. Who is 'signification'

for? How can one grasp a signification from inside? How can one grasp it from outside? Perhaps a god can, as a Mind, or simply the 'I' of the thinker. There can only be signifying structures in an imminent or transcendental way, and neither make very much sense.

3 The Specific Categories

1. See H. Lefebvre, 'Justice et vérité selon Nietzsche', *Arguments*, no. 15, 1959, pp. 13–19.

2. (*Trans.*) Lukács, *History and Class Consciousness*, trans. R. Livingstone, Merlin Press, London 1968, p. 27.

3. See Merton, *Elements of Sociological Method*, which is a study of political operations in the electoral 'machine' in the USA, with the 'boss', corruption, brutality and illegality, etc. According to Merton, moralistic criticism loses its validity when faced with what the 'functions' of the machine actually are. The 'boss' maintains the machine in good and effective working order by deliberately sharing power via a democratic constitution determined to uphold freedom. The 'boss' makes the law personal, and even humanizes it by adapting it to the real concerns of the population: inner-city areas, underprivileged groups which need assistance or advice. 'The Machine knits the links between men and women together with the complicated links of personal relationships.' Even backhanders have a function in the chaos of competition. 'Rackets' and 'gangs' facilitate social mobility, etc.

4. Merton, one of the few American sociologists before the 'New Wave' (Mills, Riesman) who penetrated the everyday life of American society, was introduced to Hegelianism via Marx and Engels, whom he quotes extensively in the book's footnotes.

5. (*Trans.*) Marx, 'Critique of Hegel's Doctrine of the State', *Early Writings*, p. 127.

6. See J. Huizinga, *Homo Ludens*, Routledge and Kegan Paul, London 1949, and the works of Roger Caillois.

7. Like the equalization of general rates of profit which Marx described and analysed as a self-regulating and stabilizing mechanism in a free-market capitalist society.

8. The existentialist thesis which defines the alienation of women as the treatment of a 'subject' as an 'object' adds very little to what Kant said, when he demanded respect for all 'subjects'. It goes back to before Hegelianism, for which objectivization is a necessity, i.e., the transformation of subjective intentions and tendencies into works, and goes so far as to condemn beauty, ornaments, fashion, and everything which makes 'woman'

beautiful and desirable, as alienating. (See A. Gorz, *La Morale de l'histoire*, Editions du Seuil, Paris 1959.) Intellectual activity is becoming misanthropic and ascetic again.

9. See, D. Riesman, *Lonely Crowd*, Doubleday Anchor Books (abridged edition) and Yale University Press, 1950; W. H. Whyte, Jr., *The Organization Man*, Penguin, Harmondsworth 1960; A. C. Spectorsky, *Exurbanites*, Berkeley Publications, 1955.

10. (*Trans.*) *Je est un autre.* Lefebvre is quoting from Rimbaud's *Une saison en enfer.* Conventionally, the translation would be 'I is another'.

11. This is implied in the work on the 'non-directive' by the American psycho-sociologist Rogers and his school in France, for example.

12. We have already published a series of articles (see notably *La Pensée*, 1956) in which we have taken this controversy up with several philosophers, in particular the late and much-missed Maurice Merleau-Ponty. We take them to task for applying the idea of ambiguity to the relations between being and consciousness, i.e., for generalizing it as an (ontological) philosophical category. In this context we consider it to be a specific (sociological) category.

13. See J. Galbraith, *The Affluent Society*.

14. (*Trans.*) A ceremonial activity among North American Indians involving the distribution of gifts.

15. According to the English historian Arnold Toynbee, every people responds victoriously to a challenge by *nature* (as long as it keeps its vitality: Egypt and the periodic Nile floods, England and sea defences, etc.), and this determines a perishable civilization. This theory is a useful and significant one. However, taken as an isolated hypothesis, and carried to the absolute, it becomes erroneous, and even dangerous. What we are considering here, sociologically, is challenge between groups.

16. See J. Duvignaud, *Pour entrer dans le XXe siècle*, Grasset, Paris 1960, where the author restricts the question (by limiting it to literature).

17. We borrow the expression (*rythmanalyse*) from Gaston Bachelard.

18. See G. Gurvitch, *Traité de sociologie*, and *La Multiplicité des temps sociaux*, Cours de la Sorbonne, 1957–8, CDU.

19. See Jean-Paul Sartre's old idea about 'to make and in making to make oneself', which is now very widely accepted as a formulation of *praxis*. (*Trans.*) In French, the verb *faire*, which means equally to make and to do.

20. The most recent example: information theory originated in telecommunications and in the transmission of telegraphic messages using a general conventional code. Zipf's Law was discovered by Estoup a long time before Zipf, in his studies of the work of shorthand typists. These important theories only developed thanks to radio and, above all, to television.

21. (*Trans.*) A reference to the 100 metre distance signs on French roads.

22. At the same time as theorems of existence were appearing, mathematicians introduced *dual* properties and demonstrated theorems of *duality*. This is connected with the influence concepts originating in physics have had on mathematics. (See Licherowicz, *Algèbre et analyse linéaires*, on the spectrum of a matrix, the inverse spectrum, etc.)

23. For Jean-Paul Sartre in *Critique of Dialectical Reason*, the stable (the 'practico-inert') is antidialectical. For Stéphane Lupasco's 'logic of contradiction', the logical level and the level of contradiction go beyond dialectical logic, and become merged. It is contradiction which produces stability.

24. This is more or less the attitude Jean-Paul Sartre adopts in *Critique*.

25. Obviously the gap between these two types of contradiction is not great. It is a distinction which already appears in the texts in which Hegel presents a kind of gradation, from distinction and difference to the alternative (antagonism), by way of contrariety, opposition, inner contradiction and antinomy. In the *Nurnberger Schriften* we are dealing with a progression which he observes empirically and turns into a general law. In Book 2 of *Greater Logic*, it is rather the result of reflection which develops the idea of dialectical movement. The Marxists have not added very much to Hegelian thought.

26. See W. H. Whyte, *The Organisation Man*.

27. (*Trans.*) Rastignac is the ambitious hero of Balzac's trilogy *Le Père Goriot: Illusions perdues* and *Splendeurs et misères des courtisanes*.

28. This essay on characterology was to appear in a projected trilogy we were to write in collaboration with Norbert Gutermann, *La Conscience mystifiée*, *La Conscience privée* and *La Conscience sociale*. Only the first of these appeared (*Les Essais*, Gallimard, Paris 1937). After the Liberation, we completed most of the project in Volume I of *Critique of Everyday Life*.

4 The Theory of the Semantic Field

1. The system of telephone numbers, for example. Each one corresponds to a possible signal (a call or a reply). They make up a rigorous set which leaves little margin for error (for 'noise', to use the vocabulary of information theory). Moreover, the set of numbers reflects a network. Each one corresponds to a determined *place* in a determined space, and to a determined *time* (linear and discontinuous, for I cannot call A or answer him until I have finished answering B, and so on and so forth, through a series of disjunctions). Since each call and answer is a possible *event*, the set of numbers defines *a space of events*.

2. Notably in the work of André Martinet, which we have already mentioned.

3. In other words, there is a certain terminology which we are unable to accept. The mathematician does not use symbols, but signs, which are as stripped of content and as formal as possible, and almost like signals of operations which are stipulated in advance.

4. We will deal with the problems of semeiology, general semantics, 'semantemes' and partial systems of social signs when we look at 'communication models'.

5. (*Trans.*) A reference to Baudelaire's poem *L'Invitation au voyage*: '*Là tout n'est qu'ordre et beauté, luxe, calme et volupté.*'

5 The Theory of Accumulative and Non-accumulative Processes

1. In *Critique of Dialectical Reason*, Jean-Paul Sartre changes rareness into a fundamental and absolute category. He 'worldifies' rareness, creating a 'world' of rareness, violence and oppression. In doing so he fails to recognize the twofold aspect of these ancient societies (in which occasionally need almost became authentic desire . . .).

2. Here we are modifying somewhat a theory we sketched out elsewhere, which suggested that *form* might be the common measure between diverse cultures, notably between antiquity and 'modernity' (by analogy with formal logic and law which subsist across differing modes of production). This theory does not seem to be inaccurate, but can only be applied to a number of limited cases.

3. Marx also demonstrates how the cycle of economic crises in the context of free-competition capitalism re-establishes proportions by eliminating excess, and allows accumulation to resume. The crisis is part of the system's process of self-regulation. Marx reveals a dialectical movement: 'balance – crisis – resumption'. Thus our study does not agree with the often remarkable views of G. G. Granger, who emphasizes factors of structure and internal balance.

4. In free-market capitalism, adjustments (of values, prices and rates of profit) and the formation of an average rate of profit play this role of self-regulation and internal balance, across a cycle of crises.

5. Work on ecology and modern demography (in particular in France, with Alfred Sauvy and Jacques Fourastié) has used mathematics to explain such processes. According to a paper presented to the Groupe d'études by A. Moles, it could be possible to study the number of publications which

have appeared in different sectors of science in order to determine the tendency towards cumulative (exponential) growth and factors of slowing down and saturation more closely.

6. The ensuing situation is so confused that the representation of society on a world scale becomes obscured at the very moment it is taking shape as a totality. And so sociology (as an ideology) appears as a substitute for an inadequate consciousness, in tandem with the vague representation of a 'social whole' which exists but which cannot be grasped by the groups and the men who constitute it.

7. Volterra's equations express these processes mathematically.

8. The difference between *digital machines* (which operate upon unlimited discontinuity with increasing scope and precision) and *analogue machines* (which operate on continuous givens and models) brings a technical argument to our hypothesis. On the level of cortical activity, the cumulative process would be linked to the dichotomy and disjunction which appear in language, arithmetic and logic.

9. In the theory of the semantic field we could already have referred to the work of Gaston Bachelard. In several books which are so well known that it is pointless to name them, this eminent philosopher has demonstrated the role of symbolisms (and above all of symbols borrowed from the elements: Fire, Water, Earth, Air) in poetry, in dreams and in language. In another area of his work Gaston Bachelard dialecticizes the concepts of scientific knowledge (see notably *Le Nouvel Esprit scientifique*). We would like to stress one specific point. There is a break between these two parts of his work and thought. Why? Because philosophy refused to come full circle and form a system? Yes, maybe. But as we see it there is something else. One part of his work is concerned with the non-accumulative (symbols and symbolisms, cycles and cosmic rhythms, nucleuses of primary or protopathic affectivity in the individual, socialized emotivity in and through language . . .). The other part is concerned with the *cumulative* (modern techniques and scientific knowledge). From the point of view of our studies, this break does not disappear, but becomes a theme, sees itself as such, and takes on a sense.

The connection of symbolisms with the elementary everyday in the work of Gaston Bachelard has been highlighted very recently by Mucchielli: 'Starting from different directions, Piaget and Bachelard have shown that very general affectivo-motor schemes corresponding to very general and very archaic human situations (being lost, concealing oneself, getting up, falling down, being attacked, mating, taking shelter, etc.) constitute the essential part of what psycho-analytic literature calls unconscious symbolism, and may be considered to be the dynamic "forms" of series of behaviour patterns which are differentiated according to epochs and cultures, as well as the generating schematic of oneiric, mythic and legendary "images" which we call "symbolic"' (*Philosophie de la médicine psycho-somatique*, p. 134). In our view Mucchielli reduces the significance of symbolisms (notably their *poetic* sense).

6   The Theory of Moments

1. (*Trans.*) Lefebvre first proposed his theory of moments in his autobiography *La Somme et le reste*, 2 vols., La Nef, Paris 1959. It can be contrasted with the theory of situations developed by Debord in the *Internationale situationniste*. The difference of view led to the intellectual rift between the two men in the 1960s.

2. This protest is also expressed in Georges Politzer's brilliant philosophical pamphlet *Le Bergsonisme, fin d'une parade philosophique*. Philosophically, the 'theory of moments' is linked to an interpretation of Leibniz. The 'substantial' link (*vinculum substantiale*) between monads is itself a monad. In so far as knowledge and love, etc., are diverse attributes or powers of being, they have a reality which would equal that of reified consciousnesses (see Henri Lefebvre, *La Somme et le reste*).

3. Hegel draws his inspiration from classic mechanics (the 'moment of inertia', etc.), but he profoundly modifies the meaning of the term.

4. See Michel Butor, 'Le roman et la poésie', *Les Lettres nouvelles*, February 1961, where he clearly spells out that 'one of the tasks of the novel will be to re-establish a continuity between marvellous moments and empty ones'.

Volume III: From Modernity to Modernism (Towards a Metaphilosophy of Daily Life)

Preface

1. For the pre-war period, readers are referred to my preface to volume one of *Critique of Everyday Life* (trans. John Moore, Verso, London and New York 1991), pp. ix–xxviii, where I refer to the article by Henri Lefebvre and Norbert Guterman, 'La mystification: notes pour une critique de la vie quotidienne', *Avant-Poste*, no. 2, August 1933, pp. 91–107. See also Henri Lefebvre, *Everyday Life in the Modern World* (1968), trans. S. Rabinowitch, Allen Lane, London 1971. Finally, let us signal that, in 1982, in an interview with Oliver Corpet and Thierry Paquot ('Henri Lefebvre philosophe du quotidien', *Le Monde Dimanche*, 19 December 1982), Lefebvre indicated that he was planning to pursue this line of inquiry with a work on rhythms, revolving around the concept of 'rhythm analysis'. The project was realized only after his death, with the publication by Catherine Régulier of *Eléments de rythmanalyse. Introduction à la connaissance des rythmes*, Syllepse, Paris 1992.

2. See Luc Ferry and Alain Renaut, *French Philosophy of the Sixties: An Essay on AntiHumanism* (1985), trans. Mary H.S. Cattani, University of Massachusetts Press, Amherst 1990.

3. Vincent Descombes, *Modern French Philosophy*, trans. Lorna Scott-Fox, Cambridge University Press, Cambridge 1980 (was the author really unaware that the French title of his work – *Le Même et l'autre* – was the same as the introduction written by Lefebvre to Schelling's *Philosophical Inquiry into the Essence of Human Freedom*, published by Rieder in 1926?); Christian Delacampagne, *A History of Philosophy in the Twentieth Century*, trans. M. B. Debevoise, Johns Hopkins University Press, Baltimore 1999.

4. Some of these concern the preface to volume one. I am especially grateful to Francis Crémieux for the information and corrections he has

provided me with on the basis of his personal archives (letter of 17 February 1996). Indicating that, as the person responsible for culture at Radio Toulouse in 1944, it was he (not Tzara) who brought in Lefebvre, he insists, sending me a copy of the Grasset contract for *Critique de la vie quotidienne* (October 1945) and several letters from Lefebvre, that it was manoeuvring and internal battles at the publisher which account for the fact that the book, delivered in February 1946, was only published in 1947. But were not these internal battles, in which Crémieux was directly involved, essentially political in character?

5. This involved a study of the everyday life of a mining community in Caen threatened with the closure of their mine (1960) and another of a wealthy agricultural community in the Oise at the beginning of the Common Agricultural Policy (1961). See Henri Lefebvre, *Writing on Cities*, ed. and trans. Eleonore Kofman and Elizabeth Lebas, Blackwell, Oxford 1996, p. 15, n. 9.

6. David Bellos, *Georges Perec: A Life in Words*, Vintage 1996. See also Derek G. Schilling, *Mémoire du quotidien: les lieux de Georges Perec*, thesis, University of Paris VII, 1997; Michael Sheringham, 'Attending to the Everyday: Blanchot, Lefebvre, Certeau, Perec', *French Studies*, vol. 54, no. 2, 2000; and Georges Perec, *Entretiens et conférences*, ed. Dominique Bertelli and Mireille Ribière, Joseph K., Nantes 2003.

7. See the intervention by Mathieu Rémy (doctoral student at the University of Nancy II), 'Georges Perec et Henri Lefebvre, critiques de la vie quotidienne', Georges Perec seminar, University of Paris VII, 24 November 2001.

8. Guy Debord, *Correspondance, juin 1957 – août 1960*, Fayard, Paris 1999; *Correspondance, septembre 1960 – décembre 1964*, Fayard, Paris 2001; and *Correspondance, janvier 1965 – décembre 1968*, Fayard, Paris 2003.

9. In particular, some rather sordid stories about the young student at Strasbourg who had become Lefebvre's companion. See Debord, *Correspondance*, vol. 2, letters to Béchir Tlili of 15 April 1964 (pp. 284–85) and Denise Cheype of 27 April (p. 287).

10. Debord, *Correspondance*, vol. 3, letter to Mustapha Khayati of 9 June 1965 (p. 40).

11. See Épistémon, *Ces idées qui ont ébranlé la France: Nanterre, novembre 1967 – juin 1968*, Fayard, Paris 1968.

12. This paragraph on May '68 in part resumes a talk given to the research seminar on 'Les années 68: événements, cultures politiques et modes de vie'

(IHTP, 17 March 1997) and 'Henri Lefebvre et la critique radicale', *Lettre d'information*, no. 23, July 1997, pp. 1–23.

13. Henri Lefebvre, *L'irruption de Nanterre au sommet*, Anthropos, Paris 1968; republished by Syllepse as *L'irruption...*, Syllepse, Paris 1998 and translated into English as *The Explosion: Marxism and the French Revolution*, trans. Alfred Ehrenfeld, Monthly Review Press, New York and London 1969.

14. Greil Marcus, *Lipstick Traces: A Secret History of the 20th Century*, Harvard University Press, Boston 1990; Bernard Brillant, *Les Clercs de 68*, Presses Universitaires de France, Paris 2000.

15. A collective letter, signed by Lefebvre, condemning repression and sketching an analysis of the crisis afflicting the university, appeared in *Le Monde*, 17 February 1967.

16. See Pascal Dumontier, *Les Situationnistes et Mai 68: théorie et pratique de la revolution, 1966–1972*, Lebovici, Paris 1990, pp. 80–97 and Jean-Pierre Duteuil, *Nanterre 1965–1966–1967–1968. Vers le Mouvement du 22 mars*, Acratie, Mauléon 1988, p. 129. An English translation can be found under the title 'On the Poverty of Student Life', in Ken Knabb, ed. and trans., *Situationist International: An Anthology*, Bureau of Public Secrets, Berkeley (CA) 1992, pp. 319–37.

17. See Hervé Hamon and Patrick Rotman, *Génération*, vol. 1, *Les Années de rêve*, Seuil, Paris 1987, p. 390.

18. Henri Lefebvre, *Le Temps des méprises*, Stock, Paris 1975, p. 117.

19. See Yvon Le Vaillant, 'Nanterre-la-folie', *Nouvel Observateur*, 21–27 February 1968; Alain Schnapp and Pierre Vidal-Naquet, *Journal de la Commune étudiante. Textes et documents, novembre 1967 – juin 1968*, Seuil, Paris 1969, p. 122; Hamon and Rotman, *Génération*, pp. 400–01; and Duteuil, *Nanterre*, p. 95.

20. Debord, *Correspondance*, vol. 3, p. 259.

21. Lefebvre, *Le Temps des méprises*, p. 120.

22. Henri Lefebvre, *Métaphilosophie*, Minuit, Paris 1965; republished by Syllepse, Paris 2000 (see p. 6 for Labica's remark).

23. Henri Lefebvre, *Position: contre les technocrats*, Gonthier, Paris 1967. We might note that the book was defended by Jean-François Revel in *L'Express* in 1967–68.

24. And also, in the summer of 1968, at the 'critical university' at Pau with workers from Péchiney de Noguères: see Brillant, *Les Clercs de 68*, p. 445.

25. Cf. Hubert Tonka, Thierry Paquot and Annie Zimmermann, 'Utopie,

la parole donnée', *Urbanisme*, May–June 1998 (special issue on May '68), pp. 49–52. See also Jean-Louis Violeau, 'L'Internationale situationniste et la ville' (pp. 41–44) and Laurent Devisme, 'Henri Lefebvre penseur de l'urbain' (pp. 45–49).

26. See Alain Touraine, 'L'apparition d'une nouvelle sensibilité sur la scène politique', in Geneviève Dreyfus-Armand and Laurent Gervereau, *Mai 68. Les mouvements étudiants en France et dans le monde*, BDIC, Paris, pp. 82–86.

27. Michel Amiot, *Les Sociologues contre l'État*, Editions de l'EHESS, Paris 1986.

28. It is all the more contemporaneous with the events in that it first appeared in *L'Homme et la société*, no. 8, April/May 1968.

29. Several yardsticks might be employed. One would be translations, of which Rémi Hess has made an inventory: see his *Henri Lefebvre et l'aventure du siècle*, A.-M. Métailié, Paris 1988, pp. 327–34. Another indicator would be the numerous radio broadcasts in which Lefebvre participated in these years, in particular a 'Radioscopie' by Jacques Chancel on 2 October 1975.

30. Manuel Castells, 'Y a-t-il une sociologie urbaine?', *Sociologie du travail*, no. 1, 1968. See also Castells, *The Urban Question: A Marxist Approach* (1972), MIT Press, Cambridge (MA) 1979.

31. See Kurt Meyer, *Henri Lefebvre. Ein romantischer Revolutionär*, Europa Verlag 1973 and Thomas Kleinspehn, *Der verdrängte Alltag. Henri Lefebvres marxistische Kritik des Alltaglebens*, Focus-Verlag, Giessen 1975. In contrast, the other authors cited by Hess (*Henri Lefebvre*, pp. 305–11) had no posterity and in any event lacked the influence he attributes to them.

32. See Mark Poster, *Existential Marxism in Postwar France: From Sartre to Althusser*, Princeton University Press, Princeton 1975; Perry Anderson, *Considerations on Western Marxism*, New Left Books, London 1976; Russell Jacoby, *Dialectic of Defeat: Contours of Western Marxism*, Cambridge University Press, New York 1981; Arthur Hirsh, *The French New Left: An Intellectual History from Sartre to Gorz*, South End Press, Boston 1981; Michael Kelly, *Modern French Marxism*, Blackwell, Oxford 1982; and Martin Jay, *Marxism and Totality: The Adventures of a Concept from Lukács to Habermas*, University of California Press, Berkeley 1984.

33. 'Henri Lefebvre philosophe du quotidien', *Le Monde Dimanche*, 19 December 1982, pp. ix–x.

34. *Le Présence et l'absence. Contribution à une théorie des représentations*, Casterman, Paris 1980; *Une Pensée devenue monde. Faut-il abandonner Marx?*,

Fayard, Paris 1980; *Qu-est-ce que penser?*, Publisud, Paris 1985; *Le Retour de la dialectique. Douze mots clefs pour le monde moderne*, Messidor-Éditions Sociales, Paris 1986.

35. 'L'être humain va toujours *au-delà* de soi': *Qu'est-ce que penser?*, p. 131.

36. See Jean-Pierre Garnier, 'La vision urbaine de Henri Lefebvre', in 'Actualités de Henri Lefebvre', *Espaces et sociétés*, no. 76, 1994, p. 123. Roland Castro, director of the programme for the suburbs in 1989, has acknowledged his debt to Lefebvre (*Civilisation urbaine ou barbarie?*, Plon, Paris 1994).

37. Olivier Corpet, 'La mort du philosophe Henri Lefebvre', *Le Monde*, 2 July 1991, p. 15.

38. Henri Lefebvre and Catherine Régulier, *La Révolution n'est plus ce qu'elle était*, Éditions Libres-Hallier, Paris 1978. There has been much comment, of a frequently abject sort, from the Parisian microcosm on Lefebvre's relations with a very young Communist whom the party had sent on an assignment to the ageing philosopher. It involves a classical vision of the plot, added to which is the tiresome reputation as a Don Juan that Lefebvre trailed after him all his life. Catherine Régulier, who was to become his wife, remained at his side to the end of his life.

39. 'Ne pas rester prisonnier du passé. Le philosophe Henri Lefebvre a rencontré le XXIIe Congrès du P.C.F.', *L'Humanité*, 2 March 1978.

40. 'L'invité de *L'Humanité*: Henri Lefebvre, sociologue, philosophe', interview with Jacques Bonis, *L'Humanité*, 2 February 1981, p. 13.

41. See Henri Lefebvre, 'Hurler contre les loups', *Le Matin*, 5 July 1984; 'Quo vadis?', interview with Jacques de Bonis, *Révolution*, no. 236, 7 September 1984; 'La société sans le PC?', *L'Humanité*, 19 November 1985. The attempt at social and political radicalism that Lefebvre still sought in the PCF would, we should note, extend to widely criticized support for the hunger strike by Action directe militants, who had (according to him) been arrested for 'political offences': *Libération*, 2 February 1988.

42. See the excellent analysis in Lefebvre, *Writing on Cities*, pp. 42–52.

43. The most recent appraisal is to be found in Stuart Elden, 'Politics, Philosophy, Geography: Henri Lefebvre in Recent Anglo-American Scholarship', *Antipode: A Radical Journal of Geography*, vol. 33, no. 5, November 2001, pp. 809–21. See also Mario Rui Martins, 'The Theory of Social Space in the Work of Henri Lefebvre', in Ray Forrest, Jeff Henderson and Peter Williams, eds, *Urban Political Economy and Social Theory: Critical Essays in Urban Studies*, Gower, Aldershot 1982; and Kristin Ross, *The*

Emergence of Social Space: Rimbaud and the Paris Commune, Macmillan, Houndmills 1988. And see especially Edward W. Soja, *Postmodern Geographies: The Reassertion of Space in Critical Social Theory*, Verso, London and New York 1989; Fredric Jameson, 'The Politics of Theory: Ideological Positions in the Postmodern Debate', in *The Ideologies of Theory: Essays 1971 – 1986*, vol. 2, *The Syntax of History*, Routledge, London 1988; Mark Gottdiener, *The Social Production of Urban Space*, University of Texas Press, Austin 1984; *The New Urban Sociology*, McGraw Hill, New York 1994; 'Lefebvre and the Bias of Academic Urbanism', *City*, no. 4/1, April 2000; 'Henri Lefebvre and the Production of Space', *Sociological Theory*, no. 11, March 1993.

44. See 'Parcours et positions', *Annales de la recherche urbaine*, no. 64, September 1994. Cf. Isaac Joseph, 'Le droit à la ville, la ville à l'oeuvre. Deux paradigmes de la recherche' (pp. 4–10) and Manuel Castells, 'L'école française de sociologie urbaine vingt ans après'. Retour ou futur?' (pp. 58–60). See also Jean-Christophe Bailly, *La Ville à l'oeuvre*, Editions J. Bertoin, Paris 1992.

45. See 'Actualités de Henri Lefebvre', *Espaces et sociétés*, no. 76, 1994 and, in particular, Michael Dear, 'Les aspects postmodernes de Henri Lefebvre' (pp. 31–39) and Pierre Hamel and Claire Poitras, 'Henri Lefebvre, penseur de la postmodernité' (pp. 41–58).

46. See 'Henri Lefebvre au présent', *Urbanisme*, no. 319, July/August 2001. See the articles by Maïté Clavel, 'La ville comme oeuvre'; Michèle Joly, 'Henri Lefebvre à Strasbourg'; 'Rencontre avec Nicole Beaurain'; Laurent Devisme, 'Henri Lefebvre, curieux sujet, non?'.

47. Donatella Carraro, *L'Avventura umana nel mundo moderno: Henri Lefebvre e l' "homo quotidianus"*, Unicopoli, Milan 1981; Philip Wander, Introduction to Henri Lefebvre, *Everyday Life in the Modern World*, Transaction, Brunswick (NJ) 1984, pp. vii–xxii; Catherine Régulier, 'Quotidienneté', in Georges Labica, ed., *Dictionnaire critique du marxisme*, second edn, Presses Universitaires de France, Paris 1985; Alice Kaplan and Kristin Ross, 'Everyday Life', *Yale French Studies*, no. 73, Fall 1987; Alberto Suarez-Rojas, *La 'Critique de la vie quotidienne' chez Henri Lefebvre. Romantisme et philosophie: genèse d'une critique du moderne*, master's thesis, University of Paris X, 1991; Rob Shields, *Lefebvre, Love and Struggle: Spatial Dialectics*, Routledge, London 1998, and 'Everyday Marxism: The Convergent Analyses of Roland Barthes and Henri Lefebvre', in James Dolamore, ed., *Making Connections: Essays in French Culture and Society in Honour of Philip Thody*, Peter Lang, Bern 1999, pp. 135–46 (see also Rob Shields's

website: Carleton.ca/~rshields/lefebvre.htm).

48. Lefebvre, *Une Pensée devenue monde*, p. 233.

49. We shall allow ourselves a risky comparison here between this disenchanted diagnosis and the works of Pierre Rosanvallon on the 'desociologization of the political', the break in the previous link between social classes and political parties, especially in *Le Peuple introuvable*, Gallimard, Paris 1998.

50. See Michel de Certeau, *L'invention du quotidien*, two vols, Gallimard, Paris 1990 and 1994.

51. Cornelius Castoriadis, *The Imaginary Institution of Society*, trans. Katherine Blamey, Polity, Cambridge 1987; Claude Lefort, *L'invention du politique*, Fayard, Paris 1981.

52. See Daniel Bensaïd, *Marx for Our Times: Adventures and Misadventures of a Critique*, trans. Gregory Elliott, Verso, London and New York 2002. And see, *inter alia*, Étienne Balibar, *The Philosophy of Marx*, trans. Chris Turner, Verso, London and New York 1995; Michel Vadée, *Marx, penseur du possible*, Méridiens Klincksieck, Paris 1993; Henri Maler, *Convoiter l'impossible. L'utopie avec Marx, malgré Marx*, Albin Michel, Paris 1995; and Yvon Quiniou, *Figures de la déraison politique*, Kimé, Paris 1995.

53. Jacques Derrida, *Specters of Marx: The State of the Debt, the Work of Mourning, and the New International*, trans. Peggy Kamuf, Routledge, New York and London 1994.

54. See François Furet, *Interpreting the French Revolution*, trans. Elborg Foster, Cambridge University Press, Cambridge 1981 and *The Passing of an Illusion: The Idea of Communism in the Twentieth Century*, trans. Deborah Furet, University of Chicago Press, Chicago 1999.

Introduction

1. See especially Michel Maffesoli, *La Conquête du présent: pour une sociologie de la vie quotidienne*, Presses Universitaires de France, Paris 1979, with a preface by Gilbert Durand.

2. See Nicolas Tertullian's remarkable book on the Hungarian philosopher, *Georg Lukács. Étapes de sa pensée esthétique*, Le Sycomore, Paris 1980.

3. See Martin Heidegger, *Being and Time*, trans. John Macquarrie and Edward Robinson, Basil Blackwell, Oxford 1962.

Part One: Continuities

1. See Siegfried Giedion, *La Mécanisation au pouvoir*, Centre Georges Pompidou, Paris 1980, p. 512 ff.

2. See Henri Lefebvre, *La Présence et l'absence. Contribution à la théorie des représentations*, Casterman, Paris 1980.

3. See Henri Lefebvre, *Une pensée devenue monde*, Fayard, Paris 1980.

Part Two: Discontinuities

1. See André Gorz, *Farewell to the Working Class*, trans. Michael Sonenscher, Pluto Press, London 1982; René Lourau, *Le Lapsus des intellectuels*, Paris 1981, esp. pp. 244 ff.

2. See Jean-Pierre Faye, *Langages totalitaires*, Herman, Paris 1973, pp. 446 ff; Lourau, *Le Lapsus des intellectuels*.

3. See, *inter alia*, G. Faye, *Le Système à tuer les peuples*, Éditions Copernic, Paris 1981.

4. See Marc Sautet, *Nietzsche et la Commune*, Le Sycomore, Paris 1981.

5. See Jean Baudrillard, *For a Critique of the Political Economy of the Sign*, trans. Charles Levin, Telos Press, St. Louis, MO 1981.

6. See John McHale, *The Changing Information Environment*, Elek, London 1976.

7. See Pierre Grémion and Haroun Gamous, *L'Ordinateur au pouvoir*, Éditions du Seuil, Paris 1978.

8. See Simon Nora and Alain Minc, *The Computerization of Society: A Report to the President of France*, MIT Press, London 1980.

9. See the works of Ilya Prigogine, Nobel Prize winner in 1977.

10. See the CORDES Report to the Commissariat du plan, 1978, pp. 147–8.

Index